THE OXFORD AUTHORS

General Editor: Frank Kermode

ROBERT BROWNING was born in 1812 at Camberwell, London. Educated privately, and (briefly) at the newly founded London University, he decided at an early age to dedicate himself to poetry. His early, experimental works met with little public recognition, and a period (1837–46) writing for the theatre led nowhere. In 1845 he met and fell in love with fellow poet Elizabeth Barrett, who was bed-ridden with a mysterious ailment. In the face of her father's tyrannical overprotectiveness the couple were forced to marry in secret and flee the country, settling in Italy. Many of Browning's most lasting dramatic monologues derive from this period, and were collected in *Men and Women* (1855), but popular success continued to elude him. After his wife's death in 1861, Browning returned to London. The public finally began acknowledging the genius of his poetry with *Dramatis Personae* (1864), and on the publication of his epic *The Ring and the Book* (1868–9) his reputation soared. In the last two, highly productive decades of his life he was venerated as the chief poetical voice of his age. A Browning Society was formed in 1881. He died in 1889.

ADAM ROBERTS is Lecturer in English at Royal Holloway, University of London. He is the author of *Robert Browning Revisited* (Twayne, 1996) and numerous articles on Browning and the Browning Circle.

DANIEL KARLIN is Professor of English at University College London. His most recent publications on Browning are *Browning's Hatreds* (Oxford University Press, 1993) and, with John Woolford, *Robert Browning* (Longman Studies in 18th and 19th Century Literature, 1996).

THE OXFORD AUTHORS

ROBERT BROWNING

EDITED BY
ADAM ROBERTS

with an introduction by Daniel Karlin

Oxford   New York
OXFORD UNIVERSITY PRESS
1997

Oxford University Press, Great Clarendon Street, Oxford OX2 6DP

Oxford New York

Athens Auckland Bangkok Bombay Bogota Buenos Aires
Calcutta Cape Town Dar es Salaam Delhi Florence Hong Kong
Istanbul Karachi Kuala Lumpur Madras Madrid Melbourne
Mexico City Nairobi Paris Singapore Taipei Tokyo Toronto

and associated companies in
Berlin Ibadan

Oxford is a trade mark of Oxford University Press

British Library Cataloguing in Publication data
Data available

Library of Congress Cataloging-in-Publication Data
Browning Robert, 1812–1889
[Selections. 1997]
Robert Browning / edited by Adam Roberts; with an introduction by Daniel Karlin.
p.   cm. — (The Oxford authors)
Includes indexes.
I. Roberts, Adam.   II. Title.   III. Series
PR4202.R67 1997   821'. 8–dc20   96–22017
ISBN 0-19-254203-6 (hardcover). — ISBN 0-19-282372-8 (pbk.)

Typeset by Pure Tech India Ltd., Pondicherry
Printed in Great Britain by
Biddles Ltd.
Guildford and King's Lynn

CONTENTS

PROSE SELECTION

INTRODUCTION
ROBERT BROWNING'S PLEASURE-HOUSE

WHY read Browning? Students are exempt from answering; he's on the reading-list, and that's (un)fair enough. There was recently an advertisement for a performance of 'Macbeth, an A-level set text by William Shakespeare'. Nor do I mean to engage in arguments about whether there should be a literary canon, and, if so, whether Browning should be in it. I know that my question derives from a larger one: why read poetry? (And that, in turn...) But if some sort of answer to the general question may be taken for granted, the particular one remains: why read *this* poetry? I have an answer, though the path to it is tortuous and bedevilled by false trails, some of them laid by Browning himself. But it matters enormously because it seems to me the only answer which allows Browning to be read, now, as a poet; which allows him to remain for us, as he was for Henry James, 'a tremendous and incomparable modern'.[1]

The historical, the 'Victorian' Browning is an unavoidable cultural fact. It is possible to find him interesting or boring according to the criteria you might apply to visiting stately homes (or Casa Guidi in Florence, which has many of the Brownings' real possessions). There is a 'period' Browning as there is a period Tennyson (though Tennyson, inevitably, gains and loses more on this measure): Browning is as much of his time as steam-engines, the Gothic Revival, Pre-Raphaelitism, the London 'season', and the Irish Question; he can be read alongside Dickens and Darwin, has things to say about faith and doubt, and Italian independence, and spiritualism, and Napoleon III; last but not least, his courtship and marriage with Elizabeth Barrett, with its touching absurdities and genuine bravery and success, have fixed an image of him as dated, splendid, and cherished as St Pancras' Station.

This image affects what a modern reader might anticipate from Browning's poetry. It is as crowded with *things* as a Victorian drawing-room, the furniture is heavy, the gardens profuse and ornate. It takes a lot of work to keep up. There is a sense of promiscuous high-mindedness in the classical and religious nudes

---

[1] 'Browning in Westminster Abbey', originally published on the occasion of Browning's funeral in 1889, repr. in *English Hours*, 1905.

which hang on the walls, and the library is intimidatingly cultured and gentlemanly. The dinners are ponderous and interminable.

Browning is truly like this, viewed from where we stand; but the perspective of historical time is not the only one available to us, or rather, that perspective is not itself uniform and stable. The poems offer us the possibility of entering their time (including their history) from a different angle.

This different point of entry begins with the question of why Browning chose to be a poet in the first place, and with the kinds of poetry which he wrote at the outset of his career. These early works have a more than chronological priority: Browning never left them behind, and he can be seen arguing about poetry, with others and with himself, on the same ground in the 1880s as in the 1830s (I am thinking especially of the magnificent 'Prologue' to *Asolando*, which revisits a literal as well as a symbolic landscape). Of course the core of most readers' knowledge of Browning will remain the central collections of shorter poems published between 1842 and 1864 (*Dramatic Lyrics, Dramatic Romances and Lyrics, Men and Women,* and *Dramatis Personae*), together with *The Ring and the Book* (1868–9); this is true even of a selection such as the present, which brings out some of the treasures from the attic of Browning's later work. But some idea of what Browning was up to in the early poems is vital if we are to understand the scope and vitality of his major achievement.

Browning's choice of poetry as a vocation happened some time in the early 1830s, and it meant more than that he would write poetry in his spare time; he meant to do nothing else. It was not an obvious choice of career for a young man born into a middle-class Noncon-formist family, even one as loving and supportive as Browning's seems to have been. His father was a gentle, humorous bibliophile, who fostered his son's talents with pride and pleasure; his mother's strong piety influenced but did not coerce him; his only and younger sister accepted from the outset a role of devoted subordination. Nevertheless we should not underestimate the strength of will which Browning showed in making poetry his life, even though he could not expect to make a living by it. Attempts were made to persuade him to enter one of the several professions with which the family had connections (banking, the law, diplomacy); Browning overcame such opposition, and went on (despite whispers of ridicule or contempt both within and outside the family circle) living at home on his father's allowance, and publishing his books at his father's expense, until his marriage and departure to Italy with Elizabeth Barrett in 1846.[2] He might have been other kinds of writer: a novelist like Dickens, an essayist and polemicist like Carlyle, a journalist and editor like John Forster, a many-handed cuttlefish of letters like Harriet Martineau or Mary Russell Mitford. All these could make a living, albeit in some cases a precarious one, from their writing. And Browning was not incapable of writing good prose, either; the letters in this selection demonstrate his range, from the nervous intensity of his courtship letters to Elizabeth Barrett to the affectionate eagerness of his invitation to Carlyle to come to Italy in 1847 ('now, at this time of times, for its own sake and the world's'); from the jovial ferocity of his rebuttal of Ruskin's criticism of *Men and Women*, to the direct, passionate conviction of his letters to Julia Wedgwood in defence of the depths of darkness in *The Ring and the Book*. The *Essay on Shelley*, the only work of criticism which he published under his own name,[3] has a rhetorical colour, subtlety of argument, and intelligent complexity of syntax worthy of his finest dramatic speakers. But the final sentence of the essay points to its being an exception in Browning's work: he wrote it as a personal tribute to Shelley, and never did anything like it again. In other words, Browning deliberately turned his back on any other work with his pen than poetry. His only concession to the demands he must have felt that he should do something professional and commercial with his talent came in the 1840s with his sustained campaign to

---

[2] Browning wrote to Elizabeth Barrett of 'this absolute independence of mine, which, if I had it not, my heart would starve and die for, I feel—and which I have fought so many good battles to preserve—for that has happened, too—this light rational life I lead, and know so well that I lead...' (16 Sept. 1845, in P. Kelley and S. Lewis (eds.), *The Brownings' Correspondence*, vol. xi (Winfield, Kan.: Wedgestone Press, 1993), 82, hereafter *Correspondence*; repr. in this edition, p. 649). There has been some debate about whether Browning's parents, as opposed to other members of the family, were opposed to his becoming a poet: see W. Craig Turner (ed.), *The Poet Robert Browning and his Kinsfolk by his Cousin Cyrus Mason* (Waco, Tex.: Baylor University Press, 1983), 65 and n. 59. I believe that Browning did have to face at least some scruples on the part of his parents. Elizabeth Barrett heard gossip about it from Mary Russell Mitford, and told Browning himself of Mrs Ann Procter's opinion 'that it was a pity he had not seven or eight hours a day of occupation' (12 Apr. 1846, *Correspondence*, xi (1994), 236). For a discussion of this issue, see D. Karlin, *The Courtship of Robert Browning and Elizabeth Barrett* (Oxford: Clarendon Press, 1985), 117–25.

[3] Browning's only other work of published criticism appeared anonymously in the *Foreign and Quarterly Review* (July 1842); it was ostensibly a review of a book on Tasso, but Browning developed it into an essay on the life and work of Chatterton. He did not acknowledge or reprint it in his lifetime.

become a successful playwright. But even if his heart was in it, the heart of his genius was not. His stage plays, though of interest to anyone who admires and studies him, are unrescuably bad, deserved to fail, and by failing did him the best turn they could.

What idea did Browning have of poetry when he chose to dedicate himself to it? Towards the end of the century stories began to circulate about this dedication, and I have found at least one poem specifically based on it, called 'Mammon and Poesy; or, The Poet's Choice', by Douglas Sladen.[4] Sladen's poem is dedicated to Browning, and depicts a 'young dreamer' who is tempted by Mammon in a scene recalling Satan's temptation of Christ: 'He took him to the mountain-top | Of Mammon, shewed him all the Earth...And said, "Bow down and worship me, | And all thou seest shall be thine..."'. The youth's rejection of this temptation is a rejection of the sordid world of work, associated with the city's 'crowded alleys trod | By hard coarse men', and with the wrong kind of writing: Mammon's devotee 'An altar of his desk must make | And missal of his ledger'. The youth turns instead to the beautiful maid Poesy, who tells him of another kind of writing, free of commerce and calculation, and which consists in writing down her 'true speech', becoming the 'singer and interpreter | Of the lost voices, which there be | Lurking within the earth and air'.

The weakness of Sladen's account is obvious: if poetry is above materialism, it risks being immaterial with a vengeance—that is, not mattering. Even more damaging—to a Victorian especially—is the notion that poetry is somehow not work. Browning stressed the contrary view as hard as he could; he wanted it known that he, too, made an altar of his desk, even if the desk was not in a counting-house. It was work for which he expected payment, too, if not in money then in reputation: as he told Elizabeth Barrett, if he grew cabbages he could sell them at Covent Garden for a penny each, and if he wrote verse he was entitled to 'a fair proportion of the

---

[4] From *In Cornwall and across the Sea: With Poems Written in Devonshire* (London, 1885), 191–200. Sladen had been inspired by an anecdote which he read in the *Century Magazine* in 1881, and which he reprints as the epigraph to his poem. According to this anecdote, when Browning's father asked him 'what he intended to be...he had the singular courage to decline to be rich. He appealed to his Father whether it would not be better for him to see life in its best sense and cultivate the powers of his mind, than to shackle himself in the very outset of his career by a laborious training foreign to that aim...so great was the confidence of the Father in the genius of the son, that the former at once acquiesced in the proposal.' The pressure of an idealizing myth is palpable here.

Reviewers' gold-currency'.[5] He could not deny the residual force of the vision which Sladen celebrates, that of poetry as divinely ordained and privileged, and of the poet as a hero or prophet set apart from his fellows, but his most extreme formulation of this principle, in a letter to Ruskin, uses a vocabulary which is economic as well as aesthetic. 'A poet's affair is with God,—to whom he is accountable, and of whom is his reward; look elsewhere, and you find misery enough.'[6] This is lofty, but it is also businesslike (*affair, accountable, reward*); the poet's divine mission has the force of a contract, which carries with it an obligation as imperative as that in any other sphere of life. The sense of a duty laid on him by God is strong in Browning, but so is the sense of being a workman who fulfils his side of the bargain by honest endeavour. 'I write from a thorough conviction that it is the duty of me, and with the belief that, after every drawback & shortcoming, I do my best'; and this emphasis on having *done his best* recurs in many places in his writings.[7]

Browning wrote to Ruskin in these terms in 1855, in the aftermath of the critical and commercial failure of *Men and Women*, a failure he felt even more deeply, perhaps, than that of *Sordello*, because he believed that this time he had done everything in his power to please his public. But with *Dramatis Personae*, in 1864, his reputation began to recover, and his rehabilitation was completed by the triumphant success of *The Ring and the Book*. It became possible to 'look elsewhere' than to God for reward, and Browning seems to have felt entitled to take his seat at the High Table of Victorian literary culture.[8] He duly became a Sage and a Great Man, and was human enough on occasion to promenade with Wisdom, rather than Knowledge, on his arm, and to mistake self-importance for dignity. The

[5] Letter of 11 Feb. 1845: *Correspondence*, x (1992), 70; repr. in this edition, p. 604.

[6] For this letter to Ruskin, see pp. 691–3.

[7] The quotation is from the letter to Elizabeth Barrett (see n. 5). In the preface to *Sordello* in the *Poetical Works* of 1863 Browning commented on the poem's failure: 'I blame nobody, least of all myself, who did my best then and since'; in the preface to a selection of his poems published in 1872, he wrote: 'Having hitherto done my utmost in the art to which my life is a devotion, I cannot engage to increase the effort.'

[8] The reference to High Table has a literal application. In 1867 Browning was awarded an honorary MA by Oxford University and an honorary fellowship by Balliol College. As a young man he had been debarred from attending either Oxford or Cambridge because his family were Nonconformists. The words 'M.A., Honorary Fellow of Balliol College, Oxford' appear beneath Browning's name on the title-page of the *Poetical Works* of 1868.

pose was inviting not simply because it represented a concession on the part of his readers and critics, but because it answered to an idea he had of himself and of his art, and confirmed a tendency which had been there from the beginning. His greatness as a poet is a factor of his resistance to this tendency, his willingness to listen to the 'lost voices' of which Sladen speaks; but it cannot be denied or forgotten, because its source is twinned with that of the dissenting spirit which informs his finest work.

'It [poetry] is all teaching,' Browning wrote to Ruskin (in the letter from which I quoted earlier), 'and the people hate to be taught.' There is no doubt that Browning allowed, even if he did not endorse, the view of him summed up by the title of a book by Henry Jones which appeared two years after his death, *Browning as a Philosophical and Religious Teacher*; nor that this view was largely responsible for his second long period of critical disparagement, the era of New Criticism from the 1920s to the 1950s.[9] It appears early in his work (though not, significantly, at the very beginning) in a long poem which Browning published before Queen Victoria came to the throne, yet which is one of his most 'Victorian' works (if we allow that epithet its conventional force); certainly Victorian readers continued to admire it and Victorian critics often exhorted Browning to return to it instead of writing such exasperating stuff as *Men and Women*. But Browning knew better than to follow the critical success of *Paracelsus* (1835) with more of the same. Had he done so you would not now be holding this book in your hands, for Robert Browning would barely command the attention of a footnote.

Paracelsus is all about teaching—it is the subject of the poem as well as its object. We first meet the hero as he is about to shake the dust of school from his feet, and later see him doing the same for the university where he has become a renowned professor. Although formal education is violently attacked in the poem (in a transparent reflection of Browning's own experiences),[10] it is itself a solemn and

---

[9] On this subject see the chapter 'Studying Browning' in J. Woolford and D. Karlin, *Robert Browning* (Harlow: Longman Studies in 18th and 19th Century Literature, 1996). The New Critics' refusal to take Browning seriously was ended by the publication of Robert Langbaum's *The Poetry of Experience* in 1957.

[10] Browning attended school until the age of 14 and didn't think much of it; Alfred Domett records him saying that 'they taught him nothing' at the school in Peckham which he attended in 1820–6, and that he had once composed an epigram on the 'damned undiluted misery' of his time there (E. A. Horsman (ed.), *The Diary of Alfred Domett* (Oxford: Oxford University Press, 1953), 73–4). From the age of 14 he was tutored at home under his father's guidance, and was otherwise self-taught, a process he

didactic work, which dramatizes the life of Paracelsus in order to demonstrate certain preconceived notions about Life and Art and other matters of capital importance. The whole poem is designed to give Paracelsus a deathbed platform from which to deliver his final, summative vision, which comes as close to a sermon as Browning ever wrote. Not until *Ferishtah's Fancies* (1884) did Browning so openly preach at his readers.

Why did Browning write a poem like *Paracelsus* at all? He had written something very different to start with—*Pauline*, published anonymously in 1833—and perhaps he was discouraged by its complete failure. (Not a single copy was sold, and Browning retrieved the unbound sheets from the publisher's and destroyed them.) Still, *Pauline* had been greeted by thirteen precious words in the *Athenaeum*: 'it... carries the stamp of no poet with whose works we are intimate'.[11] After *Paracelsus* Browning published *Sordello*—all too nonymously.[12] By 1840 the critics were unfortunately intimate with *Paracelsus*. Browning had gone backwards, everyone agreed; they didn't know that *Sordello* was really the successor to *Pauline* (Browning's authorship of that poem did not become generally known until much later) and if they had it might have made things worse. *Tait's Edinburgh Magazine*, after all, had dismissed *Pauline* as 'a piece of pure bewilderment'. But that had just been a careless quip; the ridicule heaped on *Sordello* for its obscurity and difficulty was consciously indignant. It has few parallels in literary history, and reminds me more of the reception given to contemporary art or music, in which there is often a note of triumph at catching the artist out, an accusation not simply of bad technique but bad faith. It is all right to bully the charlatan, as Mr Sludge discovers, and *Sordello* was mercilessly teased and cuffed. It became, as Guido in *The Ring and the Book* describes his own fate, 'a common hackblock to try edge of jokes'. (This doesn't stop some of the jokes

sketches in the late poem 'Development'. He had been eager to enter the new London University, but dropped out after a year (1828–9); his disillusion with the dry, formal curriculum, and his scorn for the herd-ignorance of his fellow-students, are virulently evident in *Paracelsus*, especially Bks. I, III, and IV. For the fullest and fairest account of Browning's education, see John Maynard, *Browning's Youth* (Cambridge, Mass.: Harvard University Press, 1977).

[11] The contemporary reviews of *Pauline* are reprinted in full in *Correspondence*, vol. iii (1985), 340–7.

[12] I pass over the intermediate publication of *Strafford* (1837); as I have suggested, I think that Browning's writing for the stage was mainly driven by the wish to justify his choice of poetry as a vocation.

from being funny, and I play my part in circulating them.)[13] The originality of *Sordello* is inseparable from its modernity, even its modernism. Ezra Pound loved and learned from it, and it reads as though Browning could hear, as he wrote, Pound's injunction to 'make it new'.

What is it about *Pauline* and *Sordello* that tell us of Browning's greatness, whereas *Paracelsus* is all too plainly, as W. J. Fox praised it for being, 'the result of thought, skill, and toil'?[14] There is nothing intrinsic to the subjects of these poems (a young man's 'fragment of a confession', the life of a Renaissance alchemist, and the life of a thirteenth-century Italian troubadour) to indicate why two of them should elicit brilliant and daring imaginative flights and the third a series of noble attitudes performed in the metrical equivalent of slow motion. Browning's range would always be eclectic: the great monologues of *Men and Women* belong to figures from the present and the past, and from different pasts (a Renaissance painter who really existed, an Arab physician interpolated into a biblical story, a 'Childe' from a chivalric phantasmagoria), and there is no recurring or characteristic situation which automatically elicits his best work. Nor does the mode of each poem (autobiography, drama, third-person narrative) in itself suggest the answer. True, the mode in *Pauline* and *Sordello* is the subject of intense self-conscious scrutiny, whereas *Paracelsus* is untroubled by irony or playfulness; and again we can trace a pattern in Browning's major work in which the artistry by which that work has been made is deliberately drawn to the reader's attention—Fra Lippo Lippi's 'self-portrait' at the end of his monologue, for example, or the ironic disclaimer of the speaker at the end of 'How It Strikes a Contemporary' ('Well, I could never write a verse,—could you?'). Some poems (among them 'A Grammarian's Funeral', 'Abt Vogler', and the 'Prologue' to *Ferishtah's Fancies*) take this reflexive turn to an extreme, becoming in formal terms the image of what they behold as their 'subjects'. It is a movement visible from the very first words of *Pauline*, which seem as though they must be spoken: 'Pauline, mine own, bend o'er me—thy soft breast | Shall

[13] The contemporary reviews of *Sordello* are in *Correspondence*, iv (1986), 420–4; the index to B. Litzinger and D. Smalley (eds.), *Browning: The Critical Heritage* (London: Routledge & Kegan Paul, 1970) will turn up enough examples of jokes and parodies, the best known of which is Tennyson's comment that he understood only two lines in the poem, the first ('Who will, may hear Sordello's story told') and the last ('Who would, has heard Sordello's story told') and that neither was true.

[14] Review in *The Monthly Repository*, Nov. 1835, repr. in *Correspondence*, iii (1985), 352–7. Fox's phrase comes from the opening paragraph, which I quote in full below.

pant to mine....' But their immediacy, like her yielding softness, is deceptive; it turns out that the young man's 'confession' is a text, written at Pauline's command and subject to her control. *Sordello* fuses the action of the poem with its form by means of rapid and bewildering shifts of focus, violent disjunctions of time and place, and above all the condensed and allusive style for which it was most attacked. Compared to these, *Paracelsus* is a perfectly conventional dramatic poem, and the apologia with which Browning prefaced it in 1835 was probably dropped from later editions because he realized that nobody had been perturbed.

Complexity and self-consciousness may be characteristic of many of Browning's best poems, but they, themselves, do not make these poems better; what does this is an idea of poetry, animating poems when it is present, and leaving them more or less for dead when it is not. Most poets start from the belief that there is something good which poetry alone can do, and most struggle to hold that belief against the prevailing current. I take 'poetry' here to mean nothing more, and nothing less, than verse fiction. 'Verse' encompasses form and language, 'fiction' content and design. A fiction in this sense can be a story, or the expression of a mood, or the articulation of an idea; its being in verse can mean that it is a drama, or a narrative, or a lyric. But the two terms should really be hyphenated, or fused: poetry is versifiction. *Sordello* is versifiction almost in pure form; *Paracelsus* is a work in which ideas are versified. Apart from one or two passages there is no reason why any of it should be in verse rather than prose (and there are several lengthy passages where the distinction is hard to draw). *Paracelsus* can be paraphrased; *Sordello*, questioned as to what it means, points to itself.

Browning's belief in the intrinsic value of poetry was powerful and enduring, but unstable; much of his work bears the traces of a characteristically Victorian struggle between faith and doubt, though of an aesthetic rather than religious nature. (Yet religion is bound up in the aesthetics, too: think of the image of the 'Four great walls in the New Jerusalem' at the end of 'Andrea del Sarto'). The origin of this instability is rooted in familiar ground for anyone studying early Victorian culture: it is the problem of Romanticism, or rather late Romanticism, the period from the mid-1820s in which Browning grew up and began to write.

It was not bliss in that dawn to be alive; it wasn't much like dawn, more a murky twilight; at best, as Fra Lippo Lippi puts it, a 'grey beginning'. The successive deaths of Keats (1821), Shelley (1822), but above all Byron (1824) left poetry in the hands of an older generation of Romantic writers whose appetite for innovation and dissent was long past. Great as Wordsworth, the leader of this generation, might be, nothing new was to be expected from him, yet he became in 1843 the first Poet Laureate appointed by Queen Victoria. By then he was famous as much for outgrowing Romanticism as for embodying it. In the best tradition of repentant sinners, he had thoroughly enjoyed himself before thinking better of it; his successors were exhorted to think better of enjoying themselves in the first place. As for his original wilderness, it was thoroughly mapped, and there were heritage trails for all to follow. From the mid-1820s he had no rivals. Southey was of no account, Coleridge had fallen silent; John Clare's standard was raised too far from the centre, on the margin where poverty and social disadvantage confined him.

All the major poets born in the first quarter of the nineteenth century (Elizabeth Barrett Browning, Tennyson, Robert Browning, Arnold) had to find their true voices, early or late, by rejecting Wordsworth's mature deliberations and going back to Romantic first principles, even though all did so with a guilty conscience. (I often think that the Austrian tyrant whom the priggish but wonderfully Romantic Luigi goes off to assassinate in the third episode of *Pippa Passes* is actually Wordsworth.) But Wordsworth was not the only figure standing in their path. Let us go back to W. J. Fox's review of *Paracelsus*. It opens with these words:

This poem is what few modern publications either are, or affect to be; it is A WORK. It is the result of thought, skill, and toil. Defects and irregularities there may be, but they are those of a building which the architect has erected for posterity, and not the capricious anomalies of the wattled pleasure house, which has served its turn when the summer day's amusement is over, and may be blown about by the next breeze, or washed away by the next torrent, to be replaced by another as fantastic and as transient.

The use of terms such as 'work' and 'toil', the architectural metaphor, the appeal from 'amusement' to 'thought', align this view of what poetry is for, and what it should be like, with a cultural discourse of seriousness, intellectual substance, and moral purpose; it's Carlylean in everything but its attribution of these values to poetry (Carlyle advised all poets of his acquaintance, Browning included, to switch to prose). Fox's emphasis on solid, permanent structures, opposed to the 'fantastic' and the 'transient', bears the mark of an anxiety that poetry might lose any cultural status it once enjoyed and become merely a frivolous pastime. Poetry had growing competition in the nineteenth century from the novel, from history, and from science, all of which claimed to describe the world better than poetry, to tell better stories, and to convey ideas with greater force. Religious doubt? Political radicalism? Social analysis? Natural history? Poetry had lost its grip on these subjects, and Romanticism might be held to blame. What remained was the life of feeling, but this too might be a bad thing. Male poets in particular might reflect with alarm that their art was being feminized, that Wordsworth's description of the poet as 'a man speaking to men' was cast in the wrong gender, and that the province of poetry was shrinking, thematically to the dimensions of the home and heart, and formally to those of the lyric. Farewell to the big wars; farewell to the idea of poetry as work, and of its capacity to engage with the public world.

I want to pause for a moment over Fox's scorn for the 'wattled pleasure house'. The fear of pleasure has brought us all the way from Coleridge's 'stately pleasure-dome' to this: pleasure is for picnickers. No fear of being amused by *Paracelsus*! Yet the hero of that poem is not easy in his mind. In Book V, on his deathbed, he remembers a Coleridgean encounter from his necromantic travels:

> In truth, my delicate witch,
> My serpent-queen, you did but well to hide
> The juggles I had else detected. Fire
> May well run harmless o'er a breast like yours!
> The cave was not so darkened by the smoke
> But that your white limbs dazzled me: oh, white,
> And panting as they twinkled, wildly dancing!
> I cared not for your passionate gestures then,
> But now I have forgotten the charm of charms,
> The foolish knowledge which I came to seek,
> While I remember that quaint dance; and thus
> I am come back, not for those mummeries,
> But to love you, and to kiss your little feet,
> Soft as an ermine's winter coat!

(ll. 192–205)

The strength and poignancy of Paracelsus' regret are signalled by poetry itself: the missed beat between 'you' and 'and' in line 204, whose extra syllable catches the very breath of desire, and the delighted observant tenderness of the final image. It is a moment which might turn the poem inside out; but Paracelsus is trapped in

Paracelsus: his outburst is immediately covered over by a coat of pious gloss from the faithful Festus.[15]

The scene in the cave is transgressive not just because it is about sex, but because sexual pleasure 're-members' the self, abolishing the ravages of time (not '*I have* come back' but '*I am* come back'). The poetry of Romanticism is a poetry of defiance and denial of the power of time over human identity: structures of authority (monarchy, religion, social custom) work through time, forming stories in which our humanity is constrained to play a part against its nature. Although Paracelsus is supposed to be a Romantic hero in his rebellion against all kinds of authority, *Paracelsus* asks that poetry itself be taken as an authoritative reading of history, and as capable of intellectual synthesis as any other discourse. The 'building' of a poem can both testify to its productive and progressive work, and be the symbol of that production and progress, factory and city hall in one. Only the 'fantastic' and the 'transient' must be sacrificed, yet these, it turns out, are what make poetry worth having. Again and again in his poetry, Browning turns (or returns) to the paradox of a moment which is time-free, which impossibly defeats or transcends its own nature; again and again the structures in which time is inscribed are beaten down, ruined, subjected to destruction or decay, yet retain their sinister potency. In many poems these structures are physical, though all have a metaphysical significance: the Dark Tower in 'Childe Roland to the Dark Tower Came', of course (and Roland's confrontation of it is the defining 'moment' of Browning's poetry), but also the 'font-tomb' in the castle of Goito where Sordello's mother is buried, the Bishop of Saint Praxed's tomb, the equestrian statue of the Duke in 'The Statue and the Bust', the house in Florence built by Andrea del Sarto with the money he embezzled from the King of France, the ruins of 'Love among the Ruins' . . . To these physical structures we can add social institutions, such as marriage and the Church, and the arts themselves; and finally we will find ourselves face to face with poetry itself, and with the paradox of its textuality.

Language is a structure of time, and written language doubly so; poems are necessarily monuments of the time it took to write them and the time it takes to read them. They commemorate themselves as well as their ostensible subjects. When Shakespeare boasts in Sonnet

---

[15] See ll. 205–8, p. 34. Festus' use of the epithet 'soft' contrasts revealingly with Paracelsus'.

55 that 'Not marble nor the gilded monuments | Of princes shall outlive this powerful rhyme', it is easy to forget that his overt intention was to flatter someone else. Every time we read the poem we confirm its power. Yet what Browning's poems secrete is un-writing, moments in which time is abolished and the 'fantastic' and the 'transient' achieve their impossible ascendancy.

If the object of writing is to overcome the power of time, then writing will always fail, will always defeat itself. Browning accepts and rejects this truth, simultaneously but, so to speak, at different creative depths. His refusal to give up the desire for transcendence is the source of the energy in his work; his acceptance of defeat is the source of its shape. Browning's characteristic plots, situations, land-scapes, poetic forms, turns of phrase, rhythmic effects, are all gov-erned by this differential working of a single impulse, which carries poetry towards moments of time-less or time-free pleasure, yet whose trajectory ensures that the moment of arrival is fatal.

The dramatic monologue, according to this interpretation, is a way of making the 'work' of poetry compatible with pleasure. Through its engagement with history, its concreteness and psychological realism, its aptness for intellectual argument and debate, its positing of the world through speech and relationship (abjuring the ecstatic inner voice of lyric), above all perhaps in its expansive openness, Browning was able to participate in the Victorian world of production and exploration, and to align himself with its energies and interests. The dramatic monologue is an unbounded form (unlike the sonnet, which Browning detested): free to be as long or short as it likes, and in any metrical pattern; free to be in any genre or style; dynamic and, by its very nature, individualistic. Browning's insistence on the dramatic quality of his writing renounces the personal in one direction but multiplies it in another: he described the poems of *Dramatic Lyrics* (1842) as 'so many utterances of so many imaginary persons, not mine', and he was delighted when Walter Savage Landor compared his multifarious creation with Chaucer's.[16]

The dramatic monologue, then, has all these features of the poem as 'work', but what readers are likely to remember of any particular monologue is something quite different. This 'something' is not always the same thing (it may be an effect of sudden concentration

---

[16] 'To Robert Browning', written in 1845 after Browning dedicated *Dramatic Romances and Lyrics* to Landor: 'Since Chaucer was alive and hale, | No man hath walkt along our roads with step | So active, so inquiring eye, or tongue | So varied in discourse.'

and intensity, or of cadence, or of a special vocabulary) but it is unmistakable and composes another nature for the dramatic monologue form. It is, for me, the reason why the dramatic monologues of other, really good, Victorian poets, such as Lord de Tabley or Augusta Webster, simply don't come close to Browning's art. There are different ways of describing this other nature of dramatic monologue, but I associate it above all with the physical sensation, the body, if you like, of Browning's language. We think of language as abstract and dimensionless, but of course it isn't so: the material of language is sound, and its contours are rhythmic. The tracing of these contours in any poem is already a physical act, already a protest against the uniformity of temporal sequence which is the principle of death-in-life. Browning's variety and command of rhythm is unmatched in English poetry, and the speakers of his greatest dramatic monologues seem to design their utterances in order to offer a pleasure (the touch of the body of language) far in excess of what their 'situations' or 'identities' require.

Many, if not most, of these speakers are engaged in describing or narrating loss, failure, frustration, and disenchantment, subjects in which Browning specialized (not always treating them with gloom, I should emphasize; some of his most painful stories are 'done' as light comedy, the supreme example being 'Youth and Art'). In several of these poems the offer of the kind of pleasure I have been describing is scandalously subversive: it undermines both the solidity of the speaker's feeling and the dutifulness of the reader's response to it. I am thinking of lines such as these, from 'In a Year':

> Was it something said,
>   Something done,
> Vexed him? was it touch of hand,
>   Turn of head?
> Strange! that very way
>   Love begun.
> I as little understand
>   Love's decay.

I can never read these lines without being disturbed by their chant: the artistry of arrangement of the short-breathed lines, and the delay of the rhymes one line further than where you expect them, are so exhilarating that they defeat any mere intention to express puzzlement at an unfortunate turn of events. I feel the same about a single line in 'My Last Duchess', in the passage where the Duke is complaining about the Duchess being too easily pleased:

> Sir, 'twas all one! My favour at her breast,
> The dropping of the daylight in the West,
> The bough of cherries some officious fool
> Broke in the orchard for her, the white mule
> She rode with round the terrace...

The second line stands out partly because so many of the sur-rounding couplets run on syntactically, whereas the one in which this line appears is end-stopped; and partly because the phenomenon it describes, the sunset, cannot be a personal gift to the Duchess, as the Duke's ribbon, or the bough of cherries, or the white mule are. Yet it is personal, because it prefigures her death: it does truly rhyme with the Duke's 'favour at her breast', which is mortal to her; it enlarges the scale of her tragedy with an ironic pathos. All this is apt, but the line itself is too beautiful to be spoken by the Duke; in the instant he delivers it the detail ceases to be 'touching' and offers itself to the touch.

But in many other poems the rhythm does not so much betray as overreach the speaker. Only the Bishop of Saint Praxed's seems to me to be a match for his creator—and a case can be made for arguing that he comes the closest of all Browning's speakers to the poet's own disguise. Let me give two examples to end with, one a single line and the other an entire poem. The single line (p. 137) comes from 'Caliban upon Setebos': 'This Quiet, all it hath a mind to, doth.' Obviously the power of this line comes from the two commas, which prevent you from saying the line all at once. By making you pause, the commas suggest Caliban's awe at the supremacy of a being which, unlike his god Setebos (let alone himself) is truly free. (The effect is strengthened by the use of the less colloquial 'hath' and 'doth' instead of 'has' and 'does'.) But these pauses are, in turn, a function of the syntax, which inverts the normal word order: 'This Quiet doth all it hath a mind to'. Put like this it loses the sense of *godlike* deliberation and inevitability with which Caliban invests the Quiet, and which is quite different from saying that it just does what it likes. A philosophical idea has become a banal attribute of beha-viour. Caliban's playful intelligence is richly suggested in 'Caliban upon Setebos', but it is not he who takes and offers the delight which this line affords.

My second example is 'A Toccata of Galuppi's'. The pleasure in this case is that of a doubleness in the 'voicing' of the poem which, as soon as you apprehend it, transforms the narrow limits within which the poem apparently works (the 'dramatic' expression of a particular mood), expanding its scope to that of Browning's art and, just as important, our art—the art of reading. By doubleness, I mean that there is an *alternative stress pattern* to the one which any reader begins by imposing on the poem. Suppose we take the first stanza:

Óh, Galuppi, Baldassaro, this is very sad to find!
I can hardly misconceive you; it would prove me deaf and blind;
But although I take your meaning, 'tis with such a heavy mind!

The rhythm here is 'dipodic', meaning that there is an alternation of strong and weak stresses; but where do you place the first strong stress? If you place it on the first syllable, you get the following pattern:

Óh, Ga | lúppi, | Bálda|ssáro, | |thís is | véry | sád to| find!
Í can| hárdly|míscon | céive you;| | ít would | próve me | déaf and | blínd;
Bút al | thóugh I|táke your|méaning,| |'tís with |súch a|héavy|mínd!

I have always read the poem this way, because the lugubrious regularity, the strong central pause, and the end-stopped thud, all seemed appropriate to the melancholic speaker. But suppose you place the first strong stress on the *third* syllable. This gives the following pattern:

Oh, Galúppi, | Baldassáro, | this is véry | sad to find!
I can hárdly | misconcéive you; | it would próve me | deaf and blínd;
But although I | take your méaning, | 'tis with súch a | heavy mínd!

There is nothing to prevent you from reading the whole poem in this way, whipping its lugubrious trot into a jaunty canter, and voicing the speaker's 'heavy mind' with subversive levity.[17] The title of the poem itself is in this metre: A Toccáta of Galúppi's.[18] But whether you take the melancholy or the jaunty rhythm to be 'given', the other will shadow and haunt it. We must remember that 'A Toccata of Galuppi's' is a poem which is itself about interpreting rhythm, and about the associations of mood with patterns of sound. The speaker, who has been playing one of Galuppi's toccatas, addresses the dead composer: and the first thing he says is that he 'can hardly misconceive' the meaning of Galuppi's music. But what if he has miscon-

---

[17] Derek Attridge reads the lines in this way (*The Rhythms of English Poetry* (London: Longman, 1982), 118); he goes on to illustrate the doubleness of the metre by reference to some lines of Byron (from whom Browning got a great deal of his metrical education).

[18] I am grateful to Pat O'Shea for this observation.

ceived it? The alternative metre of the poem is like an ironic rejoinder from the dead composer, and may also 'voice' the scepticism of his fellow-composer, also dead, whose poem we are 'playing'—Browning himself. Its presence radically disconcerts the reader's own confidence as an interpreter, and warns us not to impose on Browning the same single-minded reading that the speaker imposes on the music of the past and the lost culture which it evokes.

CHRONOLOGY

1812   Robert Browning born at Camberwell (7 May).

1824   R.B.'s parents try without success to publish his first collection of poems, *Incondita*. The manuscript is later destroyed.

1828   R.B. enters London University, but does not last the year.

1833   *Pauline* published anonymously. Not a single copy is sold.

1834   R.B. travels to Russia. Applies unsuccessfully for a diplomatic post.

1835   *Paracelsus* published at the expense of R.B.'s father.

1837   *Stafford* unsuccessfully performed at Covent Garden.

1838   First journey to Italy.

1840   *Sordello* published. General outcry at its obscurity.

1841   Begins publishing a series of poetic pamphlets, *Bells and Pomegranates*, aimed at reaching a popular audience. The first comprises *Pippa Passes*.

1842   *Bells and Pomegranates* II (*King Victor and King Charles*) and III (*Dramatic Lyrics*).

1843   *Bells and Pomegranates* IV (*The Return of the Druses*) and V (*A Blot in the Scutcheon*).

1844   Second journey to Italy. *Bells and Pomegranates* VI (*Colombe's Birthday*).

1845   *Bells and Pomegranates* VII (*Dramatic Romances and Lyrics*). Begins correspondence with Elizabeth Barrett on 10 January. The courtship proper begins with Browning's first visit on 20 May.

1846   *Bells and Pomegranates* VIII (*Luria* and *A Soul's Tragedy*). R.B. and Elizabeth Barrett secretly marry on 12 September. The couple leave England for Italy 19 September.

1847   The couple settle in Florence (at 'Casa Guidi').

1849   First collected edition of *Poems*. R.B.'s only child, Robert Weidemann Barrett Browning (known as 'Pen') born, 9 March.

1850   *Christmas-Eve and Easter-Day*.

1852   The 'Essay on Shelley'.

1855   *Men and Women* (in two volumes).

1857   John Kenyon's legacy of £11,000 ensures financial security for the Brownings.

1860   Comes across the *Old Yellow Book* at a bookstall in Florence.

1861   Death of Elizabeth Barrett Browning (29 June). R.B. leaves Florence, eventually settling in London.

1863   *The Poetical Works* (3 vols.).

1864   *Dramatis Personae.* R.B.'s first unqualified popular and critical success. Begins work on *The Ring and the Book*.

1868   *The Poetical Works* (4 vols.).

1868–9 *The Ring and the Book* is published in four instalments (November–February). Browning's popularity rivals Tennyson's.

1871   *Balaustion's Adventure; Prince Hohenstiel-Schwangau.*

1872   *Fifine at the Fair.*

1873   *Red Cotton Night-Cap Country.*

1874   *Aristophanes' Apology; The Inn Album.*

1876   *Pacchiarotto and How He Worked In Distemper.*

1877   Translates *The Agamemnon of Aeschylus.*

1878   *La Saisiaz* and *The Two Poets of Croisic.*

1879   *Dramatic Idyls, First Series.*

1880   *Dramatic Idyls, Second Series.*

1881   The Browning Society founded.

1883   *Jocoseria.*

1884   *Ferishtah's Fancies.*

1887   *Parleyings with Certain People of Importance in Their Day.*

1888–9 *Poetical Works* (16 vols.).

1889   *Asolando, Fancies and Facts* published 12 December. A copy is placed in Browning's hands in Venice; he dies the same evening. Burial in Westminster Abbey, 31 December.

NOTE ON THE TEXT

SELECTING representatively from a writer as productive as Browning, particularly where a great amount of his best poetry is by today's standards very long, is an almost impossible task. This selection aims to print only complete works; complete books are printed from *Paracelsus*, *The Ring and the Book*, and *Parleyings with Certain People*, and the complete text of all other works selected. This necessarily means that some of Browning's greatest achievements (for instance *Fifine at the Fair*) are not represented here. On the other hand, this selection aims to be more comprehensive than any which has yet appeared. As much of Browning's work as practicable has been included, from the complete range of his writing career, including the often neglected post-*Ring and the Book* period. The prose selection includes Browning's *Essay on Shelley* (in which he outlines his own theory of poetry), as well as a variety of letters that relate both to his courtship of Elizabeth Barrett and his broader range of friends. Most of the letters selected for this edition contain important remarks upon works in progress, on poetry in general, or otherwise reflect upon Browning's own developing sense of himself as a poet.

In the matter of copy-text, the choice facing the editor of Browning's poetry is between the poem as it first appeared in published form and as it appeared in the 'fourth and complete edition' of *Poetical Works* (sixteen volumes in 1888-9, with a seventeenth volume containing *Asolando* appearing in 1894). The choice is not a trifling one; texts of certain poems (particularly *Pauline*) are very different in the later edition. This edition prints the text of the 1888 edition as embodying Browning's last revisions and therefore his ultimate desires as to the shape of his poetry, modified only by the silent correction of errors or misprints, the modernization of the printer's house style from Smith and Elder to Oxford, and the accommodation of those of Browning's wishes that were not incorporated into the 1888 edition (for which see Philip Kelley and William S. Peterson's tabulation of Browning's final revisions, *Browning Institute Studies*, 1 (1973), 109-17). The texts of those of Browning's fugitive and uncollected poems included here are taken from the first appearances of these poems in print.

The case for printing Browning's text from first editions, however, is strong, and there is some point in spending a little time here defending my choice of 1888. Objections from those editors who favour the first-edition text touch on several points. One has to do with the fact that the order of the shorter poems printed in 1888 is in large part different from the order in which they originally appeared. Browning took the poems that had appeared in the collections *Dramatic Lyrics* (1842), *Dramatic Romances and Lyrics* (1845), and *Men and Women* (1855) and redistributed them under three headings 'Dramatic Romances', 'Dramatic Lyrics', and 'Men and Women', irrespective of their original place of publication or of chronology. In this edition the poems have been rearranged into their original place of publication, partly to give more of a sense of the author's development, and partly to correspond to works of secondary criticism (which all treat the poems in the order in which they originally appeared). Any edition has to be in part a compromise, and an editor's job must be to find the best and most workable compromise possible. To mix the first-edition order with the 1888 edition text might seem arbitrary, but seems to this editor to combine the best of both worlds whilst having only minimal disadvantages. In the notes I record the date on which the poem was first published, and, where known, the date of composition.

A thornier question is whether Browning's revisions for the 1888 edition actually improved his text or not. On this opinion is divided, and the interested reader can do no better than seek out a variorum edition of the poems to decide for himself. Richard Altick (for instance) prints the first edition of *The Ring and the Book* rather than the revised 1888 edition on the grounds that Browning's revision often diminished the text: 'his concentration on minutiae frequently drifted into a profitless concern with trivia, and more than a few of his emendations actually left the text worse off.' To disagree with this judgement by any means except bald assertion would require a lengthy citation of examples, so I must limit myself to saying that I really do not think this is the case. There has long been a critical prejudice against Browning's later poetry (the work he published after 1869's *The Ring and the Book*), founded on the sense that Browning's poetical abilities declined in the last thirty years of his life. So far from concurring with this judgement, it seems to me that some of Browning's very finest work was the product of this later period, and that his ear for poetry was if anything more acute in the 1880s than it had been in the 1830s. This edition tries to go some way towards correcting this assessment by printing fairly generously from the later poetry, and the quality of this work should partly explain why this editor has decided to trust Browning's amending judgement as it shows itself in the 1888 edition.

The annotation has been of necessity fairly thorough, although it has been kept to a minimum. The more general headnotes to individual poems are not cued.

PAULINE (1833)

Plus ne suis ce que j'ai été,
Et ne le sçaurois jamais être.—Marot°

NON dubito, quin titulus libri nostri raritate sua quamplurimos alliciat ad legendum: inter quos nonnulli obliquæ opinionis, mente languidi, multi etiam maligni, et in ingenium nostrum ingrati accedent, qui temeraria sua ignorantia, vix conspecto titulo clamabunt: Nos vetita docere, hæresium semina jacere: piis auribus offendiculo, præclaris ingeniis scandalo esse: . . . . adeo conscientiæ suæ consulentes, ut nec Apollo, nec Musæ omnes, neque Angelus de cœlo me ab illorum execratione vindicare queant: quibus et ego nunc consulo, ne scripta nostra legant, nec intelligant, nec meminerint: nam noxia sunt, venenosa sunt: Acherontis ostium est in hoc libro, lapides loquitur, caveant, ne cerebrum illis excutiat. Vos autem, qui æqua mente ad legendum venitis, si tantam prudentiæ discretionem adhibueritis, quantam in melle legendo apes, jam securi legite. Puto namque vos et utilitatis haud parum et voluptatis plurimum accepturos. Quod si qua repereritis, quæ vobis non placeant, mittite illa, nec utimini. NAM ET EGO VOBIS ILLA NON PROBO, SED NARRO. Cætera tamen propterea non respuite. . . . . Ideo, si quid liberius dictum sit, ignoscite adolescentiæ nostræ, qui minor quam adolescens hoc opus composui.—*Hen. Corn. Agrippa, De Occult. Philosoph. in Præfat.*°

LONDON: *January* 1833.
V. A. XX.

[This introduction would appear less absurdly pretentious did it apply, as was intended, to a completed structure of which the poem was meant for only a beginning and remains a fragment.]

Pauline, mine own, bend o'er me—thy soft breast
Shall pant to mine—bend o'er me—thy sweet eyes,
And loosened hair and breathing lips, and arms
Drawing me to thee—these build up a screen
To shut me in with thee, and from all fear;
So that I might unlock the sleepless brood
Of fancies from my soul, their lurking-place,
Nor doubt that each would pass, ne'er to return
To one so watched, so loved and so secured.

But what can guard thee but thy naked love?   10
Ah dearest, whoso sucks a poisoned wound
Envenoms his own veins! Thou art so good,
So calm—if thou shouldst wear a brow less light
For some wild thought which, but for me, were kept
From out thy soul as from a sacred star!
Yet till I have unlocked them it were vain
To hope to sing; some woe would light on me;
Nature would point at one whose quivering lip
Was bathed in her enchantments, whose brow burned
Beneath the crown to which her secrets knelt,   20
Who learned the spell which can call up the dead,
And then departed smiling like a fiend
Who has deceived God,—if such one should seek
Again her altars and stand robed and crowned
Amid the faithful! Sad confession first,
Remorse and pardon and old claims renewed,
Ere I can be—as I shall be no more.

I had been spared this shame if I had sat
By thee for ever from the first, in place
Of my wild dreams of beauty and of good,   30
Or with them, as an earnest of their truth:
No thought nor hope having been shut from thee,
No vague wish unexplained, no wandering aim
Sent back to bind on fancy's wings and seek°
Some strange fair world where it might be a law;
But, doubting nothing, had been led by thee,
Thro' youth, and saved, as one at length awaked
Who has slept through a peril. Ah vain, vain!

Thou lovest me; the past is in its grave
Tho' its ghost haunts us; still this much is ours,   40
To cast away restraint, lest a worse thing
Wait for us in the dark. Thou lovest me;
And thou art to receive not love but faith,
For which thou wilt be mine, and smile and take
All shapes and shames, and veil without a fear
That form which music follows like a slave:
And I look to thee and I trust in thee,
As in a Northern night one looks alway
Unto the East for morn and spring and joy.

Thou seest then my aimless, hopeless state,   50
And, resting on some few old feelings won
Back by thy beauty, wouldst that I essay
The task which was to me what now thou art:
And why should I conceal one weakness more?

Thou wilt remember one warm morn when winter
Crept aged from the earth, and spring's first breath
Blew soft from the moist hills; the black-thorn boughs,
So dark in the bare wood, when glistening
In the sunshine were white with coming buds,
Like the bright side of a sorrow, and the banks   60
Had violets opening from sleep like eyes.
I walked with thee who knew'st not a deep shame
Lurked beneath smiles and careless words which sought
To hide it till they wandered and were mute,
As we stood listening on a sunny mound
To the wind murmuring in the damp copse,
Like heavy breathings of some hidden thing
Betrayed by sleep; until the feeling rushed
That I was low indeed, yet not so low
As to endure the calmness of thine eyes.   70
And so I told thee all, while the cool breast
I leaned on altered not its quiet beating:
And long ere words like a hurt bird's complaint
Bade me look up and be what I had been,
I felt despair could never live by thee:
Thou wilt remember. Thou art not more dear
Than song was once to me; and I ne'er sung
But as one entering bright halls where all
Will rise and shout for him: sure I must own
That I am fallen, having chosen gifts   80
Distinct from theirs—that I am sad and fain
Would give up all to be but where I was,
Not high as I had been if faithful found,
But low and weak yet full of hope, and sure
Of goodness as of life—that I would lose
All this gay mastery of mind, to sit
Once more with them, trusting in truth and love
And with an aim—not being what I am.

Oh Pauline, I am ruined who believed
That though my soul had floated from its sphere   90
Of wide dominion into the dim orb
Of self—that it was strong and free as ever!
It has conformed itself to that dim orb,
Reflecting all its shades and shapes, and now
Must stay where it alone can be adored.
I have felt this in dreams—in dreams in which
I seemed the fate from which I fled; I felt
A strange delight in causing my decay.
I was a fiend in darkness chained for ever
Within some ocean-cave; and ages rolled,   100
Till through the cleft rock, like a moonbeam, came
A white swan to remain with me; and ages
Rolled, yet I tired not of my first free joy
In gazing on the peace of its pure wings:
And then I said 'It is most fair to me,
Yet its soft wings must sure have suffered change
From the thick darkness, sure its eyes are dim,
Its silver pinions must be cramped and numbed
With sleeping ages here; it cannot leave me,
For it would seem, in light beside its kind,   110
Withered, tho' here to me most beautiful.'
And then I was a young witch whose blue eyes,°
As she stood naked by the river springs,
Drew down a god: I watched his radiant form°
Growing less radiant, and it gladdened me;
Till one morn, as he sat in the sunshine
Upon my knees, singing to me of heaven,
He turned to look at me, ere I could lose
The grin with which I viewed his perishing:
And he shrieked and departed and sat long   120
By his deserted throne, but sunk at last
Murmuring, as I kissed his lips and curled
Around him, 'I am still a god—to thee.'

Still I can lay my soul bare in its fall,
Since all the wandering and all the weakness
Will be a saddest comment on the song:
And if, that done, I can be young again,
I will give up all gained, as willingly

As one gives up a charm which shuts him out
From hope or part or care in human kind.   130
As life wanes, all its care and strife and toil
Seem strangely valueless, while the old trees
Which grew by our youth's home, the waving mass
Of climbing plants heavy with bloom and dew,
The morning swallows with their songs like words,
All these seem clear and only worth our thoughts:
So, aught connected with my early life,
My rude songs or my wild imaginings,
How I look on them—most distinct amid
The fever and the stir of after years!   140

I ne'er had ventured e'en to hope for this,
Had not the glow I felt at HIS award,°
Assured me all was not extinct within:
HIS whom all honour, whose renown springs up
Like sunlight which will visit all the world,
So that e'en they who sneered at him at first,
Come out to it, as some dark spider crawls
From his foul nets which some lit torch invades,
Yet spinning still new films for his retreat.
Thou didst smile, poet, but can we forgive?   150

Sun-treader, life and light be thine for ever!°
Thou art gone from us; years go by and spring
Gladdens and the young earth is beautiful,
Yet thy songs come not, other bards arise,
But none like thee: they stand, thy majesties,
Like mighty works which tell some spirit there
Hath sat regardless of neglect and scorn,
Till, its long task completed, it hath risen
And left us, never to return, and all
Rush in to peer and praise when all in vain.   160
The air seems bright with thy past presence yet,
But thou art still for me as thou hast been
When I have stood with thee as on a throne
With all thy dim creations gathered round
Like mountains, and I felt of mould like them,
And with them creatures of my own were mixed,
Like things half-lived, catching and giving life.
But thou art still for me who have adored

Tho' single, panting but to hear thy name
Which I believed a spell to me alone,   170
Scarce deeming thou wast as a star to men!
As one should worship long a sacred spring
Scarce worth a moth's flitting, which long grasses cross,
And one small tree embowers droopingly—
Joying to see some wandering insect won
To live in its few rushes, or some locust
To pasture on its boughs, or some wild bird
Stoop for its freshness from the trackless air:
And then should find it but the fountain-head,
Long lost, of some great river washing towns   180
And towers, and seeing old woods which will live
But by its banks untrod of human foot,
Which, when the great sun sinks, lie quivering
In light as some thing lieth half of life
Before God's foot, waiting a wondrous change;
Then girt with rocks which seek to turn or stay
Its course in vain, for it does ever spread
Like a sea's arm as it goes rolling on,
Being the pulse of some great country—so
Wast thou to me, and art thou to the world!   190
And I, perchance, half feel a strange regret
That I am not what I have been to thee:
Like a girl one has silently loved long
In her first loneliness in some retreat,
When, late emerged, all gaze and glow to view
Her fresh eyes and soft hair and lips which bloom
Like a mountain berry: doubtless it is sweet
To see her thus adored, but there have been
Moments when all the world was in our praise,
Sweeter than any pride of after hours.   200
Yet, sun-treader, all hail! From my heart's heart
I bid thee hail! E'en in my wildest dreams,
I proudly feel I would have thrown to dust
The wreaths of fame which seemed o'erhanging me,
To see thee for a moment as thou art.

And if thou livest, if thou lovest, spirit!
Remember me who set this final seal
To wandering thought—that one so pure as thou

Could never die. Remember me who flung
All honour from my soul, yet paused and said   210
'There is one spark of love remaining yet,
For I have nought in common with him, shapes
Which followed him avoid me, and foul forms
Seek me, which ne'er could fasten on his mind;
And though I feel how low I am to him,
Yet I aim not even to catch a tone
Of harmonies he called profusely up;
So, one gleam still remains, although the last.'
Remember me who praise thee e'en with tears,
For never more shall I walk calm with thee;   220
Thy sweet imaginings are as an air,
A melody some wondrous singer sings,
Which, though it haunt men oft in the still eve,
They dream not to essay; yet it no less
But more is honoured. I was thine in shame,
And now when all thy proud renown is out,
I am a watcher whose eyes have grown dim
With looking for some star which breaks on him
Altered and worn and weak and full of tears.

Autumn has come like spring returned to us,   230
Won from her girlishness; like one returned
A friend that was a lover, nor forgets
The first warm love, but full of sober thoughts
Of fading years; whose soft mouth quivers yet
With the old smile, but yet so changed and still!
And here am I the scoffer, who have probed
Life's vanity, won by a word again
Into my old life—by one little word
Of this sweet friend who lives in loving me,
Lives strangely on my thoughts and looks and words,   240
As fathoms down some nameless ocean thing
Its silent course of quietness and joy.
O dearest, if indeed I tell the past,
May'st thou forget it as a sad sick dream!
Or if it linger—my lost soul too soon
Sinks to itself and whispers we shall be
But closer linked, two creatures whom the earth
Bears singly, with strange feelings unrevealed

Save to each other; or two lonely things
Created by some power whose reign is done,   250
Having no part in God or his bright world.°
I am to sing whilst ebbing day dies soft,
As a lean scholar dies worn o'er his book,
And in the heaven stars steal out one by one
As hunted men steal to their mountain watch.
I must not think, lest this new impulse die
In which I trust; I have no confidence:
So, I will sing on fast as fancies come;
Rudely, the verse being as the mood it paints

I strip my mind bare, whose first elements   260
I shall unveil—not as they struggled forth
In infancy, nor as they now exist,
When I am grown above them and can rule
But in that middle stage when they were full
Yet ere I had disposed them to my will;
And then I shall show how these elements
Produced my present state, and what it is.

I am made up of an intensest life,
Of a most clear idea of consciousness
Of self, distinct from all its qualities,
From all affections, passions, feelings, powers;   270
And thus far it exists, if tracked, in all:
But linked, in me, to self-supremacy,
Existing as a centre to all things,
Most potent to create and rule and call
Upon all things to minister to it;
And to a principle of restlessness
Which would be all, have, see, know, taste, feel, all—
This is myself; and I should thus have been
Though gifted lower than the meanest soul.   280

And of my powers, one springs up to save
From utter death a soul with such desire
Confined to clay—of powers the only one
Which marks me—an imagination which
Has been a very angel, coming not
In fitful visions but beside me ever
And never failing me; so, though my mind

Forgets not, not a shred of life forgets,
Yet I can take a secret pride in calling
The dark past up to quell it regally.   290

A mind like this must dissipate itself,
But I have always had one lode-star; now,
As I look back, I see that I have halted
Or hastened as I looked towards that star—
A need, a trust, a yearning after God:
A feeling I have analysed but late,
But it existed, and was reconciled
With a neglect of all I deemed his laws,
Which yet, when seen in others, I abhorred.
I felt as one beloved, and so shut in   300
From fear: and thence I date my trust in signs
And omens, for I saw God everywhere;
And I can only lay it to the fruit
Of a sad after-time that I could doubt
Even his being—e'en the while I felt
His presence, never acted from myself,
Still trusted in a hand to lead me through
All danger; and this feeling ever fought
Against my weakest reason and resolve.

And I can love nothing—and this dull truth   310
Has come the last: but sense supplies a love
Encircling me and mingling with my life.

These make myself: I have long sought in vain°
To trace how they were formed by circumstance,
Yet ever found them mould my wildest youth
Where they alone displayed themselves, converted
All objects to their use: now see their course!

They came to me in my first dawn of life
Which passed alone with wisest ancient books
All halo-girt with fancies of my own;   320
And I myself went with the tale—a god
Wandering after beauty, or a giant
Standing vast in the sunset—an old hunter
Talking with gods, or a high-crested chief
Sailing with troops of friends to Tenedos.°
I tell you, nought has ever been so clear

As the place, the time, the fashion of those lives:
I had not seen a work of lofty art,
Nor woman's beauty nor sweet nature's face,
Yet, I say, never morn broke clear as those   330
On the dim clustered isles in the blue sea,
The deep groves and white temples and wet caves
And nothing ever will surprise me now—
Who stood beside the naked Swift-footed,
Who bound my forehead with Proserpine's hair.°

And strange it is that I who could so dream
Should e'er have stooped to aim at aught beneath—
Aught low or painful; but I never doubted:
So, as I grew, I rudely shaped my life
To my immediate wants; yet strong beneath   340
Was a vague sense of power though folded up—
A sense that, though those shades and times were past,
Their spirit dwelt in me, with them should rule.

Then came a pause, and long restraint chained down
My soul till it was changed. I lost myself,
And were it not that I so loathe that loss,
I could recall how first I learned to turn
My mind against itself; and the effects
In deeds for which remorse were vain as for
The wanderings of delirious dream; yet thence   350
Came cunning, envy, falsehood, all world's wrong
That spotted me: at length I cleansed my soul.
Yet long world's influence remained; and nought
But the still life I led, apart once more,
Which left me free to seek soul's old delights,
Could e'er have brought me thus far back to peace.

As peace returned, I sought out some pursuit;
And song rose, no new impulse but the one
With which all others best could be combined.
My life has not been that of those whose heaven   360
Was lampless save where poesy shone out;
But as a clime where glittering mountain-tops
And glancing sea and forests steeped in light
Give back reflected the far-flashing sun;
For music (which is earnest of a heaven,
Seeing we know emotions strange by it,

Not else to be revealed,) is like a voice,
A low voice calling fancy, as a friend,
To the green woods in the gay summer time:
And she fills all the way with dancing shapes   370
Which have made painters pale, and they go on
Till stars look at them and winds call to them
As they leave life's path for the twilight world
Where the dead gather. This was not at first,
For I scarce knew what I would do. I had
An impulse but no yearning—only sang.

And first I sang as I in dream have seen
Music wait on a lyrist for some thought,
Yet singing to herself until it came.
I turned to those old times and scenes where all   380
That's beautiful had birth for me, and made
Rude verses on them all; and then I paused—
I had done nothing, so I sought to know
What other minds achieved. No fear outbroke
As on the works of mighty bards I gazed,
In the first joy at finding my own thoughts
Recorded, my own fancies justified,
And their aspirings but my very own.
With them I first explored passion and mind,—
All to begin afresh! I rather sought   390
To rival what I wondered at than form
Creations of my own; if much was light
Lent by the others, much was yet my own.

I paused again: a change was coming—came:
I was no more a boy, the past was breaking
Before the future and like fever worked.
I thought on my new self, and all my powers
Burst out. I dreamed not of restraint, but gazed
On all things: schemes and systems went and came,
And I was proud (being vainest of the weak)   400
In wandering o'er thought's world to seek some one
To be my prize, as if you wandered o'er
The White Way for a star.°

                              And my choice fell
Not so much on a system as a man—°

On one, whom praise of mine shall not offend,
Who was as calm as beauty, being such
Unto mankind as thou to me, Pauline,—
Believing in them and devoting all
His soul's strength to their winning back to peace;
Who sent forth hopes and longings for their sake,   410
Clothed in all passion's melodies: such first
Caught me and set me, slave of a sweet task,
To disentangle, gather sense from song:
Since, song-inwoven, lurked there words which seemed
A key to a new world, the muttering
Of angels, something yet unguessed by man.
How my heart leapt as still I sought and found
Much there, I felt my own soul had conceived,
But there living and burning! Soon the orb
Of his conceptions dawned on me; its praise   420
Lives in the tongues of men, men's brows are high
When his name means a triumph and a pride,
So, my weak voice may well forbear to shame
What seemed decreed my fate: I threw myself
To meet it, I was vowed to liberty,
Men were to be as gods and earth as heaven,
And I—ah, what a life was mine to prove!
My whole soul rose to meet it. Now, Pauline,
I shall go mad, if I recall that time!

  Oh let me look back ere I leave for ever   430
The time which was an hour one fondly waits
For a fair girl that comes a withered hag!
And I was lonely, far from woods and fields,
And amid dullest sights, who should be loose
As a stag; yet I was full of bliss, who lived
With Plato and who had the key to life;°
And I had dimly shaped my first attempt,
And many a thought did I build up on thought,
As the wild bee hangs cell to cell; in vain,
For I must still advance, no rest for mind.   440

'Twas in my plan to look on real life,
The life all new to me; my theories
Were firm, so them I left, to look and learn
Mankind, its cares, hopes, fears, its woes and joys;

And, as I pondered on their ways, I sought
How best life's end might be attained—an end
Comprising every joy. I deeply mused.

And suddenly without heart-wreck I awoke
As from a dream: I said ''Twas beautiful,
Yet but a dream, and so adieu to it!'   450
As some world-wanderer sees in a far meadow
Strange towers and high-walled gardens thick with trees,
Where song takes shelter and delicious mirth
From laughing fairy creatures peeping over,
And on the morrow when he comes to lie
For ever 'neath those garden-trees fruit-flushed
Sung round by fairies, all his search is vain.
First went my hopes of perfecting mankind,
Next—faith in them, and then in freedom's self
And virtue's self, then my own motives, ends   460
And aims and loves, and human love went last.
I felt this no decay, because new powers
Rose as old feelings left—wit, mockery,
Light-heartedness; for I had oft been sad,
Mistrusting my resolves, but now I cast
Hope joyously away: I laughed and said
'No more of this!' I must not think: at length
I looked again to see if all went well.

My powers were greater: as some temple seemed
My soul, where nought is changed and incense rolls   470
Around the altar, only God is gone
And some dark spirit sitteth in his seat.
So, I passed through the temple and to me
Knelt troops of shadows, and they cried 'Hail, king!
We serve thee now and thou shalt serve no more!
Call on us, prove us, let us worship thee!'
And I said 'Are ye strong? Let fancy bear me
Far from the past!' And I was borne away,
As Arab birds float sleeping in the wind,°
O'er deserts, towers and forests, I being calm.   480
And I said 'I have nursed up energies,
They will prey on me.' And a band knelt low
And cried 'Lord, we are here and we will make
Safe way for thee in thine appointed life!

But look on us!' And I said 'Ye will worship
Me; should my heart not worship too?' They shouted
'Thyself, thou art our king!' So, I stood there
Smiling—oh, vanity of vanities!
For buoyant and rejoicing was the spirit
With which I looked out how to end my course;   490
I felt once more myself, my powers—all mine;
I knew while youth and health so lifted me
That, spite of all life's nothingness, no grief
Came nigh me, I must ever be light-hearted;
And that this knowledge was the only veil
Betwixt joy and despair: so, if age came,
I should be left—a wreck linked to a soul
Yet fluttering, or mind-broken and aware°
Of my decay. So a long summer morn
Found me; and ere noon came, I had resolved   500
No age should come on me ere youth was spent,
For I would wear myself out, like that morn
Which wasted not a sunbeam; every hour
I would make mine, and die.

                              And thus I sought
To chain my spirit down which erst I freed°
For flights to fame: I said 'The troubled life
Of genius, seen so gay when working forth
Some trusted end, grows sad when all proves vain—
How sad when men have parted with truth's peace
For falsest fancy's sake, which waited first   510
As an obedient spirit when delight
Came without fancy's call: but alters soon,
Comes darkened, seldom, hastens to depart,
Leaving a heavy darkness and warm tears.
But I shall never lose her; she will live
Dearer for such seclusion. I but catch
A hue, a glance of what I sing: so, pain
Is linked with pleasure, for I ne'er may tell
Half the bright sights which dazzle me; but now
Mine shall be all the radiance: let them fade   520
Untold—others shall rise as fair, as fast!
And when all's done, the few dim gleams transferred,'—
(For a new thought sprang up how well it were,

Discarding shadowy hope, to weave such lays
As straight encircle men with praise and love,
So, I should not die utterly,—should bring
One branch from the gold forest, like the knight
Of old tales, witnessing I had been there)—
'And when all's done, how vain seems e'en success—
The vaunted influence poets have o'er men! 530
'Tis a fine thing that one weak as myself
Should sit in his lone room, knowing the words
He utters in his solitude shall move
Men like a swift wind—that tho' dead and gone,
New eyes shall glisten when his beauteous dreams
Of love come true in happier frames than his.
Ay, the still night brings thoughts like these, but morn
Comes and the mockery again laughs out
At hollow praises, smiles allied to sneers;
And my soul's idol ever whispers me 540
To dwell with him and his unhonoured song:
And I foreknow my spirit, that would press
First in the struggle, fail again to make
All bow enslaved, and I again should sink.

'And then know that this curse will come on us,
To see our idols perish; we may wither,
No marvel, we are clay, but our low fate
Should not extend to those whom trustingly
We sent before into time's yawning gulf
To face what dread may lurk in darkness there. 550
To find the painter's glory pass, and feel
Music can move us not as once, or, worst,
To weep decaying wits ere the frail body
Decays! Nought makes me trust some love is true,
But the delight of the contented lowness
With which I gaze on him I keep for ever
Above me; I to rise and rival him?
Feed his fame rather from my heart's best blood,
Wither unseen that he may flourish still.'

Pauline, my soul's friend, thou dost pity yet 560
How this mood swayed me when that soul found thine,
When I had set myself to live this life,
Defying all past glory. Ere thou camest

I seemed defiant, sweet, for old delights
Had flocked like birds again; music, my life,
Nourished me more than ever; then the lore
Loved for itself and all it shows—that king
Treading the purple calmly to his death,
While round him, like the clouds of eve, all dusk,
The giant shades of fate, silently flitting,   570
Pile the dim outline of the coming doom;°
And him sitting alone in blood while friends°
Are hunting far in the sunshine; and the boy°
With his white breast and brow and clustering curls
Streaked with his mother's blood, but striving hard
To tell his story ere his reason goes.
And when I loved thee as love seemed so oft,
Thou lovedst me indeed: I wondering searched
My heart to find some feeling like such love,
Believing I was still much I had been.   580
Too soon I found all faith had gone from me,
And the late glow of life, like change on clouds,
Proved not the morn-blush widening into day,
But eve faint-coloured by the dying sun
While darkness hastens quickly. I will tell
My state as though 'twere none of mine—despair
Cannot come near us—this it is, my state.

Souls alter not, and mine must still advance;
Strange that I knew not, when I flung away
My youth's chief aims, their loss might lead to loss   590
Of what few I retained, and no resource
Be left me: for behold how changed is all!
I cannot chain my soul: it will not rest
In its clay prison, this most narrow sphere:
It has strange impulse, tendency, desire,
Which nowise I account for nor explain,
But cannot stifle, being bound to trust
All feelings equally, to hear all sides:
How can my life indulge them? yet they live,
Referring to some state of life unknown.   600

My selfishness is satiated not,
It wears me like a flame; my hunger for
All pleasure, howsoe'er minute, grows pain;

I envy—how I envy him whose soul
Turns its whole energies to some one end,
To elevate an aim, pursue success
However mean! So, my still baffled hope
Seeks out abstractions; I would have one joy,
But one in life, so it were wholly mine,
One rapture all my soul could fill: and this   610
Wild feeling places me in dream afar
In some vast country where the eye can see
No end to the far hills and dales bestrewn
With shining towers and towns, till I grow mad
Well-nigh, to know not one abode but holds
Some pleasure, while my soul could grasp the world,
But must remain this vile form's slave. I look
With hope to age at last, which quenching much,
May let me concentrate what sparks it spares.

This restlessness of passion meets in me   620
A craving after knowledge: the sole proof
Of yet commanding will is in that power
Repressed; for I beheld it in its dawn,
The sleepless harpy with just-budding wings,°
And I considered whether to forego
All happy ignorant hopes and fears, to live,
Finding a recompense in its wild eyes.
And when I found that I should perish so,
I bade its wild eyes close from me for ever,
And I am left alone with old delights;   630
See! it lies in me a chained thing, still prompt
To serve me if I loose its slightest bond:
I cannot but be proud of my bright slave.
How should this earth's life prove my only sphere?
Can I so narrow sense but that in life
Soul still exceeds it? In their elements
My love outsoars my reason; but since love
Perforce receives its object from this earth
While reason wanders chainless, the few truths
Caught from its wanderings have sufficed to quell   640
Love chained below; then what were love, set free,
Which, with the object it demands, would pass
Reason companioning the seraphim?°

No, what I feel may pass all human love
Yet fall far short of what my love should be.
And yet I seem more warped in this than aught,
Myself stands out more hideously: of old
I could forget myself in friendship, fame,
Liberty, nay, in love of mightier souls;°
But I begin to know what thing hate is—   650
To sicken and to quiver and grow white—
And I myself have furnished its first prey.
Hate of the weak and ever-wavering will,
The selfishness, the still-decaying frame...
But I must never grieve whom wing can waft
Far from such thoughts—as now. Andromeda!°
And she is with me: years roll, I shall change,
But change can touch her not—so beautiful
With her fixed eyes, earnest and still, and hair
Lifted and spread by the salt-sweeping breeze,   660
And one red beam, all the storm leaves in heaven,
Resting upon her eyes and hair, such hair,
As she awaits the snake on the wet beach
By the dark rock and the white wave just breaking
At her feet; quite naked and alone; a thing
I doubt not, nor fear for, secure some god
To save will come in thunder from the stars.
Let it pass! Soul requires another change.
I will be gifted with a wondrous mind,
Yet sunk by error to men's sympathy,   670
And in the wane of life, yet only so
As to call up their fears; and there shall come
A time requiring youth's best energies;
And lo, I fling age, sorrow, sickness off,
And rise triumphant, triumph through decay.°

And thus it is that I supply the chasm
'Twixt what I am and all I fain would be:
But then to know nothing, to hope for nothing,
To seize on life's dull joys from a strange fear
Lest, losing them, all's lost and nought remains!°   680

There's some vile juggle with my reason here;
I feel I but explain to my own loss
These impulses: they live no less the same.

Liberty! what though I despair? my blood
Rose never at a slave's name proud as now.
Oh sympathies, obscured by sophistries!—
Why else have I sought refuge in myself,
But from the woes I saw and could not stay?
Love! is not this to love thee, my Pauline?
I cherish prejudice, lest I be left°   690
Utterly loveless? witness my belief
In poets, though sad change has come there too;
No more I leave myself to follow them—
Unconsciously I measure me by them—
Let me forget it: and I cherish most
My love of England—how her name, a word
Of hers in a strange tongue makes my heart beat!

Pauline, could I but break the spell! Not now—
All's fever—but when calm shall come again,
I am prepared: I have made life my own.   700
I would not be content with all the change
One frame should feel, but I have gone in thought
Thro' all conjuncture, I have lived all life
When it is most alive, where strangest fate
New-shapes it past surmise—the throes of men
Bit by some curse or in the grasps of doom
Half-visible and still-increasing round,
Or crowning their wide being's general aim.

These are wild fancies, but I feel, sweet friend,
As one breathing his weakness to the ear   710
Of pitying angel—dear as a winter flower,
A slight flower growing alone, and offering
Its frail cup of three leaves to the cold sun,
Yet joyous and confiding like the triumph
Of a child: and why am I not worthy thee?
I can live all the life of plants, and gaze
Drowsily on the bees that flit and play,
Or bare my breast for sunbeams which will kill,
Or open in the night of sounds, to look
For the dim stars; I can mount with the bird   720
Leaping airily his pyramid of leaves
And twisted boughs of some tall mountain tree,
Or rise cheerfully springing to the heavens;

Or like a fish breathe deep the morning air
In the misty sun-warm water; or with flower
And tree can smile in light at the sinking sun
Just as the storm comes, as a girl would look
On a departing lover—most serene.

Pauline, come with me, see how I could build
A home for us, out of the world, in thought!   730
I am uplifted: fly with me, Pauline!

Night, and one single ridge of narrow path
Between the sullen river and the woods
Waving and muttering, for the moonless night
Has shaped them into images of life,
Like the uprising of the giant-ghosts,
Looking on earth to know how their sons fare:
Thou art so close by me, the roughest swell
Of wind in the tree-tops hides not the panting
Of thy soft breasts. No, we will pass to morning—   740
Morning, the rocks and valleys and old woods.
How the sun brightens in the mist, and here,
Half in the air, like creatures of the place,
Trusting the element, living on high boughs
That swing in the wind—look at the silver spray
Flung from the foam-sheet of the cataract
Amid the broken rocks! Shall we stay here
With the wild hawks? No, ere the hot noon come,
Dive we down—safe! See this our new retreat
Walled in with a sloped mound of matted shrubs,   750
Dark, tangled, old and green, still sloping down
To a small pool whose waters lie asleep
Amid the trailing boughs turned water-plants:
And tall trees overarch to keep us in,
Breaking the sunbeams into emerald shafts,
And in the dreamy water one small group
Of two or three strange trees are got together
Wondering at all around, as strange beasts herd
Together far from their own land: all wildness,
No turf nor moss, for boughs and plants pave all,   760
And tongues of bank go shelving in the lymph,
Where the pale-throated snake reclines his head,
And old grey stones lie making eddies there,

The wild-mice cross them dry-shod. Deeper in!
Shut thy soft eyes—now look—still deeper in!
This is the very heart of the woods all round
Mountain-like heaped above us; yet even here
One pond of water gleams; far off the river
Sweeps like a sea, barred out from land; but one—
One thin clear sheet has overleaped and wound   770
Into this silent depth, which gained, it lies
Still, as but let by sufferance; the trees bend
O'er it as wild men watch a sleeping girl,
And through their roots long creeping plants out-stretch
Their twined hair, steeped and sparkling; farther on,
Tall rushes and thick flag-knots have combined
To narrow it; so, at length, a silver thread,
It winds, all noiselessly through the deep wood
Till thro' a cleft-way, thro' the moss and stone,
It joins its parent-river with a shout.   780

Up for the glowing day, leave the old woods!
See, they part, like a ruined arch: the sky!
Nothing but sky appears, so close the roots
And grass of the hill-top level with the air—
Blue sunny air, where a great cloud floats laden
With light, like a dead whale that white birds pick,
Floating away in the sun in some north sea.
Air, air, fresh life-blood, thin and searching air,
The clear, dear breath of God that loveth us,
Where small birds reel and winds take their delight!   790
Water is beautiful, but not like air:
See, where the solid azure waters lie
Made as of thickened air, and down below,
The fern-ranks like a forest spread themselves
As though each pore could feel the element;
Where the quick glancing serpent winds his way,
Float with me there, Pauline!—but not like air.

Down the hill! Stop—a clump of trees, see, set
On a heap of rock, which look o'er the far plain:
So, envious climbing shrubs would mount to rest   800
And peer from their spread boughs; wide they wave, looking
At the muleteers who whistle on their way,
To the merry chime of morning bells, past all

The little smoking cots, mid fields and banks
And copses bright in the sun. My spirit wanders:
Hedgerows for me—those living hedgerows where
The bushes close and clasp above and keep
Thought in—I am concentrated—I feel;
But my soul saddens when it looks beyond:
I cannot be immortal, taste all joy.   810

O God, where do they tend—these struggling aims?*
What would I have? What is this 'sleep' which seems
To bound all? can there be a 'waking' point
Of crowning life? The soul would never rule;
It would be first in all things, it would have
Its utmost pleasure filled, but, that complete,
Commanding, for commanding, sickens it.
The last point I can trace is—rest beneath
Some better essence than itself, in weakness;
This is 'myself,' not what I think should be: 820
And what is that I hunger for but God?

*Je crains bien que mon pauvre ami ne soit pas toujours parfaitement compris dans
ce qui reste à lire de cet étrange fragment, mais il est moins propre que tout autre à
éclaircir ce qui de sa nature ne peut jamais être que songe et confusion. D'ailleurs je ne
sais trop si en cherchant à mieux co-ordonner certaines parties l'on ne courrait pas le
risque de nuire au seul mérite auquel une production si singulière peut prétendre, celui
de donner une idée assez précise du genre qu'elle n'a fait qu'ébaucher. Ce début sans
prétention, ce remuement des passions qui va d'abord en accroissant et puis s'apaise par
degrés, ces élans de l'âme, ce retour soudain sur soi-même, et par-dessus tout, la
tournure d'esprit tout particulière de mon ami, rendent les changemens presque impos-
sibles. Les raisons qu'il fait valoir ailleurs, et d'autres encore plus puissantes, ont fait
trouver grâce à mes yeux pour cet écrit qu'autrement je lui eusse conseillé de jeter au
feu. Je n'en crois pas moins au grand principe de toute composition—à ce principe de
Shakespeare, de Rafaelle, de Beethoven, d'où il suit que la concentration des idées est
due bien plus à leur conception qu'à leur mise en exécution: j'ai tout lieu de craindre
que la première de ces qualités ne soit encore étrangère à mon ami, et je doute fort
qu'un redoublement de travail lui fasse acquérir la seconde. Le mieux serait de brûler
ceci; mais que faire?

Je crois que dans ce qui suit il fait allusion à un certain examen qu'il fit autrefois de
l'âme, ou plutôt de son âme, pour découvrir la suite des objets auxquels il lui serait
possible d'atteindre, et dont chacun une fois obtenu devait former une espèce de plateau
d'où l'on pouvait apercevoir d'autres buts, d'autres projets, d'autres jouissances qui, à
leur tour, devaient être surmontés. Il en résultait que l'oubli et le sommeil devaient tout
terminer. Cette idée, que je ne saisis pas parfaitement, lui est peut-être aussi inintelli-
gible qu'à moi.

                                                        PAULINE.°

My God, my God, let me for once look on thee
As though nought else existed, we alone!
And as creation crumbles, my soul's spark
Expands till I can say,—Even from myself
I need thee and I feel thee and I love thee.
I do not plead my rapture in thy works
For love of thee, nor that I feel as one
Who cannot die: but there is that in me
Which turns to thee, which loves or which should love.   830

Why have I girt myself with this hell-dress?
Why have I laboured to put out my life?
Is it not in my nature to adore,
And e'en for all my reason do I not
Feel him, and thank him, and pray to him—now?
Can I forego the trust that he loves me?
Do I not feel a love which only ONE ...
O thou pale form, so dimly seen, deep-eyed!
I have denied thee calmly—do I not
Pant when I read of thy consummate power,   840
And burn to see thy calm pure truths out-flash
The brightest gleams of earth's philosophy?
Do I not shake to hear aught question thee?
If I am erring save me, madden me,
Take from me powers and pleasures, let me die
Ages, so I see thee! I am knit round
As with a charm by sin and lust and pride,
Yet though my wandering dreams have seen all shapes
Of strange delight, oft have I stood by thee—
Have I been keeping lonely watch with thee   850
In the damp night by weeping Olivet,°
Or leaning on thy bosom, proudly less,
Or dying with thee on the lonely cross,
Or witnessing thine outburst from the tomb.

A mortal, sin's familiar friend, doth here
Avow that he will give all earth's reward,
But to believe and humbly teach the faith,
In suffering and poverty and shame,
Only believing he is not unloved.

And now, my Pauline, I am thine for ever!°   860
I feel the spirit which has buoyed me up
Desert me, and old shades are gathering fast;
Yet while the last light waits, I would say much,
This chiefly, it is gain that I have said
Somewhat of love I ever felt for thee
But seldom told; our hearts so beat together
That speech seemed mockery; but when dark hours come,
And joy departs, and thou, sweet, deem'st it strange
A sorrow moves me, thou canst not remove,
Look on this lay I dedicate to thee,   870
Which through thee I began, which thus I end,
Collecting the last gleams to strive to tell
How I am thine, and more than ever now
That I sink fast: yet though I deeplier sink,
No less song proves one word has brought me bliss,
Another still may win bliss surely back.
Thou knowest, dear, I could not think all calm,
For fancies followed thought and bore me off,
And left all indistinct; ere one was caught
Another glanced; so, dazzled by my wealth,   880
I knew not which to leave nor which to choose,
For all so floated, nought was fixed and firm.
And then thou said'st a perfect bard was one
Who chronicled the stages of all life,
And so thou bad'st me shadow this first stage.
'Tis done, and even now I recognize
The shift, the change from last to past—discern
Faintly how life is truth and truth is good.
And why thou must be mine is, that e'en now
In the dim hush of night, that I have done,   890
Despite the sad forebodings, love looks through—
Whispers,—E'en at the last I have her still,
With her delicious eyes as clear as heaven
When rain in a quick shower has beat down mist,
And clouds float white above like broods of swans.
How the blood lies upon her cheek, outspread
As thinned by kisses! only in her lips
It wells and pulses like a living thing,
And her neck looks like marble misted o'er
With love-breath,—a Pauline from heights above,   900

Stooping beneath me, looking up—one look
As I might kill her and be loved the more.

So, love me—me, Pauline, and nought but me,
Never leave loving! Words are wild and weak,
Believe them not, Pauline! I stained myself
But to behold thee purer by my side,
To show thou art my breath, my life, a last
Resource, an extreme want: never believe
Aught better could so look on thee; nor seek
Again the world of good thoughts left for mine!   910
There were bright troops of undiscovered suns,
Each equal in their radiant course; there were
Clusters of far fair isles which ocean kept
For his own joy, and his waves broke on them
Without a choice; and there was a dim crowd
Of visions, each a part of some grand whole:
And one star left his peers and came with peace
Upon a storm, and all eyes pined for him;
And one isle harboured a sea-beaten ship,
And the crew wandered in its bowers and plucked   920
Its fruits and gave up all their hopes of home;°
And one dream came to a pale poet's sleep,
And he said, 'I am singled out by God,
No sin must touch me.' Words are wild and weak,
But what they would express is,—Leave me not,
Still sit by me with beating breast and hair
Loosened, be watching earnest by my side,
Turning my books or kissing me when I
Look up—like summer wind! Be still to me
A help to music's mystery which mind fails   930
To fathom, its solution, no mere clue!
O reason's pedantry, life's rule prescribed!
I hopeless, I the loveless, hope and love.
Wiser and better, know me now, not when
You loved me as I was. Smile not! I have
Much yet to dawn on you, to gladden you.
No more of the past! I'll look within no more.
I have too trusted my own lawless wants,
Too trusted my vain self, vague intuition—
Draining soul's wine alone in the still night,   940

And seeing how, as gathering films arose,
As by an inspiration life seemed bare
And grinning in its vanity, while ends
Foul to be dreamed of, smiled at me as fixed
And fair, while others changed from fair to foul
As a young witch turns an old hag at night.
No more of this! We will go hand in hand,
I with thee, even as a child—love's slave,
Looking no farther than his liege commands.

And thou hast chosen where this life shall be: 950
The land which gave me thee shall be our home,°
Where nature lies all wild amid her lakes
And snow-swathed mountains and vast pines begirt
With ropes of snow—where nature lies all bare,
Suffering none to view her but a race
Or stinted or deformed, like the mute dwarfs
Which wait upon a naked Indian queen.
And there (the time being when the heavens are thick
With storm) I'll sit with thee while thou dost sing
Thy native songs, gay as a desert bird   960
Which crieth as it flies for perfect joy,
Or telling me old stories of dead knights;
Or I will read great lays to thee—how she,
The fair pale sister, went to her chill grave°
With power to love and to be loved and live:
Or we will go together, like twin gods
Of the infernal world, with scented lamp
Over the dead, to call and to awake,
Over the unshaped images which lie
Within my mind's cave: only leaving all,   970
That tells of the past doubt. So, when spring comes
With sunshine back again like an old smile,
And the fresh waters and awakened birds
And budding woods await us, I shall be
Prepared, and we will question life once more,°
Till its old sense shall come renewed by change,
Like some clear thought which harsh words veiled before;
Feeling God loves us, and that all which errs
Is but a dream which death will dissipate.
And then what need of longer exile? Seek   980

My England, and, again there, calm approach
All I once fled from, calmly look on those
The works of my past weakness, as one views
Some scene where danger met him long before.
Ah that such pleasant life should be but dreamed!

But whate'er come of it, and though it fade,
And though ere the cold morning all be gone,
As it may be;—tho' music wait to wile,
And strange eyes and bright wine lure, laugh like sin
Which steals back softly on a soul half saved,   990
And I the first deny, decry, despise,
With this avowal, these intents so fair,—
Still be it all my own, this moment's pride!
No less I make an end in perfect joy.
E'en in my brightest time, a lurking fear
Possessed me: I well knew my weak resolves,
I felt the witchery that makes mind sleep
Over its treasure, as one half afraid
To make his riches definite: but now
These feelings shall not utterly be lost,   1000
I shall not know again that nameless care
Lest, leaving all undone in youth, some new
And undreamed end reveal itself too late:
For this song shall remain to tell for ever
That when I lost all hope of such a change,
Suddenly beauty rose on me again.
No less I make an end in perfect joy,
For I, who thus again was visited,
Shall doubt not many another bliss awaits,
And, though this weak soul sink and darkness whelm,   1010
Some little word shall light it, raise aloft,
To where I clearlier see and better love,
As I again go o'er the tracts of thought
Like one who has a right, and I shall live
With poets, calmer, purer still each time,
And beauteous shapes will come for me to seize,
And unknown secrets will be trusted me
Which were denied the waverer once; but now
I shall be priest and prophet as of old.

Sun-treader, I believe in God and truth   1020
And love; and as one just escaped from death
Would bind himself in bands of friends to feel
He lives indeed, so, I would lean on thee!
Thou must be ever with me, most in gloom
If such must come, but chiefly when I die,
For I seem, dying, as one going in the dark
To fight a giant: but live thou for ever,
And be to all what thou hast been to me!
All in whom this wakes pleasant thoughts of me
Know my last state is happy, free from doubt   1030
Or touch of fear. Love me and wish me well.

RICHMOND:
October 22, 1832.

from PARACELSUS (1835)

Part V

Paracelsus attains

SCENE.—*Salzburg; a cell in the Hospital of St Sebastian.*
1541.

Festus, Paracelsus.

Festus. No change! The weary night is well-nigh spent,
The lamp burns low, and through the casement-bars
Grey morning glimmers feebly: yet no change!
Another night, and still no sigh has stirred
That fallen discoloured mouth, no pang relit
Those fixed eyes, quenched by the decaying body,
Like torch-flame choked in dust. While all beside
Was breaking, to the last they held out bright,
As a stronghold where life intrenched itself;
But they are dead now—very blind and dead: 10
He will drowse into death without a groan.

My Aureole—my forgotten, ruined Aureole!
The days are gone, are gone! How grand thou wast!
And now not one of those who struck thee down—
Poor glorious spirit—concerns him even to stay
And satisfy himself his little hand
Could turn God's image to a livid thing.

Another night, and yet no change! 'Tis much
That I should sit by him, and bathe his brow,
And chafe his hands; 'tis much: but he will sure   20
Know me, and look on me, and speak to me
Once more—but only once! His hollow cheek
Looked all night long as though a creeping laugh
At his own state were just about to break
From the dying man: my brain swam, my throat swelled,

And yet I could not turn away. In truth,
They told me how, when first brought here, he seemed
Resolved to live, to lose no faculty;
Thus striving to keep up his shattered strength,
Until they bore him to this stifling cell: 30
When straight his features fell, an hour made white
The flushed face, and relaxed the quivering limb,
Only the eye remained intense awhile
As though it recognized the tomb-like place,
And then he lay as here he lies.
                                        Ay, here!
Here is earth's noblest, nobly garlanded—
Her bravest champion with his well-won prize—
Her best achievement, her sublime amends
For countless generations fleeting fast
And followed by no trace;—the creature-god   40
She instances when angels would dispute
The title of her brood to rank with them.
Angels, this is our angel! Those bright forms
We clothe with purple, crown and call to thrones,
Are human, but not his; those are but men
Whom other men press round and kneel before;
Those palaces are dwelt in by mankind;
Higher provision is for him you seek
Amid our pomps and glories: see it here!
Behold earth's paragon! Now, raise thee, clay!   50

God! Thou art love! I build my faith on that
Even as I watch beside thy tortured child
Unconscious whose hot tears fall fast by him,
So doth thy right hand guide us through the world
Wherein we stumble. God! what shall we say?
How has he sinned? How else should he have done?
Surely he sought thy praise—thy praise, for all
He might be busied by the task so much
As half forget awhile its proper end.
Dost thou well, Lord? Thou canst not but prefer   60
That I should range myself upon his side—
How could he stop at every step to set
Thy glory forth? Hadst thou but granted him
Success, thy honour would have crowned success,

A halo round a star. Or, say he erred,—
Save him, dear God; it will be like thee: bathe him
In light and life! Thou art not made like us;
We should be wroth in such a case; but thou
Forgivest—so, forgive these passionate thoughts
Which come unsought and will not pass away!   70
I know thee, who hast kept my path, and made
Light for me in the darkness, tempering sorrow
So that it reached me like a solemn joy;
It were too strange that I should doubt thy love.
But what am I? Thou madest him and knowest
How he was fashioned. I could never err
That way: the quiet place beside thy feet,
Reserved for me, was ever in my thoughts:
But he—thou shouldst have favoured him as well!

Ah! he wakes! Aureole, I am here! 'tis Festus!   80
I cast away all wishes save one wish—
Let him but know me, only speak to me!
He mutters; louder and louder; any other
Than I, with brain less laden, could collect
What he pours forth. Dear Aureole, do but look!
Is it talking or singing, this he utters fast?
Misery that he should fix me with his eye,
Quick talking to some other all the while!
If he would husband this wild vehemence
Which frustrates its intent!—I heard, I know   90
I heard my name amid those rapid words.
Oh, he will know me yet! Could I divert
This current, lead it somehow gently back
Into the channels of the past!—His eye
Brighter than ever! It must recognize me!

I am Erasmus: I am here to pray°
That Paracelsus use his skill for me.
The schools of Paris and of Padua send
These questions for your learning to resolve.
We are your students, noble master: leave   100
This wretched cell, what business have you here?
Our class awaits you; come to us once more!
(O agony! the utmost I can do
Touches him not; how else arrest his ear?)

I am commissioned . . . I shall craze like him.
Better be mute and see what God shall send.
    Paracelsus. Stay, stay with me!
    Festus.   I will; I am come here
To stay with you—Festus, you loved of old;
Festus, you know, you must know!
    Paracelsus.   Festus! Where's
Aprile, then? Has he not chanted softly   110
The melodies I heard all night? I could not
Get to him for a cold hand on my breast,
But I made out his music well enough,
O well enough! If they have filled him full
With magical music, as they freight a star
With light, and have remitted all his sin,
They will forgive me too, I too shall know!
    Festus. Festus, your Festus!
    Paracelsus.   Ask him if Aprile
Knows as he Loves—if I shall Love and Know?
I try; but that cold hand, like lead—so cold!   120
    Festus. My hand, see!
    Paracelsus.   Ah, the curse, Aprile, Aprile!
We get so near—so very, very near!
'Tis an old tale: Jove strikes the Titans down,°
Not when they set about their mountain-piling
But when another rock would crown the work.
And Phaeton—doubtless his first radiant plunge°
Astonished mortals, though the gods were calm,
And Jove prepared his thunder: all old tales!
    Festus. And what are these to you?
    Paracelsus.   Ay, fiends must laugh
So cruelly, so well! most like I never   130
Could tread a single pleasure underfoot,
But they were grinning by my side, were chuckling
To see me toil and drop away by flakes!
Hell-spawn! I am glad, most glad, that thus I fail!
Your cunning has o'ershot its aim. One year,
One month, perhaps, and I had served your turn!
You should have curbed your spite awhile. But now,
Who will believe 'twas you that held me back?
Listen: there's shame and hissing and contempt,
And none but laughs who names me, none but spits   140

Measureless scorn upon me, me alone,
The quack, the cheat, the liar,—all on me!
And thus your famous plan to sink mankind
In silence and despair, by teaching them
One of their race had probed the inmost truth,
Had done all man could do, yet failed no less—
Your wise plan proves abortive. Men despair?
Ha, ha! why, they are hooting the empiric,°
The ignorant and incapable fool who rushed
Madly upon a work beyond his wits;   150
Nor doubt they but the simplest of themselves
Could bring the matter to triumphant issue.
So, pick and choose among them all, accursed!
Try now, persuade some other to slave for you,
To ruin body and soul to work your ends!
No, no; I am the first and last, I think.
    Festus. Dear friend, who are accursed? who has done...
    Paracelsus. What have I done? Fiends dare ask that? or you,
Brave men? Oh, you can chime in boldly, backed
By the others! What had you to do, sage peers?   160
Here stand my rivals; Latin, Arab, Jew,
Greek, join dead hands against me: all I ask
Is, that the world enrol my name with theirs,
And even this poor privilege, it seems,
They range themselves, prepared to disallow.
Only observe! why, fiends may learn from them!
How they talk calmly of my throes, my fierce
Aspirings, terrible watchings, each one claiming
Its price of blood and brain; how they dissect
And sneeringly disparage the few truths   170
Got at a life's cost; they too hanging the while
About my neck, their lies misleading me
And their dead names browbeating me! Grey crew,
Yet steeped in fresh malevolence from hell,
Is there a reason for your hate? My truths
Have shaken a little the palm about each prince?
Just think, Aprile, all these leering dotards
Were bent on nothing less than to be crowned
As we! That yellow blear-eyed wretch in chief
To whom the rest cringe low with feigned respect,   180
Galen of Pergamos and hell—nay speak°

The tale, old man! We met there face to face:
I said the crown should fall from thee. Once more
We meet as in that ghastly vestibule:
Look to my brow! Have I redeemed my pledge?
   Festus. Peace, peace; ah, see!
   Paracelsus.   Oh, emptiness of fame!
Oh Persic Zoroaster, lord of stars!°
—Who said these old renowns, dead long ago,
Could make me overlook the living world
To gaze through gloom at where they stood, indeed,   190
But stand no longer? What a warm light life
After the shade! In truth, my delicate witch,
My serpent-queen, you did but well to hide
The juggles I had else detected. Fire
May well run harmless o'er a breast like yours!
The cave was not so darkened by the smoke
But that your white limbs dazzled me: oh, white,
And panting as they twinkled, wildly dancing!
I cared not for your passionate gestures then,
But now I have forgotten the charm of charms,   200
The foolish knowledge which I came to seek,
While I remember that quaint dance; and thus
I am come back, not for those mummeries,
But to love you, and to kiss your little feet
Soft as an ermine's winter coat!
   Festus.   A light
Will struggle through these thronging words at last.
As in the angry and tumultuous West
A soft star trembles through the drifting clouds.
These are the strivings of a spirit which hates
So sad a vault should coop it, and calls up   210
The past to stand between it and its fate.
Were he at Einsiedeln—or Michal here!
   Paracelsus. Cruel! I seek her now—I kneel—I shriek—
I clasp her vesture—but she fades, still fades;
And she is gone; sweet human love is gone!
'Tis only when they spring to heaven that angels
Reveal themselves to you; they sit all day
Beside you, and lie down at night by you
Who care not for their presence, muse or sleep,
And all at once they leave you, and you know them!   220

We are so fooled, so cheated! Why, even now
I am not too secure against foul play;
The shadows deepen and the walls contract:
No doubt some treachery is going on.
'Tis very dusk. Where are we put, Aprile?
Have they left us in the lurch? This murky loathsome
Death-trap, this slaughter-house, is not the hall
In the golden city! Keep by me, Aprile!
There is a hand groping amid the blackness
To catch us. Have the spider-fingers got you,   230
Poet? Hold on me for your life! If once
They pull you!—Hold!
               'Tis but a dream—no more!
I have you still; the sun comes out again;
Let us be happy: all will yet go well!
Let us confer: is it not like, Aprile,
That spite of trouble, this ordeal passed,
The value of my labours ascertained,
Just as some stream foams long among the rocks
But after glideth glassy to the sea,
So, full content shall henceforth be my lot?   240
What think you, poet? Louder! Your clear voice
Vibrates too like a harp-string. Do you ask
How could I still remain on earth, should God
Grant me the great approval which I seek?
I, you, and God can comprehend each other,
But men would murmur, and with cause enough;
For when they saw me, stainless of all sin,
Preserved and sanctified by inward light,
They would complain that comfort, shut from them,
I drank thus unespied; that they live on,   250
Nor taste the quiet of a constant joy,
For ache and care and doubt and weariness,
While I am calm; help being vouchsafed to me,
And hid from them.—'Twere best consider that!
You reason well, Aprile; but at least
Let me know this, and die! Is this too much?
I will learn this, if God so please, and die!

If thou shalt please, dear God, if thou shalt please!
We are so weak, we know our motives least

In their confused beginning. If at first   260
I sought...but wherefore bare my heart to thee?
I know thy mercy; and already thoughts
Flock fast about my soul to comfort it,
And intimate I cannot wholly fail,
For love and praise would clasp me willingly
Could I resolve to seek them. Thou art good,
And I should be content. Yet—yet first show
I have done wrong in daring! Rather give
The supernatural consciousness of strength
Which fed my youth! Only one hour of that   270
With thee to help—O what should bar me then!

Lost, lost! Thus things are ordered here! God's creatures,
And yet he takes no pride in us!—none, none!
Truly there needs another life to come!
If this be all—(I must tell Festus that)
And other life await us not—for one,
I say 'tis a poor cheat, a stupid bungle,
A wretched failure. I, for one, protest
Against it, and I hurl it back with scorn.

Well, onward though alone! Small time remains,   280
And much to do: I must have fruit, must reap
Some profit from my toils. I doubt my body
Will hardly serve me through; while I have laboured
It has decayed; and now that I demand
Its best assistance, it will crumble fast:
A sad thought, a sad fate! How very full
Of wormwood 'tis, that just at altar-service,
The rapt hymn rising with the rolling smoke,
When glory dawns and all is at the best,
The sacred fire may flicker and grow faint   290
And die for want of a wood-piler's help!
Thus fades the flagging body, and the soul
Is pulled down in the overthrow. Well, well—
Let men catch every word, let them lose nought
Of what I say; something may yet be done.

They are ruins! Trust me who am one of you!
All ruins, glorious once, but lonely now.
It makes my heart sick to behold you crouch

Beside your desolate fane: the arches dim,
The crumbling columns grand against the moon,   300
Could I but rear them up once more—but that
May never be, so leave them! Trust me, friends,
Why should you linger here when I have built
A far resplendent temple, all your own?
Trust me, they are but ruins! See, Aprile,
Men will not heed! Yet were I not prepared
With better refuge for them, tongue of mine
Should ne'er reveal how blank their dwelling is:
I would sit down in silence with the rest.

Ha, what? you spit at me, you grin and shriek   310
Contempt into my ear—my ear which drank
God's accents once? you curse me? Why men, men,
I am not formed for it! Those hideous eyes
Will be before me sleeping, waking, praying,
They will not let me even die. Spare, spare me,
Sinning or no, forget that, only spare me
The horrible scorn! You thought I could support it.
But now you see what silly fragile creature
Cowers thus. I am not good nor bad enough,
Not Christ nor Cain, yet even Cain was saved   320
From Hate like this. Let me but totter back!
Perhaps I shall elude those jeers which creep
Into my very brain, and shut these scorched
Eyelids and keep those mocking faces out.

Listen, Aprile! I am very calm:
Be not deceived, there is no passion here
Where the blood leaps like an imprisoned thing:
I am calm: I will exterminate the race!
Enough of that: 'tis said and it shall be.
And now be merry: safe and sound am I   330
Who broke through their best ranks to get at you.
And such a havoc, such a rout, Aprile!
    Festus. Have you no thought, no memory for me,
Aureole? I am so wretched—my pure Michal
Is gone, and you alone are left me now,
And even you forget me. Take my hand—
Lean on me thus. Do you not know me, Aureole?
    Paracelsus. Festus, my own friend, you are come at last?

As you say, 'tis an awful enterprise;
But you believe I shall go through with it: 340
'Tis like you, and I thank you. Thank him for me,
Dear Michal! See how bright St. Saviour's spire
Flames in the sunset; all its figures quaint
Gay in the glancing light: you might conceive them
A troop of yellow-vested white-haired Jews
Bound for their own land where redemption dawns.
    Festus. Not that blest time—not our youth's time, dear God!
    Paracelsus. Ha—stay! true, I forget—all is done since,
And he is come to judge me. How he speaks,
How calm, how well! yes, it is true, all true;   350
All quackery; all deceit; myself can laugh
The first at it, if you desire: but still
You know the obstacles which taught me tricks
So foreign to my nature—envy and hate,
Blind opposition, brutal prejudice,
Bald ignorance—what wonder if I sunk
To humour men the way they most approved?
My cheats were never palmed on such as you,
Dear Festus! I will kneel if you require me,
Impart the meagre knowledge I possess,   360
Explain its bounded nature, and avow
My insufficiency—whate'er you will:
I give the fight up: let there be an end,
A privacy, an obscure nook for me.
I want to be forgotten even by God.
But if that cannot be, dear Festus, lay me,
When I shall die, within some narrow grave,
Not by itself—for that would be too proud—
But where such graves are thickest; let it look
Nowise distinguished from the hillocks round,   370
So that the peasant at his brother's bed
May tread upon my own and know it not;
And we shall all be equal at the last,
Or classed according to life's natural ranks,
Fathers, sons, brothers, friends—not rich, nor wise,
Nor gifted: lay me thus, then say, 'He lived
Too much advanced before his brother men;
They kept him still in front: 'twas for their good
But yet a dangerous station. It were strange

That he should tell God he had never ranked 380
With men: so, here at least he is a man.'
　Festus. That God shall take thee to his breast, dear spirit,
Unto his breast, be sure! and here on earth
Shall splendour sit upon thy name for ever.
Sun! all the heaven is glad for thee: what care
If lower mountains light their snowy phares°
At thine effulgence, yet acknowledge not
The source of day? Their theft shall be their bale:°
For after-ages shall retrack thy beams,
And put aside the crowd of busy ones 390
And worship thee alone—the master-mind,
The thinker, the explorer, the creator!
Then, who should sneer at the convulsive throes
With which thy deeds were born, would scorn as well
The sheet of winding subterraneous fire
Which, pent and writhing, sends no less at last
Huge islands up amid the simmering sea.
Behold thy might in me! thou hast infused
Thy soul in mine; and I am grand as thou,
Seeing I comprehend thee—I so simple, 400
Thou so august. I recognize thee first;
I saw thee rise, I watched thee early and late,
And though no glance reveal thou dost accept
My homage—thus no less I proffer it,
And bid thee enter gloriously thy rest.
　Paracelsus. Festus!
　Festus. 　　　　　I am for noble Aureole, God!
I am upon his side, come weal or woe.
His portion shall be mine. He has done well.
I would have sinned, had I been strong enough,
As he has sinned. Reward him or I waive 410
Reward! If thou canst find no place for him,
He shall be king elsewhere, and I will be
His slave for ever. There are two of us.
　Paracelsus. Dear Festus!
　Festus. 　　　　　　Here, dear Aureole! ever by you!
　Paracelsus. Nay, speak on, or I dream again. Speak on!
Some story, anything—only your voice.
I shall dream else. Speak on! ay, leaning so!
　Festus. Thus the Mayne glideth

Where my Love abideth.
Sleep's no softer: it proceeds   420
On through lawns, on through meads,
On and on, whate'er befall,
Meandering and musical,
Though the niggard pasturage
Bears not on its shaven ledge
Aught but weeds and waving grasses
To view the river as it passes,
Save here and there a scanty patch
Of primroses too faint to catch
A weary bee.   430

Paracelsus. More, more; say on!
Festus.   And scarce it pushes
Its gentle way through strangling rushes
Where the glossy kingfisher
Flutters when noon-heats are near,
Glad the shelving banks to shun,
Red and steaming in the sun,
Where the shrew-mouse with pale throat
Burrows, and the speckled stoat;
Where the quick sandpipers flit
In and out the marl and grit   440
That seems to breed them, brown as they:
Nought disturbs its quiet way,
Save some lazy stork that springs,
Trailing it with legs and wings,
Whom the shy fox from the hill
Rouses, creep he ne'er so still.

Paracelsus. My heart! they loose my heart, those simple words;
Its darkness passes, which nought else could touch:
Like some dark snake that force may not expel,
Which glideth out to music sweet and low.   450
What were you doing when your voice broke through
A chaos of ugly images? You, indeed!
Are you alone here?
Festus.   All alone: you know me?
This cell?
Paracelsus. An unexceptionable vault:
Good brick and stone: the bats kept out, the rats
Kept in: a snug nook: how should I mistake it?

Festus. But wherefore am I here?

Paracelsus.   Ah, well remembered!
Why, for a purpose—for a purpose, Festus!
'Tis like me: here I trifle while time fleets,
And this occasion, lost, will ne'er return.   460
You are here to be instructed. I will tell
God's message; but I have so much to say,
I fear to leave half out. All is confused
No doubt; but doubtless you will learn in time.
He would not else have brought you here: no doubt
I shall see clearer soon.

Festus.   Tell me but this—
You are not in despair?

Paracelsus.   I? and for what?

Festus. Alas, alas! he knows not, as I feared!

Paracelsus. What is it you would ask me with that earnest
Dear searching face?   470

Festus.   How feel you, Aureole?

Paracelsus.   Well:
Well. 'Tis a strange thing: I am dying, Festus,
And now that fast the storm of life subsides,
I first perceive how great the whirl has been.
I was calm then, who am so dizzy now—
Calm in the thick of the tempest, but no less
A partner of its motion and mixed up
With its career. The hurricane is spent,
And the good boat speeds through the brightening weather;
But is it earth or sea that heaves below?
The gulf rolls like a meadow-swell, o'erstrewn   480
With ravaged boughs and remnants of the shore;
And now some slet, loosened from the land,
Swims past with all its trees, sailing to ocean;
And now the air is full of uptorn canes,
Light strippings from the fan-trees, tamarisks
Unrooted, with their birds still clinging to them,
All high in the wind. Even so my varied life
Drifts by me; I am young, old, happy, sad,
Hoping, desponding, acting, taking rest,
And all at once: that is, those past conditions   490
Float back at once on me. If I select
Some special epoch from the crowd, 'tis but

To will, and straight the rest dissolve away,
And only that particular state is present
With all its long-forgotten circumstance
Distinct and vivid as at first—myself
A careless looker-on and nothing more,
Indifferent and amused, but nothing more.
And this is death: I understand it all.
New being waits me; new perceptions must   500
Be born in me before I plunge therein;
Which last is Death's affair; and while I speak,
Minute by minute he is filling me
With power; and while my foot is on the threshold
Of boundless life—the doors unopened yet,
All preparations not complete within—
I turn new knowledge upon old events,
And the effect is...but I must not tell;
It is not lawful. Your own turn will come
One day. Wait, Festus! You will die like me.   510
    Festus. 'Tis of that past life that I burn to hear.
    Paracelsus. You wonder it engages me just now?
In truth, I wonder too. What's life to me?
Where'er I look is fire, where'er I listen
Music, and where I tend bliss evermore.
Yet how can I refrain? 'Tis a refined
Delight to view those chances,—one last view.
I am so near the perils I escape,
That I must play with them and turn them over,
To feel how fully they are past and gone.   520
Still, it is like, some further cause exists
For this peculiar mood—some hidden purpose;
Did I not tell you something of it, Festus?
I had it fast, but it has somehow slipt
Away from me; it will return anon.
    Festus. (Indeed his cheek seems young again, his voice
Complete with its old tones: that little laugh
Concluding every phrase, with upturned eye,
As though one stooped above his head to whom
He looked for confirmation and approval,   530
Where was it gone so long, so well preserved?
Then, the fore-finger pointing as he speaks,
Like one who traces in an open book

The matter he declares; 'tis many a year
Since I remarked it last: and this in him,
But now a ghastly wreck!)
                              And can it be,
Dear Aureole, you have then found out at last
That worldly things are utter vanity?
That man is made for weakness, and should wait
In patient ignorance, till God appoint...   540
   Paracelsus. Ha, the purpose: the true purpose: that is it!
How could I fail to apprehend! You here,
I thus! But no more trifling: I see all,
I know all: my last mission shall be done
If strength suffice. No trifling! Stay; this posture
Hardly befits one thus about to speak:
I will arise.
   Festus.   Nay, Aureole, are you wild?
You cannot leave your couch.
   Paracelsus.   No help; no help;
Not even your hand. So! there, I stand once more!
Speak from a couch? I never lectured thus.   550
My gown—the scarlet lined with fur; now put
The chain about my neck; my signet-ring
Is still upon my hand, I think—even so;
Last, my good sword; ah, trusty Azoth, leapest°
Beneath thy master's grasp for the last time?
This couch shall be my throne: I bid these walls
Be consecrate, this wretched cell become
A shrine, for here God speaks to men through me.
Now, Festus, I am ready to begin.
   Festus. I am dumb with wonder.
   Paracelsus.   Listen, therefore, Festus!   560
There will be time enough, but none to spare.
I must content myself with telling only
The most important points. You doubtless feel
That I am happy, Festus; very happy.
   Festus. 'Tis no delusion which uplifts him thus!
Then you are pardoned, Aureole, all your sin?
   Paracelsus. Ay, pardoned: yet why pardoned?
   Festus.   'Tis God's praise
That man is bound to seek, and you...
   Paracelsus. .   Have lived!

We have to live alone to set forth well
God's praise. 'Tis true, I sinned much, as I thought,   570
And in effect need mercy, for I strove
To do that very thing; but, do your best
Or worst, praise rises, and will rise for ever
Pardon from him, because of praise denied—
Who calls me to himself to exalt himself?
He might laugh as I laugh!
    Festus.   But all comes
To the same thing. 'Tis fruitless for mankind
To fret themselves with what concerns them not;
They are no use that way: they should lie down
Content as God has made them, nor go mad   580
In thriveless cares to better what is ill.
    Paracelsus. No, no; mistake me not; let me not work
More harm than I have worked! This is my case:
If I go joyous back to God, yet bring
No offering, if I render up my soul
Without the fruits it was ordained to bear,
If I appear the better to love God
For sin, as one who has no claim on him,—
Be not deceived! It may be surely thus
With me, while higher prizes still await   590
The mortal persevering to the end.
Beside I am not all so valueless:
I have been something, though too soon I left
Following the instincts of that happy time.
    Festus. What happy time? For God's sake, for man's sake,
What time was happy? All I hope to know
That answer will decide. What happy time?
    Paracelsus. When but the time I vowed myself to man?
    Festus. Great God, thy judgments are inscrutable!
    Paracelsus. Yes, it was in me; I was born for it—   600
I, Paracelsus: it was mine by right.
Doubtless a searching and impetuous soul
Might learn from its own motions that some task
Like this awaited it about the world;
Might seek somewhere in this blank life of ours
For fit delights to stay its longings vast;
And, grappling Nature, so prevail on her
To fill the creature full she dared thus frame

Hungry for joy; and, bravely tyrannous,
Grow in demand, still craving more and more,   610
And make each joy conceded prove a pledge
Of other joy to follow—bating nought
Of its desires, still seizing fresh pretence
To turn the knowledge and the rapture wrung
As an extreme, last boon, from destiny,
Into occasion for new covetings,
New strifes, new triumphs:—doubtless a strong soul,
Alone, unaided might attain to this,
So glorious is our nature, so august
Man's inborn uninstructed impulses,   620
His naked spirit so majestical!
But this was born in me; I was made so;
Thus much time saved: the feverish appetites,
The tumult of unproved desire, the unaimed
Uncertain yearnings, aspirations blind,
Distrust, mistake, and all that ends in tears
Were saved me; thus I entered on my course.
You may be sure I was not all exempt
From human trouble; just so much of doubt
As bade me plant a surer foot upon   630
The sun-road, kept my eye unruined 'mid
The fierce and flashing splendour, set my heart
Trembling so much as warned me I stood there
On sufferance—not to idly gaze, but cast
Light on a darkling race; save for that doubt,
I stood at first where all aspire at last
To stand: the secret of the world was mine.
I knew, I felt, (perception unexpressed,
Uncomprehended by our narrow thought,
But somehow felt and known in every shift   640
And change in the spirit,—nay, in every pore
Of the body, even,)—what God is, what we are,°
What life is—how God tastes an infinite joy
In infinite ways—one everlasting bliss,
From whom all being emanates, all power
Proceeds; in whom is life for evermore,
Yet whom existence in its lowest form
Includes; where dwells enjoyment there is he:
With still a flying point of bliss remote,

A happiness in store afar, a sphere   650
Of distant glory in full view; thus climbs
Pleasure its heights for ever and for ever.
The centre-fire heaves underneath the earth,
And the earth changes like a human face;
The molten ore bursts up among the rocks,
Winds into the stone's heart, outbranches bright
In hidden mines, spots barren river-beds,
Crumbles into fine sand where sunbeams bask—
God joys therein. The wroth sea's waves are edged
With foam, white as the bitten lip of hate,   660
When, in the solitary waste, strange groups
Of young volcanos come up, cyclops-like,
Staring together with their eyes on flame—
God tastes a pleasure in their uncouth pride.
Then all is still; earth is a wintry clod:
But spring-wind, like a dancing psaltress, passes°
Over its breast to waken it, rare verdure
Buds tenderly upon rough banks, between
The withered tree-roots and the cracks of frost,
Like a smile striving with a wrinkled face;   670
The grass grows bright, the boughs are swoln with blooms
Like chrysalids impatient for the air,
The shining dorrs are busy, beetles run°
Along the furrows, ants make their ado;
Above, birds fly in merry flocks, the lark
Soars up and up, shivering for very joy;
Afar the ocean sleeps; white fishing-gulls
Flit where the strand is purple with its tribe
Of nested limpets; savage creatures seek
Their loves in wood and plain—and God renews   680
His ancient rapture. Thus he dwells in all,
From life's minute beginnings, up at last
To man—the consummation of this scheme
Of being, the completion of this sphere
Of life: whose attributes had here and there
Been scattered o'er the visible world before,
Asking to be combined, dim fragments meant
To be united in some wondrous whole,
Imperfect qualities throughout creation,
Suggesting some one creature yet to make,   690

Some point where all those scattered rays should meet
Convergent in the faculties of man.
Power—neither put forth blindly, nor controlled
Calmly by perfect knowledge; to be used
At risk, inspired or checked by hope and fear:
Knowledge—not intuition, but the slow
Uncertain fruit of an enhancing toil,
Strengthened by love: love—not serenely pure,
But strong from weakness, like a chance-sown plant
Which, cast on stubborn soil, puts forth changed buds   700
And softer stains, unknown in happier climes;
Love which endures and doubts and is oppressed
And cherished, suffering much and much sustained,
And blind, oft-failing, yet believing love,
A half-enlightened, often-chequered trust:—
Hints and previsions of which faculties,
Are strewn confusedly everywhere about
The inferior natures, and all lead up higher,
All shape out dimly the superior race,
The heir of hopes too fair to turn out false,   710
And man appears at last. So far the seal
Is put on life; one stage of being complete,
One scheme wound up: and from the grand result
A supplementary reflux of light,
Illustrates all the inferior grades, explains
Each back step in the circle. Not alone
For their possessor dawn those qualities,
But the new glory mixes with the heaven
And earth; man, once descried, imprints for ever°
His presence on all lifeless things: the winds   720
Are henceforth voices, wailing or a shout,
A querulous mutter or a quick gay laugh,
Never a senseless gust now man is born.
The herded pines commune and have deep thoughts
A secret they assemble to discuss
When the sun drops behind their trunks which glare
Like grates of hell: the peerless cup afloat
Of the lake-lily is an urn, some nymph
Swims bearing high above her head: no bird
Whistles unseen, but through the gaps above   730
That let light in upon the gloomy woods,

A shape peeps from the breezy forest-top,
Arch with small puckered mouth and mocking eye.
The morn has enterprise, deep quiet droops
With evening, triumph takes the sunset hour,
Voluptuous transport ripens with the corn
Beneath a warm moon like a happy face:
—And this to fill us with regard for man.
With apprehension of his passing worth,
Desire to work his proper nature out,   740
And ascertain his rank and final place,
For these things tend still upward, progress is
The law of life, man is not Man as yet.
Nor shall I deem his object served, his end
Attained, his genuine strength put fairly forth,
While only here and there a star dispels
The darkness, here and there a towering mind
O'erlooks its prostrate fellows: when the host
Is out at once to the despair of night,
When all mankind alike is perfected,   750
Equal in full-blown powers—then, not till then,
I say, begins man's general infancy.
For wherefore make account of feverish starts
Of restless members of a dormant whole,
Impatient nerves which quiver while the body
Slumbers as in a grave? Oh long ago
The brow was twitched, the tremulous lids astir,
The peaceful mouth disturbed; half-uttered speech
Ruffled the lip, and then the teeth were set,
The breath drawn sharp, the strong right-hand clenched
        stronger,   760
As it would pluck a lion by the jaw;
The glorious creature laughed out even in sleep!
But when full roused, each giant-limb awake,
Each sinew strung, the great heart pulsing fast,
He shall start up and stand on his own earth,
Then shall his long triumphant march begin,
Thence shall his being date,—thus wholly roused,
What he achieves shall be set down to him.
When all the race is perfected alike
As man, that is; all tended to mankind,   770
And, man produced, all has its end thus far:

But in completed man begins anew
A tendency to God. Prognostics told
Man's near approach; so in man's self arise
August anticipations, symbols, types
Of a dim splendour ever on before
In that eternal circle life pursues.
For men begin to pass their nature's bound,
And find new hopes and cares which fast supplant
Their proper joys and griefs; they grow too great   780
For narrow creeds of right and wrong, which fade
Before the unmeasured thirst for good: while peace
Rises within them ever more and more.
Such men are even now upon the earth,
Serene amid the half-formed creatures round
Who should be saved by them and joined with them.
Such was my task, and I was born to it—
Free, as I said but now, from much that chains
Spirits, high-dowered but limited and vexed
By a divided and delusive aim,   790
A shadow mocking a reality
Whose truth avails not wholly to disperse
The flitting mimic called up by itself,
And so remains perplexed and nigh put out
By its fantastic fellow's wavering gleam.
I, from the first, was never cheated thus;
I never fashioned out a fancied good
Distinct from man's; a service to be done,
A glory to be ministered unto
With powers put forth at man's expense, withdrawn   800
From labouring in his behalf; a strength
Denied that might avail him. I cared not
Lest his success ran counter to success
Elsewhere: for God is glorified in man,
And to man's glory vowed I soul and limb.
Yet, constituted thus, and thus endowed,
I failed: I gazed on power till I grew blind.
Power; I could not take my eyes from that:
That only, I thought, should be preserved, increased
At any risk, displayed, struck out at once—   810
The sign and note and character of man.
I saw no use in the past: only a scene

Of degradation, ugliness and tears,
The record of disgraces best forgotten,
A sullen page in human chronicles
Fit to erase. I saw no cause why man
Should not stand all-sufficient even now,
Or why his annals should be forced to tell
That once the tide of light, about to break
Upon the world, was sealed within its spring: 820
I would have had one day, one moment's space,
Change man's condition, push each slumbering claim
Of mastery o'er the elemental world
At once to full maturity, then roll
Oblivion o'er the work, and hide from man
What night had ushered morn. Not so, dear child
Of after-days, wilt thou reject the past
Big with deep warnings of the proper tenure
By which thou hast the earth: for thee the present
Shall have distinct and trembling beauty, seen   830
Beside that past's own shade when, in relief,
Its brightness shall stand out: nor yet on thee
Shall burst the future, as successive zones
Of several wonder open on some spirit
Flying secure and glad from heaven to heaven:
But thou shalt painfully attain to joy,
While hope and fear and love shall keep thee man!
All this was hid from me: as one by one
My dreams grew dim, my wide aims circumscribed,
As actual good within my reach decreased,   840
While obstacles sprung up this way and that
To keep me from effecting half the sum,
Small as it proved; as objects, mean within
The primal aggregate, seemed, even the least,
Itself a match for my concentred strength—
What wonder if I saw no way to shun
Despair? The power I sought for man, seemed God's.
In this conjuncture, as I prayed to die,
A strange adventure made me know, one sin
Had spotted my career from its uprise;   850
I saw Aprile—my Aprile there!
And as the poor melodious wretch disburthened
His heart, and moaned his weakness in my ear,

I learned my own deep error; love's undoing
Taught me the worth of love in man's estate,
And what proportion love should hold with power
In his right constitution; love preceding
Power, and with much power, always much more love;
Love still too straitened in his present means,
And earnest for new power to set love free. 860
I learned this, and supposed the whole was learned:
And thus, when men received with stupid wonder
My first revealings, would have worshipped me,
And I despised and loathed their proffered praise—
When, with awakened eyes, they took revenge
For past credulity in casting shame
On my real knowledge, and I hated them—
It was not strange I saw no good in man,
To overbalance all the wear and waste
Of faculties, displayed in vain, but born 870
To prosper in some better sphere: and why?
In my own heart love had not been made wise
To trace love's faint beginnings in mankind,
To know even hate is but a mask of love's,
To see a good in evil, and a hope
In ill-success; to sympathize, be proud
Of their half-reasons, faint aspirings, dim
Struggles for truth, their poorest fallacies,
Their prejudice and fears and cares and doubts;
All with a touch of nobleness, despite 880
Their error, upward tending all though weak,
Like plants in mines which never saw the sun,
But dream of him, and guess where he may be,
And do their best to climb and get to him.
All this I knew not, and I failed. Let men
Regard me, and the poet dead long ago
Who loved too rashly; and shape forth a third
And better-tempered spirit, warned by both:
As from the over-radiant star too mad
To drink the life-springs, beamless thence itself— 890
And the dark orb which borders the abyss,
Ingulfed in icy night,—might have its course
A temperate and equidistant world.
Meanwhile, I have done well, though not all well.

As yet men cannot do without contempt;
'Tis for their good, and therefore fit awhile
That they reject the weak, and scorn the false,
Rather than praise the strong and true, in me:
But after, they will know me. If I stoop
Into a dark tremendous sea of cloud,   900
It is but for a time; I press God's lamp
Close to my breast; its splendour, soon or late,
Will pierce the gloom: I shall emerge one day.
You understand me? I have said enough?
 Festus. Now die, dear Aureole!
 Paracelsus.   Festus, let my hand—
This hand, lie in your own, my own true friend!
Aprile! Hand in hand with you, Aprile!

 Festus. And this was Paracelsus!

PIPPA PASSES (1841)

Persons

PIPPA.
OTTIMA.
SEBALD.
Foreign Students.
GOTTLIEB.
SCHRAMM.
JULES.
PHENE.
Austrian Police.
BLUPHOCKS.
LUIGI *and his* Mother.
Poor Girls.
MONSIGNOR *and his Attendants.*

Introduction

New Year's Day at Asolo in the Trevisan

SCENE.—*A large mean airy chamber. A girl,* PIPPA, *from the Silk-mills, springing out of bed.*

Day!
Faster and more fast,
O'er night's brim, day boils at last:
Boils, pure gold, o'er the cloud-cup's brim
Where spurting and suppressed it lay,
For not a froth-flake touched the rim
Of yonder gap in the solid gray
Of the eastern cloud, an hour away;
But forth one wavelet, then another, curled,
Till the whole sunrise, not to be suppressed,   10
Rose, reddened, and its seething breast
Flickered in bounds, grew gold, then overflowed the world.

Oh, Day, if I squander a wavelet of thee,
A mite of my twelve hours' treasure,
The least of thy gazes or glances,
(Be they grants thou art bound to or gifts above measure)
One of thy choices or one of thy chances,
(Be they tasks God imposed thee or freaks at thy pleasure)
—My Day, if I squander such labour or leisure,
Then shame fall on Asolo, mischief on me!   20

Thy long blue solemn hours serenely flowing,
Whence earth, we feel, gets steady help and good—
Thy fitful sunshine-minutes, coming, going,
As if earth turned from work in gamesome mood—
All shall be mine! But thou must treat me not
As prosperous ones are treated, those who live
At hand here, and enjoy the higher lot,
In readiness to take what thou wilt give,
And free to let alone what thou refusest;
For, Day, my holiday, if thou ill-usest   30
Me, who am only Pippa,—old-year's sorrow,
Cast off last night, will come again to-morrow:
Whereas, if thou prove gentle, I shall borrow
Sufficient strength of thee for new-year's sorrow.
All other men and women that this earth
Belongs to, who all days alike possess,
Make general plenty cure particular dearth,
Get more joy one way, if another, less:
Thou art my single day, God lends to leaven
What were all earth else, with a feel of heaven,—   40
Sole light that helps me through the year, thy sun's!
Try now! Take Asolo's Four Happiest Ones—
And let thy morning rain on that superb
Great haughty Ottima; can rain disturb
Her Sebald's homage? All the while thy rain
Beats fiercest on her shrub-house window-pane,
He will but press the closer, breathe more warm
Against her cheek; how should she mind the storm?
And, morning past, if mid-day shed a gloom
O'er Jules and Phene,—what care bride and groom   50
Save for their dear selves? 'Tis their marriage-day;

And while they leave church and go home their way,
Hand clasping hand, within each breast would be
Sunbeams and pleasant weather spite of thee.
Then, for another trial, obscure thy eve
With mist,—will Luigi and his mother grieve—
The lady and her child, unmatched, forsooth,
She in her age, as Luigi in his youth,
For true content? The cheerful town, warm, close
And safe, the sooner that thou art morose,   60
Receives them. And yet once again, outbreak
In storm at night on Monsignor, they make
Such stir about,—whom they expect from Rome
To visit Asolo, his brothers' home,
And say here masses proper to release
A soul from pain,—what storm dares hurt his peace?
Calm would he pray, with his own thoughts to ward
Thy thunder off, nor want the angels' guard.
But Pippa—just one such mischance would spoil
Her day that lightens the next twelvemonth's toil   70
At wearisome silk-winding, coil on coil!
    And here I let time slip for nought!
Aha, you foolhardy sunbeam, caught
With a single splash from my ewer!
You that would mock the best pursuer,
Was my basin over-deep?
One splash of water ruins you asleep,
And up, up, fleet your brilliant bits
Wheeling and counterwheeling,
Reeling, broken beyond healing: 80
Now grow together on the ceiling!
That will task your wits.
Whoever it was quenched fire first, hoped to see
Morsel after morsel flee
As merrily, as giddily . . .
Meantime, what lights my sunbeam on,
Where settles by degrees the radiant cripple?
Oh, is it surely blown, my martagon?°
New-blown and ruddy as St Agnes' nipple,°
Plump as the flesh-bunch on some Turk bird's poll!°   90
Be sure if corals, branching 'neath the ripple
Of ocean, bud there,—fairies watch unroll

Such turban-flowers; I say, such lamps disperse
Thick red flame through that dusk green universe!
I am queen of thee, floweret!
And each fleshy blossom
Preserve I not—(safer
Than leaves that embower it,
Or shells that embosom)
—From weevil and chafer?°   100
Laugh through my pane then; solicit the bee;
Gibe him, be sure; and, in midst of thy glee,
Love thy queen, worship me!

—Worship whom else? For am I not, this day,
Whate'er I please? What shall I please to-day?
My morn, noon, eve and night—how spend my day?
To-morrow I must be Pippa who winds silk,
The whole year round, to earn just bread and milk:
But, this one day, I have leave to go,
And play out my fancy's fullest games;   110
I may fancy all day—and it shall be so—
That I taste of the pleasures, am called by the names
Of the Happiest Four in our Asolo!
See! Up the hill-side yonder, through the morning,
Some one shall love me, as the world calls love:
I am no less than Ottima, take warning!
The gardens, and the great stone house above,
And other house for shrubs, all glass in front,
Are mine; where Sebald steals, as he is wont,
To court me, while old Luca yet reposes: 120
And therefore, till the shrub-house door uncloses,
I . . . what now?—give abundant cause for prate
About me—Ottima, I mean—of late,
Too bold, too confident she'll still face down
The spitefullest of talkers in our town.
How we talk in the little town below!
    But love, love, love—there's better love, I know!
This foolish love was only day's first offer;
I choose my next love to defy the scoffer:
For do not our Bride and Bridegroom sally   130
Out of Possagno church at noon?°
Their house looks over Orcana valley:

Why should not I be the bride as soon
As Ottima? For I saw, beside,
Arrive last night that little bride—
Saw, if you call it seeing her, one flash
Of the pale snow-pure cheek and black bright tresses,
Blacker than all except the black eyelash;
I wonder she contrives those lids no dresses!
—So strict was she, the veil   140
Should cover close her pale
Pure cheeks—a bride to look at and scarce touch,
Scarce touch, remember, Jules! For are not such
Used to be tended, flower-like, every feature,
As if one's breath would fray the lily of a creature?
A soft and easy life these ladies lead:
Whiteness in us were wonderful indeed.
Oh, save that brow its virgin dimness,
Keep that foot its lady primness,
Let those ankles never swerve   150
From their exquisite reserve,
Yet have to trip along the streets like me,
All but naked to the knee!
How will she ever grant her Jules a bliss
So startling as her real first infant kiss?
Oh, no—not envy, this!

—Not envy, sure!—for if you gave me
Leave to take or to refuse,
In earnest, do you think I'd choose
That sort of new love to enslave me?   160
Mine should have lapped me round from the beginning;
As little fear of losing it as winning:
Lovers grow cold, men learn to hate their wives,
And only parents' love can last our lives.
At eve the Son and Mother, gentle pair,
Commune inside our turret: what prevents
My being Luigi? While that mossy lair
Of lizards through the winter-time is stirred
With each to each imparting sweet intents
For this new-year, as brooding bird to bird—   170
(For I observe of late, the evening walk
Of Luigi and his mother, always ends

Inside our ruined turret, where they talk,
Calmer than lovers, yet more kind than friends)
—Let me be cared about, kept out of harm,
And schemed for, safe in love as with a charm;
Let me be Luigi! If I only knew
What was my mother's face—my father, too!
    Nay, if you come to that, best love of all
Is God's; then why not have God's love befall   180
Myself as, in the palace by the Dome,°
Monsignor?—who to-night will bless the home
Of his dead brother; and God bless in turn
That heart which beats, those eyes which mildly burn
With love for all men! I, to-night at least,
Would be that holy and beloved priest.

Now wait!—even I already seem to share
In God's love: what does New-year's hymn declare?
What other meaning do these verses bear?

>   *All service ranks the same with God:*   190
>   *If now, as formerly he trod*
>   *Paradise, his presence fills*
>   *Our earth, each only as God wills*
>   *Can work—God's puppets, best and worst,*
>   *Are we; there is no last nor first.*
>
>   *Say not 'a small event!' Why 'small'?*
>   *Costs it more pain that this, ye call*
>   *A 'great event,' should come to pass,*
>   *Than that? Untwine me from the mass*
>   *Of deeds which make up life, one deed*   200
>   *Power shall fall short in or exceed!*

And more of it, and more of it!—oh yes—
I will pass each, and see their happiness,
And envy none—being just as great, no doubt,
Useful to men, and dear to God, as they!
A pretty thing to care about
So mightily, this single holiday!
But let the sun shine! Wherefore repine?
—With thee to lead me, O Day of mine,
Down the grass path grey with dew,   210
Under the pine-wood, blind with boughs,

Where the swallow never flew
Nor yet cicala dared carouse—°
No, dared carouse!   [*She enters the street.*

Part I

Morning

SCENE.—*Up the Hill-side, inside the Shrub-house.* LUCA'S *wife,*
OTTIMA, *and her paramour, the German* SEBALD.

Sebald [*sings*].

> *Let the watching lids wink!*
> *Day's a-blaze with eyes, think!*
> *Deep into the night, drink!*

Ottima. Night? Such may be your Rhine-land nights perhaps;
But this blood-red beam through the shutter's chink
—We call such light, the morning: let us see!
Mind how you grope your way, though! How these tall
Naked geraniums straggle! Push the lattice
Behind that frame!—Nay, do I bid you?—Sebald,
It shakes the dust down on me! Why, of course   10
The slide-bolt catches. Well, are you content.
Or must I find you something else to spoil?
Kiss and be friends, my Sebald! Is't full morning?
Oh, don't speak then!
Sebald.   Ay, thus it used to be.
Ever your house was, I remember, shut
Till mid-day; I observed that, as I strolled
On mornings through the vale here; country girls
Were noisy, washing garments in the brook,
Hinds drove the slow white oxen up the hills:
But no, your house was mute, would ope no eye.   20
And wisely: you were plotting one thing there,
Nature, another outside. I looked up—
Rough white wood shutters, rusty iron bars,
Silent as death, blind in a flood of light.
Oh, I remember!—and the peasants laughed
And said, 'The old man sleeps with the young wife.'

This house was his, this chair, this window—his.
  Ottima. Ah, the clear morning! I can see St Mark's;°
That black streak is the belfry. Stop: Vicenza
Should lie...there's Padua, plain enough, that blue!°   30
Look o'er my shoulder, follow my finger!
  Sebald.   Morning?
It seems to me a night with a sun added.
Where's dew, where's freshness? That bruised plant, I bruised
In getting through the lattice yestereve,
Droops as it did. See, here's my elbow's mark
I' the dust o' the sill.
  Ottima.   Oh, shut the lattice, pray!
  Sebald. Let me lean out. I cannot scent blood here,
Foul as the morn may be.
                         There, shut the world out!
How do you feel now, Ottima? There, curse
The world and all outside! Let us throw off   40
This mask: how do you bear yourself? Let's out
With all of it.
  Ottima.   Best never speak of it.
  Sebald. Best speak again and yet again of it,
Till words cease to be more than words. 'His blood,'
For instance—let those two words mean 'His blood'
And nothing more. Notice, I'll say them now,
'His blood.'
  Ottima.   Assuredly if I repented
The deed—
  Sebald.   Repent? Who should repent, or why?
What puts that in your head? Did I once say
That I repented?
  Ottima.   No, I said the deed...   50
  Sebald. 'The deed' and 'the event'—just now it was
'Our passion's fruit'—the devil take such cant!
Say, once and always, Luca was a wittol,°
I am his cut-throat, you are...
  Ottima.   Here's the wine;
I brought it when we left the house above,
And glasses too—wine of both sorts. Black? White then?°
  Sebald. But am not I his cut-throat? What are you?
  Ottima. There trudges on his business from the Duomo°
Benet the Capuchin, with his brown hood°

And bare feet; always in one place at church,   60
Close under the stone wall by the south entry.
I used to take him for a brown cold piece
Of the wall's self, as out of it he rose
To let me pass—at first, I say, I used:
Now, so has that dumb figure fastened on me,
I rather should account the plastered wall
A piece of him, so chilly does it strike.
This, Sebald?
    Sebald.   No, the white wine—the white wine!
Well, Ottima, I promised no new year
Should rise on us the ancient shameful way;   70
Nor does it rise. Pour on! To your black eyes!
Do you remember last damned New Year's day?
    Ottima. You brought those foreign prints. We looked at them
Over the wine and fruit. I had to scheme
To get him from the fire. Nothing but saying
His own set wants the proof-mark, roused him up°
To hunt them out.
    Sebald.   'Faith, he is not alive
To fondle you before my face.
    Ottima.   Do you
Fondle me then! Who means to take your life
For that, my Sebald?
    Sebald.   Hark you, Ottima!   80
One thing to guard against. We'll not make much
One of the other—that is, not make more
Parade of warmth, childish officious coil,°
Than yesterday: as if, sweet, I supposed
Proof upon proof were needed now, now first,
To show I love you—yes, still love you—love you
In spite of Luca and what's come to him
—Sure sign we had him ever in our thoughts,
White sneering old reproachful face and all!
We'll even quarrel, love, at times, as if   90
We still could lose each other, were not tied
By this: conceive you?
    Ottima.   Love!
    Sebald.   Not tied so sure.
Because though I was wrought upon, have struck
His insolence back into him—am I

So surely yours?—therefore forever yours?
   Ottima. Love, to be wise, (one counsel pays another)
Should we have—months ago, when first we loved,
For instance that May morning we two stole
Under the green ascent of sycamores—
If we had come upon a thing like that   100
Suddenly...
    Sebald.   'A thing'—there again—'a thing!'
   Ottima. Then, Venus' body, had we come upon°
My husband Luca Gaddi's murdered corpse
Within there, at his couch-foot, covered close—
Would you have pored upon it? Why persist
In poring now upon it? For 'tis here
As much as there in the deserted house:
You cannot rid your eyes of it. For me,
Now he is dead I hate him worse: I hate...
Dare you stay here? I would go back and hold   110
His two dead hands, and say, 'I hate you worse,
Luca, than...'
    Sebald.   Off, off—take your hands off mine,
'Tis the hot evening—off! oh, morning is it?
   Ottima. There's one thing must be done; you know what
      thing.
Come in and help to carry. We may sleep
Anywhere in the whole wide house to-night.
   Sebald. What would come, think you, if we let him lie
Just as he is? Let him lie there until
The angels take him! He is turned by this
Off from his face beside, as you will see.   120
   Ottima. This dusty pane might serve for looking glass.
Three, four—four grey hairs! Is it so you said
A plait of hair should wave across my neck?
No—this way.
    Sebald.   Ottima, I would give your neck,
Each splendid shoulder, both those breasts of yours,
That this were undone! Killing! Kill the world,
So Luca lives again!—ay, lives to sputter
His fulsome dotage on you—yes, and feign
Surprise that I return at eve to sup,
When all the morning I was loitering here—   130
Bid me despatch my business and begone.

I would . . .
   Ottima.   See!
   Sebald.   No, I'll finish. Do you think
I fear to speak the bare truth once for all?
All we have talked of, is, at bottom, fine
To suffer; there's a recompense in guilt;
One must be venturous and fortunate:
What is one young for, else? In age we'll sigh
O'er the wild reckless wicked days flown over;
Still, we have lived: the vice was in its place.
But to have eaten Luca's bread, have worn   140
His clothes, have felt his money swell my purse—
Do lovers in romances sin that way?
Why, I was starving when I used to call
And teach you music, starving while you plucked me
These flowers to smell!
   Ottima.   My poor lost friend!
   Sebald.   He gave me
Life, nothing less: what if he did reproach
My perfidy, and threaten, and do more—
Had he no right? What was to wonder at?
He sat by us at table quietly:
Why must you lean across till our cheeks touched?   150
Could he do less than make pretence to strike?
'Tis not the crime's sake—I'd commit ten crimes
Greater, to have this crime wiped out, undone!
And you—O how feel you? Feel you for me?
   Ottima. Well then, I love you better now than ever,
And best (look at me while I speak to you)—
Best for the crime; nor do I grieve, in truth,
This mask, this simulated ignorance,
This affectation of simplicity,
Falls off our crime; this naked crime of ours   160
May not now be looked over: look it down!
Great? let it be great; but the joys it brought,
Pay they or no its price? Come: they or it!
Speak not! The past, would you give up the past
Such as it is, pleasure and crime together?
Give up that noon I owned my love for you?
The garden's silence: even the single bee
Persisting in his toil, suddenly stopped,

And where he hid you only could surmise
By some campanula chalice set a-swing.°   170
Who stammered—'Yes, I love you?'
    Sebald.   And I drew
Back; put far back your face with both my hands
Lest you should grow too full of me—your face
So seemed athirst for my whole soul and body!
    Ottima. And when I ventured to receive you here,
Made you steal hither in the mornings—
    Sebald.   When
I used to look up 'neath the shrub-house here,
Till the red fire on its glazed windows spread
To a yellow haze?
    Ottima.   Ah—my sign was, the sun
Inflamed the sere side of yon chestnut-tree   180
Nipped by the first frost.
    Sebald.   You would always laugh
At my wet boots: I had to stride thro' grass
Over my ankles.
    Ottima.   Then our crowning night!
    Sebald. The July night?
    Ottima.   The day of it too, Sebald!
When heaven's pillars seemed o'erbowed with heat,
Its black-blue canopy suffered descend
Close on us both, to weigh down each to each,
And smother up all life except our life.
So lay we till the storm came.
    Sebald.   How it came!
    Ottima. Buried in woods we lay, you recollect;   190
Swift ran the searching tempest overhead;
And ever and anon some bright white shaft
Burned thro' the pine-tree roof, here burned and there,
As if God's messenger thro' the close wood screen
Plunged and replunged his weapon at a venture,
Feeling for guilty thee and me: then broke
The thunder like a whole sea overhead—
    Sebald. Yes!
    Ottima. —While I stretched myself upon you, hands
To hands, my mouth to your hot mouth, and shook
All my locks loose, and covered you with them—   200
You, Sebald, the same you!

Sebald.   Slower, Ottima!
Ottima. And as we lay—
Sebald.   Less vehemently! Love me!
Forgive me! Take not words, mere words, to heart!
Your breath is worse than wine! Breathe slow, speak slow!
Do not lean on me!
    Ottima.   Sebald, as we lay,
Rising and falling only with our pants,
Who said, 'Let death come now! 'Tis right to die!
Right to be punished! Nought completes such bliss
But woe!' Who said that?
    Sebald.   How did we ever rise?
Was't that we slept? Why did it end?
    Ottima.   I felt you   210
Taper into a point the ruffled ends
Of my loose locks 'twixt both your humid lips.
My hair is fallen now: knot it again!
    Sebald. I kiss you now, dear Ottima, now and now!
This way? Will you forgive me—be once more
My great queen?
    Ottima.   Bind it thrice about my brow;
Crown me your queen, your spirit's arbitress,
Magnificent in sin. Say that!
    Sebald.   I crown you
My great white queen, my spirit's arbitress,
Magnificent...   220
       [*From without is heard the voice of* PIPPA, *singing*—
         The year's at the spring
         And day's at the morn;
         Morning's at seven;
         The hill-side's dew-pearled;
         The lark's on the wing;
         The snail's on the thorn:
         God's in his heaven—
         All's right with the world!

                           [PIPPA *passes.*
    Sebald. God's in his heaven! Do you hear that?
      Who spoke?
You, you spoke!
    Ottima.   Oh—that little ragged girl!   230
She must have rested on the step: we give them

But this one holiday the whole year round.
Did you ever see our silk-mills—their inside?
There are ten silk-mills now belong to you.
She stoops to pick my double heartsease . . . Sh!°
She does not hear: call you out louder!
    Sebald.   Leave me!
Go, get your clothes on—dress those shoulders!
Ottima.   Sebald?
    Sebald. Wipe off that paint! I hate you.
    Ottima.   Miserable!
    Sebald. My God, and she is emptied of it now!
Outright now!—how miraculously gone   240
All of the grace—had she not strange grace once?
Why, the blank cheek hangs listless as it likes,
No purpose holds the features up together,
Only the cloven brow and puckered chin
Stay in their places: and the very hair,
That seemed to have a sort of life in it,
Drops, a dead web!
    Ottima.   Speak to me—not of me!
    Sebald.—That round great full-orbed face, where not an angle
Broke the delicious indolence—all broken!
    Ottima. To me—not of me! Ungrateful, perjured cheat!   250
A coward too: but ingrate's worse than all.
Beggar—my slave—a fawning, cringing lie!
Leave me! Betray me! I can see your drift!
A lie that walks and eats and drinks!
    Sebald.   My God!
Those morbid olive faultless shoulder-blades—
I should have known there was no blood beneath!
    Ottima. You hate me then? You hate me then?
    Sebald.   To think
She would succeed in her absurd attempt,
And fascinate by sinning, show herself
Superior—guilt from its excess superior   260
To innocence! That little peasant's voice
Has righted all again. Though I be lost,
I know which is the better, never fear,
Of vice or virtue, purity or lust,
Nature or trick! I see what I have done,
Entirely now! Oh I am proud to feel

Such torments—let the world take credit thence—
I, having done my deed, pay too its price!
I hate, hate—curse you! God's in his heaven!
   Ottima.—   Me!
Me! no, no, Sebald, not yourself—kill me!   270
Mine is the whole crime. Do but kill me—then
Yourself—then—presently—first hear me speak!
I always meant to kill myself—wait, you!
Lean on my breast—not as a breast; don't love me
The more because you lean on me, my own
Heart's Sebald! There, there, both deaths presently!
   Sebald. My brain is drowned now—quite drowned: all I feel
Is ... is, at swift-recurring intervals,
A hurry-down within me, as of waters
Loosened to smother up some ghastly pit: 280
There they go—whirls from a black fiery sea!
   Ottima. Not me—to him, O God, be merciful!

Talk by the way, while PIPPA *is passing from the hill-side to
Orcana. Foreign* Students *of painting and sculpture, from
Venice, assembled opposite the house of* JULES, *a young French
statuary, at Possagno.*

   1st Student. Attention! My own post is beneath this window,
but the pomegranate clump yonder will hide three or four of you
with a little squeezing, and Schramm and his pipe must lie flat in
the balcony. Four, five—who's a defaulter? We want everybody,
for Jules must not be suffered to hurt his bride when the jest's
found out.
   2nd Student. All here! Only our poet's away—never having
much meant to be present, moonstrike him! The airs of that   290
fellow, that Giovacchino! He was in violent love with himself,
and had a fair prospect of thriving in his suit, so unmolested was
it,—when suddenly a woman falls in love with him, too; and out
of pure jealousy he takes himself off to Trieste,° immortal poem
and all: whereto is this prophetical epitaph appended already, as
Bluphocks assures me,—'*Here a mammoth-poem lies, Fouled to
death by butterflies.*' His own fault, the simpleton! Instead of
cramp couplets, each like a knife in your entrails, he should
write, says Bluphocks, both classically and intelligibly.—*Æscu-
lapius, an Epic. Catalogue of the drugs: Hebe's plaister—One strip*   300

Cools your lip. Phœbus' emulsion—One bottle Clears your throttle.
Mercury's bolus—One box Cures...°

3rd Student. Subside, my fine fellow! If the marriage was over
by ten o'clock, Jules will certainly be here in a minute with his
bride.

2nd Student. Good!—only, so should the poet's muse have
been universally acceptable, says Bluphocks, *et canibus nostris*°
...and Delia not better known to our literary dogs than the boy
Giovacchino!

1st Student. To the point, now. Where's Gottlieb, the new-   310
comer? Oh,—listen, Gottlieb, to what has called down this piece
of friendly vengeance on Jules, of which we now assemble to
witness the winding-up. We are all agreed, all in a tale, observe,
when Jules shall burst out on us in a fury by and by: I am
spokesman—the verses that are to undeceive Jules bear my name
of Lutwyche—but each professes himself alike insulted by this
strutting stone-squarer, who came alone from Paris to Munich,
and thence with a crowd of us to Venice and Possagno here, but
proceeds in a day or two alone again—oh, alone indubitably!—to
Rome and Florence. He, forsooth, take up his portion with these   320
dissolute, brutalized, heartless bunglers!— so he was heard to
call us all: now, is Schramm brutalized, I should like to know?
Am I heartless?

Gottlieb. Why, somewhat heartless; for, suppose Jules a cox-
comb as much as you choose, still, for this mere coxcombry, you
will have brushed off—what do folks style it?—the bloom of his
life. Is it too late to alter? These love-letters now, you call his—I
can't laugh at them.

4th Student. Because you never read the sham letters of our
inditing which drew forth these.   330

Gottlieb. His discovery of the truth will be frightful.

4th Student. That's the joke. But you should have joined us at
the beginning: there's no doubt he loves the girl—loves a model
he might hire by the hour!

Gottlieb. See here! 'He has been accustomed,' he writes, 'to have
Canova's women about him, in stone, and the world's women
beside him, in flesh; these being as much below, as those above,
his soul's aspiration: but now he is to have the reality.' There you
laugh again! I say, you wipe off the very dew of his youth.

1st Student. Schramm! (Take the pipe out of his mouth,   340
somebody!) Will Jules lose the bloom of his youth?

Schramm. Nothing worth keeping is ever lost in this world: look at a blossom—it drops presently, having done its service and lasted its time; but fruits succeed, and where would be the blossom's place could it continue? As well affirm that your eye is no longer in your body, because its earliest favourite, whatever it may have first loved to look on, is dead and done with—as that any affection is lost to the soul when its first object, whatever happened first to satisfy it, is superseded in due course. Keep but ever looking, whether with the body's eye or the mind's, and you   350
will soon find something to look on! Has a man done wondering at women?—there follow men, dead and alive, to wonder at. Has he done wondering at men?—there's God to wonder at: and the faculty of wonder may be, at the same time, old and tired enough with respect to its first object, and yet young and fresh suffi-ciently, so far as concerns its novel one. Thus...

1st Student. Put Schramm's pipe into his mouth again! There, you see! Well, this Jules...a wretched fribble°—oh, I watched his disportings at Possagno, the other day! Canova's gallery— you know: there he marches first resolvedly past great works by   360
the dozen without vouchsafing an eye: all at once he stops full at the *Psiche-fanciulla*°—cannot pass that old acquaintance without a nod of encouragement—'In your new place, beauty? Then behave yourself as well here as at Munich—I see you!' Next he posts himself deliberately before the unfinished *Pietà*° for half an hour without moving, till up he starts of a sudden, and thrusts his very nose into—I say, into—the group; by which gesture you are informed that precisely the sole point he had not fully mas-tered in Canova's practice was a certain method of using the drill in the articulation of the knee-joint—and that, likewise, has he   370
mastered at length! Good-bye, therefore, to poor Canova— whose gallery no longer needs detain his successor Jules, the predestinated novel thinker in marble!

5th Student. Tell him about the women: go on to the women!

1st Student. Why, on that matter he could never be super-cilious enough. How should we be other (he said) than the poor devils you see, with those debasing habits we cherish? He was not to wallow in that mire, at least: he would wait, and love only at the proper time; and meanwhile put up with the *Psiche-fanciulla*. Now, I happened to hear of a young Greek—real   380
Greek girl at Malamocco;° a true Islander, do you see, with Alciphron's° 'hair like sea-moss'—Schramm knows!—white and

quiet as an apparition, and fourteen years old at farthest,—a
daughter of Natalia, so she swears—that hag Natalia, who helps
us to models at three *lire* an hour. We selected this girl for the
heroine of our jest. So first, Jules received a scented letter—
somebody had seen his Tydeus° at the Academy, and my picture
was nothing to it: a profound admirer bade him persevere—
would make herself known to him ere long. (Paolina, my little
friend of the *Fenice*°, transcribes divinely.) And in due time, the   390
mysterious correspondent gave certain hints of her peculiar
charms—the pale cheeks, the black hair—whatever, in short,
had struck us in our Malamocco model: we retained her name,
too—Phene, which is, by interpretation, sea-eagle. Now, think of
Jules finding himself distinguished from the herd of us by such a
creature! In his very first answer he proposed marrying his
monitress: and fancy us over these letters, two, three times a
day, to receive and despatch! I concocted the main of it: relations
were in the way—secrecy must be observed—in fine, would he
wed her on trust, and only speak to her when they were indis-   400
solubly united? St—st—Here they come!

    6th Student. Both of them! Heaven's love, speak softly, speak
within yourselves!

    5th Student. Look at the bridegroom! Half his hair in storm
and half in calm,—patted down over the left temple,— like a
frothy cup one blows on to cool it: and the same old blouse that
he murders the marble in.

    2nd Student. Not a rich vest like yours, Hannibal Scratchy!°—
rich, that your face may the better set it off.

    6th Student. And the bride! Yes, sure enough, our Phene!   410
Should you have known her in her clothes? How magnificently
pale!

    Gottlieb. She does not also take it for earnest, I hope?

    1st Student. Oh, Natalia's concern, that is! We settle with
Natalia.

    6th Student. She does not speak—has evidently let out no
word. The only thing is, will she equally remember the rest of
her lesson, and repeat correctly all those verses which are to
break the secret to Jules?

    Gottlieb. How he gazes on her! Pity—pity!   420

    1st Student. They go in: now, silence! You three,—not nearer
the window, mind, than that pomegranate: just where the little
girl, who a few minutes ago passed us singing, is seated!

Part II

Noon

SCENE.—*Over Orcana. The house of* JULES, *who crosses its threshold with* PHENE: *she is silent, on which* JULES *begins*—

Do not die, Phene! I am yours now, you
Are mine now; let fate reach me how she likes,
If you'll not die: so, never die! Sit here—
My work-room's single seat. I over-lean
This length of hair and lustrous front; they turn
Like an entire flower upward: eyes, lips, last
Your chin—no, last your throat turns: 'tis their scent
Pulls down my face upon you. Nay, look ever
This one way till I change, grow you—I could
Change into you, beloved!
               You by me,   10
And I by you; this is your hand in mine,
And side by side we sit: all's true. Thank God!
I have spoken: speak you!
             O my life to come!
My Tydeus must be carved that's there in clay;
Yet how be carved, with you about the room?
Where must I place you? When I think that once
This room-full of rough block-work seemed my heaven
Without you! Shall I ever work again,
Get fairly into my old ways again,
Bid each conception stand while, trait by trait,   20
My hand transfers its lineaments to stone?
Will my mere fancies live near you, their truth—
The live truth, passing and repassing me,
Sitting beside me?
           Now speak!
               Only first,
See, all your letters! Was't not well contrived?
Their hiding-place is Psyche's robe; she keeps
Your letters next her skin: which drops out foremost?
Ah,—this that swam down like a first moonbeam
Into my world!
          Again those eyes complete

Their melancholy survey, sweet and slow,   30
Of all my room holds; to return and rest
On me, with pity, yet some wonder too:
As if God bade some spirit plague a world,
And this were the one moment of surprise
And sorrow while she took her station, pausing
O'er what she sees, finds good, and must destroy!
What gaze you at? Those? Books, I told you of;
Let your first word to me rejoice them, too:
This minion, a Coluthus, writ in red°
Bistre and azure by Bessarion's scribe—°   40
Read this line . . . no, shame—Homer's be the Greek
First breathed me from the lips of my Greek girl!
This Odyssey in coarse black vivid type
With faded yellow blossoms 'twixt page and page,
To mark great places with due gratitude;
'*He said, and on Antinous directed*
A bitter shaft' . . . a flower blots out the rest!°
Again upon your search? My statues, then!
—Ah, do not mind that—better that will look
When cast in bronze—an Almaign Kaiser, that,°   50
Swart-green and gold, with truncheon based on hip.
This, rather, turn to! What, unrecognized?
I thought you would have seen that here you sit
As I imagined you,—Hippolyta,°
Naked upon her bright Numidian horse.
Recall you this then? 'Carve in bold relief '—
So you commanded—'carve, against I come,
A Greek, in Athens, as our fashion was,
Feasting, bay-filleted and thunder-free,°
Who rises 'neath the lifted myrtle-branch.   60
"Praise those who slew Hipparchus!" cry the guests,°
"While o'er thy head the singer's myrtle waves
As erst above our champion: stand up, all!"'
See, I have laboured to express your thought.
Quite round, a cluster of mere hands and arms,
(Thrust in all senses, all ways, from all sides,
Only consenting at the branch's end
They strain toward) serves for frame to a sole face,
The Praiser's, in the centre: who with eyes
Sightless, so bend they back to light inside   70

His brain where visionary forms throng up,
Sings, minding not that palpitating arch
Of hands and arms, nor the quick drip of wine
From the drenched leaves o'erhead, nor crowns cast off,
Violet and parsley crowns to trample on—
Sings, pausing as the patron-ghosts approve,
Devoutly their unconquerable hymn.
But you must say a 'well' to that—say 'well!'
Because you gaze—am I fantastic, sweet?
Gaze like my very life's-stuff, marble—marbly
Even to the silence! Why, before I found   80
The real flesh Phene, I inured myself
To see, throughout all nature, varied stuff
For better nature's birth by means of art:
With me, each substance tended to one form
Of beauty—to the human archetype.
On every side occurred suggestive germs
Of that—the tree, the flower—or take the fruit,—
Some rosy shape, continuing the peach,
Curved beewise o'er its bough; as rosy limbs,   90
Depending, nestled in the leaves; and just
From a cleft rose-peach the whole Dryad sprang.°
But of the stuffs one can be master of,
How I divined their capabilities!
From the soft-rinded smoothening facile chalk
That yields your outline to the air's embrace,
Half-softened by a halo's pearly gloom;
Down to the crisp imperious steel, so sure
To cut its one confided thought clean out
Of all the world. But marble!—'neath my tools   100
More pliable than jelly—as it were
Some clear primordial creature dug from depths
In the earth's heart, where itself breeds itself,
And whence all baser substance may be worked;
Refine it off to air, you may,—condense it
Down to the diamond;—is not metal there,
When o'er the sudden speck my chisel trips?
—Not flesh, as flake off flake I scale, approach,
Lay bare those bluish veins of blood asleep?
Lurks flame in no strange windings where; surprised   110
By the swift implement sent home at once,

Flushes and glowings radiate and hover
About its track?

             Phene? what—why is this?
That whitening cheek, those still dilating eyes!
Ah, you will die—I knew that you would die!

    PHENE *begins, on his having long remained silent.*

Now the end's coming; to be sure, it must
Have ended sometime! Tush, why need I speak
Their foolish speech? I cannot bring to mind
One half of it, beside; and do not care
For old Natalia now, nor any of them.   120
Oh, you—what are you?—if I do not try
To say the words Natalia made me learn,
To please your friends,—it is to keep myself
Where your voice lifted me, by letting that
Proceed: but can it? Even you, perhaps,
Cannot take up, now you have once let fall,
The music's life, and me along with that—
No, or you would! We'll stay, then, as we are:
Above the world.

           You creature with the eyes!
If I could look for ever up to them,   130
As now you let me,—I believe, all sin,
All memory of wrong done, suffering borne,
Would drop down, low and lower, to the earth
Whence all that's low comes, and there touch and stay
—Never to overtake the rest of me,
All that, unspotted, reaches up to you,
Drawn by those eyes! What rises is myself,
Not me the shame and suffering; but they sink,
Are left, I rise above them. Keep me so,
Above the world!

         But you sink, for your eyes   140
Are altering—altered! Stay—'I love you, love' ...
I could prevent it if I understood:
More of your words to me: was't in the tone
Or the words, your power?

           Or stay—I will repeat
Their speech, if that contents you! Only change
No more, and I shall find it presently

Far back here, in the brain yourself filled up.
Natalia threatened me that harm should follow
Unless I spoke their lesson to the end,
But harm to me, I thought she meant, not you.   150
Your friends,—Natalia said they were your friends
And meant you well,—because, I doubted it,
Observing (what was very strange to see)
On every face, so different in all else,
The same smile girls like me are used to bear,
But never men, men cannot stoop so low;
Yet your friends, speaking of you, used that smile,
That hateful smirk of boundless self-conceit
Which seems to take possession of the world
And make of God a tame confederate,   160
Purveyor to their appetites... you know!
But still Natalia said they were your friends,
And they assented though they smiled the more,
And all came round me,—that thin Englishman
With light lank hair seemed leader of the rest;
He held a paper—'What we want,' said he,
Ending some explanation to his friends—
'Is something slow, involved and mystical,
To hold Jules long in doubt, yet take his taste
And lure him on until, at innermost   170
Where he seeks sweetness' soul, he may find—this!
—As in the apple's core, the noisome fly:
For insects on the rind are seen at once,
And brushed aside as soon, but this is found
Only when on the lips or loathing tongue.'
And so he read what I have got by heart:
I'll speak it,—'Do not die, love! I am yours.'
No—is not that, or like that, part of words
Yourself began by speaking? Strange to lose
What cost such pains to learn! Is this more right?   180

> I am a painter who cannot paint;
> In my life, a devil rather than saint;
> In my brain, as poor a creature too:
> No end to all I cannot do!
> Yet do one thing at least I can—
> Love a man or hate a man

Supremely: thus my lore began.
Through the Valley of Love I went,
In the lovingest spot to abide,
And just on the verge where I pitched my tent,   190
I found Hate dwelling beside.
(Let the Bridegroom ask what the painter meant,
Of his Bride, of the peerless Bride!)
And further, I traversed Hate's grove,
In the hatefullest nook to dwell;
But lo, where I flung myself prone, couched Love
Where the shadow threefold fell.
(The meaning—those black bride's-eyes above,
Not a painter's lip should tell!)

'And here,' said he, 'Jules probably will ask,   200
"You have black eyes, Love,—you are, sure enough,
My peerless bride,—then do you tell indeed
What needs some explanation! What means this?"'
—And I am to go on, without a word—

So, I grew wise in Love and Hate,
From simple that I was of late.
Once, when I loved, I would enlace
Breast, eyelids, hands, feet, form and face
Of her I loved, in one embrace—
As if by mere love I could love immensely!   210
Once, when I hated, I would plunge
My sword, and wipe with the first lunge
My foe's whole life out like a sponge—
As if by mere hate I could hate intensely!
But now I am wiser, know better the fashion
How passion seeks aid from its opposite passion:
And if I see cause to love more, hate more
Than ever man loved, ever hated before—
And seek in the Valley of Love,
The nest, or the nook in Hate's Grove,   220
Where my soul may surely reach
The essence, nought less, of each,
The Hate of all Hates, the Love
Of all Loves, in the Valley or Grove,—
I find them the very warders
Each of the other's borders.

When I love most, Love is disguised
In Hate; and when Hate is surprised
In Love, then I hate most: ask
How Love smiles through Hate's iron casque,   230
Hate grins through Love's rose-braided mask,—
And how, having hated thee,
I sought long and painfully
To reach thy heart, nor prick
The skin but pierce to the quick—
Ask this, my Jules, and be answered straight
By thy bride—how the painter Lutwyche can hate!

JULES *interposes.*

Lutwyche! Who else? But all of them, no doubt,
Hated me: they at Venice—presently
Their turn, however! You I shall not meet: 240
If I dreamed, saying this would wake me.
                                        Keep
What's here, the gold—we cannot meet again,
Consider! and the money was but meant
For two years' travel, which is over now,
All chance or hope or care or need of it.
This—and what comes from selling these, my casts
And books and medals, except... let them go
Together, so the produce keeps you safe
Out of Natalia's clutches! If by chance
(For all's chance here) I should survive the gang
At Venice, root out all fifteen of them,   250
We might meet somewhere, since the world is wide.
      [*From without is heard the voice of* PIPPA, *singing—*

   Give her but a least excuse to love me!
   When—where—
   How—can this arm establish her above me,
   If fortune fixed her as my lady there,
   There already, to eternally reprove me?
      ('Hist!'—said Kate the Queen;°
      But 'Oh!'—cried the maiden, binding her tresses,
      ''Tis only a page that carols unseen,
      Crumbling your hounds their messes!')   260

Is she wronged?—To the rescue of her honour,
My heart!
Is she poor?—What costs it to be styled a donor?
Merely an earth to cleave, a sea to part.
But that fortune should have thrust all this upon her!
   ('Nay, list!'—bade Kate the Queen;
   And still cried the maiden, binding her tresses,
   ''Tis only a page that carols unseen,
   Fitting your hawks their jesses!')°   270
                                   [PIPPA *passes.*

                        JULES *resumes.*

What name was that the little girl sang forth?
Kate? The Cornaro, doubtless, who renounced
The crown of Cyprus to be lady here
At Asolo, where still her memory stays,
And peasants sing how once a certain page
Pined for the grace of her so far above
His power of doing good to, 'Kate the Queen—
She never could be wronged, be poor,' he sighed,
'Need him to help her!'
                        Yes, a bitter thing
To see our lady above all need of us;   280
Yet so we look ere we will love; not I,
But the world looks so. If whoever loves
Must be, in some sort, god or worshipper,
The blessing or the blest one, queen or page,
Why should we always choose the page's part?
Here is a woman with utter need of me,—
I find myself queen here, it seems!
                                   How strange!
Look at the woman here with the new soul,
Like my own Psyche,—fresh upon her lips
Alit, the visionary butterfly,   290
Waiting my word to enter and make bright,
Or flutter off and leave all blank as first.
This body had no soul before, but slept
Or stirred, was beauteous or ungainly, free
From taint or foul with stain, as outward things
Fastened their image on its passiveness:
Now, it will wake, feel, live—or die again!

Shall to produce form out of unshaped stuff
Be Art—and further, to evoke a soul
From form be nothing? This new soul is mine!   300

Now, to kill Lutwyche, what would that do?—save
A wretched dauber, men will hoot to death
Without me, from their hooting. Oh, to hear
God's voice plain as I heard it first, before
They broke in with their laughter! I heard them
Henceforth, not God.
                To Ancona—Greece—some isle!°
I wanted silence only; there is clay
Everywhere. One may do whate'er one likes
In Art: the only thing is, to make sure
That one does like it—which takes pains to know.   310
   Scatter all this, my Phene—this mad dream!
Who, what is Lutwyche, what Natalia's friends,
What the whole world except our love—my own,
Own Phene? But I told you, did I not,
Ere night we travel for your land—some isle
With the sea's silence on it? Stand aside—
I do but break these paltry models up
To begin Art afresh. Meet Lutwyche, I—
And save him from my statue meeting him?
Some unsuspected isle in the far seas!   320
Like a god going through his world, there stands
One mountain for a moment in the dusk,
Whole brotherhoods of cedars on its brow:
And you are ever by me while I gaze
—Are in my arms as now—as now—as now!
Some unsuspected isle in the far seas!
Some unsuspected isle in far-off seas!

Talk by the way, while PIPPA *is passing from Orcana to the Turret.
Two or three of the Austrian Police loitering with* BLUPHOCKS,
an English vagabond, just in view of the Turret.

Bluphocks.*° So, that is your Pippa, the little girl who passed
us singing? Well, your Bishop's Intendant's° money shall be
honestly earned:—now, don't make me that sour face because I   330

* 'He maketh his sun to rise on the evil and on the good, and sendeth rain on the
just and on the unjust.'

bring the Bishop's name into the business; we know he can have
nothing to do with such horrors: we know that he is a saint and
all that a bishop should be, who is a great man beside. *Oh were
but every worm a maggot, Every fly a grig,*° *Every bough a
Christmas faggot, Every tune a jig!* In fact, I have abjured all
religions; but the last I inclined to, was the Armenian: for I have
travelled, do you see, and at Koenigsberg,° Prussia Improper (so
styled because there's a sort of bleak hungry sun there), you
might remark over a venerable house-porch, a certain Chaldee°
inscription; and brief as it is, a mere glance at it used absolutely   340
to change the mood of every bearded passenger. In they turned,
one and all; the young and lightsome, with no irreverent pause,
the aged and decrepit, with a sensible alacrity: 'twas the Grand
Rabbi's abode, in short. Struck with curiosity, I lost no time in
learning Syriac—(these are vowels, you dogs,—follow my
stick's end in the mud—*Celarent, Darii, Ferio!*°) and one
morning presented myself, spelling-book in hand, a, b, c,—I
picked it out letter by letter, and what was the purport of this
miraculous posy? Some cherished legend of the past, you'll
say—'*How Moses hocus-pocussed Egypt's land with fly and*   350
locust,'—or, '*How to Jonah sounded harshish, Get thee up and go
to Tarshish,*'—or, '*How the angel meeting Balaam, Straight his ass
returned a salaam,*'° In no wise! '*Shackabrack—Boach—somebody
or other—Isaach, Re-cei-ver, Pur-cha-ser and Ex-chan-ger of—
Stolen Goods!*' So, talk to me of the religion of a bishop! I have
renounced all bishops save Bishop Beveridge°—mean to live
so—and die—*As some Greek dog-sage,*° *dead and merry, Hellward
bound in Charon's wherry,*° *With food for both worlds, under and
upper, Lupine-seed and Hecate's*° *supper, And never an obolus* . . .
(Though thanks to you, or this Intendant through you, or this   360
Bishop through his Intendant—I possess a burning pocketful of
zwanzigers°) . . . *To pay the Stygian Ferry!*

  1st Policeman. There is the girl, then; go and deserve them the
moment you have pointed out to us Signor Luigi and his
mother. [*To the rest.*] I have been noticing a house yonder, this
long while: not a shutter unclosed since morning!

  2nd Policeman. Old Luca Gaddi's, that owns the silk-mills
here: he dozes by the hour, wakes up, sighs deeply, says he
should like to be Prince Metternich,° and then dozes again, after
having bidden young Sebald, the foreigner, set his wife to playing   370
draughts. Never molest such a household, they mean well.

Bluphocks. Only, cannot you tell me something of this little Pippa, I must have to do with? One could make something of that name. Pippa—that is, short for Felippa—rhyming to *Panurge consults Hertrippa*°—*Believest thou, King Agrippa?* Something might be done with that name.

2nd Policeman. Put into rhyme that your head and a ripe musk-melon would not be dear at half a *zwanziger!* Leave this fooling, and look out; the afternoon's over or nearly so.

3rd Policeman. Where in this passport of Signor Luigi does 380
our Principal instruct you to watch him so narrowly? There? What's there beside a simple signature? (That English fool's busy watching.)

2nd Policeman. Flourish all round—'Put all possible obstacles in his way;' oblong dot at the end—'Detain him till further advices reach you;' scratch at bottom—'Send him back on pretence of some informality in the above;' ink-spirt on right-hand side (which is the case here)—'Arrest him at once.' Why and wherefore, I don't concern myself, but my instructions amount to this: if Signor Luigi leaves home to-night for Vienna—well 390
and good, the passport deposed with us for our *visa* is really for his own use, they have misinformed the Office, and he means well; but let him stay over to-night—there has been the pretence we suspect, the accounts of his corresponding and holding intelligence with the Carbonari° are correct, we arrest him at once, to-morrow comes Venice, and presently Spielberg.° Bluphocks makes the signal, sure enough! That is he, entering the turret with his mother, no doubt.

Part III

Evening

Scene.—*Inside the Turret on the Hill above Asolo.*
Luigi *and his* Mother *entering.*

Mother. If there blew wind, you'd hear a long sigh, easing
The utmost heaviness of music's heart.
Luigi. Here in the archway?
Mother.   Oh no, no—in farther,
Where the echo is made, on the ridge.
Luigi.   Here surely, then.

How plain the tap of my heel as I leaped up!
Hark—'Lucius Junius!' The very ghost of a voice°
Whose body is caught and kept by . . . what are those?
Mere withered wallflowers, waving overhead?
They seem an elvish group with thin bleached hair
That lean out of their topmost fortress—look   10
And listen, mountain men, to what we say,
Hand under chin of each grave earthy face.
Up and show faces all of you!—'All of you!'
That's the king dwarf with the scarlet comb; old Franz,°
Come down and meet your fate? Hark—'Meet your fate!'
　　Mother. Let him not meet it, my Luigi—do not
Go to his City! Putting crime aside,
Half of these ills of Italy are feigned:
Your Pellicos and writers for effect,°
Write for effect.
　　Luigi.　　　　Hush! Say A. writes, and B.   20
　　Mother. These A.s and B.s write for effect, I say.
Then, evil is in its nature loud, while good
Is silent; you hear each petty injury,
None of his virtues; he is old beside,
Quiet and kind, and densely stupid. Why
Do A. and B. not kill him themselves?
　　Luigi.　　　　　　　　　　They teach
Others to kill him—me—and, if I fail,
Others to succeed; now, if A. tried and failed,
I could not teach that: mine's the lesser task.
Mother, they visit night by night . . .
　　Mother.　　　　　　　　—You, Luigi?   30
Ah, will you let me tell you what you are?
　　Luigi. Why not? Oh, the one thing you fear to hint,
You may assure yourself I say and say
Ever to myself! At times—nay, even as now
We sit—I think my mind is touched, suspect
All is not sound: but is not knowing that,
What constitutes one sane or otherwise?
I know I am thus—so, all is right again.
I laugh at myself as through the town I walk.
And see men merry as if no Italy   40
Were suffering; then I ponder—'I am rich,
Young, healthy; why should this fact trouble me,

More than it troubles these?' But it does trouble.
No, trouble's a bad word: for as I walk
There's springing and melody and giddiness,
And old quaint turns and passages of my youth,
Dreams long forgotten, little in themselves,
Return to me—whatever may amuse me:
And earth seems in a truce with me, and heaven
Accords with me, all things suspend their strife,   50
The very cicala laughs 'There goes he, and there!
Feast him, the time is short; he is on his way
For the world's sake: feast him this once, our friend!'
And in return for all this, I can trip
Cheerfully up the scaffold-steps. I go
This evening, mother!
     Mother.   But mistrust yourself—
Mistrust the judgment you pronounce on him!
     Luigi. Oh, there I feel—am sure that I am right!
     Mother. Mistrust your judgment then, of the mere means
To this wild enterprise. Say, you are right,—   60
How should one in your state e'er bring to pass
What would require a cool head, a cold heart,
And a calm hand? You never will escape.
     Luigi. Escape? To even wish that, would spoil all.
The dying is best part of it. Too much
Have I enjoyed these fifteen years of mine,
To leave myself excuse for longer life:
Was not life pressed down, running o'er with joy,
That I might finish with it ere my fellows
Who, sparelier feasted, make a longer stay?   70
I was put at the board-head, helped to all
At first; I rise up happy and content.
God must be glad one loves his world so much.
I can give news of earth to all the dead
Who ask me:—last year's sunsets, and great stars
Which had a right to come first and see ebb
The crimson wave that drifts the sun away—
Those crescent moons with notched and burning rims
That strengthened into sharp fire, and there stood,
Impatient of the azure—and that day   80
In March, a double rainbow stopped the storm—
May's warm slow yellow moonlit summer nights—

Gone are they, but I have them in my soul!
   Mother. (He will not go!)
   Luigi.   You smile at me? 'Tis true,—
Voluptuousness, grotesqueness, ghastliness,
Environ my devotedness as quaintly
As round about some antique altar wreathe
The rose festoons, goats' horns, and oxen's skulls.
   Mother. See now: you reach the city, you must cross
His threshold—how?
   Luigi   Oh, that's if we conspired!   90
Then would come pains in plenty, as you guess—
But guess not how the qualities most fit
For such an office, qualities I have,
Would little stead me, otherwise employed,
Yet prove of rarest merit only here.
Every one knows for what his excellence
Will serve, but no one ever will consider
For what his worst defect might serve: and yet
Have you not seen me range our coppice yonder
In search of a distorted ash?—I find   100
The wry spoilt branch a natural perfect bow.
Fancy the thrice-sage, thrice-precautioned man
Arriving at the palace on my errand!
No, no! I have a handsome dress packed up—
White satin here, to set off my black hair;
In I shall march—for you may watch your life out
Behind thick walls, make friends there to betray you;
More than one man spoils everything. March straight—
Only, no clumsy knife to fumble for.
Take the great gate, and walk (not saunter) on   110
Thro' guards and guards—I have rehearsed it all
Inside the turret here a hundred times.
Don't ask the way of whom you meet, observe!
But where they cluster thickliest is the door
Of doors; they'll let you pass—they'll never blab
Each to the other, he knows not the favourite,
Whence he is bound and what's his business now.
Walk in—straight up to him; you have no knife:
Be prompt, how should he scream? Then, out with you!
Italy, Italy, my Italy!   120
You're free, you're free! Oh mother, I could dream

They got about me—Andrea from his exile,
Pier from his dungeon, Gualtier from his grave!°
    Mother. Well, you shall go. Yet seems this patriotism
The easiest virtue for a selfish man
To acquire: he loves himself—and next, the world—
If he must love beyond,—but nought between:
As a short-sighted man sees nought midway
His body and the sun above. But you
Are my adored Luigi, ever obedient   130
To my least wish, and running o'er with love:
I could not call you cruel or unkind.
Once more, your ground for killing him!—then go!
    Luigi. Now do you try me, or make sport of me?
How first the Austrians got these provinces...
(If that is all, I'll satisfy you soon)
—Never by conquest but by cunning, for
That treaty whereby...°
    Mother.   Well?
    Luigi.   (Sure, he's arrived,
The tell-tale cuckoo: spring's his confidant,
And he lets out her April purposes!)   140
Or...better go at once to modern time,
He has...they have...in fact, I understand
But can't restate the matter; that's my boast:
Others could reason it out to you, and prove
Things they have made me feel.
    Mother.   Why go to-night?
Morn's for adventure. Jupiter is now
A morning-star. I cannot hear you, Luigi!
    Luigi. 'I am the bright and morning-star,' saith God—°
And, 'to such an one I give the morning-star.'°
The gift of the morning-star! Have I God's gift   150
Of the morning-star?
    Mother.   Chiara will love to see
That Jupiter an evening-star next June.
    Luigi. True, mother. Well for those who live through June!
Great noontides, thunder-storms, all glaring pomps
That triumph at the heels of June the god
Leading his revel through our leafy world.
Yes, Chiara will be here.
    Mother.   In June: remember,

Yourself appointed that month for her coming.
    Luigi. Was that low noise the echo?
    Mother.   The night-wind.
She must be grown—with her blue eyes upturned   160
As if life were one long and sweet surprise:
In June she comes.
    Luigi.   We were to see together
The Titian at Treviso. There, again!°
        [*From without is heard the voice of* PIPPA, *singing—*

      A king lived long ago,
      In the morning of the world,
      When earth was nigher heaven than now:
      And the king's locks curled,
      Disparting o'er a forehead full
      As the milk-white space 'twixt horn and horn
      Of some sacrificial bull—   170
      Only calm as a babe new-born:
      For he was got to a sleepy mood,
      So safe from all decrepitude,
      Age with its bane, so sure gone by,
      (The gods so loved him while he dreamed)
      That, having lived thus long, there seemed
      No need the king should ever die.

Luigi. No need that sort of king should ever die!

      Among the rocks his city was:
      Before his palace, in the sun,   180
      He sat to see his people pass,
      And judge them every one
      From its threshold of smooth stone.
      They haled him many a valley-thief
      Caught in the sheep-pens, robber-chief
      Swarthy and shameless, beggar-cheat,
      Spy-prowler, or rough pirate found
      On the sea-sand left aground;
      And sometimes clung about his feet,
      With bleeding lip and burning cheek,   190
      A woman, bitterest wrong to speak
      Of one with sullen thickset brows:
      And sometimes from the prison-house
      The angry priests a pale wretch brought,

Who through some chink had pushed and pressed
On knees and elbows, belly and breast,
Worm-like into the temple,—caught
He was by the very god,
Who ever in the darkness strode
Backward and forward, keeping watch   200
O'er his brazen bowls, such rogues to catch!
These, all and every one,
The king judged, sitting in the sun.

Luigi. That king should still judge sitting in the sun!

His councillors, on left and right,
Looked anxious up,—but no surprise
Disturbed the king's old smiling eyes
Where the very blue had turned to white.
'Tis said, a Python scared one day
The breathless city, till he came,   210
With forky tongue and eyes on flame
Where the old king sat to judge alway,
But when he saw the sweepy hair
Girt with a crown of berries rare
Which the god will hardly give to wear
To the maiden who singeth, dancing bare
In the altar-smoke by the pine-torch lights,
At his wondrous forest rites,—
Seeing this, he did not dare
Approach that threshold in the sun,   220
Assault the old king smiling there.
Such grace had kings when the world begun!

[PIPPA *passes.*

Luigi. And such grace have they, now that the world ends!
The Python at the city, on the throne,°
And brave men, God would crown for slaying him,
Lurk in bye-corners lest they fall his prey.
Are crowns yet to be won in this late time,
Which weakness makes me hesitate to reach?
'Tis God's voice calls: how could I stay? Farewell!

———————

Talk by the way, while PIPPA *is passing from the Turret to the*
Bishop's Brother's House, close to the Duomo S. Maria. Poor
Girls *sitting on the steps.*

1st Girl. There goes a swallow to Venice—the stout seafarer!   230
Seeing those birds fly, makes one wish for wings.
Let us all wish; you wish first!
    2nd Girl.   I? This sunset
To finish.
    3rd Girl. That old—somebody I know,
Greyer and older than my grandfather,
To give me the same treat he gave last week—
Feeding me on his knee with fig-peckers,°
Lampreys and red Breganze-wine, and mumbling
The while some folly about how well I fare,
Let sit and eat my supper quietly:
Since had he not himself been late this morning   240
Detained at—never mind where,—had he not...
'Eh, baggage, had I not!'
    2nd Girl.   How she can lie!
    3rd Girl. Look there—by the nails!
    2nd Girl.   What makes your fingers red?
    3rd Girl. Dipping them into wine to write bad words with
On the bright table: how he laughed!
    1st Girl.   My turn.
Spring's come and summer's coming. I would wear
A long loose gown, down to the feet and hands,
With plaits here, close about the throat, all day;
And all night lie, the cool long nights, in bed;
And have new milk to drink, apples to eat,   250
Deuzans and junetings, leather-coats..ah, I should say,°
This is away in the fields—miles!
    3rd Girl.   Say at once
You'd be at home: she'd always be at home!
Now comes the story of the farm among
The cherry orchards, and how April snowed
White blossoms on her as she ran. Why, fool,
They've rubbed the chalk-mark out, how tall you were
Twisted your starling's neck, broken his cage,
Made a dung-hill of your garden!
    1st Girl.   They, destroy
My garden since I left them? well—perhaps!   260
I would have done so: so I hope they have!
A fig-tree curled out of our cottage wall;
They called it mine, I have forgotten why,

It must have been there long ere I was born:
Cric—cric—I think I hear the wasps o'erhead
Pricking the papers strung to flutter there
And keep off birds in fruit-time—coarse long papers,
And the wasps eat them, prick them through and through.
   3rd Girl. How her mouth twitches! Where was I?—before
She broke in with her wishes and long gowns   270
And wasps—would I be such a fool!—Oh, here!
This is my way: I answer every one
Who asks me why I make so much of him—
(If you say, 'you love him'—straight 'he'll not be gulled!')
'He that seduced me when I was a girl
Thus high—had eyes like yours, or hair like yours,
Brown, red, white,'—as the case may be: that pleases!
See how that beetle burnishes in the path!
There sparkles he along the dust: and, there—
Your journey to that maize-tuft spoiled at least!   280
   1st Girl. When I was young, they said if you killed one
Of those sunshiny beetles, that his friend
Up there, would shine no more that day nor next.
   2nd Girl. When you were young? Nor are you young, that's
          true.
How your plump arms, that were, have dropped away!
Why, I can span them. Cecco beats you still?
No matter, so you keep your curious hair.
I wish they'd find a way to dye our hair
Your colour—any lighter tint, indeed,
Than black: the men say they are sick of black,   290
Black eyes, black hair!
   4th Girl.   Sick of yours, like enough.
Do you pretend you ever tasted lampreys
And ortolans? Giovita, of the palace,°
Engaged (but there's no trusting him) to slice me
Polenta with a knife that had cut up°
An ortolan.
   2nd Girl. Why, there! Is not that Pippa
We are to talk to, under the window,—quick,—
Where the lights are?
   1st Girl.   That she? No, or she would sing.
For the Intendant said...
   3rd Girl.   Oh, you sing first!

Then, if she listens and comes close...I'll tell you,—   300
Sing that song the young English noble made,
Who took you for the purest of the pure,
And meant to leave the world for you—what fun!
   2nd Girl [*sings*].

> *You'll love me yet!—and I can tarry*
>   *Your love's protracted growing:*
> *June reared that bunch of flowers you carry,*
>   *From seeds of April's sowing.*
>
> *I plant a heartful now: some seed*
>   *At least is sure to strike,*
> *And yield—what you'll not pluck indeed,*   310
>   *Not love, but, may be, like.*
>
> *You'll look at least on love's remains,*
>   *A grave's one violet:*
> *Your look?—that pays a thousand pains.*
>   *What's death? You'll love me yet!*

3rd Girl [*to* PIPPA *who approaches*]. Oh, you may come closer—we shall not eat you! Why, you seem the very person that the great rich handsome Englishman has fallen so violently in love with. I'll tell you all about it.

Part IV

Night

SCENE.—*Inside the Palace by the Duomo.* MONSIGNOR, *dismissing his* Attendants.

Monsignor. Thanks, friends, many thanks! I chiefly desire life now, that I may recompense every one of you. Most I know something of already. What, a repast prepared? *Benedicto bene-dicatur*°...ugh, ugh! Where was I? Oh, as you were remarking, Ugo, the weather is mild, very unlike winter-weather: but I am a Sicilian, you know, and shiver in your Julys here. To be sure, when 'twas full summer at Messina,° as we priests used to cross in procession the great square on Assumption Day,° you might see our thickest yellow tapers twist suddenly in two, each like a

falling star, or sink down on themselves in a gore of wax. But   10
go, my friends, but go! [*To the* Intendant.] Not you, Ugo! [*The
others leave the apartment*.] I have long wanted to converse with
you, Ugo.

Intendant. Uguccio—

Monsignor . . . 'guccio Stefani, man! of Ascoli, Fermo and Fos-
sombruno;°—what I do need instructing about, are these
accounts of your administration of my poor brother's affairs.
Ugh! I shall never get through a third part of your accounts:
take some of these dainties before we attempt it, however. Are
you bashful to that degree? For me, a crust and water suffice.   20

Intendant. Do you choose this especial night to question me?

Monsignor. This night, Ugo. You have managed my late
brother's affairs since the death of our elder brother: fourteen
years and a month, all but three days. On the Third of
December, I find him . . .

Intendant. If you have so intimate an acquaintance with your
brother's affairs, you will be tender of turning so far back: they
will hardly bear looking into, so far back.

Monsignor. Ay, ay, ugh, ugh,—nothing but disappointments
here below! I remark a considerable payment made to yourself   30
on this Third of December. Talk of disappointments! There was
a young fellow here, Jules, a foreign sculptor I did my utmost to
advance, that the Church might be a gainer by us both: he was
going on hopefully enough, and of a sudden he notifies to me
some marvellous change that has happened in his notions of Art.
Here's his letter,—'He never had a clearly conceived Ideal
within his brain till to-day. Yet since his hand could manage a
chisel, he has practised expressing other men's Ideals; and, in the
very perfection he has attained to, he foresees an ultimate failure:
his unconscious hand will pursue its prescribed course of old   40
years, and will reproduce with a fatal expertness the ancient
types, let the novel one appear never so palpably to his spirit.
There is but one method of escape: confiding the virgin type to
as chaste a hand, he will turn painter instead of sculptor, and
paint, not carve, its characteristics,'—strike out, I dare say, a
school like Correggio:° how think you, Ugo?

Intendant. Is Correggio a painter?

Monsignor. Foolish Jules! and yet, after all, why foolish? He
may—probably will—fail egregiously; but if there should arise a
new painter, will it not be in some such way, by a poet now, or a   50

musician (spirits who have conceived and perfected an Ideal
through some other channel), transferring it to this, and escaping
our conventional roads by pure ignorance of them; eh, Ugo? If
you have no appetite, talk at least, Ugo!

Intendant. Sir, I can submit no longer to this course of yours.
First, you select the group of which I formed one,—next you
thin it gradually,—always retaining me with your smile,—and so
do you proceed till you have fairly got me alone with you
between four stone walls. And now then? Let this farce, this
chatter end now: what is it you want with me?   60

Monsignor. Ugo!

Intendant. From the instant you arrived, I felt your smile on
me as you questioned me about this and the other article in those
papers—why your brother should have given me this villa, that
podere,°—and your nod at the end meant,—what?

Monsignor. Possibly that I wished for no loud talk here. If once
you set me coughing, Ugo!—

Intendant. I have your brother's hand and seal to all I possess:
now ask me what for! what service I did him—ask me!

Monsignor. I would better not: I should rip up old disgraces,   70
let out my poor brother's weaknesses. By the way, Maffeo of
Forli (which, I forgot to observe, is your true name), was the
interdict ever taken off you, for robbing that church at Cesena?

Intendant. No, nor needs be: for when I murdered your
brother's friend, Pasquale, for him . . .

Monsignor. Ah, he employed you in that business, did he?
Well, I must let you keep, as you say, this villa and that *podere,*
for fear the world should find out my relations were of so
indifferent a stamp? Maffeo, my family is the oldest in Messina,
and century after century have my progenitors gone on polluting   80
themselves with every wickedness under heaven: my own
father . . . rest his soul!—I have, I know, a chapel to support that
it may rest: my dear two dead brothers were,—what you know
tolerably well; I, the youngest, might have rivalled them in vice,
if not in wealth: but from my boyhood I came out from among
them, and so am not partaker of their plagues. My glory springs
from another source; or if from this, by contrast only,—for I, the
bishop, am the brother of your employers, Ugo. I hope to repair
some of their wrong, however; so far as my brothers' ill-gotten
treasure reverts to me, I can stop the consequences of his crime: 90
and not one *soldo*° shall escape me. Maffeo, the sword we quiet

men spurn away, you shrewd knaves pick up and commit mur-
ders with; what opportunities the virtuous forego, the villanous
seize. Because, to pleasure myself apart from other considera-
tions, my food would be millet-cake, my dress sackcloth, and my
couch straw,—am I therefore to let you, the offscouring of the
earth, seduce the poor and ignorant by appropriating a pomp
these will be sure to think lessens the abominations so unac-
countably and exclusively associated with it? Must I let villas and
poderi go to you, a murderer and thief, that you may beget by   100
means of them other murderers and thieves? No—if my cough
would but allow me to speak!

Intendant. What am I to expect? You are going to punish me?

Monsignor. —Must punish you, Maffeo. I cannot afford to cast
away a chance. I have whole centuries of sin to redeem, and only
a month or two of life to do it in. How should I dare to say...

Intendant. 'Forgive us our trespasses'?

Monsignor. My friend, it is because I avow myself a very
worm, sinful beyond measure, that I reject a line of conduct you
would applaud perhaps. Shall I proceed, as it were, a-par-   110
doning?—I?—who have no symptom of reason to assume that
aught less than my strenuousest efforts will keep myself out of
mortal sin, much less keep others out. No: I do trespass, but will
not double that by allowing you to trespass.

Intendant. And suppose the villas are not your brother's to
give, nor yours to take? Oh, you are hasty enough just now!

Monsignor. 1, 2—No. 3!—ay, can you read the substance of a
letter, No. 3, I have received from Rome? It is precisely on the
ground there mentioned, of the suspicion I have that a certain
child of my late elder brother, who would have succeeded to his   120
estates, was murdered in infancy by you, Maffeo, at the instiga-
tion of my late younger brother—that the Pontiff enjoins on me
not merely the bringing that Maffeo to condign punishment, but
the taking all pains, as guardian of the infant's heritage for the
Church, to recover it parcel by parcel, howsoever, whensoever,
and wheresoever. While you are now gnawing those fingers, the
police are engaged in sealing up your papers, Maffeo, and the
mere raising my voice brings my people from the next room to
dispose of yourself. But I want you to confess quietly, and save
me raising my voice. Why, man, do I not know the old story?   130
The heir between the succeeding heir, and this heir's ruffianly
instrument, and their complot's° effect, and the life of fear and

bribes and ominous smiling silence? Did you throttle or stab my
brother's infant? Come now

Intendant. So old a story, and tell it no better? When did such
an instrument ever produce such an effect? Either the child
smiles in his face; or, most likely, he is not fool enough to put
himself in the employer's power so thoroughly: the child is
always ready to produce—as you say—howsoever, wheresoever,
and whensoever.   140

Monsignor. Liar!

Intendant. Strike me? Ah, so might a father chastise! I shall
sleep soundly to-night at least, though the gallows await me to-
morrow; for what a life did I lead! Carlo of Cesena reminds me
of his connivance, every time I pay his annuity; which happens
commonly thrice a year. If I remonstrate, he will confess all to
the good bishop—you!

Monsignor. I see through the trick, caitiff! I would you spoke
truth for once. All shall be sifted, however—seven times sifted.

Intendant. And how my absurd riches encumbered me! I   150
dared not lay claim to above half my possessions. Let me but
once unbosom myself, glorify Heaven, and die!

Sir, you are no brutal dastardly idiot like your brother I
frightened to death: let us understand one another. Sir, I will
make away with her for you—the girl—here close at hand; not
the stupid obvious kind of killing; do not speak—know nothing
of her nor of me! I see her every day—saw her this morning: of
course there is to be no killing; but at Rome the courtesans
perish off every three years, and I can entice her thither—have
indeed begun operations already. There's a certain lusty blue-   160
eyed florid-complexioned English knave, I and the Police employ
occasionally. You assent, I perceive—no, that's not it—assent I
do not say—but you will let me convert my present havings and
holdings into cash, and give me time to cross the Alps? 'Tis but a
little black-eyed pretty singing Felippa, gay silk-winding girl. I
have kept her out of harm's way up to this present; for I always
intended to make your life a plague to you with her. 'Tis as well
settled once and for ever. Some women I have procured will pass
Bluphocks, my handsome scoundrel, off for somebody; and once
Pippa entangled!—you conceive? Through her singing? Is it a   170
bargain?

[*From without is heard the voice of* PIPPA, *singing*—

Overhead the tree-tops meet,
Flowers and grass spring 'neath one's feet;
There was nought above me, nought below,
My childhood had not learned to know:
For, what are the voices of birds
—Ay, and of beasts,—but words, our words,
Only so much more sweet?
The knowledge of that with my life begun.
But I had so near made out the sun,   180
And counted your stars, the seven and one,
Like the fingers of my hand:
Nay, I could all but understand
Wherefore through heaven the white moon ranges;
And just when out of her soft fifty changes
No unfamiliar face might overlook me—
Suddenly God took me.

[PIPPA *passes.*

Monsignor [*springing up*]. My people—one and all—all—
within there! Gag this villain—tie him hand and foot! He
dares...I know not half he dares—but remove him—quick! 190
Miserere mei, Domine!° Quick, I say!

Epilogue

SCENE.—PIPPA'S *chamber again. She enters it.*

The bee with his comb,
The mouse at her dray,°
The grub in his tomb,
Wile winter away;
But the fire-fly and hedge-shrew and lob-worm, I pray,°
How fare they?
Ha, ha, thanks for your counsel, my Zanze!
'Feast upon lampreys, quaff Breganze'—
The summer of life so easy to spend,
And care for to-morrow so soon put away!   10
But winter hastens at summer's end,

And fire-fly, hedge-shrew, lob-worm, pray,
How fare they?
No bidding me then to...what did Zanze say?
'Pare your nails pearlwise, get your small feet shoes
More like'...(what said she?)—'and less like canoes!'
How pert that girl was!—would I be those pert
Impudent staring women! It had done me,
However, surely no such mighty hurt
To learn his name who passed that jest upon me: 20
No foreigner, that I can recollect,
Came, as she says, a month since, to inspect
Our silk-mills—none with blue eyes and thick rings
Of raw-silk-coloured hair, at all events.
Well, if old Luca keep his good intents,
We shall do better, see what next year brings.
I may buy shoes, my Zanze, not appear
More destitute than you perhaps next year!
Bluph...something! I had caught the uncouth name
But for Monsignor's people's sudden clatter   30
Above us—bound to spoil such idle chatter
As ours: it were indeed a serious matter
If silly talk like ours should put to shame
The pious man, the man devoid of blame,
The...ah but—ah but, all the same,
No mere mortal has a right
To carry that exalted air;
Best people are not angels quite:
While—not the worst of people's doings scare
The devil; so there's that proud look to spare!   40
    Which is mere counsel to myself, mind! for
I have just been the holy Monsignor:
And I was you too, Luigi's gentle mother,
And you too, Luigi!—how that Luigi started
Out of the turret—doubtlessly departed
On some good errand or another,
For he passed just now in a traveller's trim,
And the sullen company that prowled
About his path, I noticed, scowled
As if they had lost a prey in him.   50
And I was Jules the sculptor's bride,
And I was Ottima beside,

And now what am I?—tired of fooling.
Day for folly, night for schooling!
New year's day is over and spent,
Ill or well, I must be content.
    Even my lily's asleep, I vow:
Wake up—here's a friend I've plucked you!
Call this flower a heart's-ease now!
Something rare, let me instruct you,   60
Is this, with petals triply swollen,
Three times spotted, thrice the pollen;
While the leaves and parts that witness
Old proportions and their fitness,
Here remain unchanged, unmoved now;
Call this pampered thing improved now!
Suppose there's a king of the flowers
And a girl-show held in his bowers—
'Look ye, buds, this growth of ours,'
Says he, 'Zanze from the Brenta,°   70
I have made her gorge polenta
Till both cheeks are near as bouncing
As her . . . name there's no pronouncing!
See this heightened colour too,
For she swilled Breganze wine
Till her nose turned deep carmine;
'Twas but white when wild she grew.
And only by this Zanze's eyes
Of which we could not change the size,
The magnitude of all achieved   80
Otherwise, may be perceived.'

Oh what a drear dark close to my poor day!
How could that red sun drop in that black cloud?
Ah Pippa, morning's rule is moved away,
Dispensed with, never more to be allowed!
Day's turn is over, now arrives the night's.
Oh lark, be day's apostle
To mavis, merle and throstle,°
Bid them their betters jostle
From day and its delights!   90
But at night, brother howlet, over the woods,°
Toll the world to thy chantry;

Sing to the bats' sleek sisterhoods
Full complines with gallantry:°
Then, owls and bats,
Cowls and twats,°
Monks and nuns, in a cloister's moods,
Adjourn to the oak-stump pantry!
                    [*After she has begun to undress herself.*
Now, one thing I should like to really know:
How near I ever might approach all these   100
I only fancied being, this long day:
—Approach, I mean, so as to touch them, so
As to . . . in some way . . . move them—if you please,
Do good or evil to them some slight way.
For instance, if I wind
Silk to-morrow, my silk may bind
                    [*Sitting on the bedside.*
And border Ottima's cloak's hem.
Ah me, and my important part with them,
This morning's hymn half promised when I rose!
True in some sense or other, I suppose.   110
                    [*As she lies down.*
God bless me! I can pray no more to-night.
No doubt, some way or other, hymns say right.

> *All service ranks the same with God—*
> *With God, whose puppets, best and worst,*
> *Are we: there is no last nor first.*

                                    [*She sleeps.*

DRAMATIC LYRICS (1842)

Cavalier Tunes

I. Marching Along

I

Kentish Sir Byng stood for his King,
Bidding the crop-headed Parliament swing:°
And, pressing a troop unable to stoop°
And see the rogues flourish and honest folk droop,
Marched them along, fifty-score strong,
Great-hearted gentlemen, singing this song.

II

God for King Charles! Pym and such carles°
To the Devil that prompts 'em their treasonous parles!
Cavaliers, up! Lips from the cup,
Hands from the pasty, nor bite take nor sup°   10
Till you're—
    CHORUS.—*Marching along, fifty-score strong,*
          Great-hearted gentlemen, singing this song.

III

Hampden to hell, and his obsequies' knell
Serve Hazelrig, Fiennes, and young Harry as well!°
England, good cheer! Rupert is near!°
Kentish and loyalists, keep we not here
    CHORUS.—*Marching along, fifty-score strong,*
          Great-hearted gentlemen, singing this song?

IV

Then, God for King Charles! Pym and his snarls
To the Devil that pricks on such pestilent carles!   20

Hold by the right, you double your might;
So, onward to Nottingham, fresh for the fight,
CHORUS.—*March we along, fifty-score strong,*
        Great-hearted gentlemen, singing this song!

II. Give A Rouse°

I

King Charles, and who'll do him right now?
King Charles, and who's ripe for fight now?
Give a rouse: here's, in hell's despite now,
King Charles!

II

Who gave me the goods that went since?
Who raised me the house that sank once?
Who helped me to gold I spent since?
Who found me in wine you drank once?
CHORUS.—*King Charles, and who'll do him right now?*
        King Charles, and who's ripe for fight now?   10
        Give a rouse: here's, in hell's despite now,
        King Charles!

III

To whom used my boy George quaff else,
By the old fool's side that begot him?
For whom did he cheer and laugh else,
While Noll's damned troopers shot him?°
CHORUS.—*King Charles, and who'll do him right now?*
        King Charles, and who's ripe for fight now?
        Give a rouse: here's, in hell's despite now,
        King Charles!   20

III. Boot and Saddle

I

Boot, saddle, to horse, and away!
Rescue my castle before the hot day
Brightens to blue from its silvery grey,
        CHORUS.—*Boot, saddle, to horse, and away!*

II

Ride past the suburbs, asleep as you'd say;
Many's the friend there, will listen and pray
'God's luck to gallants that strike up the lay—
        CHORUS.—*Boot, saddle, to horse, and away!*'

III

Forty miles off, like a roebuck at bay,
Flouts Castle Brancepeth the Roundheads' array:°   10
Who laughs, 'Good fellows ere this, by my fay,°
        CHORUS.—*Boot, saddle, to horse, and away!*'

IV

Who? My wife Gertrude; that, honest and gay,
Laughs when you talk of surrendering, 'Nay!
I've better counsellors; what counsel they?
        CHORUS.—*Boot, saddle, to horse, and away!*'

My Last Duchess

Ferrara

That's my last Duchess painted on the wall,
Looking as if she were alive. I call
That piece a wonder, now: Frà Pandolf's hands°
Worked busily a day, and there she stands.
Will't please you sit and look at her? I said
'Frà Pandolf' by design, for never read
Strangers like you that pictured countenance,
The depth and passion of its earnest glance,
But to myself they turned (since none puts by
The curtain I have drawn for you, but I)   10
And seemed as they would ask me, if they durst,
How such a glance came there; so, not the first
Are you to turn and ask thus. Sir, 'twas not
Her husband's presence only, called that spot
Of joy into the Duchess' cheek: perhaps
Frà Pandolf chanced to say 'Her mantle laps

Over my lady's wrist too much,' or 'Paint
Must never hope to reproduce the faint
Half-flush that dies along her throat:' such stuff
Was courtesy, she thought, and cause enough   20
For calling up that spot of joy. She had
A heart—how shall I say?—too soon made glad,
Too easily impressed; she liked whate'er
She looked on, and her looks went everywhere.
Sir, 'twas all one! My favour at her breast,
The dropping of the daylight in the West,
The bough of cherries some officious fool
Broke in the orchard for her, the white mule
She rode with round the terrace—all and each
Would draw from her alike the approving speech,   30
Or blush, at least. She thanked men,—good! but thanked
Somehow—I know not how—as if she ranked
My gift of a nine-hundred-years-old name
With anybody's gift. Who'd stoop to blame
This sort of trifling? Even had you skill
In speech—(which I have not)—to make your will
Quite clear to such an one, and say, 'Just this
Or that in you disgusts me; here you miss,
Or there exceed the mark'—and if she let
Herself be lessoned so, nor plainly set   40
Her wits to yours, forsooth, and made excuse,
—E'en then would be some stooping; and I choose
Never to stoop. Oh sir, she smiled, no doubt,
Whene'er I passed her; but who passed without
Much the same smile? This grew; I gave commands;
Then all smiles stopped together. There she stands°
As if alive. Will't please you rise? We'll meet
The company below, then. I repeat,
The Count your master's known munificence
Is ample warrant that no just pretence   50
Of mine for dowry will be disallowed;
Though his fair daughter's self, as I avowed
At starting, is my object. Nay, we'll go
Together down, sir. Notice Neptune, though,
Taming a sea-horse, thought a rarity,
Which Claus of Innsbruck cast in bronze for me!°

Count Gismond

Aix in Provence

I

Christ God who savest man, save most
   Of men Count Gismond who saved me!
Count Gauthier, when he chose his post,
   Chose time and place and company
To suit it; when he struck at length
My honour, 'twas with all his strength.

II

And doubtlessly ere he could draw
   All points to one, he must have schemed!
That miserable morning saw
   Few half so happy as I seemed,   10
While being dressed in queen's array°
To give our tourney prize away.

III

I thought they loved me, did me grace
   To please themselves; 'twas all their deed;
God makes, or fair or foul, our face;
   If showing mine so caused to bleed
My cousins' hearts, they should have dropped
A word, and straight the play had stopped.

IV

They, too, so beauteous! Each a queen
   By virtue of her brow and breast;   20
Not needing to be crowned, I mean,
   As I do. E'en when I was dressed,
Had either of them spoke, instead
Of glancing sideways with still head!

V

But no: they let me laugh, and sing
   My birthday song quite through, adjust

The last rose in my garland, fling
  A last look on the mirror, trust
My arms to each an arm of theirs,
  And so descend the castle-stairs—   30

VI

And come out on the morning-troop
  Of merry friends who kissed my cheek,
And called me queen, and made me stoop
  Under the canopy—(a streak
That pierced it, of the outside sun,
Powdered with gold its gloom's soft dun)—°

VII

And they could let me take my state
  And foolish throne amid applause
Of all come there to celebrate
  My queen's-day—Oh I think the cause   40
Of much was, they forgot no crowd
Makes up for parents in their shroud!

VIII

However that be, all eyes were bent
  Upon me, when my cousins cast
Theirs down; 'twas time I should present
  The victor's crown, but . . . there, 't will last
No long time . . . the old mist again
Blinds me as then it did. How vain!

IX

See! Gismond's at the gate, in talk
  With his two boys: I can proceed.   50
Well, at that moment, who should stalk
  Forth boldly—to my face, indeed—
But Gauthier, and he thundered 'Stay!'
And all stayed. 'Bring no crowns, I say!

X

'Bring torches! Wind the penance-sheet
  About her! Let her shun the chaste,

Or lay herself before their feet!
    Shall she whose body I embraced
A night long, queen it in the day?
For honour's sake no crowns, I say!'   60

XI

I? What I answered? As I live,
    I never fancied such a thing
As answer possible to give.
    What says the body when they spring
Some monstrous torture-engine's whole
Strength on it? No more says the soul.

XII

Till out strode Gismond; then I knew
    That I was saved. I never met
His face before, but, at first view,
    I felt quite sure that God had set   70
Himself to Satan; who would spend
A minute's mistrust on the end?

XIII

He strode to Gauthier, in his throat
    Gave him the lie, then struck his mouth
With one back-handed blow that wrote
    In blood men's verdict there. North, South,
East, West, I looked. The lie was dead,
And damned, and truth stood up instead.

XIV

This glads me most, that I enjoyed
    The heart of the joy, with my content   80
In watching Gismond unalloyed
    By any doubt of the event:
God took that on him—I was bid
Watch Gismond for my part: I did.

XV

Did I not watch him while he let
    His armourer just brace his greaves,

Rivet his hauberk, on the fret°
   The while! His foot . . . my memory leaves
No least stamp out, nor how anon
He pulled his ringing gauntlets on.   90

XVI

And e'en before the trumpet's sound
   Was finished, prone lay the false knight,
Prone as his lie, upon the ground:
   Gismond flew at him, used no sleight
O' the sword, but open-breasted drove,
Cleaving till out the truth he clove.

XVII

Which done, he dragged him to my feet
   And said 'Here die, but end thy breath
In full confession, lest thou fleet
   From my first, to God's second death!   100
Say, hast thou lied?' And, 'I have lied
To God and her,' he said, and died.

XVIII

Then Gismond, kneeling to me, asked
   —What safe my heart holds, though no word
Could I repeat now, if I tasked
   My powers for ever, to a third
Dear even as you are. Pass the rest
Until I sank upon his breast.

XIX

Over my head his arm he flung
   Against the world; and scarce I felt   110
His sword (that dripped by me and swung)
   A little shifted in its belt:
For he began to say the while
How South our home lay many a mile.

XX

So 'mid the shouting multitude
   We two walked forth to never more

Return. My cousins have pursued
   Their life, untroubled as before
I vexed them. Gauthier's dwelling-place
God lighten! May his soul find grace!   120

XXI

Our elder boy has got the clear
   Great brow; tho' when his brother's black
Full eye shows scorn, it ... Gismond here?
   And have you brought my tercel back?°
I just was telling Adela
How many birds it struck since May.

Incident of the French Camp

I

You know, we French stormed Ratisbon:
   A mile or so away,
On a little mound, Napoleon
   Stood on our storming-day;
With neck out-thrust, you fancy how,
   Legs wide, arms locked behind,
As if to balance the prone brow
   Oppressive with its mind.

II

Just as perhaps he mused 'My plans
   That soar, to earth may fall,   10
Let once my army-leader Lannes
   Waver at yonder wall,'—
Out 'twixt the battery-smokes there flew
   A rider, bound on bound
Full-galloping; nor bridle drew
   Until he reached the mound.

III

Then off there flung in smiling joy,
   And held himself erect

By just his horse's mane, a boy:
    You hardly could suspect—   20
(So tight he kept his lips compressed,
    Scarce any blood came through)
You looked twice ere you saw his breast
    Was all but shot in two.

IV

'Well,' cried he, 'Emperor, by God's grace
    We've got you Ratisbon!
The Marshal's in the market-place,
    And you'll be there anon
To see your flag-bird flap his vans
    Where I, to heart's desire,   30
Perched him!' The chief's eye flashed; his plans
    Soared up again like fire.

V

The chief's eye flashed; but presently
    Softened itself, as sheathes
A film the mother-eagle's eye
    When her bruised eaglet breathes;
'You're wounded!' 'Nay,' the soldier's pride
    Touched to the quick, he said:
'I'm killed, Sire!' And his chief beside
    Smiling the boy fell dead.   40

Soliloquy of the Spanish Cloister

I

Gr-r-r—there go, my heart's abhorrence!
    Water your damned flower-pots, do!
If hate killed men, Brother Lawrence,
    God's blood, would not mine kill you!
What? your myrtle-bush wants trimming?
    Oh, that rose has prior claims—
Needs its leaden vase filled brimming?
    Hell dry you up with its flames!

II

At the meal we sit together:
    Salve tibi! I must hear°   10
Wise talk of the kind of weather,
    Sort of season, time of year:
Not a plenteous cork-crop: scarcely
    Dare we hope oak-galls, I doubt:°
What's the Latin name for 'parsley'?
    What's the Greek name for Swine's Snout?°

III

Whew! We'll have our platter burnished,
    Laid with care on our own shelf!
With a fire-new spoon we're furnished,
    And a goblet for ourself,   20
Rinsed like something sacrificial
    Ere 'tis fit to touch our chaps—°
Marked with L. for our initial!
    (He-he! There his lily snaps!)

IV

Saint, forsooth! While brown Dolores
    Squats outside the Convent bank
With Sanchicha, telling stories,
    Steeping tresses in the tank,
Blue-black, lustrous, thick like horsehairs,
    —Can't I see his dead eye glow,   30
Bright as 'twere a Barbary corsair's?
    (That is, if he'd let it show!)

V

When he finishes refection,
    Knife and fork he never lays
Cross-wise, to my recollection,
    As do I, in Jesu's praise.
I the Trinity illustrate,
    Drinking watered orange-pulp—
In three sips the Arian frustrate;
    While he drains his at one gulp.°   40

VI

Oh, those melons? If he's able
    We're to have a feast! so nice!
One goes to the Abbot's table,
    All of us get each a slice.
How go on your flowers? None double?
    Not one fruit-sort can you spy?
Strange!—And I, too, at such trouble,
    Keep them close-nipped on the sly!

VII

There's a great text in Galatians,°
    Once you trip on it, entails   50
Twenty-nine distinct damnations,
    One sure, if another fails:
If I trip him just a-dying,
    Sure of heaven as sure can be,
Spin him round and send him flying
    Off to hell, a Manichee?°

VIII

Or, my scrofulous French novel°
    On grey paper with blunt type!
Simply glance at it, you grovel
    Hand and foot in Belial's gripe:°   60
If I double down its pages
    At the woeful sixteenth print,°
When he gathers his greengages,
    Ope a sieve and slip it in't?

IX

Or, there's Satan!—one might venture
    Pledge one's soul to him, yet leave
Such a flaw in the indenture
    As he'd miss till, past retrieve,
Blasted lay that rose-acacia
    We're so proud of! *Hy, Zy, Hine* ...°   70
'St, there's Vespers! *Plena gratiâ*
    Ave, Virgo! Gr-r-r—you swine!°

In a Gondola

He sings

I send my heart up to thee, all my heart
  In this my singing.
For the stars help me, and the sea bears part;
  The very night is clinging
Closer to Venice' streets to leave one space
  Above me, whence thy face
May light my joyous heart to thee its dwelling-place.

She speaks

Say after me, and try to say
My very words, as if each word
Came from you of your own accord,
In your own voice, in your own way: 10
'This woman's heart and soul and brain
Are mine as much as this gold chain
She bids me wear; which' (say again)
'I choose to make by cherishing
A precious thing, or choose to fling
Over the boat-side, ring by ring.'
And yet once more say ... no word more!
Since words are only words. Give o'er!

Unless you call me, all the same,   20
Familiarly by my pet name,
Which if the Three should hear you call,°
And me reply to, would proclaim
At once our secret to them all.
Ask of me, too, command me, blame—
Do, break down the partition-wall
'Twixt us, the daylight world beholds
Curtained in dusk and splendid folds!
What's left but—all of me to take?
I am the Three's: prevent them, slake   30
Your thirst! 'Tis said, the Arab sage,
In practising with gems, can loose
Their subtle spirit in his cruce°

And leave but ashes: so, sweet mage,°
Leave them my ashes when thy use
Sucks out my soul, thy heritage!

He sings

I

Past we glide, and past, and past!
  What's that poor Agnese doing
Where they make the shutters fast?
  Grey Zanobi's just a-wooing   40
To his couch the purchased bride:
  Past we glide!

II

Past we glide, and past, and past!
  Why's the Pucci Palace flaring
Like a beacon to the blast?
  Guests by hundreds, not one caring
If the dear host's neck were wried:
  Past we glide!

She sings

I

The moth's kiss, first!
Kiss me as if you made believe   50
You were not sure, this eve,
How my face, your flower, had pursed
Its petals up; so, here and there
You brush it, till I grow aware
Who wants me, and wide ope I burst.

II

The bee's kiss, now!
Kiss me as if you entered gay
My heart at some noonday,
A bud that dares not disallow
The claim, so all is rendered up,   60
And passively its shattered cup
Over your head to sleep I bow.

He sings

I

What are we two?
I am a Jew,
And carry thee, farther than friends can pursue,
To a feast of our tribe;
Where they need thee to bribe
The devil that blasts them unless he imbibe
Thy...Scatter the vision for ever! And now,
As of old, I am I, thou art thou!   70

II

Say again, what we are?
The sprite of a star,°
I lure thee above where the destinies bar
My plumes their full play
Till a ruddier ray
Than my pale one announce there is withering away
Some...Scatter the vision for ever! And now.
As of old, I am I, thou art thou!

He muses

Oh, which were best, to roam or rest?
The land's lap or the water's breast?   80
To sleep on yellow millet-sheaves,
Or swim in lucid shallows just
Eluding water-lily leaves,
An inch from Death's black fingers, thrust
To lock you, whom release he must;
Which life were best on Summer eves?

He speaks, musing

Lie back; could thought of mine improve you?
From this shoulder let there spring
A wing; from this, another wing;
Wings, not legs and feet, shall move you!   90
Snow-white must they spring, to blend
With your flesh, but I intend
They shall deepen to the end,

Broader, into burning gold,
Till both wings crescent-wise enfold
Your perfect self, from 'neath your feet
To o'er your head, where, lo, they meet
As if a million sword-blades hurled
Defiance from you to the world!

Rescue me thou, the only real!   100
And scare away this mad ideal
That came, nor motions to depart!
Thanks! Now, stay ever as thou art!

Still he muses

I

What if the Three should catch at last
Thy serenader? While there's cast
Paul's cloak about my head, and fast
Gian pinions me, Himself has past
His stylet thro' my back; I reel;°
And . . . is it thou I feel?

II

They trail me, these three godless knaves,   110
Past every church that saints and saves,°
Nor stop till, where the cold sea raves
By Lido's wet accursed graves,°
They scoop mine, roll me to its brink,
And . . . on thy breast I sink!

She replies, musing

Dip your arm o'er the boat-side, elbow-deep,
As I do: thus: were death so unlike sleep,
Caught this way? Death's to fear from flame or steel,
Or poison doubtless; but from water—feel!

Go find the bottom! Would you stay me? There!   120
Now pluck a great blade of that ribbon-grass
To plait in where the foolish jewel was,
I flung away: since you have praised my hair,
'Tis proper to be choice in what I wear.

He speaks

Row home? must we row home? Too surely
Know I where its front's demurely
Over the Giudecca piled;°
Window just with window mating,
Door on door exactly waiting,
All's the set face of a child: 130
But behind it, where's a trace
Of the staidness and reserve,
And formal lines without a curve,
In the same child's playing-face?
No two windows look one way
O'er the small sea-water thread
Below them. Ah, the autumn day
I, passing, saw you overhead!
First, out a cloud of curtain blew,
Then a sweet cry, and last came you—   140
To catch your lory that must needs°
Escape just then, of all times then,
To peck a tall plant's fleecy seeds,
And make me happiest of men.
I scarce could breathe to see you reach
So far back o'er the balcony
To catch him ere he climbed too high
Above you in the Smyrna peach
That quick the round smooth cord of gold,
This coiled hair on your head, unrolled,   150
Fell down you like a gorgeous snake
The Roman girls were wont, of old,
When Rome there was, for coolness' sake
To let lie curling o'er their bosoms.
Dear lory, may his beak retain
Ever its delicate rose stain
As if the wounded lotus-blossoms
Had marked their thief to know again!

Stay longer yet, for others' sake
Than mine! What should your chamber do?   160
—With all its rarities that ache
In silence while day lasts, but wake
At night-time and their life renew,

Suspended just to pleasure you
Who brought against their will together
These objects, and, while day lasts, weave
Around them such a magic tether
That dumb they look: your harp, believe,
With all the sensitive tight strings
Which dare not speak, now to itself   170
Breathes slumberously, as if some elf
Went in and out the chords, his wings
Make murmur wheresoe'er they graze,
As an angel may, between the maze
Of midnight palace-pillars, on
And on, to sow God's plagues, have gone
Through guilty glorious Babylon.
And while such murmurs flow, the nymph
Bends o'er the harp-top from her shell
As the dry limpet for the lymph°   180
Come with a tune he knows so well.
And how your statues' hearts must swell!
And how your pictures must descend
To see each other, friend with friend!
Oh, could you take them by surprise,
You'd find Schidone's eager Duke
Doing the quaintest courtesies
To that prim saint by Haste-thee-Luke!
And, deeper into her rock den,
Bold Castelfranco's Magdalen   190
You'd find retreated from the ken
Of that robed counsel-keeping Ser—
As if the Tizian thinks of her,°
And is not, rather, gravely bent
On seeing for himself what toys
Are these, his progeny invent,
What litter now the board employs
Whereon he signed a document
That got him murdered! Each enjoys
Its night so well, you cannot break   200
The sport up, so, indeed must make
More stay with me, for others' sake.

She speaks

I

To-morrow, if a harp-string, say,
Is used to tie the jasmine back
That overfloods my room with sweets,
Contrive your Zorzi somehow meets
My Zanze! If the ribbon's black,°
The Three are watching: keep away!

II

Your gondola—let Zorzi wreathe
A mesh of water-weeds about   210
Its prow, as if he unaware
Had struck some quay or bridge-foot stair!
That I may throw a paper out
As you and he go underneath.

There's Zanze's vigilant taper; safe are we.
Only one minute more to-night with me?
Resume your past self of a month ago!
Be you the bashful gallant, I will be
The lady with the colder breast than snow.
Now bow you, as becomes, nor touch my hand   220
More than I touch yours when I step to land,
And say, 'All thanks, Siora!'—°
                              Heart to heart
And lips to lips! Yet once more, ere we part,
Clasp me and make me thine, as mine thou art!
                              [*He is surprised, and stabbed.*
It was ordained to be so, sweet!—and best
Comes now, beneath thine eyes, upon thy breast.
Still kiss me! Care not for the cowards! Care
Only to put aside thy beauteous hair
My blood will hurt! The Three, I do not scorn
To death, because they never lived: but I   230
Have lived indeed, and so—(yet one more kiss)—can die!

Artemis Prologizes

I am a goddess of the ambrosial courts,
And save by Here, Queen of Pride, surpassed°
By none whose temples whiten this the world.
Through heaven I roll my lucid moon along;
I shed in hell o'er my pale people peace;
On earth I, caring for the creatures, guard
Each pregnant yellow wolf and fox-bitch sleek,
And every feathered mother's callow brood,
And all that love green haunts and loneliness.
Of men, the chaste adore me, hanging crowns°   10
Of poppies red to blackness, bell and stem,
Upon my image at Athenai here;°
And this dead Youth, Asclepios bends above,°
Was dearest to me. He, my buskined step
To follow through the wild-wood leafy ways,
And chase the panting stag, or swift with darts
Stop the swift ounce, or lay the leopard low,°
Neglected homage to another god:
Whence Aphrodite, by no midnight smoke
Of tapers lulled, in jealousy despatched   20
A noisome lust that, as the gadbee stings,
Possessed his stepdame Phaidra for himself°
The son of Theseus her great absent spouse.
Hippolutos exclaiming in his rage
Against the fury of the Queen, she judged
Life insupportable; and, pricked at heart
An Amazonian stranger's race should dare°
To scorn her, perished by the murderous cord:
Yet, ere she perished, blasted in a scroll
The fame of him her swerving made not swerve.   30
And Theseus, read, returning, and believed,
And exiled, in the blindness of his wrath,
The man without a crime who, last as first,
Loyal, divulged not to his sire the truth.
Now Theseus from Poseidon had obtained
That of his wishes should be granted three,°
And one he imprecated straight—'Alive
May ne'er Hippolutos reach other lands!'

Poseidon heard, ai ai! And scarce the prince°
Had stepped into the fixed boots of the car   40
That give the feet a stay against the strength
Of the Henetian horses, and around°
His body flung the rein, and urged their speed
Along the rocks and shingles of the shore,
When from the gaping wave a monster flung
His obscene body in the coursers' path.
These, mad with terror, as the sea-bull sprawled
Wallowing about their feet, lost care of him
That reared them; and the master-chariot-pole
Snapping beneath their plunges like a reed,   50
Hippolutos, whose feet were trammelled fast,
Was yet dragged forward by the circling rein
Which either hand directed; nor they quenched
The frenzy of their flight before each trace,
Wheel-spoke and splinter of the woeful car,
Each boulder-stone, sharp stub and spiny shell,
Huge fish-bone wrecked and wreathed amid the sands
On that detested beach, was bright with blood
And morsels of his flesh: then fell the steeds
Head-foremost, crashing in their mooned fronts,   60
Shivering with sweat, each white eye horror-fixed.
His people, who had witnessed all afar,
Bore back the ruins of Hippolutos.
But when his sire, too swoln with pride, rejoiced
(Indomitable as a man foredoomed)
That vast Poseidon had fulfilled his prayer,
I, in a flood of glory visible,
Stood o'er my dying votary and, deed
By deed, revealed, as all took place, the truth.
Then Theseus lay the woefullest of men,   70
And worthily; but ere the death-veils hid
His face, the murdered prince full pardon breathed
To his rash sire. Whereat Athenai wails.

    So I, who ne'er forsake my votaries,
Lest in the cross-way none the honey-cake°
Should tender, nor pour out the dog's hot life;
Lest at my fane the priests disconsolate
Should dress my image with some faded poor

Few crowns, made favours of, nor dare object
Such slackness to my worshippers who turn   80
Elsewhere the trusting heart and loaded hand,
As they had climbed Olumpos to report
Of Artemis and nowhere found her throne—
I interposed: and, this eventful night,—
(While round the funeral pyre the populace
Stood with fierce light on their black robes which bound
Each sobbing head, while yet their hair they clipped
O'er the dead body of their withered prince,
And, in his palace, Theseus prostrated
On the cold hearth, his brow cold as the slab   90
'Twas bruised on, groaned away the heavy grief—
As the pyre fell, and down the cross logs crashed
Sending a crowd of sparkles through the night,
And the gay fire, elate with mastery,
Towered like a serpent o'er the clotted jars
Of wine, dissolving oils and frankincense,
And splendid gums like gold),—my potency
Conveyed the perished man to my retreat
In the thrice-venerable forest here.
And this white-bearded sage who squeezes now   100
The berried plant, is Phoibos' son of fame,
Asclepios, whom my radiant brother taught°
The doctrine of each herb and flower and root,
To know their secret'st virtue and express
The saving soul of all: who so has soothed
With lavers the torn brow and murdered cheeks,
Composed the hair and brought its gloss again,
And called the red bloom to the pale skin back,
And laid the strips and jagged ends of flesh
Even once more, and slacked the sinew's knot   110
Of every tortured limb—that now he lies
As if mere sleep possessed him underneath
These interwoven oaks and pines. Oh cheer,
Divine presenter of the healing rod,
Thy snake, with ardent throat and lulling eye,°
Twines his lithe spires around! I say, much cheer!
Proceed thou with thy wisest pharmacies!
And ye, white crowd of woodland sister-nymphs,
Ply, as the sage directs, these buds and leaves

That strew the turf around the twain! While I   120
Await, in fitting silence, the event.

Johannes Agricola in Meditation

There's heaven above, and night by night
    I look right through its gorgeous roof;
No suns and moons though e'er so bright
    Avail to stop me; splendour-proof
    I keep the broods of stars aloof:
For I intend to get to God,
    For 'tis to God I speed so fast,
For in God's breast, my own abode,
    Those shoals of dazzling glory, passed.
    I lay my spirit down at last.   10
I lie where I have always lain,
    God smiles as he has always smiled;
Ere suns and moons could wax and wane,
    Ere stars were thundergirt, or piled
    The heavens, God thought on me his child;
Ordained a life for me, arrayed
    Its circumstances every one
To the minutest; ay, God said
    This head this hand should rest upon
    Thus, ere he fashioned star or sun.   20
And having thus created me,
    Thus rooted me, he bade me grow,
Guiltless for ever, like a tree
    That buds and blooms, nor seeks to know
    The law by which it prospers so:
But sure that thought and word and deed
    All go to swell his love for me,
Me, made because that love had need
    Of something irreversibly
    Pledged solely its content to be.   30
Yes, yes, a tree which must ascend,
    No poison-gourd foredoomed to stoop!
I have God's warrant, could I blend
    All hideous sins, as in a cup,

To drink the mingled venoms up;
Secure my nature will convert
    The draught to blossoming gladness fast:
While sweet dews turn to the gourd's hurt,
    And bloat, and while they bloat it, blast,
    As from the first its lot was cast.   40
For as I lie, smiled on, full-fed
    By unexhausted power to bless,
I gaze below on hell's fierce bed,
    And those its waves of flame oppress,
    Swarming in ghastly wretchedness;
Whose life on earth aspired to be
    One altar-smoke, so pure!—to win
If not love like God's love for me,
    At least to keep his anger in;
    And all their striving turned to sin.   50
Priest, doctor, hermit, monk grown white
    With prayer, the broken-hearted nun,
The martyr, the wan acolyte,
    The incense-swinging child,—undone
    Before God fashioned star or sun!
God, whom I praise; how could I praise,
    If such as I might understand,
Make out and reckon on his ways,
    And bargain for his love, and stand,
    Paying a price, at his right hand?   60

Porphyria's Lover

The rain set early in to-night,
    The sullen wind was soon awake,
It tore the elm-tops down for spite,
    And did its worst to vex the lake:
    I listened with heart fit to break.
When glided in Porphyria; straight
    She shut the cold out and the storm,
And kneeled and made the cheerless grate
    Blaze up, and all the cottage warm;
    Which done, she rose, and from her form   10

Withdrew the dripping cloak and shawl,
   And laid her soiled gloves by, untied
Her hat and let the damp hair fall,
   And, last, she sat down by my side
   And called me. When no voice replied,
She put my arm about her waist,
   And made her smooth white shoulder bare,
And all her yellow hair displaced,
   And, stooping, made my cheek lie there,
   And spread, o'er all, her yellow hair,   20
Murmuring how she loved me—she
   Too weak, for all her heart's endeavour,
To set its struggling passion free
   From pride, and vainer ties dissever,
   And give herself to me for ever.
But passion sometimes would prevail,
   Nor could to-night's gay feast restrain
A sudden thought of one so pale
   For love of her, and all in vain:
   So, she was come through wind and rain.   30
Be sure I looked up at her eyes
   Happy and proud; at last I knew
Porphyria worshipped me; surprise
   Made my heart swell, and still it grew
   While I debated what to do.
That moment she was mine, mine, fair,
   Perfectly pure and good: I found
A thing to do, and all her hair
   In one long yellow string I wound
   Three times her little throat around,   40
And strangled her. No pain felt she;
   I am quite sure she felt no pain.
As a shut bud that holds a bee,
   I warily oped her lids: again
   Laughed the blue eyes without a stain.
And I untightened next the tress
   About her neck; her cheek once more
Blushed bright beneath my burning kiss:
   I propped her head up as before,
   Only, this time my shoulder bore   50
Her head, which droops upon it still:

The smiling rosy little head,
So glad it has its utmost will,
    That all it scorned at once is fled,
    And I, its love, am gained instead!
Porphyria's love: she guessed not how
    Her darling one wish would be heard.
And thus we sit together now,
    And all night long we have not stirred,
    And yet God has not said a word!   60

The Pied Piper of Hamelin

A Child's Story

(Written for, and inscribed to, W. M. the Younger)

I

Hamelin Town's in Brunswick,
    By famous Hanover city;
The river Weser, deep and wide,
Washes its wall on the southern side;
A pleasanter spot you never spied;
    But, when begins my ditty,
Almost five hundred years ago,
To see the townsfolk suffer so
    From vermin, was a pity.

II

    Rats!   10
They fought the dogs and killed the cats,
    And bit the babies in the cradles,
And ate the cheeses out of the vats,
    And licked the soup from the cooks' own ladles,
Split open the kegs of salted sprats,
Made nests inside men's Sunday hats,
And even spoiled the women's chats
    By drowning their speaking

With shrieking and squeaking
In fifty different sharps and flats.   20

III

At last the people in a body
   To the Town Hall came flocking:
' 'Tis clear,' cried they, 'our Mayor's a noddy;
   And as for our Corporation—shocking
To think we buy gowns lined with ermine
For dolts that can't or won't determine
What's best to rid us of our vermin!
You hope, because you're old and obese,
To find in the furry civic robe ease?
Rouse up, sirs! Give your brains a racking   30
To find the remedy we're lacking,
Or, sure as fate, we'll send you packing!'
At this the Mayor and Corporation
Quaked with a mighty consternation.

IV

An hour they sat in council,
   At length the Mayor broke silence:
'For a guilder I'd my ermine gown sell,
   I wish I were a mile hence!
It's easy to bid one rack one's brain—
I'm sure my poor head aches again,   40
I've scratched it so, and all in vain.
Oh for a trap, a trap, a trap!'
Just as he said this, what should hap
At the chamber door but a gentle tap?
'Bless us,' cried the Mayor, 'what's that?'
(With the Corporation as he sat,
Looking little though wondrous fat;
Nor brighter was his eye, nor moister
Than a too-long-opened oyster,
Save when at noon his paunch grew mutinous   50
For a plate of turtle green and glutinous)
'Only a scraping of shoes on the mat?
Anything like the sound of a rat
Makes my heart go pit-a-pat!'

V

'Come in!'—the Mayor cried, looking bigger:
And in did come the strangest figure!
His queer long coat from heel to head
Was half of yellow and half of red,
And he himself was tall and thin,
With sharp blue eyes, each like a pin,   60
And light loose hair, yet swarthy skin,
No tuft on cheek nor beard on chin,
But lips where smiles went out and in;
There was no guessing his kith and kin:
And nobody could enough admire
The tall man and his quaint attire.
Quoth one: 'It's as my great-grandsire,
Starting up at the Trump of Doom's tone,
Had walked this way from his painted tombstone!'

VI

He advanced to the council-table: 70
And, 'Please your honours,' said he, 'I'm able,
By means of a secret charm, to draw
    All creatures living beneath the sun,
    That creep or swim or fly or run,
After me so as you never saw!
And I chiefly use my charm
On creatures that do people harm,
The mole and toad and newt and viper;
And people call me the Pied Piper.'
(And here they noticed round his neck   80
    A scarf of red and yellow stripe,
To match with his coat of the self-same cheque;
    And at the scarf's end hung a pipe;
And his fingers, they noticed, were ever straying
As if impatient to be playing
Upon this pipe, as low it dangled
Over his vesture so old-fangled.)
'Yet,' said he, 'poor piper as I am,
In Tartary I freed the Cham,°
    Last June, from his huge swarms of gnats;   90
I eased in Asia the Nizam°

Of a monstrous brood of vampyre-bats:
And as for what your brain bewilders,
   If I can rid your town of rats
Will you give me a thousand guilders?'
'One? fifty thousand!'—was the exclamation
Of the astonished Mayor and Corporation.

VII

Into the street the Piper stept,
   Smiling first a little smile,
As if he knew what magic slept
   In his quiet pipe the while;   100
Then, like a musical adept,
To blow the pipe his lips he wrinkled,
And green and blue his sharp eyes twinkled,
Like a candle-flame where salt is sprinkled;
And ere three shrill notes the pipe uttered,
You heard as if an army muttered;
And the muttering grew to a grumbling;
And the grumbling grew to a mighty rumbling;
And out of the houses the rats came tumbling.   110
Great rats, small rats, lean rats, brawny rats,
Brown rats, black rats, grey rats, tawny rats,
Grave old plodders, gay young friskers,
   Fathers, mothers, uncles, cousins,
Cocking tails and pricking whiskers,
   Families by tens and dozens,
Brothers, sisters, husbands, wives—
Followed the Piper for their lives.
From street to street he piped advancing,
And step for step they followed dancing,   120
Until they came to the river Weser,
   Wherein all plunged and perished!
—Save one who, stout as Julius Caesar,
Swam across and lived to carry
   (As he, the manuscript he cherished)°
To Rat-land home his commentary:
Which was, 'At the first shrill notes of the pipe,
I heard a sound as of scraping tripe,
And putting apples, wondrous ripe,

Into a cider-press's gripe:
And a moving away of pickle-tub-boards,
And a leaving ajar of conserve-cupboards,
And a drawing the corks of train-oil-flasks,°
And a breaking the hoops of butter-casks:
And it seemed as if a voice
   (Sweeter far than bý harp or bý psaltery
Is breathed) called out, Oh rats, rejoice!
   The world is grown to one vast drysaltery!°
So munch on, crunch on, take your nuncheon,°
Breakfast, supper, dinner, luncheon!'   140
And just as a bulky sugar-puncheon,°
All ready staved, like a great sun shone
Glorious scarce an inch before me,
Just as methought it said, "Come, bore me!"
—I found the Weser rolling o'er me.'

VIII

You should have heard the Hamelin people
Ringing the bells till they rocked the steeple.
'Go,' cried the Mayor, 'and get long poles,
Poke out the nests and block up the holes!
Consult with carpenters and builders,   150
And leave in our town not even a trace
Of the rats!'—when suddenly, up the face
Of the Piper perked in the market-place,
With a, 'First, if you please, my thousand guilders!'

IX

A thousand guilders! The Mayor looked blue;
So did the Corporation too.
For council dinners made rare havoc
With Claret, Moselle, Vin-de-Grave, Hock;
And half the money would replenish
Their cellar's biggest butt with Rhenish.   160
To pay this sum to a wandering fellow
With a gipsy coat of red and yellow!
'Beside,' quoth the Mayor with a knowing wink,
'Our business was done at the river's brink;
We saw with our eyes the vermin sink,

And what's dead can't come to life, I think.
So, friend, we're not the folks to shrink
From the duty of giving you something for drink,
And a matter of money to put in your poke;
But as for the guilders, what we spoke   170
Of them, as you very well know, was in joke.
Beside, our losses have made us thrifty.
A thousand guilders! Come, take fifty!'

X

The Piper's face fell, and he cried
'No trifling! I can't wait, beside!
I've promised to visit by dinnertime
Bagdat, and accept the prime°
Of the Head-Cook's pottage, all he's rich in,
For having left, in the Caliph's kitchen,
Of a nest of scorpions no survivor: 180
With him I proved no bargain-driver,
With you, don't think I'll bate a stiver!°
And folks who put me in a passion
May find me pipe after another fashion.'

XI

'How?' cried the Mayor, 'd'ye think I brook
Being worse treated than a Cook?
Insulted by a lazy ribald
With idle pipe and vesture piebald?
You threaten us, fellow? Do your worst,
Blow your pipe there till you burst!'   190

XII

Once more he stept into the street
    And to his lips again
    Laid his long pipe of smooth straight cane;
And ere he blew three notes (such sweet
Soft notes as yet musician's cunning
    Never gave the enraptured air)
There was a rustling that seemed like a bustling
Of merry crowds justling at pitching and hustling,
Small feet were pattering, wooden shoes clattering,

Little hands clapping and little tongues chattering,   200
And, like fowls in a farm-yard when barley is scattering,
Out came the children running.
All the little boys and girls,
With rosy cheeks and flaxen curls,
And sparkling eyes and teeth like pearls,
Tripping and skipping, ran merrily after
The wonderful music with shouting and laughter.

XIII

The Mayor was dumb, and the Council stood
As if they were changed into blocks of wood,
Unable to move a step, or cry   210
To the children merrily skipping by,
—Could only follow with the eye
That joyous crowd at the Piper's back.
But how the Mayor was on the rack,
And the wretched Council's bosoms beat,
As the Piper turned from the High Street
To where the Weser rolled its waters
Right in the way of their sons and daughters!
However he turned from South to West,
And to Koppelberg Hill his steps addressed,   220
And after him the children pressed;
Great was the joy in every breast.
'He never can cross that mighty top!
He's forced to let the piping drop,
And we shall see our children stop!'
When, lo, as they reached the mountain-side,
A wondrous portal opened wide,
As if a cavern was suddenly hollowed;
And the Piper advanced and the children followed,
And when all were in to the very last,   230
The door in the mountain-side shut fast.
Did I say, all? No! One was lame,
    And could not dance the whole of the way;
And in after years, if you would blame
    His sadness, he was used to say,—
'It's dull in our town since my playmates left!
I can't forget that I'm bereft

Of all the pleasant sights they see,
Which the Piper also promised me.
For he led us, he said, to a joyous land,   240
Joining the town and just at hand,
Where waters gushed and fruit-trees grew
And flowers put forth a fairer hue,
And everything was strange and new;
The sparrows were brighter than peacocks here,
And their dogs outran our fallow deer,
And honey-bees had lost their stings,
And horses were born with eagles' wings:
And just as I became assured
My lame foot would be speedily cured,   250
The music stopped and I stood still,
And found myself outside the hill,
Left alone against my will,
To go now limping as before,
And never hear of that country more!'

XIV

Alas, alas for Hamelin!
    There came into many a burgher's pate
    A text which says that heaven's gate
    Opes to the rich at as easy rate
As the needle's eye takes a camel in!°   260
The mayor sent East, West, North and South,
To offer the Piper, by word of mouth,
    Wherever it was men's lot to find him,
Silver and gold to his heart's content,
If he'd only return the way he went,
    And bring the children behind him.
But when they saw 'twas a lost endeavour,
And Piper and dancers were gone for ever,
They made a decree that lawyers never
    Should think their records dated duly   270
If, after the day of the month and year,
These words did not as well appear,
'And so long after what happened here
    On the Twenty-second of July,
Thirteen hundred and seventy-six:'

And the better in memory to fix
The place of the children's last retreat,
They called it, the Pied Piper's Street—
Where any one playing on pipe or tabor
Was sure for the future to lose his labour.   280
Nor suffered they hostelry or tavern
     To shock with mirth a street so solemn;
But opposite the place of the cavern
     They wrote the story on a column,
And on the great church-window painted
The same, to make the world acquainted
How their children were stolen away,
And there it stands to this very day.
And I must not omit to say
That in Transylvania there's a tribe   290
Of alien people who ascribe
The outlandish ways and dress
On which their neighbours lay such stress,
To their fathers and mothers having risen
Out of some subterraneous prison
Into which they were trepanned°
Long time ago in a mighty band
Out of Hamelin town in Brunswick land,
But how or why, they don't understand.

XV

So, Willy, let me and you be wipers   300
Of scores out with all men—especially pipers!
And, whether they pipe us free from rats or from mice,
If we've promised them aught, let us keep our promise!

DRAMATIC ROMANCES AND LYRICS (1845)

'How They Brought the Good News from Ghent to Aix'

[16–]

I

I sprang to the stirrup, and Joris, and he;
I galloped, Dirck galloped, we galloped all three;
'Good speed!' cried the watch, as the gate-bolts undrew;
'Speed!' echoed the wall to us galloping through;
Behind shut the postern, the lights sank to rest,
And into the midnight we galloped abreast.

II

Not a word to each other; we kept the great pace
Neck by neck, stride by stride, never changing our place;
I turned in my saddle and made its girths tight,
Then shortened each stirrup, and set the pique right,°
Rebuckled the cheek-strap, chained slacker the bit,   10
Nor galloped less steadily Roland a whit.

III

'Twas moonset at starting; but while we drew near
Lokeren, the cocks crew and twilight dawned clear;
At Boom, a great yellow star came out to see;
At Düffeld, 'twas morning as plain as could be;
And from Mecheln church-steeple we heard the half-chime,
So, Joris broke silence with, 'Yet there is time!'

IV

At Aershot, up leaped of a sudden the sun,
And against him the cattle stood black every one,   20

To stare thro' the mist at us galloping past,
And I saw my stout galloper Roland at last,
With resolute shoulders, each butting away
The haze, as some bluff river headland its spray:

V

And his low head and crest, just one sharp ear bent back
For my voice, and the other pricked out on his track;
And one eye's black intelligence,—ever that glance
O'er its white edge at me, his own master, askance!
And the thick heavy spume-flakes which aye and anon
His fierce lips shook upwards in galloping on.   30

VI

By Hasselt, Dirck groaned; and cried Joris, 'Stay spur!
Your Roos galloped bravely, the fault's not in her,
We'll remember at Aix'—for one heard the quick wheeze
Of her chest, saw the stretched neck and staggering knees,
And sunk tail, and horrible heave of the flank,
As down on her haunches she shuddered and sank.

VII

So, we were left galloping, Joris and I,
Past Looz and past Tongres, no cloud in the sky;
The broad sun above laughed a pitiless laugh,
'Neath our feet broke the brittle bright stubble like chaff;   40
Till over by Dalhem a dome-spire sprang white,
And 'Gallop,' gasped Joris, 'for Aix is in sight!'

VIII

'How they'll greet us!'—and all in a moment his roan
Rolled neck and croup over, lay dead as a stone;
And there was my Roland to bear the whole weight
Of the news which alone could save Aix from her fate,
With his nostrils like pits full of blood to the brim,
And with circles of red for his eye-sockets' rim.

IX

Then I cast loose my buffcoat, each holster let fall,
Shook off both my jack-boots, let go belt and all,   50

Stood up in the stirrup, leaned, patted his ear,
Called my Roland his pet-name, my horse without peer;
Clapped my hands, laughed and sang, any noise, bad or good,
Till at length into Aix Roland galloped and stood.

X

And all I remember is—friends flocking round
As I sat with his head 'twixt my knees on the ground;
And no voice but was praising this Roland of mine,
As I poured down his throat our last measure of wine,
Which (the burgesses voted by common consent)
Was no more than his due who brought good news from Ghent.   60

Pictor Ignotus

Florence, 15–

I could have painted pictures like that youth's
   Ye praise so. How my soul springs up! No bar
Stayed me—ah, thought which saddens while it soothes!
   —Never did fate forbid me, star by star,
To outburst on your night with all my gift
   Of fires from God: nor would my flesh have shrunk
From seconding my soul, with eyes uplift
   And wide to heaven, or, straight like thunder, sunk
To the centre, of an instant; or around
   Turned calmly and inquisitive, to scan   10
The licence and the limit, space and bound,
   Allowed to truth made visible in man.
And, like that youth ye praise so, all I saw,
   Over the canvas could my hand have flung,
Each face obedient to its passion's law,
   Each passion clear proclaimed without a tongue;
Whether Hope rose at once in all the blood,
   A-tiptoe for the blessing of embrace,
Or Rapture drooped the eyes, as when her brood
   Pull down the nesting dove's heart to its place;
Or Confidence lit swift the forehead up,   20
   And locked the mouth fast, like a castle braved,—
O human faces, hath it spilt, my cup?

What did ye give me that I have not saved?
Nor will I say I have not dreamed (how well!)
    Of going—I, in each new picture,—forth,
As, making new hearts beat and bosoms swell,
    To Pope or Kaiser, East, West, South, or North,
Bound for the calmly-satisfied great State,
    Or glad aspiring little burgh, it went,   30
Flowers cast upon the car which bore the freight,
    Through old streets named afresh from the event,
Till it reached home, where learned age should greet
    My face, and youth, the star not yet distinct
Above his hair, lie learning at my feet!—
    Oh, thus to live, I and my picture, linked
With love about, and praise, till life should end,
    And then not go to heaven, but linger here,
Here on my earth, earth's every man my friend,—
    The thought grew frightful, 'twas so wildly dear!   40
But a voice changed it. Glimpses of such sights
    Have scared me, like the revels through a door
Of some strange house of idols at its rites!
    This world seemed not the world it was before:
Mixed with my loving trusting ones, there trooped
    ... Who summoned those cold faces that begun
To press on me and judge me? Though I stooped
    Shrinking, as from the soldiery a nun,
They drew me forth, and spite of me ... enough!
    These buy and sell our pictures, take and give,   50
Count them for garniture and household-stuff,
    And where they live needs must our pictures live
And see their faces, listen to their prate,
    Partakers of their daily pettiness,
Discussed of,—'This I love, or this I hate,
    This likes me more, and this affects me less!'
Wherefore I chose my portion. If at whiles
    My heart sinks, as monotonous I paint
These endless cloisters and eternal aisles
    With the same series, Virgin, Babe and Saint,   60
With the same cold calm beautiful regard,—
    At least no merchant traffics in my heart;
The sanctuary's gloom at least shall ward
    Vain tongues from where my pictures stand apart:
Only prayer breaks the silence of the shrine

While, blackening in the daily candle-smoke,
They moulder on the damp wall's travertine,°
  'Mid echoes the light footstep never woke.
So, die my pictures! surely, gently die!
  O youth, men praise so,—holds their praise its worth? 70
Blown harshly, keeps the trump its golden cry?
  Tastes sweet the water with such specks of earth?

The Englishman in Italy

Piano di Sorrento

Fortù, Fortù, my beloved one,°
  Sit here by my side,
On my knees put up both little feet!
  I was sure, if I tried,
I could make you laugh spite of Scirocco.°
  Now, open your eyes,
Let me keep you amused till he vanish
  In black from the skies,
With telling my memories over
  As you tell your beads;
All the Plain saw me gather, I garland   10
  —The flowers or the weeds.

Time for rain! for your long hot dry Autumn
  Had net-worked with brown
The white skin of each grape on the bunches,
  Marked like a quail's crown,
Those creatures you make such account of,
  Whose heads,—speckled white
Over brown like a great spider's back,
  As I told you last night,—   20
Your mother bites off for her supper.
  Red-ripe as could be,
Pomegranates were chapping and splitting
  In halves on the tree:
And betwixt the loose walls of great flintstone,
  Or in the thick dust
On the path, or straight out of the rock-side,
  Wherever could thrust

Some burnt sprig of bold hardy rock-flower
    Its yellow face up,   30
For the prize were great butterflies fighting,
    Some five for one cup.
So, I guessed, ere I got up this morning,
    What change was in store,
By the quick rustle-down of the quail-nets
    Which woke me before
I could open my shutter, made fast
    With a bough and a stone,
And look thro' the twisted dead vine-twigs,
    Sole lattice that's known.   40
Quick and sharp rang the rings down the net-poles,
    While, busy beneath,
Your priest and his brother tugged at them,
    The rain in their teeth.
And out upon all the flat house-roofs
    Where split figs lay drying,
The girls took the frails under cover:°
    Nor use seemed in trying
To get out the boats and go fishing,
    For, under the cliff,   50
Fierce the black water frothed o'er the blind-rock.
    No seeing our skiff
Arrive about noon from Amalfi,
    —Our fisher arrive,
And pitch down his basket before us,
    All trembling alive
With pink and grey jellies, your sea-fruit;
    You touch the strange lumps,
And mouths gape there, eyes open, all manner
    Of horns and of humps,   60
Which only the fisher looks grave at,
    While round him like imps
Cling screaming the children as naked
    And brown as his shrimps;
Himself too as bare to the middle
    —You see round his neck
The string and its brass coin suspended,
    That saves him from wreck.
But to-day not a boat reached Salerno,

So back, to a man,   70
Came our friends, with whose help in the vineyards
   Grape-harvest began.
In the vat, halfway up in our house-side,
   Like blood the juice spins,
While your brother all bare-legged is dancing
   Till breathless he grins
Dead-beaten in effort on effort
   To keep the grapes under,
Since still when he seems all but master,
   In pours the fresh plunder   80
From girls who keep coming and going
   With basket on shoulder,
And eyes shut against the rain's driving;
   Your girls that are older,—
For under the hedges of aloe,
   And where, on its bed
Of the orchard's black mould, the love-apple°
   Lies pulpy and red,
All the young ones are kneeling and filling
   Their laps with the snails
Tempted out by this first rainy weather,—   90
   Your best of regales,°
As to-night will be proved to my sorrow,
   When, supping in state,
We shall feast our grape-gleaners (two dozen,
   Three over one plate)
With lasagne so tempting to swallow
   In slippery ropes,
And gourds fried in great purple slices,
   That colour of popes.
Meantime, see the grape bunch they've brought you: 100
   The rain-water slips
O'er the heavy blue bloom on each globe
   Which the wasp to your lips
Still follows with fretful persistence:
   Nay, taste, while awake,
This half of a curd-white smooth cheese-ball
   That peels, flake by flake,
Like an onion, each smoother and whiter;
   Next, sip this weak wine   110

From the thin green glass flask, with its stopper,
    A leaf of the vine;
And end with the prickly-pear's red flesh
    That leaves thro' its juice
The stony black seeds on your pearl-teeth.
    Scirocco is loose!
Hark, the quick, whistling pelt of the olives
    Which, thick in one's track,
Tempt the stranger to pick up and bite them,
    Tho' not yet half black!   120
How the old twisted olive trunks shudder,
    The medlars let fall°
Their hard fruit, and the brittle great fig-trees
    Snap off, figs and all,
For here comes the whole of the tempest!
    No refuge, but creep
Back again to my side and my shoulder,
    And listen or sleep.

O how will your country show next week,
    When all the vine-boughs   130
Have been stripped of their foliage to pasture
    The mules and the cows?
Last eve, I rode over the mountains;
    Your brother, my guide,
Soon left me, to feast on the myrtles
    That offered, each side,
Their fruit-balls, black, glossy and luscious,—
    Or strip from the sorbs°
A treasure, or, rosy and wondrous,
    Those hairy gold orbs!   140
But my mule picked his sure sober path out,
    Just stopping to neigh
When he recognized down in the valley
    His mates on their way
With the faggots and barrels of water;
    And soon we emerged
From the plain, where the woods could scarce follow;
    And still as we urged
Our way, the woods wondered, and left us,
    As up still we trudged   150

Though the wild path grew wilder each instant,
    And place was e'en grudged
'Mid the rock-chasms and piles of loose stones
    Like the loose broken teeth
Of some monster which climbed there to die
    From the ocean beneath—
Place was grudged to the silver-grey fume-weed°
    That clung to the path,
And dark rosemary ever a-dying
    That, 'spite the wind's wrath,   160
So loves the salt rock's face to seaward,
    And lentisks as staunch°
To the stone where they root and bear berries,
    And . . . what shows a branch
Coral-coloured, transparent, with circlets
    Of pale seagreen leaves;
Over all trod my mule with the caution
    Of gleaners o'er sheaves,
Still, foot after foot like a lady,
    Till, round after round,   170
He climbed to the top of Calvano,°
    And God's own profound
Was above me, and round me the mountains,
    And under, the sea,
And within me my heart to bear witness
    What was and shall be.
Oh, heaven and the terrible crystal!°
    No rampart excludes
Your eye from the life to be lived
    In the blue solitudes.   180
Oh, those mountains, their infinite movement!
    Still moving with you;
For, ever some new head and breast of them
    Thrusts into view
To observe the intruder; you see it
    If quickly you turn
And, before they escape you, surprise them.
    They grudge you should learn
How the soft plains they look on, lean over
    And love (they pretend)   190
—Cower beneath them, the flat sea-pine crouches,

The wild fruit-trees bend,
E'en the myrtle-leaves curl, shrink and shut:
   All is silent and grave:
'Tis a sensual and timorous beauty,
   How fair! but a slave.
So, I turned to the sea; and there slumbered
   As greenly as ever
Those isles of the siren, your Galli;°
   No ages can sever   200
The Three, nor enable their sister
   To join them,—halfway
On the voyage, she looked at Ulysses—
   No farther to-day,
Tho' the small one, just launched in the wave,
   Watches breast-high and steady
From under the rock, her bold sister
   Swum halfway already.
Fortù, shall we sail there together
   And see from the sides   210
Quite new rocks show their faces, new haunts
   Where the siren abides?
Shall we sail round and round them, close over
   The rocks, tho' unseen,
That ruffle the grey glassy water
   To glorious green?
Then scramble from splinter to splinter,
   Reach land and explore,
On the largest, the strange square black turret
   With never a door,   220
Just a loop to admit the quick lizards;
   Then, stand there and hear
The birds' quiet singing, that tells us
   What life is, so clear?
—The secret they sang to Ulysses
   When, ages ago,
He heard and he knew this life's secret
   I hear and I know.

Ah, see! The sun breaks o'er Calvano;
   He strikes the great gloom   230
And flutters it o'er the mount's summit

In airy gold fume.
All is over. Look out, see the gipsy,
    Our tinker and smith,
Has arrived, set up bellows and forge,
    And down-squatted forthwith
To his hammering, under the wall there;
    One eye keeps aloof
The urchins that itch to be putting
    His jews'-harps to proof,   240
While the other, thro' locks of curled wire,
    Is watching how sleek
Shines the hog, come to share in the windfall
    —Chew, abbot's own cheek!
All is over. Wake up and come out now,
    And down let us go,
And see the fine things got in order
    At church for the show
Of the Sacrament, set forth this evening.
    To-morrow's the Feast   250
Of the Rosary's Virgin, by no means°
    Of Virgins the least,
As you'll hear in the off-hand discourse
    Which (all nature, no art)
The Dominican brother, these three weeks,
    Was getting by heart.
Not a pillar nor post but is dizened°
    With red and blue papers;
All the roof waves with ribbons, each altar
    A-blaze with long tapers;   260
But the great masterpiece is the scaffold
    Rigged glorious to hold
All the fiddlers and fifers and drummers
    And trumpeters bold,
Not afraid of Bellini nor Auber,°
    Who, when the priest's hoarse,
Will strike us up something that's brisk
    For the feast's second course.
And then will the flaxen-wigged Image°
    Be carried in pomp   270
Thro' the plain, while in gallant procession
    The priests mean to stomp.

All round the glad church lie old bottles
    With gunpowder stopped,
    Which will be, when the Image re-enters,
    Religiously popped;
And at night from the crest of Calvano
    Great bonfires will hang,
On the plain will the trumpets join chorus,
    And more poppers bang.   280
At all events, come—to the garden
    As far as the wall;
See me tap with a hoe on the plaster
    Till out there shall fall
A scorpion with wide angry nippers!

    —'Such trifles!' you say?
Fortù, in my England at home,
    Men meet gravely to-day
And debate, if abolishing Corn-laws
    Be righteous and wise   290
—If 'twere proper, Scirocco should vanish
    In black from the skies!°

The Lost Leader

I

Just for a handful of silver he left us,
    Just for a riband to stick in his coat—
Found the one gift of which fortune bereft us,
    Lost all the others she lets us devote;
They, with the gold to give, doled him out silver,
    So much was theirs who so little allowed:
How all our copper had gone for his service!
    Rags—were they purple, his heart had been proud!
We that had loved him so, followed him, honoured him,
    Lived in his mild and magnificent eye,   10
Learned his great language, caught his clear accents,
    Made him our pattern to live and to die!
Shakespeare was of us, Milton was for us,
    Burns, Shelley, were with us,—they watch from their graves!

He alone breaks from the van and the freemen,
  —He alone sinks to the rear and the slaves!

II

We shall march prospering,—not thro' his presence;
  Songs may inspirit us,—not from his lyre;
Deeds will be done,—while he boasts his quiescence,
  Still bidding crouch whom the rest bade aspire: 20
Blot out his name, then, record one lost soul more,
  One task more declined, one more footpath untrod,
One more devils'-triumph and sorrow for angels,
  One wrong more to man, one more insult to God!
Life's night begins: let him never come back to us!
  There would be doubt, hesitation and pain,
Forced praise on our part—the glimmer of twilight,
  Never glad confident morning again!
Best fight on well, for we taught him—strike gallantly,
  Menace our heart ere we master his own;   30
Then let him receive the new knowledge and wait us,
  Pardoned in heaven, the first by the throne!

The Laboratory

Ancien Régime

I

Now that I, tying thy glass mask tightly,
May gaze thro' these faint smokes curling whitely,
As thou pliest thy trade in this devil's-smithy—
Which is the poison to poison her, prithee?

II

He is with her, and they know that I know
Where they are, what they do: they believe my tears flow
While they laugh, laugh at me, at me fled to the drear
Empty church, to pray God in, for them!—I am here.

III

Grind away, moisten and mash up thy paste,
Pound at thy powder,—I am not in haste!   10
Better sit thus, and observe thy strange things,
Than go where men wait me and dance at the King's.

IV

That in the mortar—you call it a gum?
Ah, the brave tree whence such gold oozings come!
And yonder soft phial, the exquisite blue,
Sure to taste sweetly,—is that poison too?

V

Had I but all of them, thee and thy treasures,
What a wild crowd of invisible pleasures!
To carry pure death in an earring, a casket,
A signet, a fan-mount, a filigree basket!   20

VI

Soon, at the King's, a mere lozenge to give,
And Pauline should have just thirty minutes to live!
But to light a pastile, and Elise, with her head°
And her breast and her arms and her hands, should drop dead!

VII

Quick—is it finished? The colour's too grim!
Why not soft like the phial's, enticing and dim?
Let it brighten her drink, let her turn it and stir,
And try it and taste, ere she fix and prefer!

VIII

What a drop! She's not little, no minion like me!°
That's why she ensnared him: this never will free   30
The soul from those masculine eyes,—say, 'no!'
To that pulse's magnificent come-and-go.

IX

For only last night, as they whispered, I brought
My own eyes to bear on her so, that I thought

Could I keep them one half minute fixed, she would fall
Shrivelled; she fell not; yet this does it all!

X

Not that I bid you spare her the pain;
Let death be felt and the proof remain:
Brand, burn up, bite into its grace—
He is sure to remember her dying face!   40

XI

Is it done? Take my mask off! Nay, be not morose;
It kills her, and this prevents seeing it close:
The delicate droplet, my whole fortune's fee!
If it hurts her, beside, can it ever hurt me?

XII

Now, take all my jewels, gorge gold to your fill,
You may kiss me, old man, on my mouth if you will!
But brush this dust off me, lest horror it brings
Ere I know it—next moment I dance at the King's!

The Bishop Orders His Tomb at Saint Praxed's Church

Rome, 15—

Vanity, saith the preacher, vanity!°
Draw round my bed: is Anselm keeping back?
Nephews—sons mine...ah God, I know not! Well—°
She, men would have to be your mother once,
Old Gandolf envied me, so fair she was!
What's done is done, and she is dead beside,
Dead long ago, and I am Bishop since,
And as she died so must we die ourselves,
And thence ye may perceive the world's a dream.
Life, how and what is it? As here I lie   10
In this state-chamber, dying by degrees,
Hours and long hours in the dead night, I ask

'Do I live, am I dead?' Peace, peace seems all.
Saint Praxed's ever was the church for peace;
And so, about this tomb of mine. I fought
With tooth and nail to save my niche, ye know:
—Old Gandolf cozened me, despite my care;
Shrewd was that snatch from out the corner South
He graced his carrion with, God curse the same!
Yet still my niche is not so cramped but thence   20
One sees the pulpit o' the epistle-side,°
And somewhat of the choir, those silent seats,
And up into the aery dome where live
The angels, and a sunbeam's sure to lurk:
And I shall fill my slab of basalt there,
And 'neath my tabernacle take my rest,°
With those nine columns round me, two and two,
The odd one at my feet where Anselm stands:
Peach-blossom marble all, the rare, the ripe
As fresh-poured red wine of a mighty pulse.   30
—Old Gandolf with his paltry onion-stone,°
Put me where I may look at him! True peach,
Rosy and flawless: how I earned the prize!
Draw close: that conflagration of my church
—What then? So much was saved if aught were missed!
My sons, ye would not be my death? Go dig
The white-grape vineyard where the oil-press stood,
Drop water gently till the surface sink,
And if ye find . . . Ah God, I know not, I! . . .
Bedded in store of rotten fig-leaves soft,   40
And corded up in a tight olive-frail,°
Some lump, ah God, of *lapis lazuli*,°
Big as a Jew's head cut off at the nape,
Blue as a vein o'er the Madonna's breast . . .
Sons, all have I bequeathed you, villas, all,
That brave Frascati villa with its bath,
So, let the blue lump poise between my knees,
Like God the Father's globe on both his hands
Ye worship in the Jesu Church so gay,
For Gandolf shall not choose but see and burst!   50
Swift as a weaver's shuttle fleet our years:
Man goeth to the grave, and where is he?
Did I say basalt for my slab, sons? Black—

'Twas ever antique-black I meant! How else
Shall ye contrast my frieze to come beneath?
The bas-relief in bronze ye promised me,
Those Pans and Nymphs ye wot of, and perchance
Some tripod, thyrsus, with a vase or so,°
The Saviour at his sermon on the mount,
Saint Praxed in a glory, and one Pan°   60
Ready to twitch the Nymph's last garment off,
And Moses with the tables...but I know
Ye mark me not! What do they whisper thee,
Child of my bowels, Anselm? Ah, ye hope
To revel down my villas while I gasp
Bricked o'er with beggar's mouldy travertine°
Which Gandolf from his tomb-top chuckles at!
Nay, boys, ye love me—all of jasper, then!°
'Tis jasper ye stand pledged to, lest I grieve
My bath must needs be left behind, alas!   70
One block, pure green as a pistachio-nut,
There's plenty jasper somewhere in the world—
And have I not Saint Praxed's ear to pray
Horses for ye, and brown Greek manuscripts,
And mistresses with great smooth marbly limbs?
—That's if ye carve my epitaph aright,
Choice Latin, picked phrase, Tully's every word,
No gaudy ware like Gandolf's second line—
Tully, my masters? Ulpian serves his need!°
And then how I shall lie through centuries,   80
And hear the blessed mutter of the mass,
And see God made and eaten all day long,
And feel the steady candle-flame, and taste
Good strong thick stupefying incense-smoke!
For as I lie here, hours of the dead night,
Dying in state and by such slow degrees,
I fold my arms as if they clasped a crook,
And stretch my feet forth straight as stone can point,
And let the bedclothes, for a mortcloth, drop°
Into great laps and folds of sculptor's-work: 90
And as yon tapers dwindle, and strange thoughts
Grow, with a certain humming in my ears,
About the life before I lived this life,
And this life too, popes, cardinals and priests,

Saint Praxed at his sermon on the mount,°
Your tall pale mother with her talking eyes,
And new-found agate urns as fresh as day,
And marble's language, Latin pure, discreet,
—Aha, ELUCESCEBAT quoth our friend?°
No Tully, said I, Ulpian at the best!   100
Evil and brief hath been my pilgrimage.
All *lapis*, all, sons! Else I give the Pope
My villas! Will ye ever eat my heart?
Ever your eyes were as a lizard's quick,
They glitter like your mother's for my soul,
Or ye would heighten my impoverished frieze,
Piece out its starved design, and fill my vase
With grapes, and add a vizor and a Term,
And to the tripod ye would tie a lynx
That in his struggle throws the thyrsus down,   110
To comfort me on my entablature°
Whereon I am to lie till I must ask
'Do I live, am I dead?' There, leave me, there!
For ye have stabbed me with ingratitude
To death—ye wish it—God, ye wish it! Stone—
Gritstone, a-crumble! Clammy squares which sweat°
As if the corpse they keep were oozing through—
And no more *lapis* to delight the world!
Well go! I bless ye. Fewer tapers there,
But in a row: and, going, turn your backs   120
—Ay, like departing altar-ministrants,
And leave me in my church, the church for peace,
That I may watch at leisure if he leers—
Old Gandolf, at me, from his onion-stone,
As still he envied me, so fair she was!

The Boy and the Angel

Morning, evening, noon and night,
'Praise God!' sang Theocrite.

Then to his poor trade he turned,
Whereby the daily meal was earned.

Hard he laboured, long and well;
O'er his work the boy's curls fell.

But ever, at each period,
He stopped and sang, 'Praise God!'

Then back again his curls he threw,
And cheerful turned to work anew.   10

Said Blaise, the listening monk, 'Well done;
I doubt not thou art heard, my son:

As well as if thy voice to-day
Were praising God, the Pope's great way.

This Easter Day, the Pope at Rome
Praises God from Peter's dome.'

Said Theocrite, 'Would God that I
Might praise him, that great way, and die!'

Night passed, day shone,
And Theocrite was gone.   20

With God a day endures alway,
A thousand years are but a day.

God said in heaven, 'Nor day nor night
Now brings the voice of my delight.'

Then Gabriel, like a rainbow's birth,
Spread his wings and sank to earth;

Entered, in flesh, the empty cell,
Lived there, and played the craftsman well;

And morning, evening, noon and night,
Praised God in place of Theocrite.   30

And from a boy, to youth he grew:
The man put off the stripling's hue:

The man matured and fell away
Into the season of decay:

And ever o'er the trade he bent,
And ever lived on earth content.

(He did God's will; to him, all one
If on the earth or in the sun.)

God said, 'A praise is in mine ear;
There is no doubt in it, no fear: 40

So sing old worlds, and so
New worlds that from my footstool go.

Clearer loves sound other ways:
I miss my little human praise.'

Then forth sprang Gabriel's wings, off fell
The flesh disguise, remained the cell.

'Twas Easter Day: he flew to Rome,
And paused above Saint Peter's dome.

In the tiring-room close by
The great outer gallery,   50

With his holy vestments dight,
Stood the new Pope, Theocrite:

And all his past career
Came back upon him clear,

Since when, a boy, he plied his trade,
Till on his life the sickness weighed;

And in his cell, when death drew near,
An angel in a dream brought cheer:

And rising from the sickness drear
He grew a priest, and now stood here.   60

To the East with praise he turned,
And on his sight the angel burned.

'I bore thee from thy craftsman's cell
And set thee here; I did not well.

Vainly I left my angel-sphere,
Vain was thy dream of many a year.

Thy voice's praise seemed weak; it dropped—
Creation's chorus stopped!

Go back and praise again
The early way, while I remain.   70

With that weak voice of our disdain,
Take up creation's pausing strain.

Back to the cell and poor employ:
Resume the craftsman and the boy!'

Theocrite grew old at home;
A new Pope dwelt in Peter's dome.

One vanished as the other died:
They sought God side by side.

Garden Fancies

II. Sibrandus Schafnaburgensis

I

Plague take all your pedants, say I!
   He who wrote what I hold in my hand,
Centuries back was so good as to die,
   Leaving this rubbish to cumber the land;
This, that was a book in its time,
   Printed on paper and bound in leather,
Last month in the white of a matin-prime°
   Just when the birds sang all together.

II

Into the garden I brought it to read,
   And under the arbute and laurustine°
Read it, so help me grace in my need,
   From title-page to closing line.
Chapter on chapter did I count,
   As a curious traveller counts Stonehenge;
Added up the mortal amount;
   And then proceeded to my revenge.

10

III

Yonder's a plum-tree with a crevice
   An owl would build in, were he but sage;
For a lap of moss, like a fine pont-levis°

In a castle of the Middle Age,   20
Joins to a lip of gum, pure amber;
   When he'd be private, there might he spend
Hours alone in his lady's chamber:
   Into this crevice I dropped our friend.

IV

Splash, went he, as under he ducked,
   —At the bottom, I knew, rain-drippings stagnate:
Next, a handful of blossoms I plucked
   To bury him with, my bookshelf's magnate;
Then I went in-doors, brought out a loaf,
   Half a cheese, and a bottle of Chablis;   30
Lay on the grass and forgot the oaf
   Over a jolly chapter of Rabelais.°

V

Now, this morning, betwixt the moss
   And gum that locked our friend in limbo,
A spider had spun his web across,
   And sat in the midst with arms akimbo:
So, I took pity, for learning's sake,
   And, *de profundis, accentibus lætis,*
Cantate! quoth I, as I got a rake;
   And up I fished his delectable treatise.   40

VI

Here you have it, dry in the sun,
   With all the binding all of a blister,
And great blue spots where the ink has run,
   And reddish streaks that wink and glister
O'er the page so beautifully yellow:
   Oh, well have the droppings played their tricks!
Did he guess how toadstools grow, this fellow?
   Here's one stuck in his chapter six!

VII

How did he like it when the live creatures
   Tickled and toused and browsed him all over,   50

And worm, slug, eft, with serious features,
  Came in, each one, for his right of trover?
—When the water-beetle with great blind deaf face
  Made of her eggs the stately deposit,
And the newt borrowed just so much of the preface
  As tiled in the top of his black wife's closet?

VIII

All that life and fun and romping,
  All that frisking and twisting and coupling,
While slowly our poor friend's leaves were swamping
  And clasps were cracking and covers suppling!   60
As if you had carried sour John Knox°
  To the play-house at Paris, Vienna or Munich,
Fastened him into a front-row box,
  And danced off the ballet with trousers and tunic.

IX

Come, old martyr! What, torment enough is it?
  Back to my room shall you take your sweet self.
Good-bye, mother-beetle; husband-eft, *sufficit!*°
  See the snug niche I have made on my shelf!
A.'s book shall prop you up, B.'s shall cover you,
  Here's C. to be grave with, or D. to be gay,   70
And with E. on each side, and F. right over you,
  Dry-rot at ease till the Judgment-day!

Meeting at Night

I

The grey sea and the long black land;
And the yellow half-moon large and low;
And the startled little waves that leap
In fiery ringlets from their sleep,
As I gain the cove with pushing prow,
And quench its speed i' the slushy sand.

II

Then a mile of warm sea-scented beach;
Three fields to cross till a farm appears;
A tap at the pane, the quick sharp scratch
And blue spurt of a lighted match,   10
And a voice less loud, thro' its joys and fears,
Than the two hearts beating each to each!

Parting at Morning

Round the cape of a sudden came the sea,
And the sun looked over the mountain's rim:
And straight was a path of gold for him,
And the need of a world of men for me.

MEN AND WOMEN (1855)

Love Among the Ruins

I

Where the quiet-coloured end of evening smiles,
     Miles and miles
On the solitary pastures where our sheep
     Half-asleep
Tinkle homeward thro' the twilight, stray or stop
     As they crop—
Was the site once of a city great and gay,
     (So they say)
Of our country's very capital, its prince
     Ages since   10
Held his court in, gathered councils, wielding far
     Peace or war.

II

Now,—the country does not even boast a tree,
     As you see,
To distinguish slopes of verdure, certain rills
     From the hills
Intersect and give a name to, (else they run
     Into one)
Where the domed and daring palace shot its spires
     Up like fires
O'er the hundred-gated circuit of a wall   20
     Bounding all,
Made of marble, men might march on nor be pressed,
     Twelve abreast.

III

And such plenty and perfection, see, of grass
     Never was!

Such a carpet as, this summer-time, o'erspreads
    And embeds
Every vestige of the city, guessed alone,
    Stock or stone—   30
Where a multitude of men breathed joy and woe
    Long ago;
Lust of glory pricked their hearts up, dread of shame
    Struck them tame;
And that glory and that shame alike, the gold
    Bought and sold.

IV

Now,—the single little turret that remains
    On the plains,
By the caper overrooted, by the gourd°
    Overscored,   40
While the patching houseleek's head of blossom winks°
    Through the chinks—
Marks the basement whence a tower in ancient time
    Sprang sublime,
And a burning ring, all round, the chariots traced
    As they raced,
And the monarch and his minions and his dames
    Viewed the games.

V

And I know, while thus the quiet-coloured eve
    Smiles to leave   50
To their folding, all our many-tinkling fleece
    In such peace,
And the slopes and rills in undistinguished grey
    Melt away—
That a girl with eager eyes and yellow hair
    Waits me there
In the turret whence the charioteers caught soul
    For the goal,
When the king looked, where she looks now, breathless, dumb
    Till I come.   60

VI

But he looked upon the city, every side,
  Far and wide,
All the mountains topped with temples, all the glades'
  Colonnades,
All the causeys, bridges, aqueducts,—and then,°
  All the men!
When I do come, she will speak not, she will stand,
  Either hand
On my shoulder, give her eyes the first embrace
  Of my face,   70
Ere we rush, ere we extinguish sight and speech
  Each on each.

VII

In one year they sent a million fighters forth
  South and North,
And they built their gods a brazen pillar high
  As the sky,
Yet reserved a thousand chariots in full force—
  Gold, of course.
Oh heart! oh blood that freezes, blood that burns!
  Earth's returns   80
For whole centuries of folly, noise and sin!
  Shut them in,
With their triumphs and their glories and the rest!
  Love is best.

Evelyn Hope

I

Beautiful Evelyn Hope is dead!
 Sit and watch by her side an hour.
That is her book-shelf, this her bed;
 She plucked that piece of geranium-flower,
Beginning to die too, in the glass;
 Little has yet been changed, I think:
The shutters are shut, no light may pass
 Save two long rays thro' the hinge's chink.

II

Sixteen years old when she died!
   Perhaps she had scarcely heard my name;   10
It was not her time to love; beside,
   Her life had many a hope and aim,
Duties enough and little cares,
   And now was quiet, now astir,
Till God's hand beckoned unawares,—
   And the sweet white brow is all of her.

III

Is it too late then, Evelyn Hope?
   What, your soul was pure and true,
The good stars met in your horoscope,
   Made you of spirit, fire and dew—   20
And, just because I was thrice as old
   And our paths in the world diverged so wide,
Each was nought to each, must I be told?
   We were fellow mortals, nought beside?

IV

No, indeed! for God above
   Is great to grant, as mighty to make,
And creates the love to reward the love:
   I claim you still, for my own love's sake!
Delayed it may be for more lives yet,
   Through worlds I shall traverse, not a few: 30
Much is to learn, much to forget
   Ere the time be come for taking you.

V

But the time will come,—at last it will,
   When, Evelyn Hope, what meant (I shall say)
In the lower earth, in the years long still,
   That body and soul so pure and gay?
Why your hair was amber, I shall divine,
   And your mouth of your own geranium's red—
And what you would do with me, in fine,
   In the new life come in the old one's stead.   40

VI

I have lived (I shall say) so much since then,
    Given up myself so many times,
Gained me the gains of various men,
    Ransacked the ages, spoiled the climes;
Yet one thing, one, in my soul's full scope,
    Either I missed or itself missed me:
And I want and find you, Evelyn Hope!
    What is the issue? let us see!

VII

I loved you, Evelyn, all the while.
    My heart seemed full as it could hold?
There was place and to spare for the frank young smile,
    And the red young mouth, and the hair's young gold.
So, hush,—I will give you this leaf to keep:
    See, I shut it inside the sweet cold hand!
There, that is our secret: go to sleep!
    You will wake, and remember, and understand.

50

Up at a Villa—Down in the City

(As Distinguished by an Italian Person of Quality)

I

Had I but plenty of money, money enough and to spare,
The house for me, no doubt, were a house in the city-square;
Ah, such a life, such a life, as one leads at the window there!

II

Something to see, by Bacchus, something to hear, at least!°
There, the whole day long, one's life is a perfect feast;
While up at a villa one lives, I maintain it, no more than a beast.

III

Well now, look at our villa! stuck like the horn of a bull
Just on a mountain-edge as bare as the creature's skull,

Save a mere shag of a bush with hardly a leaf to pull!
—I scratch my own, sometimes, to see if the hair's turned wool.   10

                                    I V

But the city, oh the city—the square with the houses! Why?
They are stone-faced, white as a curd, there's something to take
      the eye!
Houses in four straight lines, not a single front awry;
You watch who crosses and gossips, who saunters, who hurries by;
Green blinds, as a matter of course, to draw when the sun gets
      high;
And the shops with fanciful signs which are painted properly.

                                    V

What of a villa? Though winter be over in March by rights,
'Tis May perhaps ere the snow shall have withered well off the
      heights:
You've the brown ploughed land before, where the oxen steam
      and wheeze,
And the hills over-smoked behind by the faint grey olive-trees.   20

                                    VI

Is it better in May, I ask you? You've summer all at once;
In a day he leaps complete with a few strong April suns.
'Mid the sharp short emerald wheat, scarce risen three fingers
      well,
The wild tulip, at end of its tube, blows out its great red bell
Like a thin clear bubble of blood, for the children to pick and sell.

                                    VII

Is it ever hot in the square? There's a fountain to spout and
      splash!
In the shade it sings and springs; in the shine such foam-bows
      flash
On the horses with curling fish-tails, that prance and paddle and
      pash°
Round the lady atop in her conch—fifty gazers do not abash,
Though all that she wears is some weeds round her waist in a
      sort of sash.   30

VIII

All the year long at the villa, nothing to see though you linger,
Except yon cypress that points like death's lean lifted forefinger.
Some think fireflies pretty, when they mix i' the corn and
    mingle,
Or thrid the stinking hemp till the stalks of it seem a-tingle.°
Late August or early September, the stunning cicala is shrill,
And the bees keep their tiresome whine round the resinous firs
    on the hill.
Enough of the seasons,—I spare you the months of the fever and
    chill.

IX

Ere you open your eyes in the city, the blessed church-bells
    begin:
No sooner the bells leave off than the diligence rattles in:°
You get the pick of the news, and it costs you never a pin.   40
By-and-by there's the travelling doctor gives pills, lets blood,
    draws teeth;
Or the Pulcinello-trumpet breaks up the market beneath.°
At the post-office such a scene-picture—the new play, piping
    hot!
And a notice how, only this morning, three liberal thieves were
    shot.
Above it, behold the Archbishop's most fatherly of rebukes,
And beneath, with his crown and his lion, some little new law of
    the Duke's!°
Or a sonnet with flowery marge, to the Reverend Don So-and-so
Who is Dante, Boccaccio, Petrarca, Saint Jerome and Cicero,
'And moreover,' (the sonnet goes rhyming,) 'the skirts of Saint
    Paul has reached,
Having preached us those six Lent-lectures more unctuous than
    ever he preached.'   50
Noon strikes,—here sweeps the procession! our Lady borne
    smiling ånd smart
With a pink gauze gown all spangles, and seven swords stuck in
    her heart!°
Bang-whang-whang goes the drum, *tootle-te-tootle* the fife;°
No keeping one's haunches still: it's the greatest pleasure in
    life.

X

But bless you, it's dear—it's dear! fowls, wine, at double the
    rate.
They have clapped a new tax upon salt, and what oil pays
    passing the gate
It's a horror to think of. And so, the villa for me, not the city!
Beggars can scarcely be choosers: but still—ah, the pity, the pity!
Look, two and two go the priests, then the monks with cowls
    and sandals,
And the penitents dressed in white shirts, a-holding the yellow
    candles;   60
One, he carries a flag up straight, and another a cross with
    handles,
And the Duke's guard brings up the rear, for the better
    prevention of scandals:
Bang-whang-whang goes the drum, *tootle-te-tootle* the fife.
Oh, a day in the city-square, there is no such pleasure in life!

By the Fire-Side

I

How well I know what I mean to do
   When the long dark autumn-evenings come;
And where, my soul, is thy pleasant hue?
   With the music of all thy voices, dumb
In life's November too!

II

I shall be found by the fire, suppose,
   O'er a great wise book as beseemeth age,
While the shutters flap as the cross-wind blows
   And I turn the page, and I turn the page,
Not verse now, only prose!   10

III

Till the young ones whisper, finger on lip,
   'There he is at it, deep in Greek:

Now then, or never, out we slip
   To cut from the hazels by the creek
A mainmast for our ship!'

IV

I shall be at it indeed, my friends:
   Greek puts already on either side
Such a branch-work forth as soon extends
   To a vista opening far and wide,
And I pass out where it ends.   20

V

The outside-frame, like your hazel-trees:
   But the inside-archway widens fast,
And a rarer sort succeeds to these,
   And we slope to Italy at last
And youth, by green degrees.

VI

I follow wherever I am led,
   Knowing so well the leader's hand:
Oh woman-country, wooed not wed,
   Loved all the more by earth's male-lands,
Laid to their hearts instead!   30

VII

Look at the ruined chapel again
   Half-way up in the Alpine gorge!
Is that a tower, I point you plain,
   Or is it a mill, or an iron-forge
Breaks solitude in vain?

VIII

A turn, and we stand in the heart of things;
   The woods are round us, heaped and dim;
From slab to slab how it slips and springs,
   The thread of water single and slim,
Through the ravage some torrent brings!   40

IX

Does it feed the little lake below?
    That speck of white just on its marge
Is Pella; see, in the evening-glow,°
    How sharp the silver spear-heads charge
When Alp meets heaven in snow!

X

On our other side is the straight-up rock;
    And a path is kept 'twixt the gorge and it
By boulder-stones where lichens mock
    The marks on a moth, and small ferns fit
Their teeth to the polished block.   50

XI

Oh the sense of the yellow mountain-flowers,
    And thorny balls, each three in one,
The chestnuts throw on our path in showers!
    For the drop of the woodland fruit's begun,
These early November hours,

XII

That crimson the creeper's leaf across
    Like a splash of blood, intense, abrupt,
O'er a shield else gold from rim to boss,°
    And lay it for show on the fairy-cupped
Elf-needled mat of moss,   60

XIII

By the rose-flesh mushrooms, undivulged
    Last evening—nay, in to-day's first dew
Yon sudden coral nipple bulged,
    Where a freaked fawn-coloured flaky crew°
Of toadstools peep indulged.

XIV

And yonder, at foot of the fronting ridge
    That takes the turn to a range beyond,

Is the chapel reached by the one-arched bridge
   Where the water is stopped in a stagnant pond
Danced over by the midge.

                                 70

XV

The chapel and bridge are of stone alike,
   Blackish-grey and mostly wet;
Cut hemp-stalks steep in the narrow dyke.
   See here again, how the lichens fret
And the roots of the ivy strike!

XVI

Poor little place, where its one priest comes
   On a festa-day, if he comes at all,
To the dozen folk from their scattered homes,
   Gathered within that precinct small
By the dozen ways one roams—

                                 80

XVII

To drop from the charcoal-burners' huts,
   Or climb from the hemp-dressers' low shed,
Leave the grange where the woodman stores his nuts,
   Or the wattled cote where the fowlers spread°
Their gear on the rock's bare juts.

XVIII

It has some pretension too, this front,
   With its bit of fresco half-moon-wise
Set over the porch, Art's early wont:
   'Tis John in the Desert, I surmise,
But has borne the weather's brunt—

                                 90

XIX

Not from the fault of the builder, though,
   For a pent-house properly projects°
Where three carved beams make a certain show,
   Dating—good thought of our architect's—
'Five, six, nine, he lets you know.

XX

And all day long a bird sings there,
  And a stray sheep drinks at the pond at times;
The place is silent and aware;
  It has had its scenes, its joys and crimes,
But that is its own affair.   100

XXI

My perfect wife, my Leonor,°
  Oh heart, my own, oh eyes, mine too,
Whom else could I dare look backward for,
  With whom beside should I dare pursue
The path grey heads abhor?

XXII

For it leads to a crag's sheer edge with them;
  Youth, flowery all the way, there stops—
Not they; age threatens and they contemn,
  Till they reach the gulf wherein youth drops,
One inch from life's safe hem!   110

XXIII

With me, youth led...I will speak now,
  No longer watch you as you sit
Reading by fire-light, that great brow
  And the spirit-small hand propping it,
Mutely, my heart knows how—

XXIV

When, if I think but deep enough,
  You are wont to answer, prompt as rhyme;
And you, too, find without rebuff
  Response your soul seeks many a time
Piercing its fine flesh-stuff.   120

XXV

My own, confirm me! If I tread
  This path back, is it not in pride

To think how little I dreamed it led
　　To an age so blest that, by its side,
Youth seems the waste instead?

XXVI

My own, see where the years conduct!
　　At first, 'twas something our two souls
Should mix as mists do; each is sucked
　　In each now: on, the new stream rolls,
Whatever rocks obstruct.   130

XXVII

Think, when our one soul understands
　　The great Word which makes all things new,°
When earth breaks up and heaven expands,
　　How will the change strike me and you
In the house not made with hands?°

XXVIII

Oh I must feel your brain prompt mine,
　　Your heart anticipate my heart,
You must be just before, in fine,
　　See and make me see, for your part,
New depths of the divine!   140

XXIX

But who could have expected this
　　When we two drew together first
Just for the obvious human bliss,
　　To satisfy life's daily thirst
With a thing men seldom miss?

XXX

Come back with me to the first of all,
　　Let us lean and love it over again,
Let us now forget and now recall,
　　Break the rosary in a pearly rain,
And gather what we let fall!   150

XXXI

What did I say?—that a small bird sings
   All day long, save when a brown pair
Of hawks from the wood float with wide wings
   Strained to a bell: 'gainst noon-day glare
You count the streaks and rings.

XXXII

But at afternoon or almost eve
   'Tis better; then the silence grows
To that degree, you half believe
   It must get rid of what it knows,
Its bosom does so heave.   160

XXXIII

Hither we walked then, side by side,
   Arm in arm and cheek to cheek,
And still I questioned or replied,
   While my heart, convulsed to really speak,
Lay choking in its pride.

XXXIV

Silent the crumbling bridge we cross,
   And pity and praise the chapel sweet,
And care about the fresco's loss,
   And wish for our souls a like retreat,
And wonder at the moss.   170

XXXV

Stoop and kneel on the settle under,°
   Look through the window's grated square:
Nothing to see! For fear of plunder,
   The cross is down and the altar bare,
As if thieves don't fear thunder.

XXXVI

We stoop and look in through the grate,
   See the little porch and rustic door,

Read duly the dead builder's date;
    Then cross the bridge that we crossed before,
Take the path again—but wait!   180

XXXVII

Oh moment, one and infinite!
    The water slips o'er stock and stone;
The West is tender, hardly bright:
    How grey at once is the evening grown—
One star, its chrysolite!°

XXXVIII

We two stood there with never a third,
    But each by each, as each knew well:
The sights we saw and the sounds we heard,
    The lights and the shades made up a spell
Till the trouble grew and stirred.   190

XXXIX

Oh, the little more, and how much it is!
    And the little less, and what worlds away!
How a sound shall quicken content to bliss,
    Or a breath suspend the blood's best play,
And life be a proof of this!

XL

Had she willed it, still had stood the screen
    So slight, so sure, 'twixt my love and her:
I could fix her face with a guard between,
    And find her soul as when friends confer,
Friends—lovers that might have been.   200

XLI

For my heart had a touch of the woodland-time,
    Wanting to sleep now over its best.
Shake the whole tree in the summer-prime,
    But bring to the last leaf no such test!
'Hold the last fast!' runs the rhyme.

XLII

For a chance to make your little much,
   To gain a lover and lose a friend,
Venture the tree and a myriad such,
   When nothing you mar but the year can mend:
But a last leaf—fear to touch!   210

XLIII

Yet should it unfasten itself and fall
   Eddying down till it find your face
At some slight wind—best chance of all!
   Be your heart henceforth its dwelling-place
You trembled to forestall!

XLIV

Worth how well, those dark grey eyes,
   That hair so dark and dear, how worth
That a man should strive and agonize,
   And taste a veriest hell on earth
For the hope of such a prize!   220

XLV

You might have turned and tried a man,
   Set him a space to weary and wear,
And prove which suited more your plan,
   His best of hope or his worst despair,
Yet end as he began.

XLVI

But you spared me this, like the heart you are,
   And filled my empty heart at a word.
If two lives join, there is oft a scar,
   They are one and one, with a shadowy third;
One near one is too far.   230

XLVII

A moment after, and hands unseen
   Were hanging the night around us fast;

But we knew that a bar was broken between
    Life and life: we were mixed at last
In spite of the mortal screen.

XLVIII

The forests had done it; there they stood;
    We caught for a moment the powers at play:
They had mingled us so, for once and good,
    Their work was done—we might go or stay,
They relapsed to their ancient mood.   240

XLIX

How the world is made for each of us!
    How all we perceive and know in it
Tends to some moment's product thus,
    When a soul declares itself—to wit,
By its fruit, the thing it does!

L

Be hate that fruit or love that fruit,
    It forwards the general deed of man,
And each of the Many helps to recruit
    The life of the race by a general plan;
Each living his own, to boot.   250

LI

I am named and known by that moment's feat;
    There took my station and degree;
So grew my own small life complete,
    As nature obtained her best of me—
One born to love you, sweet!

LII

And to watch you sink by the fire-side now
    Back again, as you mutely sit
Musing by fire-light, that great brow
    And the spirit-small hand propping it,
Yonder, my heart knows how!   260

LIII

So, earth has gained by one man the more,
   And the gain of earth must be heaven's gain too;
And the whole is well worth thinking o'er
   When autumn comes: which I mean to do
One day, as I said before.

Fra Lippo Lippi

I am poor brother Lippo, by your leave!
You need not clap your torches to my face.
Zooks, what's to blame? you think you see a monk!°
What, 'tis past midnight, and you go the rounds,
And here you catch me at an alley's end
Where sportive ladies leave their doors ajar?°
The Carmine's my cloister: hunt it up,
Do,—harry out, if you must show your zeal,
Whatever rat, there, haps on his wrong hole,
And nip each softling of a wee white mouse,   10
Weke, weke, that's crept to keep him company!
Aha, you know your betters! Then, you'll take
Your hand away that's fiddling on my throat,
And please to know me likewise. Who am I?
Why, one, sir, who is lodging with a friend
Three streets off—he's a certain . . . how d'ye call?
Master—a . . . Cosimo of the Medici,
I' the house that caps the corner. Boh! you were best!
Remember and tell me, the day you're hanged,
How you affected such a gullet's-gripe!°   20
But you, sir, it concerns you that your knaves
Pick up a manner nor discredit you:
Zooks, are we pilchards, that they sweep the streets
And count fair prize what comes into their net?
He's Judas to a tittle, that man is!
Just such a face! Why, sir, you make amends.
Lord, I'm not angry! Bid your hangdogs go
Drink out this quarter-florin to the health
Of the munificent House that harbours me
(And many more beside, lads! more beside!)   30

And all's come square again. I'd like his face—
His, elbowing on his comrade in the door
With the pike and lantern,—for the slave that holds
John Baptist's head a-dangle by the hair
With one hand ('Look you, now,' as who should say)
And his weapon in the other, yet unwiped!
It's not your chance to have a bit of chalk,
A wood-coal or the like? or you should see!
Yes, I'm the painter, since you style me so.
What, brother Lippo's doings, up and down,   40
You know them and they take you? like enough!°
I saw the proper twinkle in your eye—
'Tell you, I liked your looks at very first.
Let's sit and set things straight now, hip to haunch.
Here's spring come, and the nights one makes up bands
To roam the town and sing out carnival,
And I've been three weeks shut within my mew,°
A-painting for the great man, saints and saints
And saints again. I could not paint all night—
Ouf! I leaned out of window for fresh air.   50
There came a hurry of feet and little feet,
A sweep of lute-strings, laughs, and whifts of song,—
Flower o' the broom,
Take away love, and our earth is a tomb!
Flower o' the quince,
I let Lisa go, and what good in life since?
Flower o' the thyme—and so on. Round they went.°
Scarce had they turned the corner when a titter
Like the skipping of rabbits by moonlight,—three slim shapes,
And a face that looked up ... zooks, sir, flesh and blood,   60
That's all I'm made of! Into shreds it went,
Curtain and counterpane and coverlet,
All the bed-furniture—a dozen knots,
There was a ladder! Down I let myself,
Hands and feet, scrambling somehow, and so dropped,
And after them. I came up with the fun
Hard by Saint Laurence, hail fellow, well met,—°
Flower o' the rose,
If I've been merry, what matter who knows?
And so as I was stealing back again   70
To get to bed and have a bit of sleep

Ere I rise up to-morrow and go work
On Jerome knocking at his poor old breast
With his great round stone to subdue the flesh,
You snap me of the sudden. Ah, I see!
Though your eye twinkles still, you shake your head—
Mine's shaved—a monk, you say—the sting's in that!
If Master Cosimo announced himself,
Mum's the word naturally; but a monk!
Come, what am I a beast for? tell us, now!   80
I was a baby when my mother died
And father died and left me in the street.
I starved there, God knows how, a year or two
On fig-skins, melon-parings, rinds and shucks,
Refuse and rubbish. One fine frosty day,
My stomach being empty as your hat,
The wind doubled me up and down I went.
Old Aunt Lapaccia trussed me with one hand,
(Its fellow was a stinger as I knew)
And so along the wall, over the bridge,   90
By the straight cut to the convent. Six words there,
While I stood munching my first bread that month:
'So, boy, you're minded,' quoth the good fat father
Wiping his own mouth, 'twas refection-time,—
'To quit this very miserable world?
Will you renounce'... 'the mouthful of bread?' thought I;
By no means! Brief, they made a monk of me;
I did renounce the world, its pride and greed,
Palace, farm, villa, shop and banking-house,
Trash, such as these poor devils of Medici   100
Have given their hearts to—all at eight years old.
Well, sir, I found in time, you may be sure,
'Twas not for nothing—the good bellyful,
The warm serge and the rope that goes all round,
And day-long blessed idleness beside!
'Let's see what the urchin's fit for'—that came next.
Not overmuch their way, I must confess.
Such a to-do! They tried me with their books:
Lord, they'd have taught me Latin in pure waste!
Flower o' the clove,   110
All the Latin I construe is, 'amo' I love!
But, mind you, when a boy starves in the streets

Eight years together, as my fortune was,
Watching folk's faces to know who will fling
The bit of half-stripped grape-bunch he desires,
And who will curse or kick him for his pains,—
Which gentleman processional and fine,°
Holding a candle to the Sacrament,
Will wink and let him lift a plate and catch
The droppings of the wax to sell again,   120
Or holla for the Eight and have him whipped,—°
How say I?—nay, which dog bites, which lets drop
His bone from the heap of offal in the street,—
Why, soul and sense of him grow sharp alike,
He learns the look of things, and none the less
For admonition from the hunger-pinch.
I had a store of such remarks, be sure,
Which, after I found leisure, turned to use.
I drew men's faces on my copy-books,
Scrawled them within the antiphonary's marge,°   130
Joined legs and arms to the long music-notes,
Found eyes and nose and chin for A's and B's,
And made a string of pictures of the world
Betwixt the ins and outs of verb and noun,
On the wall, the bench, the door. The monks looked black.
'Nay,' quoth the Prior, 'turn him out, d'ye say?
In no wise. Lose a crow and catch a lark.
What if at last we get our man of parts,
We Carmelites, like those Camaldolese
And Preaching Friars, to do our church up fine   140
And put the front on it that ought to be!'
And hereupon he bade me daub away.
Thank you! my head being crammed, the walls a blank,
Never was such prompt disemburdening.
First, every sort of monk, the black and white,°
I drew them, fat and lean: then, folk at church,
From good old gossips waiting to confess
Their cribs of barrel-droppings, candle-ends,—°
To the breathless fellow at the altar-foot,
Fresh from his murder, safe and sitting there°   150
With the little children round him in a row
Of admiration, half for his beard and half
For that white anger of his victim's son

Shaking a fist at him with one fierce arm,
Signing himself with the other because of Christ
(Whose sad face on the cross sees only this
After the passion of a thousand years)
Till some poor girl, her apron o'er her head,
(Which the intense eyes looked through) came at eve
On tiptoe, said a word, dropped in a loaf,   160
Her pair of earrings and a bunch of flowers
(The brute took growling), prayed, and so was gone.
I painted all, then cried ''Tis ask and have;
Choose, for more's ready!'—laid the ladder flat,
And showed my covered bit of cloister-wall.
The monks closed in a circle and praised loud
Till checked, taught what to see and not to see,
Being simple bodies,—'That's the very man!
Look at the boy who stoops to pat the dog!
That woman's like the Prior's niece who comes°   170
To care about his asthma: it's the life!'
But there my triumph's straw-fire flared and funked;°
Their betters took their turn to see and say:
The Prior and the learned pulled a face
And stopped all that in no time. 'How? what's here?
Quite from the mark of painting, bless us all!
Faces, arms, legs and bodies like the true
As much as pea and pea! it's devil's-game!
Your business is not to catch men with show,
With homage to the perishable clay,   180
But lift them over it, ignore it all,
Make them forget there's such a thing as flesh.
Your business is to paint the souls of men—
Man's soul, and it's a fire, smoke . . . no, it's not . . .
It's vapour done up like a new-born babe—
(In that shape when you die it leaves your mouth)
It's . . . well, what matters talking, it's the soul!
Give us no more of body than shows soul!
Here's Giotto, with his Saint a-praising God,
That sets us praising,—why not stop with him?   190
Why put all thoughts of praise out of our head
With wonder at lines, colours, and what not?
Paint the soul, never mind the legs and arms!
Rub all out, try at it a second time.

Oh, that white smallish female with the breasts,
She's just my niece...Herodias, I would say,—°
Who went and danced and got men's heads cut off!
Have it all out!' Now, is this sense, I ask?°
A fine way to paint soul, by painting body
So ill, the eye can't stop there, must go further   200
And can't fare worse! Thus, yellow does for white
When what you put for yellow's simply black,
And any sort of meaning looks intense
When all beside itself means and looks nought.
Why can't a painter lift each foot in turn,
Left foot and right foot, go a double step,
Make his flesh liker and his soul more like,
Both in their order? Take the prettiest face,
The Prior's niece...patron-saint—is it so pretty
You can't discover if it means hope, fear,   210
Sorrow or joy? won't beauty go with these?
Suppose I've made her eyes all right and blue,
Can't I take breath and try to add life's flash,
And then add soul and heighten them threefold?
Or say there's beauty with no soul at all—
(I never saw it—put the case the same—)
If you get simple beauty and nought else,
You get about the best thing God invents:
That's somewhat: and you'll find the soul you have missed,
Within yourself, when you return him thanks.   220
'Rub all out!' Well, well, there's my life, in short,
And so the thing has gone on ever since.
I'm grown a man no doubt, I've broken bounds:
You should not take a fellow eight years old
And make him swear to never kiss the girls.
I'm my own master, paint now as I please—
Having a friend, you see, in the Corner-house!
Lord, it's fast holding by the rings in front—
Those great rings serve more purposes than just
To plant a flag in, or tie up a horse!   230
And yet the old schooling sticks, the old grave eyes
Are peeping o'er my shoulder as I work,
The heads shake still—'It's art's decline, my son!
You're not of the true painters, great and old;
Brother Angelico's the man, you'll find;°

Brother Lorenzo stands his single peer:°
Fag on at flesh, you'll never make the third!'
Flower o' the pine,
You keep your mistr... manners, and I'll stick to mine!
I'm not the third, then: bless us, they must know!   240
Don't you think they're the likeliest to know,
They with their Latin? So, I swallow my rage,
Clench my teeth, suck my lips in tight, and paint
To please them—sometimes do and sometimes don't;
For, doing most, there's pretty sure to come
A turn, some warm eve finds me at my saints—
A laugh, a cry, the business of the world—
(*Flower o' the peach,*
Death for us all, and his own life for each!)
And my whole soul revolves, the cup runs over,   250
The world and life's too big to pass for a dream,
And I do these wild things in sheer despite,
And play the fooleries you catch me at,
In pure rage! The old mill-horse, out at grass
After hard years, throws up his stiff heels so,
Although the miller does not preach to him
The only good of grass is to make chaff.
What would men have? Do they like grass or no—
May they or mayn't they? all I want's the thing
Settled for ever one way. As it is,   260
You tell too many lies and hurt yourself:
You don't like what you only like too much,
You do like what, if given you at your word,
You find abundantly detestable.
For me, I think I speak as I was taught;
I always see the garden and God there°
A-making man's wife: and, my lesson learned,
The value and significance of flesh,
I can't unlearn ten minutes afterwards.

    You understand me: I'm a beast, I know.   270
But see, now—why, I see as certainly
As that the morning-star's about to shine,
What will hap some day. We've a youngster here
Comes to our convent, studies what I do,
Slouches and stares and lets no atom drop:

His name is Guidi—he'll not mind the monks—°
They call him Hulking Tom, he lets them talk—
He picks my practice up—he'll paint apace,
I hope so—though I never live so long,
I know what's sure to follow. You be judge!   280
You speak no Latin more than I, belike;
However, you're my man, you've seen the world
—The beauty and the wonder and the power,
The shapes of things, their colours, lights and shades,
Changes, surprises,—and God made it all!
—For what? Do you feel thankful, ay or no,
For this fair town's face, yonder river's line,
The mountain round it and the sky above,
Much more the figures of man, woman, child,
These are the frame to? What's it all about?   290
To be passed over, despised? or dwelt upon,
Wondered at? oh, this last of course!—you say.
But why not do as well as say,—paint these
Just as they are, careless what comes of it?
God's works—paint anyone, and count it crime
To let a truth slip. Don't object, 'His works
Are here already; nature is complete:
Suppose you reproduce her—(which you can't)
There's no advantage! you must beat her, then.'
For, don't you mark? we're made so that we love   300
First when we see them painted, things we have passed
Perhaps a hundred times nor cared to see;
And so they are better, painted—better to us,
Which is the same thing. Art was given for that;
God uses us to help each other so,
Lending our minds out. Have you noticed, now,
Your cullion's hanging face? A bit of chalk,°
And trust me but you should, though! How much more,
If I drew higher things with the same truth!
That were to take the Prior's pulpit-place,   310
Interpret God to all of you! Oh, oh,
It makes me mad to see what men shall do
And we in our graves! This world's no blot for us,
Nor blank; it means intensely, and means good:
To find its meaning is my meat and drink.
'Ay, but you don't so instigate to prayer!'

Strikes in the Prior: 'when your meaning's plain
It does not say to folk—remember matins,
Or, mind you fast next Friday!' Why, for this
What need of art at all? A skull and bones,   320
Two bits of stick nailed crosswise, or, what's best,
A bell to chime the hour with, does as well.
I painted a Saint Laurence six months since
At Prato, splashed the fresco in fine style:
'How looks my painting, now the scaffold's down?'
I ask a brother: 'Hugely,' he returns—
'Already not one phiz of your three slaves°
Who turn the Deacon off his toasted side,°
But's scratched and prodded to our heart's content,
The pious people have so eased their own   330
With coming to say prayers there in a rage:
We get on fast to see the bricks beneath.
Expect another job this time next year,
For pity and religion grow i' the crowd—°
Your painting serves its purpose!' Hang the fools!

—That is—you'll not mistake an idle word
Spoke in a huff by a poor monk, God wot,
Tasting the air this spicy night which turns
The unaccustomed head like Chianti wine!
Oh, the church knows! don't misreport me, now!   340
It's natural a poor monk out of bounds
Should have his apt word to excuse himself:
And hearken how I plot to make amends.
I have bethought me: I shall paint a piece
... There's for you! Give me six months, then go, see
Something in Sant' Ambrogio's! Bless the nuns!
They want a cast o' my office. I shall paint°
God in the midst, Madonna and her babe,
Ringed by a bowery flowery angel-brood,
Lilies and vestments and white faces, sweet   350
As puff on puff of grated orris-root°
When ladies crowd to Church at midsummer.
And then i' the front, of course a saint or two—
Saint John, because he saves the Florentines,
Saint Ambrose, who puts down in black and white
The convent's friends and gives them a long day,

And Job, I must have him there past mistake,
The man of Uz (and Us without the z,°
Painters who need his patience). Well, all these
Secured at their devotion, up shall come   360
Out of a corner when you least expect,
As one by a dark stair into a great light,
Music and talking, who but Lippo! I!—
Mazed, motionless and moonstruck—I'm the man!
Back I shrink—what is this I see and hear?
I, caught up with my monk's-things by mistake,
My old serge gown and rope that goes all round,
I, in this presence, this pure company!
Where's a hole, where's a corner for escape?
Then steps a sweet angelic slip of a thing   370
Forward, puts out a soft palm—'Not so fast!'
—Addresses the celestial presence, 'nay—
He made you and devised you, after all,
Though he's none of you! Could Saint John there draw—
His camel-hair make up a painting-brush?°
We come to brother Lippo for all that,
Iste perfecit opus!' So, all smile—°
I shuffle sideways with my blushing face
Under the cover of a hundred wings
Thrown like a spread of kirtles when you're gay°   380
And play hot cockles, all the doors being shut,°
Till, wholly unexpected, in there pops
The hothead husband! Thus I scuttle off
To some safe bench behind, not letting go
The palm of her, the little lily thing
That spoke the good word for me in the nick,
Like the Prior's niece . . . Saint Lucy, I would say.
And so all's saved for me, and for the church
A pretty picture gained. Go, six months hence!
Your hand, sir, and good-bye: no lights, no lights!   390
The street's hushed, and I know my own way back,
Don't fear me! There's the grey beginning. Zooks!

A Toccata of Galuppi's

I

Oh Galuppi, Baldassaro, this is very sad to find!
I can hardly misconceive you; it would prove me deaf and blind;
But although I take your meaning, 'tis with such a heavy mind!

II

Here you come with your old music, and here's all the good it
    brings.
What, they lived once thus at Venice where the merchants were
    the kings,
Where Saint Mark's is, where the Doges used to wed the sea
    with rings?°

III

Ay, because the sea's the street there; and 'tis arched by . . . what
    you call
. . . Shylock's bridge with houses on it, where they kept the
    carnival:°
I was never out of England—it's as if I saw it all.

IV

Did young people take their pleasure when the sea was warm in
    May?   10
Balls and masks begun at midnight, burning ever to mid-day,
When they made up fresh adventures for the morrow, do you say?

V

Was a lady such a lady, cheeks so round and lips so red,—
On her neck the small face buoyant, like a bell-flower on its bed,
O'er the breast's superb abundance where a man might base his
    head?

VI

Well, and it was graceful of them—they'd break talk off and afford
—She, to bite her mask's black velvet—he, to finger on his sword,
While you sat and played Toccatas, stately at the clavichord?°

VII

What? Those lesser thirds so plaintive, sixths diminished, sigh
    on sigh,
Told them something? Those suspensions, those solutions—
    'Must we die?'
Those commiserating sevenths—'Life might last! we can but
    try!'°

      20

VIII

'Were you happy?'—'Yes.'—'And are you still as happy?'—
    'Yes. And you?'
—'Then, more kisses!'—'Did *I* stop them, when a million
    seemed so few?'
Hark, the dominant's persistence till it must be answered to!

IX

So, an octave struck the answer. Oh, they praised you, I dare say!
'Brave Galuppi! that was music! good alike at grave and gay!
I can always leave off talking when I hear a master play!'

X

Then they left you for their pleasure: till in due time, one by one,
Some with lives that came to nothing, some with deeds as well
    undone,
Death stepped tacitly and took them where they never see the
    sun.

      30

XI

But when I sit down to reason, think to take my stand nor
    swerve,
While I triumph o'er a secret wrung from nature's close reserve,
In you come with your cold music till I creep thro' every nerve.

XII

Yes, you, like a ghostly cricket, creaking where a house was
    burned:
'Dust and ashes, dead and done with, Venice spent what Venice
    earned.
The soul, doubtless, is immortal—where a soul can be discerned.

XIII

'Yours for instance: you know physics, something of geology,
Mathematics are your pastime; souls shall rise in their degree;
Butterflies may dread extinction,—you'll not die, it cannot be!

XIV

'As for Venice and her people, merely born to bloom and drop,   40
Here on earth they bore their fruitage, mirth and folly were the
      crop:
What of soul was left, I wonder, when the kissing had to stop?

XV

'Dust and ashes!' So you creak it, and I want the heart to scold.
Dear dead women, with such hair, too—what's become of all the
      gold
Used to hang and brush their bosoms? I feel chilly and grown
      old.

An Epistle

Containing the Strange Medical Experience of Karshish, the Arab Physician

Karshish, the picker-up of learning's crumbs,
The not-incurious in God's handiwork
(This man's-flesh he hath admirably made,
Blown like a bubble, kneaded like a paste,
To coop up and keep down on earth a space
That puff of vapour from his mouth, man's soul)
—To Abib, all-sagacious in our art,
Breeder in me of what poor skill I boast,
Like me inquisitive how pricks and cracks
Befall the flesh through too much stress and strain,   10
Whereby the wily vapour fain would slip
Back and rejoin its source before the term,—
And aptest in contrivance (under God)
To baffle it by deftly stopping such:—
The vagrant Scholar to his Sage at home

Sends greeting (health and knowledge, fame with peace)
Three samples of true snakestone—rarer still,°
One of the other sort, the melon-shaped,
(But fitter, pounded fine, for charms than drugs)
And writeth now the twenty-second time.   20

    My journeyings were brought to Jericho:
Thus I resume. Who studious in our art
Shall count a little labour unrepaid?
I have shed sweat enough, left flesh and bone
On many a flinty furlong of this land.
Also, the country-side is all on fire
With rumours of a marching hitherward:
Some say Vespasian cometh, some, his son.°
A black lynx snarled and pricked a tufted ear;
Lust of my blood inflamed his yellow balls:
I cried and threw my staff and he was gone.   30
Twice have the robbers stripped and beaten me,
And once a town declared me for a spy;
But at the end, I reach Jerusalem,
Since this poor covert where I pass the night,
This Bethany, lies scarce the distance thence
A man with plague-sores at the third degree
Runs till he drops down dead. Thou laughest here!
'Sooth, it elates me, thus reposed and safe,
To void the stuffing of my travel-scrip°
And share with thee whatever Jewry yields.   40
A viscid choler is observable
In tertians, I was nearly bold to say;
And falling-sickness hath a happier cure°
Than our school wots of: there's a spider here
Weaves no web, watches on the ledge of tombs,
Sprinkled with mottles on an ash-grey back;
Take five and drop them ... but who knows his mind,
The Syrian runagate I trust this to?
His service payeth me a sublimate°
Blown up his nose to help the ailing eye.   50
Best wait: I reach Jerusalem at morn,
There set in order my experiences,
Gather what most deserves, and give thee all—
Or I might add, Judæa's gum-tragacanth°

Scales off in purer flakes, shines clearer-grained,
Cracks 'twixt the pestle and the porphyry,°
In fine exceeds our produce. Scalp-disease
Confounds me, crossing so with leprosy—
Thou hadst admired one sort I gained at Zoar—   60
But zeal outruns discretion. Here I end.

Yet stay: my Syrian blinketh gratefully,
Protesteth his devotion is my price—
Suppose I write what harms not, though he steal?
I half resolve to tell thee, yet I blush,
What set me off a-writing first of all.
An itch I had, a sting to write, a tang!
For, be it this town's barrenness—or else
The Man had something in the look of him—
His case has struck me far more than 'tis worth.   70
So, pardon if—(lest presently I lose
In the great press of novelty at hand
The care and pains this somehow stole from me)
I bid thee take the thing while fresh in mind,
Almost in sight—for, wilt thou have the truth?
The very man is gone from me but now,
Whose ailment is the subject of discourse.
Thus then, and let thy better wit help all!

'Tis but a case of mania—subinduced
By epilepsy, at the turning-point   80
Of trance prolonged unduly some three days:
When, by the exhibition of some drug
Or spell, exorcization, stroke of art
Unknown to me and which 'twere well to know,
The evil thing out-breaking all at once
Left the man whole and sound of body indeed,—
But, flinging (so to speak) life's gates too wide,
Making a clear house of it too suddenly,
The first conceit that entered might inscribe°
Whatever it was minded on the wall   90
So plainly at that vantage, as it were,
(First come, first served) that nothing subsequent
Attaineth to erase those fancy-scrawls
The just-returned and new-established soul
Hath gotten now so thoroughly by heart

That henceforth she will read or these or none.
And first—the man's own firm conviction rests
That he was dead (in fact they buried him)
—That he was dead and then restored to life
By a Nazarene physician of his tribe: 100
—'Sayeth, the same bade 'Rise,' and he did rise.
'Such cases are diurnal,' thou wilt cry.°
Not so this figment!—not, that such a fume,°
Instead of giving way to time and health,
Should eat itself into the life of life,
As saffron tingeth flesh, blood, bones and all!°
For see, how he takes up the after-life.
The man—it is one Lazarus a Jew,
Sanguine, proportioned, fifty years of age,
The body's habit wholly laudable,   110
As much, indeed, beyond the common health
As he were made and put aside to show.
Think, could we penetrate by any drug
And bathe the wearied soul and worried flesh,
And bring it clear and fair, by three days' sleep!
Whence has the man the balm that brightens all?
This grown man eyes the world now like a child.
Some elders of his tribe, I should premise,
Led in their friend, obedient as a sheep,
To bear my inquisition. While they spoke,   120
Now sharply, now with sorrow,—told the case,—
He listened not except I spoke to him,
But folded his two hands and let them talk,
Watching the flies that buzzed: and yet no fool.
And that's a sample how his years must go.
Look, if a beggar, in fixed middle-life,
Should find a treasure,—can he use the same
With straitened habits and with tastes starved small,
And take at once to his impoverished brain
The sudden element that changes things,   130
That sets the undreamed-of rapture at his hand
And puts the cheap old joy in the scorned dust?
Is he not such an one as moves to mirth—
Warily parsimonious, when no need,
Wasteful as drunkenness at undue times?
All prudent counsel as to what befits

The golden mean, is lost on such an one:
The man's fantastic will is the man's law.
So here—we call the treasure knowledge, say,
Increased beyond the fleshly faculty—   140
Heaven opened to a soul while yet on earth,
Earth forced on a soul's use while seeing heaven:
The man is witless of the size, the sum,
The value in proportion of all things,
Or whether it be little or be much.
Discourse to him of prodigious armaments
Assembled to besiege his city now,
And of the passing of a mule with gourds—
'Tis one! Then take it on the other side,
Speak of some trifling fact,—he will gaze rapt   150
With stupor at its very littleness,
(Far as I see) as if in that indeed
He caught prodigious import, whole results;
And so will turn to us the bystanders
In ever the same stupor (note this point)
That we too see not with his opened eyes.
Wonder and doubt come wrongly into play,
Preposterously, at cross purposes.
Should his child sicken unto death,—why, look
For scarce abatement of his cheerfulness,   160
Or pretermission of the daily craft!°
While a word, gesture, glance from that same child
At play or in the school or laid asleep,
Will startle him to an agony of fear
Exasperation, just as like. Demand
The reason why—' 'tis but a word,' object—
'A gesture'—he regards thee as our lord
Who lived there in the pyramid alone,
Looked at us (dost thou mind?) when, being young,
We both would unadvisedly recite   170
Some charm's beginning, from that book of his,
Able to bid the sun throb wide and burst
All into stars, as suns grown old are wont.
Thou and the child have each a veil alike
Thrown o'er your heads, from under which ye both
Stretch your blind hands and trifle with a match
Over a mine of Greek fire, did ye know!°

He holds on firmly to some thread of life—
(It is the life to lead perforcedly)
Which runs across some vast distracting orb   180
Of glory on either side that meagre thread,
Which, conscious of, he must not enter yet—
The spiritual life around the earthly life:
The law of that is known to him as this,
His heart and brain move there, his feet stay here.
So is the man perplext with impulses
Sudden to start off crosswise, not straight on,
Proclaiming what is right and wrong across,
And not along, this black thread through the blaze—
'It should be' baulked by 'here it cannot be.'   190
And oft the man's soul springs into his face
As if he saw again and heard again
His sage that bade him 'Rise' and he did rise.
Something, a word, a tick o' the blood within
Admonishes: then back he sinks at once
To ashes, who was very fire before,
In sedulous recurrence to his trade
Whereby he earneth him the daily bread;
And studiously the humbler for that pride,
Professedly the faultier that he knows   200
God's secret, while he holds the thread of life.
Indeed the especial marking of the man
Is prone submission to the heavenly will—
Seeing it, what it is, and why it is.
'Sayeth, he will wait patient to the last
For that same death which must restore his being
To equilibrium, body loosening soul
Divorced even now by premature full growth:
He will live, nay, it pleaseth him to live
So long as God please, and just how God please.   210
He even seeketh not to please God more
(Which meaneth, otherwise) than as God please.
Hence, I perceive not he affects to preach
The doctrine of his sect whate'er it be,
Make proselytes as madmen thirst to do:
How can he give his neighbour the real ground,
His own conviction? Ardent as he is—
Call his great truth a lie, why, still the old

'Be it as God please' reassureth him.
I probed the sore as thy disciple should: 220
'How, beast,' said I, 'this stolid carelessness
Sufficeth thee, when Rome is on her march
To stamp out like a little spark thy town,
Thy tribe, thy crazy tale and thee at once?'
He merely looked with his large eyes on me.
The man is apathetic, you deduce?
Contrariwise, he loves both old and young,
Able and weak, affects the very brutes
And birds—how say I? flowers of the field—
As a wise workman recognizes tools   230
In a master's workshop, loving what they make.
Thus is the man as harmless as a lamb:
Only impatient, let him do his best,
At ignorance and carelessness and sin—
An indignation which is promptly curbed:
As when in certain travel I have feigned
To be an ignoramus in our art
According to some preconceived design,
And happed to hear the land's practitioners
Steeped in conceit sublimed by ignorance,°   240
Prattle fantastically on disease,
Its cause and cure—and I must hold my peace!

    Thou wilt object—Why have I not ere this
Sought out the sage himself, the Nazarene
Who wrought this cure, inquiring at the source,
Conferring with the frankness that befits?
Alas! it grieveth me, the learned leech°
Perished in a tumult many years ago,
Accused,—our learning's fate,—of wizardry,
Rebellion, to the setting up a rule   250
And creed prodigious as described to me.
His death, which happened when the earthquake fell
(Prefiguring, as soon appeared, the loss
To occult learning in our lord the sage
Who lived there in the pyramid alone)
Was wrought by the mad people—that's their wont!
On vain recourse, as I conjecture it,
To his tried virtue, for miraculous help—

How could he stop the earthquake? That's their way!°
The other imputations must be lies: 260
But take one, though I loathe to give it thee,
In mere respect for any good man's fame.
(And after all, our patient Lazarus
Is stark mad; should we count on what he says?
Perhaps not: though in writing to a leech
'Tis well to keep back nothing of a case.)
This man so cured regards the curer, then,
As—God forgive me! who but God himself,
Creator and sustainer of the world,
That came and dwelt in flesh on it awhile!   270
—'Sayeth that such an one was born and lived,
Taught, healed the sick, broke bread at his own house,
Then died, with Lazarus by, for aught I know,
And yet was . . . what I said nor choose repeat,
And must have so avouched himself, in fact,
In hearing of this very Lazarus
Who saith—but why all this of what he saith?
Why write of trivial matters, things of price
Calling at every moment for remark?
I noticed on the margin of a pool   280
Blue-flowering borage, the Aleppo sort,°
Aboundeth, very nitrous. It is strange!

    Thy pardon for this long and tedious case,
Which, now that I review it, needs must seem
Unduly dwelt on, prolixly set forth!
Nor I myself discern in what is writ
Good cause for the peculiar interest
And awe indeed this man has touched me with.
Perhaps the journey's end, the weariness
Had wrought upon me first. I met him thus: 290
I crossed a ridge of short sharp broken hills
Like an old lion's cheek teeth. Out there came
A moon made like a face with certain spots
Multiform, manifold and menacing:
Then a wind rose behind me. So we met
In this old sleepy town at unaware,
The man and I. I send thee what is writ.
Regard it as a chance, a matter risked

To this ambiguous Syrian—he may lose,
Or steal, or give it thee with equal good.   300
Jerusalem's repose shall make amends
For time this letter wastes, thy time and mine;
Till when, once more thy pardon and farewell!

    The very God! think, Abib; dost thou think?
So, the All-Great, were the All-Loving too—
So, through the thunder comes a human voice
Saying, 'O heart I made, a heart beats here!
Face, my hands fashioned, see it in myself!
Thou hast no power nor mayst conceive of mine,
But love I gave thee, with myself to love,   310
And thou must love me who have died for thee!'
The madman saith He said so: it is strange.

'Childe Roland to the Dark Tower Came'

(See Edgar's song in *Lear*)

I

My first thought was, he lied in every word,
    That hoary cripple, with malicious eye
    Askance to watch the working of his lie
On mine, and mouth scarce able to afford
Suppression of the glee, that pursed and scored
    Its edge, at one more victim gained thereby.

II

What else should he be set for, with his staff?
    What, save to waylay with his lies, ensnare
    All travellers who might find him posted there,
And ask the road? I guessed what skull-like laugh   10
Would break, what crutch 'gin write my epitaph
    For pastime in the dusty thoroughfare,

III

If at his counsel I should turn aside
    Into that ominous tract which, all agree,
    Hides the Dark Tower. Yet acquiescingly

I did turn as he pointed: neither pride
Nor hope rekindling at the end descried,
  So much as gladness that some end might be.

IV

For, what with my whole world-wide wandering,
  What with my search drawn out thro' years, my hope   20
  Dwindled into a ghost not fit to cope
With that obstreperous joy success would bring,—°
I hardly tried now to rebuke the spring
  My heart made, finding failure in its scope.

V

As when a sick man very near to death
  Seems dead indeed, and feels begin and end
  The tears and takes the farewell of each friend,
And hears one bid the other go, draw breath
Freelier outside, ('since all is o'er,' he saith,
  'And the blow fallen no grieving can amend;')°   30

VI

While some discuss if near the other graves
  Be room enough for this, and when a day
  Suits best for carrying the corpse away,
With care about the banners, scarves and staves:
And still the man hears all, and only craves
  He may not shame such tender love and stay.

VII

Thus, I had so long suffered in this quest,
  Heard failure prophesied so oft, been writ
  So many times among 'The Band'—to wit,
The knights who to the Dark Tower's search addressed   40
Their steps—that just to fail as they, seemed best,
  And all the doubt was now—should I be fit?

VIII

So, quiet as despair, I turned from him,
  That hateful cripple, out of his highway
  Into the path he pointed. All the day

Had been a dreary one at best, and dim
Was settling to its close, yet shot one grim
　　Red leer to see the plain catch its estray.°

IX

For mark! no sooner was I fairly found
　　Pledged to the plain, after a pace or two,   50
　　Than, pausing to throw backward a last view
O'er the safe road, 'twas gone; grey plain all round:
Nothing but plain to the horizon's bound.
　　I might go on; nought else remained to do.

X

So, on I went. I think I never saw
　　Such starved ignoble nature; nothing throve:
　　For flowers—as well expect a cedar grove!
But cockle, spurge, according to their law
Might propagate their kind, with none to awe,°
　　You'd think; a burr had been a treasure-trove.   60

XI

No! penury, inertness and grimace,
　　In some strange sort, were the land's portion. 'See
　　Or shut your eyes,' said Nature peevishly,
'It nothing skills: I cannot help my case:°
'Tis the Last Judgment's fire must cure this place,
　　Calcine its clods and set my prisoners free.'°

XII

If there pushed any ragged thistle-stalk
　　Above its mates, the head was chopped; the bents°
　　Were jealous else. What made those holes and rents
In the dock's harsh swarth leaves, bruised as to baulk   70
All hope of greenness? 'tis a brute must walk
　　Pashing their life out, with a brute's intents.

XIII

As for the grass, it grew as scant as hair
　　In leprosy; thin dry blades pricked the mud
　　Which underneath looked kneaded up with blood.

One stiff blind horse, his every bone a-stare,
Stood stupefied, however he came there:
   Thrust out past service from the devil's stud!

XIV

Alive? he might be dead for aught I know,
   With that red gaunt and colloped neck a-strain,°   80
   And shut eyes underneath the rusty mane;
Seldom went such grotesqueness with such woe;
I never saw a brute I hated so;
   He must be wicked to deserve such pain.

XV

I shut my eyes and turned them on my heart.
   As a man calls for wine before he fights,
   I asked one draught of earlier, happier sights,
Ere fitly I could hope to play my part.
Think first, fight afterwards—the soldier's art:
   One taste of the old time sets all to rights.   90

XVI

Not it! I fancied Cuthbert's reddening face
   Beneath its garniture of curly gold,
   Dear fellow, till I almost felt him fold
An arm in mine to fix me to the place,
That way he used. Alas, one night's disgrace!
   Out went my heart's new fire and left it cold.

XVII

Giles then, the soul of honour—there he stands
   Frank as ten years ago when knighted first.
   What honest man should dare (he said) he durst.
Good—but the scene shifts—faugh! what hangman hands   100
Pin to his breast a parchment? His own bands
   Read it. Poor traitor, spit upon and curst!

XVIII

Better this present than a past like that;
   Back therefore to my darkening path again!
   No sound, no sight as far as eye could strain.

Will the night send a howlet or a bat?°
I asked: when something on the dismal flat
   Came to arrest my thoughts and change their train.

XIX

A sudden little river crossed my path
   As unexpected as a serpent comes.   110
   No sluggish tide congenial to the glooms;
This, as it frothed by, might have been a bath
For the fiend's glowing hoof—to see the wrath
   Of its black eddy bespate with flakes and spumes.°

XX

So petty yet so spiteful! All along,
   Low scrubby alders kneeled down over it;
   Drenched willows flung them headlong in a fit
Of mute despair, a suicidal throng:
The river which had done them all the wrong,
   Whate'er that was, rolled by, deterred no whit.   120

XXI

Which, while I forded,—good saints, how I feared
   To set my foot upon a dead man's cheek,
   Each step, or feel the spear I thrust to seek
For hollows, tangled in his hair or beard!
—It may have been a water-rat I speared,
   But, ugh! it sounded like a baby's shriek.

XXII

Glad was I when I reached the other bank.
   Now for a better country. Vain presage!
   Who were the strugglers, what war did they wage,
Whose savage trample thus could pad the dank   130
Soil to a plash? Toads in a poisoned tank,°
   Or wild cats in a red-hot iron cage—

XXIII

The fight must so have seemed in that fell cirque.°
   What penned them there, with all the plain to choose?
   No foot-print leading to that horrid mews,°

None out of it. Mad brewage set to work
Their brains, no doubt, like galley-slaves the Turk
   Pits for his pastime, Christians against Jews.

XXIV

And more than that—a furlong on—why, there!
   What bad use was that engine for, that wheel,   140
   Or brake, not wheel—that harrow fit to reel°
Men's bodies out like silk? with all the air
Of Tophet's tool, on earth left unaware,°
   Or brought to sharpen its rusty teeth of steel.

XXV

Then came a bit of stubbed ground, once a wood,
   Next a marsh, it would seem, and now mere earth
   Desperate and done with; (so a fool finds mirth,
Makes a thing and then mars it, till his mood
Changes and off he goes!) within a rood—°
   Bog, clay and rubble, sand and stark black dearth.   150

XXVI

Now blotches rankling, coloured gay and grim,
   Now patches where some leanness of the soil's
   Broke into moss or substances like boils;
Then came some palsied oak, a cleft in him
Like a distorted mouth that splits its rim
   Gaping at death, and dies while it recoils.

XXVII

And just as far as ever from the end!
   Nought in the distance but the evening, nought
   To point my footstep further! At the thought,
A great black bird, Apollyon's bosom-friend,°   160
Sailed past, nor beat his wide wing dragon-penned
   That brushed my cap—perchance the guide I sought.

XXVIII

For, looking up, aware I somehow grew,
   'Spite of the dusk, the plain had given place
   All round to mountains—with such name to grace

Mere ugly heights and heaps now stolen in view.
How thus they had surprised me,—solve it, you!
　　How to get from them was no clearer case.

XXIX

Yet half I seemed to recognize some trick
　　Of mischief happened to me, God knows when—　　　170
　　In a bad dream perhaps. Here ended, then,
Progress this way. When, in the very nick
Of giving up, one time more, came a click
　　As when a trap shuts—you're inside the den!

XXX

Burningly it came on me all at once,
　　This was the place! those two hills on the right,
　　Crouched like two bulls locked horn in horn in fight;
While to the left, a tall scalped mountain . . . Dunce,
Dotard, a-dozing at the very nonce,°
　　After a life spent training for the sight!　　　180

XXXI

What in the midst lay but the Tower itself?
　　The round squat turret, blind as the fool's heart,°
　　Built of brown stone, without a counterpart
In the whole world. The tempest's mocking elf
Points to the shipman thus the unseen shelf
　　He strikes on, only when the timbers start.

XXXII

Not see? because of night perhaps?—why, day
　　Came back again for that! before it left,
　　The dying sunset kindled through a cleft:
The hills, like giants at a hunting, lay,　　　190
Chin upon hand, to see the game at bay,—
　　'Now stab and end the creature—to the heft!'°

XXXIII

Not hear? when noise was everywhere! it tolled
　　Increasing like a bell. Names in my ears
　　Of all the lost adventurers my peers,—

How such a one was strong, and such was bold,
And such was fortunate, yet each of old
  Lost, lost! one moment knelled the woe of years.

XXXIV

There they stood, ranged along the hill-sides, met
  To view the last of me, a living frame
  For one more picture! in a sheet of flame
I saw them and I knew them all. And yet
Dauntless the slug-horn to my lips I set,°
  And blew. '*Childe Roland to the Dark Tower came.*'

200

Respectability

I

Dear, had the world in its caprice
  Deigned to proclaim 'I know you both,
  Have recognized your plighted troth,
Am sponsor for you: live in peace!'—
How many precious months and years
  Of youth had passed, that speed so fast,
  Before we found it out at last,
The world, and what it fears?

II

How much of priceless life were spent
  With men that every virtue decks,
  And women models of their sex,
Society's true ornament,—
Ere we dared wander, nights like this,
  Thro' wind and rain, and watch the Seine,
  And feel the Boulevart break again°
To warmth and light and bliss?

10

III

I know! the world proscribes not love;
  Allows my finger to caress
  Your lips' contour and downiness,

Provided it supply a glove.   20
The world's good word!—the Institute!°
  Guizot receives Montalembert!°
  Eh? Down the court three lampions flare:°
Put forward your best foot!

The Statue and the Bust

There's a palace in Florence, the world knows well,
And a statue watches it from the square,
And this story of both do our townsmen tell.

Ages ago, a lady there,
At the farthest window facing the East
Asked, 'Who rides by with the royal air?'

The bridesmaids' prattle around her ceased;
She leaned forth, one on either hand;
They saw how the blush of the bride increased—

They felt by its beats her heart expand—   10
As one at each ear and both in a breath
Whispered, 'The Great-Duke Ferdinand.'

That self-same instant, underneath,
The Duke rode past in his idle way,
Empty and fine like a swordless sheath.

Gay he rode, with a friend as gay,
Till he threw his head back—'Who is she?'
—'A bride the Riccardi brings home to-day.'

Hair in heaps lay heavily
Over a pale brow spirit-pure—   20
Carved like the heart of the coal-black tree,

Crisped like a war-steed's encolure—°
And vainly sought to dissemble her eyes
Of the blackest black our eyes endure.

And lo, a blade for a knight's emprise
Filled the fine empty sheath of a man,—
The Duke grew straightway brave and wise.

He looked at her, as a lover can;
She looked at him, as one who awakes:
The past was a sleep, and her life began.   30

Now, love so ordered for both their sakes,
A feast was held that selfsame night
In the pile which the mighty shadow makes.

(For Via Larga is three-parts light,
But the palace overshadows one,
Because of a crime which may God requite!

To Florence and God the wrong was done,
Through the first republic's murder there
By Cosimo and his cursed son.)°

The Duke (with the statue's face in the square)   40
Turned in the midst of his multitude
At the bright approach of the bridal pair.

Face to face the lovers stood
A single minute and no more,
While the bridegroom bent as a man subdued—

Bowed till his bonnet brushed the floor—
For the Duke on the lady a kiss conferred,
As the courtly custom was of yore.

In a minute can lovers exchange a word?
If a word did pass, which I do not think,   50
Only one out of the thousand heard.

That was the bridegroom. At day's brink
He and his bride were alone at last
In a bedchamber by a taper's blink.

Calmly he said that her lot was cast,
That the door she had passed was shut on her
Till the final catafalk repassed.°

The world meanwhile, its noise and stir,
Through a certain window facing the East,
She could watch like a convent's chronicler.   60

Since passing the door might lead to a feast,
And a feast might lead to so much beside,
He, of many evils, chose the least.

'Freely I choose too,' said the bride—
'Your window and its world suffice,'
Replied the tongue, while the heart replied—

'If I spend the night with that devil twice,
May his window serve as my loop of hell°
Whence a damned soul looks on paradise!

'I fly to the Duke who loves me well,   70
Sit by his side and laugh at sorrow
Ere I count another ave-bell.°

' 'Tis only the coat of a page to borrow,
And tie my hair in a horse-boy's trim,
And I save my soul—but not to-morrow'—

(She checked herself and her eye grew dim)
'My father tarries to bless my state:
I must keep it one day more for him.

'Is one day more so long to wait?
Moreover the Duke rides past, I know;   80
We shall see each other, sure as fate.'

She turned on her side and slept. Just so!
So we resolve on a thing and sleep:
So did the lady, ages ago.

That night the Duke said, 'Dear or cheap
As the cost of this cup of bliss may prove
To body or soul, I will drain it deep.'

And on the morrow, bold with love,
He beckoned the bridegroom (close on call,
As his duty bade, by the Duke's alcove)   90

And smiled ' 'Twas a very funeral,
Your lady will think, this feast of ours,—
A shame to efface, whate'er befall!

'What if we break from the Arno bowers,°
And try if Petraja, cool and green,°
Cure last night's fault with this morning's flowers?'

The bridegroom, not a thought to be seen
On his steady brow and quiet mouth,
Said, 'Too much favour for me so mean!

'But, alas! my lady leaves the South;°
Each wind that comes from the Apennine
Is a menace to her tender youth:

'Nor a way exists, the wise opine,
If she quits her palace twice this year,
To avert the flower of life's decline.'

Quoth the Duke, 'A sage and a kindly fear.
Moreover Petraja is cold this spring:
Be our feast to-night as usual here!'

And then to himself—'Which night shall bring
Thy bride to her lover's embraces, fool—   110
Or I am the fool, and thou art the king!

'Yet my passion must wait a night, nor cool—
For to-night the Envoy arrives from France
Whose heart I unlock with thyself, my tool.

'I need thee still and might miss perchance.
To-day is not wholly lost, beside,
With its hope of my lady's countenance:

'For I ride—what should I do but ride?
And passing her palace, if I list,°
May glance at its window—well betide!'   120

So said, so done: nor the lady missed
One ray that broke from the ardent brow,
Nor a curl of the lips where the spirit kissed.

Be sure that each renewed the vow,
No morrow's sun should arise and set
And leave them then as it left them now.

But next day passed, and next day yet,
With still fresh cause to wait one day more
Ere each leaped over the parapet.

And still, as love's brief morning wore,   130
With a gentle start, half smile, half sigh,
They found love not as it seemed before.

They thought it would work infallibly,
But not in despite of heaven and earth:
The rose would blow when the storm passed by.°

Meantime they could profit in winter's dearth
By store of fruits that supplant the rose:
The world and its ways have a certain worth:

And to press a point while these oppose
Were simple policy; better wait: 140
We lose no friends and we gain no foes.

Meantime, worse fates than a lover's fate,
Who daily may ride and pass and look
Where his lady watches behind the grate!

And she—she watched the square like a book
Holding one picture and only one,
Which daily to find she undertook:

When the picture was reached the book was done,
And she turned from the picture at night to scheme
Of tearing it out for herself next sun.   150

So weeks grew months, years; gleam by gleam
The glory dropped from their youth and love,
And both perceived they had dreamed a dream;

Which hovered as dreams do, still above:
But who can take a dream for a truth?
Oh, hide our eyes from the next remove!

One day as the lady saw her youth
Depart, and the silver thread that streaked
Her hair, and, worn by the serpent's tooth,

The brow so puckered, the chin so peaked,—   160
And wondered who the woman was,
Hollow-eyed and haggard-cheeked,

Fronting her silent in the glass—
'Summon here,' she suddenly said,
'Before the rest of my old self pass,

'Him, the Carver, a hand to aid,
Who fashions the clay no love will change,
And fixes a beauty never to fade.

'Let Robbia's craft so apt and strange°
Arrest the remains of young and fair,   170
And rivet them while the seasons range.

'Make me a face on the window there,
Waiting as ever, mute the while,
My love to pass below in the square!

'And let me think that it may beguile
Dreary days which the dead must spend
Down in their darkness under the aisle,

'To say, "What matters it at the end?
I did no more while my heart was warm
Than does that image, my pale-faced friend."   180

'Where is the use of the lip's red charm,
The heaven of hair, the pride of the brow,
And the blood that blues the inside arm—

'Unless we turn, as the soul knows how,
The earthly gift to an end divine?
A lady of clay is as good, I trow.'

But long ere Robbia's cornice, fine,
With flowers and fruits which leaves enlace,
Was set where now is the empty shrine—

(And, leaning out of a bright blue space,   190
As a ghost might lean from a chink of sky,
The passionate pale lady's face—

Eyeing ever, with earnest eye
And quick-turned neck at its breathless stretch,
Some one who ever is passing by—)

The Duke had sighed like the simplest wretch
In Florence, 'Youth—my dream escapes!
Will its record stay?' And he bade them fetch

Some subtle moulder of brazen shapes—
'Can the soul, the will, die out of a man   200
Ere his body find the grave that gapes?

'John of Douay shall effect my plan,
Set me on horseback here aloft,
Alive, as the crafty sculptor can,

'In the very square I have crossed so oft:
That men may admire, when future suns
Shall touch the eyes to a purpose soft,

'While the mouth and the brow stay brave in bronze—
Admire and say, "When he was alive
How he would take his pleasure once!"   210

'And it shall go hard but I contrive
To listen the while, and laugh in my tomb
At idleness which aspires to strive.'

——————————

So! While these wait the trump of doom,
How do their spirits pass, I wonder,
Nights and days in the narrow room?

Still, I suppose, they sit and ponder
What a gift life was, ages ago,
Six steps out of the chapel yonder.

Only they see not God, I know,   220
Nor all that chivalry of his,
The soldier-saints who, row on row,

Burn upward each to his point of bliss—
Since, the end of life being manifest,
He had burned his way thro' the world to this.

I hear you reproach, 'But delay was best,
For their end was a crime.'—Oh, a crime will do
As well, I reply, to serve for a test,

As a virtue golden through and through,
Sufficient to vindicate itself   230
And prove its worth at a moment's view!

Must a game be played for the sake of pelf?°
Where a button goes, 'twere an epigram
To offer the stamp of the very Guelph.°

The true has no value beyond the sham:
As well the counter as coin, I submit,
When your table's a hat, and your prize a dram.

Stake your counter as boldly every whit,
Venture as warily, use the same skill,
Do your best, whether winning or losing it,   240

If you choose to play!—is my principle.
Let a man contend to the uttermost
For his life's set prize, be it what it will!

The counter our lovers staked was lost
As surely as if itwere lawful coin:
And the sin I impute to each frustrate ghost

Is—the unlit lamp and the ungirt loin,°
Though the end in sight was a vice, I say.
You of the virtue (we issue join)°
How strive you? *De te, fabula.*°

250

How It Strikes a Contemporary

I only knew one poet in my life:
And this, or something like it, was his way.

   You saw go up and down Valladolid,
A man of mark, to know next time you saw.
His very serviceable suit of black
Was courtly once and conscientious still,
And many might have worn it, though none did:
The cloak, that somewhat shone and showed the threads,
Had purpose, and the ruff, significance.
He walked and tapped the pavement with his cane,
Scenting the world, looking it full in face,
An old dog, bald and blindish, at his heels.
They turned up, now, the alley by the church,
That leads nowhither; now, they breathed themselves
On the main promenade just at the wrong time:
You'd come upon his scrutinizing hat,
Making a peaked shade blacker than itself
Against the single window spared some house
Intact yet with its mouldered Moorish work,—
Or else surprise the ferrel of his stick°
Trying the mortar's temper 'tween the chinks
Of some new shop a-building, French and fine.
He stood and watched the cobbler at his trade,
The man who slices lemons into drink,
The coffee-roaster's brazier, and the boys

10

20

That volunteer to help him turn its winch.
He glanced o'er books on stalls with half an eye,
And fly-leaf ballads on the vendor's string,°
And broad-edge bold-print posters by the wall.
He took such cognizance of men and things,   30
If any beat a horse, you felt he saw;
If any cursed a woman, he took note;
Yet stared at nobody,—you stared at him,
And found, less to your pleasure than surprise,
He seemed to know you and expect as much.
So, next time that a neighbour's tongue was loosed,
It marked the shameful and notorious fact,
We had among us, not so much a spy,
As a recording chief-inquisitor,
The town's true master if the town but knew!   40
We merely kept a governor for form,
While this man walked about and took account
Of all thought, said and acted, then went home,
And wrote it fully to our Lord the King
Who has an itch to know things, he knows why,
And reads them in his bedroom of a night.
Oh, you might smile! there wanted not a touch,
A tang of... well, it was not wholly ease
As back into your mind the man's look came.
Stricken in years a little,—such a brow   50
His eyes had to live under!—clear as flint
On either side the formidable nose
Curved, cut and coloured like an eagle's claw.
Had he to do with A.'s surprising fate?
When altogether old B. disappeared
And young C. got his mistress,—was't our friend,
His letter to the King, that did it all?
What paid the bloodless man for so much pains?
Our Lord the King has favourites manifold,
And shifts his ministry some once a month;   60
Our city gets new governors at whiles,—
But never word or sign, that I could hear,
Notified to this man about the streets
The King's approval of those letters conned
The last thing duly at the dead of night.
Did the man love his office? Frowned our Lord,

Exhorting when none heard—'Beseech me not!
Too far above my people,—beneath me!
I set the watch,—how should the people know?
Forget them, keep me all the more in mind!'   70
Was some such understanding 'twixt the two?

   I found no truth in one report at least—
That if you tracked him to his home, down lanes
Beyond the Jewry, and as clean to pace,°
You found he ate his supper in a room
Blazing with lights, four Titians on the wall,°
And twenty naked girls to change his plate!
Poor man, he lived another kind of life
In that new stuccoed third house by the bridge,
Fresh-painted, rather smart than otherwise!   80
The whole street might o'erlook him as he sat,
Leg crossing leg, one foot on the dog's back,
Playing a decent cribbage with his maid
(Jacynth, you're sure her name was) o'er the cheese
And fruit, three red halves of starved winter-pears,
Or treat of radishes in April. Nine,
Ten, struck the church clock, straight to bed went he.

   My father, like the man of sense he was,
Would point him out to me a dozen times;
' 'St—'St,' he'd whisper, 'the Corregidor!'°   90
I had been used to think that personage
Was one with lacquered breeches, lustrous belt,
And feathers like a forest in his hat,
Who blew a trumpet and proclaimed the news,
Announced the bull-fights, gave each church its turn,
And memorized the miracle in vogue!°
He had a great observance from us boys;
We were in error; that was not the man.

   I'd like now, yet had haply been afraid,
To have just looked, when this man came to die,   100
And seen who lined the clean gay garret-sides
And stood about the neat low truckle-bed,
With the heavenly manner of relieving guard.
Here had been, mark, the general-in-chief,
Thro' a whole campaign of the world's life and death,

Doing the King's work all the dim day long,
In his old coat and up to knees in mud,
Smoked like a herring, dining on a crust,—
And, now the day was won, relieved at once!
No further show or need for that old coat,   110
You are sure, for one thing! Bless us, all the while
How sprucely we are dressed out, you and I!
A second, and the angels alter that.
Well, I could never write a verse,—could you?
Let's to the Prado and make the most of time.°

Bishop Blougram's Apology

No more wine? then we'll push back chairs and talk.
A final glass for me, though: cool, i' faith!
We ought to have our Abbey back, you see.°
It's different, preaching in basilicas,
And doing duty in some masterpiece
Like this of brother Pugin's, bless his heart!°
I doubt if they're half baked, those chalk rosettes,
Ciphers and stucco-twiddlings everywhere;
It's just like breathing in a lime-kiln: eh?
These hot long ceremonies of our church   10
Cost us a little—oh, they pay the price,
You take me—amply pay it! Now, we'll talk.°

So, you despise me, Mr Gigadibs.°
No deprecation,—nay, I beg you, sir!
Beside 'tis our engagement: don't you know,
I promised, if you'd watch a dinner out,
We'd see truth dawn together?—truth that peeps
Over the glasses' edge when dinner's done,
And body gets its sop and holds its noise
And leaves soul free a little. Now's the time: 20
Truth's break of day! You do despise me then.
And if I say, 'despise me,'—never fear!
I know you do not in a certain sense—
Not in my arm-chair, for example: here,
I well imagine you respect my place
(*Status, entourage*, worldly circumstance)

Quite to its value—very much indeed:
—Are up to the protesting eyes of you
In pride at being seated here for once—
You'll turn it to such capital account!
When somebody, through years and years to come,   30
Hints of the bishop,—names me—that's enough:
'Blougram? I knew him'—(into it you slide)
'Dined with him once, a Corpus Christi Day,°
All alone, we two; he's a clever man:
And after dinner,—why, the wine you know,—
Oh, there was wine, and good!—what with the wine...
'Faith, we began upon all sorts of talk!
He's no bad fellow, Blougram; he had seen
Something of mine he relished, some review:
He's quite above their humbug in his heart,°   40
Half-said as much, indeed—the thing's his trade.
I warrant, Blougram's sceptical at times:
How otherwise? I liked him, I confess!'
Che che, my dear sir, as we say at Rome,°
Don't you protest now! It's fair give and take;
You have had your turn and spoken your home-truths:
The hand's mine now, and here you follow suit.

    Thus much conceded, still the first fact stays—
You do despise me; your ideal of life
Is not the bishop's: you would not be I.   50
You would like better to be Goethe, now,
Or Buonaparte, or, bless me, lower still,
Count D'Orsay,—so you did what you preferred,°
Spoke as you thought, and, as you cannot help,
Believed or disbelieved, no matter what,
So long as on that point, what'er it was,
You loosed your mind, were whole and sole yourself.
—That, my ideal never can include,
Upon that element of truth and worth   60
Never be based! for say they make me Pope—
(They can't—suppose it for our argument!)°
Why, there I'm at my tether's end, I've reached
My height, and not a height which pleases you:
An unbelieving Pope won't do, you say.
It's like those eerie stories nurses tell,

Of how some actor on a stage played Death,
With pasteboard crown, sham orb and tinselled dart,
And called himself the monarch of the world;
Then, going in the tire-room afterward,°   70
Because the play was done, to shift himself,
Got touched upon the sleeve familiarly,
The moment he had shut the closet door,
By Death himself. Thus God might touch a Pope
At unawares, ask what his baubles mean,
And whose part he presumed to play just now.
Best be yourself, imperial, plain and true!

So, drawing comfortable breath again,
You weigh and find, whatever more or less   80
I boast of my ideal realized
Is nothing in the balance when opposed
To your ideal, your grand simple life,
Of which you will not realize one jot.
I am much, you are nothing; you would be all,
I would be merely much: you beat me there.

No, friend, you do not beat me: hearken why!
The common problem, yours, mine, every one's,
Is—not to fancy what were fair in life
Provided it could be,—but, finding first
What may be, then find how to make it fair   90
Up to our means: a very different thing!
No abstract intellectual plan of life
Quite irrespective of life's plainest laws,
But one, a man, who is man and nothing more,
May lead within a world which (by your leave)
Is Rome or London, not Fool's-paradise.
Embellish Rome, idealize away,
Make paradise of London if you can,
You're welcome, nay, you're wise.

                              A simile!

We mortals cross the ocean of this world   100
Each in his average cabin of a life;
The best's not big, the worst yields elbow-room.
Now for our six months' voyage—how prepare?
You come on shipboard with a landsman's list
Of things he calls convenient: so they are!

An India screen is pretty furniture,
A piano-forte is a fine resource,
All Balzac's novels occupy one shelf,°
The new edition fifty volumes long;
And little Greek books, with the funny type   110
They get up well at Leipsic, fill the next:°
Go on! slabbed marble, what a bath it makes!
And Parma's pride, the Jerome, let us add!
'Twere pleasant could Correggio's fleeting glow°
Hang full in face of one where'er one roams,
Since he more than the others brings with him
Italy's self,—the marvellous Modenese!—
Yet was not on your list before, perhaps.
—Alas, friend, here's the agent . . . is't the name?
The captain, or whoever's master here—   120
You see him screw his face up; what's his cry
Ere you set foot on shipboard? 'Six feet square!'
If you won't understand what six feet mean,
Compute and purchase stores accordingly—
And if, in pique because he overhauls°
Your Jerome, piano, bath, you come on board
Bare—why, you cut a figure at the first
While sympathetic landsmen see you off;
Not afterward, when long ere half seas over,
You peep up from your utterly naked boards   130
Into some snug and well-appointed berth,
Like mine for instance (try the cooler jug—
Put back the other, but don't jog the ice!)
And mortified you mutter 'Well and good;
He sits enjoying his sea-furniture;
'Tis stout and proper, and there's store of it:
Though I've the better notion, all agree,
Of fitting rooms up. Hang the carpenter,
Neat ship-shape fixings and contrivances—
I would have brought my Jerome, frame and all!'   140
And meantime you bring nothing: never mind—
You've proved your artist-nature: what you don't
You might bring, so despise me, as I say.

    Now come, let's backward to the starting-place.
See my way: we're two college friends, suppose.

Prepare together for our voyage, then;
Each note and check the other in his work,—
Here's mine, a bishop's outfit; criticize!
What's wrong? why won't you be a bishop too?

Why first, you don't believe, you don't and can't,   150
(Not statedly, that is, and fixedly
And absolutely and exclusively)
In any revelation called divine.
No dogmas nail your faith; and what remains
But say so, like the honest man you are?
First, therefore, overhaul theology!
Nay, I too, not a fool, you please to think,
Must find believing every whit as hard:
And if I do not frankly say as much,
The ugly consequence is clear enough.   160

Now wait, my friend: well, I do not believe—
If you'll accept no faith that is not fixed,
Absolute and exclusive, as you say.
You're wrong—I mean to prove it in due time.
Meanwhile, I know where difficulties lie
I could not, cannot solve, nor ever shall,
So give up hope accordingly to solve—
(To you, and over the wine). Our dogmas then
With both of us, though in unlike degree,
Missing full credence—overboard with them!   170
I mean to meet you on your own premise:
Good, there go mine in company with yours!

And now what are we? unbelievers both,
Calm and complete, determinately fixed
To-day, to-morrow and for ever, pray?
You'll guarantee me that? Not so, I think!
In no wise! all we've gained is, that belief,
As unbelief before, shakes us by fits,
Confounds us like its predecessor. Where's
The gain? how can we guard our unbelief,   180
Make it bear fruit to us?—the problem here.
Just when we are safest, there's a sunset-touch,
A fancy from a flower-bell, some one's death,
A chorus-ending from Euripides,—°

And that's enough for fifty hopes and fears
As old and new at once as nature's self,
To rap and knock and enter in our soul,
Take hands and dance there, a fantastic ring,
Round the ancient idol, on his base again,—
The grand Perhaps! We look on helplessly.°   190
There the old misgivings, crooked questions are—
This good God,—what he could do, if he would,
Would, if he could—then must have done long since:
If so, when, where and how? some way must be,—
Once feel about, and soon or late you hit
Some sense, in which it might be, after all.
Why not, 'The Way, the Truth, the Life?'°

                                        —That way
Over the mountain, which who stands upon
Is apt to doubt if it be meant for a road;
While, if he views it from the waste itself,
Up goes the line there, plain from base to brow,   200
Not vague, mistakeable! what's a break or two
Seen from the unbroken desert either side?
And then (to bring in fresh philosophy)
What if the breaks themselves should prove at last
The most consummate of contrivances
To train a man's eye, teach him what is faith?
And so we stumble at truth's very test!
All we have gained then by our unbelief
Is a life of doubt diversified by faith,
For one of faith diversified by doubt: 210
We called the chess-board white,—we call it black.

    'Well,' you rejoin, 'the end's no worse, at least;
We've reason for both colours on the board:
Why not confess then, where I drop the faith
And you the doubt, that I'm as right as you?'

    Because, friend, in the next place, this being so,
And both things even,—faith and unbelief
Left to a man's choice,—we'll proceed a step,
Returning to our image, which I like.   220

    A man's choice, yes—but a cabin-passenger's—
The man made for the special life o' the world—

Do you forget him? I remember though!
Consult our ship's conditions and you find
One and but one choice suitable to all;
The choice, that you unluckily prefer,
Turning things topsy-turvy—they or it
Going to the ground. Belief or unbelief
Bears upon life, determines its whole course,
Begins at its beginning. See the world   230
Such as it is,—you made it not, nor I;
I mean to take it as it is,—and you,
Not so you'll take it,—though you get nought else.
I know the special kind of life I like,
What suits the most my idiosyncrasy,
Brings out the best of me and bears me fruit
In power, peace, pleasantness and length of days.
I find that positive belief does this
For me, and unbelief, no whit of this.
—For you, it does, however?—that, we'll try!   240
'Tis clear, I cannot lead my life, at least,
Induce the world to let me peaceably,
Without declaring at the outset, 'Friends,
I absolutely and peremptorily
Believe!'—I say, faith is my waking life:
One sleeps, indeed, and dreams at intervals,
We know, but waking's the main point with us
And my provision's for life's waking part.
Accordingly, I use heart, head and hand
All day, I build, scheme, study, and make friends;   250
And when night overtakes me, down I lie,
Sleep, dream a little, and get done with it,
The sooner the better, to begin afresh.
What's midnight doubt before the dayspring's faith?
You, the philosopher, that disbelieve,
That recognize the night, give dreams their weight—
To be consistent you should keep your bed,
Abstain from healthy acts that prove you man,
For fear you drowse perhaps at unawares!
And certainly at night you'll sleep and dream,   260
Live through the day and bustle as you please.
And so you live to sleep as I to wake,
To unbelieve as I to still believe?

Well, and the common sense o' the world calls you
Bed-ridden,—and its good things come to me.
Its estimation, which is half the fight,
That's the first-cabin comfort I secure:°
The next...but you perceive with half an eye!
Come, come, it's best believing, if we may;
You can't but own that!

                            Next, concede again,   270
If once we choose belief, on all accounts
We can't be too decisive in our faith,
Conclusive and exclusive in its terms,
To suit the world which gives us the good things.
In every man's career are certain points
Whereon he dares not be indifferent;
The world detects him clearly, if he dare,
As baffled at the game, and losing life.
He may care little or he may care much
For riches, honour, pleasure, work, repose,   280
Since various theories of life and life's
Success are extant which might easily
Comport with either estimate of these;
And whoso chooses wealth or poverty,
Labour or quiet, is not judged a fool
Because his fellow would choose otherwise:
We let him choose upon his own account
So long as he's consistent with his choice.
But certain points, left wholly to himself,
When once a man has arbitrated on,   290
We say he must succeed there or go hang.
Thus, he should wed the woman he loves most
Or needs most, whatsoe'er the love or need—
For he can't wed twice. Then, he must avouch,
Or follow, at the least, sufficiently,
The form of faith his conscience holds the best,
Whate'er the process of conviction was:
For nothing can compensate his mistake
On such a point, the man himself being judge:
He cannot wed twice, nor twice lose his soul.   300

    Well now, there's one great form of Christian faith
I happened to be born in—which to teach

Was given me as I grew up, on all hands,
As best and readiest means of living by;
The same on examination being proved
The most pronounced moreover, fixed, precise
And absolute form of faith in the whole world—
Accordingly, most potent of all forms
For working on the world. Observe, my friend!
Such as you know me, I am free to say,   310
In these hard latter days which hamper one,
Myself—by no immoderate exercise
Of intellect and learning, but the tact
To let external forces work for me,
—Bid the street's stones be bread and they are bread;°
Bid Peter's creed, or rather, Hildebrand's,°
Exalt me o'er my fellows in the world
And make my life an ease and joy and pride;
It does so,—which for me's a great point gained,
Who have a soul and body that exact   320
A comfortable care in many ways.
There's power in me and will to dominate
Which I must exercise, they hurt me else:
In many ways I need mankind's respect,
Obedience, and the love that's born of fear:
While at the same time, there's a taste I have,
A toy of soul, a titillating thing,
Refuses to digest these dainties crude.
The naked life is gross till clothed upon:
I must take what men offer, with a grace   330
As though I would not, could I help it, take!
An uniform I wear though over-rich—
Something imposed on me, no choice of mine;
No fancy-dress worn for pure fancy's sake
And despicable therefore! now folk kneel
And kiss my hand—of course the Church's hand.
Thus I am made, thus life is best for me,
And thus that it should be I have procured;
And thus it could not be another way,
I venture to imagine.
                          You'll reply,   340
So far my choice, no doubt, is a success;
But were I made of better elements,

With nobler instincts, purer tastes, like you,
I hardly would account the thing success
Though it did all for me I say.

                              But, friend,
We speak of what is; not of what might be,
And how 'twere better if 'twere otherwise.
I am the man you see here plain enough:
Grant I'm a beast, why, beasts must lead beasts' lives!
Suppose I own at once to tail and claws;
The tailless man exceeds me: but being tailed   350
I'll lash out lion fashion, and leave apes
To dock their stump and dress their haunches up.°
My business is not to remake myself,
But make the absolute best of what God made.
Or—our first simile—though you prove me doomed
To a viler berth still, to the steerage-hole,
The sheep-pen or the pig-stye, I should strive
To make what use of each were possible;
And as this cabin gets upholstery,   360
That hutch should rustle with sufficient straw.

    But, friend, I don't acknowledge quite so fast
I fail of all your manhood's lofty tastes
Enumerated so complacently,
On the mere ground that you forsooth can find
In this particular life I choose to lead
No fit provision for them. Can you not?
Say you, my fault is I address myself
To grosser estimators than should judge?
And that's no way of holding up the soul,   370
Which, nobler, needs men's praise perhaps, yet knows
One wise man's verdict outweighs all the fools'—
Would like the two, but, forced to choose, takes that.
I pine among my million imbeciles
(You think) aware some dozen men of sense
Eye me and know me, whether I believe
In the last winking Virgin, as I vow,°
And am a fool, or disbelieve in her
And am a knave,—approve in neither case,
Withhold their voices though I look their way;   380

Like Verdi when, at his worst opera's end
(The thing they gave at Florence,—what's its name?)
While the mad houseful's plaudits near out-bang
His orchestra of salt-box, tongs and bones,
He looks through all the roaring and the wreaths
Where sits Rossini patient in his stall.°

    Nay, friend, I meet you with an answer here—
That even your prime men who appraise their kind
Are men still, catch a wheel within a wheel,
See more in a truth than the truth's simple self,   390
Confuse themselves. You see lads walk the street
Sixty the minute; what's to note in that?°
You see one lad o'erstride a chimney-stack;
Him you must watch—he's sure to fall, yet stands!
Our interest's on the dangerous edge of things.
The honest thief, the tender murderer,
The superstitious atheist, demirep°
That loves and saves her soul in new French books—
We watch while these in equilibrium keep
The giddy line midway: one step aside,   400
They're classed and done with. I, then, keep the line
Before your sages,—just the men to shrink
From the gross weights, coarse scales and labels broad
You offer their refinement. Fool or knave?
Why needs a bishop be a fool or knave
When there's a thousand diamond weights between?
So, I enlist them. Your picked twelve, you'll find,°
Profess themselves indignant, scandalized
At thus being held unable to explain
How a superior man who disbelieves   410
May not believe as well: that's Schelling's way!°
It's through my coming in the tail of time,
Nicking the minute with a happy tact.
Had I been born three hundred years ago
They'd say, 'What's strange? Blougram of course believes;'
And, seventy years since, 'disbelieves of course.'
But now, 'He may believe; and yet, and yet
How can he?' All eyes turn with interest.
Whereas, step off the line on either side—
You, for example, clever to a fault,   420

The rough and ready man who write apace,
Read somewhat seldomer, think perhaps even less—
You disbelieve! Who wonders and who cares?
Lord So-and-so—his coat bedropped with wax,
All Peter's chains about his waist, his back°
Brave with the needlework of Noodledom—°
Believes! Again, who wonders and who cares?
But I, the man of sense and learning too,
The able to think yet act, the this, the that,
I, to believe at this late time of day!   430
Enough; you see, I need not fear contempt.

　　—Except it's yours! Admire me as these may,
You don't. But whom at least do you admire?
Present your own perfection, your ideal,
Your pattern man for a minute—oh, make haste,
Is it Napoleon you would have us grow?
Concede the means; allow his head and hand,
(A large concession, clever as you are)
Good! In our common primal element
Of unbelief (we can't believe, you know—   440
We're still at that admission, recollect!)
Where do you find—apart from, towering o'er
The secondary temporary aims
Which satisfy the gross taste you despise—
Where do you find his star?—his crazy trust
God knows through what or in what? it's alive
And shines and leads him, and that's all we want.
Have we aught in our sober night shall point
Such ends as his were, and direct the means
Of working out our purpose straight as his,   450
Nor bring a moment's trouble on success
With after-care to justify the same?
—Be a Napoleon, and yet disbelieve—
Why, the man's mad, friend, take his light away!
What's the vague good o' the world, for which you dare
With comfort to yourself blow millions up?
We neither of us see it! we do see
The blown-up millions—spatter of their brains
And writhing of their bowels and so forth,
In that bewildering entanglement   460

Of horrible eventualities
Past calculation to the end of time!
Can I mistake for some clear word of God
(Which were my ample warrant for it all)
His puff of hazy instinct, idle talk,
'The State, that's I,' quack-nonsense about crowns,°
And (when one beats the man to his last hold)
A vague idea of setting things to rights,
Policing people efficaciously,
More to their profit, most of all to his own;   470
The whole to end that dismallest of ends
By an Austrian marriage, cant to us the Church,°
And resurrection of the old *régime?*
Would I, who hope to live a dozen years,
Fight Austerlitz for reasons such and such?°
No: for, concede me but the merest chance
Doubt may be wrong—there's judgment, life to come!
With just that chance, I dare not. Doubt proves right?
This present life is all?—you offer me
Its dozen noisy years, without a chance   480
That wedding an archduchess, wearing lace,
And getting called by divers new-coined names,
Will drive off ugly thoughts and let me dine,
Sleep, read and chat in quiet as I like!
Therefore I will not.

                              Take another case;
Fit up the cabin yet another way.
What say you to the poets? shall we write
Hamlet, Othello—make the world our own,
Without a risk to run of either sort?
I can't!—to put the strongest reason first.   490
'But try,' you urge, 'the trying shall suffice;
The aim, if reached or not, makes great the life:
Try to be Shakespeare, leave the rest to fate!'
Spare my self-knowledge—there's no fooling me!
If I prefer remaining my poor self,
I say so not in self-dispraise but praise.
If I'm a Shakespeare, let the well alone;
Why should I try to be what now I am?
If I'm no Shakespeare, as too probable,—

His power and consciousness and self-delight   500
And all we want in common, shall I find—
Trying for ever? while on points of taste
Wherewith, to speak it humbly, he and I
Are dowered alike—I'll ask you, I or he,
Which in our two lives realizes most?
Much, he imagined—somewhat, I possess.
He had the imagination; stick to that!
Let him say, 'In the face of my soul's works
Your world is worthless and I touch it not
Lest I should wrong them'—I'll withdraw my plea.   510
But does he say so? look upon his life!
Himself, who only can, gives judgment there.
He leaves his towers and gorgeous palaces
To build the trimmest house in Stratford town;°
Saves money, spends it, owns the worth of things,
Giulio Romano's pictures, Dowland's lute;
Enjoys a show, respects the puppets, too,
And none more, had he seen its entry once,
Than 'Pandulph, of fair Milan cardinal.'°
Why then should I who play that personage,   520
The very Pandulph Shakespeare's fancy made,
Be told that had the poet chanced to start
From where I stand now (some degree like mine
Being just the goal he ran his race to reach)
He would have run the whole race back, forsooth,
And left being Pandulph, to begin write plays?
Ah, the earth's best can be but the earth's best!
Did Shakespeare live, he could but sit at home
And get himself in dreams the Vatican,
Greek busts, Venetian paintings, Roman walls,   530
And English books, none equal to his own,
Which I read, bound in gold (he never did).
—Terni's fall, Naples' bay and Gothard's top—°
Eh, friend? I could not fancy one of these;
But, as I pour this claret, there they are:
I've gained them—crossed St Gothard last July
With ten mules to the carriage and a bed
Slung inside; is my hap the worse for that?
We want the same things, Shakespeare and myself,
And what I want, I have: he, gifted more,   540

Could fancy he too had them when he liked,
But not so thoroughly that, if fate allowed,
He would not have them also in my sense.
We play one game; I send the ball aloft
No less adroitly that of fifty strokes
Scarce five go o'er the wall so wide and high
Which sends them back to me: I wish and get.
He struck balls higher and with better skill,
But at a poor fence level with his head,
And hit—his Stratford house, a coat of arms,   550
Successful dealings in his grain and wool,—
While I receive heaven's incense in my nose
And style myself the cousin of Queen Bess.
Ask him, if this life's all, who wins the game?

        Believe—and our whole argument breaks up.
Enthusiasm's the best thing, I repeat;
Only, we can't command it; fire and life
Are all, dead matter's nothing, we agree:
And be it a mad dream or God's very breath,
The fact's the same,—belief's fire, once in us,   560
Makes of all else mere stuff to show itself:
We penetrate our life with such a glow
As fire lends wood and iron—this turns steel,
That burns to ash—all's one, fire proves its power
For good or ill, since men call flare success.
But paint a fire, it will not therefore burn.
Light one in me, I'll find it food enough!
Why, to be Luther—that's a life to lead,°
Incomparably better than my own.
He comes, reclaims God's earth for God, he says,   570
Sets up God's rule again by simple means,
Re-opens a shut book, and all is done.
He flared out in the flaring of mankind;
Such Luther's luck was: how shall such be mine?
If he succeeded, nothing's left to do:
And if he did not altogether—well,
Strauss is the next advance. All Strauss should be°
I might be also. But to what result?
He looks upon no future: Luther did.
What can I gain on the denying side?   580

Ice makes no conflagration. State the facts,
Read the text right, emancipate the world—
The emancipated world enjoys itself
With scarce a thank-you: Blougram told it first
It could not owe a farthing,—not to him
More than Saint Paul! 'twould press its pay, you think?
Then add there's still that plaguy hundredth chance
Strauss may be wrong. And so a risk is run—
For what gain? not for Luther's, who secured
A real heaven in his heart throughout his life,   590
Supposing death a little altered things.

'Ay, but since really you lack faith,' you cry,
'You run the same risk really on all sides,
In cool indifference as bold unbelief.
As well be Strauss as swing 'twixt Paul and him.
It's not worth having, such imperfect faith,
No more available to do faith's work
Than unbelief like mine. Whole faith, or none!'

Softly, my friend! I must dispute that point.
Once own the use of faith, I'll find you faith.   600
We're back on Christian ground. You call for faith:
I show you doubt, to prove that faith exists.
The more of doubt, the stronger faith, I say,
If faith o'ercomes doubt. How I know it does?
By life and man's free will, God gave for that!
To mould life as we choose it, shows our choice:
That's our one act, the previous work's his own.
You criticize the soil? it reared this tree—
This broad life and whatever fruit it bears!
What matter though I doubt at every pore,   610
Head-doubts, heart-doubts, doubts at my fingers' ends,
Doubts in the trivial work of every day,
Doubts at the very bases of my soul
In the grand moments when she probes herself—
If finally I have a life to show,
The thing I did, brought out in evidence
Against the thing done to me underground
By hell and all its brood, for aught I know?
I say, whence sprang this? shows it faith or doubt?
All's doubt in me; where's break of faith in this?   620

It is the idea, the feeling and the love,
God means mankind should strive for and show forth
Whatever be the process to that end,—
And not historic knowledge, logic sound,
And metaphysical acumen, sure!
'What think ye of Christ,' friend? when all's done and said,°
Like you this Christianity or not?
It may be false, but will you wish it true?
Has it your vote to be so if it can?
Trust you an instinct silenced long ago   630
That will break silence and enjoin you love
What mortified philosophy is hoarse,
And all in vain, with bidding you despise?
If you desire faith—then you've faith enough:
What else seeks God—nay, what else seek ourselves?
You form a notion of me, we'll suppose,
On hearsay; it's a favourable one:
'But still' (you add), 'there was no such good man,
Because of contradiction in the facts.
One proves, for instance, he was born in Rome,   640
This Blougram; yet throughout the tales of him
I see he figures as an Englishman.'
Well, the two things are reconcileable.
But would I rather you discovered that,
Subjoining—'Still, what matter though they be?
Blougram concerns me nought, born here or there.'

    Pure faith indeed—you know not what you ask!
Naked belief in God the Omnipotent,
Omniscient, Omnipresent, sears too much
The sense of conscious creatures to be borne.   650
It were the seeing him, no flesh shall dare.
Some think, Creation's meant to show him forth:
I say it's meant to hide him all it can,
And that's what all the blessed evil's for.
Its use in Time is to environ us,
Our breath, our drop of dew, with shield enough
Against that sight till we can bear its stress.
Under a vertical sun, the exposed brain
And lidless eye and disemprisoned heart
Less certainly would wither up at once   660

Than mind, confronted with the truth of him.
But time and earth case-harden us to live;
The feeblest sense is trusted most; the child
Feels God a moment, ichors o'er the place,°
Plays on and grows to be a man like us.
With me, faith means perpetual unbelief
Kept quiet like the snake 'neath Michael's foot
Who stands calm just because he feels it writhe.
Or, if that's too ambitious,—here's my box—°
I need the excitation of a pinch   670
Threatening the torpor of the inside-nose
Nigh on the imminent sneeze that never comes.
'Leave it in peace' advise the simple folk:
Make it aware of peace by itching-fits,
Say I—let doubt occasion still more faith!

You'll say, once all believed, man, woman, child,
In that dear middle-age these noodles praise.
How you'd exult if I could put you back
Six hundred years, blot out cosmogony,
Geology, ethnology, what not,   680
(Greek endings, each the little passing-bell
That signifies some faith's about to die),
And set you square with Genesis again,—
When such a traveller told you his last news,
He saw the ark a-top of Ararat°
But did not climb there since 'twas getting dusk
And robber-bands infest the mountain's foot!
How should you feel, I ask, in such an age,
How act? As other people felt and did;
With soul more blank than this decanter's knob,   690
Believe—and yet lie, kill, rob, fornicate
Full in belief's face, like the beast you'd be!

No, when the fight begins within himself,
A man's worth something. God stoops o'er his head,
Satan looks up between his feet—both tug—
He's left, himself, i' the middle: the soul wakes
And grows. Prolong that battle through his life!
Never leave growing till the life to come!
Here, we've got callous to the Virgin's winks
That used to puzzle people wholesomely: 700

Men have outgrown the shame of being fools.
What are the laws of nature, not to bend
If the Church bid them?—brother Newman asks.
Up with the Immaculate Conception, then—°
On to the rack with faith!—is my advice.
Will not that hurry us upon our knees,
Knocking our breasts, 'It can't be—yet it shall!
Who am I, the worm, to argue with my Pope?
Low things confound the high things!' and so forth.
That's better than acquitting God with grace   710
As some folk do. He's tried—no case is proved,
Philosophy is lenient—he may go!

    You'll say, the old system's not so obsolete
But men believe still: ay, but who and where?
King Bomba's lazzaroni foster yet°
The sacred flame, so Antonelli writes;°
But even of these, what ragamuffin-saint
Believes God watches him continually,
As he believes in fire that it will burn,
Or rain that it will drench him? Break fire's law,   720
Sin against rain, although the penalty
Be just a singe or soaking? 'No,' he smiles;
'Those laws are laws that can enforce themselves.'

    The sum of all is—yes, my doubt is great,
My faith's still greater, then my faith's enough.
I have read much, thought much, experienced much,
Yet would die rather than avow my fear
The Naples' liquefaction may be false,°
When set to happen by the palace-clock
According to the clouds or dinner-time.   730
I hear you recommend, I might at least
Eliminate, decrassify my faith°
Since I adopt it; keeping what I must
And leaving what I can—such points as this.
I won't—that is, I can't throw one away.
Supposing there's no truth in what I hold
About the need of trial to man's faith,
Still, when you bid me purify the same,
To such a process I discern no end.
Clearing off one excrescence to see two,   740

There's ever a next in size, now grown as big,
That meets the knife: I cut and cut again!
First cut the Liquefaction, what comes last
But Fichte's clever cut at God himself?°
Experimentalize on sacred things!
I trust nor hand nor eye nor heart nor brain
To stop betimes: they all get drunk alike.
The first step, I am master not to take.

   You'd find the cutting-process to your taste
As much as leaving growths of lies unpruned,   750
Nor see more danger in it,—you retort.
Your taste's worth mine; but my taste proves more wise
When we consider that the steadfast hold
On the extreme end of the chain of faith
Gives all the advantage, makes the difference
With the rough purblind mass we seek to rule:
We are their lords, or they are free of us,
Just as we tighten or relax our hold.
So, other matters equal, we'll revert
To the first problem—which, if solved my way   760
And thrown into the balance, turns the scale—
How we may lead a comfortable life,
How suit our luggage to the cabin's size.

   Of course you are remarking all this time
How narrowly and grossly I view life,
Respect the creature-comforts, care to rule
The masses, and regard complacently
'The cabin,' in our old phrase. Well, I do.
I act for, talk for, live for this world now,
As this world prizes action, life and talk: 770
No prejudice to what next world may prove,
Whose new laws and requirements, my best pledge
To observe then, is that I observe these now,
Shall do hereafter what I do meanwhile.
Let us concede (gratuitously though)
Next life relieves the soul of body, yields
Pure spiritual enjoyment: well, my friend,
Why lose this life i' the meantime, since its use
May be to make the next life more intense?

Do you know, I have often had a dream   780
(Work it up in your next month's article)
Of man's poor spirit in its progress, still
Losing true life for ever and a day
Through ever trying to be and ever being—
In the evolution of successive spheres—
Before its actual sphere and place of life,
Halfway into the next, which having reached,
It shoots with corresponding foolery
Halfway into the next still, on and off!
As when a traveller, bound from North to South,   790
Scouts fur in Russia: what's its use in France?°
In France spurns flannel: where's its need in Spain?
In Spain drops cloth, too cumbrous for Algiers!
Linen goes next, and last the skin itself,
A superfluity at Timbuctoo.
When, through his journey, was the fool at ease?
I'm at ease now, friend; worldly in this world,
I take and like its way of life; I think
My brothers, who administer the means,
Live better for my comfort—that's good too;   800
And God, if he pronounce upon such life,
Approves my service, which is better still.
If he keep silence,—why, for you or me
Or that brute beast pulled-up in to-day's 'Times,'
What odds is't, save to ourselves, what life we lead?

You meet me at this issue: you declare,—
All special-pleading done with—truth is truth,
And justifies itself by undreamed ways.
You don't fear but it's better, if we doubt,
To say so, act up to our truth perceived   810
However feebly. Do then,—act away!
'Tis there I'm on the watch for you. How one acts
Is, both of us agree, our chief concern:
And how you'll act is what I fain would see
If, like the candid person you appear,
You dare to make the most of your life's scheme
As I of mine, live up to its full law
Since there's no higher law that counterchecks.
Put natural religion to the test

You've just demolished the revealed with—quick, 820
Down to the root of all that checks your will,
All prohibition to lie, kill and thieve,
Or even to be an atheistic priest!
Suppose a pricking to incontinence—
Philosophers deduce you chastity
Or shame, from just the fact that at the first
Whoso embraced a woman in the field,
Threw club down and forewent his brains beside,
So, stood a ready victim in the reach
Of any brother savage, club in hand; 830
Hence saw the use of going out of sight
In wood or cave to prosecute his loves:
I read this in a French book t'other day.
Does law so analysed coerce you much?
Oh, men spin clouds of fuzz where matters end,
But you who reach where the first thread begins,
You'll soon cut that!—which means you can, but won't,
Through certain instincts, blind, unreasoned-out,
You dare not set aside, you can't tell why,
But there they are, and so you let them rule. 840
Then, friend, you seem as much a slave as I,
A liar, conscious coward and hypocrite,
Without the good the slave expects to get,
In case he has a master after all!
You own your instincts? why, what else do I,
Who want, am made for, and must have a God
Ere I can be aught, do aught?—no mere name
Want, but the true thing with what proves its truth,
To wit, a relation from that thing to me,
Touching from head to foot—which touch I feel, 850
And with it take the rest, this life of ours!
I live my life here; yours you dare not live.

—Not as I state it, who (you please subjoin)
Disfigure such a life and call it names,
While, to your mind, remains another way
For simple men: knowledge and power have rights,
But ignorance and weakness have rights too.
There needs no crucial effort to find truth
If here or there or anywhere about:

We ought to turn each side, try hard and see,   860
And if we can't, be glad we've earned at least
The right, by one laborious proof the more,
To graze in peace earth's pleasant pasturage.
Men are not angels, neither are they brutes:
Something we may see, all we cannot see.
What need of lying? I say, I see all,
And swear to each detail the most minute
In what I think a Pan's face—you, mere cloud:°
I swear I hear him speak and see him wink,
For fear, if once I drop the emphasis,   870
Mankind may doubt there's any cloud at all.
You take the simple life—ready to see,
Willing to see (for no cloud's worth a face)—
And leaving quiet what no strength can move,
And which, who bids you move? who has the right?
I bid you; but you are God's sheep, not mine:
'*Pastor est tui Dominus.*' You find°
In this the pleasant pasture of our life
Much you may eat without the least offence,
Much you don't eat because your maw objects,   880
Much you would eat but that your fellow-flock
Open great eyes at you and even butt,
And thereupon you like your mates so well
You cannot please yourself, offending them;
Though when they seem exorbitantly sheep,
You weigh your pleasure with their butts and bleats
And strike the balance. Sometimes certain fears
Restrain you, real checks since you find them so;
Sometimes you please yourself and nothing checks:
And thus you graze through life with not one lie,   890
And like it best.

                    But do you, in truth's name?
If so, you beat—which means you are not I—
Who needs must make earth mine and feed my fill
Not simply unbutted at, unbickered with,
But motioned to the velvet of the sward
By those obsequious wethers' very selves.
Look at me, sir; my age is double yours:
At yours, I knew beforehand, so enjoyed,

What now I should be—as, permit the word,
I pretty well imagine your whole range   900
And stretch of tether twenty years to come.
We both have minds and bodies much alike:
In truth's name, don't you want my bishopric,
My daily bread, my influence and my state?
You're young. I'm old; you must be old one day;
Will you find then, as I do hour by hour,
Women their lovers kneel to, who cut curls
From your fat lap-dog's ear to grace a brooch—
Dukes, who petition just to kiss your ring—
With much beside you know or may conceive?   910
Suppose we die to-night: well, here am I,
Such were my gains, life bore this fruit to me,
While writing all the same my articles
On music, poetry, the fictile vase°
Found at Albano, chess, Anacreon's Greek.°
But you—the highest honour in your life,
The thing you'll crown yourself with, all your days,
Is—dining here and drinking this last glass
I pour you out in sign of amity
Before we part for ever. Of your power   920
And social influence, worldly worth in short,
Judge what's my estimation by the fact,
I do not condescend to enjoin, beseech,
Hint secrecy on one of all these words!
You're shrewd and know that should you publish one
The world would brand the lie—my enemies first,
Who'd sneer—'the bishop's an arch-hypocrite
And knave perhaps, but not so frank a fool.'
Whereas I should not dare for both my ears
Breathe one such syllable, smile one such smile,   930
Before the chaplain who reflects myself—
My shade's so much more potent than your flesh.
What's your reward, self-abnegating friend?
Stood you confessed of those exceptional
And privileged great natures that dwarf mine—
A zealot with a mad ideal in reach,
A poet just about to print his ode,
A statesman with a scheme to stop this war,°
An artist whose religion is his art—

I should have nothing to object: such men   940
Carry the fire, all things grow warm to them,
Their drugget's worth my purple, they beat me.°
But you,—you're just as little those as I—
You, Gigadibs, who, thirty years of age,
Write stately for Blackwood's Magazine,°
Believe you see two points in Hamlet's soul
Unseized by the Germans yet—which view you'll print—°
Meantime the best you have to show being still
That lively lightsome article we took
Almost for the true Dickens,—what's its name?   950
'The Slum and Cellar, or Whitechapel life°
Limned after dark!' it made me laugh, I know,
And pleased a month, and brought you in ten pounds.
—Success I recognize and compliment,
And therefore give you, if you choose, three words
(The card and pencil-scratch is quite enough)
Which whether here, in Dublin or New York,
Will get you, prompt as at my eyebrow's wink,
Such terms as never you aspired to get
In all our own reviews and some not ours.   960
Go write your lively sketches! be the first
'Blougram, or The Eccentric Confidence'—
Or better simply say, 'The Outward-bound.'
Why, men as soon would throw it in my teeth
As copy and quote the infamy chalked broad
About me on the church-door opposite.
You will not wait for that experience though,
I fancy, howsoever you decide,
To discontinue—not detesting, not
Defaming, but at least—despising me!   970

    Over his wine so smiled and talked his hour
Sylvester Blougram, styled *in partibus*
Episcopus, nec non—(the deuce knows what°
It's changed to by our novel hierarchy)
With Gigadibs the literary man,
Who played with spoons, explored his plate's design,
And ranged the olive-stones about its edge,

While the great bishop rolled him out a mind
Long crumpled, till creased consciousness lay smooth.

For Blougram, he believed, say, half he spoke.   980
The other portion, as he shaped it thus
For argumentatory purposes,
He felt his foe was foolish to dispute.
Some arbitrary accidental thoughts
That crossed his mind, amusing because new,
He chose to represent as fixtures there,
Invariable convictions (such they seemed
Beside his interlocutor's loose cards
Flung daily down, and not the same way twice)
While certain hell-deep instincts, man's weak tongue   990
Is never bold to utter in their truth
Because styled hell-deep ('tis an old mistake
To place hell at the bottom of the earth)
He ignored these,—not having in readiness
Their nomenclature and philosophy:
He said true things, but called them by wrong names.
'On the whole,' he thought, 'I justify myself
On every point where cavillers like this
Oppugn my life: he tries one kind of fence,°
I close, he's worsted, that's enough for him.   1000
He's on the ground: if ground should break away
I take my stand on, there's a firmer yet
Beneath it, both of us may sink and reach.
His ground was over mine and broke the first:
So, let him sit with me this many a year!'

He did not sit five minutes. Just a week
Sufficed his sudden healthy vehemence.
Something had struck him in the 'Outward-bound'
Another way than Blougram's purpose was:
And having bought, not cabin-furniture   1010
But settler's-implements (enough for three)
And started for Australia—there, I hope,
By this time he has tested his first plough,
And studied his last chapter of St John.°

Memorabilia

I

Ah, did you once see Shelley plain,
    And did he stop and speak to you
And did you speak to him again?
    How strange it seems and new!

II

But you were living before that,
    And also you are living after;
And the memory I started at—
    My starting moves your laughter.

III

I crossed a moor, with a name of its own
    And a certain use in the world no doubt,   10
Yet a hand's-breath of it shines alone
    'Mid the blank miles round about:

IV

For there I picked up on the heather
    And there I put inside my breast
A moulted feather, an eagle-feather!
    Well, I forget the rest.

Love in a Life

I

Room after room,
I hunt the house through
We inhabit together.
Heart, fear nothing, for, heart, thou shalt find her—
Next time, herself!—not the trouble behind her
Left in the curtain, the couch's perfume!

As she brushed it, the cornice-wreath blossomed anew:
Yon looking-glass gleamed at the wave of her feather.

II

Yet the day wears,
And door succeeds door;   10
I try the fresh fortune—
Range the wide house from the wing to the centre.
Still the same chance! she goes out as I enter.
Spend my whole day in the quest,—who cares?
But 'tis twilight, you see,—with such suites to explore,
Such closets to search, such alcoves to importune!

Life in a Love

Escape me?
Never—
Beloved!
While I am I, and you are you,
    So long as the world contains us both,
    Me the loving and you the loth,
While the one eludes, must the other pursue.
My life is a fault at last, I fear:
    It seems too much like a fate, indeed!
    Though I do my best I shall scarce succeed.   10
But what if I fail of my purpose here?
It is but to keep the nerves at strain,
    To dry one's eyes and laugh at a fall,
And, baffled, get up and begin again,—
    So the chace takes up one's life, that's all.
While, look but once from your farthest bound
    At me so deep in the dust and dark,
No sooner the old hope goes to ground
    Than a new one, straight to the self-same mark,
I shape me—
Ever   20
Removed!

Andrea del Sarto

(Called 'The Faultless Painter')

But do not let us quarrel any more,
No, my Lucrezia; bear with me for once:
Sit down and all shall happen as you wish.
You turn your face, but does it bring your heart?
I'll work then for your friend's friend, never fear,
Treat his own subject after his own way,
Fix his own time, accept too his own price,
And shut the money into this small hand
When next it takes mine. Will it? tenderly?   10
Oh, I'll content him,—but to-morrow, Love!
I often am much wearier than you think,
This evening more than usual, and it seems
As if—forgive now—should you let me sit
Here by the window with your hand in mine
And look a half-hour forth on Fiesole,°
Both of one mind, as married people use,
Quietly, quietly the evening through,
I might get up to-morrow to my work
Cheerful and fresh as ever. Let us try.   20
To-morrow, how you shall be glad for this!
Your soft hand is a woman of itself,
And mine the man's bared breast she curls inside.
Don't count the time lost, neither; you must serve
For each of the five pictures we require:
It saves a model. So! keep looking so—
My serpentining beauty, rounds on rounds!
—How could you ever prick those perfect ears,
Even to put the pearl there! oh, so sweet—
My face, my moon, my everybody's moon,   30
Which everybody looks on and calls his,
And, I suppose, is looked on by in turn,
While she looks—no one's: very dear, no less.
You smile? why, there's my picture ready made,
There's what we painters call our harmony!
A common greyness silvers everything,—
All in a twilight, you and I alike
—You, at the point of your first pride in me

(That's gone you know),—but I, at every point;
My youth, my hope, my art, being all toned down   40
To yonder sober pleasant Fiesole.
There's the bell clinking from the chapel-top;
That length of convent-wall across the way
Holds the trees safer, huddled more inside;
The last monk leaves the garden; days decrease,
And autumn grows, autumn in everything.
Eh? the whole seems to fall into a shape
As if I saw alike my work and self
And all that I was born to be and do,
A twilight-piece. Love, we are in God's hand.   50
How strange now, looks the life he makes us lead;
So free we seem, so fettered fast we are!
I feel he laid the fetter: let it lie!
This chamber for example—turn your head—
All that's behind us! You don't understand
Nor care to understand about my art,
But you can hear at least when people speak:
And that cartoon, the second from the door°
—It is the thing, Love! so such things should be—
Behold Madonna!—I am bold to say.   60
I can do with my pencil what I know,
What I see, what at bottom of my heart
I wish for, if I ever wish so deep—
Do easily, too—when I say, perfectly,
I do not boast, perhaps: yourself are judge,
Who listened to the Legate's talk last week,
And just as much they used to say in France.
At any rate 'tis easy, all of it!
No sketches first, no studies, that's long past:
I do what many dream of, all their lives,   70
—Dream? strive to do, and agonize to do,
And fail in doing. I could count twenty such
On twice your fingers, and not leave this town,
Who strive—you don't know how the others strive
To paint a little thing like that you smeared
Carelessly passing with your robes afloat,—
Yet do much less, so much less, Someone says,
(I know his name, no matter)—so much less!
Well, less is more, Lucrezia: I am judged.

There burns a truer light of God in them,
In their vexed beating stuffed and stopped-up brain,
Heart, or whate'er else, than goes on to prompt
This low-pulsed forthright craftsman's hand of mine.
Their works drop groundward, but themselves, I know,
Reach many a time a heaven that's shut to me,
Enter and take their place there sure enough,
Though they come back and cannot tell the world.
My works are nearer heaven, but I sit here.
The sudden blood of these men! at a word—
Praise them, it boils, or blame them, it boils too.   90
I, painting from myself and to myself,
Know what I do, am unmoved by men's blame
Or their praise either. Somebody remarks
Morello's outline there is wrongly traced,°
His hue mistaken; what of that? or else,
Rightly traced and well ordered; what of that?
Speak as they please, what does the mountain care?
Ah, but a man's reach should exceed his grasp,
Or what's a heaven for? All is silver-grey
Placid and perfect with my art: the worse!   100
I know both what I want and what might gain,
And yet how profitless to know, to sigh
'Had I been two, another and myself,
Our head would have o'erlooked the world!' No doubt.
Yonder's a work now, of that famous youth
The Urbinate who died five years ago.°
('Tis copied, George Vasari sent it me.)°
Well, I can fancy how he did it all,
Pouring his soul, with kings and popes to see,
Reaching, that heaven might so replenish him,   110
Above and through his art—for it gives way;
That arm is wrongly put—and there again—
A fault to pardon in the drawing's lines,
Its body, so to speak: its soul is right,
He means right—that, a child may understand.
Still, what an arm! and I could alter it:
But all the play, the insight and the stretch—
Out of me, out of me! And wherefore out?
Had you enjoined them on me, given me soul,
We might have risen to Rafael, I and you!   120

Nay, Love, you did give all I asked, I think—
More than I merit, yes, by many times.
But had you—oh, with the same perfect brow,
And perfect eyes, and more than perfect mouth,
And the low voice my soul hears, as a bird
The fowler's pipe, and follows to the snare—
Had you, with these the same, but brought a mind!
Some women do so. Had the mouth there urged
'God and the glory! never care for gain.
The present by the future, what is that?   130
Live for fame, side by side with Agnolo!°
Rafael is waiting: up to God, all three!'
I might have done it for you. So it seems:
Perhaps not. All is as God over-rules.
Beside, incentives come from the soul's self;
The rest avail not. Why do I need you?
What wife had Rafael, or has Agnolo?
In this world, who can do a thing, will not;
And who would do it, cannot, I perceive:
Yet the will's somewhat—somewhat, too, the power—   140
And thus we half-men struggle. At the end,
God, I conclude, compensates, punishes.
'Tis safer for me, if the award be strict,
That I am something underrated here,
Poor this long while, despised, to speak the truth.
I dared not, do you know, leave home all day,
For fear of chancing on the Paris lords.°
The best is when they pass and look aside;
But they speak sometimes; I must bear it all.
Well may they speak! That Francis, that first time,   150
And that long festal year at Fontainebleau!
I surely then could sometimes leave the ground,
Put on the glory, Rafael's daily wear,
In that humane great monarch's golden look,—
One finger in his beard or twisted curl
Over his mouth's good mark that made the smile,
One arm about my shoulder, round my neck,
The jingle of his gold chain in my ear,
I painting proudly with his breath on me,
All his court round him, seeing with his eyes,   160
Such frank French eyes, and such a fire of souls

Profuse, my hand kept plying by those hearts,—
And, best of all, this, this, this face beyond,
This in the background, waiting on my work,
To crown the issue with a last reward!
A good time, was it not, my kingly days?
And had you not grown restless... but I know—
'Tis done and past; 'twas right, my instinct said;
Too live the life grew, golden and not grey,
And I'm the weak-eyed bat no sun should tempt   170
Out of the grange whose four walls make his world.°
How could it end in any other way?
You called me, and I came home to your heart.
The triumph was—to reach and stay there; since
I reached it ere the triumph, what is lost?
Let my hands frame your face in your hair's gold,
You beautiful Lucrezia that are mine!
'Rafael did this, Andrea painted that;
The Roman's is the better when you pray,°
But still the other's Virgin was his wife—'   180
Men will excuse me. I am glad to judge
Both pictures in your presence; clearer grows
My better fortune, I resolve to think.
For, do you know, Lucrezia, as God lives,
Said one day Agnolo, his very self,
To Rafael... I have known it all these years...
(When the young man was flaming out his thoughts
Upon a palace-wall for Rome to see,
Too lifted up in heart because of it)
'Friend, there's a certain sorry little scrub   190
Goes up and down our Florence, none cares how,
Who, were he set to plan and execute
As you are, pricked on by your popes and kings,
Would bring the sweat into that brow of yours!'
To Rafael's!—And indeed the arm is wrong.
I hardly dare... yet, only you to see,
Give the chalk here—quick, thus the line should go!
Ay, but the soul! he's Rafael! rub it out!
Still, all I care for, if he spoke the truth,
(What he? why, who but Michael Agnolo?   200
Do you forget already words like those?)
If really there was such a chance, so lost,—

Is, whether you're—not grateful—but more pleased.
Well, let me think so. And you smile indeed!
This hour has been an hour! Another smile?
If you would sit thus by me every night
I should work better, do you comprehend?
I mean that I should earn more, give you more.
See, it is settled dusk now; there's a star;
Morello's gone, the watch-lights show the wall,   210
The cue-owls speak the name we call them by.
Come from the window, love,—come in, at last,
Inside the melancholy little house
We built to be so gay with. God is just.
King Francis may forgive me: oft at nights°
When I look up from painting, eyes tired out,
The walls become illumined, brick from brick
Distinct, instead of mortar, fierce bright gold,
That gold of his I did cement them with!
Let us but love each other. Must you go?   220
That Cousin here again? he waits outside?°
Must see you—you, and not with me? Those loans?
More gaming debts to pay? you smiled for that?
Well, let smiles buy me! have you more to spend?
While hand and eye and something of a heart
Are left me, work's my ware, and what's it worth?
I'll pay my fancy. Only let me sit
The grey remainder of the evening out,
Idle, you call it, and muse perfectly
How I could paint, were I but back in France,   230
One picture, just one more—the Virgin's face,
Not yours this time! I want you at my side
To hear them—that is, Michael Agnolo—
Judge all I do and tell you of its worth.
Will you? To-morrow, satisfy your friend.
I take the subjects for his corridor,
Finish the portrait out of hand—there, there,
And throw him in another thing or two
If he demurs; the whole should prove enough
To pay for this same Cousin's freak. Beside,   240
What's better and what's all I care about,
Get you the thirteen scudi for the ruff!°
Love, does that please you? Ah, but what does he,

The Cousin! what does he to please you more?

I am grown peaceful as old age to-night.
I regret little, I would change still less.
Since there my past life lies, why alter it?
The very wrong to Francis!—it is true
I took his coin, was tempted and complied,
And built this house and sinned, and all is said.   250
My father and my mother died of want.
Well, had I riches of my own? you see
How one gets rich! Let each one bear his lot.
They were born poor, lived poor, and poor they died:
And I have laboured somewhat in my time
And not been paid profusely. Some good son
Paint my two hundred pictures—let him try!
No doubt, there's something strikes a balance. Yes,
You loved me quite enough, it seems to-night.
This must suffice me here. What would one have?   260
In heaven, perhaps, new chances, one more chance—
Four great walls in the New Jerusalem,
Meted on each side by the angel's reed,°
For Leonard, Rafael, Agnolo and me
To cover—the three first without a wife,
While I have mine! So—still they overcome
Because there's still Lucrezia,—as I choose.

Again the Cousin's whistle! Go, my Love.

In a Year

I

Never any more,
    While I live,
Need I hope to see his face
    As before.
Once his love grown chill,
    Mine may strive:
Bitterly we re-embrace,
    Single still.

II

Was it something said,   10
  Something done,
Vexed him? was it touch of hand,
  Turn of head?
Strange! that very way
  Love begun:
I as little understand
  Love's decay.

III

When I sewed or drew,
  I recall
How he looked as if I sung,   20
  —Sweetly too.
If I spoke a word,
  First of all
Up his cheek the colour sprung,
  Then he heard.

IV

Sitting by my side,
  At my feet,
So he breathed but air I breathed,
  Satisfied!
I, too, at love's brim   30
  Touched the sweet:
I would die if death bequeathed
  Sweet to him.

V

'Speak, I love thee best!'
  He exclaimed:
'Let thy love my own foretell!'
  I confessed:
'Clasp my heart on thine
  Now unblamed,
Since upon thy soul as well   40
  Hangeth mine!'

VI

Was it wrong to own,
    Being truth?
Why should all the giving prove
    His alone?
I had wealth and ease,
    Beauty, youth:
Since my lover gave me love,
    I gave these.

VII

That was all I meant,   50
    —To be just,
And the passion I had raised,
    To content.
Since he chose to change
    Gold for dust,
If I gave him what he praised
    Was it strange?

VIII

Would he loved me yet,
    On and on,
While I found some way undreamed   60
    —Paid my debt!
Gave more life and more,
    Till, all gone,
He should smile 'She never seemed
    Mine before.

IX

'What, she felt the while,
    Must I think?
Love's so different with us men!'
    He should smile:
'Dying for my sake—   70
    White and pink!
Can't we touch these bubbles then
    But they break?'

X

Dear, the pang is brief,
   Do thy part,
Have thy pleasure! How perplexed
   Grows belief!
Well, this cold clay clod
   Was man's heart:
Crumble it, and what comes next?   80
   Is it God?

Saul

I

Said Abner, 'At last thou art come! Ere I tell, ere thou speak,°
Kiss my cheek, wish me well!' Then I wished it, and did kiss
   his cheek.
And he, 'Since the King, O my friend, for thy countenance
   sent,
Neither drunken nor eaten have we; nor until from his tent
Thou return with the joyful assurance the King liveth yet,
Shall our lip with the honey be bright, with the water be wet.
For out of the black mid-tent's silence, a space of three days,
Not a sound hath escaped to thy servants, of prayer nor of
   praise,
To betoken that Saul and the Spirit have ended their strife,°
And that, faint in his triumph, the monarch sinks back upon   10
   life.

II

'Yet now my heart leaps, O beloved! God's child with his dew
On thy gracious gold hair, and those lilies still living and blue
Just broken to twine round thy harp-strings, as if no wild heat
Were now raging to torture the desert!'

III

                 Then I, as was meet,
Knelt down to the God of my fathers, and rose on my feet,

And ran o'er the sand burnt to powder. The tent was unlooped;
I pulled up the spear that obstructed, and under I stooped;
Hands and knees on the slippery grass-patch, all withered and
    gone,
That extends to the second enclosure, I groped my way on
Till I felt where the foldskirts fly open. Then once more I
    prayed,   20
And opened the foldskirts and entered, and was not afraid
But spoke, 'Here is David, thy servant!' And no voice replied.
At the first I saw nought but the blackness; but soon I descried
A something more black than the blackness—the vast, the
    upright
Main prop which sustains the pavilion: and slow into sight
Grew a figure against it, gigantic and blackest of all.
Then a sunbeam, that burst thro' the tent-roof, showed Saul.

IV

He stood as erect as that tent-prop, both arms stretched out wide
On the great cross-support in the centre, that goes to each side;
He relaxed not a muscle, but hung there as, caught in his pangs   30
And waiting his change, the king-serpent all heavily hangs,
Far away from his kind, in the pine, till deliverance come
With the spring-time,—so agonized Saul, drear and stark, blind
    and dumb.

V

Then I turned my harp,—took off the lilies we twine round its
    chords
Lest they snap 'neath the stress of the noontide—those
    sunbeams like swords!
And I first played the tune all our sheep know, as, one after
    one,
So docile they come to the pen-door till folding be done.
They are white and untorn by the bushes, for lo, they have
    fed
Where the long grasses stifle the water within the stream's bed;
And now one after one seeks its lodging, as star follows star   40
Into eve and the blue far above us,—so blue and so far!

VI

—Then the tune, for which quails on the cornland will each
    leave his mate
To fly after the player; then, what makes the crickets elate
Till for boldness they fight one another: and then, what has weight
To set the quick jerboa a-musing outside his sand house—°
There are none such as he for a wonder, half bird and half mouse!
God made all the creatures and gave them our love and our fear,
To give sign, we and they are his children, one family here.

VII

Then I played the help-tune of our reapers, their wine-song,
    when hand
Grasps at hand, eye lights eye in good friendship, and great
    hearts expand
                                                  50
And grow one in the sense of this world's life.—And then, the
    last song
When the dead man is praised on his journey—'Bear, bear him
    along
With his few faults shut up like dead flowerets! Are balm-seeds
    not here°
To console us? The land has none left such as he on the bier.
Oh, would we might keep thee, my brother!'—And then, the
    glad chaunt
Of the marriage,—first go the young maidens, next, she whom
    we vaunt
As the beauty, the pride of our dwelling.—And then, the great
    march
Wherein man runs to man to assist him and buttress an arch°
Nought can break; who shall harm them, our friends?—
    Then, the chorus intoned
As the Levites go up to the altar in glory enthroned.°   60
But I stopped here: for here in the darkness Saul groaned.

VIII

And I paused, held my breath in such silence, and listened apart;
And the tent shook, for mighty Saul shuddered: and sparkles
    'gan dart
From the jewels that woke in his turban, at once with a start,

All its lordly male-sapphires, and rubies courageous at heart.
So the head: but the body still moved not, still hung there erect.
And I bent once again to my playing, pursued it unchecked,
As I sang,—

IX

'Oh, our manhood's prime vigour! No spirit feels waste,
Not a muscle is stopped in its playing nor sinew unbraced.
Oh, the wild joys of living! the leaping from rock up to rock,   70
The strong rending of boughs from the fir-tree, the cool silver
     shock
Of the plunge in a pool's living water, the hunt of the bear,
And the sultriness showing the lion is couched in his lair.
And the meal, the rich dates yellowed over with gold dust
     divine,
And the locust-flesh steeped in the pitcher, the full draught of
     wine,
And the sleep in the dried river-channel where bulrushes tell
That the water was wont to go warbling so softly and well.
How good is man's life, the mere living! how fit to employ
All the heart and the soul and the senses for ever in joy!
Hast thou loved the white locks of thy father, whose sword thou
     didst guard   80
When he trusted thee forth with the armies, for glorious
     reward?
Didst thou see the thin hands of thy mother, held up as men
     sung
The low song of the nearly-departed, and hear her faint tongue
Joining in while it could to the witness, "Let one more attest,
I have lived, seen God's hand thro' a lifetime, and all was for
     best"?
Then they sung thro' their tears in strong triumph, not much,
     but the rest.
And thy brothers, the help and the contest, the working whence
     grew
Such result as, from seething grape-bundles, the spirit strained
     true:
And the friends of thy boyhood—that boyhood of wonder and
     hope,
Present promise and wealth of the future beyond the eye's   90
     scope,—

Till lo, thou art grown to a monarch; a people is thine;
And all gifts, which the world offers singly, on one head
    combine!
On one head, all the beauty and strength, love and rage (like the
    throe
That, a-work in the rock, helps its labour and lets the gold go)
High ambition and deeds which surpass it, fame crowning
    them,— all
Brought to blaze on the head of one creature—King Saul!'

                    X

And lo, with that leap of my spirit,—heart, hand, harp and
    voice,
Each lifting Saul's name out of sorrow, each bidding rejoice
Saul's fame in the light it was made for—as when, dare I say,
The Lord's army, in rapture of service, strains through its array,   100
And upsoareth the cherubim-chariot—'Saul!' cried I, and
    stopped,°
And waited the thing that should follow. Then Saul, who hung
    propped
By the tent's cross-support in the centre, was struck by his
    name.
Have ye seen when Spring's arrowy summons goes right to the
    aim,
And some mountain, the last to withstand her, that held (he
    alone,
While the vale laughed in freedom and flowers) on a broad bust
    of stone
A year's snow bound about for a breastplate,—leaves grasp of
    the sheet?
Fold on fold all at once it crowds thunderously down to his feet,
And there fronts you, stark, black, but alive yet, your mountain
    of old,
With his rents, the successive bequeathings of ages untold—   110
Yea, each harm got in fighting your battles, each furrow and scar
Of his head thrust 'twixt you and the tempest—all hail, there
    they are!
—Now again to be softened with verdure, again hold the nest
Of the dove, tempt the goat and its young to the green on his
    crest

For their food in the ardours of summer. One long shudder thrilled
All the tent till the very air tingled, then sank and was stilled
At the King's self left standing before me, released and aware.
What was gone, what remained? All to traverse, 'twixt hope and despair;
Death was past, life not come: so he waited. Awhile his right hand
Held the brow, helped the eyes left too vacant forthwith to remand   120
To their place what new objects should enter: 'twas Saul as before.
I looked up and dared gaze at those eyes, nor was hurt any more
Than by slow pallid sunsets in autumn, ye watch from the shore,
At their sad level gaze o'er the ocean—a sun's slow decline
Over hills which, resolved in stern silence, o'erlap and entwine
Base with base to knit strength more intensely: so, arm folded arm
O'er the chest whose slow heavings subsided.

XI

                What spell or what charm,
(For, awhile there was trouble within me) what next should I urge
To sustain him where song had restored him?—Song filled to the verge
His cup with the wine of this life, pressing all that it yields   130
Of mere fruitage, the strength and the beauty: beyond, on what fields,
Glean a vintage more potent and perfect to brighten the eye
And bring blood to the lip, and commend them the cup they put by?
He saith, 'It is good;' still he drinks not: he lets me praise life,
Gives assent, yet would die for his own part.

XII

                Then fancies grew rife
Which had come long ago on the pasture, when round me the sheep
Fed in silence—above, the one eagle wheeled slow as in sleep;

And I lay in my hollow and mused on the world that might lie
'Neath his ken, though I saw but the strip 'twixt the hill and the
    sky:
And I laughed—'Since my days are ordained to be passed with
    my flocks,
Let me people at least, with my fancies, the plains and the   140
    rocks,
Dream the life I am never to mix with, and image the show
Of mankind as they live in those fashions I hardly shall know!
Schemes of life, its best rules and right uses, the courage that
    gains,
And the prudence that keeps what men strive for.'
    And now these old trains
Of vague thought came again; I grew surer; so, once more the
    string
Of my harp made response to my spirit, as thus—

XIII

                    'Yea, my King,'
I began—'thou dost well in rejecting mere comforts that spring
From the mere mortal life held in common by man and by
    brute:
In our flesh grows the branch of this life, in our soul it bears
    fruit.
Thou hast marked the slow rise of the tree,—how its stem   150
    trembled first
Till it passed the kid's lip, the stag's antler; then safely outburst
The fan-branches all round; and thou mindest when these too,
    in turn
Broke a-bloom and the palm-tree seemed perfect: yet more was
    to learn,
E'en the good that comes in with the palm-fruit. Our dates shall
    we slight,
When their juice brings a cure for all sorrow? or care for the
    plight
Of the palm's self whose slow growth produced them? Not so!
    stem and branch
Shall decay, nor be known in their place, while the palm-wine
    shall staunch
Every wound of man's spirit in winter. I pour thee such wine.

Leave the flesh to the fate it was fit for! the spirit be thine!   160
By the spirit, when age shall o'ercome thee, thou still shalt enjoy
More indeed, than at first when inconscious, the life of a boy.
Crush that life, and behold its wine running! Each deed thou
    hast done
Dies, revives, goes to work in the world; until e'en as the sun
Looking down on the earth, though clouds spoil him, though
    tempests efface,
Can find nothing his own deed produced not, must everywhere
    trace
The results of his past summer-prime,—so, each ray of thy will,
Every flash of thy passion and prowess, long over, shall thrill
Thy whole people, the countless, with ardour, till they too give
    forth
A like cheer to their sons, who in turn, fill the South and the
    North   170
With the radiance thy deed was the germ of. Carouse in the
    past!
But the license of age has its limit; thou diest at last:
As the lion when age dims his eyeball, the rose at her height
So with man—so his power and his beauty for ever take flight.
No! Again a long draught of my soul-wine! Look forth o'er the
    years!
Thou hast done now with eyes for the actual; begin with the
    seer's!
Is Saul dead? In the depth of the vale make his tomb—bid arise
A grey mountain of marble heaped four-square, till, built to the
    skies,
Let it mark where the great First King slumbers: whose fame
    would ye know?°   ·
Up above see the rock's naked face, where the record shall go   180
In great characters cut by the scribe,—Such was Saul, so he did;
With the sages directing the work, by the populace chid,—
For not half, they'll affirm, is comprised there! Which fault to
    amend,
In the grove with his kind grows the cedar, whereon they shall
    spend
(See, in tablets 'tis level before them) their praise, and record
With the gold of the graver, Saul's story,—the statesman's great
    word
Side by side with the poet's sweet comment. The river's a-wave

With smooth paper-reeds grazing each other when prophet-
    winds rave:
So the pen gives unborn generations their due and their part
In thy being! Then, first of the mighty, thank God that thou
    art!'

190

XIV

And behold while I sang ... but O Thou who didst grant me that
    day,
And before it not seldom hast granted thy help to essay,
Carry on and complete an adventure,—my shield and my sword
In that act where my soul was thy servant, thy word was my
    word,—
Still be with me, who then at the summit of human endeavour
And scaling the highest, man's thought could, gazed hopeless as
    ever
On the new stretch of heaven above me—till, mighty to save,
Just one lift of thy hand cleared that distance—God's throne
    from man's grave!
Let me tell out my tale to its ending—my voice to my heart
Which can scarce dare believe in what marvels last night I took
    part,
As this morning I gather the fragments, alone with my sheep,
And still fear lest the terrible glory evanish like sleep!
For I wake in the grey dewy covert, while Hebron up-heaves°
The dawn struggling with night on his shoulder, and Kidron
    retrieves°
Slow the damage of yesterday's sunshine.

200

XV

                      I say then,—my song
While I sang thus, assuring the monarch, and ever more strong
Made a proffer of good to console him—he slowly resumed
His old motions and habitudes kingly. The right-hand replumed
His black locks to their wonted composure, adjusted the swathes
Of his turban, and see—the huge sweat that his countenance
    bathes,
He wipes off with the robe; and he girds now his loins as of yore,
And feels slow for the armlets of price, with the clasp set before.
He is Saul, ye remember in glory,—ere error had bent

210

The broad brow from the daily communion; and still, though
    much spent
Be the life and the bearing that front you, the same, God did
    choose,
To receive what a man may waste, desecrate, never quite lose.
So sank he along by the tent-prop till, stayed by the pile
Of his armour and war-cloak and garments, he leaned there
    awhile,
And sat out my singing,—one arm round the tent-prop, to raise
His bent head, and the other hung slack—till I touched on the
    praise   220
I foresaw from all men in all time, to the man patient there;
And thus ended, the harp falling forward. Then first I was 'ware
That he sat, as I say, with my head just above his vast knees
Which were thrust out on each side around me, like oak-roots
    which please
To encircle a lamb when it slumbers. I looked up to know
If the best I could do had brought solace: he spoke not, but slow
Lifted up the hand slack at his side, till he laid it with care
Soft and grave, but in mild settled will, on my brow: thro' my
    hair
The large fingers were pushed, and he bent back my head, with
    kind power—
All my face back, intent to peruse it, as men do a flower.   230
Thus held he me there with his great eyes that scrutinized
    mine—
And oh, all my heart how it loved him! but where was the sign?
I yearned—'Could I help thee, my father, inventing a bliss,
I would add, to that life of the past, both the future and this;
I would give thee new life altogether, as good, ages hence,
As this moment,—had love but the warrant, love's heart to
    dispense!'

XVI

Then the truth came upon me. No harp more—no song more!
    outbroke—

XVII

'I have gone the whole round of creation: I saw and I spoke:
I, a work of God's hand for that purpose, received in my brain

And pronounced on the rest of his handwork—returned him
    again   240
His creation's approval or censure: I spoke as I saw:
I report, as a man may of God's work—all's love, yet all's law.
Now I lay down the judgeship he lent me. Each faculty tasked
To perceive him, has gained an abyss, where a dewdrop was
    asked.°
Have I knowledge? confounded it shrivels at Wisdom laid bare.
Have I forethought? how purblind, how blank, to the Infinite
    Care!
Do I task any faculty highest, to image success?
I but open my eyes,—and perfection, no more and no less,
In the kind I imagined, full-fronts me, and God is seen God
In the star, in the stone, in the flesh, in the soul and the clod.   250
And thus looking within and around me, I ever renew
(With that stoop of the soul which in bending upraises it too)
The submission of man's nothing-perfect to God's all-complete,
As by each new obeisance in spirit, I climb to his feet.
Yet with all this abounding experience, this deity known,
I shall dare to discover some province, some gift of my own.
There's a faculty pleasant to exercise, hard to hood-wink,
I am fain to keep still in abeyance, (I laugh as I think)
Lest, insisting to claim and parade in it, wot ye, I worst
E'en the Giver in one gift.—Behold, I could love if I durst!   260
But I sink the pretension as fearing a man may o'ertake
God's own speed in the one way of love: I abstain for love's
    sake.
—What, my soul? see thus far and no farther? when doors great
    and small,
Nine-and-ninety flew ope at our touch, should the hundredth
    appal?
In the least things have faith, yet distrust in the greatest of all?
Do I find love so full in my nature, God's ultimate gift,
That I doubt his own love can compete with it? Here, the parts
    shift?
Here, the creature surpass the Creator,—the end, what Began?
Would I fain in my impotent yearning do all for this man,
And dare doubt he alone shall not help him, who yet alone can?   270
Would it ever have entered my mind, the bare will, much less
    power,
To bestow on this Saul what I sang of, the marvellous dower

Of the life he was gifted and filled with? to make such a soul,
Such a body, and then such an earth for insphering the whole?
And doth it not enter my mind (as my warm tears attest)
These good things being given, to go on, and give one more, the
     best?
Ay, to save and redeem and restore him, maintain at the height
This perfection,—succeed with life's dayspring, death's minute
     of night?°
Interpose at the difficult minute, snatch Saul the mistake,
Saul the failure, the ruin he seems now,—and bid him awake   280
From the dream, the probation, the prelude, to find himself set
Clear and safe in new light and new life,—a new harmony yet
To be run, and continued, and ended—who knows?—or
     endure!
The man taught enough, by life's dream, of the rest to make
     sure;
By the pain-throb, triumphantly winning intensified bliss,
And the next world's reward and repose, by the struggles in
     this.

XVIII

'I believe it! 'Tis thou, God, that givest, 'tis I who receive:
In the first is the last, in thy will is my power to believe.
All's one gift: thou canst grant it moreover, as prompt to my
     prayer
As I breathe out this breath, as I open these arms to the air.   290
From thy will, stream the worlds, life and nature, thy dread
     Sabaoth:°
I will?—the mere atoms despise me! Why am I not loth
To look that, even that in the face too? Why is it I dare
Think but lightly of such impuissance? What stops my despair?
This;—'tis not what man Does which exalts him, but what man
     Would do!
See the King—I would help him but cannot, the wishes fall
     through.
Could I wrestle to raise him from sorrow, grow poor to enrich,
To fill up his life, starve my own out, I would—knowing which,
I know that my service is perfect. Oh, speak through me now!
Would I suffer for him that I love? So wouldst thou—so wilt
     thou!   300
So shall crown thee the topmost, ineffablest, uttermost crown—

And thy love fill infinitude wholly, nor leave up nor down
One spot for the creature to stand in! It is by no breath,
Turn of eye, wave of hand, that salvation joins issue with death!
As thy Love is discovered almighty, almighty be proved
Thy power, that exists with and for it, of being Beloved!
He who did most, shall bear most; the strongest shall stand the
　　most weak.
'Tis the weakness in strength, that I cry for! my flesh, that I
　　seek
In the Godhead! I seek and I find it. O Saul, it shall be
A Face like my face that receives thee; a Man like to me,　　310
Thou shalt love and be loved by, for ever: a Hand like this hand
Shall throw open the gates of new life to thee! See the Christ
　　stand!'

XIX

I know not too well how I found my way home in the night.
There were witnesses, cohorts about me, to left and to right,
Angels, powers, the unuttered, unseen, the alive, the aware:
I repressed, I got through them as hardly, as strugglingly there,
As a runner beset by the populace famished for news—
Life or death. The whole earth was awakened, hell loosed with
　　her crews;
And the stars of night beat with emotion, and tingled and shot
Out in fire the strong pain of pent knowledge: but I fainted not,　320
For the Hand still impelled me at once and supported, sup-
　　pressed
All the tumult, and quenched it with quiet, and holy behest,
Till the rapture was shut in itself, and the earth sank to rest.
Anon at the dawn, all that trouble had withered from earth—
Not so much, but I saw it die out in the day's tender birth;
In the gathered intensity brought to the grey of the hills;
In the shuddering forests' held breath; in the sudden wind-
　　thrills;
In the startled wild beasts that bore oft, each with eye sidling
　　still
Though averted with wonder and dread; in the birds stiff and
　　chill
That rose heavily, as I approached them, made stupid with awe:　330
E'en the serpent that slid away silent,—he felt the new law.

The same stared in the white humid faces upturned by the
    flowers;
The same worked in the heart of the cedar and moved the vine-
    bowers:
And the little brooks witnessing murmured, persistent and low,
With their obstinate, all but hushed voices—'E'en so, it is so!'

'De Gustibus—'

I

Your ghost will walk, you lover of trees,
    (If our loves remain)
    In an English lane,
By a cornfield-side a-flutter with poppies.
Hark, those two in the hazel coppice—
A boy and a girl, if the good fates please,
    Making love, say,—
    The happier they!
Draw yourself up from the light of the moon,°
And let them pass, as they will too soon,   10
    With the bean-flowers' boon,
    And the blackbird's tune,
    And May, and June!

II

What I love best in all the world
Is a castle, precipice-encurled,
In a gash of the wind-grieved Apennine.
Or look for me, old fellow of mine,
(If I get my head from out the mouth
O' the grave, and loose my spirit's bands,
And come again to the land of lands)—   20
In a sea-side house to the farther South,
Where the baked cicala dies of drouth,
And one sharp tree—'tis a cypress—stands,
By the many hundred years red-rusted,
Rough iron-spiked, ripe fruit-o'ercrusted,
My sentinel to guard the sands

To the water's edge. For, what expands
Before the house, but the great opaque
Blue breadth of sea without a break?
While, in the house, for ever crumbles   30
Some fragment of the frescoed walls,
From blisters where a scorpion sprawls.
A girl bare-footed brings, and tumbles
Down on the pavement, green-flesh melons,
And says there's news to-day—the king°
Was shot at, touched in the liver-wing,
Goes with his Bourbon arm in a sling:
—She hopes they have not caught the felons.
Italy, my Italy!
Queen Mary's saying serves for me—   40
    (When fortune's malice
      Lost her—Calais)—
Open my heart and you will see
Graved inside of it, 'Italy.'°
Such lovers old are I and she:
So it always was, so shall ever be!

Women and Roses

I

I dream of a red-rose tree.
And which of its roses three
Is the dearest rose to me?

II

Round and round, like a dance of snow
In a dazzling drift, as its guardians, go
Floating the women faded for ages,
Sculptured in stone, on the poet's pages.
Then follow women fresh and gay,
Living and loving and loved to-day.
Last, in the rear, flee the multitude of maidens,   10
Beauties yet unborn. And all, to one cadence,
They circle their rose on my rose tree.

III

Dear rose, thy term is reached,
Thy leaf hangs loose and bleached:
Bees pass it unimpeached.°

IV

Stay then, stoop, since I cannot climb,
You, great shapes of the antique time!
How shall I fix you, fire you, freeze you,
Break my heart at your feet to please you?
Oh, to possess and be possessed!   20
Hearts that beat 'neath each pallid breast!
Once but of love, the poesy, the passion,
Drink but once and die!—In vain, the same fashion,
They circle their rose on my rose tree.

V

Dear rose, thy joy's undimmed,
Thy cup is ruby-rimmed,
Thy cup's heart nectar-brimmed.

VI

Deep, as drops from a statue's plinth
The bee sucked in by the hyacinth,
So will I bury me while burning,   30
Quench like him at a plunge my yearning,
Eyes in your eyes, lips on your lips!
Fold me fast where the cincture slips,°
Prison all my soul in eternities of pleasure,
Girdle me for once! But no—the old measure,
They circle their rose on my rose tree.

VII

Dear rose without a thorn,
Thy bud's the babe unborn:
First streak of a new morn.

VIII

Wings, lend wings for the cold, the clear!   40
What is far conquers what is near.

Roses will bloom nor want beholders,
Sprung from the dust where our flesh moulders.
What shall arrive with the cycle's change?
A novel grace and a beauty strange.
I will make an Eve, be the artist that began her,
Shaped her to his mind!—Alas! in like manner
They circle their rose on my rose tree.

Holy-Cross Day

On which the Jews were forced to attend an annual Christian sermon in Rome

['Now was come about Holy-Cross Day, and now must my lord preach his first sermon to the Jews: as it was of old cared for in the merciful bowels of the Church, that, so to speak, a crumb at least from her conspicuous table here in Rome should be, though but once yearly, cast to the famishing dogs, under-trampled and bespitten-upon beneath the feet of the guests. And a moving sight in truth, this, of so many of the besotted blind restif and ready-to-perish Hebrews! now maternally brought—nay (for He saith, "Compel them to come in") haled, as it were, by the head and hair, and against their obstinate hearts, to partake of the heavenly grace. What awakening, what striving with tears, what working of a yeasty conscience! Nor was my lord wanting to himself on so apt an occasion; witness the abundance of conversions which did incontinently reward him: though not to my lord be altogether the glory.'—*Diary by the Bishop's Secretary*, 1600.]

What the Jews really said, on thus being driven to church, was rather to this effect:—

I

Fee, faw, fum! bubble and squeak!°
Blessedest Thursday's the fat of the week.
Rumble and tumble, sleek and rough,
Stinking and savoury, smug and gruff,
Take the church-road, for the bell's due chime
Gives us the summons—'tis sermon-time!

II

Boh, here's Barnabas! Job, that's you?
Up stumps Solomon—bustling too?

Shame, man! greedy beyond your years
To handsel the bishop's shaving-shears?°   10
Fair play's a jewel! Leave friends in the lurch?
Stand on a line ere you start for the church!

III

Higgledy piggledy, packed we lie,
Rats in a hamper, swine in a stye,
Wasps in a bottle, frogs in a sieve,
Worms in a carcase, fleas in a sleeve.
Hist! square shoulders, settle your thumbs
And buzz for the bishop—here he comes.

IV

Bow, wow, wow—a bone for the dog!
I liken his Grace to an acorned hog.°   20
What, a boy at his side, with the bloom of a lass,
To help and handle my lord's hour-glass!
Didst ever behold so lithe a chine?°
His cheek hath laps like a fresh-singed swine.

V

Aaron's asleep—shove hip to haunch,
Or somebody deal him a dig in the paunch!
Look at the purse with the tassel and knob,
And the gown with the angel and thingumbob!
What's he at, quotha? reading his text!°
Now you've his curtsey—and what comes next.   30

VI

See to our converts—you doomed black dozen—
No stealing away—nor cog nor cozen!°
You five, that were thieves, deserve it fairly;
You seven, that were beggars, will live less sparely;
You took your turn and dipped in the hat,
Got fortune—and fortune gets you; mind that!

VII

Give your first groan—compunction's at work;
And soft! from a Jew you mount to a Turk.°

Lo, Micah,—the selfsame beard on chin
He was four times already converted in!
Here's a knife, clip quick—it's a sign of grace—
Or he ruins us all with his hanging-face.

VIII

Whom now is the bishop a-leering at?
I know a point where his text falls pat.
I'll tell him to-morrow, a word just now
Went to my heart and made me vow
I meddle no more with the worst of trades—
Let somebody else pay his serenades.°

IX

Groan all together now, whee—hee—hee!
It's a-work, it's a-work, ah, woe is me!
It began, when a herd of us, picked and placed,
Were spurred through the Corso, stripped to the waist;°
Jew brutes, with sweat and blood well spent
To usher in worthily Christian Lent.

X

It grew, when the hangman entered our bounds,
Yelled, pricked us out to his church like hounds:
It got to a pitch, when the hand indeed
Which gutted my purse would throttle my creed:
And it overflows when, to even the odd,
Men I helped to their sins help me to their God.

XI

But now, while the scapegoats leave our flock,
And the rest sit silent and count the clock,
Since forced to muse the appointed time
On these precious facts and truths sublime,—
Let us fitly employ it, under our breath,
In saying Ben Ezra's Song of Death.°

XII

For Rabbi Ben Ezra, the night he died,
Called sons and sons' sons to his side,

40

50

60

And spoke, 'This world has been harsh and strange;
Something is wrong: there needeth a change. 70
But what, or where? at the last or first?
In one point only we sinned, at worst.

XIII

'The Lord will have mercy on Jacob yet,
And again in his border see Israel set.
When Judah beholds Jerusalem,
The stranger-seed shall be joined to them:
To Jacob's House shall the Gentiles cleave.
So the Prophet saith and his sons believe.

XIV

'Ay, the children of the chosen race
Shall carry and bring them to their place: 80
In the land of the Lord shall lead the same,
Bondsmen and handmaids. Who shall blame,
When the slaves enslave, the oppressed ones o'er
The oppressor triumph for evermore?

XV

'God spoke, and gave us the word to keep,
Bade never fold the hands nor sleep
'Mid a faithless world,—at watch and ward,
Till Christ at the end relieve our guard.
By His servant Moses the watch was set:
Though near upon cock-crow, we keep it yet. 90

XVI

'Thou! if thou wast He, who at mid-watch came,
By the starlight, naming a dubious name!°
And if, too heavy with sleep—too rash
With fear—O Thou, if that martyr-gash
Fell on Thee coming to take thine own,
And we gave the Cross, when we owed the Throne—

XVII

'Thou art the Judge. We are bruised thus.
But, the Judgment over, join sides with us!

Thine too is the cause! and not more thine
Than ours, is the work of these dogs and swine,   100
Whose life laughs through and spits at their creed!
Who maintain Thee in word, and defy Thee in deed!

XVIII

'We withstood Christ then? Be mindful how
At least we withstand Barabbas now!
Was our outrage sore? But the worst we spared,
To have called these—Christians, had we dared!
Let defiance to them pay mistrust of Thee,
And Rome make amends for Calvary!

XIX

'By the torture, prolonged from age to age,
By the infamy, Israel's heritage,   110
By the Ghetto's plague, by the garb's disgrace,
By the badge of shame, by the felon's place,
By the branding-tool, the bloody whip,
And the summons to Christian fellowship,—

XX

'We boast our proof that at least the Jew
Would wrest Christ's name from the Devil's crew.
Thy face took never so deep a shade
But we fought them in it, God our aid!
A trophy to bear, as we march, thy band,
South, East, and on to the Pleasant Land!'   120

[*Pope Gregory XVI. abolished this bad business of
the Sermon.*—R. B.]

Cleon

'As certain also of your own poets have said'—

Cleon the poet (from the sprinkled isles,°
Lily on lily, that o'erlace the sea,
And laugh their pride when the light wave lisps 'Greece')—
To Protus in his Tyranny: much health!°

They give thy letter to me, even now:
I read and seem as if I heard thee speak.
The master of thy galley still unlades
Gift after gift; they block my court at last
And pile themselves along its portico
Royal with sunset, like a thought of thee: 10
And one white she-slave from the group dispersed
Of black and white slaves (like the chequer-work
Pavement, at once my nation's work and gift,
Now covered with this settle-down of doves),
One lyric woman, in her crocus vest°
Woven of sea-wools, with her two white hands
Commends to me the strainer and the cup
Thy lip hath bettered ere it blesses mine.

Well-counselled, king, in thy munificence!
For so shall men remark, in such an act   20
Of love for him whose song gives life its joy,
Thy recognition of the use of life;
Nor call thy spirit barely adequate
To help on life in straight ways, broad enough
For vulgar souls, by ruling and the rest.
Thou, in the daily building of thy tower,—
Whether in fierce and sudden spasms of toil,
Or through dim lulls of unapparent growth,
Or when the general work 'mid good acclaim
Climbed with the eye to cheer the architect,—   30
Didst ne'er engage in work for mere work's sake—
Hadst ever in thy heart the luring hope
Of some eventual rest a-top of it,
Whence, all the tumult of the building hushed,
Thou first of men mightst look out to the East:
The vulgar saw thy tower, thou sawest the sun.
For this, I promise on thy festival
To pour libation, looking o'er the sea,
Making this slave narrate thy fortunes, speak
Thy great words, and describe thy royal face—   40
Wishing thee wholly where Zeus lives the most,
Within the eventual element of calm.

Thy letter's first requirement meets me here.°
It is as thou hast heard: in one short life

I, Cleon, have effected all those things
Thou wonderingly dost enumerate.
That epos on thy hundred plates of gold°
Is mine,—and also mine the little chant,
So sure to rise from every fishing-bark
When, lights at prow, the seamen haul their net.   50
The image of the sun-god on the phare,°
Men turn from the sun's self to see, is mine;
The Pœcile, o'er-storied its whole length,°
As thou didst hear, with painting, is mine too.
I know the true proportions of a man
And woman also, not observed before;
And I have written three books on the soul,
Proving absurd all written hitherto,
And putting us to ignorance again.
For music,—why, I have combined the moods,°   60
Inventing one. In brief, all arts are mine;
Thus much the people know and recognize,
Throughout our seventeen islands. Marvel not.
We of these latter days, with greater mind
Than our forerunners, since more composite,
Look not so great, beside their simple way,
To a judge who only sees one way at once,
One mind-point and no other at a time,—
Compares the small part of a man of us
With some whole man of the heroic age,
Great in his way—not ours, nor meant for ours.   70
And ours is greater, had we skill to know:
For, what we call this life of men on earth,
This sequence of the soul's achievements here
Being, as I find much reason to conceive,
Intended to be viewed eventually
As a great whole, not analyzed to parts,
But each part having reference to all,—
How shall a certain part, pronounced complete,
Endure effacement by another part?
Was the thing done?—then, what's to do again?   80
See, in the chequered pavement opposite,
Suppose the artist made a perfect rhomb,°
And next a lozenge, then a trapezoid—°
He did not overlay them, superimpose

The new upon the old and blot it out,
But laid them on a level in his work,
Making at last a picture; there it lies.
So, first the perfect separate forms were made,
The portions of mankind; and after, so,　　　　　　90
Occurred the combination of the same.
For where had been a progress, otherwise?
Mankind, made up of all the single men,—
In such a synthesis the labour ends.
Now mark me! those divine men of old time
Have reached, thou sayest well, each at one point
The outside verge that rounds our faculty;
And where they reached, who can do more than reach?
It takes but little water just to touch
At some one point the inside of a sphere,　　　　　　100
And, as we turn the sphere, touch all the rest
In due succession: but the finer air
Which not so palpably nor obviously,
Though no less universally, can touch
The whole circumference of that emptied sphere,
Fills it more fully than the water did;
Holds thrice the weight of water in itself
Resolved into a subtler element.
And yet the vulgar call the sphere first full
Up to the visible height—and after, void;　　　　　　110
Not knowing air's more hidden properties.
And thus our soul, misknown, cries out to Zeus
To vindicate his purpose in our life:
Why stay we on the earth unless to grow?
Long since, I imaged, wrote the fiction out,°
That he or other god descended here
And, once for all, showed simultaneously
What, in its nature, never can be shown,
Piecemeal or in succession;—showed, I say,
The worth both absolute and relative　　　　　　120
Of all his children from the birth of time,
His instruments for all appointed work.
I now go on to image,—might we hear
The judgment which should give the due to each,
Show where the labour lay and where the ease,
And prove Zeus' self, the latent everywhere!

This is a dream:—but no dream, let us hope,
That years and days, the summers and the springs,
Follow each other with unwaning powers.
The grapes which dye thy wine are richer far,   130
Through culture, than the wild wealth of the rock;
The suave plum than the savage-tasted drupe;°
The pastured honey-bee drops choicer sweet;
The flowers turn double, and the leaves turn flowers;
That young and tender crescent-moon, thy slave,
Sleeping above her robe as buoyed by clouds,
Refines upon the women of my youth.
What, and the soul alone deteriorates?
I have not chanted verse like Homer, no—°
Nor swept string like Terpander, no—nor carved°   140
And painted men like Phidias and his friend:°
I am not great as they are, point by point.
But I have entered into sympathy
With these four, running these into one soul,
Who, separate, ignored each other's art.
Say, is it nothing that I know them all?
The wild flower was the larger; I have dashed
Rose-blood upon its petals, pricked its cup's
Honey with wine, and driven its seed to fruit,
And show a better flower if not so large: 150
I stand myself. Refer this to the gods
Whose gift alone it is! which, shall I dare
(All pride apart) upon the absurd pretext
That such a gift by chance lay in my hand,
Discourse of lightly or depreciate?
It might have fallen to another's hand: what then?
I pass too surely: let at least truth stay!

    And next, of what thou followest on to ask.
This being with me as I declare, O king,
My works, in all these varicoloured kinds,   160
So done by me, accepted so by men—
Thou askest, if (my soul thus in men's hearts)
I must not be accounted to attain
The very crown and proper end of life?
Inquiring thence how, now life closeth up,
I face death with success in my right hand:

Whether I fear death less than dost thyself
The fortunate of men? 'For' (writest thou)
'Thou leavest much behind, while I leave nought.
Thy life stays in the poems men shall sing,   170
The pictures men shall study; while my life,
Complete and whole now in its power and joy,
Dies altogether with my brain and arm,
Is lost indeed; since, what survives myself?
The brazen statue to o'erlook my grave,
Set on the promontory which I named.
And that—some supple courtier of my heir
Shall use its robed and sceptred arm, perhaps,
To fix the rope to, which best drags it down.
I go then: triumph thou, who dost not go!'   180

    Nay, thou art worthy of hearing my whole mind.
Is this apparent, when thou turn'st to muse
Upon the scheme of earth and man in chief,
That admiration grows as knowledge grows?
That imperfection means perfection hid,
Reserved in part, to grace the after-time?
If, in the morning of philosophy,
Ere aught had been recorded, nay perceived,
Thou, with the light now in thee, couldst have looked
On all earth's tenantry, from worm to bird,   190
Ere man, her last, appeared upon the stage—
Thou wouldst have seen them perfect, and deduced
The perfectness of others yet unseen.
Conceding which,—had Zeus then questioned thee
'Shall I go on a step, improve on this,
Do more for visible creatures than is done?'
Thou wouldst have answered, 'Ay, by making each
Grow conscious in himself—by that alone.
All's perfect else: the shell sucks fast the rock,
The fish strikes through the sea, the snake both swims   200
And slides, forth range the beasts, the birds take flight,
Till life's mechanics can no further go—
And all this joy in natural life is put
Like fire from off thy finger into each,
So exquisitely perfect is the same.
But 'tis pure fire, and they mere matter are;

It has them, not they it: and so I choose
For man, thy last premeditated work
(If I might add a glory to the scheme)
That a third thing should stand apart from both,   210
A quality arise within his soul,
Which, intro-active, made to supervise
And feel the force it has, may view itself,
And so be happy.' Man might live at first
The animal life: but is there nothing more?
In due time, let him critically learn
How he lives; and, the more he gets to know
Of his own life's adaptabilities,
The more joy-giving will his life become.
Thus man, who hath this quality, is best.   220

        But thou, king, hadst more reasonably said:
'Let progress end at once,—man make no step
Beyond the natural man, the better beast,
Using his senses, not the sense of sense.'
In man there's failure, only since he left
The lower and inconscious forms of life.
We called it an advance, the rendering plain
Man's spirit might grow conscious of man's life,
And, by new lore so added to the old,
Take each step higher over the brute's head.   230
This grew the only life, the pleasure-house,
Watch-tower and treasure-fortress of the soul,
Which whole surrounding flats of natural life
Seemed only fit to yield subsistence to;
A tower that crowns a country. But alas,
The soul now climbs it just to perish there!
For thence we have discovered ('tis no dream—
We know this, which we had not else perceived)
That there's a world of capability
For joy, spread round about us, meant for us,   240
Inviting us; and still the soul craves all,
And still the flesh replies, 'Take no jot more
Than ere thou clombst the tower to look abroad!
Nay, so much less as that fatigue has brought
Deduction to it.' We struggle, fain to enlarge
Our bounded physical recipiency,

Increase our power, supply fresh oil to life,
Repair the waste of age and sickness: no,
It skills not! life's inadequate to joy,°
As the soul sees joy, tempting life to take.   250
They praise a fountain in my garden here
Wherein a Naiad sends the water-bow°
Thin from her tube; she smiles to see it rise.
What if I told her, it is just a thread
From that great river which the hills shut up,
And mock her with my leave to take the same?
The artificer has given her one small tube
Past power to widen or exchange—what boots
To know she might spout oceans if she could?
She cannot lift beyond her first thin thread: 260
And so a man can use but a man's joy
While he sees God's. Is it for Zeus to boast,
'See, man, how happy I live, and despair—
That I may be still happier—for thy use!'
If this were so, we could not thank our lord,
As hearts beat on to doing; 'tis not so—
Malice it is not. Is it carelessness?
Still, no. If care—where is the sign? I ask,
And get no answer, and agree in sum,
O king, with thy profound discouragement,   270
Who seest the wider but to sigh the more.
Most progress is most failure: thou sayest well.

    The last point now:—thou dost except a case—
Holding joy not impossible to one
With artist-gifts—to such a man as I
Who leave behind me living works indeed;
For, such a poem, such a painting lives.°
What? dost thou verily trip upon a word,
Confound the accurate view of what joy is
(Caught somewhat clearer by my eyes than thine)   280
With feeling joy? confound the knowing how
And showing how to live (my faculty)
With actually living?—Otherwise
Where is the artist's vantage o'er the king?
Because in my great epos I display
How divers men young, strong, fair, wise, can act—

Is this as though I acted? if I paint,
Carve the young Phœbus, am I therefore young?°
Methinks I'm older that I bowed myself
The many years of pain that taught me art!   290
Indeed, to know is something, and to prove
How all this beauty might be enjoyed, is more:
But, knowing nought, to enjoy is something too.
Yon rower, with the moulded muscles there,
Lowering the sail, is nearer it than I.
I can write love-odes: thy fair slave's an ode.
I get to sing of love, when grown too grey
For being beloved: she turns to that young man,
The muscles all a-ripple on his back.
I know the joy of kingship: well, thou art king!   300

      'But,' sayest thou—(and I marvel, I repeat
To find thee trip on such a mere word) 'what
Thou writest, paintest, stays; that does not die:
Sappho survives, because we sing her songs,°
And Æschylus, because we read his plays!'°
Why, if they live still, let them come and take
Thy slave in my despite, drink from thy cup,
Speak in my place. Thou diest while I survive?
Say rather that my fate is deadlier still,
In this, that every day my sense of joy   310
Grows more acute, my soul (intensified
By power and insight) more enlarged, more keen;
While every day my hairs fall more and more,
My hand shakes, and the heavy years increase—
The horror quickening still from year to year,
The consummation coming past escape
When I shall know most, and yet least enjoy—
When all my works wherein I prove my worth,
Being present still to mock me in men's mouths,
Alive still, in the praise of such as thou,   320
I, I the feeling, thinking, acting man,
The man who loved his life so over-much,
Sleep in my urn. It is so horrible,
I dare at times imagine to my need
Some future state revealed to us by Zeus,
Unlimited in capability

For joy, as this is in desire for joy,
—To seek which, the joy-hunger forces us:
That, stung by straitness of our life, made strait
On purpose to make prized the life at large—   330
Freed by the throbbing impulse we call death,
We burst there as the worm into the fly,
Who, while a worm still, wants his wings. But no!
Zeus has not yet revealed it; and alas,
He must have done so, were it possible!

    Live long and happy, and in that thought die:
Glad for what was! Farewell. And for the rest,°
I cannot tell thy messenger aright
Where to deliver what he bears of thine
To one called Paulus; we have heard his fame   340
Indeed, if Christus be not one with him—°
I know not, nor am troubled much to know.
Thou canst not think a mere barbarian Jew
As Paulus proves to be, one circumcized,
Hath access to a secret shut from us?
Thou wrongest our philosophy, O king,
In stooping to inquire of such an one,
As if his answer could impose at all!
He writeth, doth he? well, and he may write.
Oh, the Jew findeth scholars! certain slaves   350
Who touched on this same isle, preached him and Christ;
And (as I gathered from a bystander)
Their doctrine could be held by no sane man.

Popularity

I

    Stand still, true poet that you are!
      I know you; let me try and draw you.
    Some night you'll fail us: when afar
      You rise, remember one man saw you,
    Knew you, and named a star!

II

My star, God's glow-worm! Why extend
   That loving hand of his which leads you,
Yet locks you safe from end to end
   Of this dark world, unless he needs you,
Just saves your light to spend?   10

III

His clenched hand shall unclose at last,
   I know, and let out all the beauty:
My poet holds the future fast,
   Accepts the coming ages' duty,
Their present for this past.

IV

That day, the earth's feast-master's brow
   Shall clear, to God the chalice raising;
'Others give best at first, but thou
   Forever set'st our table praising,
Keep'st the good wine till now!'°   20

V

Meantime, I'll draw you as you stand,
   With few or none to watch and wonder:
I'll say—a fisher, on the sand
   By Tyre the old, with ocean-plunder,°
A netful, brought to land.

VI

Who has not heard how Tyrian shells
   Enclosed the blue, that dye of dyes
Whereof one drop worked miracles,
   And coloured like Astarte's eyes°
Raw silk the merchant sells?   30

VII

And each bystander of them all
   Could criticize, and quote tradition

How depths of blue sublimed some pall°
    —To get which, pricked a king's ambition;
Worth sceptre, crown and ball.

VIII

Yet there's the dye, in that rough mesh,
    The sea has only just o'erwhispered!
Live whelks, each lip's beard dripping fresh,
    As if they still the water's lisp heard
Through foam the rock-weeds thresh.   40

IX

Enough to furnish Solomon
    Such hangings for his cedar-house,°
That, when gold-robed he took the throne
    In that abyss of blue, the Spouse
Might swear his presence shone

X

Most like the centre-spike of gold
    Which burns deep in the blue-bell's womb,
What time, with ardours manifold,
    The bee goes singing to her groom,
Drunken and overbold.   50

XI

Mere conchs! not fit for warp or woof!
    Till cunning come to pound and squeeze
And clarify,—refine to proof°
    The liquor filtered by degrees,
While the world stands aloof.

XII

And there's the extract, flasked and fine,
    And priced and saleable at last!
And Hobbs, Nobbs, Stokes and Nokes combine
    To paint the future from the past,
Put blue into their line.   60

XIII

Hobbs hints blue,—straight he turtle eats:
    Nobbs prints blue,—claret crowns his cup:
Nokes outdares Stokes in azure feats,—
    Both gorge. Who fished the murex up?
What porridge had John Keats?°

Two in the Campagna

I

I wonder do you feel to-day
    As I have felt since, hand in hand,
We sat down on the grass, to stray
    In spirit better through the land,
This morn of Rome and May?

II

For me, I touched a thought, I know,
    Has tantalized me many times,
(Like turns of thread the spiders throw
    Mocking across our path) for rhymes
To catch at and let go.   10

III

Help me to hold it! First it left
    The yellowing fennel, run to seed
There, branching from the brickwork's cleft,
    Some old tomb's ruin: yonder weed
Took up the floating weft,°

IV

Where one small orange cup amassed
    Five beetles,—blind and green they grope
Among the honey-meal: and last,
    Everywhere on the grassy slope
I traced it. Hold it fast!   20

V

The champaign with its endless fleece
    Of feathery grasses everywhere!
Silence and passion, joy and peace,
    An everlasting wash of air—
Rome's ghost since her decease.

VI

Such life here, through such lengths of hours,
    Such miracles performed in play,
Such primal naked forms of flowers,
    Such letting nature have her way
While heaven looks from its towers!   30

VII

How say you? Let us, O my dove,
    Let us be unashamed of soul,
As earth lies bare to heaven above!
    How is it under our control
To love or not to love?

VIII

I would that you were all to me,
    You that are just so much, no more.
Nor yours nor mine, nor slave nor free!
    Where does the fault lie? What the core
O' the wound, since wound must be?   40

IX

I would I could adopt your will,
    See with your eyes, and set my heart
Beating by yours, and drink my fill
    At your soul's springs,—your part my part
In life, for good and ill.

X

No. I yearn upward, touch you close,
    Then stand away. I kiss your cheek,

Catch your soul's warmth,—I pluck the rose
    And love it more than tongue can speak—
Then the good minute goes. 50

XI

Already how am I so far
    Out of that minute? Must I go
Still like the thistle-ball, no bar,
    Onward, whenever light winds blow,
Fixed by no friendly star?°

XII

Just when I seemed about to learn!
    Where is the thread now? Off again!
The old trick! Only I discern—
    Infinite passion, and the pain
Of finite hearts that yearn. 60

A Grammarian's Funeral

Shortly after the Revival of Learning in Europe

Let us begin and carry up this corpse,
    Singing together.
Leave we the common crofts, the vulgar thorpes°
    Each in its tether
Sleeping safe on the bosom of the plain,
    Cared-for till cock-crow:
Look out if yonder be not day again
    Rimming the rock-row!
That's the appropriate country; there, man's thought,
    Rarer, intenser, 10
Self-gathered for an outbreak, as it ought,
    Chafes in the censer.°
Leave we the unlettered plain its herd and crop;
    Seek we sepulture°
On a tall mountain, citied to the top,
    Crowded with culture!

All the peaks soar, but one the rest excels;
    Clouds overcome it;
No! yonder sparkle is the citadel's
    Circling its summit.   20
Thither our path lies; wind we up the heights:
    Wait ye the warning?°
Our low life was the level's and the night's;
    He's for the morning.
Step to a tune, square chests, erect each head,
    'Ware the beholders!
This is our master, famous calm and dead,
    Borne on our shoulders.

Sleep, crop and herd! sleep, darkling thorpe and croft,
    Safe from the weather!   30
He, whom we convoy to his grave aloft,
    Singing together,
He was a man born with thy face and throat,
    Lyric Apollo!°
Long he lived nameless: how should spring take note
    Winter would follow?
Till lo, the little touch, and youth was gone!
    Cramped and diminished,
Moaned he, 'New measures, other feet anon!
    My dance is finished?'   40
No, that's the world's way: (keep the mountain-side,
    Make for the city!)
He knew the signal, and stepped on with pride
    Over men's pity;
Left play for work, and grappled with the world
    Bent on escaping:
'What's in the scroll,' quoth he, 'thou keepest furled?
    Show me their shaping,
'Theirs who most studied man, the bard and sage,—
    Give!'—So, he gowned him,°   50
Straight got by heart that book to its last page:
    Learned, we found him.
Yea, but we found him bald too, eyes like lead,
    Accents uncertain:
'Time to taste life,' another would have said,
    'Up with the curtain!'

This man said rather, 'Actual life comes next?
    Patience a moment!
Grant I have mastered learning's crabbed text,
    Still there's the comment.
Let me know all! Prate not of most or least,   60
    Painful or easy!
Even to the crumbs I'd fain eat up the feast,
    Ay, nor feel queasy.'
Oh, such a life as he resolved to live,
    When he had learned it,
When he had gathered all books had to give!
    Sooner, he spurned it.
Image the whole, then execute the parts—
    Fancy the fabric°
Quite, ere you build, ere steel strike fire from quartz,   70
    Ere mortar dab brick!

(Here's the town-gate reached: there's the market-place
    Gaping before us.)
Yea, this in him was the peculiar grace
    (Hearten our chorus!)
That before living he'd learn how to live—
    No end to learning:
Earn the means first—God surely will contrive
    Use for our earning.   80
Others mistrust and say, 'But time escapes:
    Live now or never!'
He said, 'What's time? Leave Now for dogs and apes!
    Man has Forever.'
Back to his book then: deeper drooped his head:
    Calculus racked him:°
Leaden before, his eyes grew dross of lead:
    Tussis attacked him.°
'Now, master, take a little rest!'—not he!
    (Caution redoubled,   90
Step two abreast, the way winds narrowly!)
    Not a whit troubled
Back to his studies, fresher than at first,
    Fierce as a dragon
He (soul-hydroptic with a sacred thirst)°
    Sucked at the flagon.

Oh, if we draw a circle premature,
    Heedless of far gain,
Greedy for quick returns of profit, sure
    Bad is our bargain!   100
Was it not great? did not he throw on God,
    (He loves the burthen)—
God's task to make the heavenly period
    Perfect the earthen?
Did not he magnify the mind, show clear
    Just what it all meant?
He would not discount life, as fools do here,
    Paid by instalment.
He ventured neck or nothing—heaven's success
    Found, or earth's failure: 110
'Wilt thou trust death or not?' He answered 'Yes:
    Hence with life's pale lure!'
That low man seeks a little thing to do,
    Sees it and does it:
This high man, with a great thing to pursue,
    Dies ere he knows it.
That low man goes on adding one to one,
    His hundred's soon hit:
This high man, aiming at a million,
    Misses an unit.   120
That, has the world here—should he need the next,
    Let the world mind him!
This, throws himself on God, and unperplexed
    Seeking shall find him.
So, with the throttling hands of death at strife,
    Ground he at grammar;
Still, thro' the rattle, parts of speech were rife:
    While he could stammer
He settled *Hoti's* business—let it be!—
    Properly based *Oun*—   130
Gave us the doctrine of the enclitic *De*,°
    Dead from the waist down.
Well, here's the platform, here's the proper place:
    Hail to your purlieus,°
All ye highfliers of the feathered race,
    Swallows and curlews!
Here's the top-peak; the multitude below

Live, for they can, there:
This man decided not to Live but Know—
        Bury this man there?
Here—here's his place, where meteors shoot, clouds form,   140
        Lightnings are loosened,
Stars come and go! Let joy break with the storm,
        Peace let the dew send!
Lofty designs must close in like effects:
        Loftily lying,
Leave him—still loftier than the world suspects,
        Living and dying.

'Transcendentalism: A Poem in Twelve Books'

Stop playing, poet! May a brother speak?
'Tis you speak, that's your error. Song's our art:
Whereas you please to speak these naked thoughts
Instead of draping them in sights and sounds.
—True thoughts, good thoughts, thoughts fit to treasure up!
But why such long prolusion and display,°
Such turning and adjustment of the harp,
And taking it upon your breast, at length,
Only to speak dry words across its strings?
Stark-naked thought is in request enough:
Speak prose and hollo it till Europe hears!   10
The six-foot Swiss tube, braced about with bark,
Which helps the hunter's voice from Alp to Alp—
Exchange our harp for that,—who hinders you?

    But here's your fault; grown men want thought, you think;
Thought's what they mean by verse, and seek in verse.
Boys seek for images and melody,
Men must have reason—so, you aim at men.
Quite otherwise! Objects throng our youth, 'tis true;
We see and hear and do not wonder much:
If you could tell us what they mean, indeed!   20
As German Boehme never cared for plants°
Until it happed, a-walking in the fields,
He noticed all at once that plants could speak,

Nay, turned with loosened tongue to talk with him.
That day the daisy had an eye indeed—
Colloquized with the cowslip on such themes!
We find them extant yet in Jacob's prose.
But by the time youth slips a stage or two
While reading prose in that tough book he wrote   30
(Collating and emendating the same
And settling on the sense most to our mind),
We shut the clasps and find life's summer past.
Then, who helps more, pray, to repair our loss—
Another Boehme with a tougher book
And subtler meanings of what roses say,—
Or some stout Mage like him of Halberstadt,°
John, who made things Boehme wrote thoughts about?
He with a 'look you!' vents a brace of rhymes,
And in there breaks the sudden rose herself,   40
Over us, under, round us every side,
Nay, in and out the tables and the chairs
And musty volumes, Boehme's book and all,—
Buries us with a glory, young once more,
Pouring heaven into this shut house of life.

　　So come, the harp back to your heart again!
You are a poem, though your poem's nought.
The best of all you showed before, believe,
Was your own boy-face o'er the finer chords
Bent, following the cherub at the top   50
That points to God with his paired half-moon wings.

One Word More

To E. B. B. 1855

I

There they are, my fifty men and women
Naming me the fifty poems finished!
Take them, Love, the book and me together:
Where the heart lies, let the brain lie also.

II

Rafael made a century of sonnets,°
Made and wrote them in a certain volume
Dinted with the silver-pointed pencil
Else he only used to draw Madonnas:
These, the world might view—but one, the volume.
Who that one, you ask? Your heart instructs you.   10
Did she live and love it all her life-time?
Did she drop, his lady of the sonnets,
Die, and let it drop beside her pillow
Where it lay in place of Rafael's glory,
Rafael's cheek so duteous and so loving—
Cheek, the world was wont to hail a painter's
Rafael's cheek, her love had turned a poet's?

III

You and I would rather read that volume,
(Taken to his beating bosom by it)
Lean and list the bosom-beats of Rafael,   20
Would we not? than wonder at Madonnas—
Her, San Sisto names, and Her, Foligno,
Her, that visits Florence in a vision,
Her, that's left with lilies in the Louvre—°
Seen by us and all the world in circle.

IV

You and I will never read that volume.
Guido Reni, like his own eye's apple
Guarded long the treasure-book and loved it.
Guido Reni dying, all Bologna
Cried, and the world cried too, 'Ours, the treasure!'   30
Suddenly, as rare things will, it vanished.°

V

Dante once prepared to paint an angel:°
Whom to please? You whisper 'Beatrice.'
While he mused and traced it and retraced it,
(Peradventure with a pen corroded
Still by drops of that hot ink he dipped for,

When, his left-hand i' the hair o' the wicked,
Back he held the brow and pricked its stigma,
Bit into the live man's flesh for parchment,
Loosed him, laughed to see the writing rankle,   40
Let the wretch go festering through Florence)—
Dante, who loved well because he hated,
Hated wickedness that hinders loving,
Dante standing, studying his angel,—
In there broke the folk of his Inferno.
Says he—'Certain people of importance'
(Such he gave his daily dreadful line to)
'Entered and would seize, forsooth, the poet.'
Says the poet—'Then I stopped my painting.'

VI

You and I would rather see that angel,   50
Painted by the tenderness of Dante,
Would we not?—than read a fresh Inferno.

VII

You and I will never see that picture.
While he mused on love and Beatrice,
While he softened o'er his outlined angel,
In they broke, those 'people of importance:'
We and Bice bear the loss for ever.°

VIII

What of Rafael's sonnets, Dante's picture?
This: no artist lives and loves, that longs not
Once, and only once, and for one only,   60
(Ah, the prize!) to find his love a language
Fit and fair and simple and sufficient—
Using nature that's an art to others,
Not, this one time, art that's turned his nature.
Ay, of all the artists living, loving,
None but would forego his proper dowry,—
Does he paint? he fain would write a poem,—
Does he write? he fain would paint a picture,
Put to proof art alien to the artist's,
Once, and only once, and for one only,   70

So to be the man and leave the artist,
Gain the man's joy, miss the artist's sorrow.

IX

Wherefore? Heaven's gift takes earth's abatement!
He who smites the rock and spreads the water,°
Bidding drink and live a crowd beneath him,
Even he, the minute makes immortal,
Proves, perchance, but mortal in the minute,
Desecrates, belike, the deed in doing.
While he smites, how can he but remember,
So he smote before, in such a peril,   80
When they stood and mocked—'Shall smiting help us?'
When they drank and sneered—'A stroke is easy!'
When they wiped their mouths and went their journey,
Throwing him for thanks—'But drought was pleasant.'
Thus old memories mar the actual triumph;
Thus the doing savours of disrelish;
Thus achievement lacks a gracious somewhat;
O'er-importuned brows becloud the mandate,
Carelessness or consciousness—the gesture.
For he bears an ancient wrong about him,   90
Sees and knows again those phalanxed faces,
Hears, yet one time more, the 'customed prelude—
'How shouldst thou, of all men, smite, and save us?'
Guesses what is like to prove the sequel—
'Egypt's flesh-pots—nay, the drought was better.'

X

Oh, the crowd must have emphatic warrant!
Theirs, the Sinai-forehead's cloven brilliance,°
Right-arm's rod-sweep, tongue's imperial fiat.°
Never dares the man put off the prophet.

XI

Did he love one face from out the thousands,   100
(Were she Jethro's daughter, white and wifely,
Were she but the Æthiopian bondslave,)°
He would envy yon dumb patient camel,
Keeping a reserve of scanty water

Meant to save his own life in the desert;
Ready in the desert to deliver
(Kneeling down to let his breast be opened)
Hoard and life together for his mistress.

                              XII

I shall never, in the years remaining,
Paint you pictures, no, nor carve you statues,   110
Make you music that should all-express me;
So it seems: I stand on my attainment.
This of verse alone, one life allows me;
Verse and nothing else have I to give you.
Other heights in other lives, God willing:
All the gifts from all the heights, your own, Love!

                              XIII

Yet a semblance of resource avails us—
Shade so finely touched, love's sense must seize it.
Take these lines, look lovingly and nearly,
Lines I write the first time and the last time.   120
He who works in fresco, steals a hair-brush,
Curbs the liberal hand, subservient proudly,
Cramps his spirit, crowds its all in little,
Makes a strange art of an art familiar,
Fills his lady's missal-marge with flowerets.
He who blows thro' bronze, may breathe thro' silver,
Fitly serenade a slumbrous princess.
He who writes, may write for once as I do.

                              XIV

Love, you saw me gather men and women,
Live or dead or fashioned by my fancy,   130
Enter each and all, and use their service,
Speak from every mouth,—the speech, a poem.
Hardly shall I tell my joys and sorrows,
Hopes and fears, belief and disbelieving:
I am mine and yours—the rest be all men's,
Karshish, Cleon, Norbert and the fifty.
Let me speak this once in my true person,
Not as Lippo, Roland or Andrea,

Though the fruit of speech be just this sentence:
Pray you, look on these my men and women,
Take and keep my fifty poems finished;   140
Where my heart lies, let my brain lie also!
Poor the speech; be how I speak, for all things.

XV

Not but that you know me! Lo, the moon's self!
Here in London, yonder late in Florence,
Still we find her face, the thrice-transfigured.
Curving on a sky imbrued with colour,
Drifted over Fiesole by twilight,°
Came she, our new crescent of a hair's-breadth.
Full she flared it, lamping Samminiato,°   150
Rounder 'twixt the cypresses and rounder,
Perfect till the nightingales applauded.
Now, a piece of her old self, impoverished,
Hard to greet, she traverses the houseroofs,
Hurries with unhandsome thrift of silver,
Goes dispiritedly, glad to finish.

XVI

What, there's nothing in the moon noteworthy?
Nay: for if that moon could love a mortal,
Use, to charm him (so to fit a fancy),
All her magic ('tis the old sweet mythos)°
She would turn a new side to her mortal,   160
Side unseen of herdsman, huntsman, steersman—
Blank to Zoroaster on his terrace,°
Blind to Galileo on his turret,°
Dumb to Homer, dumb to Keats—him, even!°
Think, the wonder of the moonstruck mortal—
When she turns round, comes again in heaven,
Opens out anew for worse or better!
Proves she like some portent of an iceberg
Swimming full upon the ship it founders,
Hungry with huge teeth of splintered crystals?   170
Proves she as the paved work of a sapphire
Seen by Moses when he climbed the mountain?
Moses, Aaron, Nadab and Abihu

Climbed and saw the very God, the Highest,
Stand upon the paved work of a sapphire.
Like the bodied heaven in his clearness
Shone the stone, the sapphire of that paved work,
When they ate and drank and saw God also!

XVII

What were seen? None knows, none ever shall know.   180
Only this is sure—the sight were other,
Not the moon's same side, born late in Florence,
Dying now impoverished here in London.
God be thanked, the meanest of his creatures
Boasts two soul-sides, one to face the world with,
One to show a woman when he loves her!

XVIII

This I say of me, but think of you, Love!
This to you—yourself my moon of poets!
Ah, but that's the world's side, there's the wonder,
Thus they see you, praise you, think they know you!   190
There, in turn I stand with them and praise you—
Out of my own self, I dare to phrase it.
But the best is when I glide from out them,
Cross a step or two of dubious twilight,
Come out on the other side, the novel
Silent silver lights and darks undreamed of,
Where I hush and bless myself with silence.

XIX

Oh, their Rafael of the dear Madonnas,
Oh, their Dante of the dread Inferno,
Wrote one song—and in my brain I sing it,   200
Drew one angel—borne, see, on my bosom!
                                     R. B.

DRAMATIS PERSONAE (1864)

Gold Hair

A Story of Pornic

I

Oh, the beautiful girl, too white,
  Who lived at Pornic, down by the sea,°
Just where the sea and the Loire unite!
  And a boasted name in Brittany
She bore, which I will not write.

II

Too white, for the flower of life is red;
  Her flesh was the soft seraphic screen°
Of a soul that is meant (her parents said)
  To just see earth, and hardly be seen,
And blossom in heaven instead.   10

III

Yet earth saw one thing, one how fair!
  One grace that grew to its full on earth:
Smiles might be sparse on her cheek so spare,
  And her waist want half a girdle's girth,
But she had her great gold hair.

IV

Hair, such a wonder of flix and floss,
  Freshness and fragrance—floods of it, too!
Gold, did I say? Nay, gold's mere dross:
  Here, Life smiled, 'Think what I meant to do!'
And Love sighed, 'Fancy my loss!'   20

V

So, when she died, it was scarce more strange
    Than that, when delicate evening dies,
And you follow its spent sun's pallid range,
    There's a shoot of colour startles the skies
With sudden, violent change,—

VI

That, while the breath was nearly to seek,
    As they put the little cross to her lips,
She changed; a spot came out on her cheek,
    A spark from her eye in mid-eclipse,
And she broke forth, 'I must speak!'   30

VII

'Not my hair!' made the girl her moan—
    'All the rest is gone or to go;
But the last, last grace, my all, my own,
    Let it stay in the grave, that the ghosts may know!
Leave my poor gold hair alone!'

VIII

The passion thus vented, dead lay she;
    Her parents sobbed their worst on that;
All friends joined in, nor observed degree:°
    For indeed the hair was to wonder at,
As it spread—not flowing free,   40

IX

But curled around her brow, like a crown,
    And coiled beside her cheeks, like a cap,
And calmed about her neck—ay, down
    To her breast, pressed flat, without a gap
I' the gold, it reached her gown.

X

All kissed that face, like a silver wedge
    'Mid the yellow wealth, nor disturbed its hair:

E'en the priest allowed death's privilege,
   As he planted the crucifix with care
On her breast, 'twixt edge and edge.   50

XI

And thus was she buried, inviolate
   Of body and soul, in the very space
By the altar; keeping saintly state
   In Pornic church, for her pride of race,
Pure life and piteous fate.

XII

And in after-time would your fresh tear fall,
   Though your mouth might twitch with a dubious smile,
As they told you of gold, both robe and pall,
   How she prayed them leave it alone awhile,
So it never was touched at all.   60

XIII

Years flew; this legend grew at last
   The life of the lady; all she had done,
All been, in the memories fading fast
   Of lover and friend, was summed in one
Sentence survivors passed:

XIV

To wit, she was meant for heaven, not earth;
   Had turned an angel before the time:
Yet, since she was mortal, in such dearth
   Of frailty, all you could count a crime°
Was—she knew her gold hair's worth.   70

XV

At little pleasant Pornic church,
   It chanced, the pavement wanted repair,
Was taken to pieces: left in the lurch,
   A certain sacred space lay bare,
And the boys began research.

XVI

'Twas the space where our sires would lay a saint,
   A benefactor,—a bishop, suppose,
A baron with armour-adornments quaint,
   Dame with chased ring and jewelled rose,°
Things sanctity saves from taint;   80

XVII

So we come to find them in after-days
   When the corpse is presumed to have done with gauds°
Of use to the living, in many ways:
   For the boys get pelf, and the town applauds,°
And the church deserves the praise.

XVIII

They grubbed with a will: and at length—*O cor*
   Humanum, pectora cæca, and the rest!—°
They found—no gaud they were prying for,
   No ring, no rose, but—who would have guessed?—
A double Louis-d'or!°   90

XIX

Here was a case for the priest: he heard,
   Marked, inwardly digested, laid
Finger on nose, smiled, 'There's a bird
   Chirps in my ear': then, 'Bring a spade,
Dig deeper!'—he gave the word.

XX

And lo, when they came to the coffin-lid,
   Or rotten planks which composed it once,
Why, there lay the girl's skull wedged amid
   A mint of money, it served for the nonce
To hold in its hair-heaps hid!   100

XXI

Hid there? Why? Could the girl be wont
   (She the stainless soul) to treasure up

Money, earth's trash and heaven's affront?
  Had a spider found out the communion-cup,
Was a toad in the christening-font?

XXII

Truth is truth: too true it was.
  Gold! She hoarded and hugged it first,
Longed for it, leaned o'er it, loved it—alas—
  Till the humour grew to a head and burst,
And she cried, at the final pass,—   110

XXIII

'Talk not of God, my heart is stone!
  Nor lover nor friend—be gold for both!
Gold I lack; and, my all, my own,
  It shall hide in my hair. I scarce die loth
If they let my hair alone!'

XXIV

Louis-d'or, some six times five,
  And duly double, every piece.
Now do you see? With the priest to shrive,
  With parents preventing her soul's release
By kisses that kept alive,—   120

XXV

With heaven's gold gates about to ope,
  With friends' praise, gold-like, lingering still,
An instinct had bidden the girl's hand grope
  For gold, the true sort—'Gold in heaven, if you will;
But I keep earth's too, I hope.'

XXVI

Enough! The priest took the grave's grim yield:
  The parents, they eyed that price of sin
As if *thirty pieces* lay revealed
  On the place *to bury strangers in*,
The hideous Potter's Field.°   130

XXVII

But the priest bethought him: ' "Milk that's spilt"°
  —You know the adage! Watch and pray!
Saints tumble to earth with so slight a tilt!
   It would build a new altar; that, we may!'
And the altar therewith was built.

XXVIII

Why I deliver this horrible verse?
  As the text of a sermon, which now I preach:
Evil or good may be better or worse
  In the human heart, but the mixture of each
Is a marvel and a curse.   140

XXIX

The candid incline to surmise of late
  That the Christian faith proves false, I find;
For our Essays-and-Reviews' debate°
  Begins to tell on the public mind,
And Colenso's words have weight:°

XXX

I still, to suppose it true, for my part,
  See reasons and reasons; this, to begin:
'Tis the faith that launched point-blank her dart
  At the head of a lie—taught Original Sin,
The Corruption of Man's Heart.   150

Abt Vogler

*(After he has been extemporizing upon the musical instrument
of his invention)*

I

Would that the structure brave, the manifold music I build,°
  Bidding my organ obey, calling its keys to their work,
Claiming each slave of the sound, at a touch, as when Solomon
    willed°

Armies of angels that soar, legions of demons that lurk,
Man, brute, reptile, fly,—alien of end and of aim,
    Adverse, each from the other heaven-high, hell-deep
      removed,—
Should rush into sight at once as he named the ineffable Name,
    And pile him a palace straight, to pleasure the princess he
      loved!

II

Would it might tarry like his, the beautiful building of mine,
    This which my keys in a crowd pressed and importuned to
      raise!
Ah, one and all, how they helped, would dispart now and now
    combine,°
    Zealous to hasten the work, heighten their master his praise!
And one would bury his brow with a blind plunge down to hell,
    Burrow awhile and build, broad on the roots of things,
Then up again swim into sight, having based me my palace well,
    Founded it, fearless of flame, flat on the nether springs.°

III

And another would mount and march, like the excellent minion
    he was,°
    Ay, another and yet another, one crowd but with many a crest,
Raising my rampired walls of gold as transparent as glass,°
    Eager to do and die, yield each his place to the rest:
For higher still and higher (as a runner tips with fire,
    When a great illumination surprises a festal night—
Outlining round and round Rome's dome from space to spire)
    Up, the pinnacled glory reached, and the pride of my soul was
      in sight.

IV

In sight? Not half! for it seemed, it was certain, to match man's
    birth,
    Nature in turn conceived, obeying an impulse as I;
And the emulous heaven yearned down, made effort to reach the
    earth,
    As the earth had done her best, in my passion, to scale the sky:
Novel splendours burst forth, grew familiar and dwelt with
    mine,

Not a point nor peak but found and fixed its wandering star;　30
Meteor-moons, balls of blaze: and they did not pale nor pine,
　For earth had attained to heaven, there was no more near nor
　　far.

V

Nay more; for there wanted not who walked in the glare and
　　glow,
　Presences plain in the place; or, fresh from the Protoplast,°
Furnished for ages to come, when a kindlier wind should blow,
　Lured now to begin and live, in a house to their liking at last;
Or else the wonderful Dead who have passed through the body
　　and gone,
　But were back once more to breathe in an old world worth
　　their new:
What never had been, was now; what was, as it shall be anon;
　And what is,—shall I say, matched both? for I was made
　　perfect too.　　40

VI

All through my keys that gave their sounds to a wish of my soul,
　All through my soul that praised as its wish flowed visibly
　　forth,
All through music and me! For think, had I painted the whole,
　Why, there it had stood, to see, nor the process so wonder-
　　worth:
Had I written the same, made verse—still, effect proceeds from
　　cause,
　Ye know why the forms are fair, ye hear how the tale is told;
It is all triumphant art, but art in obedience to laws,
　Painter and poet are proud in the artist-list enrolled:—

VII

But here is the finger of God, a flash of the will that can,
　Existent behind all laws, that made them and, lo, they are!　50
And I know not if, save in this, such gift be allowed to man,
　That out of three sounds he frame, not a fourth sound, but a
　　star.
Consider it well: each tone of our scale in itself is nought;
　It is everywhere in the world—loud, soft, and all is said:

Give it to me to use! I mix it with two in my thought:
  And, there! Ye have heard and seen: consider and bow the
    head!

VIII

Well, it is gone at last, the palace of music I reared;
  Gone! and the good tears start, the praises that come too slow;
For one is assured at first, one scarce can say that he feared,
  That he even gave it a thought, the gone thing was to go.   60
Never to be again! But many more of the kind
  As good, nay, better perchance: is this your comfort to me?
To me, who must be saved because I cling with my mind
  To the same, same self, same love, same God: ay, what was,
    shall be.

IX

Therefore to whom turn I but to thee, the ineffable Name?
  Builder and maker, thou, of houses not made with hands!°
What, have fear of change from thee who art ever the same?
  Doubt that thy power can fill the heart that thy power
    expands?
There shall never be one lost good! What was, shall live as
    before;
  The evil is null, is nought, is silence implying sound;   70
What was good shall be good, with, for evil, so much good more;
  On the earth the broken arcs; in the heaven, a perfect round.

X

All we have willed or hoped or dreamed of good shall exist;
  Not its semblance, but itself; no beauty, nor good, nor power
Whose voice has gone forth, but each survives for the melodist
  When eternity affirms the conception of an hour.
The high that proved too high, the heroic for earth too hard,
  The passion that left the ground to lose itself in the sky,
Are music sent up to God by the lover and the bard;
  Enough that he heard it once: we shall hear it by-and-by.   80

XI

And what is our failure here but a triumph's evidence
  For the fulness of the days? Have we withered or agonized?

Why else was the pause prolonged but that singing might issue
        thence?
  Why rushed the discords in but that harmony should be
        prized?
Sorrow is hard to bear, and doubt is slow to clear,
  Each sufferer says his say, his scheme of the weal and woe:
But God has a few of us whom he whispers in the ear;
  The rest may reason and welcome: 'tis we musicians know.

XII

Well, it is earth with me; silence resumes her reign:
  I will be patient and proud, and soberly acquiesce.   90
Give me the keys. I feel for the common chord again,
  Sliding by semitones, till I sink to the minor,—yes,
And I blunt it into a ninth, and I stand on alien ground,
  Surveying awhile the heights I rolled from into the deep;
Which, hark, I have dared and done, for my resting-place is
        found,
  The C Major of this life: so, now I will try to sleep.°

Rabbi Ben Ezra

I

        Grow old along with me!
        The best is yet to be,
The last of life, for which the first was made:
        Our times are in His hand
        Who saith 'A whole I planned,
Youth shows but half; trust God: see all nor be afraid!'

II

        Not that, amassing flowers,
        Youth sighed 'Which rose make ours,
Which lily leave and then as best recall?'
        Not that, admiring stars,   10
        It yearned 'Nor Jove, nor Mars;
Mine be some figured flame which blends, transcends them all!'

III

Not for such hopes and fears
　　Annulling youth's brief years,
Do I remonstrate: folly wide the mark!
　　Rather I prize the doubt
　　Low kinds exist without,
Finished and finite clods, untroubled by a spark.

IV

Poor vaunt of life indeed,
　　Were man but formed to feed
On joy, to solely seek and find and feast: 20
　　Such feasting ended, then
　　As sure an end to men;
Irks care the crop-full bird? Frets doubt the maw-crammed
　　beast?°

V

Rejoice we are allied
　　To That which doth provide
And not partake, effect and not receive!
　　A spark disturbs our clod;
　　Nearer we hold of God
Who gives, than of His tribes that take, I must believe.   30

VI

Then, welcome each rebuff
　　That turns earth's smoothness rough,
Each sting that bids nor sit nor stand but go!
　　Be our joys three-parts pain!
　　Strive, and hold cheap the strain;
Learn, nor account the pang; dare, never grudge the throe!

VII

For thence,—a paradox
　　Which comforts while it mocks,—
Shall life succeed in that it seems to fail:
　　What I aspired to be,
　　And was not, comforts me: 40
A brute I might have been, but would not sink i' the scale.

VIII

What is he but a brute
Whose flesh has soul to suit,
Whose spirit works lest arms and legs want play?
To man, propose this test—
Thy body at its best,
How far can that project thy soul on its lone way?

IX

Yet gifts should prove their use:
I own the Past profuse   50
Of power each side, perfection every turn:
Eyes, ears took in their dole,
Brain treasured up the whole;
Should not the heart beat once 'How good to live and learn?'

X

Not once beat 'Praise be Thine!
I see the whole design,
I, who saw power, see now love perfect too:
Perfect I call Thy plan:
Thanks that I was a man!
Maker, remake, complete,—I trust what Thou shalt do!'   60

XI

For pleasant is this flesh;
Our soul, in its rose-mesh°
Pulled ever to the earth, still yearns for rest;
Would we some prize might hold
To match those manifold
Possessions of the brute,—gain most, as we did best!

XII

Let us not always say
'Spite of this flesh to-day
I strove, made head, gained ground upon the whole!'
As the bird wings and sings,   70
Let us cry 'All good things
Are ours, nor soul helps flesh more, now, than flesh helps soul!'

XIII

Therefore I summon age
To grant youth's heritage,
Life's struggle having so far reached its term:
Thence shall I pass, approved
A man, for aye removed
From the developed brute; a god though in the germ.

XIV

And I shall thereupon
Take rest, ere I be gone   80
Once more on my adventure brave and new:
Fearless and unperplexed,
When I wage battle next,
What weapons to select, what armour to indue.°

XV

Youth ended, I shall try
My gain or loss thereby;
Leave the fire ashes, what survives is gold:
And I shall weigh the same,
Give life its praise or blame:
Young, all lay in dispute; I shall know, being old.   90

XVI

For note, when evening shuts,
A certain moment cuts
The deed off, calls the glory from the grey:
A whisper from the west
Shoots—'Add this to the rest,
Take it and try its worth: here dies another day.'

XVII

So, still within this life,
Though lifted o'er its strife,
Let me discern, compare, pronounce at last,
'This rage was right i' the main,
That acquiescence vain: 100
The Future I may face now I have proved the Past.'

XVIII

For more is not reserved
To man, with soul just nerved
To act to-morrow what he learns to-day:
Here, work enough to watch
The Master work, and catch
Hints of the proper craft, tricks of the tool's true play.

XIX

As it was better, youth
Should strive, through acts uncouth,   110
Toward making, than repose on aught found made:
So, better, age, exempt
From strife, should know, than tempt°
Further. Thou waitedest age: wait death nor be afraid!

XX

Enough now, if the Right
And Good and Infinite
Be named here, as thou callest thy hand thine own,
With knowledge absolute,
Subject to no dispute
From fools that crowded youth, nor let thee feel alone.   120

XXI

Be there, for once and all,
Severed great minds from small,
Announced to each his station in the Past!
Was I, the world arraigned,°
Were they, my soul disdained,
Right? Let age speak the truth and give us peace at last!

XXII

Now, who shall arbitrate?
Ten men love what I hate,
Shun what I follow, slight what I receive;
Ten, who in ears and eyes   130
Match me: we all surmise,
They this thing, and I that: whom shall my soul believe?

XXIII

Not on the vulgar mass
Called 'work,' must sentence pass,
Things done, that took the eye and had the price;
O'er which, from level stand,
The low world laid its hand,
Found straightway to its mind, could value in a trice:

XXIV

But all, the world's coarse thumb
And finger failed to plumb,
So passed in making up the main account;
All instincts immature,
All purposes unsure,
That weighed not as his work, yet swelled the man's amount:

XXV

Thoughts hardly to be packed
Into a narrow act,
Fancies that broke through language and escaped;
All I could never be,
All, men ignored in me,
This, I was worth to God, whose wheel the pitcher shaped.

XXVI

Ay, note that Potter's wheel,
That metaphor! and feel
Why time spins fast, why passive lies our clay,—
Thou, to whom fools propound,
When the wine makes its round,
'Since life fleets, all is change; the Past gone, seize to-day!'

XXVII

Fool! All that is, at all,
Lasts ever, past recall;
Earth changes, but thy soul and God stand sure:
What entered into thee,
That was, is, and shall be:
Time's wheel runs back or stops: Potter and clay endure.

XXVIII

He fixed thee mid this dance
Of plastic circumstance,°
This Present, thou, forsooth, wouldst fain arrest:
    Machinery just meant
    To give thy soul its bent,
Try thee and turn thee forth, sufficiently impressed.

XXIX

What though the earlier grooves
Which ran the laughing loves   170
Around thy base, no longer pause and press?
    What though, about thy rim,
    Scull-things in order grim
Grow out, in graver mood, obey the sterner stress?

XXX

Look not thou down but up!
To uses of a cup,
The festal board, lamp's flash and trumpet's peal,
    The new wine's foaming flow,
    The Master's lips a-glow!
Thou, heaven's consummate cup, what need'st thou with earth's
        wheel?   180

XXXI

But I need, now as then,
    Thee, God, who mouldest men;
And since, not even while the whirl was worst,
    Did I,—to the wheel of life
    With shapes and colours rife,
Bound dizzily,—mistake my end, to slake Thy thirst:

XXXII

So, take and use Thy work:
    Amend what flaws may lurk,
What strain o' the stuff, what warpings past the aim!
    My times be in Thy hand!   190
    Perfect the cup as planned!
Let age approve of youth, and death complete the same!

A Death in the Desert

[Supposed of Pamphylax the Antiochene:
It is a parchment, of my rolls the fifth,
Hath three skins glued together, is all Greek
And goeth from *Epsilon* down to *Mu*:
Lies second in the surnamed Chosen Chest,
Stained and conserved with juice of terebinth,°
Covered with cloth of hair, and lettered *Xi*,
From Xanthus, my wife's uncle, now at peace:
Mu and *Epsilon* stand for my own name.
I may not write it, but I make a cross   10
To show I wait His coming, with the rest,
And leave off here: beginneth Pamphylax.]°

I said, 'If one should wet his lips with wine,
And slip the broadest plantain-leaf we find,
Or else the lappet of a linen robe,
Into the water-vessel, lay it right,
And cool his forehead just above the eyes,
The while a brother, kneeling either side,
Should chafe each hand and try to make it warm,—
He is not so far gone but he might speak.'   20

This did not happen in the outer cave,
Nor in the secret chamber of the rock
Where, sixty days since the decree was out,°
We had him, bedded on a camel-skin,
And waited for his dying all the while;
But in the midmost grotto: since noon's light
Reached there a little, and we would not lose
The last of what might happen on his face.

I at the head, and Xanthus at the feet,
With Valens and the Boy, had lifted him,   30
And brought him from the chamber in the depths,
And laid him in the light where we might see
For certain smiles began about his mouth,
And his lids moved, presageful of the end.

Beyond, and half way up the mouth o' the cave,
The Bactrian convert, having his desire,°

Kept watch, and made pretence to graze a goat
That gave us milk, on rags of various herb,
Plantain and quitch, the rocks' shade keeps alive:°
So that if any thief or soldier passed,   40
(Because the persecution was aware)
Yielding the goat up promptly with his life,
Such man might pass on, joyful at a prize,
Nor care to pry into the cool o' the cave.
Outside was all noon and the burning blue.

'Here is wine,' answered Xanthus,—dropped a drop;
I stooped and placed the lap of cloth aright,
Then chafed his right hand, and the Boy his left:
But Valens had bethought him, and produced
And broke a ball of nard, and made perfume.°   50
Only, he did—not so much wake, as—turn
And smile a little, as a sleeper does
If any dear one call him, touch his face—
And smiles and loves, but will not be disturbed.

Then Xanthus said a prayer, but still he slept:
It is the Xanthus that escaped to Rome,
Was burned, and could not write the chronicle.

Then the Boy sprang up from his knees, and ran,
Stung by the splendour of a sudden thought,
And fetched the seventh plate of graven lead   60
Out of the secret chamber, found a place,
Pressing with finger on the deeper dints,
And spoke, as 'twere his mouth proclaiming first,
'I am the Resurrection and the Life.'°

Whereat he opened his eyes wide at once,
And sat up of himself, and looked at us;
And thenceforth nobody pronounced a word:
Only, outside, the Bactrian cried his cry
Like the lone desert-bird that wears the ruff,
As signal we were safe, from time to time.   70

First he said, 'If a friend declared to me,
This my son Valens, this my other son,
Were James and Peter,—nay, declared as well
This lad was very John,—I could believe!

—Could, for a moment, doubtlessly believe:
So is myself withdrawn into my depths,
The soul retreated from the perished brain
Whence it was wont to feel and use the world
Through these dull members, done with long ago.
Yet I myself remain; I feel myself: 80
And there is nothing lost. Let be, awhile!'

[This is the doctrine he was wont to teach,
How divers persons witness in each man,
Three souls which make up one soul: first, to wit,
A soul of each and all the bodily parts,
Seated therein, which works, and is what Does,
And has the use of earth, and ends the man
Downward: but, tending upward for advice,
Grows into, and again is grown into
By the next soul, which, seated in the brain,   90
Useth the first with its collected use,
And feeleth, thinketh, willeth,—is what Knows:
Which, duly tending upward in its turn,
Grows into, and again is grown into
By the last soul, that uses both the first,
Subsisting whether they assist or no,
And, constituting man's self, is what Is—
And leans upon the former, makes it play,
As that played off the first: and, tending up,
Holds, is upheld by, God, and ends the man   100
Upward in that dread point of intercourse,
Nor needs a place, for it returns to Him.
What Does, what Knows, what Is; three souls, one man.
I give the glossa of Theotypas.]°

And then, 'A stick, once fire from end to end;
Now, ashes save the tip that holds a spark!
Yet, blow the spark, it runs back, spreads itself
A little where the fire was: thus I urge
The soul that served me, till it task once more
What ashes of my brain have kept their shape,   110
And these make effort on the last o' the flesh,
Trying to taste again the truth of things—'
(He smiled)—'their very superficial truth;
As that ye are my sons, that it is long

Since James and Peter had release by death,°
And I am only he, your brother John,
Who saw and heard, and could remember all.
Remember all! It is not much to say.
What if the truth broke on me from above
As once and oft-times? Such might hap again: 120
Doubtlessly He might stand in presence here,
With head wool-white, eyes flame, and feet like brass,
The sword and the seven stars, as I have seen—°
I who now shudder only and surmise
"How did your brother bear that sight and live?"

'If I live yet, it is for good, more love
Through me to men: be nought but ashes here
That keep awhile my semblance, who was John,—
Still, when they scatter, there is left on earth
No one alive who knew (consider this!)   130
—Saw with his eyes and handled with his hands
That which was from the first, the Word of Life.
How will it be when none more saith "I saw"?

'Such ever was love's way: to rise, it stoops.
Since I, whom Christ's mouth taught, was bidden teach,
I went, for many years, about the world,
Saying "It was so; so I heard and saw,"
Speaking as the case asked: and men believed.
Afterward came the message to myself
In Patmos isle; I was not bidden teach,   140
But simply listen, take a book and write,
Nor set down other than the given word,
With nothing left to my arbitrament
To choose or change: I wrote, and men believed.
Then, for my time grew brief, no message more,
No call to write again, I found a way,
And, reasoning from my knowledge, merely taught
Men should, for love's sake, in love's strength believe;
Or I would pen a letter to a friend
And urge the same as friend, nor less nor more: 150
Friends said I reasoned rightly, and believed.
But at the last, why, I seemed left alive
Like a sea-jelly weak on Patmos strand,
To tell dry sea-beach gazers how I fared

When there was mid-sea, and the mighty things;
Left to repeat, "I saw, I heard, I knew,"
And go all over the old ground again,
With Antichrist already in the world,°
And many Antichrists, who answered prompt
"Am I not Jasper as thyself art John?   160
Nay, young, whereas through age thou mayest forget:
Wherefore, explain, or how shall we believe?"
I never thought to call down fire on such,
Or, as in wonderful and early days,
Pick up the scorpion, tread the serpent dumb;°
But patient stated much of the Lord's life
Forgotten or misdelivered, and let it work:
Since much that at the first, in deed and word,
Lay simply and sufficiently exposed,
Had grown (or else my soul was grown to match,
Fed through such years, familiar with such light,   170
Guarded and guided still to see and speak)
Of new significance and fresh result;
What first were guessed as points, I now knew stars,
And named them in the Gospel I have writ.
For men said, "It is getting long ago:
Where is the promise of His coming?"—asked°
These young ones in their strength, as loth to wait,
Of me who, when their sires were born, was old.
I, for I loved them, answered, joyfully,
Since I was there, and helpful in my age;   180
And, in the main, I think such men believed.
Finally, thus endeavouring, I fell sick,
Ye brought me here, and I supposed the end,
And went to sleep with one thought that, at least,
Though the whole earth should lie in wickedness,°
We had the truth, might leave the rest to God.
Yet now I wake in such decrepitude
As I had slidden down and fallen afar,
Past even the presence of my former self,
Grasping the while for stay at facts which snap,   190
Till I am found away from my own world,
Feeling for foot-hold through a blank profound,
Along with unborn people in strange lands,
Who say—I hear said or conceive they say—

"Was John at all, and did he say he saw?
Assure us, ere we ask what he might see!"

'And how shall I assure them? Can they share
—They, who have flesh, a veil of youth and strength
About each spirit, that needs must bide its time,   200
Living and learning still as years assist
Which wear the thickness thin, and let man see—
With me who hardly am withheld at all,
But shudderingly, scarce a shred between,
Lie bare to the universal prick of light?
Is it for nothing we grow old and weak,
We whom God loves? When pain ends, gain ends too.
To me, that story—ay, that Life and Death
Of which I wrote "it was"—to me, it is;
—Is, here and now: I apprehend nought else.   210
Is not God now i' the world His power first made?
Is not His love at issue still with sin
Visibly when a wrong is done on earth?
Love, wrong, and pain, what see I else around?
Yea, and the Resurrection and Uprise
To the right hand of the throne—what is it beside,
When such truth, breaking bounds, o'erfloods my soul,
And, as I saw the sin and death, even so
See I the need yet transiency of both,
The good and glory consummated thence?   220
I saw the power; I see the Love, once weak,
Resume the Power: and in this word "I see,"
Lo, there is recognized the Spirit of both
That moving o'er the spirit of man, unblinds
His eye and bids him look. These are, I see;
But ye, the children, His beloved ones too,
Ye need,—as I should use an optic glass°
I wondered at erewhile, somewhere i' the world,
It had been given a crafty smith to make;
A tube, he turned on objects brought too close,   230
Lying confusedly insubordinate
For the unassisted eye to master once:
Look through his tube, at distance now they lay,
Become succinct, distinct, so small, so clear!
Just thus, ye needs must apprehend what truth

I see, reduced to plain historic fact,
Diminished into clearness, proved a point
And far away: ye would withdraw your sense
From out eternity, strain it upon time,
Then stand before that fact, that Life and Death,   240
Stay there at gaze, till it dispart, dispread,°
As though a star should open out, all sides,
Grow the world on you, as it is my world.

'For life, with all it yields of joy and woe,
And hope and fear,—believe the aged friend,—
Is just our chance o' the prize of learning love,
How love might be, hath been indeed, and is;
And that we hold thenceforth to the uttermost
Such prize despite the envy of the world,
And, having gained truth, keep truth: that is all.   250
But see the double way wherein we are led,
How the soul learns diversely from the flesh!
With flesh, that hath so little time to stay,
And yields mere basement for the soul's emprise,°
Expect prompt teaching. Helpful was the light,
And warmth was cherishing and food was choice
To every man's flesh, thousand years ago,
As now to yours and mine; the body sprang
At once to the height, and stayed: but the soul,—no!
Since sages who, this noontide, meditate   260
In Rome or Athens, may descry some point
Of the eternal power, hid yestereve;
And, as thereby the power's whole mass extends,
So much extends the æther floating o'er,
The love that tops the might, the Christ in God.
Then, as new lessons shall be learned in these
Till earth's work stop and useless time run out,
So duly, daily, needs provision be
For keeping the soul's prowess possible,
Building new barriers as the old decay,   270
Saving us from evasion of life's proof,
Putting the question ever, "Does God love,
And will ye hold that truth against the world?"
Ye know there needs no second proof with good
Gained for our flesh from any earthly source:

We might go freezing, ages,—give us fire,
Thereafter we judge fire at its full worth,
And guard it safe through every chance, ye know!
That fable of Prometheus and his theft,°
How mortals gained Jove's fiery flower, grows old   280
(I have been used to hear the pagans own)
And out of mind; but fire, howe'er its birth,
Here is it, precious to the sophist now
Who laughs the myth of Æschylus to scorn,°
As precious to those satyrs of his play,
Who touched it in gay wonder at the thing.
While were it so with the soul,—this gift of truth
Once grasped, were this our soul's gain safe, and sure
To prosper as the body's gain is wont,—
Why, man's probation would conclude, his earth   290
Crumble; for he both reasons and decides,
Weighs first, then chooses: will he give up fire
For gold or purple once he knows its worth?
Could he give Christ up were His worth as plain?
Therefore, I say, to test man, the proofs shift,
Nor may he grasp that fact like other fact,
And straightway in his life acknowledge it,
As, say, the indubitable bliss of fire.
Sigh ye, "It had been easier once than now"?
To give you answer I am left alive;   300
Look at me who was present from the first!
Ye know what things I saw; then came a test,
My first, befitting me who so had seen:
"Forsake the Christ thou sawest transfigured, Him
Who trod the sea and brought the dead to life?
What should wring this from thee!"—ye laugh and ask.
What wrung it? Even a torchlight and a noise,
The sudden Roman faces, violent hands,
And fear of what the Jews might do! Just that,
And it is written, "I forsook and fled:"°   310
There was my trial, and it ended thus.
Ay, but my soul had gained its truth, could grow:
Another year or two,—what little child,
What tender woman that had seen no least
Of all my sights, but barely heard them told,
Who did not clasp the cross with a light laugh,

Or wrap the burning robe round, thanking God?
Well, was truth safe for ever, then? Not so.
Already had begun the silent work
Whereby truth, deadened of its absolute blaze,
Might need love's eye to pierce the o'erstretched doubt.   320
Teachers were busy, whispering "All is true
As the aged ones report; but youth can reach
Where age gropes dimly, weak with stir and strain,
And the full doctrine slumbers till to-day."
Thus, what the Roman's lowered spear was found,
A bar to me who touched and handled truth,
Now proved the glozing of some new shrewd tongue,°
This Ebion, this Cerinthus or their mates,°
Till imminent was the outcry "Save our Christ!"   330
Whereon I stated much of the Lord's life
Forgotten or misdelivered, and let it work.
Such work done, as it will be, what comes next?
What do I hear say, or conceive men say,
"Was John at all, and did he say he saw?
Assure us, ere we ask what he might see!"

'Is this indeed a burthen for late days,
And may I help to bear it with you all,
Using my weakness which becomes your strength?
For if a babe were born inside this grot,   340
Grew to a boy here, heard us praise the sun,
Yet had but yon sole glimmer in light's place,—
One loving him and wishful he should learn,
Would much rejoice himself was blinded first
Month by month here, so made to understand
How eyes, born darkling, apprehend amiss:
I think I could explain to such a child
There was more glow outside than gleams he caught,
Ay, nor need urge "I saw it, so believe!"
It is a heavy burthen you shall bear   350
In latter days, new lands, or old grown strange,
Left without me, which must be very soon.
What is the doubt, my brothers? Quick with it!
I see you stand conversing, each new face,
Either in fields, of yellow summer eves,
On islets yet unnamed amid the sea;

Or pace for shelter 'neath a portico
Out of the crowd in some enormous town
Where now the larks sing in a solitude;
Or muse upon blank heaps of stone and sand 360
Idly conjectured to be Ephesus:°
And no one asks his fellow any more
"Where is the promise of His coming?" but
"Was he revealed in any of His lives,
As Power, as Love, as Influencing Soul?"

'Quick, for time presses, tell the whole mind out,
And let us ask and answer and be saved!
My book speaks on, because it cannot pass;
One listens quietly, nor scoffs but pleads
"Here is a tale of things done ages since; 370
What truth was ever told the second day?
Wonders, that would prove doctrine, go for nought.
Remains the doctrine, love; well, we must love,
And what we love most, power and love in one,
Let us acknowledge on the record here,
Accepting these in Christ: must Christ then be?
Has He been? Did not we ourselves make Him?
Our mind receives but what it holds, no more.
First of the love, then; we acknowledge Christ—
A proof we comprehend His love, a proof 380
We had such love already in ourselves,
Knew first what else we should not recognize.
'Tis mere projection from man's inmost mind,
And, what he loves, thus falls reflected back,
Becomes accounted somewhat out of him;
He throws it up in air, it drops down earth's,
With shape, name, story added, man's old way.
How prove you Christ came otherwise at least?
Next try the power: He made and rules the world:
Certes there is a world once made, now ruled, 390
Unless things have been ever as we see.
Our sires declared a charioteer's yoked steeds
Brought the sun up the east and down the west,
Which only of itself now rises, sets,
As if a hand impelled it and a will,—
Thus they long thought, they who had will and hands:

But the new question's whisper is distinct,
Wherefore must all force needs be like ourselves?
We have the hands, the will; what made and drives
The sun is force, is law, is named, not known,   400
While will and love we do know; marks of these,
Eye-witnesses attest, so books declare—
As that, to punish or reward our race,
The sun at undue times arose or set
Or else stood still: what do not men affirm?
But earth requires as urgently reward
Or punishment to-day as years ago,
And none expects the sun will interpose:
Therefore it was mere passion and mistake,
Or erring zeal for right, which changed the truth.   410
Go back, far, farther, to the birth of things;
Ever the will, the intelligence, the love,
Man's!—which he gives, supposing he but finds,
As late he gave head, body, hands and feet,
To help these in what forms he called his gods.
First, Jove's brow, Juno's eyes were swept away,
But Jove's wrath, Juno's pride continued long;
As last, will, power, and love discarded these,
So law in turn discards power, love, and will.
What proveth God is otherwise at least?   420
All else, projection from the mind of man!"

'Nay, do not give me wine, for I am strong,
But place my gospel where I put my hands.

'I say that man was made to grow, not stop;
That help, he needed once, and needs no more,
Having grown but an inch by, is withdrawn:
For he hath new needs, and new helps to these.
This imports solely, man should mount on each
New height in view; the help whereby he mounts,
The ladder-rung his foot has left, may fall,   430
Since all things suffer change save God the Truth.
Man apprehends Him newly at each stage
Whereat earth's ladder drops, its service done;
And nothing shall prove twice what once was proved.
You stick a garden-plot with ordered twigs
To show inside lie germs of herbs unborn,

And check the careless step would spoil their birth;
But when herbs wave, the guardian twigs may go,
Since should ye doubt of virtues, question kinds,
It is no longer for old twigs ye look,   440
Which proved once underneath lay store of seed,
But to the herb's self, by what light ye boast,
For what fruit's signs are. This book's fruit is plain,
Nor miracles need prove it any more.
Doth the fruit show? Then miracles bade 'ware
At first of root and stem, saved both till now
From trampling ox, rough boar and wanton goat.
What? Was man made a wheelwork to wind up,°
And be discharged, and straight wound up anew?
No!—grown, his growth lasts; taught, he ne'er forgets: 450
May learn a thousand things, not twice the same.

'This might be pagan teaching: now hear mine.

'I say, that as the babe, you feed awhile,
Becomes a boy and fit to feed himself,
So, minds at first must be spoon-fed with truth:
When they can eat, babe's-nurture is withdrawn.
I fed the babe whether it would or no:
I bid the boy or feed himself or starve.
I cried once, "That ye may believe in Christ,
Behold this blind man shall receive his sight!"   460
I cry now, "Urgest thou, *for I am shrewd
And smile at stories how John's word could cure—
Repeat that miracle and take my faith?*"
I say, that miracle was duly wrought
When, save for it, no faith was possible.
Whether a change were wrought i' the shows o' the world,
Whether the change came from our minds which see
Of shows o' the world so much as and no more
Than God wills for His purpose,—(what do I
See now, suppose you, there where you see rock   470
Round us?)—I know not; such was the effect,
So faith grew, making void more miracles
Because too much: they would compel, not help.
I say, the acknowledgment of God in Christ
Accepted by thy reason, solves for thee
All questions in the earth and out of it,

And has so far advanced thee to be wise.
Wouldst thou unprove this to re-prove the proved?
In life's mere minute, with power to use that proof,
Leave knowledge and revert to how it sprung?   480
Thou hast it; use it and forthwith, or die!

'For I say, this is death and the sole death,
When a man's loss comes to him from his gain,
Darkness from light, from knowledge ignorance,
And lack of love from love made manifest;
A lamp's death when, replete with oil, it chokes;
A stomach's when, surcharged with food, it starves.
With ignorance was surety of a cure.
When man, appalled at nature, questioned first
"What if there lurk a might behind this might?"   490
He needed satisfaction God could give,
And did give, as ye have the written word:
But when he finds might still redouble might,
Yet asks, "Since all is might, what use of will?"
—Will, the one source of might,—he being man
With a man's will and a man's might, to teach
In little how the two combine in large,—
That man has turned round on himself and stands,
Which in the course of nature is, to die.

'And when man questioned, "What if there be love   500
Behind the will and might, as real as they?"—
He needed satisfaction God could give,
And did give, as ye have the written word:
But when, beholding that love everywhere,
He reasons, "Since such love is everywhere,
And since ourselves can love and would be loved,
We ourselves make the love, and Christ was not,"—
How shall ye help this man who knows himself,
That he must love and would be loved again,
Yet, owning his own love that proveth Christ,   510
Rejecteth Christ through very need of Him?
The lamp o'erswims with oil, the stomach flags
Loaded with nurture, and that man's soul dies.

'If he rejoin, "But this was all the while
A trick; the fault was, first of all, in thee,

Thy story of the places, names and dates,
Where, when and how the ultimate truth had rise,
—Thy prior truth, at last discovered none,
Whence now the second suffers detriment.
What good of giving knowledge if, because   520
O' the manner of the gift, its profit fail?
And why refuse what modicum of help
Had stopped the after-doubt, impossible
I' the face of truth—truth absolute, uniform?
Why must I hit of this and miss of that,
Distinguish just as I be weak or strong,
And not ask of thee and have answer prompt,
Was this once, was it not once?—then and now
And evermore, plain truth from man to man.
Is John's procedure just the heathen bard's?°   530
Put question of his famous play again
How for the ephemerals' sake Jove's fire was filched,
And carried in a cane and brought to earth:
The fact is in the fable, cry the wise,
Mortals obtained the boon, so much is fact,
Though fire be spirit and produced on earth.
As with the Titan's, so now with thy tale:
Why breed in us perplexity, mistake,
Nor tell the whole truth in the proper words?"

'I answer, Have ye yet to argue out   540
The very primal thesis, plainest law,
—Man is not God but hath God's end to serve,
A master to obey, a course to take,
Somewhat to cast off, somewhat to become?
Grant this, then man must pass from old to new,
From vain to real, from mistake to fact,
From what once seemed good, to what now proves best.
How could man have progression otherwise?
Before the point was mooted "What is God?"
No savage man inquired "What am myself?"   550
Much less replied, "First, last, and best of things."
Man takes that title now if he believes
Might can exist with neither will nor love,
In God's case—what he names now Nature's Law—
While in himself he recognizes love

No less than might and will: and rightly takes.
Since if man prove the sole existent thing
Where these combine, whatever their degree,
However weak the might or will or love,
So they be found there, put in evidence,—   560
He is as surely higher in the scale
Than any might with neither love nor will,
As life, apparent in the poorest midge,
(When the faint dust-speck flits, ye guess its wing)
Is marvellous beyond dead Atlas' self—°
Given to the nobler midge for resting-place!
Thus, man proves best and highest—God, in fine,
And thus the victory leads but to defeat,
The gain to loss, best rise to the worst fall,
His life becomes impossible, which is death.   570

'But if, appealing thence, he cower, avouch
He is mere man, and in humility
Neither may know God nor mistake himself;
I point to the immediate consequence
And say, by such confession straight he falls
Into man's place, a thing nor God nor beast,
Made to know that he can know and not more:
Lower than God who knows all and can all,
Higher than beasts which know and can so far
As each beast's limit, perfect to an end,   580
Nor conscious that they know, nor craving more;
While man knows partly but conceives beside,
Creeps ever on from fancies to the fact,
And in this striving, this converting air
Into a solid he may grasp and use,
Finds progress, man's distinctive mark alone,
Not God's, and not the beasts': God is, they are,
Man partly is and wholly hopes to be.
Such progress could no more attend his soul
Were all it struggles after found at first   590
And guesses changed to knowledge absolute,
Than motion wait his body, were all else
Than it the solid earth on every side,
Where now through space he moves from rest to rest.
Man, therefore, thus conditioned, must expect

He could not, what he knows now, know at first;
What he considers that he knows to-day,
Come but to-morrow, he will find misknown;
Getting increase of knowledge, since he learns
Because he lives, which is to be a man,   600
Set to instruct himself by his past self:
First, like the brute, obliged by facts to learn,
Next, as man may, obliged by his own mind,
Bent, habit, nature, knowledge turned to law.
God's gift was that man should conceive of truth
And yearn to gain it, catching at mistake,
As midway help till he reach fact indeed.
The statuary ere he mould a shape
Boasts a like gift, the shape's idea, and next
The aspiration to produce the same;   610
So, taking clay, he calls his shape thereout,
Cries ever "Now I have the thing I see":
Yet all the while goes changing what was wrought,
From falsehood like the truth, to truth itself.
How were it had he cried "I see no face,
No breast, no feet i' the ineffectual clay"?
Rather commend him that he clapped his hands,
And laughed "It is my shape and lives again!"
Enjoyed the falsehood, touched it on to truth,
Until yourselves applaud the flesh indeed   620
In what is still flesh-imitating clay.
Right in you, right in him, such way be man's!
God only makes the live shape at a jet.°
Will ye renounce this pact of creatureship?
The pattern on the Mount subsists no more,°
Seemed awhile, then returned to nothingness;
But copies, Moses strove to make thereby,
Serve still and are replaced as time requires:
By these, make newest vessels, reach the type!°
If ye demur, this judgment on your head,   630
Never to reach the ultimate, angels' law,
Indulging every instinct of the soul
There where law, life, joy, impulse are one thing!

'Such is the burthen of the latest time.
I have survived to hear it with my ears,

Answer it with my lips: does this suffice?
For if there be a further woe than such,
Wherein my brothers struggling need a hand,
So long as any pulse is left in mine,
May I be absent even longer yet, 640
Plucking the blind ones back from the abyss,
Though I should tarry a new hundred years!'

But he was dead; 'twas about noon, the day
Somewhat declining: we five buried him
That eve, and then, dividing, went five ways,
And I, disguised, returned to Ephesus.

By this, the cave's mouth must be filled with sand.
Valens is lost, I know not of his trace;
The Bactrian was but a wild childish man,
And could not write nor speak, but only loved: 650
So, lest the memory of this go quite,
Seeing that I to-morrow fight the beasts,°
I tell the same of Phœbas, whom believe!
For many look again to find that face,
Beloved John's to whom I ministered,
Somewhere in life about the world; they err:
Either mistaking what was darkly spoke
At ending of his book, as he relates,
Or misconceiving somewhat of this speech
Scattered from mouth to mouth, as I suppose. 660
Believe ye will not see him any more
About the world with his divine regard!
For all was as I say, and now the man
Lies as he lay once, breast to breast with God.

[Cerinthus read and mused; one added this:

'If Christ, as thou affirmest, be of men
Mere man, the first and best but nothing more,—
Account Him, for reward of what He was,
Now and for ever, wretchedest of all.
For see; Himself conceived of life as love, 670
Conceived of love as what must enter in,
Fill up, make one with His each soul He loved:
Thus much for man's joy, all men's joy for Him.

Well, He is gone, thou sayest, to fit reward.
But by this time are many souls set free,
And very many still retained alive:
Nay, should His coming be delayed awhile,
Say, ten years longer (twelve years, some compute)
See if, for every finger of thy hands,
There be not found, that day the world shall end,   680
Hundreds of souls, each holding by Christ's word
That He will grow incorporate with all,
With me as Pamphylax, with him as John,
Groom for each bride! Can a mere man do this?
Yet Christ saith, this He lived and died to do.
Call Christ, then, the illimitable God,
Or lost!'
                           But 'twas Cerinthus that is lost.]

Caliban upon Setebos; or, Natural Theology in the Island

'Thou thoughtest that I was altogether such a one as thyself.'

['Will sprawl, now that the heat of day is best,°
Flat on his belly in the pit's much mire,
With elbows wide, fists clenched to prop his chin.
And, while he kicks both feet in the cool slush,
And feels about his spine small eft-things course,°
Run in and out each arm, and make him laugh:
And while above his head a pompion-plant,°
Coating the cave-top as a brow its eye,
Creeps down to touch and tickle hair and beard,
And now a flower drops with a bee inside,   10
And now a fruit to snap at, catch and crunch,—
He looks out o'er yon sea which sunbeams cross
And recross till they weave a spider-web
(Meshes of fire, some great fish breaks at times)
And talks to his own self, howe'er he please,
Touching that other, whom his dam called God.°
Because to talk about Him, vexes—ha,

Could He but know! and time to vex is now,
When talk is safer than in winter-time.
Moreover Prosper and Miranda sleep°   20
In confidence he drudges at their task,
And it is good to cheat the pair, and gibe,
Letting the rank tongue blossom into speech.]°

Setebos, Setebos, and Setebos!
'Thinketh, He dwelleth i' the cold o' the moon.

'Thinketh He made it, with the sun to match,
But not the stars; the stars came otherwise;
Only made clouds, winds, meteors, such as that:
Also this isle, what lives and grows thereon,
And snaky sea which rounds and ends the same.   30

'Thinketh, it came of being ill at ease:
He hated that He cannot change His cold,
Nor cure its ache. 'Hath spied an icy fish
That longed to 'scape the rock-stream where she lived,
And thaw herself within the lukewarm brine
O' the lazy sea her stream thrusts far amid,
A crystal spike 'twixt two warm walls of wave;
Only, she ever sickened, found repulse
At the other kind of water, not her life,
(Green-dense and dim-delicious, bred o' the sun)   40
Flounced back from bliss she was not born to breathe,
And in her old bounds buried her despair,
Hating and loving warmth alike: so He.

'Thinketh, He made thereat the sun, this isle,
Trees and the fowls here, beast and creeping thing.
Yon otter, sleek-wet, black, lithe as a leech;
Yon auk, one fire-eye in a ball of foam,
That floats and feeds; a certain badger brown
He hath watched hunt with that slant white-wedge eye
By moonlight; and the pie with the long tongue°
That pricks deep into oakwarts for a worm,°   50
And says a plain word when she finds her prize,
But will not eat the ants; the ants themselves
That build a wall of seeds and settled stalks
About their hole—He made all these and more,
Made all we see, and us, in spite: how else?

He could not, Himself, make a second self
To be His mate; as well have made Himself:
He would not make what he mislikes or slights,
An eyesore to Him, or not worth His pains: 60
But did, in envy, listlessness or sport,
Make what Himself would fain, in a manner, be—
Weaker in most points, stronger in a few,
Worthy, and yet mere playthings all the while,
Things He admires and mocks too,—that is it.
Because, so brave, so better though they be,
It nothing skills if He begin to plague.
Look now, I melt a gourd-fruit into mash,
Add honeycomb and pods, I have perceived,
Which bite like finches when they bill and kiss,—   70
Then, when froth rises bladdery, drink up all,°
Quick, quick, till maggots scamper through my brain;
Last, throw me on my back i' the seeded thyme,
And wanton, wishing I were born a bird.
Put case, unable to be what I wish,
I yet could make a live bird out of clay:
Would not I take clay, pinch my Caliban
Able to fly?—for, there, see, he hath wings,
And great comb like the hoopoe's to admire,°
And there, a sting to do his foes offence,   80
There, and I will that he begin to live,
Fly to yon rock-top, nip me off the horns
Of grigs high up that make the merry din,°
Saucy through their veined wings, and mind me not.
In which feat, if his leg snapped, brittle clay,
And he lay stupid-like,—why, I should laugh;
And if he, spying me, should fall to weep,
Beseech me to be good, repair his wrong,
Bid his poor leg smart less or grow again,—
Well, as the chance were, this might take or else   90
Not take my fancy: I might hear his cry,
And give the mankin three sound legs for one,
Or pluck the other off, leave him like an egg,
And lessoned he was mine and merely clay.
Were this no pleasure, lying in the thyme,
Drinking the mash, with brain become alive,
Making and marring clay at will? So He.

'Thinketh, such shows nor right nor wrong in Him,
Nor kind, nor cruel: He is strong and Lord.
'Am strong myself compared to yonder crabs
That march now from the mountain to the sea,   100
'Let twenty pass, and stone the twenty-first,
Loving not, hating not, just choosing so.
'Say, the first straggler that boasts purple spots
Shall join the file, one pincer twisted off;
'Say, this bruised fellow shall receive a worm,
And two worms he whose nippers end in red;
As it likes me each time, I do: so He.

Well then, 'supposeth He is good i' the main,
Placable if His mind and ways were guessed,
But rougher than His handiwork, be sure!   110
Oh, He hath made things worthier than Himself,
And envieth that, so helped, such things do more
Than He who made them! What consoles but this?
That they, unless through Him, do nought at all,
And must submit: what other use in things?
'Hath cut a pipe of pithless elder joint
That, blown through, gives exact the scream o' the jay
When from her wing you twitch the feathers blue:
Sound this, and little birds that hate the jay   120
Flock within stone's throw, glad their foe is hurt:
Put case such pipe could prattle and boast forsooth
'I catch the birds, I am the crafty thing,
I make the cry my maker cannot make
With his great round mouth; he must blow through mine!'
Would not I smash it with my foot? So He.

But wherefore rough, why cold and ill at ease?
Aha, that is a question! Ask, for that,
What knows,—the something over Setebos
That made Him, or He, may be, found and fought,   130
Worsted, drove off and did to nothing, perchance.
There may be something quiet o'er His head,
Out of His reach, that feels nor joy nor grief,
Since both derive from weakness in some way.
I joy because the quails come; would not joy
Could I bring quails here when I have a mind:
This Quiet, all it hath a mind to, doth.

'Esteemeth stars the outposts of its couch,
But never spends much thought nor care that way.
It may look up, work up,—the worse for those   140
It works on! 'Careth but for Setebos
The many-handed as a cuttle-fish,°
Who, making Himself feared through what He does,
Looks up, first, and perceives he cannot soar
To what is quiet and hath happy life;
Next looks down here, and out of very spite
Makes this a bauble-world to ape yon real,
These good things to match those as hips do grapes.°
'Tis solace making baubles, ay, and sport.
Himself peeped late, eyed Prosper at his books   150
Careless and lofty, lord now of the isle:
Vexed, 'stitched a book of broad leaves, arrow-shaped,
Wrote thereon, he knows what, prodigious words;
Has peeled a wand and called it by a name;
Weareth at whiles for an enchanter's robe
The eyed skin of a supple oncelot;°
And hath an ounce sleeker than youngling mole,°
A four-legged serpent he makes cower and couch,
Now snarl, now hold its breath and mind his eye,
And saith she is Miranda and my wife: 160
'Keeps for his Ariel a tall pouch-bill crane°
He bids go wade for fish and straight disgorge;
Also a sea-beast, lumpish, which he snared,
Blinded the eyes of, and brought somewhat tame,
And split its toe-webs, and now pens the drudge
In a hole o' the rock and calls him Caliban;
A bitter heart that bides its time and bites.
'Plays thus at being Prosper in a way,
Taketh his mirth with make-believes: so He.

His dam held that the Quiet made all things   170
Which Setebos vexed only: 'holds not so.
Who made them weak, meant weakness He might vex.
Had He meant other, while His hand was in,
Why not make horny eyes no thorn could prick,
Or plate my scalp with bone against the snow,
Or overscale my flesh 'neath joint and joint,
Like an orc's armour? Ay,—so spoil His sport!°
He is the One now: only He doth all.

'Saith, He may like, perchance, what profits Him.
Ay, himself loves what does him good; but why?   180
'Gets good no otherwise. This blinded beast
Loves whoso places flesh-meat on his nose,
But, had he eyes, would want no help, but hate
Or love, just as it liked him: He hath eyes.
Also it pleaseth Setebos to work,
Use all His hands, and exercise much craft,
By no means for the love of what is worked.
'Tasteth, himself, no finer good i' the world
When all goes right, in this safe summer-time,
And he wants little, hungers, aches not much,   190
Than trying what to do with wit and strength.
'Falls to make something: 'piled yon pile of turfs,
And squared and stuck there squares of soft white chalk,
And, with a fish-tooth, scratched a moon on each,
And set up endwise certain spikes of tree,
And crowned the whole with a sloth's skull a-top,
Found dead i' the woods, too hard for one to kill.
No use at all i' the work, for work's sole sake;
'Shall some day knock it down again: so He.

'Saith He is terrible: watch His feats in proof!   200
One hurricane will spoil six good months' hope.
He hath a spite against me, that I know,
Just as He favours Prosper, who knows why?
So it is, all the same, as well I find.
'Wove wattles half the winter, fenced them firm°
With stone and stake to stop she-tortoises
Crawling to lay their eggs here: well, one wave,
Feeling the foot of Him upon its neck,
Gaped as a snake does, lolled out its large tongue,
And licked the whole labour flat: so much for spite.   210
'Saw a ball flame down late (yonder it lies)°
Where, half an hour before, I slept i' the shade:
Often they scatter sparkles: there is force!
'Dug up a newt He may have envied once
And turned to stone, shut up inside a stone.
Please Him and hinder this?—What Prosper does?
Aha, if He would tell me how! Not He!
There is the sport: discover how or die!

All need not die, for of the things o' the isle
Some flee afar, some dive, some run up trees;   220
Those at His mercy,—why, they please Him most
When... when... well, never try the same way twice!
Repeat what act has pleased, He may grow wroth.
You must not know His ways, and play Him off,
Sure of the issue. 'Doth the like himself:
'Spareth a squirrel that it nothing fears
But steals the nut from underneath my thumb,
And when I threat, bites stoutly in defence:
'Spareth an urchin that contrariwise,°
Curls up into a ball, pretending death   230
For fright at my approach: the two ways please.
But what would move my choler more than this,
That either creature counted on its life
To-morrow and next day and all days to come,
Saying, forsooth, in the inmost of its heart,
'Because he did so yesterday with me,
And otherwise with such another brute,
So must he do henceforth and always.'—Ay?
Would teach the reasoning couple what 'must' means!
'Doth as he likes, or wherefore Lord? So He.   240

'Conceiveth all things will continue thus,
And we shall have to live in fear of Him
So long as He lives, keeps His strength: no change,
If He have done His best, make no new world
To please Him more, so leave off watching this,—
If He surprise not even the Quiet's self°
Some strange day,—or, suppose, grow into it
As grubs grow butterflies: else, here are we,
And there is He, and nowhere help at all.

'Believeth with the life, the pain shall stop.   250
His dam held different, that after death
He both plagued enemies and feasted friends:
Idly! He doth His worst in this our life,
Giving just respite lest we die through pain,
Saving last pain for worst,—with which, an end.
Meanwhile, the best way to escape His ire
Is, not to seem too happy. 'Sees, himself,
Yonder two flies, with purple films and pink,°

Bask on the pompion-bell above: kills both.
'Sees two black painful beetles roll their ball   260
On head and tail as if to save their lives:
Moves them the stick away they strive to clear.

Even so, 'would have Him misconceive, suppose
This Caliban strives hard and ails no less,
And always, above all else, envies Him;
Wherefore he mainly dances on dark nights,
Moans in the sun, gets under holes to laugh,
And never speaks his mind save housed as now:
Outside, 'groans, curses. If He caught me here,
O'erheard this speech, and asked 'What chucklest at?'   270
'Would, to appease Him, cut a finger off,
Or of my three kid yearlings burn the best,
Or let the toothsome apples rot on tree,
Or push my tame beast for the orc to taste:
While myself lit a fire, and made a song
And sung it, '*What I hate, be consecrate*
To celebrate Thee and Thy state, no mate
For Thee; what see for envy in poor me?'
Hoping the while, since evils sometimes mend,
Warts rub away and sores are cured with slime,
That some strange day, will either the Quiet catch   280
And conquer Setebos, or likelier He
Decrepit may doze, doze, as good as die.

[What, what? A curtain o'er the world at once!
Crickets stop hissing; not a bird—or, yes,
There scuds His raven that has told Him all!
It was fool's play, this prattling! Ha! The wind
Shoulders the pillared dust, death's house o' the move,
And fast invading fires begin! White blaze—
A tree's head snaps—and there, there, there, there, there,   290
His thunder follows! Fool to gibe at Him!°
Lo! 'Lieth flat and loveth Setebos!
'Maketh his teeth meet through his upper lip,
Will let those quails fly, will not eat this month
One little mess of whelks, so he may 'scape!]

Confessions

I

What is he buzzing in my ears?
   'Now that I come to die,
Do I view the world as a vale of tears?'
   Ah, reverend sir, not I!

II

What I viewed there once, what I view again
   Where the physic bottles stand
On the table's edge,—is a suburb lane,
   With a wall to my bedside hand.

III

That lane sloped, much as the bottles do,
   From a house you could descry
O'er the garden-wall: is the curtain blue
   Or green to a healthy eye?

IV

To mine, it serves for the old June weather
   Blue above lane and wall;
And that farthest bottle labelled 'Ether'
   Is the house o'ertopping all.

V

At a terrace, somewhere near the stopper,
   There watched for me, one June,
A girl: I know, sir, it's improper,
   My poor mind's out of tune.

VI

Only, there was a way . . . you crept
   Close by the side, to dodge
Eyes in the house, two eyes except:
   They styled their house 'The Lodge.'

VII

What right had a lounger up their lane?
   But, by creeping very close,
With the good wall's help,—their eyes might strain
   And stretch themselves to Oes,

VIII

Yet never catch her and me together,
   As she left the attic, there,
By the rim of the bottle labelled 'Ether,'   30
   And stole from stair to stair,

IX

And stood by the rose-wreathed gate. Alas,
   We loved, sir—used to meet:
How sad and bad and mad it was—
   But then, how it was sweet!

Prospice

Fear death?—to feel the fog in my throat,
   The mist in my face,
When the snows begin, and the blasts denote
   I am nearing the place,
The power of the night, the press of the storm,
   The post of the foe;
Where he stands, the Arch Fear in a visible form,
   Yet the strong man must go:
For the journey is done and the summit attained,
   And the barriers fall,   10
Though a battle's to fight ere the guerdon be gained,
   The reward of it all.
I was ever a fighter, so—one fight more,
   The best and the last!
I would hate that death bandaged my eyes, and forbore,
   And bade me creep past.
No! let me taste the whole of it, fare like my peers
   The heroes of old,

Bear the brunt, in a minute pay glad life's arrears
    Of pain, darkness and cold.   20
For sudden the worst turns the best to the brave,
    The black minute's at end,
And the elements' rage, the fiend-voices that rave,
    Shall dwindle, shall blend,
Shall change, shall become first a peace out of pain,
    Then a light, then thy breast,
O thou soul of my soul! I shall clasp thee again,
    And with God be the rest!

Youth and Art

I

It once might have been, once only:
    We lodged in a street together,
You, a sparrow on the housetop lonely,
    I, a lone she-bird of his feather.

II

Your trade was with sticks and clay,
    You thumbed, thrust, patted and polished,
Then laughed 'They will see some day
    Smith made, and Gibson demolished.'°

III

My business was song, song, song;
    I chirped, cheeped, trilled and twittered,   10
'Kate Brown's on the boards ere long,
    And Grisi's existence embittered!'°

IV

I earned no more by a warble
    Than you by a sketch in plaster;
You wanted a piece of marble,
    I needed a music-master.

V

We studied hard in our styles,
　Chipped each at a crust like Hindoos,°
For air looked out on the tiles,
　For fun watched each other's windows.   20

VI

You lounged, like a boy of the South,
　Cap and blouse—nay, a bit of beard too;
Or you got it, rubbing your mouth
　With fingers the clay adhered to.

VII

And I—soon managed to find
　Weak points in the flower-fence facing,
Was forced to put up a blind
　And be safe in my corset-lacing.

VIII

No harm! It was not my fault
　If you never turned your eye's tail up   30
As I shook upon E *in alt*,°
　Or ran the chromatic scale up:

IX

For spring bade the sparrows pair,
　And the boys and girls gave guesses,
And stalls in our street looked rare
　With bulrush and watercresses.

X

Why did not you pinch a flower
　In a pellet of clay and fling it?
Why did not I put a power
　Of thanks in a look, or sing it?   40

XI

I did look, sharp as a lynx,
　(And yet the memory rankles)

When models arrived, some minx
    Tripped up-stairs, she and her ankles.

XII

But I think I gave you as good!
    'That foreign fellow,—who can know
How she pays, in a playful mood,
    For his tuning her that piano?'

XIII

Could you say so, and never say
    'Suppose we join hands and fortunes,   50
And I fetch her from over the way,
    Her, piano, and long tunes and short tunes?'

XIV

No, no: you would not be rash,
    Nor I rasher and something over:
You've to settle yet Gibson's hash,
    And Grisi yet lives in clover.

XV

But you meet the Prince at the Board,°
    I'm queen myself at *bals-paré*,°
I've married a rich old lord,
    And you're dubbed knight and an R.A.°   60

XVI

Each life unfulfilled, you see;
    It hangs still, patchy and scrappy:
We have not sighed deep, laughed free,
    Starved, feasted, despaired,—been happy.

XVII

And nobody calls you a dunce,
    And people suppose me clever:
This could but have happened once,
    And we missed it, lost it for ever.

A Likeness

Some people hang portraits up
In a room where they dine or sup:
    And the wife clinks tea-things under,
And her cousin, he stirs his cup,
    Asks, 'Who was the lady, I wonder?'
' 'Tis a daub John bought at a sale,'
    Quoth the wife,—looks black as thunder:
'What a shade beneath her nose!
'Snuff-taking, I suppose,—'
Adds the cousin, while John's corns ail.°   10

Or else, there's no wife in the case,
But the portrait's queen of the place,
Alone mid the other spoils
Of youth,—masks, gloves and foils,
And pipe-sticks, rose, cherry-tree, jasmine,
    And the long whip, the tandem-lasher,°
And the cast from a fist ('not, alas! mine,
    But my master's, the Tipton Slasher'),°
And the cards where pistol-balls mark ace,°
And a satin shoe used for cigar-case,   20
And the chamois-horns ('shot in the Chablais')
    And prints—Rarey drumming on Cruiser,°
    And Sayers, our champion, the bruiser,°
And the little edition of Rabelais:
Where a friend, with both hands in his pockets,
    May saunter up close to examine it,
    And remark a good deal of Jane Lamb in it,°
'But the eyes are half out of their sockets;
That hair's not so bad, where the gloss is,
But they've made the girl's nose a proboscis: 30
Jane Lamb, that we danced with at Vichy!
What, is not she Jane? Then, who is she?'

All that I own is a print,
An etching, a mezzotint;
'Tis a study, a fancy, a fiction,
Yet a fact (take my conviction)

Because it has more than a hint
　Of a certain face, I never
Saw elsewhere touch or trace of
In women I've seen the face of:　　　　　　　　　40
　　Just an etching, and, so far, clever.

I keep my prints, an imbroglio,°
Fifty in one portfolio.
When somebody tries my claret,
We turn round chairs to the fire,
Chirp over days in a garret,
　　Chuckle o'er increase of salary,
Taste the good fruits of our leisure,
Talk about pencil and lyre,
　　And the National Portrait Gallery:　　　　　　50
Then I exhibit my treasure.
After we've turned over twenty,
　　And the debt of wonder my crony owes
　　Is paid to my Marc Antonios,°
He stops me—'*Festina lentè!*°
What's that sweet thing there, the etching?'
How my waistcoat-strings want stretching,
　　How my cheeks grow red as tomatos,
How my heart leaps! But hearts, after leaps, ache.

'By the by, you must take, for a keepsake,　　　　　60
　　That other, you praised, of Volpato's.'°
The fool! would he try a flight further and say—
He never saw, never before to-day,
What was able to take his breath away,
A face to lose youth for, to occupy age
With the dream of, meet death with,—why, I'll not engage
But that, half in a rapture and half in a rage,
I should toss him the thing's self—''Tis only a duplicate,
A thing of no value! Take it, I supplicate!'

Apparent Failure

'We shall soon lose a celebrated building.'
Paris Newspaper.

I

No, for I'll save it! Seven years since,
　I passed through Paris, stopped a day
To see the baptism of your Prince;°
　Saw, made my bow, and went my way:
Walking the heat and headache off,
　I took the Seine-side, you surmise,°
Thought of the Congress, Gortschakoff,
　Cavour's appeal and Buol's replies,°
So sauntered till—what met my eyes?

II

Only the Doric little Morgue!°
　The dead-house where you show your drowned:
Petrarch's Vaucluse makes proud the Sorgue,°
　Your Morgue has made the Seine renowned.
One pays one's debt in such a case;
　I plucked up heart and entered,—stalked,
Keeping a tolerable face
　Compared with some whose cheeks were chalked:
Let them! No Briton's to be baulked!

III

First came the silent gazers; next,
　A screen of glass, we're thankful for;
Last, the sight's self, the sermon's text,
　The three men who did most abhor
Their life in Paris yesterday,
　So killed themselves: and now, enthroned
Each on his copper couch, they lay
　Fronting me, waiting to be owned.
I thought, and think, their sin's atoned.

IV

Poor men, God made, and all for that!
   The reverence struck me; o'er each head
Religiously was hung its hat,   30
   Each coat dripped by the owner's bed,
Sacred from touch: each had his berth,
   His bounds, his proper place of rest,
Who last night tenanted on earth
   Some arch, where twelve such slept abreast,—
Unless the plain asphalte seemed best.

V

How did it happen, my poor boy?
   You wanted to be Buonaparte
And have the Tuileries for toy,°
   And could not, so it broke your heart?   40
You, old one by his side, I judge,
   Were, red as blood, a socialist,
A leveller! Does the Empire grudge°
   You've gained what no Republic missed?
Be quiet, and unclench your fist!

VI

And this—why, he was red in vain,°
   Or black,—poor fellow that is blue!
What fancy was it turned your brain?
   Oh, women were the prize for you!
Money gets women, cards and dice   50
   Get money, and ill-luck gets just
The copper couch and one clear nice
   Cool squirt of water o'er your bust,
The right thing to extinguish lust!

VII

It's wiser being good than bad;
   It's safer being meek than fierce:
It's fitter being sane than mad.
   My own hope is, a sun will pierce
The thickest cloud earth ever stretched;

That, after Last, returns the First,
Though a wide compass round be fetched;
  That what began best, can't end worst,
Nor what God blessed once, prove accurst.

Epilogue

FIRST SPEAKER, *as David*

I

On the first of the Feast of Feasts,
  The Dedication Day,°
When the Levites joined the Priests°
  At the Altar in robed array,
Gave signal to sound and say,—

II

When the thousands, rear and van,°
  Swarming with one accord
Became as a single man
  (Look, gesture, thought and word)
In praising and thanking the Lord,—   10

III

When the singers lift up their voice,
  And the trumpets made endeavour,
Sounding, 'In God rejoice!'
  Saying, 'In Him rejoice
Whose mercy endureth for ever!'

IV

Then the Temple filled with a cloud,
  Even the House of the Lord;
Porch bent and pillar bowed:
  For the presence of the Lord,
In the glory of His cloud,
  Had filled the House of the Lord.   20

SECOND SPEAKER, *as Renan*

Gone now! All gone across the dark so far,
   Sharpening fast, shuddering ever, shutting still,
Dwindling into the distance, dies that star°
   Which came, stood, opened once! We gazed our fill
With upturned faces on as real a Face°
   That, stooping from grave music and mild fire,
Took in our homage, made a visible place
   Through many a depth of glory, gyre on gyre,°
For the dim human tribute. Was this true?   30
   Could man indeed avail, mere praise of his,
To help by rapture God's own rapture too,
   Thrill with a heart's red tinge that pure pale bliss?
Why did it end? Who failed to beat the breast,
   And shriek, and throw the arms protesting wide,
When a first shadow showed the star addressed
   Itself to motion, and on either side
The rims contracted as the rays retired;
   The music, like a fountain's sickening pulse,
Subsided on itself; awhile transpired   40
   Some vestige of a Face no pangs convulse,
No prayers retard; then even this was gone,
   Lost in the night at last. We, lone and left
Silent through centuries, ever and anon
   Venture to probe again the vault bereft
Of all now save the lesser lights, a mist
   Of multitudinous points, yet suns, men say—
And this leaps ruby, this lurks amethyst,
   But where may hide what came and loved our clay?
How shall the sage detect in yon expanse   50
   The star which chose to stoop and stay for us?
Unroll the records! Hailed ye such advance
   Indeed, and did your hope evanish thus?
Watchers of twilight, is the worst averred?
   We shall not look up, know ourselves are seen,
Speak, and be sure that we again are heard,
   Acting or suffering, have the disk's serene°
Reflect our life, absorb an earthly flame,
   Nor doubt that, were mankind inert and numb,
Its core had never crimsoned all the same,   60

Nor, missing ours, its music fallen dumb?
Oh, dread succession to a dizzy post,
  Sad sway of sceptre whose mere touch appals,
Ghastly dethronement, cursed by those the most
  On whose repugnant brow the crown next falls!

THIRD SPEAKER

I

Witless alike of will and way divine,
How heaven's high with earth's low should intertwine!
Friends, I have seen through your eyes: now use mine!

II

Take the least man of all mankind, as I;
Look at his head and heart, find how and why
He differs from his fellows utterly:

70

III

Then, like me, watch when nature by degrees
Grows alive round him, as in Arctic seas
(They said of old) the instinctive water flees

IV

Toward some elected point of central rock,
As though, for its sake only, roamed the flock
Of waves about the waste: awhile they mock

V

With radiance caught for the occasion,—hues
Of blackest hell now, now such reds and blues
As only heaven could fitly interfuse,—

80

VI

The mimic monarch of the whirlpool, king
O' the current for a minute: then they wring
Up by the roots and oversweep the thing,

VII

And hasten off, to play again elsewhere
The same part, choose another peak as bare,
They find and flatter, feast and finish there.

VIII

When you see what I tell you,—nature dance
About each man of us, retire, advance,
As though the pageant's end were to enhance

IX

His worth, and—once the life, his product, gained—   90
Roll away elsewhere, keep the strife sustained,
And show thus real, a thing the North but feigned—

X

When you acknowledge that one world could do
All the diverse work, old yet ever new,
Divide us, each from other, me from you,—

XI

Why, where's the need of Temple, when the walls
O' the world are that? What use of swells and falls
From Levites' choir, Priests' cries, and trumpet-calls?

XII

That one Face, far from vanish, rather grows,
Or decomposes but to recompose,   100
Become my universe that feels and knows.

from THE RING AND THE BOOK
(1868–9)

Book I
The Ring and the Book

Do you see this Ring?
                    'Tis Rome-work, made to match°
(By Castellani's imitative craft)
Etrurian circlets found, some happy morn,
After a dropping April; found alive
Spark-like 'mid unearthed slope-side figtree-roots
That roof old tombs at Chiusi: soft, you see,
Yet crisp as jewel-cutting. There's one trick,
(Craftsmen instruct me) one approved device
And but one, fits such slivers of pure gold
As this was,—such mere oozings from the mine,   10
Virgin as oval tawny pendent tear
At beehive-edge when ripened combs o'erflow,—
To bear the file's tooth and the hammer's tap:
Since hammer needs must widen out the round,
And file emboss it fine with lily-flowers,
Ere the stuff grow a ring-thing right to wear.
That trick is, the artificer melts up wax
With honey, so to speak; he mingles gold
With gold's alloy, and, duly tempering both,
Effects a manageable mass, then works: 20
But his work ended, once the thing a ring,
Oh, there's repristination! Just a spirt°
O' the proper fiery acid o'er its face,
And forth the alloy unfastened flies in fume;
While, self-sufficient now, the shape remains,
The rondure brave, the lilied loveliness,
Gold as it was, is, shall be evermore:
Prime nature with an added artistry—
No carat lost, and you have gained a ring.

What of it? 'Tis a figure, a symbol, say;   30
A thing's sign: now for the thing signified.

Do you see this square old yellow Book, I toss
I' the air, and catch again, and twirl about
By the crumpled vellum covers,—pure crude fact
Secreted from man's life when hearts beat hard,
And brains, high-blooded, ticked two centuries since?°
Examine it yourselves! I found this book,
Gave a *lira* for it, eightpence English just,
(Mark the predestination!) when a Hand,
Always above my shoulder, pushed me once,   40
One day still fierce 'mid many a day struck calm,
Across a Square in Florence, crammed with booths,
Buzzing and blaze, noontide and market-time,
Toward Baccio's marble,—ay, the basement-ledge
O' the pedestal where sits and menaces
John of the Black Bands with the upright spear,
'Twixt palace and church,—Riccardi where they lived,
His race, and San Lorenzo where they lie.°
This book,—precisely on that palace-step
Which, meant for lounging knaves o' the Medici,°   50
Now serves re-venders to display their ware,—
'Mongst odds and ends of ravage, picture-frames
White through the worn gilt, mirror-sconces chipped,
Bronze angel-heads once knobs attached to chests,
(Handled when ancient dames chose forth brocade)
Modern chalk drawings, studies from the nude,
Samples of stone, jet, breccia, porphyry,
Polished and rough, sundry amazing busts
In baked earth, (broken, Providence be praised!)
A wreck of tapestry, proudly-purposed web   60
When reds and blues were indeed red and blue,
Now offered as a mat to save bare feet
(Since carpets constitute a cruel cost)
Treading the chill scagliola bedward: then°
A pile of brown-etched prints, two *crazie* each,°
Stopped by a conch a-top from fluttering forth
—Sowing the Square with works of one and the same
Master, the imaginative Sienese°
Great in the scenic backgrounds—(name and fame

None of you know, nor does he fare the worse:)   70
From these...Oh, with a Lionard going cheap°
If it should prove, as promised, that Joconde°
Whereof a copy contents the Louvre!—these
I picked this book from. Five compeers in flank
Stood left and right of it as tempting more—
A dogseared Spicilegium, the fond tale°
O' the Frail one of the Flower, by young Dumas,°
Vulgarized Horace for the use of schools,
The Life, Death, Miracles of Saint Somebody,
Saint Somebody Else, his Miracles, Death and Life,—   80
With this, one glance at the lettered back of which,
And 'Stall!' cried I: a *lira* made it mine.

Here it is, this I toss and take again;
Small-quarto size, part print part manuscript:
A book in shape but, really, pure crude fact
Secreted from man's life when hearts beat hard,
And brains, high-blooded, ticked two centuries since.
Give it me back! The thing's restorative
I' the touch and sight.

        That memorable day,
(June was the month, Lorenzo named the Square)   90
I leaned a little and overlooked my prize
By the low railing round the fountain-source
Close to the statue, where a step descends:
While clinked the cans of copper, as stooped and rose
Thick-ankled girls who brimmed them, and made place
For marketmen glad to pitch basket down,
Dip a broad melon-leaf that holds the wet,
And whisk their faded fresh. And on I read
Presently, though my path grew perilous
Between the outspread straw-work, piles of plait   100
Soon to be flapping, each o'er two black eyes
And swathe of Tuscan hair, on festas fine:
Through fire-irons, tribes of tongs, shovels in sheaves,
Skeleton bedsteads, wardrobe-drawers agape,
Rows of tall slim brass lamps with dangling gear,—
And worse, cast clothes a-sweetening in the sun:
None of them took my eye from off my prize.

Still read I on, from written title-page
To written index, on, through street and street,
At the Strozzi, at the Pillar, at the Bridge;   110
Till, by the time I stood at home again
In Casa Guidi by Felice Church,°
Under the doorway where the black begins
With the first stone-slab of the staircase cold,
I had mastered the contents, knew the whole truth
Gathered together, bound up in this book,
Print three-fifths, written supplement the rest.
'*Romana Homicidiorum*'—nay,
Better translate—'A Roman murder-case:
Position of the entire criminal cause   120
Of Guido Franceschini, nobleman,
With certain Four the cutthroats in his pay,
Tried, all five, and found guilty and put to death
By heading or hanging as befitted ranks,
At Rome on February Twenty Two,
Since our salvation Sixteen Ninety Eight:
Wherein it is disputed if, and when,
Husbands may kill adulterous wives, yet 'scape
The customary forfeit.'

                    Word for word,
So ran the title-page: murder, or else   130
Legitimate punishment of the other crime,
Accounted murder by mistake,—just that
And no more, in a Latin cramp enough
When the law had her eloquence to launch,
But interfilleted with Italian streaks
When testimony stooped to mother-tongue,—
That, was this old square yellow book about.

Now, as the ingot, ere the ring was forged,
Lay gold, (beseech you, hold that figure fast!)
So, in this book lay absolutely truth,   140
Fanciless fact, the documents indeed,
Primary lawyer-pleadings for, against,
The aforesaid Five; real summed-up circumstance
Adduced in proof of these on either side,
Put forth and printed, as the practice was,
At Rome, in the Apostolic Chamber's type,

And so submitted to the eye o' the Court
Presided over by His Reverence
Rome's Governor and Criminal Judge,—the trial
Itself, to all intents, being then as now   150
Here in the book and nowise out of it;
Seeing, there properly was no judgment-bar,
No bringing of accuser and accused,
And whoso judged both parties, face to face
Before some court, as we conceive of courts.
There was a Hall of Justice; that came last:
For Justice had a chamber by the hall
Where she took evidence first, summed up the same,
Then sent accuser and accused alike,
In person of the advocate of each,   160
To weigh its worth, thereby arrange, array
The battle. 'Twas the so-styled Fisc began,
Pleaded (and since he only spoke in print
The printed voice of him lives now as then)
The public Prosecutor—'Murder's proved;
With five ... what we call qualities of bad,
Worse, worst, and yet worse still, and still worse yet;
Crest over crest crowning the cockatrice,°
That beggar hell's regalia to enrich
Count Guido Franceschini: punish him!'   170
Thus was the paper put before the court
In the next stage, (no noisy work at all,)
To study at ease. In due time like reply
Came from the so-styled Patron of the Poor,
Official mouthpiece of the five accused
Too poor to fee a better,—Guido's luck
Or else his fellows',—which, I hardly know,—
An outbreak as of wonder at the world,
A fury-fit of outraged innocence,
A passion of betrayed simplicity: 180
'Punish Count Guido? For what crime, what hint
O' the colour of a crime, inform us first!
Reward him rather! Recognize, we say,
In the deed done, a righteous judgment dealt!
All conscience and all courage,—there's our Count
Charactered in a word; and, what's more strange,
He had companionship in privilege,

Found four courageous conscientious friends:
Absolve, applaud all five, as props of law,
Sustainers of society!—perchance   190
A trifle over-hasty with the hand
To hold her tottering ark, had tumbled else;°
But that's a splendid fault whereat we wink,
Wishing your cold correctness sparkled so!'
Thus paper second followed paper first,
Thus did the two join issue—nay, the four,
Each pleader having an adjunct. 'True, he killed
—So to speak—in a certain sort—his wife,
But laudably, since thus it happed!' quoth one:
Whereat, more witness and the case postponed.   200
'Thus it happed not, since thus he did the deed,
And proved himself thereby portentousest
Of cutthroats and a prodigy of crime,
As the woman that he slaughtered was a saint,
Martyr and miracle!' quoth the other to match:
Again, more witness, and the case postponed.
'A miracle, ay—of lust and impudence;
Hear my new reasons!' interposed the first:
'—Coupled with more of mine!' pursued his peer.
'Beside, the precedents, the authorities!'   210
From both at once a cry with an echo, that!
That was a firebrand at each fox's tail
Unleashed in a cornfield: soon spread flare enough,°
As hurtled thither and there heaped themselves
From earth's four corners, all authority
And precedent for putting wives to death,
Or letting wives live, sinful as they seem.
How legislated, now, in this respect,
Solon and his Athenians? Quote the code
Of Romulus and Rome! Justinian speak!   220
Nor modern Baldo, Bartolo be dumb!
The Roman voice was potent, plentiful;
Cornelia de Sicariis hurried to help
Pompeia de Parricidiis; Julia de
Something-or-other jostled *Lex* this-and-that;
King Solomon confirmed Apostle Paul:
That nice decision of Dolabella, eh?
That pregnant instance of Theodoric, oh!

Down to that choice example Ælian gives°
(An instance I find much insisted on)   230
Of the elephant who, brute-beast though he were,
Yet understood and punished on the spot
His master's naughty spouse and faithless friend;
A true tale which has edified each child,
Much more shall flourish favoured by our court!
Pages of proof this way, and that way proof,
And always—once again the case postponed.

Thus wrangled, brangled, jangled they a month,
—Only on paper, pleadings all in print,
Nor ever was, except i' the brains of men,   240
More noise by word of mouth than you hear now—
Till the court cut all short with 'Judged, your cause.
Receive our sentence! Praise God! We pronounce
Count Guido devilish and damnable:
His wife Pompilia in thought, word and deed,
Was perfect pure, he murdered her for that:
As for the Four who helped the One, all Five—
Why, let employer and hirelings share alike
In guilt and guilt's reward, the death their due!'

So was the trial at end, do you suppose?   250
'Guilty you find him, death you doom him to?
Ay, were not Guido, more than needs, a priest,
Priest and to spare!'—this was a shot reserved;
I learn this from epistles which begin
Here where the print ends,—see the pen and ink
Of the advocate, the ready at a pinch!—
'My client boasts the clerkly privilege,°
Has taken minor orders many enough,
Shows still sufficient chrism upon his pate
To neutralize a blood-stain: presbyter,   260
Primæ tonsuræ, subdiaconus,
Sacerdos, so he slips from underneath°
Your power, the temporal, slides inside the robe
Of mother Church: to her we make appeal
By the Pope, the Church's head!'

                              A parlous plea,
Put in with noticeable effect, it seems;
'Since straight,'—resumes the zealous orator,

Making a friend acquainted with the facts,—
'Once the word "clericality" let fall,
Procedure stopped and freer breath was drawn   270
By all considerate and responsible Rome.'
Quality took the decent part, of course;°
Held by the husband, who was noble too:
Or, for the matter of that, a churl would side
With too-refined susceptibility,
And honour which, tender in the extreme,
Stung to the quick, must roughly right itself
At all risks, not sit still and whine for law
As a Jew would, if you squeezed him to the wall,
Brisk-trotting through the Ghetto. Nay, it seems,   280
Even the Emperor's Envoy had his say
To say on the subject; might not see, unmoved,
Civility menaced throughout Christendom
By too harsh measure dealt her champion here.
Lastly, what made all safe, the Pope was kind,
From his youth up, reluctant to take life,
If mercy might be just and yet show grace;
Much more unlikely then, in extreme age,
To take a life the general sense bade spare.
'Twas plain that Guido would go scatheless yet.   290

But human promise, oh, how short of shine!
How topple down the piles of hope we rear!
How history proves . . . nay, read Herodotus!°
Suddenly starting from a nap, as it were,
A dog-sleep with one shut, one open orb,
Cried the Pope's great self,—Innocent by name
And nature too, and eighty-six years old,
Antonio Pignatelli of Naples, Pope
Who had trod many lands, known many deeds,
Probed many hearts, beginning with his own,   300
And now was far in readiness for God,—
'Twas he who first bade leave those souls in peace,
Those Jansenists, re-nicknamed Molinists,°
('Gainst whom the cry went, like a frowsy tune,
Tickling men's ears—the sect for a quarter of an hour
I' the teeth of the world which, clown-like, loves to chew
Be it but a straw 'twixt work and whistling-while,

Taste some vituperation, bite away,
Whether at marjoram-sprig or garlic-clove,
Aught it may sport with, spoil, and then spit forth)   310
'Leave them alone,' bade he, 'those Molinists!
Who may have other light than we perceive,
Or why is it the whole world hates them thus?'
Also he peeled off that last scandal-rag
Of Nepotism; and so observed the poor
That men would merrily say, 'Halt, deaf and blind,
Who feed on fat things, leave the master's self
To gather up the fragments of his feast,
These be the nephews of Pope Innocent!—
His own meal costs but five carlines a day,°   320
Poor-priest's allowance, for he claims no more.'
—He cried of a sudden, this great good old Pope,
When they appealed in last resort to him,
'I have mastered the whole matter: I nothing doubt.
Though Guido stood forth priest from head to heel,
Instead of, as alleged, a piece of one,—
And further, were he, from the tonsured scalp
To the sandaled sole of him, my son and Christ's,
Instead of touching us by finger-tip
As you assert, and pressing up so close   330
Only to set a blood-smutch on our robe,—
I and Christ would renounce all right in him.
Am I not Pope, and presently to die,
And busied how to render my account,
And shall I wait a day ere I decide
On doing or not doing justice here?
Cut off his head to-morrow by this time,
Hang up his four mates, two on either hand,
And end one business more!'

                           So said, so done—
Rather so writ, for the old Pope bade this,   340
I find, with his particular chirograph,°
His own no such infirm hand, Friday night;
And next day, February Twenty Two,
Since our salvation Sixteen Ninety Eight,
—Not at the proper head-and-hanging-place
On bridge-foot close by Castle Angelo,

Where custom somewhat staled the spectacle,
('Twas not so well i' the way of Rome, beside,
The noble Rome, the Rome of Guido's rank)
But at the city's newer gayer end,—   350
The cavalcading promenading place
Beside the gate and opposite the church
Under the Pincian gardens green with Spring,
'Neath the obelisk 'twixt the fountains in the Square,
Did Guido and his fellows find their fate,
All Rome for witness, and—my writer adds—
Remonstrant in its universal grief,
Since Guido had the suffrage of all Rome.°

This is the bookful; thus far take the truth,
The untempered gold, the fact untampered with,   360
The mere ring-metal ere the ring be made!
And what has hitherto come of it? Who preserves
The memory of this Guido, and his wife
Pompilia, more than Ademollo's name,°
The etcher of those prints, two *crazie* each,
Saved by a stone from snowing broad the Square
With scenic backgrounds? Was this truth of force?
Able to take its own part as truth should,
Sufficient, self-sustaining? Why, if so—
Yonder's a fire, into it goes my book,   370
As who shall say me nay, and what the loss?
You know the tale already: I may ask,
Rather than think to tell you, more thereof,—
Ask you not merely who were he and she,
Husband and wife, what manner of mankind,
But how you hold concerning this and that
Other yet-unnamed actor in the piece.
The young frank handsome courtly Canon, now,
The priest, declared the lover of the wife,
He who, no question, did elope with her,   380
For certain bring the tragedy about,
Giuseppe Caponsacchi;—his strange course
I' the matter, was it right or wrong or both?
Then the old couple, slaughtered with the wife
By the husband as accomplices in crime,
Those Comparini, Pietro and his spouse,—

What say you to the right or wrong of that,
When, at a known name whispered through the door
Of a lone villa on a Christmas night,
It opened that the joyous hearts inside   390
Might welcome as it were an angel-guest
Come in Christ's name to knock and enter, sup
And satisfy the loving ones he saved,
And so did welcome devils and their death?
I have been silent on that circumstance
Although the couple passed for close of kin
To wife and husband, were by some accounts
Pompilia's very parents: you know best.
Also that infant the great joy was for,
That Gaetano, the wife's two-weeks' babe,°   400
The husband's first-born child, his son and heir,
Whose birth and being turned his night to day—
Why must the father kill the mother thus
Because she bore his son and saved himself?

Well, British Public, ye who like me not,
(God love you!) and will have your proper laugh
At the dark question, laugh it! I laugh first.
Truth must prevail, the proverb vows; and truth°
—Here is it all i' the book at last, as first
There it was all i' the heads and hearts of Rome   410
Gentle and simple, never to fall nor fade
Nor be forgotten. Yet, a little while,
The passage of a century or so,
Decads thrice five, and here's time paid his tax,
Oblivion gone home with her harvesting,
And all left smooth again as scythe could shave.
Far from beginning with you London folk,
I took my book to Rome first, tried truth's power
On likely people. 'Have you met such names?
Is a tradition extant of such facts?   420
Your law-courts stand, your records frown a-row:
What if I rove and rummage?' '—Why, you'll waste
Your pains and end as wise as you began!'
Everyone snickered: 'names and facts thus old
Are newer much than Europe news we find
Down in to-day's *Diario*. Records, quotha?°

Why, the French burned them, what else do the French?°
The rap-and-rending nation! And it tells
Against the Church, no doubt,—another gird
At the Temporality, your Trial, of course?'   430
'—Quite otherwise this time,' submitted I;
'Clean for the Church and dead against the world,
The flesh and the devil, does it tell for once.'
'—The rarer and the happier! All the same,
Content you with your treasure of a book,
And waive what's wanting! Take a friend's advice!
It's not the custom of the country. Mend
Your ways indeed and we may stretch a point:
Go get you manned by Manning and new-manned
By Newman and, mayhap, wise-manned to boot   440
By Wiseman, and we'll see or else we won't!°
Thanks meantime for the story, long and strong,
A pretty piece of narrative enough,
Which scarce ought so to drop out, one would think,
From the more curious annals of our kind.
Do you tell the story, now, in off-hand style,
Straight from the book? Or simply here and there,
(The while you vault it through the loose and large)
Hang to a hint? Or is there book at all,
And don't you deal in poetry, make-believe,   450
And the white lies it sounds like?'

                        Yes and no!
From the book, yes; thence bit by bit I dug
The lingot truth, that memorable day,°
Assayed and knew my piecemeal gain was gold,—
Yes; but from something else surpassing that,
Something of mine which, mixed up with the mass,
Made it bear hammer and be firm to file.
Fancy with fact is just one fact the more;
To-wit, that fancy has informed, transpierced,
Thridded and so thrown fast the facts else free,   460
As right through ring and ring runs the djereed°
And binds the loose, one bar without a break.
I fused my live soul and that inert stuff,
Before attempting smithcraft, on the night
After the day when,—truth thus grasped and gained,—

The book was shut and done with and laid by
On the cream-coloured massive agate, broad
'Neath the twin cherubs in the tarnished frame
O' the mirror, tall thence to the ceiling-top.
And from the reading, and that slab I leant   470
My elbow on, the while I read and read,
I turned, to free myself and find the world,
And stepped out on the narrow terrace, built
Over the street and opposite the church,
And paced its lozenge-brickwork sprinkled cool;
Because Felice-church-side stretched, a-glow°
Through each square window fringed for festival,
Whence came the clear voice of the cloistered ones
Chanting a chant made for midsummer nights—
I know not what particular praise of God,   480
It always came and went with June. Beneath
I' the street, quick shown by openings of the sky
When flame fell silently from cloud to cloud,
Richer than that gold snow Jove rained on Rhodes,°
The townsmen walked by twos and threes, and talked,
Drinking the blackness in default of air—
A busy human sense beneath my feet:
While in and out the terrace-plants, and round
One branch of tall datura, waxed and waned°
The lamp-fly lured there, wanting the white flower.   490
Over the roof o' the lighted church I looked
A bowshot to the street's end, north away
Out of the Roman gate to the Roman road
By the river, till I felt the Apennine.
And there would lie Arezzo, the man's town,°
The woman's trap and cage and torture-place,
Also the stage where the priest played his part,
A spectacle for angels,—ay, indeed,
There lay Arezzo! Farther then I fared,
Feeling my way on through the hot and dense,   500
Romeward, until I found the wayside inn
By Castelnuovo's few mean hut-like homes°
Huddled together on the hill-foot bleak,
Bare, broken only by that tree or two
Against the sudden bloody splendour poured
Cursewise in day's departure by the sun

O'er the low house-roof of that squalid inn
Where they three, for the first time and the last,
Husband and wife and priest, met face to face.
Whence I went on again, the end was near,   510
Step by step, missing none and marking all,
Till Rome itself, the ghastly goal, I reached.
Why, all the while,—how could it otherwise?—
The life in me abolished the death of things,
Deep calling unto deep: as then and there
Acted itself over again once more
The tragic piece. I saw with my own eyes
In Florence as I trod the terrace, breathed
The beauty and the fearfulness of night,
How it had run, this round from Rome to Rome—   520
Because, you are to know, they lived at Rome,
Pompilia's parents, as they thought themselves,
Two poor ignoble hearts who did their best
Part God's way, part the other way than God's,
To somehow make a shift and scramble through
The world's mud, careless if it splashed and spoiled,
Provided they might so hold high, keep clean
Their child's soul, one soul white enough for three,
And lift it to whatever star should stoop,
What possible sphere of purer life than theirs   530
Should come in aid of whiteness hard to save.
I saw the star stoop, that they strained to touch,
And did touch and depose their treasure on,
As Guido Franceschini took away
Pompilia to be his for evermore,
While they sang 'Now let us depart in peace,
Having beheld thy glory, Guido's wife!'
I saw the star supposed, but fog o' the fen,
Gilded star-fashion by a glint from hell;
Having been heaved up, haled on its gross way,   540
By hands unguessed before, invisible help
From a dark brotherhood, and specially
Two obscure goblin creatures, fox-faced this,
Cat-clawed the other, called his next of kin
By Guido the main monster,—cloaked and caped,
Making as they were priests, to mock God more,—
Abate Paul, Canon Girolamo.°

These who had rolled the starlike pest to Rome
And stationed it to suck up and absorb
The sweetness of Pompilia, rolled again   550
That bloated bubble, with her soul inside,
Back to Arezzo and a palace there—
Or say, a fissure in the honest earth
Whence long ago had curled the vapour first,
Blown big by nether fires to appal day:
It touched home, broke, and blasted far and wide.
I saw the cheated couple find the cheat
And guess what foul rite they were captured for,—
Too fain to follow over hill and dale
That child of theirs caught up thus in the cloud   560
And carried by the Prince o' the Power of the Air°
Whither he would, to wilderness or sea.
I saw them, in the potency of fear,
Break somehow through the satyr-family
(For a grey mother with a monkey-mien,
Mopping and mowing, was apparent too,°
As, confident of capture, all took hands
And danced about the captives in a ring)
—Saw them break through, breathe safe, at Rome again,
Saved by the selfish instinct, losing so   570
Their loved one left with haters. These I saw,
In recrudescency of baffled hate,
Prepare to wring the uttermost revenge
From body and soul thus left them: all was sure,
Fire laid and cauldron set, the obscene ring traced,
The victim stripped and prostrate: what of God?
The cleaving of a cloud, a cry, a crash,
Quenched lay their cauldron, cowered i' the dust the crew,
As, in a glory of armour like Saint George,°
Out again sprang the young good beauteous priest   580
Bearing away the lady in his arms,
Saved for a splendid minute and no more.
For, whom i' the path did that priest come upon,
He and the poor lost lady borne so brave,
—Checking the song of praise in me, had else
Swelled to the full for God's will done on earth—
Whom but a dusk misfeatured messenger,
No other than the angel of this life,

Whose care is lest men see too much at once.
He made the sign, such God glimpse must suffice,   590
Nor prejudice the Prince o' the Power of the Air,
Whose ministration piles us overhead
What we call, first, earth's roof and, last, heaven's floor,
Now grate o' the trap, then outlet of the cage:
So took the lady, left the priest alone,
And once more canopied the world with black.
But through the blackness I saw Rome again,
And where a solitary villa stood
In a lone garden-quarter: it was eve,
The second of the year, and oh so cold!   600
Ever and anon there flittered through the air
A snow-flake, and a scanty couch of snow
Crusted the grass-walk and the garden-mould.
All was grave, silent, sinister,—when, ha?
Glimmeringly did a pack of were-wolves pad
The snow, those flames were Guido's eyes in front,
And all five found and footed it, the track,
To where a threshold-streak of warmth and light
Betrayed the villa-door with life inside,
While an inch outside were those blood-bright eyes,   610
And black lips wrinkling o'er the flash of teeth,
And tongues that lolled—Oh God that madest man!
They parleyed in their language. Then one whined—
That was the policy and master-stroke—
Deep in his throat whispered what seemed a name—
'Open to Caponsacchi!' Guido cried:
'Gabriel!' cried Lucifer at Eden-gate.°
Wide as a heart, opened the door at once,
Showing the joyous couple, and their child
The two-weeks' mother, to the wolves, the wolves   620
To them. Close eyes! And when the corpses lay
Stark-stretched, and those the wolves, their wolf-work done,
Were safe-embosomed by the night again,
I knew a necessary change in things;
As when the worst watch of the night gives way,
And there comes duly, to take cognizance,
The scrutinizing eye-point of some star—
And who despairs of a new daybreak now?
Lo, the first ray protruded on those five!

It reached them, and each felon writhed transfixed 630
Awhile they palpitated on the spear
Motionless over Tophet: stand or fall?°
'I say, the spear should fall—should stand, I say!'
Cried the world come to judgment, granting grace
Or dealing doom according to world's wont,
Those world's-bystanders grouped on Rome's cross-road
At prick and summons of the primal curse
Which bids man love as well as make a lie.
There prattled they, discoursed the right and wrong,
Turned wrong to right, proved wolves sheep and sheep wolves, 640
So that you scarce distinguished fell from fleece;°
Till out spoke a great guardian of the fold,
Stood up, put forth his hand that held the crook,
And motioned that the arrested point decline:
Horribly off, the wriggling dead-weight reeled,
Rushed to the bottom and lay ruined there.
Though still at the pit's mouth, despite the smoke
O' the burning, tarriers turned again to talk
And trim the balance, and detect at least
A touch of wolf in what showed whitest sheep, 650
A cross of sheep redeeming the whole wolf,—
Vex truth a little longer:—less and less,
Because years came and went, and more and more
Brought new lies with them to be loved in turn.
Till all at once the memory of the thing,—
The fact that, wolves or sheep, such creatures were,—
Which hitherto, however men supposed,
Had somehow plain and pillar-like prevailed
I' the midst of them, indisputably fact,
Granite, time's tooth should grate against, not graze,— 660
Why, this proved sandstone, friable, fast to fly
And give its grain away at wish o' the wind.
Ever and ever more diminutive,
Base gone, shaft lost, only entablature,°
Dwindled into no bigger than a book,
Lay of the column; and that little, left
By the roadside 'mid the ordure, shards and weeds.
Until I haply, wandering that lone way,
Kicked it up, turned it over, and recognized,
For all the crumblement, this abacus, 670

This square old yellow book,—could calculate
By this the lost proportions of the style.

This was it from, my fancy with those facts,
I used to tell the tale, turned gay to grave,
But lacked a listener seldom; such alloy,
Such substance of me interfused the gold
Which, wrought into a shapely ring therewith,
Hammered and filed, fingered and favoured, last°
Lay ready for the renovating wash
O' the water. 'How much of the tale was true?'   680
I disappeared; the book grew all in all;
The lawyers' pleadings swelled back to their size,—
Doubled in two, the crease upon them yet,
For more commodity of carriage, see!—°
And these are letters, veritable sheets
That brought posthaste the news to Florence, writ
At Rome the day Count Guido died, we find,
To stay the craving of a client there,
Who bound the same and so produced my book.
Lovers of dead truth, did ye fare the worse?   690
Lovers of live truth, found ye false my tale?

Well, now; there's nothing in nor out o' the world
Good except truth: yet this, the something else,
What's this then, which proves good yet seems untrue?
This that I mixed with truth, motions of mine
That quickened, made the inertness malleolable
O' the gold was not mine,—what's your name for this?
Are means to the end, themselves in part the end?
Is fiction which makes fact alive, fact too?
The somehow may be thishow.
                          I find first   700
Writ down for very A B C of fact,
'In the beginning God made heaven and earth;'
From which, no matter with what lisp, I spell
And speak you out a consequence—that man,
Man,—as befits the made, the inferior thing,—
Purposed, since made, to grow, not make in turn,
Yet forced to try and make, else fail to grow,—
Formed to rise, reach at, if not grasp and gain
The good beyond him,—which attempt is growth,—

Repeats God's process in man's due degree,   710
Attaining man's proportionate result,—
Creates, no, but resuscitates, perhaps.
Inalienable, the arch-prerogative
Which turns thought, act—conceives, expresses too!
No less, man, bounded, yearning to be free,
May so project his surplusage of soul
In search of body, so add self to self
By owning what lay ownerless before,—
So find, so fill full, so appropriate forms—
That, although nothing which had never life   720
Shall get life from him, be, not having been,
Yet, something dead may get to live again,
Something with too much life or not enough,
Which, either way imperfect, ended once:
An end whereat man's impulse intervenes,
Makes new beginning, starts the dead alive,
Completes the incomplete and saves the thing.
Man's breath were vain to light a virgin wick,—
Half-burned-out, all but quite-quenched wicks o' the lamp
Stationed for temple-service on this earth,°
These indeed let him breathe on and relume!   730
For such man's feat is, in the due degree,
—Mimic creation, galvanism for life,
But still a glory portioned in the scale.
Why did the mage say,—feeling as we are wont
For truth, and stopping midway short of truth,
And resting on a lie,—'I raise a ghost'?
'Because,' he taught adepts, 'man makes not man.
Yet by a special gift, an art of arts,
More insight and more outsight and much more   740
Will to use both of these than boast my mates,
I can detach from me, commission forth
Half of my soul; which in its pilgrimage
O'er old unwandered waste ways of the world,
May chance upon some fragment of a whole,
Rag of flesh, scrap of bone in dim disuse,
Smoking flax that fed fire once: prompt therein
I enter, spark-like, put old powers to play,
Push lines out to the limit, lead forth last
(By a moonrise through a ruin of a crypt)   750

What shall be mistily seen, murmuringly heard,
Mistakenly felt: then write my name with Faust's!'°
Oh, Faust, why Faust? Was not Elisha once?—
Who bade them lay his staff on a corpse-face.
There was no voice, no hearing: he went in
Therefore, and shut the door upon them twain,
And prayed unto the Lord: and he went up
And lay upon the corpse, dead on the couch,
And put his mouth upon its mouth, his eyes
Upon its eyes, his hands upon its hands,   760
And stretched him on the flesh; the flesh waxed warm:
And he returned, walked to and fro the house,
And went up, stretched him on the flesh again,
And the eyes opened. 'Tis a credible feat°
With the right man and way.
                              Enough of me!
The Book! I turn its medicinable leaves
In London now till, as in Florence erst,
A spirit laughs and leaps through every limb,
And lights my eye, and lifts me by the hair,
Letting me have my will again with these   770
—How title I the dead alive once more?

Count Guido Franceschini the Aretine,
Descended of an ancient house, though poor,
A beak-nosed bushy-bearded black-haired lord,
Lean, pallid, low of stature yet robust,
Fifty years old,—having four years ago
Married Pompilia Comparini, young,
Good, beautiful, at Rome, where she was born,
And brought her to Arezzo, where they lived
Unhappy lives, whatever curse the cause,—   780
This husband, taking four accomplices,
Followed this wife to Rome, where she was fled
From their Arezzo to find peace again,
In convoy, eight months earlier, of a priest,
Aretine also, of still nobler birth,
Giuseppe Caponsacchi,—caught her there
Quiet in a villa on a Christmas night,
With only Pietro and Violante by,
Both her putative parents; killed the three,

Aged, they, seventy each, and she, seventeen,   790
And, two weeks since, the mother of his babe
First-born and heir to what the style was worth
O' the Guido who determined, dared and did
This deed just as he purposed point by point.
Then, bent upon escape, but hotly pressed,
And captured with his co-mates that same night,
He, brought to trial, stood on this defence—
Injury to his honour caused the act;
And since his wife was false, (as manifest
By flight from home in such companionship,)   800
Death, punishment deserved of the false wife
And faithless parents who abetted her
I' the flight aforesaid, wronged nor God nor man.
'Nor false she, nor yet faithless they,' replied
The accuser; 'cloaked and masked this murder glooms;
True was Pompilia, loyal too the pair;
Out of the man's own heart a monster curled
Which—crime coiled with connivancy at crime—
His victim's breast, he tells you, hatched and reared;
Uncoil we and stretch stark the worm of hell!'   810
A month the trial swayed this way and that
Ere judgment settled down on Guido's guilt;
Then was the Pope, that good Twelfth Innocent,
Appealed to: who well weighed what went before,
Affirmed the guilt and gave the guilty doom.

Let this old woe step on the stage again!
Act itself o'er anew for men to judge,
Not by the very sense and sight indeed—
(Which take at best imperfect cognizance,
Since, how heart moves brain, and how both move hand,   820
What mortal ever in entirety saw?)
—No dose of purer truth than man digests,
But truth with falsehood, milk that feeds him now,
Not strong meat he may get to bear some day—
To-wit, by voices we call evidence,
Uproar in the echo, live fact deadened down,
Talked over, bruited abroad, whispered away,
Yet helping us to all we seem to hear:
For how else know we save by worth of word?

Here are the voices presently shall sound   830
In due succession. First, the world's outcry
Around the rush and ripple of any fact
Fallen stonewise, plumb on the smooth face of things;
The world's guess, as it crowds the bank o' the pool,
At what were figure and substance, by their splash:
Then, by vibrations in the general mind,
At depth of deed already out of reach.
This threefold murder of the day before,—
Say, Half-Rome's feel after the vanished truth;
Honest enough, as the way is: all the same,   840
Harbouring in the centre of its sense
A hidden germ of failure, shy but sure,
To neutralize that honesty and leave
That feel for truth at fault, as the way is too.
Some prepossession such as starts amiss,
By but a hair's breadth at the shoulder-blade,
The arm o' the feeler, dip he ne'er so bold;
So leads arm waveringly, lets fall wide
O' the mark its finger, sent to find and fix
Truth at the bottom, that deceptive speck.   850
With this Half-Rome,—the source of swerving, call
Over-belief in Guido's right and wrong
Rather than in Pompilia's wrong and right:
Who shall say how, who shall say why? 'Tis there—
The instinctive theorizing whence a fact
Looks to the eye as the eye likes the look.
Gossip in a public place, a sample-speech.
Some worthy, with his previous hint to find
A husband's side the safer, and no whit
Aware he is not Æacus the while,—°   860
How such an one supposes and states fact
To whosoever of a multitude
Will listen, and perhaps prolong thereby
The not-unpleasant flutter at the breast,
Born of a certain spectacle shut in
By the church Lorenzo opposite. So, they lounge
Midway the mouth o' the street, on Corso side,
'Twixt palace Fiano and palace Ruspoli,
Linger and listen; keeping clear o' the crowd,
Yet wishful one could lend that crowd one's eyes,   870

(So universal is its plague of squint)
And make hearts beat our time that flutter false:
—All for the truth's sake, mere truth, nothing else!
How Half-Rome found for Guido much excuse.°

Next, from Rome's other half, the opposite feel
For truth with a like swerve, like unsuccess,—
Or if success, by no skill but more luck
This time, through siding rather with the wife,
Because a fancy-fit inclined that way,
Than with the husband. One wears drab, one pink;   880
Who wears pink, ask him 'Which shall win the race,
Of coupled runners like as egg and egg?'
'—Why, if I must choose, he with the pink scarf.'
Doubtless for some such reason choice fell here.
A piece of public talk to correspond
At the next stage of the story; just a day
Let pass and new day brings the proper change.
Another sample-speech i' the market-place
O' the Barberini by the Capucins;
Where the old Triton, at his fountain-sport,°   890
Bernini's creature plated to the paps,
Puffs up steel sleet which breaks to diamond dust,
A spray of sparkles snorted from his conch,
High over the caritellas, out o' the way°
O' the motley merchandizing multitude.
Our murder has been done three days ago,
The frost is over and gone, the south wind laughs,
And, to the very tiles of each red roof
A-smoke i' the sunshine, Rome lies gold and glad:
So, listen how, to the other half of Rome,   900
Pompilia seemed a saint and martyr both!°

Then, yet another day let come and go,
With pause prelusive still of novelty,
Hear a fresh speaker!—neither this nor that
Half-Rome aforesaid; something bred of both:
One and one breed the inevitable three.
Such is the personage harangues you next;
The elaborated product, *tertium quid:*
Rome's first commotion in subsidence gives
The curd o' the cream, flower o' the wheat, as it were,   910

And finer sense o' the city. Is this plain?
You get a reasoned statement of the case,
Eventual verdict of the curious few
Who care to sift a business to the bran
Nor coarsely bolt it like the simpler sort.
Here, after ignorance, instruction speaks;
Here, clarity of candour, history's soul,
The critical mind, in short: no gossip-guess.
What the superior social section thinks,
In person of some man of quality   920
Who,—breathing musk from lace-work and brocade,
His solitaire amid the flow of frill,
Powdered peruke on nose, and bag at back,
And cane dependent from the ruffled wrist,—
Harangues in silvery and selectest phrase
'Neath waxlight in a glorified saloon
Where mirrors multiply the girandole:°
Courting the approbation of no mob,
But Eminence This and All-Illustrious That
Who take snuff softly, range in well-bred ring,   930
Card-table-quitters for observance' sake,
Around the argument, the rational word—
Still, spite its weight and worth, a sample-speech.
How Quality dissertated on the case.°

So much for Rome and rumour; smoke comes first:
Once let smoke rise untroubled, we descry
Clearlier what tongues of flame may spire and spit
To eye and ear, each with appropriate tinge
According to its food, or pure or foul.
The actors, no mere rumours of the act,   940
Intervene. First you hear Count Guido's voice,
In a small chamber that adjoins the court,
Where Governor and Judges, summoned thence,
Tommati, Venturini and the rest,
Find the accused ripe for declaring truth.
Soft-cushioned sits he; yet shifts seat, shirks touch,
As, with a twitchy brow and wincing lip
And cheek that changes to all kinds of white,
He proffers his defence, in tones subdued
Near to mock-mildness now, so mournful seems   950

The obtuser sense truth fails to satisfy;
Now, moved, from pathos at the wrong endured,
To passion; for the natural man is roused
At fools who first do wrong then pour the blame
Of their wrong-doing, Satan-like, on Job.
Also his tongue at times is hard to curb;
Incisive, nigh satiric bites the phrase,
Rough-raw, yet somehow claiming privilege
—It is so hard for shrewdness to admit
Folly means no harm when she calls black white!   960
—Eruption momentary at the most,
Modified forthwith by a fall o' the fire,
Sage acquiescence; for the world's the world,
And, what it errs in, Judges rectify:
He feels he has a fist, then folds his arms
Crosswise and makes his mind up to be meek.
And never once does he detach his eye
From those ranged there to slay him or to save,
But does his best man's-service for himself,
Despite,—what twitches brow and makes lip wince,—   970
His limbs' late taste of what was called the Cord,°
Or Vigil-torture more facetiously.
Even so; they were wont to tease the truth
Out of loth witness (toying, trifling time)
By torture: 'twas a trick, a vice of the age,
Here, there and everywhere, what would you have?
Religion used to tell Humanity
She gave him warrant or denied him course.
And since the course was much to his own mind,
Of pinching flesh and pulling bone from bone   980
To unhusk truth a-hiding in its hulls,
Nor whisper of a warning stopped the way,
He, in their joint behalf, the burly slave,
Bestirred him, mauled and maimed all recusants,
While, prim in place, Religion overlooked;
And so had done till doomsday, never a sign
Nor sound of interference from her mouth,
But that at last the burly slave wiped brow,
Let eye give notice as if soul were there,
Muttered ''Tis a vile trick, foolish more than vile,   990
Should have been counted sin; I make it so:

At any rate no more of it for me—
Nay, for I break the torture-engine thus!'
Then did Religion start up, stare amain,
Look round for help and see none, smile and say
'What, broken is the rack? Well done of thee!
Did I forget to abrogate its use?
Be the mistake in common with us both!
—One more fault our blind age shall answer for,
Down in my book denounced though it must be   1000
Somewhere. Henceforth find truth by milder means!'
Ah but, Religion, did we wait for thee
To ope the book, that serves to sit upon,
And pick such place out, we should wait indeed!
Thatis all history: and what is not now,
Was then, defendants found it to their cost.
How Guido, after being tortured, spoke.°

Also hear Caponsacchi who comes next,
Man and priest—could you comprehend the coil!—
In days when that was rife which now is rare.   1010
How, mingling each its multifarious wires,
Now heaven, now earth, now heaven and earth at once,
Had plucked at and perplexed their puppet here,
Played off the young frank personable priest;
Sworn fast and tonsured plain heaven's celibate,
And yet earth's clear-accepted servitor,
A courtly spiritual Cupid, squire of dames
By law of love and mandate of the mode.
The Church's own, or why parade her seal,
Wherefore that chrism and consecrative work?°   1020
Yet verily the world's, or why go badged
A prince of sonneteers and lutanists,
Show colour of each vanity in vogue
Borne with decorum due on blameless breast?
All that is changed now, as he tells the court
How he had played the part excepted at;
Tells it, moreover, now the second time:
Since, for his cause of scandal, his own share
I' the flight from home and husband of the wife,
He has been censured, punished in a sort   1030
By relegation,—exile, we should say,

To a short distance for a little time,—
Whence he is summoned on a sudden now,
Informed that she, he thought to save, is lost,
And, in a breath, bidden re-tell his tale,
Since the first telling somehow missed effect,
And then advise in the matter. There stands he,
While the same grim black-panelled chamber blinks
As though rubbed shiny with the sins of Rome
Told the same oak for ages—wave-washed wall   1040
Against which sets a sea of wickedness.
There, where you yesterday heard Guido speak,
Speaks Caponsacchi; and there face him too
Tommati, Venturini and the rest°
Who, eight months earlier, scarce repressed the smile,
Forewent the wink; waived recognition so
Of peccadillos incident to youth,
Especially youth high-born; for youth means love,
Vows can't change nature, priests are only men,
And love likes stratagem and subterfuge   1050
Which age, that once was youth, should recognize,
May blame, but needs not press too hard upon.
Here sit the old Judges then, but with no grace
Of reverend carriage, magisterial port:
For why? The accused of eight months since,—the same
Who cut the conscious figure of a fool,
Changed countenance, dropped bashful gaze to ground,
While hesitating for an answer then,—
Now is grown judge himself, terrifies now
This, now the other culprit called a judge,   1060
Whose turn it is to stammer and look strange,
As he speaks rapidly, angrily, speech that smites:
And they keep silence, bear blow after blow,
Because the seeming-solitary man,
Speaking for God, may have an audience too,
Invisible, no discreet judge provokes.
How the priest Caponsacchi said his say.°

Then a soul sighs its lowest and its last
After the loud ones,—so much breath remains
Unused by the four-days'-dying; for she lived   1070
Thus long, miraculously long, 'twas thought,

Just that Pompilia might defend herself.
How, while the hireling and the alien stoop,
Comfort, yet question,—since the time is brief,
And folk, allowably inquisitive,
Encircle the low pallet where she lies
In the good house that helps the poor to die,—
Pompilia tells the story of her life.
For friend and lover,—leech and man of law   1080
Do service; busy helpful ministrants
As varied in their calling as their mind,
Temper and age: and yet from all of these,
About the white bed under the arched roof,
Is somehow, as it were, evolved a one,—
Small separate sympathies combined and large,
Nothings that were, grown something very much:
As if the bystanders gave each his straw,
All he had, though a trifle in itself,
Which, plaited all together, made a Cross
Fit to die looking on and praying with,   1090
Just as well as if ivory or gold.
So, to the common kindliness she speaks,
There being scarce more privacy at the last
For mind than body: but she is used to bear,
And only unused to the brotherly look.
How she endeavoured to explain her life.°

Then, since a Trial ensued, a touch o' the same
To sober us, flustered with frothy talk,
And teach our common sense its helplessness.
For why deal simply with divining-rod,   1100
Scrape where we fancy secret sources flow,
And ignore law, the recognized machine,
Elaborate display of pipe and wheel
Framed to unchoke, pump up and pour apace
Truth till a flowery foam shall wash the world?
The patent truth-extracting process,—ha?
Let us make that grave mystery turn one wheel,
Give you a single grind of law at least!
One orator, of two on either side,
Shall teach us the puissance of the tongue   1110
—That is, o' the pen which simulated tongue

On paper and saved all except the sound
Which never was. Law's speech beside law's thought?
That were too stunning, too immense an odds:
That point of vantage law lets nobly pass.
One lawyer shall admit us to behold
The manner of the making out a case,
First fashion of a speech; the chick in egg,
The masterpiece law's bosom incubates.
How Don Giacinto of the Arcangeli,   1120
Called Procurator of the Poor at Rome,
Now advocate for Guido and his mates,—
The jolly learned man of middle age,
Cheek and jowl all in laps with fat and law,
Mirthful as mighty, yet, as great hearts use,
Despite the name and fame that tempt our flesh,
Constant to that devotion of the hearth,
Still captive in those dear domestic ties!—
How he,—having a cause to triumph with,
All kind of interests to keep intact,   1130
More than one efficacious personage
To tranquillize, conciliate and secure,
And above all, public anxiety
To quiet, show its Guido in good hands,—
Also, as if such burdens were too light,
A certain family-feast to claim his care,
The birthday-banquet for the only son—
Paternity at smiling strife with law—
How he brings both to buckle in one bond;
And, thick at throat, with waterish under-eye,   1140
Turns to his task and settles in his seat
And puts his utmost means in practice now:
Wheezes out law-phrase, whiffles Latin forth,
And, just as though roast lamb would never be,
Makes logic levigate the big crime small:°
Rubs palm on palm, rakes foot with itchy foot,
Conceives and inchoates the argument,°
Sprinkling each flower appropriate to the time,
—Ovidian quip or Ciceronian crank,°
A-bubble in the larynx while he laughs,   1150
As he had fritters deep down frying there.
How he turns, twists, and tries the oily thing

Shall be—first speech for Guido 'gainst the Fisc.°
Then with a skip as it were from heel to head,
Leaving yourselves fill up the middle bulk
O' the Trial, reconstruct its shape august,
From such exordium clap we to the close;°
Give you, if we dare wing to such a height,
The absolute glory in some full-grown speech
On the other side, some finished butterfly,   1160
Some breathing diamond-flake with leaf-gold fans,
That takes the air, no trace of worm it was,
Or cabbage-bed it had production from.
Giovambattista o' the Bottini, Fisc,
Pompilia's patron by the chance of the hour,
To-morrow her persecutor,—composite, he,
As becomes who must meet such various calls—
Odds of age joined in him with ends of youth.
A man of ready smile and facile tear,
Improvised hopes, despairs at nod and beck,   1170
And language—ah, the gift of eloquence!
Language that goes, goes, easy as a glove,
O'er good and evil, smoothens both to one.
Rashness helps caution with him, fires the straw,
In free enthusiastic careless fit,
On the first proper pinnacle of rock
Which offers, as reward for all that zeal,
To lure some bark to founder and bring gain:
While calm sits Caution, rapt with heavenward eye,
A true confessor's gaze, amid the glare   1180
Beaconing to the breaker, death and hell.
'Well done, thou good and faithful!' she approves:°
'Hadst thou let slip a faggot to the beach,
The crew might surely spy thy precipice
And save their boat; the simple and the slow
Might so, forsooth, forestall the wrecker's fee!
Let the next crew be wise and hail in time!'
Just so compounded is the outside man,
Blue juvenile pure eye and pippin cheek,
And brow all prematurely soiled and seamed   1190
With sudden age, bright devastated hair.
Ah, but you miss the very tones o' the voice,
The scrannel pipe that screams in heights of head,°

As, in his modest studio, all alone,°
The tall wight stands a-tiptoe, strives and strains,
Both eyes shut, like the cockerel that would crow,
Tries to his own self amorously o'er
What never will be uttered else than so—
Since to the four walls, Forum and Mars' Hill,
Speaks out the poesy which, penned, turns prose.   1200
Clavecinist debarred his instrument,°
He yet thrums—shirking neither turn nor trill,
With desperate finger on dumb table-edge—
The sovereign rondo, shall conclude his *Suite*,
Charm an imaginary audience there,
From old Corelli to young Haendel, both°
I' the flesh at Rome, ere he perforce go print
The cold black score, mere music for the mind—
The last speech against Guido and his gang,
With special end to prove Pompilia pure.   1210
How the Fisc vindicates Pompilia's fame.°

Then comes the all but end, the ultimate
Judgment save yours. Pope Innocent the Twelfth,
Simple, sagacious, mild yet resolute,
With prudence, probity and—what beside
From the other world he feels impress at times,
Having attained to fourscore years and six,—
How, when the court found Guido and the rest
Guilty, but law supplied a subterfuge
And passed the final sentence to the Pope,   1220
He, bringing his intelligence to bear
This last time on what ball behoves him drop
In the urn, or white or black, does drop a black,
Send five souls more to just precede his own,
Stand him in stead and witness, if need were,
How he is wont to do God's work on earth.
The manner of his sitting out the dim
Droop of a sombre February day
In the plain closet where he does such work,
With, from all Peter's treasury, one stool,   1230
One table and one lathen crucifix.°
There sits the Pope, his thoughts for company;
Grave but not sad,—nay, something like a cheer

Leaves the lips free to be benevolent,
Which, all day long, did duty firm and fast.
A cherishing there is of foot and knee,
A chafing loose-skinned large-veined hand with hand,—
What steward but knows when stewardship earns its wage,
May levy praise, anticipate the lord?
He reads, notes, lays the papers down at last,   1240
Muses, then takes a turn about the room;
Unclasps a huge tome in an antique guise,
Primitive print and tongue half obsolete,
That stands him in diurnal stead; opes page,°
Finds place where falls the passage to be conned
According to an order long in use:
And, as he comes upon the evening's chance,
Starts somewhat, solemnizes straight his smile,
Then reads aloud that portion first to last,
And at the end lets flow his own thoughts forth   1250
Likewise aloud, for respite and relief,
Till by the dreary relics of the west
Wan through the half-moon window, all his light,
He bows the head while the lips move in prayer,
Writes some three brief lines, signs and seals the same,
Tinkles a hand-bell, bids the obsequious Sir
Who puts foot presently o' the closet-sill
He watched outside of, bear as superscribed
That mandate to the Governor forthwith:
Then heaves abroad his cares in one good sigh,   1260
Traverses corridor with no arm's help,
And so to sup as a clear conscience should.
The manner of the judgment of the Pope.°

Then must speak Guido yet a second time,
Satan's old saw being apt here—skin for skin,°
All a man hath that will he give for life.
While life was graspable and gainable,
And bird-like buzzed her wings round Guido's brow,
Not much truth stiffened out the web of words
He wove to catch her: when away she flew   1270
And death came, death's breath rivelled up the lies,
Left bare the metal thread, the fibre fine
Of truth, i' the spinning: the true words shone last.

How Guido, to another purpose quite,
Speaks and despairs, the last night of his life,
In that New Prison by Castle Angelo
At the bridge foot: the same man, another voice.
On a stone bench in a close fetid cell,
Where the hot vapour of an agony,
Struck into drops on the cold wall, runs down—   1280
Horrible worms made out of sweat and tears—
There crouch, well nigh to the knees in dungeon-straw,
Lit by the sole lamp suffered for their sake,
Two awe-struck figures, this a Cardinal,
That an Abate, both of old styled friends
O' the thing part man part monster in the midst,
So changed is Franceschini's gentle blood.
The tiger-cat screams now, that whined before,
That pried and tried and trod so gingerly,
Till in its silkiness the trap-teeth joined;   1290
Then you know how the bristling fury foams.
They listen, this wrapped in his folds of red,
While his feet fumble for the filth below;
The other, as beseems a stouter heart,
Working his best with beads and cross to ban
The enemy that comes in like a flood°
Spite of the standard set up, verily
And in no trope at all, against him there;
For at the prison-gate, just a few steps
Outside, already, in the doubtful dawn,   1300
Thither, from this side and from that, slow sweep
And settle down in silence solidly,
Crow-wise, the frightful Brotherhood of Death.
Black-hatted and black-hooded huddle they,
Black rosaries a-dangling from each waist;
So take they their grim station at the door,
Torches lit, skull-and-cross-bones-banner spread,
And that gigantic Christ with open arms,
Grounded. Nor lacks there aught but that the group
Break forth, intone the lamentable psalm,   1310
'Out of the deeps, Lord, have I cried to thee!'—°
When inside, from the true profound, a sign
Shall bear intelligence that the foe is foiled,
Count Guido Franceschini has confessed,

And is absolved and reconciled with God.
Then they, intoning, may begin their march,
Make by the longest way for the People's Square,
Carry the criminal to his crime's award:
A mob to cleave, a scaffolding to reach,
Two gallows and Mannaia crowning all.°   1320
How Guido made defence a second time.°

Finally, even as thus by step and step
I led you from the level of to-day
Up to the summit of so long ago,
Here, whence I point you the wide prospect round—
Let me, by like steps, slope you back to smooth,
Land you on mother-earth, no whit the worse,
To feed o' the fat o' the furrow: free to dwell,
Taste our time's better things profusely spread
For all who love the level, corn and wine,   1330
Much cattle and the many-folded fleece.
Shall not my friends go feast again on sward,°
Though cognizant of country in the clouds
Higher than wistful eagle's horny eye
Ever unclosed for, 'mid ancestral crags,
When morning broke and Spring was back once more,
And he died, heaven, save by his heart, unreached?
Yet heaven my fancy lifts to, ladder-like,—
As Jack reached, holpen of his beanstalk-rungs!

A novel country: I might make it mine   1340
By choosing which one aspect of the year
Suited mood best, and putting solely that
On panel somewhere in the House of Fame,°
Landscaping what I saved, not what I saw:
—Might fix you, whether frost in goblin-time
Startled the moon with his abrupt bright laugh,
Or, August's hair afloat in filmy fire,
She fell, arms wide, face foremost on the world,
Swooned there and so singed out the strength of things.
Thus were abolished Spring and Autumn both,   1350
The land dwarfed to one likeness of the land,
Life cramped corpse-fashion. Rather learn and love
Each facet-flash of the revolving year!—
Red, green and blue that whirl into a white,

The variance now, the eventual unity,
Which make the miracle. See it for yourselves,
This man's act, changeable because alive!
Action now shrouds, nor shows the informing thought;
Man, like a glass ball with a spark a-top,°
Out of the magic fire that lurks inside,   1360
Shows one tint at a time to take the eye:
Which, let a finger touch the silent sleep,
Shifted a hair's-breadth shoots you dark for bright,
Suffuses bright with dark, and baffles so
Your sentence absolute for shine or shade.
Once set such orbs,—white styled, black stigmatized,—
A-rolling, see them once on the other side
Your good men and your bad men every one
From Guido Franceschini to Guy Faux,°
Oft would you rub your eyes and change your names.   1370

Such, British Public, ye who like me not,
(God love you!)—whom I yet have laboured for,
Perchance more careful whoso runs may read
Than erst when all, it seemed, could read who ran,—
Perchance more careless whoso reads may praise
Than late when he who praised and read and wrote
Was apt to find himself the self-same me,—
Such labour had such issue, so I wrought
This arc, by furtherance of such alloy,
And so, by one spirt, take away its trace   1380
Till, justifiably golden, rounds my ring.

A ring without a posy, and that ring mine?°

O lyric Love, half angel and half bird°
And all a wonder and a wild desire,—
Boldest of hearts that ever braved the sun,
Took sanctuary within the holier blue,
And sang a kindred soul out to his face,—
Yet human at the red-ripe of the heart—
When the first summons from the darkling earth
Reached thee amid thy chambers, blanched their blue,   1390
And bared them of the glory—to drop down,
To toil for man, to suffer or to die,—
This is the same voice: can thy soul know change?

Hail then, and hearken from the realms of help!
Never may I commence my song, my due
To God who best taught song by gift of thee,
Except with bent head and beseeching hand—
That still, despite the distance and the dark,
What was, again may be; some interchange
Of grace, some splendour once thy very thought,   1400
Some benediction anciently thy smile:
—Never conclude, but raising hand and head
Thither where eyes, that cannot reach, yet yearn
For all hope, all sustainment, all reward,
Their utmost up and on,—so blessing back
In those thy realms of help, that heaven thy home,
Some whiteness which, I judge, thy face makes proud,
Some wanness where, I think, thy foot may fall!

Book X

The Pope

Like to Ahasuerus, that shrewd prince,°
I will begin,—as is, these seven years now,
My daily wont,—and read a History
(Written by one whose deft right hand was dust
To the last digit, ages ere my birth)
Of all my predecessors, Popes of Rome:
For though mine ancient early dropped the pen,
Yet others picked it up and wrote it dry,
Since of the making books there is no end.°
And so I have the Papacy complete   10
From Peter first to Alexander last;°
Can question each and take instruction so.
Have I to dare?—I ask, how dared this Pope?
To suffer?—Suchanone, how suffered he?
Being about to judge, as now, I seek
How judged once, well or ill, some other Pope;
Study some signal judgment that subsists
To blaze on, or else blot, the page which seals
The sum up of what gain or loss to God

Came of His one more Vicar in the world.
So, do I find example, rule of life;
So, square and set in order the next page,
Shall be stretched smooth o'er my own funeral cyst.°

Eight hundred years exact before the year
I was made Pope, men made Formosus Pope,
Say Sigebert and other chroniclers.
Ere I confirm or quash the Trial here
Of Guido Franceschini and his friends,
Read,—How there was a ghastly Trial once
Of a dead man by a live man, and both, Popes: 30
Thus—in the antique penman's very phrase.

'Then Stephen, Pope and seventh of the name,
Cried out, in synod as he sat in state,
While choler quivered on his brow and beard,
"Come into court, Formosus, thou lost wretch,
That claimedst to be late Pope as even I!"

'And at the word the great door of the church
Flew wide, and in they brought Formosus' self,
The body of him, dead, even as embalmed
And buried duly in the Vatican
Eight months before, exhumed thus for the nonce.   40
They set it, that dead body of a Pope,
Clothed in pontific vesture now again,
Upright on Peter's chair as if alive.

'And Stephen, springing up, cried furiously
"Bishop of Porto, wherefore didst presume
To leave that see and take this Roman see,
Exchange the lesser for the greater see,
—A thing against the canons of the Church?"

'Then one—(a Deacon who, observing forms,   50
Was placed by Stephen to repel the charge,
Be advocate and mouthpiece of the corpse)—
Spoke as he dared, set stammeringly forth
With white lips and dry tongue,—as but a youth,
For frightful was the corpse-face to behold,—
How nowise lacked there precedent for this.

'But when, for his last precedent of all,
Emboldened by the Spirit, out he blurts
"And, Holy Father, didst not thou thyself
Vacate the lesser for the greater see,   60
Half a year since change Arago for Rome?"
"—Ye have the sin's defence now, Synod mine!"
Shrieks Stephen in a beastly froth of rage:
"Judge now betwixt him dead and me alive!
Hath he intruded, or do I pretend?
Judge, judge!"—breaks wavelike one whole foam of wrath.

'Whereupon they, being friends and followers,
Said "Ay, thou art Christ's Vicar, and not he!
Away with what is frightful to behold!
This act was uncanonic and a fault."   70

'Then, swallowed up in rage, Stephen exclaimed
"So, guilty! So, remains I punish guilt!
He is unpoped, and all he did I damn:
The Bishop, that ordained him, I degrade:
Depose to laics those he raised to priests:
What they have wrought is mischief nor shall stand,
It is confusion, let it vex no more!
Since I revoke, annul and abrogate
All his decrees in all kinds: they are void!
In token whereof and warning to the world,   80
Strip me yon miscreant of those robes usurped,
And clothe him with vile serge befitting such!
Then hale the carrion to the market-place:
Let the town-hangman chop from his right hand
Those same three fingers which he blessed withal;
Next cut the head off once was crowned forsooth:
And last go fling them, fingers, head and trunk,
To Tiber that my Christian fish may sup!"
—Either because of ΙΧΘΥΣ which means Fish°
And very aptly symbolizes Christ,   90
Or else because the Pope is Fisherman,
And seals with Fisher's-signet.

                                    'Anyway,
So said, so done: himself, to see it done,
Followed the corpse they trailed from street to street

Till into Tiber wave they threw the thing.
The people, crowded on the banks to see,
Were loud or mute, wept or laughed, cursed or jeered,
According as the deed addressed their sense;
A scandal verily: and out spake a Jew
"Wot ye your Christ had vexed our Herod thus?"   100

'Now when, Formosus being dead a year,
His judge Pope Stephen tasted death in turn,
Made captive by the mob and strangled straight,
Romanus, his successor for a month,
Did make protest Formosus was with God,
Holy, just, true in thought and word and deed.
Next Theodore, who reigned but twenty days,
Therein convoked a synod, whose decree
Did reinstate, repope the late unpoped,
And do away with Stephen as accursed.   110
So that when presently certain fisher-folk
(As if the queasy river could not hold
Its swallowed Jonas, but discharged the meal)
Produced the timely product of their nets,
The mutilated man, Formosus,—saved
From putrefaction by the embalmer's spice,
Or, as some said, by sanctity of flesh,—
"Why, lay the body again," bade Theodore,
"Among his predecessors, in the church
And burial-place of Peter!" which was done.   120
"And," addeth Luitprand, "many of repute,
Pious and still alive, avouch to me
That, as they bore the body up the aisle,
The saints in imaged row bowed each his head
For welcome to a brother-saint come back."
As for Romanus and this Theodore,
These two Popes, through the brief reign granted each,
Could but initiate what John came to close
And give the final stamp to: he it was
Ninth of the name, (I follow the best guides)   130
Who,—in full synod at Ravenna held
With Bishops seventy-four, and present too
Eude King of France with his Archbishopry,—
Did condemn Stephen, anathematize

The disinterment, and make all blots blank,
"For," argueth here Auxilius in a place
De Ordinationibus, "precedents
Had been, no lack, before Formosus long,
Of Bishops so transferred from see to see,—
Marinus, for example:" read the tract.   140

'But, after John, came Sergius, reaffirmed
The right of Stephen, cursed Formosus, nay
Cast out, some say, his corpse a second time.
And here,—because the matter went to ground,
Fretted by new griefs, other cares of the age,—
Here is the last pronouncing of the Church,
Her sentence that subsists unto this day.
Yet constantly opinion hath prevailed
I' the Church, Formosus was a holy man.'°

Which of the judgments was infallible?°   150
Which of my predecessors spoke for God?
And what availed Formosus that this cursed,
That blessed, and then this other cursed again?
'Fear ye not those whose power can kill the body
And not the soul,' saith Christ, 'but rather those
Can cast both soul and body into hell!'°

John judged thus in Eight Hundred Ninety Eight,
Exact eight hundred years ago to-day
When, sitting in his stead, Vice-gerent here,
I must give judgment on my own behoof.   160
So worked the predecessor: now, my turn!

In God's name! Once more on this earth of God's,
While twilight lasts and time wherein to work,°
I take His staff with my uncertain hand,
And stay my six and fourscore years, my due
Labour and sorrow, on His judgment-seat,
And forthwith think, speak, act, in place of Him—
The Pope for Christ. Once more appeal is made
From man's assize to mine: I sit and see°
Another poor weak trembling human wretch   170
Pushed by his fellows, who pretend the right,
Up to the gulf which, where I gaze, begins
From this world to the next,—gives way and way,

Just on the edge over the awful dark:
With nothing to arrest him but my feet.
He catches at me with convulsive face,
Cries 'Leave to live the natural minute more!'
While hollowly the avengers echo 'Leave?
None! So has he exceeded man's due share
In man's fit license, wrung by Adam's fall,   180
To sin and yet not surely die,—that we,
All of us sinful, all with need of grace,
All chary of our life,—the minute more
Or minute less of grace which saves a soul,—
Bound to make common cause with who craves time,
—We yet protest against the exorbitance
Of sin in this one sinner, and demand
That his poor sole remaining piece of time
Be plucked from out his clutch: put him to death!
Punish him now! As for the weal or woe   190
Hereafter, God grant mercy! Man be just,
Nor let the felon boast he went scot-free!'
And I am bound, the solitary judge,
To weigh the worth, decide upon the plea,
And either hold a hand out, or withdraw
A foot and let the wretch drift to the fall.
Ay, and while thus I dally, dare perchance
Put fancies for a comfort 'twixt this calm
And yonder passion that I have to bear,—
As if reprieve were possible for both   200
Prisoner and Pope,—how easy were reprieve!
A touch o' the hand-bell here, a hasty word
To those who wait, and wonder they wait long,
I' the passage there, and I should gain the life!—
Yea, though I flatter me with fancy thus,
I know it is but nature's craven-trick.
The case is over, judgment at an end,
And all things done now and irrevocable:
A mere dead man is Franceschini here,
Even as Formosus centuries ago.   210
I have worn through this sombre wintry day,
With winter in my soul beyond the world's,
Over these dismalest of documents
Which drew night down on me ere eve befell,—

Pleadings and counter-pleadings, figure of fact
Beside fact's self, these summaries to-wit,—
How certain three were slain by certain five:
I read here why it was, and how it went,
And how the chief o' the five preferred excuse,
And how law rather chose defence should lie,—   220
What argument he urged by wary word
When free to play off wile, start subterfuge,
And what the unguarded groan told, torture's feat
When law grew brutal, outbroke, overbore
And glutted hunger on the truth, at last,—
No matter for the flesh and blood between.
All's a clear rede and no more riddle now.°
Truth, nowhere, lies yet everywhere in these—
Not absolutely in a portion, yet
Evolvible from the whole: evolved at last   230
Painfully, held tenaciously by me.
Therefore there is not any doubt to clear
When I shall write the brief word presently
And chink the hand-bell, which I pause to do.
Irresolute? Not I, more than the mound
With the pine-trees on it yonder! Some surmise,
Perchance, that since man's wit is fallible,
Mine may fail here? Suppose it so,—what then?
Say,—Guido, I count guilty, there's no babe
So guiltless, for I misconceive the man!   240
What's in the chance should move me from my mind?
If, as I walk in a rough country-side,
Peasants of mine cry 'Thou art he can help,
Lord of the land and counted wise to boot:
Look at our brother, strangling in his foam,
He fell so where we find him,—prove thy worth!'
I may presume, pronounce, 'A frenzy-fit,
A falling-sickness or a fever-stroke!
Breathe a vein, copiously let blood at once!'
So perishes the patient, and anon   250
I hear my peasants—'All was error, lord!
Our story, thy prescription: for there crawled
In due time from our hapless brother's breast
The serpent which had stung him: bleeding slew
Whom a prompt cordial had restored to health.'

What other should I say than 'God so willed:
Mankind is ignorant, a man am I:
Call ignorance my sorrow, not my sin!'
So and not otherwise, in after-time,
If some acuter wit, fresh probing, sound   260
This multifarious mass of words and deeds
Deeper, and reach through guilt to innocence,
I shall face Guido's ghost nor blench a jot.
'God who set me to judge thee, meted out
So much of judging faculty, no more:
Ask Him if I was slack in use thereof!'
I hold a heavier fault imputable
Inasmuch as I changed a chaplain once,
For no cause,—no, if I must bare my heart,—
Save that he snuffled somewhat saying mass.
For I am ware it is the seed of act,   270
God holds appraising in His hollow palm,
Not act grown great thence on the world below,
Leafage and branchage, vulgar eyes admire.
Therefore I stand on my integrity,
Nor fear at all: and if I hesitate,
It is because I need to breathe awhile,
Rest, as the human right allows, review
Intent the little seeds of act, my tree,—
The thought, which, clothed in deed, I give the world   280
At chink of bell and push of arrased door.

O pale departure, dim disgrace of day!
Winter's in wane, his vengeful worst art thou,
To dash the boldness of advancing March!
Thy chill persistent rain has purged our streets
Of gossipry; pert tongue and idle ear
By this, consort 'neath archway, portico.
But wheresoe'er Rome gathers in the grey,
Two names now snap and flash from mouth to mouth—
(Sparks, flint and steel strike) Guido and the Pope.   290
By this same hour to-morrow eve—aha,
How do they call him?—the sagacious Swede°
Who finds by figures how the chances prove,
Why one comes rather than another thing,
As, say, such dots turn up by throw of dice,

Or, if we dip in Virgil here and there
And prick for such a verse, when such shall point.
Take this Swede, tell him, hiding name and rank,
Two men are in our city this dull eve;
One doomed to death,—but hundreds in such plight   300
Slip aside, clean escape by leave of law
Which leans to mercy in this latter time;
Moreover in the plenitude of life
Is he, with strength of limb and brain adroit,
Presumably of service here: beside,
The man is noble, backed by nobler friends:
Nay, they so wish him well, the city's self
Makes common cause with who—house-magistrate,
Patron of hearth and home, domestic lord—
But ruled his own, let aliens cavil. Die?   310
He'll bribe a gaoler or break prison first!
Nay, a sedition may be helpful, give
Hint to the mob to batter wall, burn gate,
And bid the favourite malefactor march.
Calculate now these chances of escape!
'It is not probable, but well may be.'
Again, there is another man, weighed now
By twice eight years beyond the seven-times-ten,
Appointed overweight to break our branch.
And this man's loaded branch lifts, more than snow,   320
All the world's cark and care, though a bird's nest
Were a superfluous burthen: notably
Hath he been pressed, as if his age were youth,
From to-day's dawn till now that day departs,
Trying one question with true sweat of soul
'Shall the said doomed man fitlier die or live?'
When a straw swallowed in his posset, stool°
Stumbled on where his path lies, any puff
That's incident to such a smoking flax,
Hurries the natural end and quenches him!°   330
Now calculate, thou sage, the chances here,
Say, which shall die the sooner, this or that?
'That, possibly, this in all likelihood.'
I thought so: yet thou tripp'st, my foreign friend!
No, it will be quite otherwise,—to-day
Is Guido's last: my term is yet to run.

But say the Swede were right, and I forthwith
Acknowledge a prompt summons and lie dead:
Why, then I stand already in God's face
And hear 'Since by its fruit a tree is judged,   340
Show me thy fruit, the latest act of thine!
For in the last is summed the first and all,—
What thy life last put heart and soul into,
There shall I taste thy product.' I must plead
This condemnation of a man to-day.

Not so! Expect nor question nor reply
At what we figure as God's judgment-bar!
None of this vile way by the barren words
Which, more than any deed, characterize
Man as made subject to a curse: no speech—   350
That still bursts o'er some lie which lurks inside,
As the split skin across the coppery snake,
And most denotes man! since, in all beside,
In hate or lust or guile or unbelief,
Out of some core of truth the excrescence comes,
And, in the last resort, the man may urge
'So was I made, a weak thing that gave way
To truth, to impulse only strong since true,
And hated, lusted, used guile, forwent faith.'
But when man walks the garden of this world   360
For his own solace, and, unchecked by law,
Speaks or keeps silence as himself sees fit,
Without the least incumbency to lie,
—Why, can he tell you what a rose is like,
Or how the birds fly, and not slip to false
Though truth serve better? Man must tell his mate
Of you, me and himself, knowing he lies,
Knowing his fellow knows the same,—will think
'He lies, it is the method of a man!'
And yet will speak for answer 'It is truth'   370
To him who shall rejoin 'Again a lie!'
Therefore these filthy rags of speech, this coil
Of statement, comment, query and response,
Tatters all too contaminate for use,
Have no renewing: He, the Truth, is, too,°
The Word. We men, in our degree, may know

There, simply, instantaneously, as here
After long time and amid many lies,
Whatever we dare think we know indeed
—That I am I, as He is He,—what else?   380
But be man's method for man's life at least!
Wherefore, Antonio Pignatelli, thou°
My ancient self, who wast no Pope so long
But studiedst God and man, the many years
I' the school, i' the cloister, in the diocese
Domestic, legate-rule in foreign lands,—
Thou other force in those old busy days
Than this grey ultimate decrepitude,—
Yet sensible of fires that more and more
Visit a soul, in passage to the sky,   390
Left nakeder than when flesh-robe was new—
Thou, not Pope but the mere old man o' the world,
Supposed inquisitive and dispassionate,
Wilt thou, the one whose speech I somewhat trust,
Question the after-me, this self now Pope,
Hear his procedure, criticize his work?
Wise in its generation is the world.

This is why Guido is found reprobate.
I see him furnished forth for his career,
On starting for the life-chance in our world,   400
With nearly all we count sufficient help:
Body and mind in balance, a sound frame,
A solid intellect: the wit to seek,
Wisdom to choose, and courage wherewithal
To deal in whatsoever circumstance
Should minister to man, make life succeed.
Oh, and much drawback! what were earth without?
Is this our ultimate stage, or starting-place
To try man's foot, if it will creep or climb,
'Mid obstacles in seeming, points that prove   410
Advantage for who vaults from low to high
And makes the stumbling-block a stepping-stone?
So, Guido, born with appetite, lacks food:
Is poor, who yet could deftly play-off wealth:
Straitened, whose limbs are restless till at large.
He, as he eyes each outlet of the cirque°

And narrow penfold for probation, pines
After the good things just outside its grate,
With less monition, fainter conscience-twitch,
Rarer instinctive qualm at the first feel
Of greed unseemly, prompting grasp undue,
Than nature furnishes her main mankind,—
Making it harder to do wrong than right
The first time, careful lest the common ear
Break measure, miss the outstep of life's march.
Wherein I see a trial fair and fit
For one else too unfairly fenced about,
Set above sin, beyond his fellows here:
Guarded from the arch-tempter all must fight,
By a great birth, traditionary name,
Diligent culture, choice companionship,
Above all, conversancy with the faith
Which puts forth for its base of doctrine just
'Man is born nowise to content himself,
But please God.' He accepted such a rule,°
Recognized man's obedience; and the Church,
Which simply is such rule's embodiment,
He clave to, he held on by,—nay, indeed,
Near pushed inside of, deep as layman durst,
Professed so much of priesthood as might sue
For priest's-exemption where the layman sinned,—
Got his arm frocked which, bare, the law would bruise.
Hence, at this moment, what's his last resource,
His extreme stay and utmost stretch of hope
But that,—convicted of such crime as law
Wipes not away save with a worldling's blood,—
Guido, the three-parts consecrate, may 'scape?
Nay, the portentous brothers of the man°
Are veritably priests, protected each
May do his murder in the Church's pale,
Abate Paul, Canon Girolamo!
This is the man proves irreligiousest
Of all mankind, religion's parasite!
This may forsooth plead dinned ear, jaded sense,
The vice o' the watcher who bides near the bell,
Sleeps sound because the clock is vigilant,
And cares not whether it be shade or shine,

420

430

440

450

Doling out day and night to all men else!
Why was the choice o' the man to niche himself
Perversely 'neath the tower where Time's own tongue   460
Thus undertakes to sermonize the world?
Why, but because the solemn is safe too,
The belfry proves a fortress of a sort,
Has other uses than to teach the hour:
Turns sunscreen, paravent and ombrifuge°
To whoso seeks a shelter in its pale,
—Ay, and attractive to unwary folk
Who gaze at storied portal, statued spire,
And go home with full head but empty purse,
Nor dare suspect the sacristan the thief!°   470
Shall Judas,—hard upon the donor's heel,
To filch the fragments of the basket,—plead
He was too near the preacher's mouth, nor sat
Attent with fifties in a company?
No,—closer to promulgated decree,
Clearer the censure of default. Proceed!

I find him bound, then, to begin life well;
Fortified by propitious circumstance,
Great birth, good breeding, with the Church for guide,
How lives he? Cased thus in a coat of proof,   480
Mailed like a man-at-arms, though all the while
A puny starveling,—does the breast pant big,
The limb swell to the limit, emptiness
Strive to become solidity indeed?
Rather, he shrinks up like the ambiguous fish,°
Detaches flesh from shell and outside show,
And steals by moonlight (I have seen the thing)
In and out, now to prey and now to skulk.
Armour he boasts when a wave breaks on beach,
Or bird stoops for the prize: with peril nigh,—   490
The man of rank, the much-befriended-man,
The man almost affiliate to the Church,
Such is to deal with, let the world beware!
Does the world recognize, pass prudently?
Do tides abate and sea-fowl hunt i' the deep?
Already is the slug from out its mew,
Ignobly faring with all loose and free,

Sand-fly and slush-worm at their garbage-feast,
A naked blotch no better than they all:
Guido has dropped nobility, slipped the Church,   500
Plays trickster if not cut-purse, body and soul
Prostrate among the filthy feeders—faugh!
And when Law takes him by surprise at last,
Catches the foul thing on its carrion-prey,
Behold, he points to shell left high and dry,
Pleads, 'But the case out yonder is myself!'
Nay, it is thou, Law prongs amid thy peers,
Congenial vermin; that was none of thee,
Thine outside,—give it to the soldier-crab!°

For I find this black mark impinge the man,   510
That he believes in just the vile of life.
Low instinct, base pretension, are these truth?
Then, that aforesaid armour, probity
He figures in, is falsehood scale on scale;
Honour and faith,—a lie and a disguise,
Probably for all livers in this world,
Certainly for himself! All say good words
To who will hear, all do thereby bad deeds
To who must undergo; so thrive mankind!
See this habitual creed exemplified   520
Most in the last deliberate act; as last,
So, very sum and substance of the soul
Of him that planned and leaves one perfect piece,
The sin brought under jurisdiction now,
Even the marriage of the man: this act
I sever from his life as sample, show
For Guido's self, intend to test him by,
As, from a cup filled fairly at the fount,
By the components we decide enough
Or to let flow as late, or staunch the source.   530

He purposes this marriage, I remark,
On no one motive that should prompt thereto—
Farthest, by consequence, from ends alleged
Appropriate to the action; so they were:
The best, he knew and feigned, the worst he took.
Not one permissible impulse moves the man,
From the mere liking of the eye and ear,

To the true longing of the heart that loves,
No trace of these: but all to instigate,
Is what sinks man past level of the brute   540
Whose appetite if brutish is a truth.
All is the lust for money: to get gold,—
Why, lie, rob, if it must be, murder! Make
Body and soul wring gold out, lured within
The clutch of hate by love, the trap's pretence!
What good else get from bodies and from souls?
This got, there were some life to lead thereby,
—What, where or how, appreciate those who tell
How the toad lives: it lives,—enough for me!
To get this good,—with but a groan or so,   550
Then, silence of the victims,—were the feat.
He foresaw, made a picture in his mind,—
Of father and mother stunned and echoless
To the blow, as they lie staring at fate's jaws
Their folly danced into, till the woe fell;
Edged in a month by strenuous cruelty
From even the poor nook whence they watched the wolf
Feast on their heart, the lamb-like child his prey;
Plundered to the last remnant of their wealth,
(What daily pittance pleased the plunderer dole)   560
Hunted forth to go hide head, starve and die,
And leave the pale awe-stricken wife, past hope
Of help i' the world now, mute and motionless,
His slave, his chattel, to first use, then destroy.
All this, he bent mind how to bring about,
Put plain in act and life, as painted plain,
So have success, reach crown of earthly good,
In this particular enterprise of man,
By marriage—undertaken in God's face
With all these lies so opposite God's truth,   570
For end so other than man's end.

                                        Thus schemes
Guido, and thus would carry out his scheme:
But when an obstacle first blocks the path,
When he finds none may boast monopoly
Of lies and trick i' the tricking lying world,—
That sorry timid natures, even this sort

O' the Comparini, want nor trick nor lie
Proper to the kind,—that as the gor-crow treats°
The bramble-finch so treats the finch the moth,
And the great Guido is minutely matched   580
By this same couple,—whether true or false
The revelation of Pompilia's birth,
Which in a moment brings his scheme to nought,—
Then, he is piqued, advances yet a stage,
Leaves the low region to the finch and fly,
Soars to the zenith whence the fiercer fowl
May dare the inimitable swoop. I see.
He draws now on the curious crime, the fine°
Felicity and flower of wickedness;
Determines, by the utmost exercise   590
Of violence, made safe and sure by craft,
To satiate malice, pluck one last arch-pang
From the parents, else would triumph out of reach,
By punishing their child, within reach yet,
Who, by thought, word or deed, could nowise wrong
I' the matter that now moves him. So plans he,
Always subordinating (note the point!)
Revenge, the manlier sin, to interest
The meaner,—would pluck pang forth, but unclench
No gripe in the act, let fall no money-piece.   600
Hence a plan for so plaguing, body and soul,
His wife, so putting, day by day, hour by hour,
The untried torture to the untouched place,
As must precipitate an end foreseen,
Goad her into some plain revolt, most like
Plunge upon patent suicidal shame,
Death to herself, damnation by rebound
To those whose hearts he, holding hers, holds still:
Such plan as, in its bad completeness, shall
Ruin the three together and alike,   610
Yet leave himself in luck and liberty,
No claim renounced, no right a forfeiture,
His person unendangered, his good fame
Without a flaw, his pristine worth intact,—
While they, with all their claims and rights that cling,
Shall forthwith crumble off him every side,
Scorched into dust, a plaything for the winds.

As when, in our Campagna, there is fired
The nest-like work that overruns a hut;
And, as the thatch burns here, there, everywhere,   620
Even to the ivy and wild vine, that bound
And blessed the home where men were happy once,
There rises gradual, black amid the blaze,
Some grim and unscathed nucleus of the nest,—
Some old malicious tower, some obscene tomb°
They thought a temple in their ignorance,
And clung about and thought to lean upon—
There laughs it o'er their ravage,—where are they?
So did his cruelty burn life about,
And lay the ruin bare in dreadfulness,   630
Try the persistency of torment so
Upon the wife, that, at extremity,
Some crisis brought about by fire and flame,
The patient frenzy-stung must needs break loose,
Fly anyhow, find refuge anywhere,
Even in the arms of who should front her first,
No monster but a man—while nature shrieked
'Or thus escape, or die!' The spasm arrived,
Not the escape by way of sin,—O God,
Who shall pluck sheep Thou holdest, from Thy hand?°   640
Therefore she lay resigned to die,—so far
The simple cruelty was foiled. Why then,
Craft to the rescue, let craft supplement
Cruelty and show hell a masterpiece!
Hence this consummate lie, this love-intrigue,
Unmanly simulation of a sin,
With place and time and circumstance to suit—
These letters false beyond all forgery—
Not just handwriting and mere authorship,
But false to body and soul they figure forth—   650
As though the man had cut out shape and shape
From fancies of that other Aretine,°
To paste below—incorporate the filth
With cherub faces on a missal-page!

Whereby the man so far attains his end
That strange temptation is permitted,—see!
Pompilia wife, and Caponsacchi priest,

Are brought together as nor priest nor wife
Should stand, and there is passion in the place,
Power in the air for evil as for good,   660
Promptings from heaven and hell, as if the stars
Fought in their courses for a fate to be.
Thus stand the wife and priest, a spectacle,
I doubt not, to unseen assemblage there.
No lamp will mark that window for a shrine,
No tablet signalize the terrace, teach
New generations which succeed the old
The pavement of the street is holy ground;
No bard describe in verse how Christ prevailed
And Satan fell like lightning! Why repine?   670
What does the world, told truth, but lie the more?

A second time the plot is foiled; nor, now,
By corresponding sin for countercheck,
No wile and trick that baffle trick and wile,—
The play o' the parents! Here the blot is blanched
By God's gift of a purity of soul
That will not take pollution, ermine-like
Armed from dishonour by its own soft snow.
Such was this gift of God who showed for once
How He would have the world go white: it seems   680
As a new attribute were born of each
Champion of truth, the priest and wife I praise,—
As a new safeguard sprang up in defence
Of their new noble nature: so a thorn
Comes to the aid of and completes the rose—
Courage to-wit, no woman's gift nor priest's,
I' the crisis; might leaps vindicating right.
See how the strong aggressor, bad and bold,
With every vantage, preconcerts surprise,°
Leaps of a sudden at his victim's throat   690
In a byeway,—how fares he when face to face
With Caponsacchi? Who fights, who fears now?
There quails Count Guido armed to the chattering teeth,
Cowers at the steadfast eye and quiet word
O' the Canon of the Pieve! There skulks crime°
Behind law called in to back cowardice:
While out of the poor trampled worm the wife,

Springs up a serpent!

But anon of these.
Him I judge now,—of him proceed to note,
Failing the first, a second chance befriends   700
Guido, gives pause ere punishment arrive.
The law he called, comes, hears, adjudicates,
Nor does amiss i' the main,—secludes the wife
From the husband, respites the oppressed one, grants
Probation to the oppressor, could he know
The mercy of a minute's fiery purge!
The furnace-coals alike of public scorn,
Private remorse, heaped glowing on his head,
What if,—the force and guile, the ore's alloy,
Eliminate, his baser soul refined—   710
The lost be saved even yet, so as by fire?°
Let him, rebuked, go softly all his days°
And, when no graver musings claim their due,
Meditate on a man's immense mistake
Who, fashioned to use feet and walk, deigns crawl—
Takes the unmanly means—ay, though to ends
Man scarce should make for, would but reach thro' wrong,—
May sin, but nowise needs shame manhood so:
Since fowlers hawk, shoot, nay and snare the game,
And yet eschew vile practice, nor find sport   720
In torch-light treachery or the luring owl.

But how hunts Guido? Why, the fraudful trap—
Late spurned to ruin by the indignant feet
Of fellows in the chase who loved fair play—
Here he picks up its fragments to the least,
Lades him and hies to the old lurking-place
Where haply he may patch again, refit
The mischief, file its blunted teeth anew,
Make sure, next time, first snap shall break the bone.
Craft, greed and violence complot revenge: 730
Craft, for its quota, schemes to bring about
And seize occasion and be safe withal:
Greed craves its act may work both far and near,
Crush the tree, branch and trunk and root, beside,
Whichever twig or leaf arrests a streak
Of possible sunshine else would coin itself,

And drop down one more gold piece in the path:
Violence stipulates 'Advantage proved
And safety sure, be pain the overplus!
Murder with jagged knife! Cut but tear too!°   740
Foiled oft, starved long, glut malice for amends!'
And what, craft's scheme? scheme sorrowful and strange
As though the elements, whom mercy checked,
Had mustered hate for one eruption more,
One final deluge to surprise the Ark
Cradled and sleeping on its mountain-top:
Their outbreak-signal—what but the dove's coo,
Back with the olive in her bill for news
Sorrow was over? 'Tis an infant's birth,°
Guido's first born, his son and heir, that gives   750
The occasion: other men cut free their souls°
From care in such a case, fly up in thanks
To God, reach, recognize His love for once:
Guido cries 'Soul, at last the mire is thine!
Lie there in likeness of a money-bag
My babe's birth so pins down past moving now,
That I dare cut adrift the lives I late
Scrupled to touch lest thou escape with them!
These parents and their child my wife,—touch one,
Lose all! Their rights determined on a head   760
I could but hate, not harm, since from each hair
Dangled a hope for me: now—chance and change!
No right was in their child but passes plain
To that child's child and through such child to me.
I am a father now,—come what, come will,
I represent my child; he comes between—
Cuts sudden off the sunshine of this life
From those three: why, the gold is in his curls!
Not with old Pietro's, Violante's head,
Not his grey horror, her more hideous black—   770
Go these, devoted to the knife!'
                              'Tis done:
Wherefore should mind misgive, heart hesitate?
He calls to counsel, fashions certain four
Colourless natures counted clean till now,
—Rustic simplicity, uncorrupted youth,
Ignorant virtue! Here's the gold o' the prime

When Saturn ruled, shall shock our leaden day—°
The clown abash the courtier! Mark it, bards!
The courtier tries his hand on clownship here,
Speaks a word, names a crime, appoints a price,—   780
Just breathes on what, suffused with all himself,
Is red-hot henceforth past distinction now
I' the common glow of hell. And thus they break
And blaze on us at Rome, Christ's birthnight-eve!°
Oh angels that sang erst 'On the earth, peace!
To man, good will!'—such peace finds earth to-day!
After the seventeen hundred years, so man
Wills good to man, so Guido makes complete
His murder! what is it I said?—cuts loose
Three lives that hitherto he suffered cling,   790
Simply because each served to nail secure,
By a corner of the money-bag, his soul,—
Therefore, lives sacred till the babe's first breath
O'erweights them in the balance,—off they fly!

So is the murder managed, sin conceived
To the full: and why not crowned with triumph too?
Why must the sin, conceived thus, bring forth death?
I note how, within hair's-breadth of escape,
Impunity and the thing supposed success,
Guido is found when the check comes, the change,   800
The monitory touch o' the tether—felt
By few, not marked by many, named by none
At the moment, only recognized aright
I' the fulness of the days, for God's, lest sin
Exceed the service, leap the line: such check—
A secret which this life finds hard to keep,
And, often guessed, is never quite revealed—
Needs must trip Guido on a stumbling-block
Too vulgar, too absurdly plain i' the path!
Study this single oversight of care,   810
This hebetude that marred sagacity,°
Forgetfulness of all the man best knew,—
How any stranger having need to fly,
Needs but to ask and have the means of flight.
Why, the first urchin tells you, to leave Rome,
Get horses, you must show the warrant, just

The banal scrap, clerk's scribble, a fair word buys,
Or foul one, if a ducat sweeten word,—°
And straight authority will back demand,
Give you the pick o' the post-house!—how should he,°   820
Then, resident at Rome for thirty years,
Guido, instruct a stranger! And himself
Forgets just this poor paper scrap, wherewith
Armed, every door he knocks at opens wide
To save him: horsed and manned, with such advance
O' the hunt behind, why, 'twere the easy task
Of hours told on the fingers of one hand,
To reach the Tuscan frontier, laugh at-home,
Light-hearted with his fellows of the place,—
Prepared by that strange shameful judgment, that   830
Satire upon a sentence just pronounced
By the Rota and confirmed by the Granduke,—°
Ready in a circle to receive their peer,
Appreciate his good story how, when Rome,
The Pope-King and the populace of priests
Made common cause with their confederate
The other priestling who seduced his wife,
He, all unaided, wiped out the affront
With decent bloodshed and could face his friends,
Frolic it in the world's eye. Ay, such tale   840
Missed such applause, and by such oversight!
So, tired and footsore, those blood-flustered five
Went reeling on the road through dark and cold,
The few permissible miles, to sink at length,
Wallow and sleep in the first wayside straw,
As the other herd quenched, i' the wash o' the wave,
—Each swine, the devil inside him: so slept they,
And so were caught and caged—all through one trip,
One touch of fool in Guido the astute!
He curses the omission, I surmise,   850
More than the murder. Why, thou fool and blind,
It is the mercy-stroke that stops thy fate,
Hamstrings and holds thee to thy hurt,—but how?
On the edge o' the precipice! One minute more,
Thou hadst gone farther and fared worse, my son,
Fathoms down on the flint and fire beneath!
Thy comrades each and all were of one mind,

Thy murder done, to straightway murder thee
In turn, because of promised pay withheld.   860
So, to the last, greed found itself at odds
With craft in thee, and, proving conqueror,
Had sent thee, the same night that crowned thy hope,
Thither where, this same day, I see thee not,
Nor, through God's mercy, need, to-morrow, see.

Such I find Guido, midmost blotch of black
Discernible in this group of clustered crimes
Huddling together in the cave they call
Their palace outraged day thus penetrates.
Around him ranged, now close and now remote,
Prominent or obscure to meet the needs   870
O' the mage and master, I detect each shape
Subsidiary i' the scene nor loathed the less,
All alike coloured, all descried akin
By one and the same pitchy furnace stirred
At the centre: see, they lick the master's hand,—
This fox-faced horrible priest, this brother-brute
The Abate,—why, mere wolfishness looks well,
Guido stands honest in the red o' the flame,
Beside this yellow that would pass for white,
Twice Guido, all craft but no violence,   880
This copier of the mien and gait and garb
Of Peter and Paul, that he may go disguised,
Rob halt and lame, sick folk i' the temple-porch!
Armed with religion, fortified by law,
A man of peace, who trims the midnight lamp
And turns the classic page—and all for craft,
All to work harm with, yet incur no scratch!
While Guido brings the struggle to a close,
Paul steps back the due distance, clear o' the trap
He builds and baits. Guido I catch and judge;   890
Paul is past reach in this world and my time:
That is a case reserved. Pass to the next,
The boy of the brood, the young Girolamo°
Priest, Canon, and what more? nor wolf nor fox,
But hybrid, neither craft nor violence
Wholly, part violence part craft: such cross
Tempts speculation—will both blend one day,

And prove hell's better product? Or subside
And let the simple quality emerge,
Go on with Satan's service the old way?
Meanwhile, what promise,—what performance too!   900
For there's a new distinctive touch, I see,
Lust—lacking in the two—hell's own blue tint
That gives a character and marks the man
More than a match for yellow and red. Once more,
A case reserved: why should I doubt? Then comes
The gaunt grey nightmare in the furthest smoke,
The hag that gave these three abortions birth,
Unmotherly mother and unwomanly
Woman, that near turns motherhood to shame,   910
Womanliness to loathing: no one word,
No gesture to curb cruelty a whit
More than the she-pard thwarts her playsome whelps
Trying their milk-teeth on the soft o' the throat
O' the first fawn, flung, with those beseeching eyes,
Flat in the covert! How should she but couch,
Lick the dry lips, unsheath the blunted claw,
Catch 'twixt her placid eyewinks at what chance
Old bloody half-forgotten dream may flit,
Born when herself was novice to the taste,   920
The while she lets youth take its pleasure. Last,
These God-abandoned wretched lumps of life,
These four companions,—country-folk this time,
Not tainted by the unwholesome civic breath,
Much less the curse o' the Court! Mere striplings too,
Fit to do human nature justice still!
Surely when impudence in Guido's shape
Shall propose crime and proffer money's-worth
To these stout tall rough bright-eyed black-haired boys,
The blood shall bound in answer to each cheek   930
Before the indignant outcry break from lip!
Are these i' the mood to murder, hardly loosed
From healthy autumn-finish of ploughed glebe,°
Grapes in the barrel, work at happy end,
And winter near with rest and Christmas play?
How greet they Guido with his final task—
(As if he but proposed 'One vineyard more
To dig, ere frost come, then relax indeed!')

'Anywhere, anyhow and anywhy,
Murder me some three people, old and young,   940
Ye never heard the names of,—and be paid
So much!' And the whole four accede at once.
Demur? Do cattle bidden march or halt?
Is it some lingering habit, old fond faith
I' the lord o' the land, instructs them,—birthright-badge
Of feudal tenure claims its slaves again?
Not so at all, thou noble human heart!
All is done purely for the pay,—which, earned,
And not forthcoming at the instant, makes
Religion heresy, and the lord o' the land   950
Fit subject for a murder in his turn.
The patron with cut throat and rifled purse,
Deposited i' the roadside-ditch, his due,
Nought hinders each good fellow trudging home,
The heavier by a piece or two in poke,
And so with new zest to the common life,
Mattock and spade, plough-tail and waggon-shaft,
Till some such other piece of luck betide,
Who knows? Since this is a mere start in life,
And none of them exceeds the twentieth year.   960
Nay, more i' the background yet? Unnoticed forms
Claim to be classed, subordinately vile?
Complacent lookers-on that laugh,—perchance
Shake head as their friend's horse-play grows too rough
With the mere child he manages amiss—
But would not interfere and make bad worse
For twice the fractious tears and prayers: thou know'st
Civility better, Marzi-Medici,°
Governor for thy kinsman the Granduke!
Fit representative of law, man's lamp   970
I' the magistrate's grasp full-flare, no rushlight-end
Sputtering 'twixt thumb and finger of the priest!
Whose answer to the couple's cry for help
Is a threat,—whose remedy of Pompilia's wrong,
A shrug o' the shoulder, and facetious word
Or wink, traditional with Tuscan wits,
To Guido in the doorway. Laud to law!
The wife is pushed back to the husband, he
Who knows how these home-squabblings persecute

People who have the public good to mind,   980
And work best with a silence in the court!

Ah, but I save my word at least for thee,
Archbishop, who art under me, i' the Church,°
As I am under God,—thou, chosen by both
To do the shepherd's office, feed the sheep—
How of this lamb that panted at thy foot
While the wolf pressed on her within crook's reach?
Wast thou the hireling that did turn and flee?°
With thee at least anon the little word!

Such denizens o' the cave now cluster round   990
And heat the furnace sevenfold: time indeed
A bolt from heaven should cleave roof and clear place,
Transfix and show the world, suspiring flame,
The main offender, scar and brand the rest
Hurrying, each miscreant to his hole: then flood
And purify the scene with outside day—
Which yet, in the absolutest drench of dark,
Ne'er wants a witness, some stray beauty-beam
To the despair of hell.

              First of the first,
Such I pronounce Pompilia, then as now   1000
Perfect in whiteness: stoop thou down, my child,
Give one good moment to the poor old Pope
Heart-sick at having all his world to blame—
Let me look at thee in the flesh as erst,
Let me enjoy the old clean linen garb,
Not the new splendid vesture! Armed and crowned,
Would Michael, yonder, be, nor crowned nor armed,°
The less pre-eminent angel? Everywhere
I see in the world the intellect of man,
That sword, the energy his subtle spear,   1010
The knowledge which defends him like a shield—
Everywhere; but they make not up, I think,
The marvel of a soul like thine, earth's flower
She holds up to the softened gaze of God!
It was not given Pompilia to know much,
Speak much, to write a book, to move mankind,
Be memorized by who records my time.

Yet if in purity and patience, if
In faith held fast despite the plucking fiend,
Safe like the signet stone with the new name   1020
That saints are known by,—if in right returned
For wrong, most pardon for worst injury,
If there be any virtue, any praise,—
Then will this woman-child have proved—who knows?—
Just the one prize vouchsafed unworthy me,
Seven years a gardener of the untoward ground,
I till,—this earth, my sweat and blood manure
All the long day that barrenly grows dusk:
At least one blossom makes me proud at eve
Born 'mid the briers of my enclosure! Still   1030
(Oh, here as elsewhere, nothingness of man!)
Those be the plants, imbedded yonder South
To mellow in the morning, those made fat
By the master's eye, that yield such timid leaf,
Uncertain bud, as product of his pains!
While—see how this mere chance-sown cleft-nursed seed
That sprang up by the wayside 'neath the foot
Of the enemy, this breaks all into blaze,
Spreads itself, one wide glory of desire
To incorporate the whole great sun it loves   1040
From the inch-height whence it looks and longs! My flower,
My rose, I gather for the breast of God,
This I praise most in thee, where all I praise,
That having been obedient to the end
According to the light allotted, law
Prescribed thy life, still tried, still standing test,—
Dutiful to the foolish parents first,
Submissive next to the bad husband,—nay,
Tolerant of those meaner miserable
That did his hests, eked out the dole of pain,—   1050
Thou, patient thus, couldst rise from law to law,
The old to the new, promoted at one cry
O' the trump of God to the new service, not
To longer bear, but henceforth fight, be found
Sublime in new impatience with the foe!
Endure man and obey God: plant firm foot
On neck of man, tread man into the hell
Meet for him, and obey God all the more!

Oh child that didst despise thy life so much
When it seemed only thine to keep or lose,   1060
How the fine ear felt fall the first low word
'Value life, and preserve life for My sake!'
Thou didst... how shall I say?...receive so long
The standing ordinance of God on earth,
What wonder if the novel claim had clashed
With old requirement, seemed to supersede
Too much the customary law? But, brave,
Thou at first prompting of what I call God,
And fools call Nature, didst hear, comprehend,
Accept the obligation laid on thee,   1070
Mother elect, to save the unborn child,
As brute and bird do, reptile and the fly,
Ay and, I nothing doubt, even tree, shrub, plant
And flower o' the field, all in a common pact
To worthily defend the trust of trusts,
Life from the Ever Living:—didst resist—
Anticipate the office that is mine—
And with his own sword stay the upraised arm,
The endeavour of the wicked, and defend
Him who,—again in my default,—was there°   1080
For visible providence: one less true than thou
To touch, i' the past, less practised in the right,
Approved less far in all docility
To all instruction,—how had such an one
Made scruple 'Is this motion a decree?'
It was authentic to the experienced ear
O' the good and faithful servant. Go past me
And get thy praise,—and be not far to seek
Presently when I follow if I may!

And surely not so very much apart   1090
Need I place thee, my warrior-priest,—in whom
What if I gain the other rose, the gold,°
We grave to imitate God's miracle,
Greet monarchs with, good rose in its degree?
Irregular noble 'scapegrace—son the same!
Faulty—and peradventure ours the fault
Who still misteach, mislead, throw hook and line,
Thinking to land leviathan forsooth,°

Tame the scaled neck, play with him as a bird,
And bind him for our maidens! Better bear   1100
The King of Pride go wantoning awhile,
Unplagued by cord in nose and thorn in jaw,
Through deep to deep, followed by all that shine,
Churning the blackness hoary: He who made
The comely terror, He shall make the sword
To match that piece of netherstone his heart,
Ay, nor miss praise thereby; who else shut fire
I' the stone, to leap from mouth at sword's first stroke,
In lamps of love and faith, the chivalry
That dares the right and disregards alike   1110
The yea and nay o' the world? Self-sacrifice,—
What if an idol took it? Ask the Church
Why she was wont to turn each Venus here,—
Poor Rome perversely lingered round, despite
Instruction, for the sake of purblind love,—
Into Madonna's shape, and waste no whit
Of aught so rare on earth as gratitude!
All this sweet savour was not ours but thine,
Nard of the rock, a natural wealth we name°
Incense, and treasure up as food for saints,   1120
When flung to us—whose function was to give
Not find the costly perfume. Do I smile?
Nay, Caponsacchi, much I find amiss,
Blameworthy, punishable in this freak
Of thine, this youth prolonged, though age was ripe,
This masquerade in sober day, with change
Of motley too,—now hypocrite's disguise,
Now fool's-costume: which lie was least like truth,
Which the ungainlier, more discordant garb
With that symmetric soul inside my son,   1130
The churchman's or the worldling's,—let him judge,
Our adversary who enjoys the task!
I rather chronicle the healthy rage,—
When the first moan broke from the martyr-maid
At that uncaging of the beasts,—made bare
My athlete on the instant, gave such good
Great undisguised leap over post and pale
Right into the mid-cirque, free fighting-place.
There may have been rash stripping—every rag

Went to the winds,—infringement manifold   1140
Of laws prescribed pudicity, I fear,°
In this impulsive and prompt self-display!
Ever such tax comes of the foolish youth;
Men mulct the wiser manhood, and suspect°
No veritable star swims out of cloud.
Bear thou such imputation, undergo
The penalty I nowise dare relax,—
Conventional chastisement and rebuke.
But for the outcome, the brave starry birth
Conciliating earth with all that cloud,   1150
Thank heaven as I do! Ay, such championship
Of God at first blush, such prompt cheery thud
Of glove on ground that answers ringingly
The challenge of the false knight,—watch we long
And wait we vainly for its gallant like
From those appointed to the service, sworn
His body-guard with pay and privilege—
White-cinct, because in white walks sanctity,°
Red-socked, how else proclaim fine scorn of flesh,
Unchariness of blood when blood faith begs!°   1160
Where are the men-at-arms with cross on coat?
Aloof, bewraying their attire: whilst thou
In mask and motley, pledged to dance not fight,
Sprang'st forth the hero! In thought, word and deed,
How throughout all thy warfare thou wast pure,
I find it easy to believe: and if
At any fateful moment of the strange
Adventure, the strong passion of that strait,
Fear and surprise, may have revealed too much,—
As when a thundrous midnight, with black air   1170
That burns, rain-drops that blister, breaks a spell,
Draws out the excessive virtue of some sheathed
Shut unsuspected flower that hoards and hides
Immensity of sweetness,—so, perchance,
Might the surprise and fear release too much
The perfect beauty of the body and soul
Thou savedst in thy passion for God's sake,
He who is Pity. Was the trial sore?
Temptation sharp? Thank God a second time!
Why comes temptation but for man to meet   1180

And master and make crouch beneath his foot,
And so be pedestaled in triumph? Pray
'Lead us into no such temptations, Lord!'
Yea, but, O Thou whose servants are the bold,
Lead such temptations by the head and hair,
Reluctant dragons, up to who dares fight,
That so he may do battle and have praise!
Do I not see the praise?—that while thy mates
Bound to deserve i' the matter, prove at need
Unprofitable through the very pains   1190
We gave to train them well and start them fair,—
Are found too stiff, with standing ranked and ranged,
For onset in good earnest, too obtuse
Of ear, through iteration of command,
For catching quick the sense of the real cry,—
Thou, whose sword-hand was used to strike the lute,
Whose sentry-station graced some wanton's gate,
Thou didst push forward and show mettle, shame
The laggards, and retrieve the day. Well done!
Be glad thou hast let light into the world   1200
Through that irregular breach o' the boundary,—see
The same upon thy path and march assured,
Learning anew the use of soldiership,
Self-abnegation, freedom from all fear,
Loyalty to the life's end! Ruminate,
Deserve the initiatory spasm,—once more°
Work, be unhappy but bear life, my son!

And troop you, somewhere 'twixt the best and worst,
Where crowd the indifferent product, all too poor
Makeshift, starved samples of humanity!   1210
Father and mother, huddle there and hide!
A gracious eye may find you! Foul and fair,
Sadly mixed natures: self-indulgent,—yet
Self-sacrificing too: how the love soars,
How the craft, avarice, vanity and spite
Sink again! So they keep the middle course,
Slide into silly crime at unaware,
Slip back upon the stupid virtue, stay
Nowhere enough for being classed, I hope
And fear. Accept the swift and rueful death,   1220

Taught, somewhat sternlier than is wont, what waits
The ambiguous creature,—how the one black tuft
Steadies the aim of the arrow just as well
As the wide faultless white on the bird's breast!
Nay, you were punished in the very part
That looked most pure of speck,—'twas honest love
Betrayed you,—did love seem most worthy pains,
Challenge such purging, since ordained survive
When all the rest of you was done with? Go!
Never again elude the choice of tints!   1230
White shall not neutralize the black, nor good
Compensate bad in man, absolve him so:
Life's business being just the terrible choice.

So do I see, pronounce on all and some
Grouped for my judgment now,—profess no doubt
While I pronounce: dark, difficult enough
The human sphere, yet eyes grow sharp by use,
I find the truth, dispart the shine from shade,
As a mere man may, with no special touch
O' the lynx-gift in each ordinary orb:°   1240
Nay, if the popular notion class me right,
One of well-nigh decayed intelligence,—
What of that? Through hard labour and good will,
And habitude that gives a blind man sight
At the practised finger-ends of him, I do
Discern, and dare decree in consequence,
Whatever prove the peril of mistake.
Whence, then, this quite new quick cold thrill,—cloud like,
This keen dread creeping from a quarter scarce
Suspected in the skies I nightly scan?   1250
What slacks the tense nerve, saps the wound-up spring
Of the act that should and shall be, sends the mount
And mass o' the whole man's-strength,—conglobed so late—
Shudderingly into dust, a moment's work?
While I stand firm, go fearless, in this world,
For this life recognize and arbitrate,
Touch and let stay, or else remove a thing,
Judge 'This is right, this object out of place,'
Candle in hand that helps me and to spare,—
What if a voice deride me, 'Perk and pry!'°   1260

Brighten each nook with thine intelligence!
Play the good householder, ply man and maid
With tasks prolonged into the midnight, test
Their work and nowise stint of the due wage
Each worthy worker: but with gyves and whip°
Pay thou misprision of a single point
Plain to thy happy self who lift'st the light,
Lament'st the darkling,—bold to all beneath!
What if thyself adventure, now the place
Is purged so well? Leave pavement and mount roof,   1270
Look round thee for the light of the upper sky,
The fire which lit thy fire which finds default
In Guido Franceschini to his cost!
What if, above in the domain of light,
Thou miss the accustomed signs, remark eclipse?
Shalt thou still gaze on ground nor lift a lid,—
Steady in thy superb prerogative,
Thy inch of inkling,—nor once face the doubt
I' the sphere above thee, darkness to be felt?'   1280

Yet my poor spark had for its source, the sun;
Thither I sent the great looks which compel
Light from its fount: all that I do and am
Comes from the truth, or seen or else surmised,
Remembered or divined, as mere man may:
I know just so, nor otherwise. As I know,
I speak,—what should I know, then, and how speak
Were there a wild mistake of eye or brain
As to recorded governance above?
If my own breath, only, blew coal alight
I styled celestial and the morning-star?   1290
I, who in this world act resolvedly,
Dispose of men, their bodies and their souls,
As they acknowledge or gainsay the light
I show them,—shall I too lack courage?—leave
I, too, the post of me, like those I blame?
Refuse, with kindred inconsistency,
To grapple danger whereby souls grow strong?
I am near the end; but still not at the end;
All to the very end is trial in life:
At this stage is the trial of my soul   1300

Danger to face, or danger to refuse?
Shall I dare try the doubt now, or not dare?

O Thou,—as represented here to me
In such conception as my soul allows,—
Under Thy measureless, my atom width!—
Man's mind, what is it but a convex glass
Wherein are gathered all the scattered points
Picked out of the immensity of sky,
To re-unite there, be our heaven for earth,
Our known unknown, our God revealed to man?   1310
Existent somewhere, somehow, as a whole;
Here, as a whole proportioned to our sense,—
There, (which is nowhere, speech must babble thus!)
In the absolute immensity, the whole
Appreciable solely by Thyself,—
Here, by the little mind of man, reduced
To littleness that suits his faculty,
In the degree appreciable too;
Between Thee and ourselves—nay even, again,
Below us, to the extreme of the minute,   1320
Appreciable by how many and what diverse
Modes of the life Thou madest be! (why live
Except for love,—how love unless they know?)
Each of them, only filling to the edge,
Insect or angel, his just length and breadth,
Due facet of reflection,—full, no less,
Angel or insect, as Thou framedst things.
I it is who have been appointed here
To represent Thee, in my turn, on earth,
Just as, if new philosophy know aught,   1330
This one earth, out of all the multitude
Of peopled worlds, as stars are now supposed,—
Was chosen, and no sun-star of the swarm,
For stage and scene of Thy transcendent act°
Beside which even the creation fades
Into a puny exercise of power.
Choice of the world, choice of the thing I am,
Both emanate alike from Thy dread play
Of operation outside this our sphere
Where things are classed and counted small or great,— 1340

Incomprehensibly the choice is Thine!
I therefore bow my head and take Thy place.
There is, beside the works, a tale of Thee
In the world's mouth, which I find credible:
I love it with my heart: unsatisfied,
I try it with my reason, nor discept
From any point I probe and pronounce sound.
Mind is not matter nor from matter, but
Above,—leave matter then, proceed with mind!
Man's be the mind recognized at the height,—   1350
Leave the inferior minds and look at man!
Is he the strong, intelligent and good
Up to his own conceivable height? Nowise.
Enough o' the low,—soar the conceivable height,
Find cause to match the effect in evidence,
The work i' the world, not man's but God's; leave man!
Conjecture of the worker by the work:
Is there strength there?—enough: intelligence?
Ample: but goodness in a like degree?
Not to the human eye in the present state,   1360
An isoscele deficient in the base.°
What lacks, then, of perfection fit for God
But just the instance which this tale supplies
Of love without a limit? So is strength,
So is intelligence; let love be so,
Unlimited in its self-sacrifice,
Then is the tale true and God shows complete.
Beyond the tale, I reach into the dark,
Feel what I cannot see, and still faith stands:
I can believe this dread machinery   1370
Of sin and sorrow, would confound me else,
Devised,—all pain, at most expenditure
Of pain by Who devised pain,—to evolve,
By new machinery in counterpart,
The moral qualities of man—how else?—
To make him love in turn and be beloved,
Creative and self-sacrificing too,
And thus eventually God-like, (ay,
'I have said ye are Gods,'—shall it be said for nought?)°
Enable man to wring, from out all pain,   1380
All pleasure for a common heritage

To all eternity: this may be surmised,
The other is revealed,—whether a fact,
Absolute, abstract, independent truth,
Historic, not reduced to suit man's mind,—
Or only truth reverberate, changed, made pass
A spectrum into mind, the narrow eye,—
The same and not the same, else unconceived—
Though quite conceivable to the next grade
Above it in intelligence,—as truth   1390
Easy to man were blindness to the beast
By parity of procedure,—the same truth
In a new form, but changed in either case:
What matter so intelligence be filled?
To a child, the sea is angry, for it roars:
Frost bites, else why the tooth-like fret on face?
Man makes acoustics deal with the sea's wrath,
Explains the choppy cheek by chymic law,—°
To man and child remains the same effect
On drum of ear and root of nose, change cause   1400
Never so thoroughly: so my heart be struck,
What care I,—by God's gloved hand or the bare?°
Nor do I much perplex me with aught hard,
Dubious in the transmitting of the tale,—
No, nor with certain riddles set to solve.
This life is training and a passage; pass,—
Still, we march over some flat obstacle
We made give way before us; solid truth
In front of it, what motion for the world?
The moral sense grows but by exercise.   1410
'Tis even as man grew probatively°
Initiated in Godship, set to make
A fairer moral world than this he finds,
Guess now what shall be known hereafter. Deal
Thus with the present problem: as we see,
A faultless creature is destroyed, and sin
Has had its way i' the world where God should rule.
Ay, but for this irrelevant circumstance
Of inquisition after blood, we see
Pompilia lost and Guido saved: how long?   1420
For his whole life: how much is that whole life?
We are not babes, but know the minute's worth,

And feel that life is large and the world small,
So, wait till life have passed from out the world.
Neither does this astonish at the end,
That whereas I can so receive and trust,
Other men, made with hearts and souls the same,
Reject and disbelieve,—subordinate
The future to the present,—sin, nor fear.
This I refer still to the foremost fact,   1430
Life is probation and the earth no goal
But starting-point of man: compel him strive,
Which means, in man, as good as reach the goal,—
Why institute that race, his life, at all?
But this does overwhelm me with surprise,
Touch me to terror,—not that faith, the pearl,
Should be let lie by fishers wanting food,—
Nor, seen and handled by a certain few
Critical and contemptuous, straight consigned
To shore and shingle for the pebble it proves,—   1440
But that, when haply found and known and named
By the residue made rich for evermore,
These,—that these favoured ones, should in a trice
Turn, and with double zest go dredge for whelks,
Mud-worms that make the savoury soup! Enough
O' the disbelievers, see the faithful few!
How do the Christians here deport them, keep
Their robes of white unspotted by the world?
What is this Aretine Archbishop, this
Man under me as I am under God,   1450
This champion of the faith, I armed and decked,
Pushed forward, put upon a pinnacle,
To show the enemy his victor,—see!
What's the best fighting when the couple close?
Pompilia cries, 'Protect me from the wolf!'
He—'No, thy Guido is rough, heady, strong,
Dangerous to disquiet: let him bide!
He needs some bone to mumble, help amuse
The darkness of his den with: so, the fawn
Which limps up bleeding to my foot and lies,   1460
—Come to me, daughter!—thus I throw him back!'
Have we misjudged here, over-armed our knight,
Given gold and silk where plain hard steel serves best,

Enfeebled whom we sought to fortify,
Made an archbishop and undone a saint?
Well, then, descend these heights, this pride of life,
Sit in the ashes with a barefoot monk
Who long ago stamped out the worldly sparks,
By fasting, watching, stone cell and wire scourge,
—No such indulgence as unknits the strength—
These breed the tight nerve and tough cuticle,°
And the world's praise or blame runs rillet-wise
Off the broad back and brawny breast, we know!
He meets the first cold sprinkle of the world,
And shudders to the marrow. 'Save this child?
Oh, my superiors, oh, the Archbishop's self!
Who was it dared lay hand upon the ark
His betters saw fall nor put finger forth?°
Great ones could help yet help not: why should small?
I break my promise: let her break her heart!'
These are the Christians not the worldlings, not
The sceptics, who thus battle for the faith!
If foolish virgins disobey and sleep,
What wonder? But, this time, the wise that watch,
Sell lamps and buy lutes, exchange oil for wine,
The mystic Spouse betrays the Bridegroom here.°
To our last resource, then! Since all flesh is weak,
Bind weaknesses together, we get strength:
The individual weighed, found wanting, try
Some institution, honest artifice
Whereby the units grow compact and firm!
Each props the other, and so stand is made
By our embodied cowards that grow brave.
The Monastery called of Convertites,°
Meant to help women because these helped Christ,—
A thing existent only while it acts,
Does as designed, else a nonentity,—
For what is an idea unrealized?—
Pompilia is consigned to these for help.
They do help: they are prompt to testify
To her pure life and saintly dying days.
She dies, and lo, who seemed so poor, proves rich.
What does the body that lives through helpfulness°
To women for Christ's sake? The kiss turns bite,

1470

1480

1490

1500

The dove's note changes to the crow's cry: judge!
'Seeing that this our Convent claims of right
What goods belong to those we succour, be
The same proved women of dishonest life,—
And seeing that this Trial made appear
Pompilia was in such predicament,—   1510
The Convent hereupon pretends to said
Succession of Pompilia, issues writ,
And takes possession by the Fisc's advice.'°
Such is their attestation to the cause
Of Christ, who had one saint at least, they hoped:
But, is a title-deed to filch, a corpse
To slander, and an infant-heir to cheat?
Christ must give up his gains then! They unsay
All the fine speeches,—who was saint is whore.
Why, scripture yields no parallel for this!   1520
The soldiers only threw dice for Christ's coat;°
We want another legend of the Twelve
Disputing if it was Christ's coat at all,
Claiming as prize the woof of price—for why?°
The Master was a thief, purloined the same,
Or paid for it out of the common bag!
Can it be this is end and outcome, all
I take with me to show as stewardship's fruit,
The best yield of the latest time, this year
The seventeen-hundredth since God died for man?   1530
Is such effect proportionate to cause?
And still the terror keeps on the increase
When I perceive...how can I blink the fact?
That the fault, the obduracy to good,
Lies not with the impracticable stuff
Whence man is made, his very nature's fault,
As if it were of ice the moon may gild
Not melt, or stone 'twas meant the sun should warm
Not make bear flowers,—nor ice nor stone to blame:
But it can melt, that ice, can bloom, that stone,   1540
Impassible to rule of day and night!
This terrifies me, thus compelled perceive,
Whatever love and faith we looked should spring
At advent of the authoritative star,
Which yet lie sluggish, curdled at the source,—

These have leapt forth profusely in old time,
These still respond with promptitude to-day,
At challenge of—what unacknowledged powers
O' the air, what uncommissioned meteors, warmth
By law, and light by rule should supersede?   1550
For see this priest, this Caponsacchi, stung
At the first summons,—'Help for honour's sake,
Play the man, pity the oppressed!'—no pause,
How does he lay about him in the midst,
Strike any foe, right wrong at any risk,
All blindness, bravery and obedience!—blind?
Ay, as a man would be inside the sun,
Delirious with the plenitude of light
Should interfuse him to the finger-ends—
Let him rush straight, and how shall he go wrong?   1560
Where are the Christians in their panoply?
The loins we girt about with truth, the breasts
Righteousness plated round, the shield of faith,
The helmet of salvation, and that sword
O' the Spirit, even the word of God,—where these?
Slunk into corners! Oh, I hear at once
Hubbub of protestation! 'What, we monks
We friars, of such an order, such a rule,
Have not we fought, bled, left our martyr-mark
At every point along the boundary-line   1570
'Twixt true and false, religion and the world,
Where this or the other dogma of our Church
Called for defence?' And I, despite myself,
How can I but speak loud what truth speaks low,
'Or better than the best, or nothing serves!
What boots deed, I can cap and cover straight
With such another doughtiness to match,
Done at an instinct of the natural man?'
Immolate body, sacrifice soul too,—
Do not these publicans the same? Outstrip!   1580
Or else stop race you boast runs neck and neck,
You with the wings, they with the feet,—for shame!
Oh, I remark your diligence and zeal!
Five years long, now, rounds faith into my ears,
'Help thou, or Christendom is done to death!'
Five years since, in the Province of To-kien,

Which is in China as some people know,
Maigrot, my Vicar Apostolic there,
Having a great qualm, issues a decree.
Alack, the converts use as God's name, not   1590
Tien-chu but plain *Tien* or else mere *Shang-ti*,
As Jesuits please to fancy politic,
While, say Dominicans, it calls down fire,—
For *Tien* means heaven, and *Shang-ti*, supreme prince,
While *Tien-chu* means the lord of heaven: all cry,
'There is no business urgent for despatch
As that thou send a legate, specially
Cardinal Tournon, straight to Pekin, there
To settle and compose the difference!'
So have I seen a potentate all fume   1600
For some infringement of his realm's just right,
Some menace to a mud-built straw-thatched farm
O' the frontier; while inside the mainland lie,
Quite undisputed-for in solitude,
Whole cities plague may waste or famine sap:
What if the sun crumble, the sands encroach,
While he looks on sublimely at his ease?
How does their ruin touch the empire's bound?°

And is this little all that was to be?
Where is the gloriously-decisive change,   1610
Metamorphosis the immeasurable
Of human clay to divine gold, we looked
Should, in some poor sort, justify its price?
Had an adept of the mere Rosy Cross°
Spent his life to consummate the Great Work,
Would not we start to see the stuff it touched
Yield not a grain more than the vulgar got
By the old smelting-process years ago?
If this were sad to see in just the sage
Who should profess so much, perform no more,   1620
What is it when suspected in that Power
Who undertook to make and made the world,
Devised and did effect man, body and soul,
Ordained salvation for them both, and yet . . .
Well, is the thing we see, salvation?

I

Put no such dreadful question to myself,
Within whose circle of experience burns
The central truth, Power, Wisdom, Goodness,—God:
I must outlive a thing ere know it dead:
When I outlive the faith there is a sun,   1630
When I lie, ashes to the very soul,—
Someone, not I, must wail above the heap,
'He died in dark whence never morn arose.'°
While I see day succeed the deepest night—
How can I speak but as I know?—my speech
Must be, throughout the darkness, 'It will end:
The light that did burn, will burn!' Clouds obscure—
But for which obscuration all were bright?
Too hastily concluded! Sun-suffused,
A cloud may soothe the eye made blind by blaze,—   1640
Better the very clarity of heaven:
The soft streaks are the beautiful and dear.
What but the weakness in a faith supplies
The incentive to humanity, no strength
Absolute, irresistible, comports?°
How can man love but what he yearns to help?
And that which men think weakness within strength,
But angels know for strength and stronger yet—
What were it else but the first things made new,
But repetition of the miracle,
The divine instance of self-sacrifice   1650
That never ends and aye begins for man?
So, never I miss footing in the maze,
No,—I have light nor fear the dark at all.

But are mankind not real, who pace outside
My petty circle, world that's measured me?
And when they stumble even as I stand,
Have I a right to stop ear when they cry,
As they were phantoms who took clouds for crags,
Tripped and fell, where man's march might safely move?   1660
Beside, the cry is other than a ghost's,
When out of the old time there pleads some bard,°
Philosopher, or both, and—whispers not,

But words it boldly. 'The inward work and worth
Of any mind, what other mind may judge
Save God who only knows the thing He made,
The veritable service He exacts?
It is the outward product men appraise.
Behold, an engine hoists a tower aloft:
"I looked that it should move the mountain too!"   1670
Or else "Had just a turret toppled down,
Success enough!"—may say the Machinist°
Who knows what less or more result might be:
But we, who see that done we cannot do,
"A feat beyond man's force," we men must say.
Regard me and that shake I gave the world!
I was born, not so long before Christ's birth
As Christ's birth haply did precede thy day,—
But many a watch before the star of dawn:
Therefore I lived,—it is thy creed affirms,   1680
Pope Innocent, who art to answer me!—
Under conditions, nowise to escape,
Whereby salvation was impossible.
Each impulse to achieve the good and fair,
Each aspiration to the pure and true,
Being without a warrant or an aim,
Was just as sterile a felicity
As if the insect, born to spend his life
Soaring his circles, stopped them to describe
(Painfully motionless in the mid-air)   1690
Some word of weighty counsel for man's sake,
Some "Know thyself" or "Take the golden mean!"
—Forwent his happy dance and the glad ray,
Died half an hour the sooner and was dust.
I, born to perish like the brutes, or worse,°
Why not live brutishly, obey brutes' law?
But I, of body as of soul complete,
A gymnast at the games, philosopher
I' the schools, who painted, and made music,—all
Glories that met upon the tragic stage   1700
When the Third Poet's tread surprised the Two,—°
Whose lot fell in a land where life was great
And sense went free and beauty lay profuse,
I, untouched by one adverse circumstance,
Adopted virtue as my rule of life,

Waived all reward, loved but for loving's sake,
And, what my heart taught me, I taught the world,
And have been teaching now two thousand years.
Witness my work,—plays that should please, forsooth!
"They might please, they may displease, they shall teach,
For truth's sake," so I said, and did, and do.   1710
Five hundred years ere Paul spoke, Felix heard,—°
How much of temperance and righteousness,
Judgment to come, did I find reason for,
Corroborate with my strong style that spared°
No sin, nor swerved the more from branding brow
Because the sinner was called Zeus and God?
How nearly did I guess at that Paul knew?
How closely come, in what I represent
As duty, to his doctrine yet a blank?
And as that limner not untruly limns   1720
Who draws an object round or square, which square
Or round seems to the unassisted eye,
Though Galileo's tube display the same
Oval or oblong,—so, who controverts
I rendered rightly what proves wrongly wrought
Beside Paul's picture? Mine was true for me.
I saw that there are, first and above all,
The hidden forces, blind necessities,
Named Nature, but the thing's self unconceived: 1730
Then follow,—how dependent upon these,
We know not, how imposed above ourselves,
We well know,—what I name the gods, a power
Various or one: for great and strong and good
Is there, and little, weak and bad there too,
Wisdom and folly: say, these make no God,—
What is it else that rules outside man's self?
A fact then,—always, to the naked eye,—
And so, the one revealment possible
Of what were unimagined else by man.
Therefore, what gods do, man may criticize,   1740
Applaud, condemn,—how should he fear the truth?—
But likewise have in awe because of power,
Venerate for the main munificence,
And give the doubtful deed its due excuse
From the acknowledged creature of a day
To the Eternal and Divine. Thus, bold

Yet self-mistrusting, should man bear himself,
Most assured on what now concerns him most—
The law of his own life, the path he prints,—   1750
Which law is virtue and not vice, I say,—
And least inquisitive where search least skills,
I' the nature we best give the clouds to keep.
What could I paint beyond a scheme like this
Out of the fragmentary truths where light
Lay fitful in a tenebrific time?°
You have the sunrise now, joins truth to truth,
Shoots life and substance into death and void;
Themselves compose the whole we made before:
The forces and necessity grow God,—   1760
The beings so contrarious that seemed gods,
Prove just His operation manifold
And multiform, translated, as must be,
Into intelligible shape so far
As suits our sense and sets us free to feel.
What if I let a child think, childhood-long,
That lightning, I would have him spare his eye,
Is a real arrow shot at naked orb?
The man knows more, but shuts his lids the same:
Lightning's cause comprehends nor man nor child.   1770
Why then, my scheme, your better knowledge broke,
Presently re-adjusts itself, the small
Proportioned largelier, parts and whole named new:
So much, no more two thousand years have done!
Pope, dost thou dare pretend to punish me,
For not descrying sunshine at midnight,
Me who crept all-fours, found my way so far—
While thou rewardest teachers of the truth,
Who miss the plain way in the blaze of noon,—
Though just a word from that strong style of mine,   1780
Grasped honestly in hand as guiding-staff,
Had pricked them a sure path across the bog,
That mire of cowardice and slush of lies
Wherein I find them wallow in wide day!'

    How should I answer this Euripides?
Paul,—'tis a legend,—answered Seneca,°
But that was in the day-spring; noon is now:

We have got too familiar with the light.
Shall I wish back once more that thrill of dawn?
When the whole truth-touched man burned up, one fire?   1790
—Assured the trial, fiery, fierce, but fleet,
Would, from his little heap of ashes, lend
Wings to that conflagration of the world
Which Christ awaits ere He makes all things new:
So should the frail become the perfect, rapt
From glory of pain to glory of joy; and so,
Even in the end,—the act renouncing earth,
Lands, houses, husbands, wives and children here,—
Begin that other act which finds all, lost,
Regained, in this time even, a hundredfold,   1800
And, in the next time, feels the finite love
Blent and embalmed with the eternal life.
So does the sun ghastlily seem to sink
In those north parts, lean all but out of life,
Desist a dread mere breathing-stop, then slow
Re-assert day, begin the endless rise.
Was this too easy for our after-stage?
Was such a lighting-up of faith, in life,
Only allowed initiate, set man's step
In the true way by help of the great glow?   1810
A way wherein it is ordained he walk,
Bearing to see the light from heaven still more
And more encroached on by the light of earth,
Tentatives earth puts forth to rival heaven,
Earthly incitements that mankind serve God
For man's sole sake, not God's and therefore man's.
Till at last, who distinguishes the sun
From a mere Druid fire on a far mount?°
More praise to him who with his subtle prism
Shall decompose both beams and name the true.   1820
In such sense, who is last proves first indeed°
For how could saints and martyrs fail see truth
Streak the night's blackness? Who is faithful now?
Who untwists heaven's white from the yellow flare
O' the world's gross torch, without night's foil that helped
Produce the Christian act so possible
When in the way stood Nero's cross and stake,—°
So hard now when the world smiles 'Right and wise!

Faith points the politic, the thrifty way,
Will make who plods it in the end returns   1830
Beyond mere fool's-sport and improvidence.
We fools dance thro' the cornfield of this life,
Pluck ears to left and right and swallow raw,
—Nay, tread, at pleasure, a sheaf underfoot,
To get the better at some poppy-flower,—
Well aware we shall have so much less wheat
In the eventual harvest: you meantime
Waste not a spike,—the richlier will you reap!
What then? There will be always garnered meal
Sufficient for our comfortable loaf,   1840
While you enjoy the undiminished sack!'
Is it not this ignoble confidence,
Cowardly hardihood, that dulls and damps,
Makes the old heroism impossible?

Unless ... what whispers me of times to come?
What if it be the mission of that age
My death will usher into life, to shake
This torpor of assurance from our creed,
Re-introduce the doubt discarded, bring
That formidable danger back, we drove   1850
Long ago to the distance and the dark?
No wild beast now prowls round the infant camp:
We have built wall and sleep in city safe:
But if some earthquake try the towers that laugh
To think they once saw lions rule outside,
And man stand out again, pale, resolute,
Prepared to die,—which means, alive at last?
As we broke up that old faith of the world,
Have we, next age, to break up this the new—
Faith, in the thing, grown faith in the report—   1860
Whence need to bravely disbelieve report
Through increased faith i' the thing reports belie?
Must we deny,—do they, these Molinists,°
At peril of their body and their soul,—
Recognized truths, obedient to some truth
Unrecognized yet, but perceptible?—
Correct the portrait by the living face,
Man's God, by God's God in the mind of man?

Then, for the few that rise to the new height,
The many that must sink to the old depth,   1870
The multitude found fall away! A few,
E'en ere new law speak clear, may keep the old,
Preserve the Christian level, call good good
And evil evil, (even though razed and blank
The old titles,) helped by custom, habitude,
And all else they mistake for finer sense
O' the fact than reason warrants,—as before,
They hope perhaps, fear not impossibly.
At least some one Pompilia left the world
Will say 'I know the right place by foot's feel,   1880
I took it and tread firm there; wherefore change?'
But what a multitude will surely fall
Quite through the crumbling truth, late subjacent,
Sink to the next discoverable base,
Rest upon human nature, settle there
On what is firm, the lust and pride of life!
A mass of men, whose very souls even now
Seem to need re-creating,—so they slink
Worm-like into the mud, light now lays bare,—
Whose future we dispose of with shut eyes   1890
And whisper—'They are grafted, barren twigs,
Into the living stock of Christ: may bear
One day, till when they lie death-like, not dead,'—
Those who with all the aid of Christ succumb,
How, without Christ, shall they, unaided, sink?
Whither but to this gulf before my eyes?
Do not we end, the century and I?
The impatient antimasque treads close on kibe°
O' the very masque's self it will mock,—on me,
Last lingering personage, the impatient mime   1900
Pushes already,—will I block the way?
Will my slow trail of garments ne'er leave space
For pantaloon, sock, plume and castanet?
Here comes the first experimentalist
In the new order of things,—he plays a priest;
Does he take inspiration from the Church,
Directly make her rule his law of life?
Not he: his own mere impulse guides the man—
Happily sometimes, since ourselves allow

He has danced, in gaiety of heart, i' the main   1910
The right step through the maze we bade him foot.
But if his heart had prompted him break loose
And mar the measure? Why, we must submit,
And thank the chance that brought him safe so far.
Will he repeat the prodigy? Perhaps.
Can he teach others how to quit themselves,
Show why this step was right while that were wrong?
How should he? 'Ask your hearts as I asked mine,
And get discreetly through the morrice too;°
If your hearts misdirect you,—quit the stage,   1920
And make amends,—be there amends to make!'
Such is, for the Augustin that was once,°
This Canon Caponsacchi we see now.
'But my heart answers to another tune,'
Puts in the Abate, second in the suite,°
'I have my taste too, and tread no such step!
You choose the glorious life, and may, for me!
I like the lowest of life's appetites,—
So you judge,—but the very truth of joy
To my own apprehension which decides.   1930
Call me knave and you get yourself called fool!
I live for greed, ambition, lust, revenge;
Attain these ends by force, guile: hypocrite,
To-day, perchance to-morrow recognized
The rational man, the type of common sense.'
There's Loyola adapted to our time!°
Under such guidance Guido plays his part,
He also influencing in the due turn
These last clods where I track intelligence
By any glimmer, these four at his beck   1940
Ready to murder any, and, at their own,
As ready to murder him,—such make the world!
And, first effect of the new cause of things,
There they lie also duly,—the old pair
Of the weak head and not so wicked heart,
With the one Christian mother, wife and girl,
—Which three gifts seem to make an angel up,—
The world's first foot o' the dance is on their heads!
Still, I stand here, not off the stage though close
On the exit: and my last act, as my first,   1950

I owe the scene, and Him who armed me thus
With Paul's sword as with Peter's key. I smite
With my whole strength once more, ere end my part,
Ending, so far as man may, this offence.
And when I raise my arm, who plucks my sleeve?
Who stops me in the righteous function,—foe
Or friend? Oh, still as ever, friends are they
Who, in the interest of outraged truth
Deprecate such rough handling of a lie!
The facts being proved and incontestable,   1960
What is the last word I must listen to?
Perchance—'Spare yet a term this barren stock
We pray thee dig about and dung and dress
Till he repent and bring forth fruit even yet!'°
Perchance—'So poor and swift a punishment
Shall throw him out of life with all that sin:
Let mercy rather pile up pain on pain
Till the flesh expiate what the soul pays else!'
Nowise! Remonstrants on each side commence
Instructing, there's a new tribunal now   1970
Higher than God's—the educated man's!
Nice sense of honour in the human breast
Supersedes here the old coarse oracle—
Confirming none the less a point or so
Wherein blind predecessors worked aright
By rule of thumb: as when Christ said,—when, where?
Enough, I find it pleaded in a place,—
'All other wrongs done, patiently I take:
But touch my honour and the case is changed!
I feel the due resentment,—*nemini*   1980
Honorem trado is my quick retort.'°
Right of Him, just as if pronounced to-day!
Still, should the old authority be mute
Or doubtful or in speaking clash with new,
The younger takes permission to decide.
At last we have the instinct of the world
Ruling its household without tutelage:
And while the two laws, human and divine,
Have busied finger with this tangled case,
In pushes the brisk junior, cuts the knot,   1990
Pronounces for acquittal. How it trips

Silverly o'er the tongue! 'Remit the death!
Forgive,... well, in the old way, if thou please,
Decency and the relics of routine
Respected,—let the Count go free as air!
Since he may plead a priest's immunity,—
The minor orders help enough for that,
With Farinacci's licence,—who decides°
That the mere implication of such man,
So privileged, in any cause, before   2000
Whatever Court except the Spiritual,
Straight quashes law-procedure,—quash it, then!
Remains a pretty loophole of escape
Moreover, that, beside the patent fact
O' the law's allowance, there's involved the weal
O' the Popedom: a son's privilege at stake,
Thou wilt pretend the Church's interest,
Ignore all finer reasons to forgive!
But herein lies the crowning cogency—
(Let thy friends teach thee while thou tellest beads)   2010
That in this case the spirit of culture speaks,
Civilization is imperative.
To her shall we remand all delicate points
Henceforth, nor take irregular advice
O' the sly, as heretofore: she used to hint
Remonstrances, when law was out of sorts
Because a saucy tongue was put to rest,
An eye that roved was cured of arrogance:
But why be forced to mumble under breath
What soon shall be acknowledged as plain fact,   2020
Outspoken, say, in thy successor's time?
Methinks we see the golden age return!
Civilization and the Emperor
Succeed to Christianity and Pope.
One Emperor then, as one Pope now: meanwhile,
Anticipate a little! We tell thee "Take
Guido's life, sapped society shall crash,
Whereof the main prop was, is, and shall be
—Supremacy of husband over wife!"
Does the man rule i' the house, and may his mate   2030
Because of any plea dispute the same?
Oh, pleas of all sorts shall abound, be sure,

One but allowed validity,—for, harsh
And savage, for, inept and silly-sooth,
For, this and that, will the ingenious sex
Demonstrate the best master e'er graced slave:
And there's but one short way to end the coil,—°
Acknowledge right and reason steadily
I' the man and master: then the wife submits
To plain truth broadly stated. Does the time   2040
Advise we shift—a pillar? nay, a stake
Out of its place i' the social tenement?°
One touch may send a shudder through the heap
And bring it toppling on our children's heads!
Moreover, if ours breed a qualm in thee,
Give thine own better feeling play for once!
Thou, whose own life winks o'er the socket-edge,
Wouldst thou it went out in such ugly snuff
As dooming sons dead, e'en though justice prompt?
Why, on a certain feast, Barabbas' self   2050
Was set free, not to cloud the general cheer:°
Neither shalt thou pollute thy Sabbath close!°
Mercy is safe and graceful. How one hears
The howl begin, scarce the three little taps
O' the silver mallet silent on thy brow,—°
"His last act was to sacrifice a Count
And thereby screen a scandal of the Church!
Guido condemned, the Canon justified
Of course,—delinquents of his cloth go free!"
And so the Luthers chuckle, Calvins scowl,   2060
So thy hand helps Molinos to the chair
Whence he may hold forth till doom's day on just
These *petit-maître* priestlings,—in the choir°
Sanctus et Benedictus, with a brush
Of soft guitar-strings that obey the thumb,
Touched by the bedside, for accompaniment!
Does this give umbrage to a husband? Death
To the fool, and to the priest impunity!
But no impunity to any friend
So simply over-loyal as these four   2070
Who made religion of their patron's cause,
Believed in him and did his bidding straight,
Asked not one question but laid down the lives

This Pope took,—all four lives together made
Just his own length of days,—so, dead they lie,
As these were times when loyalty's a drug,
And zeal in a subordinate too cheap
And common to be saved when we spend life!
Come, 'tis too much good breath we waste in words:
The pardon, Holy Father! Spare grimace,   2080
Shrugs and reluctance! Are not we the world,
Art not thou Priam? Let soft culture plead°
Hecuba-like, "*non tali*" (Virgil serves)
"*Auxilio*" and the rest! Enough, it works!
The Pope relaxes, and the Prince is loth,
The father's bowels yearn, the man's will bends,
Reply is apt. Our tears on tremble, hearts
Big with a benediction, wait the word
Shall circulate thro' the city in a trice,
Set every window flaring, give each man   2090
O' the mob his torch to wave for gratitude.
Pronounce then, for our breath and patience fail!'

I will, Sirs: but a voice other than yours
Quickens my spirit. '*Quis pro Domino?*
Who is upon the Lord's side?' asked the Count.°
I, who write—
                'On receipt of this command,
Acquaint Count Guido and his fellows four
They die to-morrow: could it be to-night,
The better, but the work to do, takes time.
Set with all diligence a scaffold up,   2100
Not in the customary place, by Bridge
Saint Angelo, where die the common sort;
But since the man is noble, and his peers
By predilection haunt the People's Square,°
There let him be beheaded in the midst,
And his companions hanged on either side:
So shall the quality see, fear and learn.
All which work takes time: till to-morrow, then,
Let there be prayer incessant for the five!'

For the main criminal I have no hope   2110
Except in such a suddenness of fate.
I stood at Naples once, a night so dark

I could have scarce conjectured there was earth
Anywhere, sky or sea or world at all:
But the night's black was burst through by a blaze—
Thunder struck blow on blow, earth groaned and bore,
Through her whole length of mountain visible:
There lay the city thick and plain with spires,
And, like a ghost disshrouded, white the sea.
So may the truth be flashed out by one blow,   2120
And Guido see, one instant, and be saved.
Else I avert my face, nor follow him
Into that sad obscure sequestered state°
Where God unmakes but to remake the soul
He else made first in vain; which must not be.
Enough, for I may die this very night
And how should I dare die, this man let live?

Carry this forthwith to the Governor!

Book XI
Guido

You are the Cardinal Acciaiuoli, and you,
Abate Panciatichi—two good Tuscan names:
Acciaiuoli—ah, your ancestor it was
Built the huge battlemented convent-block
Over the little forky flashing Greve
That takes the quick turn at the foot o' the hill
Just as one first sees Florence: oh those days!
'Tis Ema, though, the other rivulet,
The one-arched brown brick bridge yawns over,—yes,
Gallop and go five minutes, and you gain   10
The Roman Gate from where the Ema's bridged:°
Kingfishers fly there: how I see the bend
O'erturreted by Certosa which he built,
That Senescal (we styled him) of your House!°
I do adjure you, help me, Sirs! My blood
Comes from as far a source: ought it to end
This way, by leakage through their scaffold-planks
Into Rome's sink where her red refuse runs?

Sirs, I beseech you by blood-sympathy,
If there be any vile experiment　　　　　　　　　　　　20
In the air,—if this your visit simply prove,
When all's done, just a well-intentioned trick
That tries for truth truer than truth itself,
By startling up a man, ere break of day,
To tell him he must die at sunset,—pshaw!
That man's a Franceschini; feel his pulse,
Laugh at your folly, and let's all go sleep!
You have my last word,—innocent am I
As Innocent my Pope and murderer,
Innocent as a babe, as Mary's own,　　　　　　　　　　30
As Mary's self,—I said, say and repeat,—
And why, then, should I die twelve hours hence? I—
Whom, not twelve hours ago, the gaoler bade
Turn to my straw-truss, settle and sleep sound
That I might wake the sooner, promptlier pay
His due of meat-and-drink-indulgence, cross
His palm with fee of the good-hand, beside,°
As gallants use who go at large again!
For why? All honest Rome approved my part;
Whoever owned wife, sister, daughter,—nay,　　　　　　40
Mistress,—had any shadow of any right
That looks like right, and, all the more resolved,
Held it with tooth and nail,—these manly men
Approved! I being for Rome, Rome was for me.
Then, there's the point reserved, the subterfuge
My lawyers held by, kept for last resource,
Firm should all else,—the impossible fancy!—fail,
And sneaking burgess-spirit win the day.
The knaves! One plea at least would hold,—they laughed,—
One grappling-iron scratch the bottom-rock　　　　　　50
Even should the middle mud let anchor go!
I hooked my cause on to the Clergy's,—plea
Which, even if law tipped off my hat and plume,°
Revealed my priestly tonsure, saved me so.
The Pope moreover, this old Innocent,
Being so meek and mild and merciful,
So fond o' the poor and so fatigued of earth,
So ... fifty thousand devils in deepest hell!
Why must he cure us of our strange conceit

Of the angel in man's likeness, that we loved   60
And looked should help us at a pinch? He help?
He pardon? Here's his mind and message—death!
Thank the good Pope! Now, is he good in this,
Never mind, Christian,—no such stuff's extant,—
But will my death do credit to his reign,
Show he both lived and let live, so was good?
Cannot I live if he but like? 'The law!'
Why, just the law gives him the very chance,
The precise leave to let my life alone,
Which the archangelic soul of him (he says)   70
Yearns after! Here they drop it in his palm,
My lawyers, capital o' the cursed kind,—
Drop life to take and hold and keep: but no!
He sighs, shakes head, refuses to shut hand,
Motions away the gift they bid him grasp,
And of the coyness comes—that off I run°
And down I go, he best knows whither! mind,
He knows, who sets me rolling all the same!
Disinterested Vicar of our Lord,
This way he abrogates and disallows,   80
Nullifies and ignores,—reverts in fine
To the good and right, in detriment of me!
Talk away! Will you have the naked truth?
He's sick of his life's supper,—swallowed lies:
So, hobbling bedward, needs must ease his maw
Just where I sit o' the door-sill. Sir Abate,
Can you do nothing? Friends, we used to frisk:
What of this sudden slash in a friend's face,
This cut across our good companionship
That showed its front so gay when both were young?   90
Were not we put into a beaten path,
Bid pace the world, we nobles born and bred,
We body of friends with each his scutcheon full
Of old achievement and impunity,—
Taking the laugh of morn and Sol's salute
As forth we fared, pricked on to breathe our steeds°
And take equestrian sport over the green
Under the blue, across the crop,—what care?
If we went prancing up hill and down dale,
In and out of the level and the straight,   100

By the bit of pleasant byeway, where was harm?
Still Sol salutes me and the morning laughs:
I see my grandsire's hoof-prints,—point the spot
Where he drew rein, slipped saddle, and stabbed knave
For daring throw gibe—much less, stone—from pale:°
Then back, and on, and up with the cavalcade.
Just so wend we, now canter, now converse,
Till, 'mid the jauncing pride and jaunty port,
Something of a sudden jerks at somebody—
A dagger is out, a flashing cut and thrust,   110
Because I play some prank my grandsire played,
And here I sprawl: where is the company? Gone!
A trot and a trample! only I lie trapped,
Writhe in a certain novel springe just set°
By the good old Pope: I'm first prize. Warn me? Why?
Apprise me that the law o' the game is changed?
Enough that I'm a warning, as I writhe,
To all and each my fellows of the file,
And make law plain henceforward past mistake,
'For such a prank, death is the penalty!'   120
Pope the Five Hundredth (what do I know or care?)
Deputes your Eminency and Abateship
To announce that, twelve hours from this time, he needs
I just essay upon my body and soul
The virtue of his brand-new engine, prove°
Represser of the pranksome! I'm the first!
Thanks. Do you know what teeth you mean to try
The sharpness of, on this soft neck and throat?
I know it,—I have seen and hate it,—ay,
As you shall, while I tell you! Let me talk,   130
Or leave me, at your pleasure! talk I must:
What is your visit but my lure to talk?
Nay, you have something to disclose?—a smile,
At end of the forced sternness, means to mock
The heart-beats here? I call your two hearts stone!
Is your charge to stay with me till I die?
Be tacit as your bench, then! Use your ears,°
I use my tongue: how glibly yours will run
At pleasant supper-time . . . God's curse! . . . to-night
When all the guests jump up, begin so brisk   140
'Welcome, his Eminence who shrived the wretch!°
Now we shall have the Abate's story!'

                                        Life!
How I could spill this overplus of mine
Among those hoar-haired, shrunk-shanked odds and ends
Of body and soul old age is chewing dry!
Those windlestraws that stare while purblind death°
Mows here, mows there, makes hay of juicy me,
And misses just the bunch of withered weed
Would brighten hell and streak its smoke with flame!
How the life I could shed yet never shrink,   150
Would drench their stalks with sap like grass in May!
Is it not terrible, I entreat you, Sirs?—
With manifold and plenitudinous life,
Prompt at death's menace to give blow for threat,
Answer his 'Be thou not!' by 'Thus I am!'—
Terrible so to be alive yet die?

How I live, how I see! so,—how I speak!
Lucidity of soul unlocks the lips:
I never had the words at will before.
How I see all my folly at a glance!   160
'A man requires a woman and a wife:'
There was my folly; I believed the saw.
I knew that just myself concerned myself,
Yet needs must look for what I seemed to lack,
In a woman,—why, the woman's in the man!
Fools we are, how we learn things when too late!
Overmuch life turns round my woman-side:
The male and female in me, mixed before,
Settle of a sudden: I'm my wife outright
In this unmanly appetite for truth,   170
This careless courage as to consequence,
This instantaneous sight through things and through,
This voluble rhetoric, if you please,—'tis she!
Here you have that Pompilia whom I slew,
Also the folly for which I slew her!
                                        Fool!
And, fool-like, what is it I wander from?
What did I say of your sharp iron tooth?
Ah,—that I know the hateful thing! this way.
I chanced to stroll forth, many a good year gone,
One warm Spring eve in Rome, and unaware   180
Looking, mayhap, to count what stars were out,

Came on your fine axe in a frame, that falls
And so cuts off a man's head underneath,
Mannaia,—thus we made acquaintance first:°
Out of the way, in a by-part o' the town,
At the Mouth-of-Truth o' the river-side, you know:°
One goes by the Capitol: and wherefore coy,
Retiring out of crowded noisy Rome?
Because a very little time ago
It had done service, chopped off head from trunk   190
Belonging to a fellow whose poor house
The thing must make a point to stand before—
Felice Whatsoever-was-the-name
Who stabled buffaloes and so gained bread,
(Our clowns unyoke them in the ground hard by)
And, after use of much improper speech,
Had struck at Duke Some-title-or-other's face,
Because he kidnapped, carried away and kept
Felice's sister who would sit and sing
I' the filthy doorway while she plaited fringe   200
To deck the brutes with,—on their gear it goes,—
The good girl with the velvet in her voice.
So did the Duke, so did Felice, so
Did Justice, intervening with her axe.
There the man-mutilating engine stood
At ease, both gay and grim, like a Swiss guard°
Off duty,—purified itself as well,
Getting dry, sweet and proper for next week,—
And doing incidental good, 'twas hoped,
To the rough lesson-lacking populace   210
Who now and then, forsooth, must right their wrongs!
There stood the twelve-foot-square of scaffold, railed
Considerately round to elbow-height,
For fear an officer should tumble thence
And sprain his ankle and be lame a month
Through starting when the axe fell and head too!
Railed likewise were the steps whereby 'twas reached.
All of it painted red: red, in the midst,
Ran up two narrow tall beams barred across,
Since from the summit, some twelve feet to reach,   220
The iron plate with the sharp shearing edge
Had slammed, jerked, shot, slid,—I shall soon find which!—

And so lay quiet, fast in its fit place,
The wooden half-moon collar, now eclipsed
By the blade which blocked its curvature: apart,
The other half,—the under half-moon board
Which, helped by this, completes a neck's embrace,—
Joined to a sort of desk that wheels aside
Out of the way when done with,—down you kneel,
In you're pushed, over you the other drops,   230
Tight you're clipped, whiz, there's the blade cleaves its best,
Out trundles body, down flops head on floor,
And where's your soul gone? That, too, I shall find!
This kneeling-place was red, red, never fear!
But only slimy-like with paint, not blood,
For why? a decent pitcher stood at hand,
A broad dish to hold sawdust, and a broom
By some unnamed utensil,—scraper-rake,—
Each with a conscious air of duty done.
Underneath, loungers,—boys and some few men,—   240
Discoursed this platter, named the other tool,
Just as, when grooms tie up and dress a steed,
Boys lounge and look on, and elucubrate°
What the round brush is used for, what the square,—
So was explained—to me the skill-less then—
The manner of the grooming for next world
Undergone by Felice What's-his-name.
There's no such lovely month in Rome as May—
May's crescent is no half-moon of red plank,
And came now tilting o'er the wave i' the west,   250
One greenish-golden sea, right 'twixt those bars
Of the engine—I began acquaintance with,
Understood, hated, hurried from before,
To have it out of sight and cleanse my soul!
Here it is all again, conserved for use:
Twelve hours hence, I may know more, not hate worse.

That young May-moon-month! Devils of the deep!
Was not a Pope then Pope as much as now?
Used not he chirrup o'er the Merry Tales,
Chuckle,—his nephew so exact the wag   260
To play a jealous cullion such a trick°

As wins the wife i' the pleasant story! Well?
Why do things change? Wherefore is Rome un-Romed?
I tell you, ere Felice's corpse was cold,
The Duke, that night, threw wide his palace-doors,
Received the compliments o' the quality
For justice done him,—bowed and smirked his best,
And in return passed round a pretty thing.
A portrait of Felice's sister's self,
Florid old rogue Albano's masterpiece,°   270
As—better than virginity in rags—
Bouncing Europa on the back o' the bull:
They laughed and took their road the safelier home.
Ah, but times change, there's quite another Pope,
I do the Duke's deed, take Felice's place,
And, being no Felice, lout and clout,
Stomach but ill the phrase 'I lose my head!'
How euphemistic! Lose what? Lose your ring,
Your snuff-box, tablets, kerchief!—but, your head?
I learnt the process at an early age;   280
'Twas useful knowledge, in those same old days,
To know the way a head is set on neck.
My fencing-master urged 'Would you excel?
Rest not content with mere bold give-and-guard,
Nor pink the antagonist somehow-anyhow!
See me dissect a little, and know your game!
Only anatomy makes a thrust the thing.'
Oh Cardinal, those lithe live necks of ours!
Here go the vertebræ, here's *Atlas*, here
Axis, and here the symphyses stop short,   290
So wisely and well,—as, o'er a corpse, we cant,—
And here's the silver cord which ... what's our word?
Depends from the gold bowl, which loosed (not 'lost')
Lets us from heaven to hell,—one chop, we're loose!°
'And not much pain i' the process,' quoth a sage:
Who told him? Not Felice's ghost, I think!
Such 'losing' is scarce Mother Nature's mode.
She fain would have cord ease itself away,
Worn to a thread by threescore years and ten,
Snap while we slumber: that seems bearable.   300
I'm told one clot of blood extravasate°
Ends one as certainly as Roland's sword,—

One drop of lymph suffused proves Oliver's mace,—°
Intruding, either of the pleasant pair,
On the arachnoid tunic of my brain.°
That's Nature's way of loosing cord!—but Art,
How of Art's process with the engine here,
When bowl and cord alike are crushed across,
Bored between, bruised through? Why, if Fagon's self,°
The French Court's pride, that famed practitioner,   310
Would pass his cold pale lightning of a knife,
Pistoja-ware, adroit 'twixt joint and joint,°
With just a 'See how facile, gentlefolk!'—
The thing were not so bad to bear! Brute force
Cuts as he comes, breaks in, breaks on, breaks out
O' the hard and soft of you: is that the same?
A lithe snake thrids the hedge, makes throb no leaf:
A heavy ox sets chest to brier and branch,
Bursts somehow through, and leaves one hideous hole
Behind him!

        And why, why must this needs be?   320
Oh, if men were but good! They are not good,
Nowise like Peter: people called him rough,
But if, as I left Rome, I spoke the Saint,
—'Petrus, quo vadis?'—doubtless, I should hear,°
'To free the prisoner and forgive his fault!
I plucked the absolute dead from God's own bar,
And raised up Dorcas,—why not rescue thee?'°
What would cost one such nullifying word?
If Innocent succeeds to Peter's place,
Let him think Peter's thought, speak Peter's speech!   330
I say, he is bound to it: friends, how say you?
Concede I be all one bloodguiltiness
And mystery of murder in the flesh,
Why should that fact keep the Pope's mouth shut fast?
He execrates my crime,—good!—sees hell yawn
One inch from the red plank's end which I press,—
Nothing is better! What's the consequence?
How should a Pope proceed that knows his cue?
Why, leave me linger out my minute here,
Since close on death comes judgment and comes doom,   340
Not crib at dawn its pittance from a sheep°

Destined ere dewfall to be butcher's-meat!
Think, Sirs, if I have done you any harm,
And you require the natural revenge,
Suppose, and so intend to poison me,
—Just as you take and slip into my draught
The paperful of powder that clears scores,
You notice on my brow a certain blue:
How you both overset the wine at once!
How you both smile! 'Our enemy has the plague!   350
Twelve hours hence he'll be scraping his bones bare
Of that intolerable flesh, and die,
Frenzied with pain: no need for poison here!
Step aside and enjoy the spectacle!'
Tender for souls are you, Pope Innocent!
Christ's maxim is—one soul outweighs the world:
Respite me, save a soul, then, curse the world!
'No,' venerable sire, I hear you smirk,
'No: for Christ's gospel changes names, not things.
Renews the obsolete, does nothing more!   360
Our fire-new gospel is re-tinkered law,
Our mercy, justice,—Jove's rechristened God,—
Nay, whereas, in the popular conceit,
'Tis pity that old harsh Law somehow limps,
Lingers on earth, although Law's day be done,
Else would benignant Gospel interpose,
Not furtively as now, but bold and frank
O'erflutter us with healing in her wings,
Law being harshness, Gospel only love—
We tell the people, on the contrary,   370
Gospel takes up the rod which Law lets fall;
Mercy is vigilant when justice sleeps!
Does Law permit a taste of Gospel-grace?
The secular arm allow the spiritual power
To act for once?—no compliment so fine
As that our Gospel handsomely turn harsh,
Thrust victim back on Law the nice and coy!'°
Yes, you do say so, else you would forgive
Me whom Law does not touch but tosses you!
Don't think to put on the professional face!   380
You know what I know: casuists as you are,
Each nerve must creep, each hair start, sting and stand,

At such illogical inconsequence!
Dear my friends, do but see! A murder's tried,
There are two parties to the cause: I'm one,
—Defend myself, as somebody must do:
I have the best o' the battle: that's a fact,
Simple fact,—fancies find no place just now.
What though half Rome condemned me? Half approved:
And, none disputes, the luck is mine at last,   390
All Rome, i' the main, acquitting me: whereon,
What has the Pope to ask but 'How finds Law?'
'I find,' replies Law, 'I have erred this while:
Guilty or guiltless, Guido proves a priest,
No layman: he is therefore yours, not mine:
I bound him: loose him, you whose will is Christ's!'
And now what does this Vicar of our Lord,
Shepherd o' the flock,—one of whose charge bleats sore
For crook's help from the quag wherein it drowns?
Law suffers him employ the crumpled end:°   400
His pleasure is to turn staff, use the point,
And thrust the shuddering sheep, he calls a wolf,
Back and back, down and down to where hell gapes!
'Guiltless,' cries Law—'Guilty' corrects the Pope!
'Guilty,' for the whim's sake! 'Guilty,' he somehow thinks,
And anyhow says: 'tis truth; he dares not lie!

Others should do the lying. That's the cause
Brings you both here: I ought in decency
Confess to you that I deserve my fate,
Am guilty, as the Pope thinks,—ay, to the end,   410
Keep up the jest, lie on, lie ever, lie
I' the latest gasp of me! What reason, Sirs?
Because to-morrow will succeed to-day
For you, though not for me: and if I stick
Still to the truth, declare with my last breath,
I die an innocent and murdered man,—
Why, there's the tongue of Rome will wag apace
This time to-morrow: don't I hear the talk!
'So, to the last he proved impenitent?
Pagans have said as much of martyred saints!   420
Law demurred, washed her hands of the whole case.
Prince Somebody said this, Duke Something, that.

Doubtless the man's dead, dead enough, don't fear!
But, hang it, what if there have been a spice,
A touch of... eh? You see, the Pope's so old,
Some of us add, obtuse: age never slips
The chance of shoving youth to face death first!'
And so on. Therefore to suppress such talk
You two come here, entreat I tell you lies,
And end, the edifying way. I end,   430
Telling the truth! Your self-styled shepherd thieves!
A thief—and how thieves hate the wolves we know:
Damage to theft, damage to thrift, all's one!
The red hand is sworn foe of the black jaw.
That's only natural, that's right enough:
But why the wolf should compliment the thief
With shepherd's title, bark out life in thanks,
And, spiteless, lick the prong that spits him,—eh,
Cardinal? My Abate, scarcely thus!
There, let my sheepskin-garb, a curse on 't, go—   440
Leave my teeth free if I must show my shag!°
Repent? What good shall follow? If I pass
Twelve hours repenting, will that fact hold fast
The thirteenth at the horrid dozen's end?
If I fall forthwith at your feet, gnash, tear,
Foam, rave, to give your story the due grace,
Will that assist the engine half-way back
Into its hiding-house?—boards, shaking now,
Bone against bone, like some old skeleton bat
That wants, at winter's end, to wake and prey!   450
Will howling put the spectre back to sleep?
Ah, but I misconceive your object, Sirs!
Since I want new life like the creature,—life,
Being done with here, begins i' the world away:
I shall next have 'Come, mortals, and be judged!'
There's but a minute betwixt this and then:
So, quick, be sorry since it saves my soul!
Sirs, truth shall save it, since no lies assist!
Hear the truth, you, whatever you style yourselves,
Civilization and society!   460
Come, one good grapple, I with all the world!
Dying in cold blood is the desperate thing;
The angry heart explodes, bears off in blaze

The indignant soul, and I'm combustion-ripe.
Why, you intend to do your worst with me!
That's in your eyes! You dare no more than death,
And mean no less. I must make up my mind.
So Pietro,—when I chased him here and there,
Morsel by morsel cut away the life
I loathed,—cried for just respite to confess   470
And save his soul: much respite did I grant!
Why grant me respite who deserve my doom?
Me—who engaged to play a prize, fight you,
Knowing your arms, and foil you, trick for trick,
At rapier-fence, your match and, maybe, more.
I knew that if I chose sin certain sins,
Solace my lusts out of the regular way
Prescribed me, I should find you in the path,
Have to try skill with a redoubted foe;
You would lunge, I would parry, and make end.   480
At last, occasion of a murder comes:
We cross blades, I, for all my brag, break guard,
And in goes the cold iron at my breast,
Out at my back, and end is made of me.
You stand confessed the adroiter swordsman,—ay,
But on your triumph you increase, it seems,
Want more of me than lying flat on face:
I ought to raise my ruined head, allege
Not simply I pushed worse blade o' the pair,
But my antagonist dispensed with steel!   490
There was no passage of arms, you looked me low,°
With brow and eye abolished cut and thrust
Nor used the vulgar weapon! This chance scratch,
This incidental hurt, this sort of hole
I' the heart of me? I stumbled, got it so!
Fell on my own sword as a bungler may!
Yourself proscribe such heathen tools, and trust
To the naked virtue: it was virtue stood
Unarmed and awed me,—on my brow there burned
Crime out so plainly intolerably red,   500
That I was fain to cry—'Down to the dust
With me, and bury there brow, brand and all!'
Law had essayed the adventure,—but what's Law?
Morality exposed the Gorgon shield!°

Morality and Religion conquer me.
If Law sufficed would you come here, entreat
I supplement law, and confess forsooth?
Did not the Trial show things plain enough?
'Ah, but a word of the man's very self
Would somehow put the keystone in its place   510
And crown the arch!' Then take the word you want!

I say that, long ago, when things began,
All the world made agreement, such and such
Were pleasure-giving profit-bearing acts,
But henceforth extra-legal, nor to be:
You must not kill the man whose death would please
And profit you, unless his life stop yours
Plainly, and need so be put aside:
Get the thing by a public course, by law,
Only no private bloodshed as of old!   520
All of us, for the good of every one,
Renounced such licence and conformed to law:
Who breaks law, breaks pact therefore, helps himself
To pleasure and profit over and above the due,
And must pay forfeit,—pain beyond his share:
For, pleasure being the sole good in the world,
Anyone's pleasure turns to someone's pain,
So, law must watch for everyone,—say we,
Who call things wicked that give too much joy,
And nickname mere reprisal, envy makes,   530
Punishment: quite right! thus the world goes round.
I, being well aware such pact there was,
I, in my time who found advantage come
Of law's observance and crime's penalty,—
Who, but for wholesome fear law bred in friends,
Had doubtless given example long ago,
Furnished forth some friend's pleasure with my pain,
And, by my death, pieced out his scanty life,—
I could not, for that foolish life of me,
Help risking law's infringement,—I broke bond,   540
And needs must pay price,—wherefore, here's my head,
Flung with a flourish! But, repentance too?
But pure and simple sorrow for law's breach
Rather than blunderer's-ineptitude?

Cardinal, no! Abate, scarcely thus!
'Tis the fault, not that I dared try a fall°
With Law and straightway am found undermost,
But that I failed to see, above man's law,
God's precept you, the Christians, recognize?
Colly my cow! Don't fidget, Cardinal!°   550
Abate, cross your breast and count your beads
And exorcize the devil, for here he stands
And stiffens in the bristly nape of neck,
Daring you drive him hence! You, Christians both?
I say, if ever was such faith at all
Born in the world, by your community
Suffered to live its little tick of time,
'Tis dead of age, now, ludicrously dead;
Honour its ashes, if you be discreet,
In epitaph only! For, concede its death,   560
Allow extinction, you may boast unchecked
What feats the thing did in a crazy land
At a fabulous epoch,—treat your faith, that way,
Just as you treat your relics: 'Here's a shred
Of saintly flesh, a scrap of blessed bone,
Raised King Cophetua, who was dead, to life°
In Mesopotamy twelve centuries since,
Such was its virtue!'—twangs the Sacristan,
Holding the shrine-box up, with hands like feet
Because of gout in every finger joint: 570
Does he bethink him to reduce one knob,
Allay one twinge by touching what he vaunts?
I think he half uncrooks fist to catch fee,
But, for the grace, the quality of cure,—
Cophetua was the man put that to proof!
Not otherwise, your faith is shrined and shown
And shamed at once: you banter while you bow!
Do you dispute this? Come, a monster-laugh,
A madman's laugh, allowed his Carnival
Later ten days than when all Rome, but he,   580
Laughed at the candle-contest: mine's alight,
'Tis just it sputter till the puff o' the Pope
End it to-morrow and the world turn Ash.°
Come, thus I wave a wand and bring to pass
In a moment, in the twinkle of an eye,

What but that—feigning everywhere grows fact,
Professors turn possessors, realize°
The faith they play with as a fancy now,
And bid it operate, have full effect
On every circumstance of life, to-day,   590
In Rome,—faith's flow set free at fountain-head!
Now, you'll own, at this present, when I speak,
Before I work the wonder, there's no man
Woman or child in Rome, faith's fountain-head,
But might, if each were minded, realize
Conversely unbelief, faith's opposite—
Set it to work on life unflinchingly,
Yet give no symptom of an outward change:
Why should things change because men disbelieve?
What's incompatible, in the whited tomb,   600
With bones and rottenness one inch below?
What saintly act is done in Rome to-day
But might be prompted by the devil,—'is'
I say not,—'has been, and again may be,—'
I do say, full i' the face o' the crucifix
You try to stop my mouth with! Off with it!
Look in your own heart, if your soul have eyes!
You shall see reason why, though faith were fled,
Unbelief still might work the wires and move
Man, the machine, to play a faithful part.   610
Preside your college, Cardinal, in your cape,
Or,—having got above his head, grown Pope,—
Abate, gird your loins and wash my feet!
Do you suppose I am at loss at all
Why you crook, why you cringe, why fast or feast?
Praise, blame, sit, stand, lie or go!—all of it,
In each of you, purest unbelief may prompt,
And wit explain to who has eyes to see.
But, lo, I wave wand, made the false the true!
Here's Rome believes in Christianity!   620
What an explosion, how the fragments fly
Of what was surface, mask and make-believe!
Begin now,—look at this Pope's-halberdier°
In wasp-like black and yellow foolery!
He, doing duty at the corridor,
Wakes from a muse and stands convinced of sin!

Down he flings halbert, leaps the passage-length,
Pushes into the presence, pantingly
Submits the extreme peril of the case
To the Pope's self,—whom in the world beside?—   630
And the Pope breaks talk with ambassador,
Bids aside bishop, wills the whole world wait
Till he secure that prize, outweighs the world,
A soul, relieve the sentry of his qualm!
His Altitude the Referendary,—°
Robed right, and ready for the usher's word
To pay devoir,—is, of all times, just then
'Ware of a master-stroke of argument
Will cut the spinal cord...ugh, ugh!...I mean,
Paralyse Molinism for evermore!   640
Straight he leaves lobby, trundles, two and two,
Down steps to reach home, write, if but a word
Shall end the impudence: he leaves who likes
Go pacify the Pope: there's Christ to serve!
How otherwise would men display their zeal?
If the same sentry had the least surmise
A powder-barrel 'neath the pavement lay
In neighbourhood with what might prove a match,
Meant to blow sky-high Pope and presence both—
Would he not break through courtiers, rank and file,   650
Bundle up, bear off and save body so,
The Pope, no matter for his priceless soul?
There's no fool's-freak here, nought to soundly swinge,
Only a man in earnest, you'll so praise
And pay and prate about, that earth shall ring!
Had thought possessed the Referendary
His jewel-case at home was left ajar,
What would be wrong in running, robes awry,
To be beforehand with the pilferer?
What talk then of indecent haste? Which means,   660
That both these, each in his degree, would do
Just that,—for a comparative nothing's sake,
And thereby gain approval and reward,—
Which, done for what Christ says is worth the world,
Procures the doer curses, cuffs and kicks.
I call such difference 'twixt act and act,
Sheer lunacy unless your truth on lip

Be recognized a lie in heart of you!
How do you all act, promptly or in doubt,
When there's a guest poisoned at supper-time   670
And he sits chatting on with spot on cheek?
'Pluck him by the skirt, and round him in the ears,
Have at him by the beard, warn anyhow!'
Good, and this other friend that's cheat and thief
And dissolute,—go stop the devil's feast,
Withdraw him from the imminent hell-fire!
Why, for your life, you dare not tell your friend
'You lie, and I admonish you for Christ!'
Who yet dare seek that same man at the Mass
To warn him—on his knees, and tinkle near,—°   680
He left a cask a-tilt, a tap unturned,
The Trebbian running: what a grateful jump°
Out of the Church rewards your vigilance!
Perform that self-same service just a thought
More maladroitly,—since a bishop sits
At function!—and he budges not, bites lip,—
'You see my case: how can I quit my post?
He has an eye to any such default.
See to it, neighbour, I beseech your love!'
He and you know the relative worth of things,   690
What is permissible or inopportune.
Contort your brows! You know I speak the truth:
Gold is called gold, and dross called dross, i' the Book:
Gold you let lie and dross pick up and prize!
—Despite your muster of some fifty monks
And nuns a-maundering here and mumping there,
Who could, and on occasion would, spurn dross,
Clutch gold, and prove their faith a fact so far,—
I grant you! Fifty times the number squeak
And gibber in the madhouse—firm of faith,   700
This fellow, that his nose supports the moon;
The other, that his straw hat crowns him Pope:
Does that prove all the world outside insane?
Do fifty miracle-mongers match the mob
That acts on the frank faithless principle,
Born-baptized-and-bred Christian-atheists, each
With just as much a right to judge as you,—
As many senses in his soul, and nerves

I' neck of him as I,—whom, soul and sense,
Neck and nerve, you abolish presently,—   710
I being the unit in creation now
Who pay the Maker, in this speech of mine,
A creature's duty, spend my last of breath
In bearing witness, even by my worst fault,
To the creature's obligation, absolute,
Perpetual: my worst fault protests, 'The faith
Claims all of me: I would give all she claims,
But for a spice of doubt: the risk's too rash:
Double or quits, I play, but, all or nought,
Exceeds my courage: therefore, I descend   720
To the next faith with no dubiety—
Faith in the present life, made last as long
And prove as full of pleasure as may hap,
Whatever pain it cause the world.' I'm wrong?
I've had my life, whate'er I lose: I'm right?
I've got the single good there was to gain.
Entire faith, or else complete unbelief!
Aught between has my loathing and contempt,
Mine and God's also, doubtless: ask yourself,
Cardinal, where and how you like a man!   730
Why, either with your feet upon his head,
Confessed your caudatory, or, at large,°
The stranger in the crowd who caps to you°
But keeps his distance,—why should he presume?
You want no hanger-on and dropper-off,
Now yours, and now not yours but quite his own,
According as the sky looks black or bright.
Just so I capped to and kept off from faith—
You promised trudge behind through fair and foul,
Yet leave i' the lurch at the first spit of rain.   740
Who holds to faith whenever rain begins?
What does the father when his son lies dead,
The merchant when his money-bags take wing,
The politician whom a rival ousts?
No case but has its conduct, faith prescribes:
Where's the obedience that shall edify?
Why, they laugh frankly in the face of faith
And take the natural course,—this rends his hair
Because his child is taken to God's breast,

That gnashes teeth and raves at loss of trash   750
Which rust corrupts and thieves break through and steal,
And this, enabled to inherit earth
Through meekness, curses till your blood runs cold!
Down they all drop to my low level, rest
Heart upon dungy earth that's warm and soft,
And let who please attempt the altitudes.
Each playing prodigal son of heavenly sire,°
Turning his nose up at the fatted calf,
Fain to fill belly with the husks, we swine
Did eat by born depravity of taste!   760

Enough of the hypocrites. But you, Sirs, you—
Who never budged from litter where I lay,
And buried snout i' the draff-box while I fed,
Cried amen to my creed's one article—
'Get pleasure, 'scape pain,—give your preference
To the immediate good, for time is brief,
And death ends good and ill and everything!
What's got is gained, what's gained soon is gained twice,
And,—inasmuch as faith gains most,—feign faith!'
So did we brother-like pass word about: 770
—You, now,—like bloody drunkards but half-drunk,
Who fool men yet perceive men find them fools,—
Vexed that a titter gains the gravest mouth,—
O' the sudden you must needs re-introduce
Solemnity, straight sober undue mirth
By a blow dealt me your boon companion here
Who, using the old licence, dreamed of harm
No more than snow in harvest: yet it falls!
You check the merriment effectually
By pushing your abrupt machine i' the midst,   780
Making me Rome's example: blood for wine!
The general good needs that you chop and change!
I may dislike the hocus-pocus,—Rome,
The laughter-loving people, won't they stare
Chap-fallen!—while serious natures sermonize°
'The magistrate, he beareth not the sword
In vain; who sins may taste its edge, we see!'
Why my sin, drunkards? Where have I abused
Liberty, scandalized you all so much?

Who called me, who crooked finger till I came,   790
Fool that I was, to join companionship?
I knew my own mind, meant to live my life,
Elude your envy, or else make a stand,
Take my own part and sell you my life dear.
But it was 'Fie! No prejudice in the world
To the proper manly instinct! Cast your lot
Into our lap, one genius ruled our births,
We'll compass joy by concert; take with us°
The regular irregular way i' the wood;
You'll miss no game through riding breast by breast,   800
In this preserve, the Church's park and pale,
Rather than outside where the world lies waste!'
Come, if you said not that, did you say this?
Give plain and terrible warning, 'Live, enjoy?
Such life begins in death and ends in hell!
Dare you bid us assist your sins, us priests
Who hurry sin and sinners from the earth?
No such delight for us, why then for you?
Leave earth, seek heaven or find its opposite!'
Had you so warned me, not in lying words   810
But veritable deeds with tongues of flame,
That had been fair, that might have struck a man,
Silenced the squabble between soul and sense,
Compelled him to make mind up, take one course
Or the other, peradventure!—wrong or right,
Foolish or wise, you would have been at least
Sincere, no question,—forced me choose, indulge
Or else renounce my instincts, still play wolf
Or find my way submissive to your fold,
Be red-crossed on my fleece, one sheep the more.   820
But you as good as bade me wear sheep's wool
Over wolf's skin, suck blood and hide the noise
By mimicry of something like a bleat,—
Whence it comes that because, despite my care,
Because I smack my tongue too loud for once,
Drop baaing, here's the village up in arms!
Have at the wolf's throat, you who hate the breed!
Oh, were it only open yet to choose—
One little time more—whether I'd be free
Your foe, or subsidized your friend forsooth!   830

Should not you get a growl through the white fangs
In answer to your beckoning! Cardinal,
Abate, managers o' the multitude,
I'd turn your gloved hands to account, be sure!
You should manipulate the coarse rough mob:
'Tis you I'd deal directly with, not them,—
Using your fears: why touch the thing myself
When I could see you hunt, and then cry 'Shares!
Quarter the carcase or we quarrel; come,
Here's the world ready to see justice done!'   840
Oh, it had been a desperate game, but game
Wherein the winner's chance were worth the pains!
We'd try conclusions!—at the worst, what worse
Than this Mannaia-machine, each minute's talk
Helps push an inch the nearer me? Fool, fool!

You understand me and forgive, sweet Sirs?
I blame you, tear my hair and tell my woe—
All's but a flourish, figure of rhetoric!
One must try each expedient to save life.
One makes fools look foolisher fifty-fold   850
By putting in their place men wise like you,
To take the full force of an argument
Would buffet their stolidity in vain.
If you should feel aggrieved by the mere wind
O' the blow that means to miss you and maul them,
That's my success! Is it not folly, now,
To say with folk, 'A plausible defence—
We see through notwithstanding, and reject?'
Reject the plausible they do, these fools,
Who never even make pretence to show   860
One point beyond its plausibility
In favour of the best belief they hold!
'Saint Somebody-or-other raised the dead:'
Did he? How do you come to know as much?
'Know it, what need? The story's plausible,
Avouched for by a martyrologist,
And why should good men sup on cheese and leeks
On such a saint's day, if there were no saint?'
I praise the wisdom of these fools, and straight
Tell them my story—'plausible, but false!'   870

False, to be sure! What else can story be
That runs—a young wife tired of an old spouse,
Found a priest whom she fled away with,—both
Took their full pleasure in the two-days' flight,
Which a grey-headed greyer-hearted pair,
(Whose best boast was, their life had been a lie)
Helped for the love they bore all liars. Oh,
Here incredulity begins! Indeed?
Allow then, were no one point strictly true,
There's that i' the tale might seem like truth at least   880
To the unlucky husband,—jaundiced patch—°
Jealousy maddens people, why not him?
Say, he was maddened, so forgivable!
Humanity pleads that though the wife were true,
The priest true, and the pair of liars true,
They might seem false to one man in the world!
A thousand gnats make up a serpent's sting,
And many sly soft stimulants to wrath
Compose a formidable wrong at last
That gets called easily by some one name   890
Not applicable to the single parts,
And so draws down a general revenge,
Excessive if you take crime, fault by fault.
Jealousy! I have known a score of plays,
Were listened to and laughed at in my time
As like the everyday-life on all sides,
Wherein the husband, mad as a March hare,
Suspected all the world contrived his shame.
What did the wife? The wife kissed both eyes blind,
Explained away ambiguous circumstance,
And while she held him captive by the hand,   900
Crowned his head,—you know what's the mockery,—
By half her body behind the curtain. That's
Nature now! That's the subject of a piece°
I saw in Vallombrosa Convent, made
Expressly to teach men what marriage was!
But say 'Just so did I misapprehend,
Imagine she deceived me to my face,'
And that's pretence too easily seen through!
All those eyes of all husbands in all plays,
At stare like one expanded peacock-tail,   910

Are laughed at for pretending to be keen
While horn-blind: but the moment I step forth—°
Oh, I must needs o' the sudden prove a lynx°
And look the heart, that stone-wall, through and through!
Such an eye, God's may be,—not yours nor mine.

Yes, presently . . . what hour is fleeting now?
When you cut earth away from under me,
I shall be left alone with, pushed beneath
Some such an apparitional dread orb   920
As the eye of God, since such an eye there glares:
I fancy it go filling up the void
Above my mote-self it devours, or what°
Proves—wrath, immensity wreaks on nothingness.
Just how I felt once, couching through the dark,
Hard by Vittiano; young I was, and gay,
And wanting to trap fieldfares: first a spark°
Tipped a bent, as a mere dew-globule might°
Any stiff grass-stalk on the meadow,—this
Grew fiercer, flamed out full, and proved the sun.   930
What do I want with proverbs, precepts here?
Away with man! What shall I say to God?
This, if I find the tongue and keep the mind—
'Do Thou wipe out the being of me, and smear
This soul from off Thy white of things, I blot!°
I am one huge and sheer mistake,—whose fault?
Not mine at least, who did not make myself!'
Someone declares my wife excused me so!
Perhaps she knew what argument to use.
Grind your teeth, Cardinal: Abate, writhe!   940
What else am I to cry out in my rage,
Unable to repent one particle
O' the past? Oh, how I wish some cold wise man
Would dig beneath the surface which you scrape,
Deal with the depths, pronounce on my desert
Groundedly! I want simple sober sense,
That asks, before it finishes with a dog,
Who taught the dog that trick you hang him for?
You both persist to call that act a crime,
Which sense would call . . . yes, I maintain it, Sirs, . . .   950
A blunder! At the worst, I stood in doubt

On cross-road, took one path of many paths:
It leads to the red thing, we all see now,
But nobody saw at first: one primrose-patch
In bank, one singing-bird in bush, the less,
Had warned me from such wayfare: let me prove!
Put me back to the cross-road, start afresh!
Advise me when I take the first false step!
Give me my wife: how should I use my wife,
Love her or hate her? Prompt my action now!   960
There she is, there she stands alive and pale,
The thirteen-years'-old child, with milk for blood,
Pompilia Comparini, as at first,
Which first is only four brief years ago!
I stand too in the little ground-floor room
O' the father's house at Via Vittoria: see!
Her so-called mother,—one arm round the waist
O' the child to keep her from the toys, let fall
At wonder I can live yet look so grim,—
Ushers her in, with deprecating wave   970
Of the other,—and she fronts me loose at last,
Held only by the mother's finger-tip.
Struck dumb,—for she was white enough before!—
She eyes me with those frightened balls of black,
As heifer—the old simile comes pat—
Eyes tremblingly the altar and the priest.
The amazed look, all one insuppressive prayer,—
Might she but breathe, set free as heretofore,
Have this cup leave her lips unblistered, bear
Any cross anywhither anyhow,   980
So but alone, so but apart from me!
You are touched? So am I, quite otherwise,
If 'tis with pity. I resent my wrong,
Being a man: I only show man's soul
Through man's flesh: she sees mine, it strikes her thus!
Is that attractive? To a youth perhaps—
Calf-creature, one-part boy to three-parts girl,
To whom it is a flattering novelty
That he, men use to motion from their path,
Can thus impose, thus terrify in turn   990
A chit whose terror shall be changed apace
To bliss unbearable when grace and glow,

Prowess and pride descend the throne and touch
Esther in all that pretty tremble, cured°
By the dove o' the sceptre! But myself am old,
O' the wane at least, in all things: what do you say
To her who frankly thus confirms my doubt?
I am past the prime, I scare the woman-world,
Done-with that way: you like this piece of news?
A little saucy rose-bud minx can strike   1000
Death-damp into the breast of doughty king
Though 'twere French Louis,—soul I understand,—°
Saying, by gesture of repugnance, just
'Sire, you are regal, puissant and so forth,
But—young you have been, are not, nor will be!'
In vain the mother nods, winks, bustles up,
'Count, girls incline to mature worth like you!
As for Pompilia, what's flesh, fish, or fowl
To one who apprehends no difference,
And would accept you even were you old   1010
As you are...youngish by her father's side?
Trim but your beard a little, thin your bush
Of eyebrow; and for presence, portliness,
And decent gravity, you beat a boy!'
Deceive yourself one minute, if you may,
In presence of the child that so loves age,
Whose neck writhes, cords itself against your kiss,
Whose hand you wring stark, rigid with despair!
Well, I resent this; I am young in soul,
Nor old in body,—thews and sinews here,—   1020
Though the vile surface be not smooth as once,—
Far beyond that first wheelwork which went wrong°
Through the untempered iron ere 'twas proof:°
I am the wrought man worth ten times the crude,
Would woman see what this declines to see,
Declines to say 'I see,'—the officious word
That makes the thing, pricks on the soul to shoot
New fire into the half-used cinder, flesh!
Therefore 'tis she begins with wronging me,
Who cannot but begin with hating her.   1030
Our marriage follows: there she stands again!
Why do I laugh? Why, in the very gripe
O' the jaws of death's gigantic skull, do I

Grin back his grin, make sport of my own pangs?
Why from each clashing of his molars, ground
To make the devil bread from out my grist,
Leaps out a spark of mirth, a hellish toy?
Take notice we are lovers in a church,
Waiting the sacrament to make us one
And happy! Just as bid, she bears herself,   1040
Comes and kneels, rises, speaks, is silent,—goes:
So have I brought my horse, by word and blow,
To stand stock-still and front the fire he dreads.
How can I other than remember this,
Resent the very obedience? Gain thereby?
Yes, I do gain my end and have my will,—
Thanks to whom? When the mother speaks the word.
She obeys it—even to enduring me!
There had been compensation in revolt—
Revolt's to quell: but martyrdom rehearsed,   1050
But predetermined saintship for the sake
O' the mother?—'Go!' thought I, 'we meet again!'
Pass the next weeks of dumb contented death,
She lives,—wakes up, installed in house and home,
Is mine, mine all day-long, all night-long mine.
Good folk begin at me with open mouth
'Now, at least, reconcile the child to life!
Study and make her love . . . that is, endure
The . . . hem! the . . . all of you though somewhat old,°
Till it amount to something, in her eye,   1060
As good as love, better a thousand times,—
Since nature helps the woman in such strait,
Makes passiveness her pleasure: failing which,
What if you give up boy-and-girl-fools'-play
And go on to wise friendship all at once?
Those boys and girls kiss themselves cold, you know,
Toy themselves tired and slink aside full soon
To friendship, as they name satiety:
Thither go you and wait their coming!' Thanks,
Considerate advisers,—but, fair play!   1070
Had you and I, friends, started fair at first,
We, keeping fair, might reach it, neck by neck,
This blessed goal, whenever fate so please:
But why am I to miss the daisied mile

The course begins with, why obtain the dust
Of the end precisely at the starting-point?
Why quaff life's cup blown free of all the beads,
The bright red froth wherein our beard should steep
Before our mouth essay the black o' the wine?
Foolish, the love-fit? Let me prove it such   1080
Like you, before like you I puff things clear!
'The best's to come, no rapture but content!
Not love's first glory but a sober glow,
Not a spontaneous outburst in pure boon,
So much as, gained by patience, care and toil,
Proper appreciation and esteem!'
Go preach that to your nephews, not to me
Who, tired i' the midway of my life, would stop
And take my first refreshment, pluck a rose:
What's this coarse woolly hip, worn smooth of leaf,   1090
You counsel I go plant in garden-plot,
Water with tears, manure with sweat and blood,
In confidence the seed shall germinate
And, for its very best, some far-off day,
Grow big, and blow me out a dog-rose bell?
Why must your nephews begin breathing spice
O' the hundred-petalled Provence prodigy?°
Nay, more and worse,—would such my root bear rose—
Prove really flower and favourite, not the kind
That's queen, but those three leaves that make one cup   1100
And hold the hedge-bird's breakfast,—then indeed
The prize though poor would pay the care and toil!
Respect we Nature that makes least as most,
Marvellous in the minim! But this bud,
Bit through and burned black by the tempter's tooth,
This bloom whose best grace was the slug outside
And the wasp inside its bosom,—call you 'rose'?
Claim no immunity from a weed's fate
For the horrible present! What you call my wife
I call a nullity in female shape,   1110
Vapid disgust, soon to be pungent plague,
When mixed with, made confusion and a curse
By two abominable nondescripts,
That father and that mother: think you see
The dreadful bronze our boast, we Aretines,

The Etruscan monster, the three-headed thing,
Bellerophon's foe! How name you the whole beast?
You choose to name the body from one head,
That of the simple kid which droops the eye,
Hangs the neck and dies tenderly enough: 1120
I rather see the griesly lion belch
Flame out i' the midst, the serpent writhe her rings,
Grafted into the common stock for tail,
And name the brute, Chimæra which I slew!°
How was there ever more to be—(concede
My wife's insipid harmless nullity)—
Dissociation from that pair of plagues—
That mother with her cunning and her cant—
The eyes with first their twinkle of conceit,
Then, dropped to earth in mock-demureness,—now,   1130
The smile self-satisfied from ear to ear,
Now, the prim pursed-up mouth's protruded lips,
With deferential duck, slow swing of head,
Tempting the sudden fist of man too much,—
That owl-like screw of lid and rock of ruff!
As for the father,—Cardinal, you know,
The kind of idiot!—such are rife in Rome,
But they wear velvet commonly; good fools,°
At the end of life, to furnish forth young folk
Who grin and bear with imbecility: 1140
Since the stalled ass, the joker, sheds from jaw
Corn, in the joke, for those who laugh or starve.
But what say we to the same solemn beast
Wagging his ears and wishful of our pat,
When turned, with holes in hide and bones laid bare,
To forage for himself i' the waste o' the world,
Sir Dignity i' the dumps? Pat him? We drub
Self-knowledge, rather, into frowzy pate,
Teach Pietro to get trappings or go hang!
Fancy this quondam oracle in vogue°   1150
At Via Vittoria, this personified
Authority when time was,—Pantaloon°
Flaunting his tom-fool tawdry just the same
As if Ash-Wednesday were mid-Carninal!
That's the extreme and unforgiveable
Of sins, as I account such. Have you stooped

For your own ends to bestialize yourself
By flattery of a fellow of this stamp?
The ends obtained or else shown out of reach,
He goes on, takes the flattery for pure truth,—   1160
'You love, and honour me, of course: what next?'
What, but the trifle of the stabbing, friend?—
Which taught you how one worships when the shrine
Has lost the relic that we bent before.
Angry! And how could I be otherwise?
'Tis plain: this pair of old pretentious fools
Meant to fool me: it happens, I fooled them.
Why could not these who sought to buy and sell
Me,—when they found themselves were bought and sold,
Make up their mind to the proved rule of right,   1170
Be chattel and not chapman any more?
Miscalculation has its consequence;
But when the shepherd crooks a sheep-like thing
And meaning to get wool, dislodges fleece
And finds the veritable wolf beneath,
(How that staunch image serves at every turn!)
Does he, by way of being politic,
Pluck the first whisker grimly visible?
Or rather grow in a trice all gratitude,
Protest this sort-of-what-one-might-name sheep   1180
Beats the old other curly-coated kind,
And shall share board and bed, if so it deign,
With its discoverer, like a royal ram?
Ay, thus, with chattering teeth and knocking knees,
Would wisdom treat the adventure! these, forsooth,
Tried whisker-plucking, and so found what trap
The whisker kept perdue, two rows of teeth—°
Sharp, as too late the prying fingers felt.
What would you have? The fools transgress, the fools
Forthwith receive appropriate punishment: 1190
They first insult me, I return the blow,
There follows noise enough: four hubbub months,
Now hue and cry, now whimpering and wail—
A perfect goose-yard cackle of complaint
Because I do not gild the geese their oats,—
I have enough of noise, ope wicket wide,
Sweep out the couple to go whine elsewhere,

Frightened a little, hurt in no respect,
And am just taking thought to breathe again,
Taste the sweet sudden silence all about,   1200
When, there they raise it, the old noise I know,
At Rome i' the distance! 'What, begun once more?
Whine on, wail ever, 'tis the loser's right!'
But eh, what sort of voice grows on the wind?
Triumph it sounds and no complaint at all!
And triumph it is. My boast was premature:
The creatures, I turned forth, clapped wing and crew
Fighting-cock-fashion,—they had filched a pearl
From dung-heap, and might boast with cause enough!
I was defrauded of all bargained for: 1210
You know, the Pope knows, not a soul but knows
My dowry was derision, my gain—muck,
My wife, (the Church declared my flesh and blood)
The nameless bastard of a common whore:
My old name turned henceforth to . . . shall I say
'He that received the ordure in his face'?
And they who planned this wrong, performed this wrong,
And then revealed this wrong to the wide world,
Rounded myself in the ears with my own wrong,—
Why, these were (note hell's lucky malice, now!)   1220
These were just they who, they alone, could act
And publish and proclaim their infamy,
Secure that men would in a breath believe
Compassionate and pardon them,—for why?
They plainly were too stupid to invent,
Too simple to distinguish wrong from right,—
Inconscious agents they, the silly-sooth,
Of heaven's retributive justice on the strong
Proud cunning violent oppressor—me!
Follow them to their fate and help your best,   1230
You Rome, Arezzo, foes called friends of me,
They gave the good long laugh to, at my cost!
Defray your share o' the cost, since you partook
The entertainment! Do!—assured the while,
That not one stab, I dealt to right and left,
But went the deeper for a fancy—this—
That each might do me two-fold service, find
A friend's face at the bottom of each wound,

And scratch its smirk a little!
                                Panciatichi!
There's a report at Florence,—is it true?—   1240
That when your relative the Cardinal
Built, only the other day, that barrack-bulk,
The palace in Via Larga, someone picked
From out the street a saucy quip enough°
That fell there from its day's flight through the town,
About the flat front and the windows wide
And bulging heap of cornice,—hitched the joke
Into a sonnet, signed his name thereto,
And forthwith pinned on post the pleasantry:
For which he's at the galleys, rowing now   1250
Up to his waist in water,—just because
Panciatic and *lymphatic* rhymed so pat!
I hope, Sir, those who passed this joke on me
Were not unduly punished? What say you,
Prince of the Church, my patron? Nay, indeed,
I shall not dare insult your wits so much
As think this problem difficult to solve.
This Pietro and Violante then, I say,
These two ambiguous insects, changing name
And nature with the season's warmth or chill,—   1260
Now, grovelled, grubbing toiling moiling ants,
A very synonym of thrift and peace,—
Anon, with lusty June to prick their heart,
Soared i' the air, winged flies for more offence,
Circled me, buzzed me deaf and stung me blind,
And stunk me dead with fetor in the face
Until I stopped the nuisance: there's my crime!
Pity I did not suffer them subside
Into some further shape and final form
Of execrable life? My masters, no!   1270
I, by one blow, wisely cut short at once
Them and their transformations of disgust,°
In the snug little Villa out of hand.
'Grant me confession, give bare time for that!'—
Shouted the sinner till his mouth was stopped.
His life confessed!—that was enough for me,
Who came to see that he did penance. 'S death!
Here's a coil raised, a pother and for what?°

Because strength, being provoked by weakness, fought
And conquered,—the world never heard the like!   1280
Pah, how I spend my breath on them, as if
'Twas their fate troubled me, too hard to range
Among the right and fit and proper things!

Ay, but Pompilia,—I await your word,—
She, unimpeached of crime, unimplicate
In folly, one of alien blood to these
I punish, why extend my claim, exact
Her portion of the penalty? Yes, friends,
I go too fast: the orator's at fault:
Yes, ere I lay her, with your leave, by them   1290
As she was laid at San Lorenzo late,°
I ought to step back, lead you by degrees,
Recounting at each step some fresh offence,
Up to the red bed,—never fear, I will!
Gaze at her, where I place her, to begin,
Confound me with her gentleness and worth!
The horrible pair have fled and left her now,
She has her husband for her sole concern:
His wife, the woman fashioned for his help,
Flesh of his flesh, bone of his bone, the bride   1300
To groom as is the Church and Spouse to Christ:
There she stands in his presence: 'Thy desire
Shall be to the husband, o'er thee shall he rule!'
—'Pompilia, who declare that you love God,
You know who said that: then, desire my love,
Yield me contentment and be ruled aright!'
She sits up, she lies down, she comes and goes,
Kneels at the couch-side, overleans the sill
O' the window, cold and pale and mute as stone,
Strong as stone also. 'Well, are they not fled?   1310
Am I not left, am I not one for all?
Speak a word, drop a tear, detach a glance,
Bless me or curse me of your own accord!
Is it the ceiling only wants your soul,
Is worth your eyes?' And then the eyes descend,
And do look at me. Is it at the meal?
'Speak!' she obeys, 'Be silent!' she obeys,
Counting the minutes till I cry 'Depart,'

As brood-bird when you saunter past her eggs.
Departs she? just the same through door and wall   1320
I see the same stone strength of white despair.
And all this will be never otherwise!
Before, the parents' presence lent her life:
She could play off her sex's armoury,
Entreat, reproach, be female to my male,
Try all the shrieking doubles of the hare,°
Go clamour to the Commissary, bid
The Archbishop hold my hands and stop my tongue,
And yield fair sport so: but the tactics change,
The hare stands stock-still to enrage the hound!   1330
Since that day when she learned she was no child
Of those she thought her parents,—that their trick
Had tricked me whom she thought sole trickster late,—
Why, I suppose she said within herself
'Then, no more struggle for my parents' sake!
And, for my own sake, why needs struggle be?'
But is there no third party to the pact?
What of her husband's relish or dislike
For this new game of giving up the game,
This worst offence of not offending more?   1340
I'll not believe but instinct wrought in this,
Set her on to conceive and execute
The preferable plague: how sure they probe—
These jades, the sensitivest soft of man!
The long black hair was wound now in a wisp,
Crowned sorrow better than the wild web late:
No more soiled dress, 'tis trimness triumphs now,
For how should malice go with negligence?
The frayed silk looked the fresher for her spite!
There was an end to springing out of bed,   1350
Praying me, with face buried on my feet,
Be hindered of my pastime,—so an end
To my rejoinder, 'What, on the ground at last?
Vanquished in fight, a supplicant for life?
What if I raise you? 'Ware the casting down
When next you fight me!' Then, she lay there, mine:
Now, mine she is if I please wring her neck,—
A moment of disquiet, working eyes,
Protruding tongue, a long sigh, then no more,—

As if one killed the horse one could not ride!   1360
Had I enjoined 'Cut off the hair!'—why, snap
The scissors, and at once a yard or so
Had fluttered in black serpents to the floor:
But till I did enjoin it, how she combs,
Uncurls and draws out to the complete length,
Plaits, places the insulting rope on head
To be an eyesore past dishevelment!
Is all done? Then sit still again and stare!
I advise—no one think to bear that look
Of steady wrong, endured as steadily   1370
—Through what sustainment of deluding hope?
Who is the friend i' the background that notes all?
Who may come presently and close accounts?
This self-possession to the uttermost,
How does it differ in aught, save degree,
From the terrible patience of God?

                              'All which just means,
She did not love you!' Again the word is launched
And the fact fronts me! What, you try the wards°
With the true key and the dead lock flies ope?
No, it sticks fast and leaves you fumbling still!   1380
You have some fifty servants, Cardinal,—
Which of them loves you? Which subordinate
But makes parade of such officiousness
That,—if there's no love prompts it,—love, the sham,
Does twice the service done by love, the true?
God bless us liars, where's one touch of truth
In what we tell the world, or world tells us,
Of how we love each other? All the same,
We calculate on word and deed, nor err,—
Bid such a man do such a loving act,   1390
Sure of effect and negligent of cause,
Just as we bid a horse, with cluck of tongue,
Stretch his legs arch-wise, crouch his saddled back
To foot-reach of the stirrup—all for love,
And some for memory of the smart of switch
On the inside of the foreleg—what care we?
Yet where's the bond obliges horse to man
Like that which binds fast wife to husband? God
Laid down the law: gave man the brawny arm

And ball of fist—woman the beardless cheek   1400
And proper place to suffer in the side:
Since it is he can strike, let her obey!
Can she feel no love? Let her show the more,
Sham the worse, damn herself praiseworthily!
Who's that soprano, Rome went mad about
Last week while I lay rotting in my straw?
The very jailer gossiped in his praise—
How,—dressed up like Armida, though a man;°
And painted to look pretty, though a fright,—
He still made love so that the ladies swooned,   1410
Being an eunuch. 'Ah, Rinaldo mine!
But to breathe by thee while Jove slays us both!'
All the poor bloodless creature never felt,
Si, do, re, mi, fa, squeak and squall—for what?
Two gold zecchines the evening. Here's my slave,°
Whose body and soul depend upon my nod,
Can't falter out the first note in the scale
For her life! Why blame me if I take the life?
All women cannot give men love, forsooth!
No, nor all pullets lay the henwife eggs—   1420
Whereat she bids them remedy the fault,
Brood on a chalk-ball: soon the nest is stocked—
Otherwise, to the plucking and the spit!
This wife of mine was of another mood—
Would not begin the lie that ends with truth,
Nor feign the love that brings real love about:
Wherefore I judged, sentenced and punished her.
But why particularize, defend the deed?
Say that I hated her for no one cause
Beyond my pleasure so to do,—what then?   1430
Just on as much incitement acts the world,
All of you! Look and like! You favour one,
Browbeat another, leave alone a third,—
Why should you master natural caprice?
Pure nature! Try: plant elm by ash in file;
Both unexceptionable trees enough,
They ought to overlean each other, pair
At top, and arch across the avenue
The whole path to the pleasaunce: do they so—°
Or loathe, lie off abhorrent each from each?   1440

Lay the fault elsewhere: since we must have faults,
Mine shall have been,—seeing there's ill in the end
Come of my course,—that I fare somehow worse
For the way I took: my fault . . . as God's my judge,
I see not where my fault lies, that's the truth!
I ought . . . oh, ought in my own interest
Have let the whole adventure go untried,
This chance by marriage: or else, trying it,
Ought to have turned it to account, some one
O' the hundred otherwises? Ay, my friend,   1450
Easy to say, easy to do: step right
Now you've stepped left and stumbled on the thing,
—The red thing! Doubt I any more than you
That practice makes man perfect? Give again
The chance,—same marriage and no other wife,
Be sure I'll edify you! That's because
I'm practised, grown fit guide for Guido's self.
You proffered guidance,—I know, none so well,—
You laid down law and rolled decorum out,
From pulpit-corner on the gospel-side,—°   1460
Wanted to make your great experience mine,
Save me the personal search and pains so: thanks!
Take your word on life's use? When I take his—
The muzzled ox that treadeth out the corn,°
Gone blind in padding round and round one path,—
As to the taste of green grass in the field!
What do you know o' the world that's trodden flat
And salted sterile with your daily dung,
Leavened into a lump of loathsomeness?
Take your opinion of the modes of life,   1470
The aims of life, life's triumph or defeat,
How to feel, how to scheme, and how to do
Or else leave undone? You preached long and loud
On high-days, 'Take our doctrine upon trust!°
Into the mill-house with you! Grind our corn,
Relish our chaff, and let the green grass grow!'
I tried chaff, found I famished on such fare,
So made this mad rush at the mill-house-door,
Buried my head up to the ears in dew,
Browsed on the best: for which you brain me, Sirs!   1480
Be it so. I conceived of life that way,

And still declare—life, without absolute use
Of the actual sweet therein, is death, not life.
Give me,—pay down,—not promise, which is air,—
Something that's out of life and better still,
Make sure reward, make certain punishment,
Entice me, scare me,—I'll forgo this life;
Otherwise, no!—the less that words, mere wind,
Would cheat me of some minutes while they plague,
Baulk fulness of revenge here,—blame yourselves   1490
For this eruption of the pent-up soul
You prisoned first and played with afterward!
'Deny myself' meant simply pleasure you,
The sacred and superior, save the mark!
You,—whose stupidity and insolence
I must defer to, soothe at every turn,—
Whose swine-like snuffling greed and grunting lust
I had to wink at or help gratify,—
While the same passions,—dared they perk in me,
Me, the immeasurably marked, by God,   1500
Master of the whole world of such as you,—
I, boast such passions? 'Twas 'Suppress them straight!
Or stay, we'll pick and choose before destroy.
Here's wrath in you, a serviceable sword,—
Beat it into a ploughshare! What's this long
Lance-like ambition? Forge a pruning-hook,
May be of service when our vines grow tall!
But—sword use swordwise, spear thrust out as spear?
Anathema! Suppression is the word!'°
My nature, when the outrage was too gross,   1510
Widened itself an outlet over-wide
By way of answer, sought its own relief
With more of fire and brimstone than you wished.
All your own doing: preachers, blame yourselves!

'Tis I preach while the hour-glass runs and runs!
God keep me patient! All I say just means—
My wife proved, whether by her fault or mine,—
That's immaterial,—a true stumbling-block
I' the way of me her husband. I but plied
The hatchet yourselves use to clear a path,   1520
Was politic, played the game you warrant wins,

Plucked at law's robe a-rustle through the courts,
Bowed down to kiss divinity's buckled shoe
Cushioned i' the church: efforts all wide the aim!
Procedures to no purpose! Then flashed truth.
The letter kills, the spirit keeps alive°
In law and gospel: there be nods and winks
Instruct a wise man to assist himself
In certain matters, nor seek aid at all.
'Ask money of me,'—quoth the clownish saw,—   1530
'And take my purse! But,—speaking with respect,—
Need you a solace for the troubled nose?
Let everybody wipe his own himself!'
Sirs, tell me free and fair! Had things gone well
At the wayside inn: had I surprised asleep
The runaways, as was so probable,
And pinned them each to other partridge-wise,
Through back and breast to breast and back, then bade
Bystanders witness if the spit, my sword,
Were loaded with unlawful game for once—   1540
Would you have interposed to damp the glow
Applauding me on every husband's cheek?
Would you have checked the cry 'A judgment, see!
A warning, note! Be henceforth chaste, ye wives,
Nor stray beyond your proper precinct, priests!'
If you had, then your house against itself
Divides, nor stands your kingdom any more.
Oh why, why was it not ordained just so?
Why fell not things out so nor otherwise?
Ask that particular devil whose task it is   1550
To trip the all-but-at perfection,—slur
The line of the painter just where paint leaves off
And life begins,—put ice into the ode
O' the poet while he cries 'Next stanza—fire!'
Inscribe all human effort with one word,
Artistry's haunting curse, the Incomplete!
Being incomplete, my act escaped success.
Easy to blame now! Every fool can swear
To hole in net that held and slipped the fish.
But, treat my act with fair unjaundiced eye,   1560
What was there wanting to a masterpiece
Except the luck that lies beyond a man?

My way with the woman, now proved grossly wrong,
Just missed of being gravely grandly right
And making mouths laugh on the other side.
Do, for the poor obstructed artist's sake,
Go with him over that spoiled work once more!
Take only its first flower, the ended act
Now in the dusty pod, dry and defunct!
I march to the Villa, and my men with me,   1570
That evening, and we reach the door and stand.
I say...no, it shoots through me lightning-like
While I pause, breathe, my hand upon the latch,
'Let me forebode! Thus far, too much success:
I want the natural failure—find it where?
Which thread will have to break and leave a loop
I' the meshy combination, my brain's loom
Wove this long while, and now next minute tests?
Of three that are to catch, two should go free,
One must: all three surprised,—impossible!   1580
Beside, I seek three and may chance on six,—
This neighbour, t' other gossip,—the babe's birth
Brings such to fireside, and folks give them wine,—
'Tis late: but when I break in presently
One will be found outlingering the rest
For promise of a posset,—one whose shout
Would raise the dead down in the catacombs,
Much more the city-watch that goes its round.
When did I ever turn adroitly up
To sun some brick embedded in the soil,   1590
And with one blow crush all three scorpions there?
Or Pietro or Violante shambles off—
It cannot be but I surprise my wife—
If only she is stopped and stamped on, good!
That shall suffice: more is improbable.
Now I may knock!' And this once for my sake
The impossible was effected: I called king,
Queen and knave in a sequence, and cards came,
All three, three only! So, I had my way,
Did my deed: so, unbrokenly lay bare   1600
Each tænia that had sucked me dry of juice,°
At last outside me, not an inch of ring
Left now to writhe about and root itself

I' the heart all powerless for revenge! Henceforth
I might thrive: these were drawn and dead and damned.
Oh Cardinal, the deep long sigh you heave
When the load's off you, ringing as it runs
All the way down the serpent-stair to hell!
No doubt the fine delirium flustered me,
Turned my brain with the influx of success   1610
As if the sole need now were to wave wand
And find doors fly wide,—wish and have my will,—
The rest o' the scheme would care for itself: escape?
Easy enough were that, and poor beside!
It all but proved so,—ought to quite have proved,
Since, half the chances had sufficed, set free
Anyone, with his senses at command,
From thrice the danger of my flight. But, drunk,
Redundantly triumphant,—some reverse
Was sure to follow! There's no other way   1620
Accounts for such prompt perfect failure then
And there on the instant. Any day o' the week,
A ducat slid discreetly into palm
O' the mute post-master, while you whisper him—
How you the Count and certain four your knaves,
Have just been mauling who was malapert,°
Suspect the kindred may prove troublesome,
Therefore, want horses in a hurry,—that
And nothing more secures you any day
The pick o' the stable! Yet I try the trick,   1630
Double the bribe, call myself Duke for Count,
And say the dead man only was a Jew,
And for my pains find I am dealing just
With the one scrupulous fellow in all Rome—
Just this immaculate official stares,
Sees I want hat on head and sword in sheath,
Am splashed with other sort of wet than wine,
Shrugs shoulder, puts my hand by, gold and all,
Stands on the strictness of the rule o' the road!
'Where's the Permission?' Where's the wretched rag   1640
With the due seal and sign of Rome's Police,
To be had for asking, half-an-hour ago?
'Gone? Get another, or no horses hence!'
He dares not stop me, we five glare too grim,

But hinders,—hacks and hamstrings sure enough,°
Gives me some twenty miles of miry road
More to march in the middle of that night
Whereof the rough beginning taxed the strength
O' the youngsters, much more mine, both soul and flesh,
Who had to think as well as act: dead-beat,   1650
We gave in ere we reached the boundary
And safe spot out of this irrational Rome,—
Where, on dismounting from our steeds next day,
We had snapped our fingers at you, safe and sound,
Tuscans once more in blessed Tuscany,
Where laws make wise allowance, understand
Civilized life and do its champions right!
Witness the sentence of the Rota there,
Arezzo uttered, the Granduke confirmed,
One week before I acted on its hint,—   1660
Giving friend Guillichini, for his love,
The galleys, and my wife your saint, Rome's saint,—
Rome manufactures saints enough to know,—
Seclusion at the Stinche for her life.
All this, that all but was, might all have been,
Yet was not! baulked by just a scrupulous knave
Whose palm was horn through handling horses' hoofs
And could not close upon my proffered gold!
What say you to the spite of fortune? Well,
The worst's in store: thus hindered, haled this way   1670
To Rome again by hangdogs, whom find I
Here, still to fight with, but my pale frail wife?
—Riddled with wounds by one not like to waste
The blows he dealt,—knowing anatomy,—
(I think I told you) bound to pick and choose
The vital parts! 'Twas learning all in vain!
She too must shimmer through the gloom o' the grave,
Come and confront me—not at judgment-seat
Where I could twist her soul, as erst her flesh,
And turn her truth into a lie,—but there,   1680
O' the death-bed, with God's hand between us both,
Striking me dumb, and helping her to speak,
Tell her own story her own way, and turn
My plausibility to nothingness!
Four whole days did Pompilia keep alive,

With the best surgery of Rome agape
At the miracle,—this cut, the other slash,
And yet the life refusing to dislodge,
Four whole extravagant impossible days,
Till she had time to finish and persuade   1690
Every man, every woman, every child
In Rome, of what she would: the selfsame she
Who, but a year ago, had wrung her hands,
Reddened her eyes and beat her breasts, rehearsed
The whole game at Arezzo, nor availed
Thereby to move one heart or raise one hand!
When destiny intends you cards like these,
What good of skill and preconcerted play?
Had she been found dead, as I left her dead,
I should have told a tale brooked no reply: 1700
You scarcely will suppose me found at fault
With that advantage! 'What brings me to Rome?
Necessity to claim and take my wife:
Better, to claim and take my new born babe,—
Strong in paternity a fortnight old,
When 'tis at strongest: warily I work,
Knowing the machinations of my foe;
I have companionship and use the night:
I seek my wife and child,—I find—no child
But wife, in the embraces of that priest   1710
Who caused her to elope from me. These two,
Backed by the pander-pair who watch the while,
Spring on me like so many tiger-cats,
Glad of the chance to end the intruder. I—
What should I do but stand on my defence,
Strike right, strike left, strike thick and threefold, slay,
Not all—because the coward priest escapes.
Last, I escape, in fear of evil tongues,
And having had my taste of Roman law.'
What's disputable, refutable here?—   1720
Save by just this one ghost-thing half on earth,
Half out of it,—as if she held God's hand
While she leant back and looked her last at me,
Forgiving me (here monks begin to weep)
Oh, from her very soul, commending mine
To heavenly mercies which are infinite,—

While fixing fast my head beneath your knife!
'Tis fate not fortune. All is of a piece!
When was it chance informed me of my youths?
My rustic four o' the family, soft swains,   1730
What sweet surprise had they in store for me,
Those of my very household,—what did Law
Twist with her rack-and-cord-contrivance late
From out their bones and marrow? What but this—
Had no one of these several stumbling-blocks
Stopped me, they yet were cherishing a scheme,
All of their honest country homespun wit,
To quietly next day at crow of cock
Cut my own throat too, for their own behoof,
Seeing I had forgot to clear accounts   1740
O' the instant, nowise slackened speed for that,—
And somehow never might find memory,
Once safe back in Arezzo, where things change,
And a court-lord needs mind no country lout.
Well, being the arch-offender, I die last,—
May, ere my head falls, have my eyesight free,
Nor miss them dangling high on either hand,
Like scarecrows in a hemp-field, for their pains!

And then my Trial,—'tis my Trial that bites
Like a corrosive, so the cards are packed,   1750
Dice loaded, and my life-stake tricked away!
Look at my lawyers, lacked they grace of law,
Latin or logic? Were not they fools to the height,
Fools to the depth, fools to the level between,
O' the foolishness set to decide the case?
They feign, they flatter; nowise does it skill,
Everything goes against me: deal each judge
His dole of flattery and feigning,—why
He turns and tries and snuffs and savours it,
As some old fly the sugar-grain, your gift;   1760
Then eyes your thumb and finger, brushes clean
The absurd old head of him, and whisks away,
Leaving your thumb and finger dirty. Faugh!

And finally, after this long-drawn range
Of affront and failure, failure and affront,—
This path, 'twixt crosses leading to a skull,°

Paced by me barefoot, bloodied by my palms
From the entry to the end,—there's light at length,
A cranny of escape: appeal may be
To the old man, to the father, to the Pope,   1770
For a little life—from one whose life is spent,
A little pity—from pity's source and seat,
A little indulgence to rank, privilege,
From one who is the thing personified,
Rank, privilege, indulgence, grown beyond
Earth's bearing, even, ask Jansenius else!°
Still the same answer, still no other tune
From the cicala perched at the tree-top
Than crickets noisy round the root: 'tis 'Die!'
Bids Law—'Be damned!' adds Gospel,—nay,   1780
No word so frank,—'tis rather, 'Save yourself!'
The Pope subjoins—'Confess and be absolved!
So shall my credit countervail your shame,
And the world see I have not lost the knack
Of trying all the spirits: yours, my son,
Wants but a fiery washing to emerge
In clarity! Come, cleanse you, ease the ache
Of these old bones, refresh our bowels, boy!'
Do I mistake your mission from the Pope?
Then, bear his Holiness the mind of me!   1790
I do get strength from being thrust to wall,
Successively wrenched from pillar and from post
By this tenacious hate of fortune, hate
Of all things in, under, and above earth.
Warfare, begun this mean unmanly mode,
Does best to end so,—gives earth spectacle
Of a brave fighter who succumbs to odds
That turn defeat to victory. Stab, I fold
My mantle round me! Rome approves my act:
Applauds the blow which costs me life but keeps   1800
My honour spotless: Rome would praise no more
Had I fallen, say, some fifteen years ago,
Helping Vienna when our Aretines°
Flocked to Duke Charles and fought Turk Mustafa;
Nor would you two be trembling o'er my corpse
With all this exquisite solicitude.
Why is it that I make such suit to live?

The popular sympathy that's round me now
Would break like bubble that o'er-domes a fly:
Solid enough while he lies quiet there,   1810
But let him want the air and ply the wing,
Why, it breaks and bespatters him, what else?
Cardinal, if the Pope had pardoned me,
And I walked out of prison through the crowd,
It would not be your arm I should dare press!
Then, if I got safe to my place again,
How sad and sapless were the years to come!
I go my old ways and find things grown grey;
You priests leer at me, old friends look askance,
The mob's in love, I'll wager, to a man,   1820
With my poor young good beauteous murdered wife:
For hearts require instruction how to beat,
And eyes, on warrant of the story, wax
Wanton at portraiture in white and black
Of dead Pompilia gracing ballad-sheet,
Which eyes, lived she unmurdered and unsung,
Would never turn though she paced street as bare
As the mad penitent ladies do in France.
My brothers quietly would edge me out
Of use and management of things called mine;   1830
Do I command? 'You stretched command before!'
Show anger? 'Anger little helped you once!'
Advise? 'How managed you affairs of old?'
My very mother, all the while they gird,°
Turns eye up, gives confirmatory groan;
For unsuccess, explain it how you will,
Disqualifies you, makes you doubt yourself,
—Much more, is found decisive by your friends.
Beside, am I not fifty years of age?
What new leap would a life take, checked like mine   1840
I' the spring at outset? Where's my second chance?
Ay, but the babe . . . I had forgot my son,
My heir! Now for a burst of gratitude!
There's some appropriate service to intone,
Some *gaudeamus* and thanksgiving-psalm!°
Old, I renew my youth in him, and poor
Possess a treasure,—is not that the phrase?
Only I must wait patient twenty years—

Nourishing all the while, as father ought,
The excrescence with my daily blood of life.   1850
Does it respond to hope, such sacrifice,—
Grows the wen plump while I myself grow lean?
Why, here's my son and heir in evidence,
Who stronger, wiser, handsomer than I
By fifty years, relieves me of each load,—
Tames my hot horse, carries my heavy gun,
Courts my coy mistress,—has his apt advice
On house-economy, expenditure,
And what not. All which good gifts and great growth
Because of my decline, he brings to bear   1860
On Guido, but half apprehensive how
He cumbers earth, crosses the brisk young Count,
Who civilly would thrust him from the scene.
Contrariwise, does the blood-offering fail?
There's an ineptitude, one blank the more
Added to earth in semblance of my child?
Then, this has been a costly piece of work,
My life exchanged for his!—why he, not I,
Enjoy the world, if no more grace accrue?
Dwarf me, what giant have you made of him?   1870
I do not dread the disobedient son:
I know how to suppress rebellion there,
Being not quite the fool my father was.
But grant the medium measure of a man,
The usual compromise 'twixt fool and sage,
—You know—the tolerably-obstinate,
The not-so-much-perverse but you may train,
The true son-servant that, when parent bids
'Go work, son, in my vineyard!' makes reply
'I go, Sir!'—Why, what profit in your son°   1880
Beyond the drudges you might subsidize,
Have the same work from, at a paul the head?°
Look at those four young precious olive-plants
Reared at Vittiano,—not on flesh and blood,
These twenty years, but black bread and sour wine!
I bade them put forth tender branch, hook, hold,
And hurt three enemies I had in Rome:
They did my hest as unreluctantly,
At promise of a dollar, as a son°

Adjured by mumping memories of the past.   1890
No, nothing repays youth expended so—
Youth, I say, who am young still: grant but leave
To live my life out, to the last I'd live
And die conceding age no right of youth!
It is the will runs the renewing nerve
Through flaccid flesh that faints before the time.
Therefore no sort of use for son have I—
Sick, not of life's feast but of steps to climb
To the house where life prepares her feast,—of means
To the end: for make the end attainable   1900
Without the means,—my relish were like yours.
A man may have an appetite enough
For a whole dish of robins ready cooked,
And yet lack courage to face sleet, pad snow,
And snare sufficiently for supper.

                                                    Thus
The time's arrived when, ancient Roman-like,
I am bound to fall on my own sword: why not
Say—Tuscan-like, more ancient, better still?
Will you hear truth can do no harm nor good?
I think I never was at any time   1910
A Christian, as you nickname all the world.
Me among others: truce to nonsense now!
Name me, a primitive religionist—
As should the aboriginary be
I boast myself, Etruscan, Aretine,°
One sprung,—your frigid Virgil's fieriest word,—
From fauns and nymphs, trunks and the heart of oak,
With,—for a visible divinity,—
The portent of a Jove Ægiochus°
Descried 'mid clouds, lightning and thunder, couched   1920
On topmost crag of your Capitoline:
'Tis in the Seventh Æneid,—what, the Eighth?
Right,—thanks, Abate,—though the Christian's dumb,
The Latinist's vivacious in you yet!
I know my grandsire had our tapestry
Marked with the motto, 'neath a certain shield,
Whereto his grandson presently will give gules
To vary azure. First we fight for faiths,°

But get to shake hands at the last of all:
Mine's your faith too,—in Jove Ægiochus! 1930
Nor do Greek gods, that serve as supplement,
Jar with the simpler scheme, if understood.
We want such intermediary race
To make communication possible;
The real thing were too lofty, we too low,
Midway hang these: we feel their use so plain
In linking height to depth, that we doff hat
And put no question nor pry narrowly
Into the nature hid behind the names.
We grudge no rite the fancy may demand; 1940
But never, more than needs, invent, refine,
Improve upon requirement, idly wise
Beyond the letter, teaching gods their trade,
Which is to teach us: we'll obey when taught.
Why should we do our duty past the need?
When the sky darkens, Jove is wroth,—say prayer!
When the sun shines and Jove is glad,—sing psalm!
But wherefore pass prescription and devise
Blood-offering for sweat-service, lend the rod
A pungency through pickle of our own? 1950
Learned Abate,—no one teaches you
What Venus means and who's Apollo here!
I spare you, Cardinal,—but, though you wince,
You know me, I know you, and both know that!
So, if Apollo bids us fast, we fast:
But where does Venus order we stop sense
When Master Pietro rhymes a pleasantry?
Give alms prescribed on Friday: but, hold hand
Because your foe lies prostrate,—where's the word
Explicit in the book debars revenge? 1960
The rationale of your scheme is just
'Pay toll here, there pursue your pleasure free!'
So do you turn to use the medium-powers,
Mars and Minerva, Bacchus and the rest,
And so are saved propitiating—whom?
What all-good, all-wise and all-potent Jove
Vexed by the very sins in man, himself
Made life's necessity when man he made?
Irrational bunglers! So, the living truth

Revealed to strike Pan dead, ducks low at last,°   1970
Prays leave to hold its own and live good days
Provided it go masque grotesquely, called
Christian not Pagan. Oh, you purged the sky
Of all gods save the One, the great and good,
Clapped hands and triumphed! But the change came fast:
The inexorable need in man for life—
(Life, you may mulct and minish to a grain°
Out of the lump, so that the grain but live)
Laughed at your substituting death for life,
And bade you do your worst: which worst was done   1980
In just that age styled primitive and pure
When Saint this, Saint that, dutifully starved,
Froze, fought with beasts, was beaten and abused
And finally ridded of his flesh by fire:
He kept life-long unspotted from the world!
Next age, how goes the game, what mortal gives
His life and emulates Saint that, Saint this?
Men mutter, make excuse or mutiny,
In fine are minded all to leave the new,
Stick to the old,—enjoy old liberty,   1990
No prejudice in enjoyment, if you please,
To the new profession: sin o' the sly, henceforth!
The law stands though the letter kills: what then?
The spirit saves as unmistakeably.
Omniscience sees, Omnipotence could stop,
Omnibenevolence pardons: it must be,
Frown law its fiercest, there's a wink somewhere!

Such was the logic in this head of mine:
I, like the rest, wrote 'poison' on my bread,
But broke and ate:—said 'Those that use the sword   2000
Shall perish by the same;' then stabbed my foe.°
I stand on solid earth, not empty air:
Dislodge me, let your Pope's crook hale me hence!
Not he, nor you! And I so pity both,
I'll make the true charge you want wit to make:
'Count Guido, who reveal our mystery,
And trace all issues to the love of life:
We having life to love and guard, like you,
Why did you put us upon self-defence?

You well knew what prompt pass-word would appease   2010
The sentry's ire when folk infringed his bounds,
And yet kept mouth shut: do you wonder then
If, in mere decency, he shot you dead?
He can't have people play such pranks as yours
Beneath his nose at noonday: you disdained
To give him an excuse before the world
By crying "I break rule to save our camp!"
Under the old rule, such offence were death;
And you had heard the Pontifex pronounce°
"Since you slay foe and violate the form,   2020
Slaying turns murder, which were sacrifice
Had you, while, say, law-suiting foe to death,
But raised an altar to the Unknown God
Or else the Genius of the Vatican."
Why then this pother?—all because the Pope,
Doing his duty, cried "A foreigner,
You scandalize the natives: here at Rome
Romano vivitur more: wise men, here,°
Put the Church forward and efface themselves.
The fit defence had been,—you stamped on wheat,   2030
Intending all the time to trample tares,—°
Were fain extirpate, then, the heretic,
You now find, in your haste was slain a fool:
Nor Pietro, nor Violante, nor your wife
Meant to breed up your babe a Molinist!
Whence you are duly contrite. Not one word
Of all this wisdom did you urge: which slip
Death must atone for."'
                        So, let death atone!
So ends mistake, so end mistakers!—end
Perhaps to recommence,—how should I know?   2040
Only, be sure, no punishment, no pain
Childish, preposterous, impossible,
But some such fate as Ovid could foresee,—
Byblis in fluvium, let the weak soul end
In water, *sed Lycaon in lupum*, but
The strong become a wolf for evermore!
Change that Pompilia to a puny stream
Fit to reflect the daisies on its bank!
Let me turn wolf, be whole, and sate, for once,—°

Wallow in what is now a wolfishness   2050
Coerced too much by the humanity°
That's half of me as well! Grow out of man,
Glut the wolf-nature,—what remains but grow
Into the man again, be man indeed
And all man? Do I ring the changes right?
Deformed, transformed, reformed, informed, conformed!
The honest instinct, pent and crossed through life,
Let surge by death into a visible flow
Of rapture: as the strangled thread of flame
Painfully winds, annoying and annoyed,   2060
Malignant and maligned, thro' stone and ore,
Till earth exclude the stranger: vented once,
It finds full play, is recognized a-top
Some mountain as no such abnormal birth,
Fire for the mount, not streamlet for the vale!
Ay, of the water was that wife of mine—
Be it for good, be it for ill, no run
O' the red thread through that insignificance!
Again, how she is at me with those eyes!
Away with the empty stare! Be holy still,   2070
And stupid ever! Occupy your patch
Of private snow that's somewhere in what world
May now be growing icy round your head,
And aguish at your foot-print,—freeze not me,
Dare follow not another step I take,
Not with so much as those detested eyes,
No, though they follow but to pray me pause
On the incline, earth's edge that's next to hell!
None of your abnegation of revenge!
Fly at me frank, tug while I tear again!   2080
There's God, go tell Him, testify your worst!
Not she! There was no touch in her of hate:
And it would prove her hell, if I reached mine!
To know I suffered, would still sadden her,
Do what the angels might to make amends!
Therefore there's either no such place as hell,
Or thence shall I be thrust forth, for her sake,
And thereby undergo three hells, not one—
I who, with outlet for escape to heaven,
Would tarry if such flight allowed my foe   2090

To raise his head, relieved of that firm foot
Had pinned him to the fiery pavement else!
So am I made, 'who did not make myself:'°
(How dared she rob my own lip of the word?)
Beware me in what other world may be!—
Pompilia, who have brought me to this pass!
All I know here, will I say there, and go
Beyond the saying with the deed. Some use
There cannot but be for a mood like mine,
Implacable, persistent in revenge.   2100
She maundered 'All is over and at end:
I go my own road, go you where God will!
Forgive you? I forget you!' There's the saint
That takes your taste, you other kind of men!
How you had loved her! Guido wanted skill
To value such a woman at her worth!
Properly the instructed criticize
'What's here, you simpleton have tossed to take
Its chance i' the gutter? This a daub, indeed?
Why, 'tis a Rafael that you kicked to rags!'°   2110
Perhaps so: some prefer the pure design:
Give me my gorge of colour, glut of gold
In a glory round the Virgin made for me!
Titian's the man, not Monk Angelico°
Who traces you some timid chalky ghost
That turns the church into a charnel: ay,
Just such a pencil might depict my wife!
She,—since she, also, would not change herself,—
Why could not she come in some heart-shaped cloud,
Rainbowed about with riches, royalty   2120
Rimming her round, as round the tintless lawn°
Guardingly runs the selvage cloth of gold?
I would have left the faint fine gauze untouched,
Needle-worked over with its lily and rose,
Let her bleach unmolested in the midst,
Chill that selected solitary spot
Of quietude she pleased to think was life.
Purity, pallor grace the lawn no doubt
When there's the costly bordure to unthread
And make again an ingot: but what's grace   2130
When you want meat and drink and clothes and fire?

A tale comes to my mind that's apposite—
Possibly true, probably false, a truth
Such as all truths we live by, Cardinal!
'Tis said, a certain ancestor of mine
Followed—whoever was the potentate,
To Paynimrie, and in some battle, broke°
Through more than due allowance of the foe,
And, risking much his own life, saved the lord's.
Battered and bruised, the Emperor scrambles up,   2140
Rubs his eyes and looks round and sees my sire,
Picks a furze-sprig from out his hauberk-joint,°
(Token how near the ground went majesty)
And says 'Take this, and if thou get safe home,
Plant the same in thy garden-ground to grow:
Run thence an hour in a straight line, and stop:
Describe a circle round (for central point)
The furze aforesaid, reaching every way
The length of that hour's run: I give it thee,—
The central point, to build a castle there,   2150
The space circumjacent, for fit demesne,°
The whole to be thy children's heritage,—
Whom, for thy sake, bid thou wear furze on cap!'
Those are my arms: we turned the furze a tree
To show more, and the greyhound tied thereto,
Straining to start, means swift and greedy both;
He stands upon a triple mount of gold—
By Jove, then, he's escaping from true gold
And trying to arrive at empty air!
Aha! the fancy never crossed my mind!   2160
My father used to tell me, and subjoin
'As for the castle, that took wings and flew:
The broad lands,—why, to traverse them to-day
Scarce tasks my gouty feet, and in my prime
I doubt not I could stand and spit so far;
But for the furze, boy, fear no lack of that,
So long as fortune leaves one field to grub!
Wherefore, hurra for furze and loyalty!'
What may I mean, where may the lesson lurk?
'Do not bestow on man, by way of gift,   2170
Furze without land for framework,—vaunt no grace
Of purity, no furze-sprig of a wife,

To me, i' the thick of battle for my bread,
Without some better dowry,—gold will do!'
No better gift than sordid muck? Yes, Sirs!
Many more gifts much better. Give them me!
O those Olimpias bold, those Biancas brave,°
That brought a husband power worth Ormuz' wealth!°
Cried 'Thou being mine, why, what but thine am I?
Be thou to me law, right, wrong, heaven and hell!   2180
Let us blend souls, blent, thou in me, to bid
Two bodies work one pleasure! What are these
Called king, priest, father, mother, stranger, friend?
They fret thee or they frustrate? Give the word—
Be certain they shall frustrate nothing more!
And who is this young florid foolishness
That holds thy fortune in his pigmy clutch,
—Being a prince and potency, forsooth!—
He hesitates to let the trifle go?
Let me but seal up eye, sing ear to sleep   2190
Sounder than Samson,—pounce thou on the prize
Shall slip from off my breast, and down couch-side,
And on to floor, and far as my lord's feet—
Where he stands in the shadow with the knife,
Waiting to see what Delilah dares do!°
Is the youth fair? What is a man to me
Who am thy call-bird? Twist his neck—my dupe's,—°
Then take the breast shall turn a breast indeed!'
Such women are there; and they marry whom?
Why, when a man has gone and hanged himself   2200
Because of what he calls a wicked wife,—
See, if the very turpitude bemoaned
Prove not mere excellence the fool ignores!
His monster is perfection,—Circe, sent°
Straight from the sun, with wand the idiot blames
As not an honest distaff to spin wool!°
O thou Lucrezia, is it long to wait°
Yonder where all the gloom is in a glow
With thy suspected presence?—virgin yet,
Virtuous again, in face of what's to teach—   2210
Sin unimagined, unimaginable,—
I come to claim my bride,—thy Borgia's self
Not half the burning bridegroom I shall be!

Cardinal, take away your crucifix!
Abate, leave my lips alone,—they bite!
Vainly you try to change what should not change,
And shall not. I have bared, you bathe my heart—
It grows the stonier for your saving dew!
You steep the substance, you would lubricate,
In waters that but touch to petrify!   2220

You too are petrifactions of a kind:
Move not a muscle that shows mercy. Rave
Another twelve hours, every word were waste!
I thought you would not slay impenitence,
But teased, from men you slew, contrition first,—
I thought you had a conscience. Cardinal,
You know I am wronged!—wronged, say, and wronged, maintain.
Was this strict inquisition made for blood
When first you showed us scarlet on your back,
Called to the College? Your straightforward way   2230
To your legitimate end,—I think it passed
Over a scantling of heads brained, hearts broke,°
Lives trodden into dust! How otherwise?
Such was the way o' the world, and so you walked.
Does memory haunt your pillow? Not a whit.
God wills you never pace your garden-path,
One appetizing hour ere dinner-time,
But your intrusion there treads out of life
A universe of happy innocent things:
Feel you remorse about that damsel-fly   2240
Which buzzed so near your mouth and flapped your face?
You blotted it from being at a blow:
It was a fly, you were a man, and more,
Lord of created things, so took your course.
Manliness, mind,—these are things fit to save,
Fit to brush fly from: why, because I take
My course, must needs the Pope kill me?—kill you!
You! for this instrument, he throws away,
Is strong to serve a master, and were yours
To have and hold and get much good from out!   2250
The Pope who dooms me needs must die next year;
I'll tell you how the chances are supposed
For his successor: first the Chamberlain,

Old San Cesario,—Colloredo, next,—
Then, one, two, three, four, I refuse to name;
After these, comes Altieri; then come you—
Seventh on the list you come, unless . . . ha, ha,°
How can a dead hand give a friend a lift?
Are you the person to despise the help
O' the head shall drop in pannier presently?   2260
So a child seesaws on or kicks away
The fulcrum-stone that's all the sage requires
To fit his lever to and move the world.°
Cardinal, I adjure you in God's name,
Save my life, fall at the Pope's feet, set forth
Things your own fashion, not in words like these
Made for a sense like yours who apprehend!
Translate into the Court-conventional
'Count Guido must not die, is innocent!
Fair, be assured! But what an he were foul,   2270
Blood-drenched and murder-crusted head to foot?
Spare one whose death insults the Emperor,
Nay, outrages the Louis you so love!
He has friends who will avenge him; enemies
Who will hate God now with impunity,
Missing the old coercive: would you send
A soul straight to perdition, dying frank
An atheist?' Go and say this, for God's sake!
—Why, you don't think I hope you'll say one word?
Neither shall I persuade you from your stand   2280
Nor you persuade me from my station: take
Your crucifix away, I tell you twice!

Come, I am tired of silence! Pause enough!
You have prayed: I have gone inside my soul
And shut its door behind me: 'tis your torch
Makes the place dark: the darkness let alone
Grows tolerable twilight: one may grope
And get to guess at length and breadth and depth.
What is this fact I feel persuaded of—
This something like a foothold in the sea,   2290
Although Saint Peter's bark scuds, billow-borne,°
Leaves me to founder where it flung me first?
Spite of your splashing, I am high and dry!

God takes his own part in each thing He made;
Made for a reason, He conserves his work,
Gives each its proper instinct of defence.
My lamblike wife could neither bark nor bite,
She bleated, bleated, till for pity pure
The village roused up, ran with pole and prong
To the rescue, and behold the wolf's at bay!   2300
Shall he try bleating?—or take turn or two,
Since the wolf owns some kinship with the fox,
And, failing to escape the foe by craft,
Give up attempt, die fighting quietly?
The last bad blow that strikes fire in at eye
And on to brain, and so out, life and all.
How can it but be cheated of a pang
If, fighting quietly, the jaws enjoy
One re-embrace in mid back-bone they break,
After their weary work thro' the foe's flesh?   2310
That's the wolf-nature. Don't mistake my trope!
A Cardinal so qualmish? Eminence,
My fight is figurative, blows i' the air,
Brain-war with powers and principalities,°
Spirit-bravado, no real fisticuffs!
I shall not presently, when the knock comes,
Cling to this bench nor claw the hangman's face,
No, trust me! I conceive worse lots than mine.
Whether it be, the old contagious fit
And plague o' the prison have surprised me too,   2320
The appropriate drunkenness of the death-hour
Crept on my sense, kind work o' the wine and myrrh,—
I know not,—I begin to taste my strength,
Careless, gay even. What's the worth of life?
The Pope's dead now, my murderous old man,
For Tozzi told me so: and you, forsooth—°
Why, you don't think, Abate, do your best,
You'll live a year more with that hacking cough
And blotch of crimson where the cheek's a pit?
Tozzi has got you also down in book!   2330
Cardinal, only seventh of seventy near,
Is not one called Albano in the lot?
Go eat your heart, you'll never be a Pope!
Inform me, is it true you left your love,

A Pucci, for promotion in the church?
She's more than in the church,—in the churchyard!
Plautilla Pucci, your affianced bride,
Has dust now in the eyes that held the love,—
And Martinez, suppose they make you Pope,°
Stops that with *veto*,—so, enjoy yourself!   2340
I see you all reel to the rock, you waves—
Some forthright, some describe a sinuous track,
Some, crested brilliantly, with heads above,
Some in a strangled swirl sunk who knows how,
But all bound whither the main-current sets,
Rockward, an end in foam for all of you!
What if I be o'ertaken, pushed to the front
By all you crowding smoother souls behind,
And reach, a minute sooner than was meant,
The boundary whereon I break to mist?   2350
Go to! the smoothest safest of you all,
Most perfect and compact wave in my train,
Spite of the blue tranquillity above,
Spite of the breadth before of lapsing peace
Where broods the halcyon and the fish leaps free,°
Will presently begin to feel the prick
At lazy heart, the push at torpid brain,
Will rock vertiginously in turn, and reel,
And, emulative, rush to death like me.
Later or sooner by a minute then,   2360
So much for the untimeliness of death!
And, as regards the manner that offends,
The rude and rough, I count the same for gain.
Be the act harsh and quick! Undoubtedly
The soul's condensed and, twice itself, expands
To burst thro' life, by alternation due,
Into the other state whate'er it prove.
You never know what life means till you die:
Even throughout life, 'tis death that makes life live,
Gives it whatever the significance.   2370
For see, on your own ground and argument,
Suppose life had no death to fear, how find
A possibility of nobleness
In man, prevented daring any more?
What's love, what's faith without a worst to dread?

Lack-lustre jewelry! but faith and love
With death behind them bidding do or die—
Put such a foil at back, the sparkle's born!
From out myself how the strange colours come!
Is there a new rule in another world?   2380
Be sure I shall resign myself: as here
I recognized no law I could not see,
There, what I see, I shall acknowledge too:
On earth I never took the Pope for God,
In heaven I shall scarce take God for the Pope.
Unmanned, remanned: I hold it probable—
With something changeless at the heart of me
To know me by, some nucleus that's myself:
Accretions did it wrong? Away with them—
You soon shall see the use of fire!

                              Till when,   2390
All that was, is; and must forever be.
Nor is it in me to unhate my hates,—
I use up my last strength to strike once more
Old Pietro in the wine-house-gossip-face,
To trample underfoot the whine and wile
Of beast Violante,—and I grow one gorge
To loathingly reject Pompilia's pale
Poison my hasty hunger took for food.
A strong tree wants no wreaths about its trunk,
No cloying cups, no sickly sweet of scent,   2400
But sustenance at root, a bucketful.
How else lived that Athenian who died so,°
Drinking hot bull's blood, fit for men like me?
I lived and died a man, and take man's chance,
Honest and bold: right will be done to such.

Who are these you have let descend my stair?
Ha, their accursed psalm! Lights at the sill!°
Is it 'Open' they dare bid you? Treachery!
Sirs, have I spoken one word all this while
Out of the world of words I had to say?   2410
Not one word! All was folly—I laughed and mocked!
Sirs, my first true word, all truth and no lie,
Is—save me notwithstanding! Life is all!
I was just stark mad,—let the madman live

Pressed by as many chains as you please pile!
Don't open! Hold me from them! I am yours,
I am the Granduke's—no, I am the Pope's!
Abate,—Cardinal,—Christ,—Maria,—God, . . .
Pompilia, will you let them murder me?

from FIFINE AT THE FAIR
(1872)

Prologue

Amphibian

I

The fancy I had to-day,
   Fancy which turned a fear!
I swam far out in the bay,
   Since waves laughed warm and clear.

II

I lay and looked at the sun,
   The noon-sun looked at me:
Between us two, no one
   Live creature, that I could see.

III

Yes! There came floating by
   Me, who lay floating too,
Such a strange butterfly!
   Creature as dear as new:

IV

Because the membraned wings
   So wonderful, so wide,
So sun-suffused, were things
   Like soul and nought beside.

V

A handbreadth over head!
   All of the sea my own,

10

It owned the sky instead;
  Both of us were alone.

20

VI

I never shall join its flight,
  For, nought buoys flesh in air.
If it touch the sea—good night!
  Death sure and swift waits there.

VII

Can the insect feel the better
  For watching the uncouth play
Of limbs that slip the fetter,
  Pretend as they were not clay?

VIII

Undoubtedly I rejoice
  That the air comports so well
With a creature which had the choice
  Of the land once. Who can tell?

30

IX

What if a certain soul
  Which early slipped its sheath,
And has for its home the whole
  Of heaven, thus look beneath,

X

Thus watch one who, in the world,
  Both lives and likes life's way,
Nor wishes the wings unfurled
  That sleep in the worm, they say?

40

XI

But sometimes when the weather
  Is blue, and warm waves tempt
To free oneself of tether,
  And try a life exempt

XII

From worldly noise and dust,
  In the sphere which overbrims
With passion and thought,—why, just
  Unable to fly, one swims!

XIII

By passion and thought upborne,
  One smiles to oneself—'They fare   50
Scarce better, they need not scorn
  Our sea, who live in the air!'

XIV

Emancipate through passion°
  And thought, with sea for sky,
We substitute, in a fashion,
  For heaven—poetry:

XV

Which sea, to all intent,
  Gives flesh such noon-disport°
As a finer element
  Affords the spirit-sort.   60

XVI

Whatever they are, we seem:
  Imagine the thing they know;
All deeds they do, we dream;
  Can heaven be else but so?

XVII

And meantime, yonder streak
  Meets the horizon's verge;
That is the land, to seek
  If we tire or dread the surge:

XVIII

Land the solid and safe—
  To welcome again (confess!)   70

When, high and dry, we chafe
 The body, and don the dress.

XIX

Does she look, pity, wonder°
 At one who mimics flight,
Swims—heaven above, sea under,
 Yet always earth in sight?

Epilogue
The Householder

I

Savage I was sitting in my house, late, lone:
 Dreary, weary with the long day's work:
Head of me, heart of me, stupid as a stone:
 Tongue-tied now, now blaspheming like a Turk;
When, in a moment, just a knock, call, cry,
 Half a pang and all a rapture, there again were we!—
'What, and is it really you again?' quoth I:
 'I again, what else did you expect?' quoth She.

II

'Never mind, hie away from this old house—
 Every crumbling brick embrowned with sin and shame!
Quick, in its corners ere certain shapes arouse!
 Let them—every devil of the night—lay claim,
Make and mend, or rap and rend, for me! Good-bye!
 God be their guard from disturbance at their glee,
Till, crash, comes down the carcass in a heap!' quoth I:
 'Nay, but there's a decency required!' quoth She.

III

'Ah, but if you knew how time has dragged, days, nights!
 All the neighbour-talk with man and maid—such men!
All the fuss and trouble of street-sounds, window-sights:

10

   All the worry of flapping door and echoing roof; and then,   20
All the fancies . . . Who were they had leave, dared try
   Darker arts that almost struck despair in me?
If you knew but how I dwelt down here!' quoth I:
   'And was I so better off up there?' quoth She.

              IV

'Help and get it over! *Re-united to his wife*
   (How draw up the paper lets the parish-people know?)
Lies M., or N., departed from this life,
   Day the this or that, month and year the so and so.
What i' the way of final flourish? Prose, verse? Try!
   Affliction sore long time he bore, or, what is it to be?   30
Till God did please to grant him ease. Do end!' quoth I:
   'I end with—Love is all and Death is nought!' quoth She.

from ARISTOPHANES' APOLOGY (1875)

'But—lend me the psalterion! Nay, for once—°
Once let my hand fall where the other's lay!
I see it, just as I were Sophokles,°
That sunrise and combustion of the east!'

And then he sang—are these unlike the words?

Thamuris marching,—lyre and song of Thrace—
(Perpend the first, the worst of woes that were°
Allotted lyre and song, ye poet-race!)   5190

Thamuris from Oichalia, feasted there
By kingly Eurutos of late, now bound
For Dorion at the uprise broad and bare

Of Mount Pangaios (ore with earth enwound°
Glittered beneath his footstep)—marching gay
And glad, Thessalia through, came, robed and crowned,°

From triumph on to triumph, mid a ray
Of early morn,—came, saw and knew the spot
Assigned him for his worst of woes, that day.

Balura—happier while its name was not—°   5200
Met him, but nowise menaced; slipt aside,
Obsequious river to pursue its lot

Of solacing the valley—say, some wide
Thick busy human cluster, house and home,
Embanked for peace, or thrift that thanks the tide.

Thamuris, marching, laughed 'Each flake of foam'
(As sparklingly the ripple raced him by)
'Mocks slower clouds adrift in the blue dome!'

For Autumn was the season; red the sky
Held morn's conclusive signet of the sun   5210
To break the mists up, bid them blaze and die.

Morn had the mastery as, one by one
All pomps produced themselves along the tract
From earth's far ending to near heaven begun.

Was there a ravaged tree? it laughed compact
With gold, a leaf-ball crisp, high-brandished now,
Tempting to onset frost which late attacked.

Was there a wizened shrub, a starveling bough,
A fleecy thistle filched from by the wind,
A weed, Pan's trampling hoof would disallow?°   5220

Each, with a glory and a rapture twined
About it, joined the rush of air and light
And force: the world was of one joyous mind.

Say not the birds flew! they forebore their right—
Swam, revelling onward in the roll of things.
Say not the beasts' mirth bounded! that was flight—

How could the creatures leap, no lift of wings?
Such earth's community of purpose, such
The ease of earth's fulfilled imaginings,—

So did the near and far appear to touch   5230
I' the moment's transport,—that an interchange
Of function, far with near, seemed scarce too much;

And had the rooted plant aspired to range
With the snake's license, while the insect yearned
To glow fixed as the flower, it were not strange—

No more than if the fluttery tree-top turned
To actual music, sang itself aloft;
Or if the wind, impassioned chantress, earned

The right to soar embodied in some soft
Fine form all fit for cloud-companionship,   5240
And, blissful, once touch beauty chased so oft.

Thamuris, marching, let no fancy slip
Born of the fiery transport; lyre and song
Were his, to smite with hand and launch from lip—

Peerless recorded, since the list grew long
Of poets (saith Homeros) free to stand
Pedestalled mid the Muses' temple-throng,

A statued service, laurelled, lyre in hand,
(Ay, for we see them)—Thamuris of Thrace
Predominating foremost of the band.   5250

Therefore the morn-ray that enriched his face,
If it gave lambent chill, took flame again
From flush of pride; he saw, he knew the place.

What wind arrived with all the rhythms from plain,
Hill, dale, and that rough wildwood interspersed?
Compounding these to one consummate strain,

It reached him, music; but his own outburst
Of victory concluded the account,
And that grew song which was mere music erst.

'Be my Parnassos, thou Pangaian mount!°   5260
And turn thee, river, nameless hitherto!
Famed shalt thou vie with famed Pieria's fount!°

'Here I await the end of this ado:
Which wins—Earth's poet or the Heavenly Muse.'...

But song broke up in laughter. 'Tell the rest
Who may! *I* have not spurned the common life,
Nor vaunted mine a lyre to match the Muse
Who sings for gods, not men! Accordingly,
I shall not decorate her vestibule—
Mute marble, blind the eyes and quenched the brain,   5270
Loose in the hand a bright, a broken lyre!
—Not Thamuris but Aristophanes!

'There! I have sung content back to myself,
And started subject for a play beside.
My next performance shall content you both.
Did "Prelude-Battle" maul "best friend" too much?°
Then "Main-Fight" be my next song, fairness' self!
Its subject—Contest for the Tragic Crown.
Ay, you shall hear none else but Aischulos
Lay down the law of Tragedy, and prove   5280
"Best friend" a stray-away,—no praise denied°

His manifold deservings, never fear—
Nor word more of the old fun! Death defends.
Sound admonition has its due effect.
Oh, you have uttered weighty words, believe!
Such as shall bear abundant fruit, next year,
In judgment, regular, legitimate.
Let Bacchos' self preside in person! Ay—°
For there's a buzz about those "Bacchanals"
Rumour attributes to your great and dead   5290
For final effort: just the prodigy
Great dead men leave, to lay survivors low!
—Until we make acquaintance with our fate
And find, fate's worst done, we, the same, survive
Perchance to honour more the patron-god,°
Fitlier inaugurate a festal year.
Now that the cloud has broken, sky laughs blue,
Earth blossoms youthfully. Athenai breathes.
After a twenty-six years' wintry blank°
Struck from her life,—war-madness, one long swoon,   5300
She wakes up: Arginousai bids good cheer.
We have disposed of Kallikratidas;°
Once more will Sparté sue for terms,—who knows?
Cede Dekeleia, as the rumour runs:°
Terms which Athenai, of right mind again,
Accepts—she can no other. Peace declared,
Have my long labours borne their fruit or no?°
Grinned coarse buffoonery so oft in vain?
Enough—it simply saved you. Saved ones, praise
Theoria's beauty and Opora's breadth!°   5310
Nor, when Peace realizes promised bliss,
Forget the Bald Bard, Envy! but go burst
As the cup goes round and the cates abound,
Collops of hare with roast spinks rare!°
Confess my pipings, dancings, posings served
A purpose: guttlings, guzzlings, had their use!
Say whether light Muse, Rosy-finger-tips,°
Or 'best friend's' heavy-hand, Melpomené,°
Touched lyre to purpose, played Amphion's part,°
And built Athenai to the skies once more!   5320
Farewell, brave couple! Next year, welcome me!'

House

I

Shall I sonnet-sing you about myself?
　Do I live in a house you would like to see?
Is it scant of gear, has it store of pelf?°
　'Unlock my heart with a sonnet-key?'°

10

II

Invite the world, as my betters have done?
　'Take notice: this building remains on view,
Its suites of reception every one,
　Its private apartment and bedroom too;

III

'For a ticket, apply to the Publisher.'
　No: thanking the public, I must decline.
A peep through my window, if folk prefer;
　But, please you, no foot over threshold of mine!

IV

I have mixed with a crowd and heard free talk
　In a foreign land where an earthquake chanced:
And a house stood gaping, nought to baulk
　Man's eye wherever he gazed or glanced.

V

The whole of the frontage shaven sheer,
　　The inside gaped: exposed to day,
Right and wrong and common and queer,
　　Bare, as the palm of your hand, it lay.   20

VI

The owner? Oh, he had been crushed, no doubt!
　　'Odd tables and chairs for a man of wealth!
What a parcel of musty old books about!
　　He smoked,—no wonder he lost his health!

VII

'I doubt if he bathed before he dressed.
　　A brasier?—the pagan, he burned perfumes!
You see it is proved, what the neighbours guessed:
　　His wife and himself had separate rooms.'

VIII

Friends, the goodman of the house at least
　　Kept house to himself till an earthquake came: 30
'Tis the fall of its frontage permits you feast
　　On the inside arrangement you praise or blame.

IX

Outside should suffice for evidence:
　　And whoso desires to penetrate
Deeper, must dive by the spirit-sense—
　　No optics like yours, at any rate!

X

'Hoity toity! A street to explore,
　　Your house the exception! "*With this same key
Shakespeare unlocked his heart,*" once more!'
　　Did Shakespeare? If so, the less Shakespeare he!   40

Numpholeptos

Still you stand, still you listen, still you smile!
Still melts your moonbeam through me, white awhile,
Softening, sweetening, till sweet and soft
Increase so round this heart of mine, that oft
I could believe your moonbeam-smile has past
The pallid limit, lies, transformed at last
To sunlight and salvation—warms the soul
It sweetens, softens! Would you pass that goal,
Gain love's birth at the limit's happier verge,
And, where an iridescence lurks, but urge   10
The hesitating pallor on to prime
Of dawn!—true blood-streaked, sun-warmth, action-time,
By heart-pulse ripened to a ruddy glow
Of gold above my clay—I scarce should know
From gold's self, thus suffused! For gold means love.
What means the sad slow silver smile above
My clay but pity, pardon?—at the best,
But acquiescence that I take my rest,
Contented to be clay, while in your heaven
The sun reserves love for the Spirit-Seven°   20
Companioning God's throne they lamp before,°
—Leaves earth a mute waste only wandered o'er
By that pale soft sweet disempassioned moon
Which smiles me slow forgiveness! Such the boon
I beg? Nay, dear, submit to this—just this
Supreme endeavour! As my lips now kiss
Your feet, my arms convulse your shrouding robe,
My eyes, acquainted with the dust, dare probe
Your eyes above for—what, if born, would blind
Mine with redundant bliss, as flash may find   30
The inert nerve, sting awake the palsied limb,
Bid with life's ecstasy sense overbrim
And suck back death in the resurging joy—
Love, the love whole and sole without alloy!

Vainly! The promise withers! I employ
Lips, arms, eyes, pray the prayer which finds the word,
Make the appeal which must be felt, not heard,

And none the more is changed your calm regard:
Rather, its sweet and soft grow harsh and hard—
Forbearance, then repulsion, then disdain.   40
Avert the rest! I rise, see!—make, again
Once more, the old departure for some track
Untried yet through a world which brings me back
Ever thus fruitlessly to find your feet,
To fix your eyes, to pray the soft and sweet
Which smile there—take from his new pilgrimage
Your outcast, once your inmate, and assuage
With love—not placid pardon now—his thirst
For a mere drop from out the ocean erst
He drank at! Well, the quest shall be renewed.   50
Fear nothing! Though I linger, unembued
With any drop, my lips thus close. I go!
So did I leave you, I have found you so,
And doubtlessly, if fated to return,
So shall my pleading persevere and earn
Pardon—not love—in that same smile, I learn,
And lose the meaning of, to learn once more,
Vainly!

          What fairy track do I explore?
What magic hall return to, like the gem
Centuply-angled o'er a diadem?°   60
You dwell there, hearted; from your midmost home°
Rays forth—through that fantastic world I roam
Ever—from centre to circumference,
Shaft upon coloured shaft: this crimsons thence,
That purples out its precinct through the waste.
Surely I had your sanction when I faced,
Fared forth upon that untried yellow ray
Whence I retrack my steps? They end to-day
Where they began—before your feet, beneath
Your eyes, your smile: the blade is shut in sheath,   70
Fire quenched in flint; irradiation, late
Triumphant through the distance, finds its fate,
Merged in your blank pure soul, alike the source°
And tomb of that prismatic glow: divorce
Absolute, all-conclusive! Forth I fared,
Treading the lambent flamelet: little cared

If now its flickering took the topaz tint,
If now my dull-caked path gave sulphury hint
Of subterranean rage—no stay nor stint
To yellow, since you sanctioned that I bathe,   80
Burnish me, soul and body, swim and swathe
In yellow license. Here I reek suffused
With crocus, saffron, orange, as I used
With scarlet, purple, every dye o' the bow°
Born of the storm-cloud. As before, you show
Scarce recognition, no approval, some
Mistrust, more wonder at a man become
Monstrous in garb, nay—flesh disguised as well,
Through his adventure. Whatso'er befell,
I followed, whereso'er it wound, that vein   90
You authorized should leave your whiteness, stain
Earth's sombre stretch beyond your midmost place
Of vantage,—trode that tint whereof the trace
On garb and flesh repel you! Yes, I plead
Your own permission—your command, indeed,
That who would worthily retain the love
Must share the knowledge shrined those eyes above,
Go boldly on adventure, break through bounds
O' the quintessential whiteness that surrounds
Your feet, obtain experience of each tinge
That bickers forth to broaden out, impinge°   100
Plainer his foot its pathway all distinct
From every other. Ah, the wonder, linked
With fear, as exploration manifests
What agency it was first tipped the crests
Of unnamed wildflower, soon protruding grew
Portentous mid the sands, as when his hue
Betrays him and the burrowing snake gleams through;
Till, last... but why parade more shame and pain?
Are not the proofs upon me? Here again
I pass into your presence, I receive   110
Your smile of pity, pardon, and I leave...
No, not this last of times I leave you, mute,
Submitted to my penance, so my foot
May yet again adventure, tread, from source
To issue, one more ray of rays which course
Each other, at your bidding, from the sphere

Silver and sweet, their birthplace, down that drear
Dark of the world,—you promise shall return
Your pilgrim jewelled as with drops o' the urn   120
The rainbow paints from, and no smatch at all°
Of ghastliness at edge of some cloud-pall
Heaven cowers before, as earth awaits the fall
O' the bolt and flash of doom. Who trusts your word
Tries the adventure: and returns—absurd
As frightful—in that sulphur-steeped disguise
Mocking the priestly cloth-of-gold, sole prize
The arch-heretic was wont to bear away
Until he reached the burning. No, I say:
No fresh adventure! No more seeking love   130
At end of toil, and finding, calm above
My passion, the old statuesque regard,
The sad petrific smile!

                    O you—less hard°
And hateful than mistaken and obtuse
Unreason of a she-intelligence!
You very woman with the pert pretence
To match the male achievement! Like enough!
Ay, you were easy victors, did the rough
Straightway efface itself to smooth, the gruff
Grind down and grow a whisper,—did man's truth   140
Subdue, for sake of chivalry and ruth,
Its rapier-edge to suit the bulrush-spear
Womanly falsehood fights with! O that ear
All fact pricks rudely, that thrice-superfine
Feminity of sense, with right divine
To waive all process, take result stain-free
From out the very muck wherein . . .

                              Ah me!
The true slave's querulous outbreak! All the rest
Be resignation! Forth at your behest
I fare. Who knows but this—the crimson-quest—   150
May deepen to a sunrise, not decay
To that cold sad sweet smile?—which I obey.

Tray

Sing me a hero! Quench my thirst
Of soul, ye bards!
          Quoth Bard the first:°
'Sir Olaf, the good knight, did don
His helm and eke his habergeon...'
Sir Olaf and his bard——!

'That sin-scathed brow' (quoth Bard the second)°
'That eye wide ope as though Fate beckoned
My hero to some steep, beneath
Which precipice smiled tempting death...'
You too without your host have reckoned!   10

'A beggar-child' (let's hear this third!)
'Sat on a quay's edge: like a bird
Sang to herself at careless play,
And fell into the stream. "Dismay!
Help, you the standers-by!" None stirred.

'Bystanders reason, think of wives
And children ere they risk their lives.
Over the balustrade has bounced
A mere instinctive dog, and pounced
Plumb on the prize. "How well he dives!   20

'"Up he comes with the child, see, tight
In mouth, alive too, clutched from quite
A depth of ten feet—twelve, I bet!
Good dog! What, off again? There's yet
Another child to save? All right!

'"How strange we saw no other fall!
It's instinct in the animal.
Good dog! But he's a long while under:
If he got drowned I should not wonder—
Strong current, that against the wall!   30

'"Here he comes, holds in mouth this time
—What may the thing be? Well, that's prime!
Now, did you ever? Reason reigns
In man alone, since all Tray's pains
Have fished—the child's doll from the slime!"

'And so, amid the laughter gay,
Trotted my hero off,—old Tray,—
Till somebody, prerogatived
With reason, reasoned: "Why he dived,
His brain would show us, I should say.   40

'"John, go and catch—or, if needs be,
Purchase—that animal for me!
By vivisection, at expense
Of half-an-hour and eighteenpence,
How brain secretes dog's soul, we'll see!"'

Clive

I and Clive were friends—and why not? Friends! I think you
    laugh, my lad.
Clive it was gave England India, while your father gives—egad,
England nothing but the graceless boy who lures him on to
    speak—
'Well, Sir, you and Clive were comrades—' with a tongue thrust
    in your cheek!
Very true: in my eyes, your eyes, all the world's eyes, Clive was
    man,
I was, am and ever shall be—mouse, nay, mouse of all its clan
Sorriest sample, if you take the kitchen's estimate for fame;
While the man Clive—he fought Plassy, spoiled the clever
    foreign game,°
Conquered and annexed and Englished!

                        Never mind! As o'er my punch
(You away) I sit of evenings,—silence, save for biscuit-crunch,   10
Black, unbroken,—thought grows busy, thrids each path-way of
    old years,
Notes this forthright, that meander, till the long-past life
    appears°
Like an outspread map of country plodded through, each mile
    and rood,°
Once, and well remembered still: I'm startled in my solitude
Ever and anon by—what's the sudden mocking light that breaks
On me as I slap the table till no rummer-glass but shakes°
While I ask—aloud, I do believe, God help me!—'Was it thus?
Can it be that so I faltered, stopped when just one step for
    us—'
(Us,—you were not born, I grant, but surely some day born
    would be)

'—One bold step had gained a province' (figurative talk, you see)   20
'Got no end of wealth and honour,—yet I stood stock still no
    less?'
—'For I was not Clive,' you comment: but it needs no Clive to
    guess
Wealth were handy, honour ticklish, did no writing on the wall
Warn me 'Trespasser, 'ware man-traps!' Him who braves that
    notice—call
Hero! none of such heroics suit myself who read plain words,
Doff my hat, and leap no barrier. Scripture says the land's the
    Lord's:
Louts then—what avail the thousand, noisy in a smock-frocked
    ring,°
All-agog to have me trespass, clear the fence, be Clive their king?
Higher warrant must you show me ere I set one foot before
T'other in that dark direction, though I stand for evermore   30
Poor as Job and meek as Moses. Evermore? No! By-and-by
Job grows rich and Moses valiant, Clive turns out less wise
    than I.
Don't object 'Why call him friend, then?' Power is power, my
    boy, and still
Marks a man,—God's gift magnific, exercised for good or ill.
You've your boot now on my hearth-rug, tread what was a
    tiger's skin:
Rarely such a royal monster as I lodged the bullet in!
True, he murdered half a village, so his own death came to pass;
Still, for size and beauty, cunning, courage—ah, the brute he
    was!
Why, that Clive,—that youth, that greenhorn, that quill-driving
    clerk, in fine,—°
He sustained a siege in Arcot…But the world knows! Pass
    the wine.°   40

Where did I break off at? How bring Clive in? Oh, you
    mentioned 'fear'!
Just so: and, said I, that minds me of a story you shall hear.

We were friends then, Clive and I: so, when the clouds, about
    the orb°
Late supreme, encroaching slowly, surely, threatened to absorb
Ray by ray its noontide brilliance,—friendship might, with
    steadier eye

Drawing near, bear what had burned else, now no blaze—all
    majesty.
Too much bee's-wing floats my figure? Well, suppose a castle's
    new:°
None presume to climb its ramparts, none find foothold sure for
    shoe
'Twixt those squares and squares of granite plating the
    impervious pile
As his scale-mail's warty iron cuirasses a crocodile.   50
Reels that castle thunder-smitten, storm-dismantled? From
    without
Scrambling up by crack and crevice, every cockney prates about
Towers—the heap he kicks now! turrets—just the measure of
    his cane!
Will that do? Observe moreover—(same similitude again)—
Such a castle seldom crumbles by sheer stress of cannonade:
'Tis when foes are foiled and fighting's finished that vile rains
    invade,
Grass o'ergrows, o'ergrows till night-birds congregating find no
    holes
Fit to build in like the topmost sockets made for banner-poles.
So Clive crumbled slow in London—crashed at last.°

                                  A week before,
Dining with him,—after trying churchyard-chat of days of
    yore,—
Both of us stopped, tired as tombstones, head-piece, footpiece,   60
    when they lean
Each to other, drowsed in fog-smoke, o'er a coffined Past between.
As I saw his head sink heavy, guessed the soul's extinguishment
By the glazing eyeball, noticed how the furtive fingers went
Where a drug-box skulked behind the honest liquor,—'One
    more throw
Try for Clive!' thought I: 'Let's venture some good rattling
    question!' So—
'Come, Clive, tell us'—out I blurted—'what to tell in turn, years
    hence,
When my boy—suppose I have one—asks me on what evidence
I maintain my friend of Plassy proved a warrior every whit°
Worth your Alexanders, Cæsars, Marlboroughs and—what said
    Pitt?—°
                                          70

Frederick the Fierce himself! Clive told me once'—I want to
    say—°
'Which feat out of all those famous doings bore the bell away°
—In his own calm estimation, mark you, not the mob's rough
    guess—
Which stood foremost as evincing what Clive called courageous-
    ness!
Come! what moment of the minute, what speck-centre in the
    wide
Circle of the action saw your mortal fairly deified?
(Let alone that filthy sleep-stuff, swallow bold this wholesome
    Port!)°
If a friend has leave to question,—when were you most brave, in
    short?'

Up he arched his brows o' the instant—formidably Clive again.
'When was I most brave? I'd answer, were the instance half as
    plain   80
As another instance that's a brain-lodged crystal—curse it!—
    here
Freezing when my memory touches—ugh!—the time I felt most
    fear.
Ugh! I cannot say for certain if I showed fear—anyhow,
Fear I felt, and, very likely, shuddered, since I shiver now.'

'Fear!' smiled I. 'Well, that's the rarer: that's a specimen to seek,
Ticket up in one's museum, *Mind-Freaks, Lord Clive's Fear,
    Unique!*'
Down his brows dropped. On the table painfully he pored as
    though
Tracing, in the stains and streaks there, thoughts encrusted long
    ago.
When he spoke 'twas like a lawyer reading word by word some
    will,
Some blind jungle of a statement,—beating on and on until   90
Out there leaps fierce life to fight with.

                          'This fell in my factor-days.°
Desk-drudge, slaving at St David's, one must game, or drink, or
    craze.°
I chose gaming: and,—because your high-flown gamesters
    hardly take

Umbrage at a factor's elbow if the factor pays his stake,—
I was winked at in a circle where the company was choice,
Captain This and Major That, men high of colour, loud of voice,
Yet indulgent, condescending to the modest juvenile
Who not merely risked but lost his hard-earned guineas with a
        smile.

'Down I sat to cards, one evening,—had for my antagonist
Somebody whose name's a secret—you'll know why—so, if you
        list,   100
Call him Cock o' the Walk, my scarlet son of Mars from head to
        heel!°
Play commenced: and, whether Cocky fancied that a clerk must
        feel
Quite sufficient honour came of bending over one green baize,
I the scribe with him the warrior,—guessed no penman dared to
        raise
Shadow of objection should the honour stay but playing end
More or less abruptly,—whether disinclined he grew to spend
Practice strictly scientific on a booby born to stare
At—not ask of—lace-and-ruffles if the hand they hide plays
        fair,—
Anyhow, I marked a movement when he bade me "Cut!"

                                                            'I rose.
"Such the new manœuvre, Captain? I'm a novice: knowledge
        grows.   110
What, you force a card, you cheat, Sir?"

                                    'Never did a thunder-clap°
Cause emotion, startle Thyrsis locked with Chloe in his lap,°
As my word and gesture (down I flung my cards to join the pack)
Fired the man of arms, whose visage, simply red before, turned
        black.
When he found his voice, he stammered "That expression once
        again!"

' "Well, you forced a card and cheated!"

                                    ' "Possibly a factor's brain,
Busied with his all-important balance of accounts, may deem
Weighing words superfluous trouble: *cheat* to clerkly ears may
        seem

Just the joke for friends to venture: but we are not friends, you see!
When a gentleman is joked with,—if he's good at repartee,   120
He rejoins, as do I—Sirrah, on your knees, withdraw in full!
Beg my pardon, or be sure a kindly bullet through your skull
Lets in light and teaches manners to what brain it finds! Choose
    quick—
Have your life snuffed out or, kneeling, pray me trim yon
    candle-wick!"

' "Well, you cheated!"
               'Then outbroke a howl from all the friends around.
To his feet sprang each in fury, fists were clenched and teeth
    were ground.
"End it! no time like the present! Captain, yours were our
    disgrace!
No delay, begin and finish! Stand back, leave the pair a space!
Let civilians be instructed: henceforth simply ply the pen,
Fly the sword! This clerk's no swordsman? Suit him with a
    pistol, then!   130
Even odds! A dozen paces 'twixt the most and least expert
Make a dwarf a giant's equal: nay, the dwarf, if he's alert,
Likelier hits the broader target!"

                'Up we stood accordingly.
As they handed me the weapon, such was my soul's thirst to try
Then and there conclusions with this bully, tread on and stamp
    out
Every spark of his existence, that,—crept close to, curled about
By that toying tempting teasing fool-forefinger's middle joint,—
Don't you guess?—the trigger yielded. Gone my chance! and at
    the point
Of such prime success moreover: scarce an inch above his head
Went my ball to hit the wainscot. He was living, I was dead.   140

'Up he marched in flaming triumph—'twas his right, mind!—
    up, within
Just an arm's length. "Now, my clerkling," chuckled Cocky with
    a grin
As the levelled piece quite touched me, "Now, Sir Counting-
    House, repeat
That expression which I told you proved bad manners! Did I
    cheat?"

' "Cheat you did, you knew you cheated, and, this moment,
    know as well.
As for me, my homely breeding bids you—fire and go to Hell!"

'Twice the muzzle touched my forehead. Heavy barrel, flurried
    wrist,°
Either spoils a steady lifting. Thrice: then, "Laugh at Hell who
    list,
I can't! God's no fable either. Did this boy's eye wink once? No!
There's no standing him and Hell and God all three against
    me,— so,   150
I did cheat!"

        'And down he threw the pistol, out rushed—by the door
Possibly, but, as for knowledge if by chimney, roof or floor,
He effected disappearance—I'll engage no glance was sent
That way by a single starer, such a blank astonishment
Swallowed up their senses: as for speaking—mute they stood as
    mice.

'Mute not long, though! Such reaction, such a hubbub in a trice!
"Rogue and rascal! Who'd have thought it? What's to be
    expected next,
When His Majesty's Commission serves a sharper as pretext
For... But where's the need of wasting time now? Nought
    requires delay:
Punishment the Service cries for: let disgrace be wiped away   160
Publicly, in good broad daylight! Resignation? No, indeed
Drum and fife must play the Rogue's March, rank and file be
    free to speed°
Tardy marching on the rogue's part by appliance in the rear
—Kicks administered shall right this wronged civilian,—never
    fear,
Mister Clive, for—though a clerk—you bore yourself—suppose
    we say—
Just as would beseem a soldier!"

                                ' "Gentlemen, attention—pray!
First, one word!"

                'I passed each speaker severally in review.
When I had precise their number, names and styles, and fully
    knew

Over whom my supervision thenceforth must extend,—why,
    then—

'"Some five minutes since, my life lay—as you all saw,
    gentlemen—   170
At the mercy of your friend there. Not a single voice was raised
In arrest of judgment, not one tongue—before my powder
    blazed—
Ventured 'Can it be the youngster blundered, really seemed to
    mark
Some irregular proceeding? We conjecture in the dark,
Guess at random,—still, for sake of fair play—what if for a
    freak,
In a fit of absence,—such things have been!—if our friend
    proved weak
—What's the phrase?—corrected fortune! Look into the case, at
    least!'
Who dared interpose between the altar's victim and the priest?
Yet he spared me! You eleven! Whosoever, all or each,
To the disadvantage of the man who spared me, utters speech   180
—To his face, behind his back,—that speaker has to do with me:
Me who promise, if positions change and mine the chance
    should be,
Not to imitate your friend and waive advantage!"

                                'Twenty-five
Years ago this matter happened: and 'tis certain,' added Clive,
'Never, to my knowledge, did Sir Cocky have a single breath
Breathed against him: lips were closed throughout his life, or
    since his death,
For if he be dead or living I can tell no more than you.
All I know is—Cocky had one chance more; how he used it,—
    grew
Out of such unlucky habits, or relapsed, and back again
Brought the late-ejected devil with a score more in his train,—   190
That's for you to judge. Reprieval I procured, at any rate.
Ugh—the memory of that minute's fear makes gooseflesh rise!
    Why prate
Longer? You've my story, there's your instance: fear I did, you
    see!'

'Well'—I hardly kept from laughing—'if I see it, thanks must be

Wholly to your Lordship's candour. Not that—in a common case—
When a bully caught at cheating thrusts a pistol in one's face,
I should underrate, believe me, such a trial to the nerve!
'Tis no joke, at one-and-twenty, for a youth to stand nor swerve.
Fear I naturally look for—unless, of all men alive,
I am forced to make exception when I come to Robert Clive.   200
Since at Arcot, Plassy, elsewhere, he and death—the whole world knows—
Came to somewhat closer quarters.'

                      Quarters? Had we come to blows,
Clive and I, you had not wondered—up he sprang so, out he rapped
Such a round of oaths—no matter! I'll endeavour to adapt
To our modern usage words he—well, 'twas friendly licence—flung
At me like so many fire-balls, fast as he could wag his tongue.

'You—a soldier? You—at Plassy? Yours the faculty to nick°
Instantaneously occasion when your foe, if lightning-quick,
—At his mercy, at his malice,—has you, through some stupid inch
Undefended in your bulwark? Thus laid open,—not to flinch   210
—That needs courage, you'll concede me. Then, look here! Suppose the man,
Checking his advance, his weapon still extended, not a span
Distant from my temple,—curse him!—quietly had bade me "There!
Keep your life, calumniator!—worthless life I freely spare:
Mine you freely would have taken—murdered me and my good fame
Both at once—and all the better! Go, and thank your own bad aim
Which permits me to forgive you!" What if, with such words as these,
He had cast away his weapon? How should I have borne me, please?
Nay, I'll spare you pains and tell you. This, and only this, remained—

Pick his weapon up and use it on myself. I so had gained   220
Sleep the earlier, leaving England probably to pay on still
Rent and taxes for half India, tenant at the Frenchman's will.'

'Such the turn,' said I, 'the matter takes with you? Then I abate
—No, by not one jot nor tittle,—of your act my estimate.
Fear—I wish I could detect there: courage fronts me, plain
    enough—
Call it desperation, madness—never mind! for here's in rough
Why, had mine been such a trial, fear had overcome disgrace.
True, disgrace were hard to bear: but such a rush against God's
    face
—None of that for me, Lord Plassy, since I go to church at
    times,
Say the creed my mother taught me! Many years in foreign
    climes   230
Rub some marks away—not all, though! We poor sinners reach
    life's brink,
Overlook what rolls beneath it, recklessly enough, but think
There's advantage in what's left us—ground to stand on, time to
    call
"Lord, have mercy!" ere we topple over—do not leap, that's all!'

Oh, he made no answer,—re-absorbed into his cloud. I caught
Something like 'Yes—courage: only fools will call it fear.'
    If aught
Comfort you, my great unhappy hero Clive, in that I heard,
Next week, how your own hand dealt you doom, and uttered just
    the word
'Fearfully courageous!'—this, be sure, and nothing else I
    groaned.
I'm no Clive, nor parson either: Clive's worst deed—we'll hope
    condoned.   240

Wanting is—what?
Summer redundant,°
Blueness abundant,
—Where is the blot?
Beamy the world, yet a blank all the same,
—Framework which waits for a picture to frame:
What of the leafage, what of the flower?
Roses embowering with nought they embower!
Come then, complete incompletion, O comer,°
Pant through the blueness, perfect the summer!   10
          Breathe but one breath
          Rose-beauty above,
          And all that was death
          Grows life, grows love,
               Grows love!

Donald

'Will you hear my story also,
     —Huge Sport, brave adventure in plenty?'
The boys were a band from Oxford,
     The oldest of whom was twenty.

The bothy we held carouse in°
     Was bright with fire and candle;
Tale followed tale like a merry-go-round
     Whereof Sport turned the handle.

In our eyes and noses—turf-smoke:
     In our ears a tune from the trivet,°   10
Whence 'Boiling, boiling,' the kettle sang,
     'And ready for fresh Glenlivet.'°

So, feat capped feat, with a vengeance:
   Truths, though,—the lads were loyal:
'Grouse, five score brace to the bag!
   Deer, ten hours' stalk of the Royal!'°

Of boasting, not one bit, boys!
   Only there seemed to settle
Somehow above your curly heads,
   —Plain through the singing kettle,   20

Palpable through the cloud,
   As each new-puffed Havanna
Rewarded the teller's well-told tale,—
   This vaunt 'To Sport—Hosanna!

'Hunt, fish, shoot,
   Would a man fulfil life's duty!
Not to the bodily frame alone
   Does Sport give strength and beauty,

'But character gains in—courage?
   Ay, Sir, and much beside it!   30
You don't sport, more's the pity:
   You soon would find, if you tried it,

'Good sportsman means good fellow,
   Sound-hearted he, to the centre;
Your mealy-mouthed mild milksops
   —There's where the rot can enter!

'There's where the dirt will breed,
   The shabbiness Sport would banish!
Oh no, Sir, no! In your honoured case
   All such objections vanish.   40

' 'Tis known how hard you studied:
   A Double-First—what, the jigger!°
Give me but half your Latin and Greek,
   I'll never again touch trigger!

'Still, tastes are tastes, allow me!
   Allow, too, where there's keenness
For Sport, there's little likelihood
   Of a man's displaying meanness!'

So, put on my mettle, I interposed.
   'Will you hear my story?' quoth I.
'Never mind how long since it happed,
   I sat, as we sit, in a bothy; 50

'With as merry a band of mates, too,
   Undergrads all on a level:
(One's a Bishop, one's gone to the Bench,
   And one's gone—well, to the Devil.)

'When, lo, a scratching and tapping!
   In hobbled a ghastly visitor.
Listen to just what he told us himself
   —No need of our playing inquisitor!' 60

Do you happen to know in Ross-shire
   Mount... Ben... but the name scarce matters:°
Of the naked fact I am sure enough,
   Though I clothe it in rags and tatters.

You may recognize Ben by description;
   Behind him—a moor's immenseness:
Up goes the middle mount of a range,
   Fringed with its firs in denseness.

Rimming the edge, its fir-fringe, mind!
   For an edge there is, though narrow;
From end to end of the range, a stripe 70
   Of path runs straight as an arrow.

And the mountaineer who takes that path
   Saves himself miles of journey
He has to plod if he crosses the moor
   Through heather, peat and burnie.°

But a mountaineer he needs must be,
   For, look you, right in the middle
Projects bluff Ben—with an end in *ich*—
   Why planted there, is a riddle: 80

Since all Ben's brothers little and big
   Keep rank, set shoulder to shoulder,
And only this burliest out must bulge
   Till it seems—to the beholder

From down in the gully,—as if Ben's breast
    To a sudden spike diminished,
Would signify to the boldest foot
    'All further passage finished!'

Yet the mountaineer who sidles on
    And on to the very bending,   90
Discovers, if heart and brain be proof,
    No necessary ending.

Foot up, foot down, to the turn abrupt
    Having trod, he, there arriving,
Finds—what he took for a point was breadth,
    A mercy of Nature's contriving.

So, he rounds what, when 'tis reached, proves straight,
    From one side gains the other:
The wee path widens—resume the march,
    And he foils you, Ben my brother!   100

But Donald—(that name, I hope, will do)—
    I wrong him if I call 'foiling'°
The tramp of the callant, whistling the while°
    As blithe as our kettle's boiling.

He had dared the danger from boyhood up,
    And now,—when perchance was waiting
A lass at the brig below,—'twixt mount°
    And moor would he stand debating?

Moreover this Donald was twenty-five,
    A glory of bone and muscle: 110
Did a fiend dispute the right of way,
    Donald would try a tussle.

Lightsomely marched he out of the broad
    On to the narrow and narrow;
A step more, rounding the angular rock,
    Reached the front straight as an arrow.

He stepped it, safe on the ledge he stood,
    When—whom found he full-facing?
What fellow in courage and wariness too,
    Had scouted ignoble pacing,   120

And left low safety to timid mates,
    And made for the dread dear danger,
And gained the height where—who could guess
    He would meet with a rival ranger?

'Twas a gold-red stag that stood and stared,
    Gigantic and magnific,
By the wonder—ay, and the peril—struck
    Intelligent and pacific:

For a red deer is no fallow deer
    Grown cowardly through park-feeding;   130
He batters you like a thunderbolt
    If you brave his haunts unheeding.

I doubt he could hardly perform *volte-face*
    Had valour advised discretion:
You may walk on a rope, but to turn on a rope
    No Blondin makes profession.°

Yet Donald must turn, would pride permit,
    Though pride ill brooks retiring:
Each eyed each—mute man, motionless beast—
    Less fearing than admiring.   140

These are the moments when quite new sense,
    To meet some need as novel,
Springs up in the brain: it inspired resource:
    —'Nor advance nor retreat but—grovel!'

And slowly, surely, never a whit
    Relaxing the steady tension
Of eye-stare which binds man to beast,—
    By an inch and inch declension,

Sank Donald sidewise down and down:
    Till flat, breast upwards, lying
At his six-foot length, no corpse more still,   150
    —'If he cross me! The trick's worth trying.'

Minutes were an eternity;
    But a new sense was created
In the stag's brain too; he resolves! Slow, sure,
    With eye-stare unabated,

Feelingly he extends a foot
   Which tastes the way ere it touches
Earth's solid and just escapes man's soft,
   Nor hold of the same unclutches   160

Till its fellow foot, light as a feather whisk,
   Lands itself no less finely:
So a mother removes a fly from the face
   Of her babe asleep supinely.

And now 'tis the haunch and hind foot's turn
   —That's hard: can the beast quite raise it?
Yes, traversing half the prostrate length,
   His hoof-tip does not graze it.

Just one more lift! But Donald, you see,
   Was sportsman first, man after: 170
A fancy lightened his caution through,
   —He well-nigh broke into laughter.

'It were nothing short of a miracle!
   Unrivalled, unexampled—
All sporting feats with this feat matched
   Were down and dead and trampled!'

The last of the legs as tenderly
   Follows the rest: or never
Or now is the time! His knife in reach,
   And his right-hand loose—how clever!   180

For this can stab up the stomach's soft,
   While the left-hand grasps the pastern.
A rise on the elbow, and—now's the time
   Or never: this turn's the last turn!

I shall dare to place myself by God
   Who scanned—for He does—each feature
Of the face thrown up in appeal to Him
   By the agonizing creature.

Nay, I hear plain words: 'Thy gift brings this!'
   Up he sprang, back he staggered,   190
Over he fell, and with him our friend
   —At following game no laggard.

Yet he was not dead when they picked next day
   From the gully's depth the wreck of him;
His fall had been stayed by the stag beneath
   Who cushioned and saved the neck of him

But the rest of his body—why, doctors said,
   Whatever could break was broken;
Legs, arms, ribs, all of him looked like a toast
   In a tumbler of port-wine soaken.   200

'That your life is left you, thank the stag!'
   Said they when—the slow cure ended—
They opened the hospital door, and thence
   —Strapped, spliced, main fractures mended,

And minor damage left wisely alone,—
   Like an old shoe clouted and cobbled,°
Out—what went in a Goliath well-nigh,—
   Some half of a David hobbled.

'You must ask an alms from house to house:
   Sell the stag's head for a bracket,°
With its grand twelve tines—I'd buy it myself—   210
   And use the skin for a jacket!'

He was wiser, made both head and hide
   His win-penny: hands and knees on,°
Would manage to crawl—poor crab—by the roads
   In the misty stalking-season.

And if he discovered a bothy like this,
   Why, harvest was sure: folk listened.
He told his tale to the lovers of Sport:
   Lips twitched, cheeks glowed, eyes glistened.   220

And when he had come to the close, and spread
   His spoils for the gazers' wonder,
With 'Gentlemen, here's the skull of the stag
   I was over, thank God, not under!'—

The company broke out in applause;
   'By Jingo, a lucky cripple!
Have a munch of grouse and a hunk of bread
   And a tug, besides, at our tipple!'

And 'There's my pay for your pluck!' cried This,
   'And mine for your jolly story!'   230
Cried That, while T'other—but he was drunk—
   Hiccupped 'A trump, a Tory!'°

I hope I gave twice as much as the rest;
   For, as Homer would say, 'within grate°
Though teeth kept tongue,' my whole soul growled
   'Rightly rewarded,—Ingrate!'

Ixion

High in the dome, suspended, of Hell, sad triumph, behold us!
   Here the revenge of a God, there the amends of a Man.
Whirling forever in torment, flesh once mortal, immortal
   Made—for a purpose of hate—able to die and revive,
Pays to the uttermost pang, then, newly for payment replenished,
   Doles out—old yet young—agonies ever afresh;
Whence the result above me: torment is bridged by a rainbow,—
   Tears, sweat, blood,—each spasm, ghastly once, glorified now.
Wrung, by the rush of the wheel ordained my place of reposing,
   Off in a sparklike spray,—flesh become vapour thro' pain,—   10
Flies the bestowment of Zeus, soul's vaunted bodily vesture,
   Made that his feats observed gain the approval of Man,—
Flesh that he fashioned with sense of the earth and the sky and
   the ocean,
   Framed should pierce to the star, fitted to pore on the
   plant,—
All, for a purpose of hate, re-framed, re-fashioned, re-fitted
   Till, consummate at length,—lo, the employment of sense!
Pain's mere minister now to the soul, once pledged to her
   pleasure—
   Soul, if untrammelled by flesh, unapprehensive of pain!
Body, professed soul's slave, which serving beguiled and
   betrayed her,
   Made things false seem true, cheated thro' eye and thro' ear,   20
Lured thus heart and brain to believe in the lying reported,—
   Spurn but the traitorous slave, uttermost atom, away,
What should obstruct soul's rush on the real, the only apparent?

Say I have erred,—how else? Was I Ixion or Zeus?
Foiled by my senses I dreamed; I doubtless awaken in wonder:
  This proves shine, that—shade? Good was the evil that
    seemed?
Shall I, with sight thus gained, by torture be taught I was blind
    once?
  Sisuphos, teaches thy stone—Tantalos, teaches thy thirst°
Aught which unaided sense, purged pure, less plainly demon-
    strates?
  No, for the past was dream: now that the dreamers awake,   30
Sisuphos scouts low fraud, and to Tantalos treason is folly.
  Ask of myself, whose form melts on the murderous wheel,
What is the sin which throe and throe prove sin to the sinner!°
  Say the false charge was true,—thus do I expiate, say,
Arrogant thought, word, deed,—mere man who conceited me
    godlike,°
  Sat beside Zeus, my friend—knelt before Heré, my love!
What were the need but of pitying power to touch and disperse it,
  Film-work—eye's and ear's—all the distraction of sense?
How should the soul not see, not hear,—perceive and as plainly
  Render, in thought, word, deed, back again truth—not a lie?   40
'Ay, but the pain is to punish thee!' Zeus, once more for a
    pastime,
  Play the familiar, the frank! Speak and have speech in return!
I was of Thessaly king, there ruled and a people obeyed me:
  Mine to establish the law, theirs to obey it or die:
Wherefore? Because of the good to the people, because of the
    honour
  Thence accruing to me, king, the king's law was supreme.
What of the weakling, the ignorant criminal? Not who, excuseless,
  Breaking my law braved death, knowing his deed and its due—
Nay, but the feeble and foolish, the poor transgressor, of purpose
  No whit more than a tree, born to erectness of bole,   50
Palm or plane or pine, we laud if lofty, columnar—
  Loathe if athwart, askew,—leave to the axe and the flame!
Where is the vision may penetrate earth and beholding acknow-
    ledge
  Just one pebble at root ruined the straightness of stem?
Whose fine vigilance follows the sapling, accounts for the failure,
  —Here blew wind, so it bent: there the snow lodged, so it
    broke?

Also the tooth of the beast, bird's bill, mere bite of the insect
　　Gnawed, gnarled, warped their worst: passive it lay to offence.
King—I was man, no more: what I recognized faulty I punished,
　　Laying it prone: be sure, more than a man had I proved,　　60
Watch and ward o'er the sapling at birthtime had saved it, nor
　　　simply
　　　Owned the distortion's excuse,—hindered it wholly: nay,
　　　　more—
Even a man, as I sat in my place to do judgment, and pallid
　　Criminals passing to doom shuddered away at my foot,
Could I have probed thro' the face to the heart, read plain a
　　　repentance,
　　　Crime confessed fools' play, virtue ascribed to the wise,
Had I not stayed the consignment to doom, not dealt the
　　　renewed ones
　　　Life to retraverse the past, light to retrieve the misdeed?
Thus had I done, and thus to have done much more it behoves
　　　thee,
　　　Zeus who madest man—flawless or faulty, thy work!　　70
What if the charge were true, as thou mouthest,—Ixion the
　　　cherished
　　　Minion of Zeus grew vain, vied with the godships and fell,
Forfeit thro' arrogance? Stranger! I clothed, with the grace of
　　　our human,
　　　Inhumanity—gods, natures I likened to ours.
Man among men I had borne me till gods forsooth must regard
　　　me
　　　—Nay, must approve, applaud, claim as a comrade at last.
Summoned to enter their circle, I sat—their equal, how other?
　　　Love should be absolute love, faith is in fulness or nought.
'I am thy friend, be mine!' smiled Zeus: 'If Heré attract thee,'
　　Blushed the imperial cheek, 'then—as thy heart may suggest!'　　80
Faith in me sprang to the faith, my love hailed love as its fellow,
　　　'Zeus, we are friends—how fast! Heré, my heart for thy
　　　　heart!'
Then broke smile into fury of frown, and the thunder of 'Hence,
　　　fool!'
　　　Then thro' the kiss laughed scorn 'Limbs or a cloud was to
　　　　clasp?'
Then from Olumpos to Erebos, then from the rapture to tor-
　　　ment,°

Then from the fellow of gods—misery's mate, to the man!
—Man henceforth and forever, who lent from the glow of his
    nature
    Warmth to the cold, with light coloured the black and the
    blank.
So did a man conceive of your passion, you passion-protesters!
    So did he trust, so love—being the truth of your lie!   90
You to aspire to be Man! Man made you who vainly would ape
    him:
    You are the hollowness, he—filling you, falsifies void.
Even as—witness the emblem, Hell's sad triumph suspended,
    Born of my tears, sweat, blood—bursting to vapour above—
Arching my torment, an iris ghostlike startles the darkness,°
    Cold white—jewelry quenched—justifies, glorifies pain.
Strive, mankind, through strife endure through endless
    obstruction,
    Stage after stage, each rise marred by as certain a fall!
Baffled forever—yet never so baffled but, e'en in the baffling,
    When Man's strength proves weak, checked in the body or
    soul—   100
Whatsoever the medium, flesh or essence,—Ixion's
    Made for a purpose of hate,—clothing the entity Thou,
—Medium whence that entity strives for the Not-Thou beyond
    it,
    Fire elemental, free, frame unencumbered, the All,—
Never so baffled but—when, on the verge of an alien existence,
    Heartened to press, by pangs burst to the infinite Pure,
Nothing is reached but the ancient weakness still that arrests
    strength,
    Circumambient still, still the poor human array,
Pride and revenge and hate and cruelty—all it has burst through,
    Thought to escape,—fresh formed, found in the fashion it
    fled,—   110
Never so baffled but—when Man pays the price of endeavour,
    Thunderstruck, downthrust, Tartaros-doomed to the
    wheel,— °
Then, ay, then, from the tears and sweat and blood of his
    torment,
    E'en from the triumph of Hell, up let him look and rejoice!
What is the influence, high o'er Hell, that turns to a rapture
    Pain—and despair's murk mists blends in a rainbow of hope?

What is beyond the obstruction, stage by stage tho' it baffle?
  Back must I fall, confess 'Ever the weakness I fled'?
No, for beyond, far, far is a Purity all-unobstructed!
  Zeus was Zeus—not Man: wrecked by his weakness, I whirl.   120
Out of the wreck I rise—past Zeus to the Potency o'er him!
  I—to have hailed him my friend! I—to have clasped her—my
    love!
Pallid birth of my pain,—where light, where light is, aspiring
  Thither I rise, whilst thou—Zeus, keep the godship and sink!

Never the Time and the Place

Never the time and the place
  And the loved one all together!
This path—how soft to pace!
  This May—what magic weather!
Where is the loved one's face?
In a dream that loved one's face meets mine,
  But the house is narrow, the place is bleak
Where, outside, rain and wind combine
  With a furtive ear, if I strive to speak,
  With a hostile eye at my flushing cheek,   10
With a malice that marks each word, each sign!
O enemy sly and serpentine,
  Uncoil thee from the waking man!
      Do I hold the Past
      Thus firm and fast
  Yet doubt if the Future hold I can?
This path so soft to pace shall lead
Thro' the magic of May to herself indeed!
Or narrow if needs the house must be,
Outside are the storms and strangers: we—   20
Oh, close, safe, warm sleep I and she,
  —I and she!

Prologue

Pray, Reader, have you eaten ortolans°
    Ever in Italy?
Recall how cooks there cook them: for my plan's
    To—Lyre with Spit ally.
They pluck the birds,—some dozen luscious lumps,
    Or more or fewer,—
Then roast them, heads by heads and rumps by rumps,
    Stuck on a skewer.
But first,—and here's the point I fain would press,—
    Don't think I'm tattling!—   10
They interpose, to curb its lusciousness,
    —What, 'twixt each fatling?°
First comes plain bread, crisp, brown, a toasted square:
    Then, a strong sage-leaf:
(So we find books with flowers dried here and there
    Lest leaf engage leaf.)°
First, food—then, piquancy—and last of all
    Follows the thirdling:
Through wholesome hard, sharp soft, your tooth must bite
    Ere reach the birdling.   20
Now, were there only crust to crunch, you'd wince:
    Unpalatable!
Sage-leaf is bitter-pungent—so's a quince:
    Eat each who's able!
But through all three bite boldly—lo, the gust!
    Flavour—no fixture—
Flies, permeating flesh and leaf and crust
    In fine admixture.
So with your meal, my poem: masticate
    Sense, sight and song there!   30
Digest these, and I praise your peptics' state,°

    Nothing found wrong there.
Whence springs my illustration who can tell?
    —The more surprising
That here eggs, milk, cheese, fruit suffice so well
    For gormandizing.
A fancy-freak by contrast born of thee,
    Delightful Gressoney!°
Who laughest 'Take what is, trust what may be!'
    That's Life's true lesson,—eh?   40

So, the head aches and the limbs are faint!
    Flesh is a burthen—even to you!
Can I force a smile with a fancy quaint?
    Why are my ailments none or few?

In the soul of me sits sluggishness:
    Body so strong and will so weak!
The slave stands fit for the labour—yes,
    But the master's mandate is still to seek.

You, now—what if the outside clay
    Helped, not hindered the inside flame?   10
My dim to-morrow—your plain to-day,
    Yours the achievement, mine the aim?

So were it rightly, so shall it be!
    Only, while earth we pace together
For the purpose apportioned you and me,
    Closer we tread for a common tether.

You shall sigh 'Wait for his sluggish soul!
    Shame he should lag, not lamed as I!'
May not I smile 'Ungained her goal:
    Body may reach her—by-and-by?'   20

Verse-making was least of my virtues: I viewed with despair
Wealth that never yet was but might be—all that verse-making
    were

If the life would but lengthen to wish, let the mind be laid bare.
So I said 'To do little is bad, to do nothing is worse'—
　　And made verse.

Love-making,—how simple a matter! No depths to explore,
No heights in a life to ascend! No disheartening Before,
No affrighting Hereafter,—love now will be love evermore.
So I felt 'To keep silence were folly:'—all language above,
　　I made love.

from PARLEYINGS WITH CERTAIN PEOPLE OF IMPORTANCE IN THEIR DAY (1887)

Apollo and the Fates

A Prologue

(Hymn. in Mercurium, v. 559. Eumenides, vv. 693–4, 697–8.
Alcestis, vv. 12, 33)

Apollo	[*From above.*

Flame at my footfall, Parnassus! Apollo,°
  Breaking a-blaze on thy topmost peak,
Burns thence, down to the depths—dread hollow—
  Haunt of the Dire Ones. Haste! They wreak°
Wrath on Admetus whose respite I seek.

The Fates	[*Below. Darkness.*

Dragonwise couched in the womb of our Mother,°
  Coiled at thy nourishing heart's core, Night!
Dominant Dreads, we, one by the other,
  Deal to each mortal his dole of light
On earth—the upper, the glad, the bright.   10

Clotho

Even so: thus from my loaded spindle
  Plucking a pinch of the fleece, lo, 'Birth'
Brays from my bronze lip: life I kindle:
  Look, 'tis a man! go, measure on earth
The minute thy portion, whatever its worth!

Lachesis

Woe-purfled, weal-prankt,—if it speed, if it linger,—°
   Life's substance and show are determined by me,
Who, meting out, mixing with sure thumb and finger,
   Lead life the due length: is all smoothness and glee,
All tangle and grief? Take the lot, my decree!   20

Atropos

—Which I make an end of: the smooth as the tangled
   My shears cut asunder: each snap shrieks 'One more
Mortal makes sport for us Moirai who dangled°
   The puppet grotesquely till earth's solid floor
Proved film he fell through, lost in Nought as before.'

Clotho

I spin thee a thread. Live, Admetus! Produce him!

Lachesis

   Go,—brave, wise, good, happy! Now chequer the thread!
He is slaved for, yet loved by a god. I unloose him
   A goddess-sent plague. He has conquered, is wed,°
Men crown him, he stands at the height,—

Atropos

He is...

Apollo   [*Entering: Light.*
                         'Dead?'   30

Nay, swart spinsters! So I surprise you
   Making and marring the fortunes of Man?
Huddling—no marvel, your enemy eyes you—
   Head by head bat-like, blots under the ban
Of daylight earth's blessing since time began!

The Fates

Back to thy blest earth, prying Apollo!
   Shaft upon shaft transpierce with thy beams
Earth to the centre,—spare but this hollow

Hewn out of Night's heart, where our mystery seems
Mewed from day's malice: wake earth from her dreams!   40

Apollo

Crones, 'tis your dusk selves I startle from slumber:
    Day's god deposes you—queens Night-crowned!°
—Plying your trade in a world ye encumber,
    Fashioning Man's web of life—spun, wound,
Left the length ye allot till a clip strews the ground!

Behold I bid truce to your doleful amusement—
    Annulled by a sunbeam!

The Fates

                                                    Boy, are not we peers?

Apollo

You with the spindle grant birth: whose inducement
    But yours—with the niggardly digits—endears
To mankind chance and change, good and evil? Your shears ...   50

Atropos

Ay, mine end the conflict: so much is no fable.
    We spin, draw to length, cut asunder: what then?
So it was, and so is, and so shall be: art able
    To alter life's law for ephemeral men?

Apollo

Nor able nor willing. To threescore and ten

Extend but the years of Admetus! Disaster
    O'ertook me, and, banished by Zeus, I became
A servant to one who forbore me though master:°
    True lovers were we. Discontinue your game,
Let him live whom I loved, then hate on, all the same!   60

The Fates

And what if we granted—law flouter, use trampler—
    His life at the suit of an upstart? Judge, thou—
Of joy were it fuller, of span because ampler?

For love's sake, not hate's, end Admetus—ay, now—
Not a gray hair on head, nor a wrinkle on brow!

For, boy, 'tis illusion: from thee comes a glimmer
   Transforming to beauty life blank at the best.
Withdraw—and how looks life at worst, when to shimmer
   Succeeds the sure shade, and Man's lot frowns—confessed
Mere blackness chance-brightened? Whereof shall attest   70

The truth this same mortal, the darling thou stylest,
   Whom love would advantage,—eke out, day by day,
A life which 'tis solely thyself reconcilest
   Thy friend to endure,—life with hope: take away
Hope's gleam from Admetus, he spurns it. For, say—

What's infancy? Ignorance, idleness, mischief:
   Youth ripens to arrogance, foolishness, greed:
Age—impotence, churlishness, rancour: call *this* chief
   Of boons for thy loved one? Much rather bid speed
Our function, let live whom thou hatest indeed!   80

Persuade thee, bright boy-thing! Our eld be instructive!

Apollo

   And certes youth owns the experience of age.°
Ye hold then, grave seniors, my beams are productive
   —They solely—of good that's mere semblance, engage
Man's eye—gilding evil, Man's true heritage?

The Fates

So, even so! From without,—at due distance
   If viewed,—set a-sparkle, reflecting thy rays,—
Life mimics the sun: but withdraw such assistance,
   The counterfeit goes, the reality stays—
An ice-ball disguised as a fire-orb.

Apollo

                What craze   90

Possesses the fool then whose fancy conceits him°
   As happy?

The Fates

Man happy?

Apollo

                                 If otherwise—solve

This doubt which besets me! What friend ever greets him
    Except with 'Live long as the seasons revolve,'
Not 'Death to thee straightway'? Your doctrines absolve

Such hailing from hatred: yet Man should know best.
    He talks it, and glibly, as life were a load
Man fain would be rid off: when put to the test,
    He whines 'Let it lie, leave me trudging the road
That is rugged so far, but methinks...'

The Fates

                           Ay, 'tis owed   100

To that glamour of thine, he bethinks him 'Once past
    The stony, some patch, nay, a smoothness of sward
Awaits my tired foot: life turns easy at last'—
    Thy largess so lures him, he looks for reward
Of the labour and sorrow.

Apollo

                      It seems, then—debarred

Of illusion—(I needs must acknowledge the plea)
    Man desponds and despairs. Yet,—still further to draw
Due profit from counsel,—suppose there should be
    Some power in himself, some compensative law
By virtue of which, independently...   110

The Fates

                       Faugh!

Strength hid in the weakling!
                     What bowl-shape hast there,
    Thus laughingly proffered? A gift to our shrine?
Thanks—worsted in argument! Not so? Declare
    Its purpose!

Apollo

I proffer earth's product, not mine.
Taste, try, and approve Man's invention of—WINE!

The Fates

We feeding suck honeycombs.

Apollo

                    Sustenance meagre!
Such fare breeds the fumes that show all things amiss.
Quaff wine,—how the spirits rise nimble and eager,
    Unscale the dim eyes! To Man's cup grant one kiss
Of your lip, then allow—no enchantment like this!   120

Clotho

Unhook wings, unhood brows! Dost hearken?

Lachesis

                              I listen:
I see—smell the food these fond mortals prefer
    To our feast, the bee's bounty!

Atropos

                    The thing leaps! But—glisten
Its best, I withstand it—unless all concur
In adventure so novel.

Apollo

Ye drink?

The Fates

                    We demur.

Apollo

Sweet Trine, be indulgent nor scout the contrivance
    Of Man—Bacchus-prompted! The juice, I uphold,°
Illuminates gloom without sunny connivance,

Turns fear into hope and makes cowardice bold,—
Touching all that is leadlike in life turns it gold!   130

The Fates

Faith foolish as false!

Apollo

But essay it, soft sisters!
Then mock as ye may. Lift the chalice to lip!
Good: thou next—and thou! Seems the web, to you twisters
    Of life's yarn, so worthless?

Clotho

Who guessed that one sip
Would impart such a lightness of limb?

Lachesis

I could skip

In a trice from the pied to the plain in my woof!
    What parts each from either? A hair's breadth, no inch.
Once learn the right method of stepping aloof,
    Though on black next foot falls, firm I fix it, nor flinch,
—Such my trust white succeeds!   140

Atropos

One could live—at a pinch!

Apollo

What beldames? Earth's yield, by Man's skill, can effect
    Such a cure of sick sense that ye spy the relation
Of evil to good? But drink deeper, correct
    Blear sight more convincingly still! Take your station
Beside me, drain dregs! Now for edification!

Whose gift have ye gulped? Thank not me but my brother,
    Blithe Bacchus, our youngest of godships. 'Twas he
Found all boons to all men, by one god or other
    Already conceded, so judged there must be
New guerdon to grace the new advent, you see!   150

Else how would a claim to Man's homage arise?
  The plan lay arranged of his mixed woe and weal,
So disposed—such Zeus' will—with design to make wise
  The witless—that false things were mingled with real,
Good with bad: such the lot whereto law set the seal.

Now, human of instinct—since Semele's son,°
  Yet minded divinely—since fathered by Zeus,
With nought Bacchus tampered, undid not things done,
  Owned wisdom anterior, would spare wont and use,
Yet change—without shock to old rule—introduce.   160

Regard how your cavern from crag-tip to base
  Frowns sheer, height and depth adamantine, one death!
I rouse with a beam the whole rampart, displace
  No splinter—yet see how my flambeau, beneath°
And above, bids this gem wink, that crystal unsheath!

Withdraw beam—disclosure once more Night forbids you
  Of spangle and sparkle—Day's chance-gift, surmised
Rock's permanent birthright: my potency rids you
  No longer of darkness, yet light—recognized—
Proves darkness a mask: day lives on though disguised.   170

If Bacchus by wine's aid avail so to fluster
  Your sense, that life's fact grows from adverse and thwart
To helpful and kindly by means of a cluster—°
  Mere hand-squeeze, earth's nature sublimed by Man's art—
Shall Bacchus claim thanks wherein Zeus has no part?

Zeus—wisdom anterior? No, maids, be admonished!
  If morn's touch at base worked such wonders, much more
Had noontide in absolute glory astonished
  Your den, filled a-top to o'erflowing. I pour
No such mad confusion. 'Tis Man's to explore   180

Up and down, inch by inch, with the taper his reason:
  No torch, it suffices—held deftly and straight.
Eyes, purblind at first, feel their way in due season,
  Accept good with bad, till unseemly debate
Turns concord—despair, acquiescence in fate.

Who works this but Zeus? Are not instinct and impulse,
  Not concept and incept his work through Man's soul

On Man's sense? Just as wine ere it reach brain must brim pulse,
   Zeus' flash stings the mind that speeds body to goal,
Bids pause at no part but press on, reach the whole.   190

For petty and poor is the part ye envisage
   When—(quaff away, cummers!)—ye view, last and first,°
As evil Man's earthly existence. Come! *Is* age,
   Is infancy—manhood—so uninterspersed
With good—some faint sprinkle?

Clotho

                I'd speak if I durst.

Apollo

Draughts dregward loose tongue-tie.

Lachesis

                I'd see, did no web
Set eyes somehow winking.

Apollo

                Drains-deep lies their purge
—True collyrium!

Atropos

            Words, surging at high-tide, soon ebb°
From starved ears.

Apollo

   Drink but down to the source, they resurge.
Join hands! Yours and yours too! A dance or a dirge?   200

Chorus

Quashed be our quarrel! Sourly and smilingly,
   Bare and gowned, bleached limbs and browned,
Drive we a dance, three and one, reconcilingly,
   Thanks to the cup where dissension is drowned,
Defeat proves triumphant and slavery crowned.

Infancy? What if the rose-streak of morning
   Pale and depart in a passion of tears?
Once to have hoped is no matter for scorning!
   Love once—e'en love's disappointment endears!
A minute's success pays the failure of years.   210

Manhood—the actual? Nay, praise the potential!
   (Bound upon bound, foot it around!)
What *is*? No, what *may* be—sing! that's Man's essential!
   (Ramp, tramp, stamp and compound
Fancy with fact—the lost secret is found!)

Age? Why, fear ends there: the contest concluded,
   Man *did* live his life, *did* escape from the fray:
Not scratchless but unscathed, he somehow eluded
   Each blow fortune dealt him, and conquers to-day:
To-morrow—new chance and fresh strength,—might we say?   220

Laud then Man's life—no defeat but a triumph!
               [*Explosion from the earth's centre.*

Clotho

Ha, loose hands!

Lachesis

I reel in a swound.°

Atropos

Horror yawns under me, while from on high—humph!
   Lightnings astound, thunders resound,
Vault-roof reverberates, groans the ground!   [*Silence.*

Apollo

I acknowledge.

The Fates

    Hence, trickster! Straight sobered are we!
  The portent assures 'twas our tongue spoke the truth,
Not thine. While the vapour encompassed us three
  We conceived and bore knowledge—a bantling uncouth,°
Old brains shudder back from: so—take it, rash youth!
                    230

Lick the lump into shape till a cry comes!

Apollo

I hear.

The Fates

Dumb music, dead eloquence! Say it, or sing!
  What was quickened in us and thee also?

Apollo

I fear.

The Fates

Half female, half male—go, ambiguous thing!
While we speak—perchance sputter—pick up what we fling!

Known yet ignored, nor divined nor unguessed,
  Such is Man's law of life. Do we strive to declare
What is ill, what is good in our spinning? Worst, best,
  Change hues of a sudden: now here and now there
Flits the sign which decides: all about yet nowhere.   240

'Tis willed so,—that Man's life be lived, first to last,
  Up and down, through and through,—not in portions, forsooth,
To pick and to choose from. Our shuttles fly fast,
  Weave living, not life sole and whole: as age—youth,
So death completes living, shows life in its truth.

Man learningly lives: till death helps him—no lore!
  It is doom and must be. Dost submit?

Apollo

I assent—
Concede but Admetus! So much if no more
  Of my prayer grant as peace-pledge! Be gracious though,
      blent,
Good and ill, love and hate streak your life-gift!

The Fates

Content!   250

Such boon we accord in due measure. Life's term
  We lengthen should any be moved for love's sake

To forego life's fulfilment, renounce in the germ
   Fruit mature—bliss or woe—either infinite. Take
Or leave thy friend's lot: on his head be the stake!

Apollo

On mine, griesly gammers! Admetus, I know thee!°
   Thou prizest the right these unwittingly give
Thy subjects to rush, pay obedience they owe thee!
   Importunate one with another they strive
For the glory to die that their king may survive.   260

Friends rush: and who first in all Pheræ appears°
   But thy father to serve as thy substitute?

Clotho

                  Bah!

Apollo

Ye wince? Then his mother, well-stricken in years,
Advances her claim—or his wife—

Lachesis

              Tra-la-la!

Apollo

But he spurns the exchange, rather dies!

Atropos

             Ha, ha, ha!
          [*Apollo ascends. Darkness.*

With Christopher Smart

I

It seems as if . . . or did the actual chance
Startle me and perplex? Let truth be said!
How might this happen? Dreaming, blindfold led

By visionary hand, did soul's advance
Precede my body's, gain inheritance
Of fact by fancy—so that when I read
At length with waking eyes your Song, instead
Of mere bewilderment, with me first glance
Was but full recognition that in trance
Or merely thought's adventure some old day   10
Of dim and done-with boyishness, or—well,
Why might it not have been, the miracle
Broke on me as I took my sober way
Through veritable regions of our earth
And made discovery, many a wondrous one?

II

Anyhow, fact or fancy, such its birth:
I was exploring some huge house, had gone
Through room and room complacently, no dearth
Anywhere of the signs of decent taste,
Adequate culture: wealth had run to waste   20
Nowise, nor penury was proved by stint:
All showed the Golden Mean without a hint
Of brave extravagance that breaks the rule.
The master of the mansion was no fool
Assuredly, no genius just as sure!
Safe mediocrity had scorned the lure
Of now too much and now too little cost,
And satisfied me sight was never lost
Of moderate design's accomplishment
In calm completeness. On and on I went,   30
With no more hope than fear of what came next,
Till lo, I push a door, sudden uplift
A hanging, enter, chance upon a shift
Indeed of scene! So—thus it is thou deck'st,
High heaven, our low earth's brick-and-mortar work?

III

It was the Chapel. That a star, from murk
Which hid, should flashingly emerge at last,
Were small surprise: but from broad day I passed
Into a presence that turned shine to shade.

There fronted me the Rafael Mother-Maid,°   40
Never to whom knelt votarist in shrine
By Nature's bounty helped, by Art's divine
More varied—beauty with magnificence—
Than this: from floor to roof one evidence
Of how far earth may rival heaven. No niche
Where glory was not prisoned to enrich
Man's gaze with gold and gems, no space but glowed
With colour, gleamed with carving—hues which owed
Their outburst to a brush the painter fed
With rainbow-substance—rare shapes never wed   50
To actual flesh and blood, which, brain-born once,
Became the sculptor's dowry, Art's response
To earth's despair. And all seemed old yet new:
Youth,—in the marble's curve, the canvas' hue,
Apparent,—wanted not the crowning thrill
Of age the consecrator. Hands long still
Had worked here—could it be, what lent them skill
Retained a power to supervise, protect,
Enforce new lessons with the old, connect
Our life with theirs? No merely modern touch   60
Told me that here the artist, doing much,
Elsewhere did more, perchance does better, lives—
So needs must learn.

IV

                              Well, these provocatives
Having fulfilled their office, forth I went
Big with anticipation—well-nigh fear—
Of what next room and next for startled eyes
Might have in store, surprise beyond surprise.
Next room and next and next—what followed here?
Why, nothing! not one object to arrest
My passage—everywhere too manifest   70
The previous decent null and void of best
And worst, mere ordinary right and fit,
Calm commonplace which neither missed, nor hit
Inch-high, inch-low, the placid mark proposed.

V

Armed with this instance, have I diagnosed
Your case, my Christopher? The man was sound
And sane at starting: all at once the ground
Gave way beneath his step, a certain smoke
Curled up and caught him, or perhaps down broke
A fireball wrapping flesh and spirit both   80
In conflagration. Then—as heaven were loth
To linger—let earth understand too well
How heaven at need can operate—off fell
The flame-robe, and the untransfigured man
Resumed sobriety,—as he began,
So did he end nor alter pace, not he!

VI

Now, what I fain would know is—could it be
That he—whoe'er he was that furnished forth
The Chapel, making thus, from South to North,°
Rafael touch Leighton, Michelagnolo   90
Join Watts, was found but once combining so°
The elder and the younger, taking stand
On Art's supreme,—or that yourself who sang°
A Song where flute-breath silvers trumpet-clang,°
And stations you for once on either hand
With Milton and with Keats, empowered to claim°
Affinity on just one point—(or blame
Or praise my judgment, thus it fronts you full)—
How came it you resume the void and null,
Subside to insignificance,—live, die   100
—Proved plainly two mere mortals who drew nigh
One moment—that, to Art's best hierarchy,
This, to the superhuman poet-pair?
What if, in one point only, then and there
The otherwise all-unapproachable
Allowed impingement? Does the sphere pretend
To span the cube's breadth, cover end to end
The plane with its embrace? No, surely! Still,
Contact is contact, sphere's touch no whit less
Than cube's superimposure. Such success   110
Befell Smart only out of throngs between

Milton and Keats that donned the singing-dress—
Smart, solely of such songmen, pierced the screen
'Twixt thing and word, lit language straight from soul,—
Left no fine film-flake on the naked coal
Live from the censer—shapely or uncouth,
Fire-suffused through and through, one blaze of truth
Undeadened by a lie,—(you have my mind)—
For, think! this blaze outleapt with black behind
And blank before, when Hayley and the rest...°   120
But let the dead successors worst and best
Bury their dead: with life be my concern—
Yours with the fire-flame: what I fain would learn
Is just—(suppose me haply ignorant
Down to the common knowledge, doctors vaunt)
Just this—why only once the fire-flame was:
No matter if the marvel came to pass
The way folk judged—if power too long suppressed
Broke loose and maddened, as the vulgar guessed,
Or simply brain-disorder (doctors said)   130
A turmoil of the particles disturbed
Brain's workaday performance in your head,
Spurred spirit to wild action health had curbed:
And so verse issued in a cataract
Whence prose, before and after, unperturbed
Was wont to wend its way. Concede the fact
That here a poet was who always could—
Never before did—never after would—
Achieve the feat: how were such fact explained?

VII

Was it that when, by rarest chance, there fell   140
Disguise from Nature, so that Truth remained
Naked, and whoso saw for once could tell
Us others of her majesty and might
In large, her lovelinesses infinite
In little,—straight you used the power wherewith
Sense, penetrating as through rind to pith
Each object, thoroughly revealed might view
And comprehend the old things thus made new,
So that while eye saw, soul to tongue could trust
Thing which struck word out, and once more adjust°   150

Real vision to right language, till heaven's vault
Pompous with sunset, storm-stirred sea's assault
On the swilled rock-ridge, earth's embosomed brood°
Of tree and flower and weed, with all the life
That flies or swims or crawls, in peace or strife,
Above, below,—each had its note and name
For Man to know by,—Man who, now—the same
As erst in Eden, needs that all he sees
Be named him ere he note by what degrees°
Of strength and beauty to its end Design   160
Ever thus operates—(your thought and mine,
No matter for the many dissident)—
So did you sing your Song, so truth found vent
In words for once with you?

VIII

                                 Then—back was furled
The robe thus thrown aside, and straight the world
Darkened into the old oft-catalogued
Repository of things that sky, wave, land,
Or show or hide, clear late, accretion-clogged
Now, just as long ago, by tellings and
Re-tellings to satiety, which strike   170
Muffled upon the ear's drum. Very like
None was so startled as yourself when friends
Came, hailed your fast-returning wits: 'Health mends
Importantly, for—to be plain with you—
This scribble on the wall was done—in lieu
Of pen and paper—with—ha, ha!—your key
Denting it on the wainscot! Do you see
How wise our caution was? Thus much we stopped
Of babble that had else grown print: and lopped
From your trim bay-tree this unsightly bough—°   180
Smart's who translated Horace! Write us now' . . .°
Why, what Smart did write—never afterward
One line to show that he, who paced the sward,°
Had reached the zenith from his madhouse cell.

IX

Was it because you judged (I know full well
You never had the fancy)—judged—as some—

That who makes poetry must reproduce
Thus ever and thus only, as they come,
Each strength, each beauty, everywhere diffuse
Throughout creation, so that eye and ear,   190
Seeing and hearing, straight shall recognize,
At touch of just a trait, the strength appear,—
Suggested by a line's lapse see arise
All evident the beauty,—fresh surprise
Startling at fresh achievement? 'So, indeed,
Wallows the whale's bulk in the waste of brine,
Nor otherwise its feather-tufts make fine
Wild Virgin's Bower when stars faint off to seed!'
(My prose—your poetry I dare not give,
Purpling too much my mere grey argument.)°   200
—Was it because you judged—when fugitive
Was glory found, and wholly gone and spent
Such power of startling up deaf ear, blind eye,
At truth's appearance,—that you humbly bent
The head and, bidding vivid work good-bye,
Doffed lyric dress and trod the world once more
A drab-clothed decent proseman as before?
Strengths, beauties, by one word's flash thus laid bare
—That was effectual service: made aware
Of strengths and beauties, Man but hears the text,°   210
Awaits your teaching. Nature? What comes next?
Why all the strength and beauty?—to be shown
Thus in one word's flash, thenceforth let alone
By Man who needs must deal with aught that's known
Never so lately and so little? Friend,
First give us knowledge, then appoint its use!
Strength, beauty are the means: ignore their end?
As well you stopped at proving how profuse
Stones, sticks, nay stubble lie to left and right
Ready to help the builder,—careless quite   220
If he should take, or leave the same to strew
Earth idly,—as by word's flash bring in view
Strength, beauty, then bid who beholds the same
Go on beholding. Why gains unemployed?
Nature was made to be by Man enjoyed
First; followed duly by enjoyment's fruit,
Instruction—haply leaving joy behind:

And you, the instructor, would you slack pursuit
Of the main prize, as poet help mankind
Just to enjoy, there leave them? Play the fool,   230
Abjuring a superior privilege?
Please simply when your function is to rule—°
By thought incite to deed? From edge to edge
Of earth's round, strength and beauty everywhere
Pullulate—and must you particularize°
All, each and every apparition? Spare
Yourself and us the trouble! Ears and eyes
Want so much strength and beauty, and no less
Nor more, to learn life's lesson by. Oh, yes—
The other method's favoured in our day!   240
The end ere the beginning: as you may,
Master the heavens before you study earth,
Make you familiar with the meteor's birth
Ere you descend to scrutinize the rose!
I say, o'erstep no least one of the rows
That lead man from the bottom where he plants
Foot first of all, to life's last ladder-top:
Arrived there, vain enough will seem the vaunts
Of those who say—'We scale the skies, then drop
To earth—to find, how all things there are loth   250
To answer heavenly law: we understand
The meteor's course, and lo, the rose's growth—
How other than should be by law's command!'
Would not you tell such—'Friends, beware lest fume
Offuscate sense: learn earth first ere presume°
To teach heaven legislation. Law must be
Active in earth or nowhere: earth you see,—
Or there or not at all, Will, Power and Love
Admit discovery,—as below, above
Seek next law's confirmation! But reverse   260
The order, where's the wonder things grow worse
Than, by the law your fancy formulates,
They should be? Cease from anger at the fates
Which thwart themselves so madly. Live and learn,
Not first learn and then live, is our concern.'

ASOLANDO (1889)

Prologue

'The Poet's age is sad: for why?
   In youth, the natural world could show
No common object but his eye
   At once involved with alien glow—
His own soul's iris-bow.°

'And now a flower is just a flower:
   Man, bird, beast are but beast, bird, man—
Simply themselves, uncinct by dower
   Of dyes which, when life's day began,°
Round each in glory ran.'°   10

Friend, did you need an optic glass,
   Which were your choice? A lens to drape
In ruby, emerald, chrysopras,°
   Each object—or reveal its shape
Clear outlined, past escape,

The naked very thing?—so clear
   That, when you had the chance to gaze,
You found its inmost self appear
   Through outer seeming—truth ablaze,
Not falsehood's fancy-haze?   20

How many a year, my Asolo,°
   Since—one step just from sea to land—
I found you, loved yet feared you so—
   For natural objects seemed to stand
Palpably fire-clothed! No—

No mastery of mine o'er these!
   Terror with beauty, like the Bush
Burning but unconsumed. Bend knees,°
   Drop eyes to earthward! Language? Tush!
Silence 'tis awe decrees.   30

And now? The lambent flame is—where?
  Lost from the naked world: earth, sky,
Hill, vale, tree, flower,—Italia's rare
  O'er-running beauty crowds the eye—
But flame? The Bush is bare.

Hill, vale, tree, flower—they stand distinct,
  Nature to know and name. What then?
A Voice spoke thence which straight unlinked
  Fancy from fact: see, all's in ken:°
Has once my eyelid winked?   40

No, for the purged ear apprehends
  Earth's import, not the eye late dazed:
The Voice said 'Call my works thy friends!
  At Nature dost thou shrink amazed?
God is it who transcends.'

                                        ASOLO: *Sept.* 6, 1889.

Bad Dreams I

Last night I saw you in my sleep:
  And how your charm of face was changed!
I asked 'Some love, some faith you keep?'
  You answered 'Faith gone, love estranged.'

Whereat I woke—a twofold bliss:
  Waking was one, but next there came
This other: 'Though I felt, for this,°
  My heart break, I loved on the same.'°

Bad Dreams II

You in the flesh and here—
  Your very self! Now, wait!   10
One word! May I hope or fear?
  Must I speak in love or hate?
Stay while I ruminate!

The fact and each circumstance
    Dare you disown? Not you!
That vast dome, that huge dance,
    And the gloom which overgrew
A—possibly festive crew!

For why should men dance at all—
    Why women—a crowd of both— 20
Unless they are gay? Strange ball—
    Hands and feet plighting troth,
Yet partners enforced and loth!

Of who danced there, no shape
    Did I recognize: thwart, perverse,°
Each grasped each, past escape
    In a whirl or weary or worse:
Man's sneer met woman's curse,

While he and she toiled as if
    Their guardian set galley-slaves 30
To supple chained limbs grown stiff:
    Unmanacled trulls and knaves—°
The lash for who misbehaves!

And a gloom was, all the while,
    Deeper and deeper yet
O'ergrowing the rank and file
    Of that army of haters—set
To mimic love's fever-fret.

By the wall-side close I crept,
    Avoiding the livid maze, 40
And, safely so far, outstepped
    On a chamber—a chapel, says
My memory or betrays—

Closet-like, kept aloof
    From unseemly witnessing
What sport made floor and roof
    Of the Devil's palace ring
While his Damned amused their king.

Ay, for a low lamp burned,
    And a silence lay about 50
What I, in the midst, discerned

Though dimly till, past doubt,
'Twas a sort of throne stood out—

High seat with steps, at least:
   And the topmost step was filled
By—whom? What vestured priest?
   A stranger to me,—his guild,
His cult, unreconciled°

To my knowledge how guild and cult
   Are clothed in this world of ours: 60
I pondered, but no result
   Came to—unless that Giaours°
So worship the Lower Powers.

When suddenly who entered?
   Who knelt—did you guess I saw?
Who—raising that face where centred
   Allegiance to love and law
So lately—off-casting awe,

Down-treading reserve, away
   Thrusting respect . . . but mine   70
Stands firm—firm still shall stay!
   Ask Satan! for I decline
To tell—what I saw, in fine!

Yet here in the flesh you come—
   Your same self, form and face,—
In the eyes, mirth still at home!
   On the lips, that commonplace
Perfection of honest grace!

Yet your errand is—needs must be—
   To palliate—well, explain,   80
Expurgate in some degree
   Your soul of its ugly stain.
Oh, you—the good in grain—

How was it your white took tinge?
   'A mere dream'—never object!
Sleep leaves a door on hinge
   Whence soul, ere our flesh suspect,
Is off and away: detect

Her vagaries when loose, who can!
    Be she pranksome, be she prude,°   90
Disguise with the day began:
    With the night—ah, what ensued
From draughts of a drink hell-brewed?°

Then She: 'What a queer wild dream!
    And perhaps the best fun is—
Myself had its fellow—I seem
    Scarce awake from yet. 'Twas this—
Shall I tell you? First, a kiss!

'For the fault was just your own,—
    'Tis myself expect apology: 100
You warned me to let alone
    (Since our studies were mere philology)
That ticklish (you said) Anthology.°

'So, I dreamed that I passed *exam*
    Till a question posed me sore:
"Who translated this epigram
    By—an author we best ignore?"
And I answered "Hannah More"!'°

Bad Dreams III

This was my dream: I saw a Forest
    Old as the earth, no track nor trace   110
Of unmade man. Thou, Soul, explorest—
    Though in a trembling rapture—space
Immeasurable! Shrubs, turned trees,
Trees that touch heaven, support its frieze
Studded with sun and moon and star:
While—oh, the enormous growths that bar
Mine eye from penetrating past
    Their tangled twine where lurks—nay, lives
Royally lone, some brute-type cast
    I' the rough, time cancels, man forgives.   120

On, Soul! I saw a lucid City
    Of architectural device

Every way perfect. Pause for pity,
   Lightning! nor leave a cicatrice°
On those bright marbles, dome and spire,
Structures palatial,—streets which mire
Dares not defile, paved all too fine
For human footstep's smirch, not thine—
Proud solitary traverser,
   My Soul, of silent lengths of way—   130
With what ecstatic dread, aver,
   Lest life start sanctioned by thy stay!

Ah, but the last sight was the hideous!
   A City, yes,—a Forest, true,—
But each devouring each. Perfidious
Snake-plants had strangled what I knew
Was a pavilion once: each oak
Held on his horns some spoil he broke
By surreptitiously beneath
Upthrusting: pavements, as with teeth,   140
Griped huge weed widening crack and split
   In squares and circles stone-work erst.
Oh, Nature—good! Oh, Art—no whit
   Less worthy! Both in one—accurst!°

Bad Dreams IV

It happened thus: my slab, though new,°
   Was getting weather-stained,—beside,
Herbage, balm, peppermint o'ergrew
   Letter and letter: till you tried
Somewhat, the Name was scarce descried.

That strong stern man my lover came: 150
   —Was he my lover? Call him, pray,
My life's cold critic bent on blame
   Of all poor I could do or say
To make me worth his love one day—

One far day when, by diligent
   And dutiful amending faults,

Foibles, all weaknesses which went
  To challenge and excuse assaults
Of culture wronged by taste that halts—°

Discrepancies should mar no plan   160
  Symmetric of the qualities
Claiming respect from—say—a man
  That's strong and stern. 'Once more he pries
Into me with those critic eyes!'

No question! so—'Conclude, condemn
  Each failure my poor self avows!
Leave to its fate all you contemn!
  There's Solomon's selected spouse:°
Earth needs must hold such maids—choose them!'

Why, he was weeping! Surely gone   170
  Sternness and strength: with eyes to ground
And voice a broken monotone—
  'Only be as you were! Abound
In foibles, faults,—laugh, robed and crowned

'As Folly's veriest queen,—care I
  One feather-fluff? Look pity, Love,
On prostrate me—your foot shall try
  This forehead's use—mount thence above,
And reach what Heaven you dignify!'

Now, what could bring such change about?   180
  The thought perplexed: till, following
His gaze upon the ground,—why, out
  Came all the secret! So, a thing
Thus simple has deposed my king!

For, spite of weeds that strove to spoil
  Plain reading on the lettered slab,
My name was clear enough—no soil
  Effaced the date when one chance stab
Of scorn . . . if only ghosts might blab!°

Inapprehensiveness

We two stood simply friend-like side by side,
Viewing a twilight country far and wide,

Till she at length broke silence. 'How it towers
Yonder, the ruin o'er this vale of ours!
The West's faint flare behind it so relieves
Its rugged outline—sight perhaps deceives,
Or I could almost fancy that I see
A branch wave plain—belike some wind-sown tree
Chance-rooted where a missing turret was.
What would I give for the perspective glass   10
At home, to make out if 'tis really so!'
'Has Ruskin noticed here at Asolo°
That certain weed-growths on the ravaged wall
Seem'... something that I could not say at all,
My thought being rather—as absorbed she sent
Look onward after look from eyes distent°
With longing to reach Heaven's gate left ajar—
'Oh, fancies that might be, oh, facts that are!
What of a wilding? By you stands, and may
So stand unnoticed till the Judgment Day,   20
One who, if once aware that your regard
Claimed what his heart holds,—woke, as from its sward
The flower, the dormant passion, so to speak—
Then what a rush of life would startling wreak
Revenge on your inapprehensive stare
While, from the ruin and the West's faint flare,
You let your eyes meet mine, touch what you term
Quietude—that's an universe in germ—
The dormant passion needing but a look   30
To burst into immense life!'
                    'No, the book
Which noticed how the wall-growths wave' said she
'Was not by Ruskin.'
                    I said 'Vernon Lee?'°

Development

My Father was a scholar and knew Greek.
When I was five years old, I asked him once
'What do you read about?'
                    'The siege of Troy.'°

'What is a siege and what is Troy?'
                                        Whereat
He piled up chairs and tables for a town,
Set me a-top for Priam, called our cat
—Helen, enticed away from home (he said)
By wicked Paris, who couched somewhere cl°ose
Under the footstool, being cowardly,
But whom—since she was worth the pains, poor puss—   10
Towzer and Tray,—our dogs, the Atreidai,—sought°
By taking Troy to get possession of
—Always when great Achilles ceased to sulk,°
(My pony in the stable)—forth would prance
And put to flight Hector—our page-boy's self.
This taught me who was who and what was what:
So far I rightly understood the case
At five years old: a huge delight it proved
And still proves—thanks to that instructor sage
My Father, who knew better than turn straight   20
Learning's full flare on weak-eyed ignorance,
Or, worse yet, leave weak eyes to grow sand-blind,
Content with darkness and vacuity.

It happened, two or three years afterward,
That—I and playmates playing at Troy's Siege—
My Father came upon our make-believe.
'How would you like to read yourself the tale
Properly told, of which I gave you first
Merely such notion as a boy could bear?
Pope, now, would give you the precise account°   30
Of what, some day, by dint of scholarship,
You'll hear—who knows?—from Homer's very mouth.
Learn Greek by all means, read the "Blind Old Man,
Sweetest of Singers"—*tuphlos* which means "blind,"
Hedistos which means "sweetest." Time enough!
Try, anyhow, to master him some day;
Until when, take what serves for substitute,
Read Pope, by all means!'
                               So I ran through Pope,
Enjoyed the tale—what history so true?
Also attacked my Primer, duly drudged,   40
Grew fitter thus for what was promised next—

The very thing itself, the actual words,
When I could turn—say, Buttmann to account.°

Time passed, I ripened somewhat: one fine day,
'Quite ready for the Iliad, nothing less?
There's Heine, where the big books block the shelf:°
Don't skip a word, thumb well the Lexicon!'

I thumbed well and skipped nowise till I learned
Who was who, what was what, from Homer's tongue,
And there an end of learning. Had you asked   50
The all-accomplished scholar, twelve years old,
'Who was it wrote the Iliad?'—what a laugh!
'Why, Homer, all the world knows: of his life
Doubtless some facts exist: it's everywhere:
We have not settled, though, his place of birth:
He begged, for certain, and was blind beside:
Seven cities claimed him—Scio, with best right,°
Thinks Byron. What he wrote? Those Hymns we have.°
Then there's the "Battle of the Frogs and Mice,"°
That's all—unless they dig "Margites" up°   60
(I'd like that) nothing more remains to know.'

Thus did youth spend a comfortable time;
Until—'What's this the Germans say is fact
That Wolf found out first? It's unpleasant work°
Their chop and change, unsettling one's belief:
All the same, while we live, we learn, that's sure.'
So, I bent brow o'er *Prolegomena*.
And, after Wolf, a dozen of his like
Proved there was never any Troy at all,
Neither Besiegers nor Besieged,—nay, worse,—   70
No actual Homer, no authentic text,
No warrant for the fiction I, as fact,
Had treasured in my heart and soul so long—
Ay, mark you! and as fact held still, still hold,
Spite of new knowledge, in my heart of hearts
And soul of souls, fact's essence freed and fixed
From accidental fancy's guardian sheath.
Assuredly thenceforward—thank my stars!—
However it got there, deprive who could—
Wring from the shrine my precious tenantry,   80

Helen, Ulysses, Hector and his Spouse,°
Achilles and his Friend?—though Wolf—ah, Wolf!°
Why must he needs come doubting, spoil a dream?

But then 'No dream's worth waking'—Browning says:°
And here's the reason why I tell thus much.
I, now mature man, you anticipate,
May blame my Father justifiably
For letting me dream out my nonage thus,°
And only by such slow and sure degrees
Permitting me to sift the grain from chaff,   90
Get truth and falsehood known and named as such.
Why did he ever let me dream at all,
Not bid me taste the story in its strength?
Suppose my childhood was scarce qualified
To rightly understand mythology,
Silence at least was in his power to keep:
I might have—somehow—correspondingly—
Well, who knows by what method, gained my gains,
Been taught, by forthrights not meanderings,
My aim should be to loathe, like Peleus' son,   100
A lie as Hell's Gate, love my wedded wife,°
Like Hector, and so on with all the rest.
Could not I have excogitated this
Without believing such men really were?
That is—he might have put into my hand
The 'Ethics'? In translation, if you please,
Exact, no pretty lying that improves,
To suit the modern taste: no more, no less—
The 'Ethics': 'tis a treatise I find hard°
To read aright now that my hair is grey,   110
And I can manage the original.
At five years old—how ill had fared its leaves!
Now, growing double o'er the Stagirite,°
At least I soil no page with bread and milk,
Nor crumple, dogsear and deface—boys' way.

Epilogue

At the midnight in the silence of the sleep-time,
    When you set your fancies free,
Will they pass to where—by death, fools think, imprisoned—
Low he lies who once so loved you, whom you loved so,
                    —Pity me?

Oh to love so, be so loved, yet so mistaken!°
    What had I on earth to do
With the slothful, with the mawkish, the unmanly?
Like the aimless, helpless, hopeless, did I drivel
                    —Being—who?   10

One who never turned his back but marched breast forward,
    Never doubted clouds would break,
Never dreamed, though right were worsted, wrong would
        triumph,
Held we fall to rise, are baffled to fight better,
                    Sleep to wake.

No, at noonday in the bustle of man's work-time
    Greet the unseen with a cheer!
Bid him forward, breast and back as either should be,
'Strive and thrive!' cry 'Speed,—fight on, fare ever
                    There as here!'   20

UNCOLLECTED POEMS

Helen's Tower

'Ελένη ἐπὶ πύργῳ

Who hears of Helen's Tower, may dream perchance
  How the Greek beauty from the Scaean gate°
  Gazed on old friends unanimous in hate,
Death-doomed because of her fair countenance.
Hearts would leap otherwise at thy advance,
  Lady, to whom this Tower is consecrate!
  Like hers, thy face once made all eyes elate,
Yet, unlike hers, was blessed by every glance.

The Tower of Hate is outworn, far and strange:
  A transitory shame of long ago,
  It dies into the sand from which it sprang;
But thine, Love's rock-built Tower, shall fear no change:
  God's self laid stable earth's foundations so,
  When all the morning stars together sang.°

10

'Oh Love, Love'

I

Oh Love, Love, thou that from the eyes diffusest
Yearning, and on the soul sweet grace inducest—
Souls against whom thy hostile march is made—
Never to me be manifest in ire,
Nor, out of time and tune, my peace invade!
Since neither from the fire—
No, nor the stars—is launched a bolt more mighty
Than that of Aphrodité
Hurled from the hands of Love, the boy with Zeus for sire.°

II

Idly, how idly, by the Alpheian river°   10
And in the Pythian shrines of Phœbus, quiver°
Blood-offerings from the bull, which Hellas heaps:°
While Love we worship not—the Lord of men!
Worship not him, the very key who keeps
Of Aphrodité, when
She closes up her dearest chamber-portals:
—Love, when he comes to mortals,
Wide-wasting, through those deeps of woes beyond the deep!

Why I Am a Liberal

'Why?' Because all I haply can and do,
    All that I am now, all I hope to be—
    Whence comes it save from fortune setting free
Body and soul the purpose to pursue,
God traced for both? If fetters, not a few,
    Of prejudice, convention, fall from me,
    These shall I bid men—each in his degree
Also God-guided—bear, and gaily too?

But little do or can the best of us:
    THAT LITTLE IS ACHIEVED THROUGH LIBERTY.   10
Who, then, dares hold—emancipated thus—
    His fellow shall continue bound? Not I,
Who live, love, labour freely, nor discuss
    A brother's right to freedom. That is 'Why.'

To Edward FitzGerald

I chanced upon a new book yesterday:
I opened it, and, where my finger lay
    'Twixt page and uncut page, these words I read
—Some six or seven at most—and learned thereby
That you, FitzGerald, whom by ear and eye
    She never knew, 'thanked God my wife was dead.'

Ay, dead! and were yourself alive, good Fitz,°
How to return you thanks would task my wits:
  Kicking you seems the common lot of curs—
While more appropriate greeting lends you grace: 10
Surely to spit there glorifies your face—
  Spitting—from lips once sanctified by Hers.

INTRODUCTORY ESSAY
[ESSAY ON SHELLEY] (1852)

An opportunity having presented itself for the acquisition of a series of unedited letters by Shelley, all more or less directly supplementary to and illustrative of the collection already published by Mr. Moxon, that gentleman has decided on securing them. They will prove an acceptable addition to a body of correspondence, the value of which towards a right understanding of its author's purpose and work, may be said to exceed that of any similar contribution exhibiting the worldly relations of a poet whose genius has operated by a different law.

Doubtless we accept gladly the biography of an objective poet, as the phrase now goes; one whose endeavour has been to reproduce things external (whether the phenomena of the scenic universe, or the manifested action of the human heart and brain) with an immediate reference, in every case, to the common eye and apprehension of his fellow men, assumed capable of receiving and profiting by this reproduction. It has been obtained through the poet's double faculty of seeing external objects more clearly, widely, and deeply, than is possible to the average mind, at the same time that he is so acquainted and in sympathy with its narrow comprehension as to be careful to supply it with no other materials than it can combine into an intelligible whole. The auditory of such a poet will include, not only the intelligences which, save for such assistance, would have missed the deeper meaning and enjoyment of the original objects, but also the spirits of a like endowment with his own, who, by means of his abstract, can forthwith pass to the reality it was made from, and either corroborate their impressions of things known already, or supply themselves with new from whatever shows in the inexhaustible variety of existence may have hitherto escaped their knowledge. Such a poet is properly the ποιητης,° the fashioner; and the thing fashioned, his poetry, will of necessity be substantive, projected from himself and distinct. We are ignorant what the inventor of 'Othello' conceived of that fact as he beheld it in completeness, how he accounted for it, under what known law he registered its nature, or to what unknown law he traced its coincidence. We learn only what he intended we should learn by that particular exercise of his power,—the fact itself,—which, with its infinite significances, each of us receives for the first time as a creation, and is hereafter left to deal with, as, in proportion to his own intelligence, he best may. We are ignorant, and would fain be otherwise.

Doubtless, with respect to such a poet, we covet his biography. We desire to look back upon the process of gathering together in a lifetime, the materials of the work we behold entire; of elaborating, perhaps under difficulty and with hindrance, all that is familiar to our admiration in the apparent facility of success. And the inner impulse of this effort and operation, what induced it? Did a soul's delight in its own extended sphere of vision set it, for the gratification of an insuppressible power, on labour, as other men are set on rest? Or did a sense of duty or of love lead it to communicate its own sensations to mankind? Did an irresistible sympathy with men compel it to bring down and suit its own provision of knowledge and beauty to their narrow scope? Did the personality of such an one stand like an open watch-tower in the midst of the territory it is erected to gaze on, and were the storms and calms, the stars and meteors, its watchman was wont to report of, the habitual variegation of his every-day life, as they glanced across its open roof or lay reflected on its four-square parapet? Or did some sunken and darkened chamber of imagery witness, in the artificial illumination of every storied compartment we are permitted to contemplate, how rare and precious were the outlooks through here and there an embrasure upon a world beyond, and how blankly would have pressed on the artificer the boundary of his daily life, except for the amorous diligence with which he had rendered permanent by art whatever came to diversify the gloom? Still, fraught with instruction and interest as such details undoubtedly are, we can, if needs be, dispense with them. The man passes, the work remains. The work speaks for itself, as we say: and the biography of the worker is no more necessary to an understanding or enjoyment of it, than is a model or anatomy of some tropical tree, to the right tasting of the fruit we are familiar with on the market-stall,—or a geologist's map and stratification, to the prompt recognition of the hill-top, our land-mark of every day.

We turn with stronger needs to the genius of an opposite tendency—the subjective poet of modern classification. He, gifted like the objective poet with the fuller perception of nature and man, is impelled to embody the thing he perceives, not so   80 much with reference to the many below, as to the One above him, the supreme Intelligence which apprehends all things in their absolute truth,—an ultimate view ever aspired to, if but partially attained, by the poet's own soul. Not what man sees, but what God sees—the *Ideas* of Plato, seeds of creation lying burningly on the Divine Hand—it is toward these that he struggles. Not with the combination of humanity in action, but with the primal elements of humanity he has to do; and he digs where he stands,—preferring to seek them in his own soul as the nearest reflex of that absolute Mind, according to the intuitions   90 of which he desires to perceive and speak. Such a poet does not deal habitually with the picturesque groupings and tempestuous tossings of the forest-trees, but with their roots and fibres naked to the chalk and stone. He does not paint pictures and hang them on the walls, but rather carries them on the retina of his own eyes: we must look deep into his human eyes, to see those pictures on them. He is rather a seer, accordingly, than a fashioner, and what he produces will be less a work than an effluence. That effluence cannot be easily considered in abstraction from his personality,—being indeed the very radiance and aroma   100 of his personality, projected from it but not separated. Therefore, in our approach to the poetry, we necessarily approach the personality of the poet; in apprehending it we apprehend him, and certainly we cannot love it without loving him. Both for love's and for understanding's sake we desire to know him, and as readers of his poetry must be readers of his biography also.

I shall observe, in passing, that it seems not so much from any essential distinction in the faculty of the two poets or in the nature of the objects contemplated by either, as in the more immediate adaptability of these objects to the distinct purpose of   110 each, that the objective poet, in his appeal to the aggregate human mind, chooses to deal with the doings of men, (the result of which dealing, in its pure form, when even description, as suggesting a describer, is dispensed with, is what we call dramatic poetry), while the subjective poet, whose study has been himself, appealing through himself to the absolute Divine mind, prefers to dwell upon those external scenic appearances which strike out most abundantly and uninterruptedly his inner light and power, selects that silence of the earth and sea in which he can best hear the beating of his individual heart, and leaves 120 the noisy, complex, yet imperfect exhibitions of nature in the manifold experience of man around him, which serve only to distract and suppress the working of his brain. These opposite tendencies of genius will be more readily descried in their artistic effect than in their moral spring and cause. Pushed to an extreme and manifested as a deformity, they will be seen plainest of all in the fault of either artist, when subsidiarily to the human interest of his work his occasional illustrations from scenic nature are introduced as in the earlier works of the originative painters— men and women filling the foreground with consummate mas- 130 tery, while mountain, grove and rivulet show like an anticipatory revenge on that succeeding race of landscape-painters whose 'figures' disturb the perfection of their earth and sky. It would be idle to inquire, of these two kinds of poetic faculty in operation, which is the higher or even rarer endowment. If the subjective might seem to be the ultimate requirement of every age, the objective, in the strictest state, must still retain its original value. For it is with this world, as starting point and basis alike, that we shall always have to concern ourselves: the world is not to be learned and thrown aside, but reverted to and relearned. The 140 spiritual comprehension may be infinitely subtilised, but the raw material it operates upon, must remain. There may be no end of the poets who communicate to us what they see in an object with reference to their own individuality; what it was before they saw it, in reference to the aggregate human mind, will be as desirable to know as ever. Nor is there any reason why these two modes of poetic faculty may not issue hereafter from the same poet in successive perfect works, examples of which, according to what are now considered the exigences of art, we have hitherto pos- sessed in distinct individuals only. A mere running-in of the one 150 faculty upon the other, is, of course, the ordinary circumstance. Far more rarely it happens that either is found so decidedly prominent and superior, as to be pronounced comparatively pure: while of the perfect shield, with the gold and the silver side set up for all comers to challenge, there has yet been no

instance. Either faculty in its eminent state is doubtless conceded
by Providence as a best gift to men, according to their especial
want. There is a time when the general eye has, so to speak,
absorbed its fill of the phenomena around it, whether spiritual or
material, and desires rather to learn the exacter significance of   160
what it possesses, than to receive any augmentation of what is
possessed. Then is the opportunity for the poet of loftier vision,
to lift his fellows, with their half-apprehensions, up to his own
sphere, by intensifying the import of details and rounding the
universal meaning. The influence of such an achievement will
not soon die out. A tribe of successors (Homerides)° working
more or less in the same spirit, dwell on his discoveries and
reinforce his doctrine; till, at unawares, the world is found to be
subsisting wholly on the shadow of a reality, on sentiments
diluted from passions, on the tradition of a fact, the convention   170
of a moral, the straw of last year's harvest. Then is the imper-
ative call for the appearance of another sort of poet, who shall at
once replace this intellectual rumination of food swallowed long
ago, by a supply of the fresh and living swathe; getting at new
substance by breaking up the assumed wholes into parts of
independent and unclassed value, careless of the unknown laws
for recombining them (it will be the business of yet another poet
to suggest those hereafter), prodigal of objects for men's outer
and not inner sight, shaping for their uses a new and different
creation from the last, which it displaces by the right of life over 180
death,—to endure until, in the inevitable process, its very suffi-
ciency to itself shall require, at length, an exposition of its
affinity to something higher,—when the positive yet conflicting
facts shall again precipitate themselves under a harmonising law,
and one more degree will be apparent for a poet to climb in that
mighty ladder, of which, however cloud-involved and undefined
may glimmer the topmost step, the world dares no longer doubt
that its gradations ascend.

Such being the two kinds of artists, it is naturally, as I have
shown, with the biography of the subjective poet that we have   190
the deeper concern. Apart from his recorded life altogether, we
might fail to determine with satisfactory precision to what class
his productions belong, and what amount of praise is assignable
to the producer. Certainly, in the face of any conspicuous
achievement of genius, philosophy, no less than sympathetic
instinct, warrants our belief in a great moral purpose having

mainly inspired even where it does not visibly look out of the
same. Greatness in a work suggests an adequate instrumentality;
and none of the lower incitements, however they may avail to
initiate or even effect many considerable displays of power, 200
simulating the nobler inspiration to which they are mistakenly
referred, have been found able, under the ordinary conditions of
humanity, to task themselves to the end of so exacting a perfor-
mance as a poet's complete work. As soon will the galvanism,
that provokes to violent action the muscles of a corpse, induce it
to cross the chamber steadily: sooner. The love of displaying
power for the display's sake, the love of riches, of distinction, of
notoriety,—the desire of a triumph over rivals, and the vanity in
the applause of friends,—each and all of such whetted appetites
grow intenser by exercise and increasingly sagacious as to the 210
best and readiest means of self-appeasement,—while for any of
their ends, whether the money or the pointed finger of the
crowd, or the flattery and hate to heart's content, there are
cheaper prices to pay, they will all find soon enough, than the
bestowment of a life upon a labour, hard, slow, and not sure.
Also, assuming the proper moral aim to have produced a work,
there are many and various states of an aim: it may be more
intense than clear-sighted, or too easily satisfied with a lower
field of activity than a steadier aspiration would reach. All the
bad poetry in the world (accounted poetry, that is, by its affin- 220
ities) will be found to result from some one of the infinite
degrees of discrepancy between the attributes of the poet's soul,
occasioning a want of correspondency between his work and the
verities of nature,—issuing in poetry, false under whatever form,
which shows a thing not as it is to mankind generally, nor as it is
to the particular describer, but as it is supposed to be for some
unreal neutral mood, midway between both and of value to
neither, and living its brief minute simply through the indolence
of whoever accepts it, or his incapacity to denounce a cheat.
Although of such depths of failure there can be no question here, 230
we must in every case betake ourselves to the review of a poet's
life ere we determine some of the nicer questions concerning his
poetry,—more especially if the performance we seek to estimate
aright, has been obstructed and cut short of completion by
circumstances,—a disastrous youth or a premature death. We
may learn from the biography whether his spirit invariably saw
and spoke from the last height to which it had attained. An

absolute vision is not for this world, but we are permitted a
continual approximation to it, every degree of which in the
individual, provided it exceed the attainment of the masses, must   240
procure him a clear advantage. Did the poet ever attain to a
higher platform than where he rested and exhibited a result? Did
he know more than he spoke of?

  I concede however, in respect to the subject of our study as
well as some few other illustrious examples, that the unmistake-
able quality of the verse would be evidence enough, under usual
circumstances, not only of the kind and degree of the intellectual
but of the moral constitution of Shelley: the whole personality of
the poet shining forward from the poems, without much need of
going further to seek it. The 'Remains'°—produced within a   250
period of ten years, and at a season of life when other men of at
all comparable genius have hardly done more than prepare the
eye for future sight and the tongue for speech—present us with
the complete enginery of a poet, as signal in the excellence of its
several adaptitudes as transcendent in the combination of
effects,—examples, in fact, of the whole poet's function of
beholding with an understanding keenness the universe, nature
and man, in their actual state of perfection in imperfection,—of
the whole poet's virtue of being untempted by the manifold
partial developments of beauty and good on every side, into   260
leaving them the ultimates he found them,—induced by the
facility of the gratification of his own sense of those qualities,
or by the pleasure of acquiescence in the short-comings of his
predecessors in art, and the pain of disturbing their convention-
alisms,—the whole poet's virtue, I repeat, of looking higher than
any manifestation yet made of both beauty and good, in order to
suggest from the utmost actual realisation of the one a corres-
ponding capability in the other, and out of the calm, purity and
energy of nature, to reconstitute and store up for the forth-
coming stage of man's being, a gift in repayment of that former   270
gift, in which man's own thought and passion had been lavished
by the poet on the else-incompleted magnificence of the sunrise,
the else-uninterpreted mystery of the lake,—so drawing out,
lifting up, and assimilating this ideal of a future man, thus
described as possible, to the present reality of the poet's soul
already arrived at the higher state of development, and still
aspirant to elevate and extend itself in conformity with its still-
improving perceptions of, no longer the eventual Human, but

the actual Divine. In conjunction with which noble and rare powers, came the subordinate power of delivering these attained results to the world in an embodiment of verse more closely answering to and indicative of the process of the informing spirit, (failing as it occasionally does, in art, only to succeed in highest art),—with a diction more adequate to the task in its natural and acquired richness, its material colour and spiritual transparency,—the whole being moved by and suffused with a music at once of the soul and the sense, expressive both of an external might of sincere passion and an internal fitness and consonancy,—than can be attributed to any other writer whose record is among us. Such was the spheric poetical faculty of Shelley, as its own self-sufficing central light, radiating equally through immaturity and accomplishment, through many fragments and occasional completion, reveals it to a competent judgment.

But the acceptance of this truth by the public, has been retarded by certain objections which cast us back on the evidence of biography, even with Shelley's poetry in our hands. Except for the particular character of these objections, indeed, the non-appreciation of his contemporaries would simply class, now that it is over, with a series of experiences which have necessarily happened and needlessly been wondered at, ever since the world began, and concerning which any present anger may well be moderated, no less in justice to our forerunners than in policy to ourselves. For the misapprehensiveness of his age is exactly what a poet is sent to remedy; and the interval between his operation and the generally perceptible effect of it, is no greater, less indeed, than in many other departments of the great human effort. The 'E pur si muove'° of the astronomer was as bitter a word as any uttered before or since by a poet over his rejected living work, in that depth of conviction which is so like despair.

But in this respect was the experience of Shelley peculiarly unfortunate—that the disbelief in him as a man, even preceded the disbelief in him as a writer; the misconstruction of his moral nature preparing the way for the misappreciation of his intellectual labours. There existed from the beginning,— simultaneous with, indeed anterior to his earliest noticeable works, and not brought forward to counteract any impression they had succeeded in making,—certain charges against his private character and life,° which, if substantiated to their whole breadth, would

materially disturb, I do not attempt to deny, our reception and 320
enjoyment of his works, however wonderful the artistic qualities
of these. For we are not sufficiently supplied with instances of
genius of his order, to be able to pronounce certainly how many
of its constituent parts have been tasked and strained to the
production of a given lie, and how high and pure a mood of the
creative mind may be dramatically simulated as the poet's habit-
ual and exclusive one. The doubts, therefore, arising from such a
question, required to be set at rest, as they were effectually, by
those early authentic notices of Shelley's career and the corrob-
orative accompaniment of his letters, in which not only the main 330
tenor and principal result of his life, but the purity and beauty of
many of the processes which had conducted to them, were made
apparent enough for the general reader's purpose,—whoever
lightly condemned Shelley first, on the evidence of reviews and
gossip, as lightly acquitting him now, on that of memoirs and
correspondence. Still, it is advisable to lose no opportunity of
strengthening and completing the chain of biographical testi-
mony; much more, of course, for the sake of the poet's original
lovers, whose volunteered sacrifice of particular principle in
favour of absorbing sympathy we might desire to dispense with, 340
than for the sake of his foolish haters, who have long since
diverted upon other objects their obtuseness or malignancy. A
full life of Shelley should be written at once, while the materials
for it continue in reach; not to minister to the curiosity of the
public, but to obliterate the last stain of that false life which was
forced on the public's attention before it had any curiosity on the
matter,—a biography, composed in harmony with the present
general disposition to have faith in him, yet not shrinking from a
candid statement of all ambiguous passages, through a reason-
able confidence that the most doubtful of them will be found 350
consistent with a belief in the eventual perfection of his char-
acter, according to the poor limits of our humanity. Nor will
men persist in confounding, any more than God confounds, with
genuine infidelity and an atheism of the heart, those passionate,
impatient struggles of a boy towards distant truth and love, made
in the dark, and ended by one sweep of the natural seas before
the full moral sunrise could shine out on him. Crude convictions
of boyhood, conveyed in imperfect and inapt forms of speech,—
for such things all boys have been pardoned. There are growing-
pains, accompanied by temporary distortion, of the soul also. 360

And it would be hard indeed upon this young Titan of genius, murmuring in divine music his human ignorances, through his very thirst for knowledge, and his rebellion, in mere aspiration to law, if the melody itself substantiated the error, and the tragic cutting short of life perpetuated into sins, such faults as, under happier circumstances, would have been left behind by the consent of the most arrogant moralist, forgotten on the lowest steps of youth.

The responsibility of presenting to the public a biography of Shelley, does not, however lie with me: I have only to make it a little easier by arranging these few supplementary letters, with a recognition of the value of the whole collection. This value I take to consist in a most truthful conformity of the Correspondence, in its limited degree, with the moral and intellectual character of the writer as displayed in the highest manifestations of his genius. Letters and poems are obviously an act of the same mind, produced by the same law, only differing in the application to the individual or collective understanding. Letters and poems may be used indifferently as the basement of our opinion upon the writer's character; the finished expression of a sentiment in the poems, giving light and significance to the rudiments of the same in the letters, and these, again, in their incipiency and unripeness, authenticating the exalted mood and reattaching it to the personality of the writer. The musician speaks on the note he sings with; there is no change in the scale, as he diminishes the volume into familiar intercourse. There is nothing of that jarring between the man and the author, which has been found so amusing or so melancholy; no dropping of the tragic mask, as the crowd melts away; no mean discovery of the real motives of a life's achievement, often, in other lives, laid bare as pitifully as when, at the close of a holiday, we catch sight of the internal lead-pipes and wood-valves, to which, and not to the ostensible conch and dominant Triton of the fountain, we have owed our admired waterwork. No breaking out, in household privacy, of hatred anger and scorn, incongruous with the higher mood and suppressed artistically in the book: no brutal return to self-delighting, when the audience of philanthropic schemes is out of hearing: no indecent stripping off the grander feeling and rule of life as too costly and cumbrous for every-day wear. Whatever Shelley was, he was with an admirable sincerity. It was not always truth that he thought and spoke; but in the purity

of truth he spoke and thought always. Everywhere is apparent
his belief in the existence of Good, to which Evil is an accident;
his faithful holding by what he assumed to be the former, going
everywhere in company with the tenderest pity for those acting
or suffering on the opposite hypothesis. For he was tender,
though tenderness is not always the characteristic of very sincere
natures; he was eminently both tender and sincere. And not only
do the same affection and yearning after the well-being of his
kind, appear in the letters as in the poems, but they express   410
themselves by the same theories and plans, however crude and
unsound. There is no reservation of a subtler, less costly, more
serviceable remedy for his own ill, than he has proposed for the
general one; nor does he ever contemplate an object on his own
account, from a less elevation than he uses in exhibiting it to the
world. How shall we help believing Shelley to have been, in his
ultimate attainment, the splendid spirit of his own best poetry,
when we find even his carnal speech to agree faithfully, at
faintest as at strongest, with the tone and rhythm of his most
oracular utterances?   420

For the rest, these new letters are not offered as presenting
any new feature of the poet's character. Regarded in themselves,
and as the substantive productions of a man, their importance
would be slight. But they possess interest beyond their limits, in
confirming the evidence just dwelt on, of the poetical mood of
Shelley being only the intensification of his habitual mood; the
same tongue only speaking, for want of the special excitement to
sing. The very first letter, as one instance for all, strikes the key-
note of the predominating sentiment of Shelley throughout his
whole life—his sympathy with the oppressed. And when we see   430
him at so early an age, casting out, under the influence of such a
sympathy, letters and pamphlets on every side, we accept it as
the simple exemplification of the sincerity, with which, at the
close of his life, he spoke of himself, as—

> 'One whose heart a stranger's tear might wear
> As water-drops the sandy fountain stone;
> Who loved and pitied all things, and could moan
> For woes which others hear not, and could see
> The absent with the glass of phantasy,
> And near the poor and trampled sit and weep,   440
> Following the captive to his dungeon deep—

One who was as a nerve o'er which do creep
The else-unfelt oppressions of this earth.'°

Such sympathy with his kind was evidently developed in him to an extraordinary and even morbid degree, at a period when the general intellectual powers it was impatient to put in motion, were immature or deficient.

I conjecture, from a review of the various publications of Shelley's youth, that one of the causes of his failure at the outset, was the peculiar *practicalness* of his mind, which was not without 450 a determinate effect on his progress in theorising. An ordinary youth, who turns his attention to similar subjects, discovers falsities, incongruities, and various points for amendment, and, in the natural advance of the purely critical spirit unchecked by considerations of remedy, keeps up before his young eyes so many instances of the same error and wrong, that he finds himself unawares arrived at the startling conclusion, that all must be changed—or nothing: in the face of which plainly impossible achievement, he is apt (looking perhaps a little more serious by the time he touches at the decisive issue), to feel, 460 either carelessly or considerately, that his own attempting a single piece of service would be worse than useless even, and to refer the whole task to another age and person—safe in proportion to his incapacity. Wanting words to speak, he has never made a fool of himself by speaking. But, in Shelley's case, the early fervour and power to *see*, was accompanied by as precocious a fertility to *contrive:* he endeavoured to realise as he went on idealising; every wrong had simultaneously its remedy, and, out of the strength of his hatred for the former, he took the strength of his confidence in the latter—till sud- 470 denly he stood pledged to the defence of a set of miserable little expedients, just as if they represented great principles, and to an attack upon various great principles, really so, without leaving himself time to examine whether, because they were antagonis- tical to the remedy he had suggested, they must therefore be identical or even essentially connected with the wrong he sought to cure,—playing with blind passion into the hands of his enem- ies, and dashing at whatever red cloak was held forth to him, as the cause of the fireball he had last been stung with—mistaking Churchdom for Christianity, and for marriage, 'the sale of love' 480 and the law of sexual oppression.

Gradually, however, he was leaving behind him this low practical dexterity, unable to keep up with his widening intellectual perception; and, in exact proportion as he did so, his true power strengthened and proved itself. Gradually he was raised above the contemplation of spots and the attempt at effacing them, to the great Abstract Light, and, through the discrepancy of the creation, to the sufficiency of the First Cause. Gradually he was learning that the best way of removing abuses is to stand fast by truth. Truth is one, as they are manifold; and innumer- 490 able negative effects are produced by the upholding of one positive principle. I shall say what I think,—had Shelley lived he would have finally ranged himself with the Christians; his very instinct for helping the weaker side (if numbers make strength), his very 'hate of hate,' which at first mistranslated itself into delirious Queen Mab notes and the like, would have got clearer-sighted by exercise. The preliminary step to following Christ, is the leaving the dead to bury their dead°—not clamouring on his doctrine for an especial solution of difficulties which are referable to the general problem of the universe. 500 Already he had attained to a profession of 'a worship to the Spirit of good within, which requires (before it sends that inspiration forth, which impresses its likeness upon all it creates) devoted and disinterested homage, *as Coleridge says*,'—and Paul likewise. And we find in one of his last exquisite fragments, avowedly a record of one of his own mornings and its experience, as it dawned on him at his soul and body's best in his boat on the Serchio—that as surely as

> 'The stars burnt out in the pale blue air,
> And the thin white moon lay withering there—   510
> Day had kindled the dewy woods,
> And the rocks above, and the stream below,
> And the vapours in their multitudes,
> And the Apennine's shroud of summer snow—
> Day had awakened all things that be;'°

just so surely, he tells us (stepping forward from this delicious dance-music, choragus-like, into the grander measure befitting the final enunciation),

> 'All rose to do the task He set to each,
> Who shaped us to his ends and not our own;   520

The million rose to learn, and One to teach
What none yet ever knew or can be known.'°

No more difference than this, from David's° pregnant con-
clusion so long ago!

Meantime, as I call Shelley a moral man, because he was true,
simple-hearted, and brave, and because what he acted corres-
ponded to what he knew, so I call him a man of religious mind,
because every audacious negative cast up by him against the
Divine, was interpenetrated with a mood of reverence and adora-
tion,—and because I find him everywhere taking for granted 530
some of the capital dogmas of Christianity, while most vehe-
mently denying their historical basement. There is such a thing
as an efficacious knowledge of and belief in the politics of
Junius,° or the poetry of Rowley,° though a man should at the
same time dispute the title of Chatterton to the one, and con-
sider the author of the other, as Byron wittily did, 'really, truly,
nobody at all.'¹ There is even such a thing, we come to learn
wonderingly in these very letters, as a profound sensibility and
adaptitude for art, while the science of the percipient is so little
advanced as to admit of his stronger admiration for Guido (and 540
Carlo Dolce!)° than for Michael Angelo. A Divine Being° has
Himself said, that 'a word against the Son of man shall be
forgiven to a man,' while 'a word against the Spirit of God'
(implying a general deliberate preference of perceived evil to
perceived good) 'shall not be forgiven to a man.' Also, in reli-
gion, one earnest and unextorted assertion of belief should out-
weigh, as a matter of testimony, many assertions of unbelief. The
fact that there is a gold-region is established by the finding of
one lump, though you miss the vein never so often.

Shelley died before his youth ended. In taking the measure of 550
him as a man, he must be considered on the whole and at his

---

¹ Or, to take our illustrations from the writings of Shelley himself, there is such
a thing as admirably appreciating a work by Andrea Verocchio°—and fancifully
characterising° the Pisan Torre Guelfa by the Ponte a Mare, black against the
sunsets,—and consummately painting the islet of San Clemente with its peni-
tentiary for rebellious priests, to the west between Venice and the Lido—while
you believe the first to be a fragment of an antique sarcophagus—the second,
Ugolino's Tower of Famine (the vestiges of which should be sought for in the
Piazza de' Cavalieri)—and the third (as I convinced myself last summer at
Venice), San Servolo with its madhouse—which, far from being 'windowless,'
is as full of windows as a barrack.

ultimate spiritual stature, and not be judged of at the immaturity and by the mistakes of ten years before: that, indeed, would be to judge of the author of 'Julian and Maddalo' by 'Zastrozzi.'° Let the whole truth be told of his worst mistake. I believe, for my own part, that if anything could now shame or grieve Shelley, it would be an attempt to vindicate him at the expense of another.

In forming a judgment, I would, however, press on the reader the simple justice of considering tenderly his constitution of body as well as mind, and how unfavourable it was to the steady 560 symmetries of conventional life; the body, in the torture of incurable disease, refusing to give repose to the bewildered soul, tossing in its hot fever of the fancy,—and the laudanum-bottle making but a perilous and pitiful truce between these two. He was constantly subject to 'that state of mind' (I quote his own note to 'Hellas'°) 'in which ideas may be supposed to assume the force of sensation, through the confusion of thought with the objects of thought, and excess of passion animating the creations of the imagination:' in other words, he was liable to remarkable delusions and hallucinations. The nocturnal attack in Wales, for 570 instance, was assuredly a delusion; and I venture to express my own conviction, derived from a little attention to the circum- stances of either story, that the idea of the enamoured lady following him to Naples, and of the 'man in the cloak' who struck him at the Pisan post-office, were equally illusory,—the mere projection, in fact, from himself, of the image of his own love and hate.

> 'To thirst and find no fill—to wail and wander
> With short unsteady steps—to pause and ponder—
> To feel the blood run through the veins and tingle 580
> What busy thought and blind sensation mingle,—
> To nurse the image of *unfelt caresses*
> Till dim imagination just possesses
> The half-created shadow'—°

of unfelt caresses,—and of unfelt blows as well: to such condi- tions was his genius subject. It was not at Rome only (where he heard a mystic voice exclaiming, 'Cenci, Cenci,' in reference to the tragic theme which occupied him at the time),—it was not at Rome only that he mistook the cry of 'old rags.' The habit of somnambulism is said to have extended to the very last days of 590 his life.

Let me conclude with a thought of Shelley as a poet. In the hierarchy of creative minds, it is the presence of the highest faculty that gives first rank, in virtue of its kind, not degree; no pretension of a lower nature, whatever the completeness of development or variety of effect, impeding the precedency of the rarer endowment though only in the germ. The contrary is sometimes maintained; it is attempted to make the lower gifts (which are potentially included in the higher faculty) of independent value, and equal to some exercise of the special func- 600 tion. For instance, should not a poet possess common sense? Then the possession of abundant common sense implies a step towards becoming a poet. Yes; such a step as the lapidary's,° when, strong in the fact of carbon entering largely into the composition of the diamond, he heaps up a sack of charcoal in order to compete with the Koh-i-noor.° I pass at once, therefore, from Shelley's minor excellencies to his noblest and predominating characteristic.

This I call his simultaneous perception of Power and Love in the absolute, and of Beauty and Good in the concrete, while he 610 throws, from his poet's station between both, swifter, subtler, and more numerous films for the connexion of each with each, than have been thrown by any modern artificer of whom I have knowledge; proving how, as he says,

'The spirit of the worm within the sod,
In love and worship blends itself with God.'°

I would rather consider Shelley's poetry as a sublime fragmentary essay towards a presentment of the correspondency of the universe to Deity, of the natural to the spiritual, and of the actual to the ideal, than I would isolate and separately appraise 620 the worth of many detachable portions which might be acknowledged as utterly perfect in a lower moral point of view, under the mere conditions of art. It would be easy to take my stand on successful instances of objectivity in Shelley: there is the unrivalled 'Cenci;' there is the 'Julian and Maddalo' too; there is the magnificent 'Ode to Naples:' why not regard, it may be said, the less organised matter as the radiant elemental foam and solution, out of which would have been evolved, eventually, creations as perfect even as those? But I prefer to look for the highest attainment, not simply the high,—and, seeing it, I hold by it. 630 There is surely enough of the work 'Shelley' to be known enduringly among men, and, I believe, to be accepted of God, as human work may; and around the imperfect proportions of such, the most elaborated productions of ordinary art must arrange themselves as inferior illustrations.

It is because I have long held these opinions in assurance and gratitude, that I catch at the opportunity offered to me of expressing them here; knowing that the alacrity to fulfil an humble office conveys more love than the acceptance of the honour of a higher one, and that better, therefore, than the 640 signal service it was the dream of my boyhood to render to his fame and memory, may be the saying of a few, inadequate words upon these scarcely more important supplementary letters of SHELLEY.

PARIS, *Dec. 4th, 1851.*

COURTSHIP
CORRESPONDENCE (1845–6)

1. R.B. to E.B.B., 10 Jan. 1845

New Cross, Hatcham, Surrey.

    I love your verses with all my heart, dear Miss Barrett,—and this is no off-hand complimentary letter that I shall write,—whatever else, no prompt matter-of-course recognition of your genius, and there a graceful and natural end of the thing: since the day last week when I first read your poems,° I quite laugh to remember how I have been turning and turning again in my mind what I should be able to tell you of their effect upon me—for in the first flush of delight I thought I would this once get out of my habit of purely passive enjoyment, when I do really enjoy, and thoroughly justify my admiration—perhaps even, as a loyal fellow-craftsman should, try and find fault and do you some little good to be proud of hereafter!— but nothing comes of it all—so into me has it gone, and part of me has it become, this great living poetry of yours, not a flower of which but took root and grew—oh how different that is from lying to be dried and pressed flat, and prized highly and put in a book with a proper account at top and bottom, and shut up and put away . . and the book called a 'Flora,' besides! After all I need not give up the thought of doing that, too, in time; because even now, talking with whoever is worthy, I can give a reason for my faith in one and another excellence, the fresh strange music, the affluent language, the exquisite pathos and true new brave thought—but in this addressing myself to you—your own self, and for the first time, my feeling rises altogether. I do, as I say, love these books with all my heart— and I love you too: do you know I was once not very far from seeing—really seeing you? Mr Kenyon said to me one morning 'Would you like to see Miss Barrett?'—then he went to announce me,—then he returned . . you were too unwell—and now it is years ago—and I feel as at some untoward passage in my travels—as if I had been close, so close, to some world's-wonder in chapel or crypt, only a screen to push and I might have entered, but there was some slight . . so it now seems . . slight and just-sufficient bar to admission; and the half-opened door shut, and I went home my thousands of miles, and the sight was never to be!

Well, these Poems were to be—and this true thankful joy and pride with which I feel myself

Yours ever faithfully,

Robert Browning

2. E.B.B. to R.B., 11 Jan. 1845

50 Wimpole Street:
Jan. 11, 1845.

I thank you, dear Mr Browning, from the bottom of my heart. You meant to give me pleasure by your letter—and even if the object had not been answered, I ought still to thank you. But it is thoroughly answered. Such a letter from such a hand! Sympathy is dear—very dear to me: but the sympathy of a poet, & of such a poet, is the quintessence of sympathy to me! Will you take back my gratitude for it?—agreeing, too, that of all the commerce done in the world, from Tyre to Carthage, the exchange of sympathy for gratitude is the most princely thing?

For the rest you draw me on with your kindness. It is difficult to get rid of people when you once have given them too much pleasure—*that* is a fact, & we will not stop for the moral of it. What I was going to say . . after a little natural hesitation . . is, that if ever you emerge without inconvenient effort from your 'passive state,' & will *tell* me of such faults as rise to the surface and strike you as important in my poems, (for of course, I do not think of troubling you with criticism in detail) you will confer a lasting obligation on me, and one which I shall value so much, that I covet it at a distance. I do not pretend to any extraordinary meekness under criticism, & it is possible enough that I might not be altogether obedient to yours. But with my high respect for your power in your Art & for your experience as an artist, it would be quite impossible for me to hear a general observation of yours on what appear to you my master-faults, without being the better for it hereafter in some way. I ask for only a sentence or two of general observation—and I do not ask even for *that*, so as to teaze you—but in the humble, low voice, which is so excellent a thing in women°—particularly when they go a-begging!

The most frequent general criticism I receive, is, I think, upon the style, 'if I *would* but change my style'! But *that* is an objection (isn't it?) to the writer bodily? Buffon says, and every sincere writer must feel, that '*Le style c'est l'homme;*' a fact, however, scarcely calculated to lessen the objection with certain critics.

It is indeed true that I was so near to the pleasure and honour of making your acquaintance?—& can it be true that you look back upon the lost opportunity with any regret? BUT . . . you know . . if you had entered the 'crypt,' you might have caught cold, or been tired to death, & *wished* yourself 'a thousand miles off'—which w^{d} have been worse than travelling them. It is not my interest however to put such thoughts in your head about its being 'all for the best'— and I would rather hope (as I do) that what I lost by one chance I may recover by some future one. Winters shut me up as they do dormouse's eyes: in the spring, *we shall see*: & I am so much better that I seem turning round to the outward world again. And in the meantime I have learnt to know your voice, not merely from the poetry but from the kindness in it. Mr Kenyon often speaks of you— dear Mr Kenyon!—who most unspeakably, or only speakably with tears in my eyes, . . has been my friend & helper, & my book's friend & helper! critic & sympathiser, true friend of all hours! You know him well enough, I think, to understand that I must be grateful to him.

I am writing too much—& notwithstanding that I am writing too much, I will write of one thing more. I will say that I am your debtor, not only for this cordial letter & for all the pleasure which came with it, but in other ways, & those the highest: & I will say that while I live to follow this divine art of poetry . . in proportion to my love for it and my devotion to it, I must be a devout admirer & student of your works. This is in my heart to say to you—& I say it.
And, for the rest, I am proud to remain
Your obliged and faithful
Elizabeth B. Barrett

3. R.B. to E.B.B., 13 Jan. 1845

New Cross, Hatcham, Surrey.
Jan. 13, 1845.

Dear Miss Barrett,
  I just shall say, in as few words as I can, that you make me very

happy, and that, now the beginning is over, I dare say I shall do better . . because my poor praise, number one, was nearly as felicitously brought out, as a certain tribute to no less a personage than Tasso, which I was amused with at Rome some weeks ago, in a neat pencilling on the plaister-wall by his tomb at Sant' Onofrio—'Alla cara memoria—di—(please fancy solemn interspaces and grave capital letters at the new lines)—di—Torquato Tasso—il Dottore Bernardini—offriva—il seguente Carme—*O tu*'° . . and no more, the good man, it should seem, breaking down with the overload of love here! But my 'O tu'—was breathed out most sincerely, and now you have taken it in gracious part, the rest will come after. Only,—and which is why I write now—it looks as if I have introduced some phrase or other about 'your faults' so cleverly as to give exactly the opposite meaning to what I meant, which was, that in my first ardour I had thought to tell you of *everything* which impressed me in your verses, down, even, to whatever 'faults' I could find—a good earnest, when I had got to *them*, that I had left out not much between: as if some Mr Fellows° were to say, in the overflow of his first enthusiasm of rewarded adventure, 'I will describe you all the outer life and ways of these Lycians, down to their very sandal-thongs,' whereto the be-corresponded one rejoins—'Shall I get next week, then, your dissertation on sandal-thongs'? Yes, and a little about the 'Olympian Horses,' and god-charioteers as well!

What 'struck me as faults,' were not matters on the removal of which, one was to have—poetry, or high poetry,—but the very highest poetry, so I thought, and that, to universal recognition: for myself, or any artist, in many of the cases there would be a positive loss of true, peculiar artist's pleasure . . for an instructed eye loves to see where the brush has dipped twice in a lustrous colour, has lain insistingly along a favorite outline, dwelt lovingly in a grand shadow—for these 'too muches' for the everybody's picture are so many helps to the making out the real painter's-picture as he had it in his brain; and all of the Titian's Naples Magdalen must have once been golden in its degree to justify that heap of hair in her hands— the *only* gold effected now!

But about this soon—for night is drawing on and I go out, yet cannot, quiet at conscience, till I repeat (to *myself* . . for I never said it to you, I think) that your poetry must be, cannot but be, infinitely more to me than mine to you—for you *do* what I always wanted, hoped to do, and only seem now likely to do for the first time. You speak out, *you*,—I only make men & women speak—give you truth

broken into prismatic hues, and fear the pure white light, even if it is
in me: but I am going to try .. so it will be no small comfort to have
your company just now,—seeing that when you have your men &
women aforesaid, you are busied with them, whereas it seems bleak
melancholy work, this talking to the wind (for I have begun)—yet I
don't think I shall let *you* hear, after all, the savage things about
Popes and imaginative religions that I must say.

See how I go on and on to you,—I who, whenever now and then
pulled, by the head and hair, into letter-writing, get sorrowfully on
for a line or two, as the cognate creature urged on by stick and string,
and then come down 'flop' upon the sweet haven of page one, line
last, as serene as the sleep of the virtuous! You will never more, I
hope, talk of 'the honor of my acquaintance,' but I will joyfully wait
for the delight of your friendship, and the spring, and my Chapel-
sight after all!

Ever yours most faithfully,

R. Browning

For Mr Kenyon—I have a convenient theory about *him*, and his
otherwise quite unaccountable kindness to me—but 'tis quite night
now, and they call me.

4. E.B.B. to R.B., 15 Jan. 1845

50 Wimpole Street:
Jan. 15, 1845.

Dear Mr Browning,

The fault was clearly with me & not with you.

When I had an Italian master, years ago, he told me that there was
an unpronounceable English word which absolutely expressed me, &
which he would say in his own tongue, as he could not in mine, ..
'*testa lunga*.' Of course, the signor meant *headlong*°—and now I have
had enough to tame me, & might be expected to stand still in my
stall. But you see I do not. Headlong I was at first, and headlong I
continue—precipitously rushing forward through all manner of net-
tles & briars instead of keeping the path,—guessing at the meaning of
unknown words instead of looking into the dictionary .. tearing open
letters, and never untying a string,—and expecting everything to be
done in a minute, & the thunder to be as quick as the lightning. And
so, at your half word I flew at the whole one, with all its possible

consequences, & wrote what you read. Our common friend, as I think he is, Mr Horne.° is often forced to entreat me into patience & coolness of purpose,—though his only intercourse with me has been by letter. And, by the way, you will be sorry to hear that during his stay in Germany *he* has been 'headlong' (out of a metaphor) twice,—once, in falling from the Drachenfels, when he only just saved himself by catching at a vine,—and once quite lately, at Christmas, in a fall on the ice of the Elbe in skating, when he dislocated his left shoulder in a very painful manner. He is doing quite well, I believe—but it was sad to have such a shadow from the German Christmas tree, & he a stranger.

In art, however, I understand that it does not do to be headlong, but patient & laborious—& there is a love strong enough, even in me, to overcome nature. I apprehend what you mean in the criticism you just intimate, & shall turn it over & over in my mind until I get practical good from it. What no mere critic sees, but what you, an artist, know, is the difference between the thing desired & the thing attained, between the idea in the writer's mind & the $\epsilon\check{\iota}\delta\omega\lambda o\nu$° cast off in his work. All the effort—the quickening of the breath & beating of the heart in pursuit, which is ruffling & injurious to the general effect of a composition; all which you call 'insistency,' & which many w^{d} call superfluity, and which *is* superfluous in a sense.. *you* can pardon, because you understand. The great chasm between the thing I say, & the thing I would say, w^{d} be quite dispiriting to me, in spite even of such kindnesses as yours, if the desire did not master the despondency. 'Oh for a horse with wings!' It is wrong of me to write so of myself—only you put your finger on the root of a fault, which has, to my fancy, been a little misapprehended. I do not *say everything I think* (as has been said of me by master-critics) but I *take every means to say what I think*, which is different!—or I fancy so!

In one thing, however, you are wrong. Why sh^{d} you deny the full measure of my delight & benefit from your writings? I could tell you why you should not. You have in your vision two worlds—or to use the language of the schools of the day, you are both subjective & objective in the habits of your mind. You can deal both with abstract thought & with human passion in the most passionate sense. Thus, you have an immense grasp in Art; and no one at all accustomed to consider the usual forms of it, could help regarding with reverence & gladness the gradual expansion of your powers. Then you are 'masculine' to the height—and I, as a woman, have studied some of your

gestures of language & intonation wistfully, as a thing beyond me far!
& the more admirable for being beyond.

Of your new work I hear with delight. How good of you to tell me.
And it is not dramatic in the strict sense I am to understand . . (am I
right in understanding so?) and you speak in your own person 'to the
winds'? no—but to the thousand living sympathies which will awake
to hear you. A great dramatic power may develop itself otherwise
than in the formal drama; & I have been guilty of wishing, before this
hour, (for reasons which I will not thrust upon you after all my
tedious writing), that you w^d give the public a poem unassociated
directly or indirectly with the stage, for a trial on the popular heart. I
reverence the drama, but—

But I break in on myself out of consideration for you. I might have
done it you will think, before. I vex your 'serene sleep of the vir-
tuous' like a nightmare. Do not say . . 'No.' I am *sure* I do! As to the
vain parlance of the world, I did not talk of the 'honor of your
acquaintance' without a true sense of honor, indeed; but I shall
willingly exchange it all (& *now*, if you please, at this moment, for
fear of worldly mutabilities) for the 'delight of your friendship.'

Believe me, therefore, dear Mr Browning.

Faithfully yours & gratefully,

Elizabeth B. Barrett

For Mr Kenyon's kindness, as *I* see it . . no 'theory' will account. I
class it with mesmerism for that reason.

5. R.B. to E.B.B., 27 Jan. 1845

New Cross, Hatcham
Monday Night

Dear Miss Barrett,

Your books lie on my table here, at arm's length from me, in this
old room where I sit all day: and when my head aches or wanders or
strikes work, as it now or then will, I take my chance for either green
covered volume, as if it were so much fresh trefoil to feel in one's
hands this winter-time,—and round I turn, and, putting a decisive
elbow on three or four half-done-with 'Bells'° of mine, read, read,
read, and just as I have shut up the book and walked to the window, I
recollect that you wanted me to find faults there, and that, in an

unwise hour, I engaged to do so. Meantime, the days go by (the whitethroat is come and sings now) and as I would not have you 'look down on me from your white heights' as promise breaker, evader, or forgetter, if I could help . . and as, if I am very candid & contrite, you may find it in your heart to write to me again . . who knows? . . I shall say at once that the said faults cannot be lost, must be *somewhere*, and shall be faithfully brought you back whenever they turn up,—as people tell one of missing matters. I am rather exacting, myself, with my own gentle audience, and get to say spiteful things about them when they are backward in their duties of appreciation—but really, *really*—could I be quite sure that anybody as good as . . I must go on, I suppose, and say—as myself, even, were honestly to feel towards me as I do, towards the writer of Bertha, and the Drama, and the Duchess, and the Page° and—the whole two volumes, I should be paid after a fashion, I know.

One thing I can do . . pencil, if you like, and annotate, and dissertate upon that I love most and least—I think I can do it, that is.

Here an odd memory comes—of a friend who,—volunteering such a service to a sonnet-writing somebody, gave him a taste of his quality in a side-column of short criticisms on sonnet the First, and starting off the beginning three lines with, of course, 'bad, worse, worst'—made by a generous mintage of words to meet the sudden run on his epithets, 'worser, worserer, worserest' pay off the second terzet in full . . no 'badder, badderer, badderest' fell to the *Second's* allowance, and 'worser' &c. answered the demands of the Third—'worster, worsterer, worsterest' supplied the emergency of the Fourth; and, bestowing his last 'worserestest and worstestest' on lines 13 and 14, my friend (slapping his forehead like an emptied strong-box) frankly declared himself bankrupt, and honourably incompetent, to satisfy the reasonable expectations of the rest of the series.

What an illustration of the law by which opposite ideas suggest opposite, and contrary images come together!

See now, how, of that 'Friendship' you offer me (and here Juliet's word rises to my lips)—I feel sure once and for ever—I have got already, I see, into this little pet-handwriting of mine (not anyone else's) which scratches on as if theatrical copyists (ah me!) and BRADBURY AND EVANS' READER° were not! But you shall get something better than this nonsense one day, if you will have patience with me . . hardly better, tho', because this does me real good, gives real relief, to write. After all, you know nothing, next to nothing of me, and that stops me. Spring is to come, however!

If you hate writing to me as I hate writing to nearly everybody, I pray you never write—if you do, as you say, care for anything I have done,—I will simply assure you, that meaning to begin work in deep earnest, BEGIN without affectation, God knows—I do not know what will help me more than hearing from you,—and therefore, if you do not so very much hate it, I know I *shall* hear from you—and very little more about your 'tiring me.'

Ever yours faithfully,

Robert Browning

6. *E.B.B. to R.B. 3 Feb. 1845*

50 Wimpole Street
Feb. 3, 1845

Why how could I hate to write to you, dear Mr Browning? Could you believe in such a thing? If nobody likes writing to everybody (except such professional letter writers as you & I are *not*) yet everybody likes writing to somebody, & it w^d be strange and contradictory if I were not always delighted both to hear from *you* and to write to *you* .. this talking upon paper being as good a social pleasure as another, when our means are somewhat straightened. As for me, I have done most of my talking by post of late years—as people shut up in dungeons, take up with scrawling mottos on the walls. Not that I write to many in the way of regular correspondence, as our friend Mr Horne predicates of me in his romances° (which is mere romancing!—) but that there are a few who will write & be written to by me without a sense of injury. Dear Miss Mitford, for instance—you do not know her, I think, personally, although she was the first to tell me (when I was very ill & insensible to all the glories of the world except poetry) of the grand scene in Pippa Passes,°—she has filled a large drawer in this room with delightful letters, heart-warm & soul-warm, .. driftings of nature (if sunshine c^d drift like snow)—& which, if they sh^d ever fall the way of all writing, into print, w^d assume the folio shape as a matter of course, & take rank on the lowest shelf of libraries, with Benedictine editions of the Fathers, κ.τ.λ.° I write this to you to show how I can have pleasure in letters, and never think them too long, nor too frequent, nor too illegible from being written in little 'pet hands.' I can read any MS. except the writing on the pyramids. And if you will only promise to treat me 'en bon camarade,' without reference to the conventionalities of 'ladies & gentlemen,' taking no thought for your sentences, (nor for mine) nor for your blots, (nor for mine), nor for your blunt speaking (nor for mine), nor for your badd speling (nor for mine), & if you agree to send me a blotted thought whenever you are in the mind for it, & with as little ceremony & less legibility than you would think it necessary to employ towards your printer .. why, *then*, I am ready to sign & seal the contract, and to rejoice in being 'articled' as your correspondent. Only *don't* let us have any constraint, any ceremony! *Don't* be civil to me when you feel rude,—nor loquacious when you incline to silence,—nor yielding in the manners when you are perverse in the mind. See how out of the world I am! Suffer me to profit by it in almost the only profitable circumstance .. & let us rest from the bowing and the courtesying, you & I, on each side. You will find me an honest man on the whole, if rather hasty & prejudging, .. which is a different thing from prejudice at the worst. And we have great sympathies in common, & I am inclined to look up to you in many things, & to learn as much of everything as you will teach me. On the other hand you must prepare yourself to forbear & to forgive—will you? While I throw off the ceremony, I hold the faster to the kindness.

Is it true, as you say, that I 'know so "little"' of you? And is it true, as others say, that the productions of an artist do not partake of his real nature, .. that in the minor sense, man is not made in the image of God? It is *not* true, to my mind—& therefore it is not true that I know little of you, except in as far as it is true (which I believe) that your greatest works are to come. Need I assure you that I shall always hear with the deepest interest every word you will say to me of what you are doing or about to do? I hear of the 'old room' & the '"bells" lying about,' with an interest .. which you may guess at, perhaps. And when you tell me besides, .. of *my poems being there*; & of your caring for them so much beyond the tide-mark of my hopes, .. the pleasure rounds itself into a charm, & prevents its own expression. Overjoyed I am with this cordial sympathy—but it is better, I feel, to try to justify it by future work, than to thank you for it now. I think,—if I may dare to name myself with you in the poetic relation,—that we both have high views of the art we follow, and steadfast purpose in the pursuit of it, & that we should not, either of *us*, be likely to be thrown from the course, by the casting of any Atalanta-ball° of speedy popularity. But I do not know, I cannot

guess, .. whether you are liable to be pained deeply by hard criticism
& cold neglect .. such as original writers like yourself, are too often
exposed to—or whether the love of Art is enough for you, & the
exercise of Art the filling joy of your life. Not that praise must not
always, of necessity, be delightful to the artist, but that it may be
redundant to his content. Do you think so? or not? It appears to me
that poets who, like Keats, are highly susceptible to criticism, must
be jealous, in their own persons, of the future honour of their works.
Because, if a work is worthy, honour must follow it— though the
worker should not live to see that following or overtaking. Now, is it
not enough that the work be honoured—enough I mean, for the
worker? And is it not enough to keep down a poets ordinary wearing
anxieties, to think, that if his work be worthy it will have honour, &,
if not, that 'Sparta must have nobler sons than he'?° I am writing
nothing applicable, I see, to anything in question—but when one
falls into a favorite train of thought, one indulges oneself in thinking
on. I began in thinking & wondering what sort of artistic constitution
you had—being determined, as you may observe (with a sarcastic
smile at the impertinence!), to set about knowing as much as possible
of you immediately. Then you spoke of your 'gentle audience'—(you
began!) & I who know that you have not one but many enthusiastic
admirers, the 'fit & few' in the intense meaning, yet not the *diffused*
fame which will come to you presently,—wrote on, down the margin
of the subject, till I parted from it altogether. But, after all, we are on
the proper matter of sympathy. And after all, & after all that has been
said and mused upon the 'natural ills,' the anxiety, & wearing out
experienced by the true artist, .. is not the *good* immeasurably greater
than the *evil*? Is it not great good, & great joy? For my part, I wonder
sometimes .. I surprise myself wondering .. how without such an
object & purpose of life, people find it worth while to live at all.
And, for happiness .. why my only idea of happiness, as far as my
personal enjoyment is concerned, (but I have been straightened in
some respects and in comparison with the majority of livers!) lies
deep in poetry & its associations. And then, the escape from pangs of
heart & bodily weakness .. when you throw off *yourself* .. what you
feel to be *yourself*, .. into another atmosphere & into other relations,
where your life may spread its wings out new, & gather on every
separate plume a brightness from the sun of the sun! Is it possible
that imaginative writers sh^d be so fond of depreciating & lamenting
over their own destiny? Possible, certainly—but reasonable, not at
all—& grateful, less than anything!

My faults, my faults—Shall I help you? Ah—you see them too well, I fear. And do you know that *I* also have something of your feeling about 'being about to *begin*'—or I should dare to praise you for having it. But in you, it is different—it is, in you, a virtue. When Prometheus had recounted a long list of sorrows to be endured by Io, & declared at last that he was μηδέπω ἐν προοιμίοις,° poor Io burst out crying. And when the author of 'Paracelsus' and the 'Bells and Pomegranates' says that he is only 'going to begin' we may well (to take 'the opposite idea' as you write) rejoice & clap our hands. Yet I believe that, whatever you may have done, you *will* do what is greater. It is my faith for you.

And how I sh^d like to know what poets have been your sponsors, 'to promise & vow' for you,—and whether you have held true to early tastes, or leapt violently from them—& what books you read, & what hours you write in. How curious I could prove myself!—(if it isn't proved already).

But this is too much indeed—past all bearing, I suspect. Well—but if I ever write to you again, . . I mean, if you wish it,—it may be in the other extreme of shortness. So do not take me for a born heroine of Richardson, or think that I sin always to this length! else,—you might indeed repent your quotation from Juliet . . which I guessed at once—& of course.

'I have no joy in this contract to-day!
It is too unadvised, too rash and sudden.'°

Ever faithfully yours,

Elizabeth B. Barrett

7. *R.B. to E.B.B., 11 Feb. 1845*

Hatcham, Tuesday.

Dear Miss Barrett,

People would hardly ever tell falsehoods about a matter, if they had been let tell truth in the beginning—for it is hard to prophane one's very self, and nobody who has, for instance, used certain words and ways to a mother or a father *could* . . even if by the devil's help he *would* . . reproduce or mimic them with any effect to anybody else that was to be won over; and so, if 'I love you' were always outspoken when it might be, there would, I suppose, be no fear of its desecration at any after time: but lo! only last night, I had to write, on the part of Mr Carlyle, to a certain ungainly foolish gentleman who keeps back from him, with all the fussy impotence of stupidity (not bad feeling, alas; for *that* we could deal with) a certain MS. letter of Cromwell's which completes the collection now going to press°—and this long-ears had to be 'dear Sir'd' and 'obedient servanted' till I *said* (to use a mild word) 'commend me to the sincerities of this kind of thing'! When I spoke of you knowing little of me, one of the senses in which I meant so was this .. that I would not well vowel-point my common-place letters and syllables with a masoretic° *other* sound and sense, make my 'dear' something intenser than 'dears' in ordinary, and 'yours ever' a thought more significant than the run of its like; and all this came of your talking of 'tiring me,' 'being too curious,' &c. &c. which I should never have heard of had the plain truth looked out of my letter with its unmistakeable eyes: *now*, what you say of the 'bowing,' and convention that is to be, and *tant de façons*° that are not to be, helps me once and for ever—for have I not a right to say simply that, for reasons I know, for other reasons I don't exactly know, but might if I chose to think a little, and for still other reasons, which, most likely, all the choosing and thinking in the world would not make me know, I had rather hear from you than see anybody else. Never you care, dear noble Carlyle, nor you, my own friend Alfred over the sea,° nor a troop of true lovers!—Are not these fates written? There! Don't you answer this, please, but, mind it is on record, and now then, with a lighter conscience I shall begin replying to your questions. First then,—what I have printed gives *no* knowledge of me—it evidences abilities of various kinds, if you will—and a dramatic sympathy with certain modifications of passion .. *that* I think: but I never have begun, even, what I hope I was born to begin and end,—'R.B. a poem.' And next, if I speak (and, God knows, feel) as if what you have read were sadly imperfect demonstrations of even mere ability, it is from no absurd vanity, though it might seem so—these scenes and song-scraps *are* such mere and very escapes of my inner power, which lives in me like the light in those crazy Mediterranean phares I have watched at sea, wherein the light is ever revolving in a dark gallery, bright and alive, and only after a weary interval leaps out, for a moment, from the one narrow chink, and then goes on with the blind wall between it and you; and, no doubt, *then*, precisely, does the poor drudge that carries the cresset set himself most busily to trim the wick—for don't think I want to say I have not worked hard—(this head of mine knows better)—but the work has been *inside*, and not when at stated times

I held up my light to you—and, that there is no self-delusion here, I would prove to you, (and nobody else) even by opening this desk I write on, and showing what stuff, in the way of wood, I *could* make a great bonfire with, if I might only knock the whole clumsy top off my tower!—Of course, every writing body says the same, so I gain nothing by the avowal; but when I remember how I have done what was published, and half done what may never be, I say with some right, you can know but little of me. Still, I *hope* sometimes, though phrenologists will have it that I *cannot*, and am doing better with this darling 'Luria'—so safe in my head, & a tiny slip of paper I cover with my thumb!

Then you inquire about my 'sensitiveness to criticism,' and I shall be glad to tell you exactly, because I have, more than once, taken a course you might else not understand. I shall live always,—that is for me—I am living here this 1845, that is for London. I write from a thorough conviction that it is the duty of me, and with the belief that, after every drawback & shortcoming, I do my best, all things considered—that is for *me*, and, so being, the not being listened to by one human creature would, I hope, in nowise affect me. But of course I must, if for merely scientific purposes, know all about this 1845, its ways and doings, and something I do know, as that for a dozen cabbages, if I pleased to grow them in the garden here, I might demand, say, a dozen pence at Covent Garden Market,—and that for a dozen scenes, of the average goodness, I may challenge as many plaudits at the theatre close by; and a dozen pages of verse, brought to the Rialto where verse-merchants most do congregate° ought to bring me a fair proportion of the Reviewers' gold-currency, seeing the other traders pouch their winnings, as I do see: well, when they won't pay me for my cabbages, nor praise me for my poems, I may, if I please, say 'more's the shame,' and bid both parties 'decamp to the crows,'° in Greek phrase, and YET go very lighthearted back to a garden-full of rose-trees, and a soul-full of comforts; if they had bought my greens I should have been able to buy the last number of 'Punch,' and go thro' the toll-gate of Waterloo Bridge, and give the blind clarionet-player a trifle, and all without changing my gold—if they had taken to my books, my father and mother would have been proud of this and the other 'favourable critique,' and .. at least so folks hold .. I should have to pay Mr Moxon less by a few pounds—whereas .. but you see! Indeed, I force myself to say ever and anon, in the interest of the market-gardeners regular, and Keats's proper,—'It's nothing to *you*,—critics & hucksters, all of you, if I *have* this

garden and this conscience,—I might go die at Rome, or take to gin
and the newspaper, for what *you* would care'! So I don't quite lay
open my resources to everybody. But it does so happen, that I have
met with much more than I could have expected in this matter of
kindly and prompt recognition. I never wanted a real set of good
hearty praisers—and no bad reviewers—I am quite content with my
share. No—what I laughed at in my 'gentle audience' is a sad trick
the real admirers have of admiring at the wrong place—enough to
make an apostle swear. *That* does make me savage,—*never* the other
kind of people; why, think now: take your own 'Drama of Exile' and
let *me* send it to the first twenty men & women that shall knock at
your door to-day and after—of whom the first five are—the
Postman, the seller of cheap sealing-wax, Mr Hawkins Junr, the
Butcher for orders, and the Tax gatherer—will you let me, by
Cornelius Agrippa's assistance,° force these five and their fellows to
read, and report on, this drama—and, when I have put these faithful
reports into fair English, do you believe they would be better than, if
as good, as, the general run of Periodical criticisms? Not they, I will
venture to affirm. But then,—once again, I get these people together
and give them your book, and persuade them, moreover, that by
praising it, the Postman will be helping its author to divide Long
Acre into two beats, one of which she will take with half the salary
and all the red collar,—that a sealing wax-vendor will see red wafers
brought into vogue, and so on with the rest—and won't you just wish
for your Spectators and Observers and Newcastle-upon-Tyne—
Hebdomadal Mercuries back again! You see the inference—I do
sincerely esteem it a perfectly providential and miraculous thing that
they are so well-behaved in ordinary, these critics; and for Keats and
Tennyson to 'go softly all their days'° for a gruff word or two is quite
inexplicable to me, and always has been. Tennyson reads the 'Quar-
terly' and does as they bid him,° with the most solemn face in
the world—out goes this, in goes that, all is changed and ranged
.. Oh me!—
   Out comes the sun, in comes the 'Times' and eleven strikes (it
does) already, and I have to go to Town, and I have no alternative but
that this story of the Critic and Poet, 'the Bear and the Fiddle,'
should 'begin but break off in the middle'°—yet I do not—nor will
you henceforth, I know, say, 'I vex you, I am sure, by this lengthy
writing'—mind that spring is coming, for all this snow; and know me
for yours ever faithfully,

                                             R. Browning

I don't dare—yet I will—ask *can* you read this? Because I *could* write a little better, but not so fast. Do you keep writing just as you do now!

8. E.B.B. to R.B., 17 Feb. 1845

50 Wimpole Street,
February 17, 1845.

Dear Mr Browning,

To begin with the end (which is only characteristic of the perverse like myself), I assure you I read your handwriting as currently as I could read the clearest type from font. If I had practised the art of reading your letters all my life, I couldn't do it better. And then I approve of small MS. upon principle. Think of what an immense quantity of physical energy must go to the making of those immense sweeping handwritings achieved by some persons . . . Mr Landor,° for instance, who writes as if he had the sky for a copybook & dotted his *i*'s in proportion. People who do such things sh^d wear gauntlets,—yes, and have none to wear,—or they wouldn't waste their strength so. People who write . . by profession . . shall I say? . . never should do it . . or what will become of them when most of their strengths retires into their head & heart, (as is the case with some of us & may be the case with all) & when they have to write a poem twelve times over, as Mr Kenyon says I should do if I were virtuous? Not that I do it. Does anybody do it, I wonder? Do *you*, ever? From what you tell me of the trimming of the light, I imagine not. And besides, one may be laborious as a writer, without copying twelve times over. I believe there are people who will tell you in a moment what three times six is, without 'doing it' on their fingers; and in the same way one may work one's verses in one's head quite as laboriously as on paper—I maintain it. I consider myself a very patient, laborious writer—though dear Mr Kenyon laughs me to scorn when I say so. And just see how it could be otherwise. If I were netting a purse I might be thinking of something else & drop my stitches,—or even if I were writing verses to please a popular taste, I might be careless in it. But the pursuit of an Ideal acknowledged by the mind, *will* draw and concentrate the powers of the mind—and Art, you know, is a jealous god & demands the whole man . . or woman. I cannot conceive of a sincere artist who is also a careless one—though one may have a quicker hand than another, in general,—& though all are liable to vicissitudes in the degree of facility .. & to entanglements in the machinery, notwithstanding every degree of facility. You may write twenty lines one day—or even three like Euripides in three days—and a hundred lines in one more day—& yet on the hundred, may have been expended as much good work, as on the twenty & the three. And also, as you say, the lamp is trimmed behind the wall—and the act of utterance is the evidence of foregone study still more than it is the occasion to study. The deep interest with which I read all that you had the kindness to write to me of yourself, you must trust me for, as I find it hard to express it. It is sympathy in one way, and interest every way! And now, see! Although you proved to me with admirable logic that, for reasons which you know & reasons which you don't know, I couldn't possibly know anything about you, .. though that is all true .. & proven (which is better than true) I really did understand of you before I was told, exactly what you told me. Yes—I did indeed. I felt sure that as a poet you fronted the future—& that your chief works, in your own apprehension, were to come. Oh—I take no credit of sagacity for it,—as I did not long ago to my sisters & brothers, when I professed to have knowledge of all their friends whom I never saw in my life, by the image coming with the name; and threw them into shouts of laughter by giving out all the blue eyes & black eyes & hazel eyes & noses Roman & Gothic ticketed aright for the Mr Smiths & Miss Hawkinses—& hit the bull's eye & the true features of the case, ten times out of twelve. But *you* are different. *You* are to be made out by the comparative anatomy system. You have thrown out fragments of bone, *os* .. *sublime* .. indicative of soul-mammothism—and you live to develop your nature, .. *if* you live. That is easy & plain. You have taken a great range—from those high faint notes of the mystics which are beyond personality .. to dramatic impersonations, gruff with nature, 'gr-r-r-you swine';° & when these are thrown into harmony, as in a manner they are in 'Pippa Passes' (which I could find in my heart to covet the authorship of, more than any of your works—), the combinations of effect must always be striking & noble—and you must feel yourself drawn on to such combinations more and more. But I do not, you say, know yourself .. you. I only know abilities and faculties. Well, then! teach me yourself .. you. I will not insist on the knowledge—and, in fact, you have not written the R. B. poem yet—your rays fall obliquely rather than directly straight. I see you only in your moon. Do tell me all of yourself that you can & will .. before the

R. B. poem comes out. And what is *Luria*? A poem and not a drama? I mean, a poem not in the dramatic form? Well! I have wondered at you sometimes, not for daring, but for bearing to trust your noble works into the great mill of the 'rank, popular' playhouse, to be ground to pieces between the teeth of vulgar actors and actresses. I, for one, would as soon have 'my soul among lions.'° 'There is a fascination in it,' says Miss Mitford, & I am sure there must be, to account for it. Publics in the mass are bad enough; but to distil the dregs of the public & baptise oneself in that acrid moisture, where can be the temptation? I could swear by Shakespeare, as was once sworn 'by those dead at Marathon,' that I do not see where. I love the drama too. I look to our old dramatists as to our Kings & princes in poetry. I love them through all the deeps of their abominations. But the theatre in those days was a better medium between the people and the poet; and the press in those days was a less sufficient medium than now. Still, the poet suffered by the theatre even then; & the reasons are very obvious.

How true—how true . . is all you say about critics. My convictions follow you in every word. And I delighted to read your views of the poet's right aspect towards criticism—I read them with the most complete appreciation & sympathy. I have sometimes thought that it would be a curious & instructive process, as illustrative of the wisdom & apprehensiveness of critics, if anyone would collect the critical soliloquies of every age touching its own literature, (as far as such may be extant) and *confer* them with the literary product of the said ages. Professor Wilson° has begun something of the kind apparently, in his initiatory paper of the last Blackwood number on critics, beginning with Dryden—but he seems to have no design in his notice—it is a mere critique on the critic. And then, he sh^d have begun earlier than Dryden—earlier even than Sir Philip Sydney, who in the noble 'Discourse on Poetry,'° gives such singular evidence of being stone-critic-blind to the gods who moved around him. As far as I can remember, he saw even Shakespeare but indifferently. Oh, it was in his eyes quite an unillumed age, that period of Elizabeth which *we* see full of suns! and few can see what is close to the eyes though they run their heads against it: the denial of contemporary genius is the rule rather than the exception. No one counts the eagles in the nest, till there is a rush of wings—and lo! they are flown. And here we speak of understanding men, such as the Sydneys and the Drydens. Of the great body of critics you observe rightly, that they are better than might be expected of their badness—only the fact of their *influence* is no less undeniable than the reason why they should not be influential. The brazen kettles will be taken for oracles all the world over. But the influence is for to-day, for this hour—not for to-morrow & the day after—unless indeed as you say, the poet do himself perpetuate the influence by submitting to it. Do you know Tennyson?—that is, with a face to face knowledge? I have great admiration for him. In execution, he is exquisite,— and, in music, a most subtle weigher out to the ear of fine airs. That such a poet sh^d submit blindly to the suggestions of his critics, (I do not say that suggestions from without may not be accepted with discrimination sometimes, to the benefit of the acceptor) blindly & implicitly to the suggestions of his critics, .. is much as if Babbage were to take my opinion & undo his calculating machine° by it. Napoleon called poetry '*science creuse*'°—which, although he was not scientific in poetry himself, is true enough. But anybody is qualified, according to everybody, for giving opinions upon poetry. It is not so in chymistry and mathematics. Nor is it so, I believe, in whist and the polka. But then these are more serious things.

Yes—and it does delight me to hear of your 'garden full of roses and soul full of comforts.' You have the right to both—you have the key to both. You have written enough to live by, though only beginning to write, as you say of yourself. And this reminds me to remind you that when I talked of coveting most of the authorship of your 'Pippa,' I did not mean to call it your finest work (you might reproach me for *that*) but just to express a personal feeling. Do you know what it is to covet your neighbour's poetry?—not his fame, but his poetry?—I dare say not. You are too generous. And, in fact, beauty is beauty, and, whether it comes by our own hand or another's, blessed be the coming of it! *I*, besides, feel *that*. And yet— and yet, I have been aware of a feeling within me which has spoken two or three times to the effect of a wish, that I had been visited with the vision of 'Pippa', before you—and *confiteor tibi*°—I confess the baseness of it. The conception is, to my mind, most exquisite & altogether original—and the contrast in the working out of the plan, singularly expressive of various faculty.

Is the poem under your thumb, emerging from it? and in what metre? May I ask such questions?

And does Mr Carlyle tell you that he has forbidden all 'singing' to this perverse & froward generation, which should work & not sing? And have you told Mr Carlyle that song is work, and also the condition of work? I am a devout sitter at his feet—and it is an effort to me to think him wrong in anything—and once when he told me to write prose and not verse, I fancied that his opinion was I had mistaken my calling, . . a fancy which in infinite kindness & gentleness he stooped immediately to correct. I never shall forget the grace of that kindness—but then! For *him* to have thought ill of *me*, would not have been strange—I often think ill of myself, as God knows. But for Carlyle to think of putting away, even for a season, the poetry of the world, was wonderful, and has left me ruffled in my thoughts ever since. I do not know him personally at all. But as his disciple I ventured (by an exceptional motive) to send him my poems, and I heard from him as a consequence. 'Dear and noble' he is indeed—and a poet unaware of himself; all but the sense of music. You feel it so—do you not? And the 'dear sir' has let him have the 'letter of Cromwell,' I hope; and satisfied 'the obedient servant.' The curious thing in this world is not the stupidity, but the upper-handism of the stupidity. The geese are in the Capitol,° and the Romans in the farmyard—and it seems all quite natural that it should be so, both to geese & Romans!

But there are things you say, which seem to me supernatural . . for reasons which I know and for reasons which I don't know. You will let me be grateful to you, . . will you not? You must, if you will or not. And also . . I would not wait for more leave . . if I could but see your desk . . as I do your death's heads and the spider-webs appertaining; but the soul of Cornelius Agrippa fades from me.

Ever faithfully yours,

Elizabeth B. Barrett

9. *R.B. to E.B.B., 26 Feb. 1845*

Wednesday morning—Spring!

Real warm Spring, dear Miss Barrett, and the birds know it; and in Spring I shall see you, surely see you . . for when did I once fail to get whatever I had set my heart upon?—as I ask myself sometimes, with a strange fear.

I took up this paper to write a great deal—now, I don't think I shall write much—'I shall see you,' I say!

That 'Luria' you enquire about, shall be my last play . . for it is but a play, woe's me! I have one done here, 'A Soul's Tragedy,' as it is properly enough called, but *that* would not do to end with—(end I will)— and Luria is a Moor, of Othello's country, and devotes himself to something he thinks Florence, and the old fortune follows—all in my brain, yet, but the bright weather helps and I will soon loosen my Braccio and Puccio (a pale discontented man), and Tiburzio (the Pisan, good true fellow, this one), and Domizia the Lady .. loosen all these on dear foolish (ravishing must his folly be) golden-hearted Luria, all these with their worldly-wisdom and Tuscan shrewd ways,—and, for me, the misfortune is, I sympathise just as much with these as with him,—so there can no good come of keeping this wild company any longer, and 'Luria' and the other sadder ruin of one Chiappino,—these got rid of, I will do as you bid me, and .. but first I have some Romances and Lyrics, all dramatic, to dispatch, and *then*, I shall stoop of a sudden under and out of this dancing ring of men & women hand in hand; and stand still awhile, should my eyes dazzle,—and when that's over, they will be gone and you will be there, *pas vrai?*—For, as I think I told you, I always shiver involuntarily when I look .. no, glance .. at this First Poem of mine to be. '*Now*,' I call it, what, upon my soul,—for a solemn matter it is,—what is to be done *now*, believed *now*,—so far as it has been revealed to me—solemn words, truly,—and to find myself writing them to any one else! Enough now.

I know Tennyson 'face to face,'—no more than that. I know Carlyle and love him—know him so well, that I would have told you he had shaken that grand head of his at 'singing,' so thoroughly does he love and live by it. When I last saw him, a fortnight ago, he turned, from I don't know what other talk, quite abruptly on me with, 'Did you never try to write a *Song?* Of all things in the world, *that* I should be proudest to do.' Then came his definition of a song—then, with an appealing look to Mrs C., 'I always say that some day in *spite of nature and my stars*, I shall burst into a song' (he is not mechanically 'musical,'—he meant, and the music is the poetry, he holds, and should enwrap the thought as Donne says 'an amber-drop enwraps a bee'),° and then he began to recite an old Scotch song, stopping at the first rude couplet, 'The beginning words are merely to set the tune, they tell me'—and then again at the couplet about—or, to the effect that—'give me' (but in broad Scotch) 'give me but my lass, I care not for my cogie.' '*He says*,' quoth Carlyle magisterially, 'that if you allow him the love of his lass, you may take away all else,—even his cogie, his cup or can, and he cares not'—just as a professor expounds Lycophron.° And just before I left England, six months ago, did not I hear him croon, if not certainly sing, 'Charlie is my darling'° ('my *darling*' with an adoring emphasis) and then he stood back, as it were, from the song, to look at it better, and said 'How must that notion of ideal wondrous perfection have impressed itself in this old Jacobite's 'young Cavalier'—('They go to save their land, and the *young Cavalier!*')—when I who care nothing about such a rag of a man, cannot but feel as he felt, in speaking his words after him!' After saying which, he would be sure to counsel everybody to get their heads clear of all singing!—Don't let me forget to clap hands—we got the letter, dearly bought as it was by the 'Dear Sirs,' &c., and insignificant scrap as it proved— but still it is got, to my encouragement in diplomacy.

Who told you of my sculls and spider webs—Horne? Last year I petted extraordinarily a fine fellow, (a *garden* spider—there was the singularity,—the thin clever-even-for a spider-sort, and they are *so* 'spirited and sly,' all of them—this kind makes a long cone of web, with a square chamber of vantage at the end, and there he sits loosely and looks about)—a great fellow that housed himself, with real gusto, in the jaws of a great scull, whence he watched me as I wrote, and I remember speaking to Horne about his good points. Phrenologists look gravely at that great scull, by the way, and hope, in their grim manner, that its owner made a good end. It looks quietly, now, out at the green little hill behind. I have no little insight to the feelings of furniture, and treat books and prints with a reasonable consideration—how some people use their pictures, for instance, is a mystery to me—very revolting all the same: portraits obliged to face each other for ever,—prints put together in portfolios . . my Polidoro's perfect Andromeda° along with 'Boors Carousing,' by Ostade,—where I found her,—my own father's doing, or I would say more.

And when I have said I like 'Pippa' better than anything else I have done yet, I shall have answered all you bade me. And now may *I* begin questioning? No,—for it is all a pure delight to me, so that you do but write. I never was without good, kind, generous friends and lovers, so they say—so they were and are—perhaps they came at the wrong time—I never wanted them,—though that makes no difference in my gratitude, I trust—but I know myself—surely—and always have done so—for is there not somewhere the little book I first printed when a boy, with John Mill,° the metaphysical head, *his* marginal note that 'the writer possesses a deeper self-consciousness than I ever knew in a sane human being'—So I never deceived myself much, nor called my feelings for people other than they were; and who has a right to say, if I have not, that I had, but I said that, supernatural or no. Pray tell me, too, of your present doings and projects, and never write yourself 'grateful' to me who *am* grateful, very grateful to you,—for none of your words but I take in earnest—and tell me if Spring *be not* coming, come—and I will take to writing the gravest of letters—because this beginning is for gladness' sake, like Carlyle's song couplet. My head aches a little to-day too and, as poor dear Kirke White said to the moon, from his heap of mathematical papers, 'I throw aside the learned sheet,—I cannot choose but gaze she looks so—mildly sweet.'° Out on the foolish phrase, but there's hard rhyming without it.

Ever yours faithfully,

Robert Browning

10. E.B.B. to R.B., 27 Feb. 1845

50 Wimpole Street
Feb. 27, 1845.

Yes, but, dear Mr Browning, I want the spring according to the new 'style' (mine), & not the old one of you & the rest of the poets. To me unhappily, the snowdrop is much the same as the snow—it feels as cold underfoot—and I have grown sceptical about 'the voice of the turtle,'° the east winds blow so loud. April is a Parthian with a dart, & May (at least the early part of it) a spy in the camp. *That* is my idea of what you call spring; mine, in the *new style!* A little later comes my spring,—and indeed after such severe weather, from which I have just escaped with my life, I may thank it for coming at all. How happy you are, to be able to listen to the 'birds' without the commentary of the east wind,—which, like other commentaries, spoils the music. And how happy I am to listen to you, when you write such kind open-hearted letters to me!—I am delighted to hear all you say to me of yourself, & 'Luria,' & the spider, & to do him no dishonour in the association, of the great teacher of the age, Carlyle, who is also yours & mine. He fills the office of a poet—does he not?—by analyzing humanity back into its elements, to the destruction of the conventions of the hour. That is—strictly speaking .. the office of the poet, is it not?—and he discharges it fully,—and with a wider intelligibility perhaps as far as the contemporary period is concerned, than if he did forthwith 'burst into a song.'

But how I do wander!—I meant to say, and I will call myself back to say, that spring will really come some day I hope & believe, & the warm settled weather with it, and that then I shall be probably fitter for certain pleasures than I can appear even to myself, now.

And, in the meantime, I seem to see 'Luria' instead of you,—I have visions & dream dreams. And the 'Soul's Tragedy,' which sounds to me like the step of a ghost of an old Drama! & you are not to think that I blaspheme the Drama, dear Mr Browning; or that I ever thought of exhorting you to give up the 'solemn robes' & tread of the buskin. It is the theatre which vulgarizes these things; the modern theatre in which we see no altar!—where the thymele° is replaced by the caprice of a popular actor. And also, I have a fancy that your great dramatic power would work more clearly & audibly in the less definite mould—but you ride your own faculty as Oceanus did his sea-horse, 'directing it by your will';° and woe to the impertinence, which would dare to say 'turn this way' or 'turn from that way'—it should not be MY impertinence. Do not think I blaspheme the Drama. I have gone through 'all such reading as should never be read' (that is, by women!)—through my love of it on the contrary. And the dramatic faculty is strong in you—& therefore, as 'I speak unto a wise man, judge what I say.'°

For myself & my own doings, you shall hear directly what I have been doing, & what I am about to do. Some years ago, as perhaps you may have heard, (but I hope not .. for the fewer who hear of it the better ..)—some years ago, I translated or rather *undid* into English, the Prometheus of Æschylus. To speak of this production moderately (not modestly), it is the most miserable of all miserable versions of the class. It was completed (in the first place) in thirteen days—the iambics thrown into blank verse, the lyrics into rhymed octosyllabics & the like—and the whole together as cold as Caucasus, & as flat as the nearest plain. To account for this, the haste may be something; but if my mind had been properly awakened at the time, I might have made still more haste & done it better. Well,—the comfort is, that the little book was unadvertised & unknown, & that most of the copies (through my entreaty of my father) are shut up in the wardrobe of his bedroom. If ever I get well I shall show my joy by making a bonfire of them. In the meantime, the recollection of this sin of mine, has been my nightmare & daymare too, and the sin has been the 'Blot on my escutcheon.' I could look in nobody's face, with a 'Thou canst not say I did it'°—I know, I did it. And so I resolved to wash away the transgression, and translate the tragedy over again. It was an honest straightforward proof of repentance—was it not? and I have completed it, except the transcription & last polishing. If Æschylus stands at the foot of my bed now, I shall have a little breath to front him. I have done my duty by him, not indeed according to his claims, but in proportion to my faculty. Whether I shall ever publish or not (remember) remains to be considered—that is a different side of the subject. If I do, it *may* be in a magazine . . or . . but this is another ground. And then, I have in my head to associate with the version . . a monodram of my own—not a long poem, . . but a monologue of Æschylus as he sate a blind exile on the flats of Sicily and recounted the past to his own soul, just before the eagle cracked his great massy skull with a stone.

But my chief *intention* just now is the writing of a sort of novel-poem°—a poem as completely modern as 'Geraldine's Courtship,' running into the midst of our conventions, & rushing into drawing-rooms & the like 'where angels fear to tread'; & so, meeting face to face & without mask the Humanity of the age, & speaking the truth as I conceive of it, out plainly. That is my intention. It is not mature enough yet to be called a plan. I am waiting for a story, & I won't take one, because I want to make one, & I like to make my own stories, because then I can take liberties with them in the treatment.

Who told me of your skulls and spiders? Why, couldn't I know it without being told? Did Cornelius Agrippa know nothing without being told? Mr Horne—never spoke it to my ears—(I never saw him face to face in my life, although we have corresponded for long and long), & he never wrote it to my eyes. Perhaps he does not know that I know it. Well, then! if I were to say that *I heard it from you yourself*, . . how would you answer? AND IT WAS SO. Why, are you not aware that these are the days of Mesmerism & clairvoyance? Are you an infidel? I have believed in your skulls for the last year, for my part.

And I have some sympathy in your habit of feeling for chairs & tables. I remember, when I was a child & wrote poems in little clasped books, I used to kiss the books & put them away tenderly because I had been happy near them, & take them out by turns when I was going from home, to cheer them by the change of air & the pleasure of the new place. This, not for the sake of the verses written in them, & not for the sake of writing more verses in them, but from pure gratitude. Other books I used to treat in a like manner—and to talk to the trees & the flowers, was a natural inclination—but between me & that time, the cypresses grow thick & dark.

Is it true that your wishes fulfil themselves?—And when they *do*, are they not bitter to your taste—do you not wish them *un*fulfilled? Oh—this life, this life! There is comfort in it, they say, & I almost believe—but the brightest place in the house, is the leaning out of the window!—at least, for me.

Of course you are *self-conscious*—How c^d you be a poet otherwise? Tell me.

Ever faithfully yours,

E. B. B.

16. *R.B. to E.B.B., 15 Apr. 1845*

Tuesday Night.

I heard of you, dear Miss Barrett, between a Polka and a Cellarius° the other evening, of Mr Kenyon—how this wind must hurt you! And yesterday I had occasion to go your way—pass, that is, Wimpole Street, the end of it,—and, do you know, I did not seem to have leave from you to go down it yet, much less count number after number till I came to yours,—much least than less, look up when I did come there. So I went on to a viperine she-friend of mine who, I think, rather loves me she does so hate me, and we talked over the chances of certain other friends who were to be balloted for at the 'Athenæum' last night,—one of whom, it seems, was in a fright about it—'to such little purpose' said my friend—'for he is so inoffensive— now, if one were to style *you* that!'—'Or you'—I said—and so we hugged ourselves in our grimness like tiger-cats. Then there is a deal in the papers to-day about Maynooth, and a meeting presided over by Lord Mayor Gibbs, and the Reverend Mr Somebody's speech— And Mrs Norton has gone and book-made at a great rate about the Prince of Wales, pleasantly putting off till his time all that used of old to be put off till his mother's time—altogether, I should dearly like to hear from you, but not till the wind goes, and sun comes—because I shall see Mr Kenyon next week and get him to tell me some more. By the way, do you suppose anybody else looks like him? If you do, the first room full of real London people you go among you will fancy to be lighted up by a saucer of burning salt & spirits of wine in the background.

Monday—Last night when I could do nothing else I began to write to you, such writing as you have seen—strange! The proper time & season for good sound sensible & profitable forms of speech—when ought it to have occurred, and how did I evade it in these letters of mine? For people begin with a graceful skittish levity, lest you should be struck all of a heap with what is to come, and *that* is sure to be the stuff and staple of the man, full of wisdom and sorrow,—and then again comes the fringe of reeds and pink little stones on the other side, that you may put foot on land, and draw breath, and think what a deep pond you have swum across. But *you* are the real deep wonder of a creature,—and I sail these paper-boats on you rather impudently. But I always mean to be very grave one day,—when I am in better spirits and can go *fuori di me.*°

And one thing I want to persuade you of, which is, that all you gain by travel is the discovery that you have gained nothing, and have done rightly in trusting to your innate ideas—or not rightly in distrusting them, as the case may be; you get, too, a little .. perhaps a considerable, good, in finding the world's accepted *moulds* everywhere, into which you may run & fix your own fused metal,—but not a grain Troy-weight do you get of new gold, silver or brass. After this, you go boldly on your own resources, and are justified to yourself, that's all. Three scratches with a pen, even with this pen,—and you have the green little Syrenusa° where I have sate and heard the quails sing. One of these days I shall describe a country I have seen in my soul only, fruits, flowers, birds and all.

Ever yours, dear Miss Barrett,

R. Browning

17. E.B.B. to R.B., 17 Apr. 1845

Thursday Morning.

If you did but know dear Mr Browning how often I have written .. not this letter I am about to write, but another better letter to you, .. in the midst of my silence, .. you w^d not think for a moment that the east wind, with all the harm it does to me, is able to do the great harm of putting out the light of the thought of you to my mind,—for this, indeed, it has no power to do. I had the pen in my hand once to write,—& why it fell out, I cannot tell you. And you see, .. all your writing will not change the wind! You wished all manner of good to me one day as the clock struck ten,—yes, & I assure you I was better that day—& I must not forget to tell you so though it is so long since. And *therefore*, I was logically bound to believe that you had never thought of me since .. unless you thought east winds of me! *That* was quite clear; was it not?—or would have been,—if it had not been for the supernatural conviction, I had above all, of your kindness, which was too large to be taken in the hinge of a syllogism. In fact I have long left off thinking that logic proves anything—it *doesn't*, you know.

But your Lamia° has taught you some subtle 'viperine' reasoning & *motiving*, for the turning down one street instead of another. It was conclusive.

Ah—but you will never persuade me that I am the better, or as well, for the thing that I have not. We look from different points of view, & yours is the point of attainment. Not that you do not truly say that, when all is done, we must come home to place our engines, & act by our own strength. I do not want material as material,—no one does. But every life requires a full experience, a various experience—& I have a profound conviction that where a poet has been shut from most of the *outward* aspects of life, he is at a lamentable disadvantage. Can you, speaking for yourself, separate the results in you from the external influences at work around you, that you say so boldly that you get nothing from the world? You do not *directly*, I know—but you do indirectly & by a rebound. Whatever acts upon you, becomes *you*—& whatever you love or hate, whatever charms you or is scorned by you, acts on you & becomes *you*. Have you read the 'Improvisatore'? or will you?—The writer seems to feel, just as I do, the good of the outward life,—and he is a poet in his soul. It is a book full of beauty & had a great charm to me.

As to the Polkas and Cellariuses, .. I do not covet them of course .. but what a strange world you seem to have, to me at a distance— what a strange husk of a world! How it looks to me like mandarin-life or something as remote; nay, not mandarin-life but mandarin *manners*, .. life, even the outer life, meaning something deeper, in my account of it. As to dear Mr Kenyon I do not make the mistake of fancying that many can look like him or talk like him or *be* like him. I know enough to know otherwise. When he spoke of me he sh^d have said that I was better notwithstanding the east wind. It is really true—I am getting slowly up from the prostration of the severe cold, & feel stronger in myself.

But Mrs Norton discourses excellent music—& for the rest, there are fruits in the world so over-ripe, that they will fall, .. without being gathered. Let Maynooth witness to it!—*if you think it worth while!*

Ever yours,

Elizabeth B. Barrett

18. R.B. to E.B.B., 30 Apr. 1845

Wednesday Morning.

If you did but know, dear Miss Barrett, how the 'full stop' after 'Morning' just above, has turned out the fullest of stops,—and how for about a quarter of an hour since the ink dried I have been reasoning out the why & wherefore of the stopping, the wisdom of it, and the folly of it...

—By this time you see what you have got in me—You ask me questions, 'if I like novels,' 'if the Improvisatore is not good,' 'if travel and sightseeing do not effect this and that for one,' and 'what I am devising—play or poem,'—and I shall not say I could not answer at all manner of lengths—but, let me only begin some good piece of writing of the kind, and .. no, you shall have it, have what I was going to tell you stops such judicious beginnings,—in a parallel case, out of which your ingenuity shall, please, pick the meaning—There is a story of D'Israeli's° an old one, with an episode of strange interest, or so I found it years ago,—well, you go breathlessly on with the people of it, page after page, till at last the end *must* come, you feel—and the tangled threads draw to one, and an out-of-door feast in the woods helps you .. that is, helps them, the people, wonderfully on,—and, lo, dinner is done, and Vivian Grey is here, and Violet Fane there,—and a detachment of the party is drafted off to go catch butterflies, and only two or three stop behind. At this moment, Mr Somebody, a good man and rather the lady's uncle, 'in answer to a question from Violet, drew from his pocket a small neatly written manuscript, and, seating himself on an inverted wine-cooler, proceeded to read the following brief remarks upon the characteristics of the Maeso-gothic literature'—this ends the page,—which you don't turn at once! But when you *do*, in bitterness of soul, turn it, you read—'On consideration, I' (Ben, himself) 'shall keep them for Mr Colburn's New Magazine'—and deeply you draw thankful breath! (Note this 'parallel case' of mine is pretty sure to meet the usual fortune of my writings—you will ask what it means,—and this it means, or should mean, all of it, instance and reasoning and all,—that I am naturally earnest, in earnest about whatever thing I do, and little able to write about one thing while I think of another)—

I think I will really write verse to you some day, *this* day, it is quite clear I had better give up trying.

No, spite of all the lines in the world, I will make an end of it, as Ophelia with her swan's-song,—for it grows too absurd. But remember that I write letters to nobody but you, and that I want method and much more. That book you like so, the Danish novel, must be full of truth & beauty, to judge from the few extracts I have seen in Reviews. That a Dane should write so, confirms me in an old belief—that Italy is stuff for the use of the North, and no more: pure Poetry there is none, nearly as possible none, in Dante even—materials for Poetry in the pitifullest romancist of their thousands, on the contrary—strange that those great wide black eyes should stare nothing out of the earth that lies before them! Alfieri,° with even grey eyes, and a life of travel, writes you some fifteen tragedies as colourless as salad grown under a garden glass with matting over it—as free, that is, from local colouring, touches of the soil they are said to spring from,—think of 'Saulle,' and his Greek attempts!

I expected to see Mr Kenyon, at a place where I was last week, but he kept away. Here is the bad wind back again, and the black sky. I am sure I never knew till now whether the East or West or South were the quarter to pray for—But surely the weather was a little better last week, and you, were you not better? And do you know—but it's all self-flattery I believe,—still I cannot help fancying the East wind does *my* head harm too!

Ever yours faithfully

R. Browning

19. E.B.B. to R.B., 1 May 1845

Thursday.

People say of you & of me, dear Mr Browning, that we love the darkness & use a sphinxine idiom in our talk,—and really you do talk a little like a sphinx in your argument drawn from Vivian Grey. Once I sate up all night to read 'Grey,'—but I never drew such an argument from him. Not that I give it up (nor *you* up) for a mere mystery. Nor that I can '*see what you have got in you*,' from a mere guess. But just observe! If I ask questions about novels, is it not because I want to know how much elbow-room there may be for our sympathies . . & whether there is room for my loose sleeves, & the lace lappets, as well as for my elbows,—& because I want to see *you* by the refracted lights as well as by the direct ones,—& because I am willing for you to know *me* from the beginning, with all my weaknesses & foolishnesses, . . as they are accounted by people who say to me 'no one would ever think, without knowing you, that you were so & so.' Now if I send all my idle questions to Colburn's Magazine, with other Gothic literature, & take to standing up in a perpendicular personality like the angel on the schoolman's needle, in my letters to come, without further leaning to the left or the right—why the end would be that *you* w^d take to 'running after the butterflies,' for change of air & exercise. And then . . oh . . then, my 'small neatly written manuscripts' might fall back into my desk . . . ! (*Not* a 'full stop'!.)

Indeed . . I do assure you . . I never for a moment thought of 'making conversation' about the 'Improvisatore' or novels in general, when I wrote what I did to you. I might, to other persons . . perhaps. Certainly not to *you*. I was not dealing round from one pack of cards to you & to others. That's what you meant to reproach me for, you know—& of that, I am not guilty at all. I never could think of 'making conversation' in a letter to *you*—never. Women are said to partake of the nature of children—& my brothers call me 'absurdly childish' sometimes: and I am capable of being childishly 'in earnest' about novels, & straws, & such 'puppydogs tails' as my Flush's!° Also I write more letters than you do, . . I write in fact almost as you pay visits, . . & one has to 'make conversation' in turn, of course. *But*— give me something to vow by—whatever you meant in the Vivian Grey argument, you were wrong in it! & you never can be much more wrong—which is a comfortable reflection.

Yet you leap very high at Dante's crown—or you do not leap, . . you simply extend your hand to it, & make a rustling among the laurel leaves, which is somewhat prophane. Dante's poetry only materials for the northern rhymers!—I must think of that . . if you please . . before I agree with you. Dante's poetry seems to come down in hail, rather than in rain—but count me the drops congealed in one hailstone! Oh! the 'Flight of the Duchess'—do let us hear more of her! Are you (I wonder) . . . not a 'self-flatterer,' . . but . . a flatterer.

Ever yours
E. B. B.

20. *R.B. to E.B.B., 3 May 1845*

Saturday Morning.

Now shall you see what you shall see—here shall be 'sound speech not to be reproved,'°—for this morning you are to know that the soul of me has it all her own way, dear Miss Barrett, this green cool nine-in-the-morning time for my chestnut-tree over there, and for me who only coaxed my good-natured—(really)—body up, after its three-hours night-rest on condition it should lounge, or creep about, incognito and without consequences—and so it shall, all but my right-hand which is half-spirit and 'cuts' its poor relation, and passes itself off for somebody (that is, some soul) and is doubly active & ready on such occasions—Now I shall tell you all about it, first what last letter meant, and then more. You are to know, then, that for some reason, that looked like an instinct, I thought I ought not to send shaft on shaft, letter-plague on letter, with such an uninterrupted clanging . . that I ought to wait, say a week at least, having killed all your mules for you, before I shot down your dogs: but not being exactly Phoibos Apollon,° you are to know further that when I *did* think I might go modestly on, . . ὤμοι,° let me get out of this slough of a simile, never mind with what dislocation of ancles! Plainly, from waiting and turning my eyes away (not from *you*, but from you in your special capacity of being *written*-to, not spoken-to) when I turned again you had grown formidable somehow—tho' that's not the word,—nor are you the person, either,—it was my fortune, my privilege of being your friend this one way, that it seemed a shame for me to make no better use of than taking it up with talk about books and I don't know what: write what I will, you would read for once, I think—well, then,—what I shall write shall be—something on this book, and the other book, and my own books, and Mary Howitt's books, and at the end of it—good bye, and I hope here is a quarter of an hour rationally spent. So the thought of what I should find in my heart to say, and the contrast with what I suppose I ought to say . . all these things are against me. But this is very foolish, all the same, I need not be told—and is part & parcel of an older—indeed primitive folly of mine, which I shall never wholly get rid of, of desiring to do nothing when I cannot do all; seeing nothing, getting, enjoying nothing, where there is no seeing & getting & enjoying *wholly*—and in this case, moreover, you are *you*, and know something about me, if not much, and have read Bos on the art of supplying Ellipses, and (after, particularly, I have confessed all this, why & how it has been) you will *subaudire*° when I pull out my Mediaeval-Gothic-Architectural-Manuscript (so it was, I remember now,) and instruct you about corbeils and ogives..tho', after all, it was none of Vivian's doing, that,—all the uncle kind of man's, which I never professed to be. Now you see how I came to say some nonsense (I very vaguely think *what*) about Dante—some desperate splash I know I made for the beginning of my picture, as when a painter at his wits' end and hunger's beginning says 'Here shall the figures hand be'—and spots *that* down, meaning to reach it naturally from the other end of his canvass,—and leaving off tired, there you see the spectral disjoined thing, and nothing between it and rationality: I intended to shade down and soften off and put in and leave out, and, before I had done, bring Italian Poets round to their old place again in my heart, giving new praise if I took old,—anyhow Dante is out of it all, as who knows but I, with all of him in my head and heart? But they do fret one, those tantalizing creatures, of fine passionate class, with such capabilities, and such a facility of being made pure mind of. And the special instance that vexed me, was that a man of sands and dog-roses and white rock and green sea-water just under, should come to Italy where my heart lives, and discover the sights and sounds..certainly discover them. And so do all Northern writers; for take up handfuls of sonetti, rime, poemetti, doings of those who never did anything else,—and try and make out, for yourself, what..say, what flowers they tread on, or trees they walk under,—as you might bid *them*, those tree & flower loving creatures, pick out of *our* North poetry a notion of what *our* daisies and harebells and furze bushes and brambles are—'Odorosi fioretti, rose porporine, bianchissimi gigli.'° And which of you eternal triflers was it called yourself 'Shelley' and so told me years ago that in the mountains it was a feast 'When one should find those globes of deep red gold—Which in the woods the strawberry-tree doth bear, Suspended in their emerald atmosphere.'° So that when my Mule walked into a sorb-tree, not to tumble sheer over Monte Calvano,° and I felt the fruit against my face, the little ragged bare-legged guide fairly laughed at my knowing them so well—'Niursi—sorbi!'° No, no,—does not all Naples-bay and half Sicily, shore and inland, come flocking once a year to the Piedigrotta fête° only to see the blessed King's Volanti, or livery servants all in their best, as tho' heaven opened? and would not I engage to bring the whole of the Piano (of Sorrento) in likeness to a red velvet dressing gown properly spangled over, before the priest that held it out on a pole had even begun his story of how Noah's son Shem, the founder of Sorrento, threw it off to swim thither, as the world knows he did? Oh, it makes one's soul angry, so enough of it. But never enough of telling you—bring all your sympathies, come with loosest sleeves and longest lace-lappets, and you and yours shall find 'elbow room,' oh, shall you not! For never did man woman or child, Greek, Hebrew, or as Danish as our friend, like a thing, not to say love it, but I liked and loved it, one liking neutralizing the rebellious stir of its fellow, so that I don't go about now wanting the fixed stars before my time; this world has not escaped me, thank God; and—what other people say is the best of it, may not escape me after all, tho' until so very lately I made up my mind to do without it;—perhaps, on that account, and to make fair amends to other people,—who, I have no right to say, complain without cause. I have been surprised, rather, with something not unlike illness of late—I have had a constant pain in the head for these two months, which only very rough exercise gets rid of, and which stops my 'Luria' and much besides. I thought I never could be unwell. Just now all of it is gone, thanks to polking all night and walking home by broad daylight to the surprise of the thrushes in the bush here. And do you know I said 'this must *go*, cannot mean to stay, so I will not tell Miss Barrett why this & this is not done,'—but I mean to tell you all, or more of the truth, because you call me 'flatterer,' so that my eyes widened again! I, and in what? And of whom, pray? not of *you*, at all events,—of whom then? *Do* tell me, because I want to stand with you—and am quite in earnest there. And 'The Flight of the Duchess,' to leave nothing out, is only the beginning of a story written some time ago, and given to poor Hood in his emergency° at a day's notice,—the true stuff and story is all to come, the '*Flight*' and what you allude to is the mere introduction— but the Magazine has passed into other hands and I must put the rest in some 'Bell' or other—it is one of my Dramatic Romances. So is a certain 'Saul' I should like to show you one day—an ominous liking,—for nobody ever sees what I do till it is printed. But as you *do* know the printed little part of me, I should not be sorry if, in justice, you knew all I have *really* done,—written in the portfolio there,—tho' that would be far enough from *this* me, that writes to you now. I should like to write something in concert with you—how I would try!

I have read your letter thro' again. Does this clear up all the difficulty, and do you see that I never dreamed of 'reproaching you for dealing out one sort of cards to me and everybody else'—but that .. why, '*that*' which I have, I hope, said, so need not resay. I will tell you—Sydney Smith laughs somewhere at some Methodist or other whose wont was, on meeting an acquaintance in the street, to open at once on him with some enquiry after the state of his soul—Sydney knows better now, and sees that one might quite as wisely ask such questions as the price of Illinois stock or the condition of glebe-land,—and I *could* say such

———

— — —'could' .. the plague of it! So no more at present from your loving .. Or, let me tell you that I am going to see Mr Kenyon on the 12 inst.—that you do not tell me how you are, and that yet if you do not continue to improve in health .. I shall not see you—not—not—not—what 'knots' to untie! Surely the wind that sets my chestnut-tree dancing, all its baby-cone-blossoms, green now, rocking like fairy castles on a hill in an earthquake,—that is South West, surely! God bless you, and me in that—and do write to me soon, and tell me who was the 'flatterer,' and how he never was

Yours

R. B.

30. *E.B.B. to R.B., 23 May 1845*

Friday Evening.

I intended to write to you last night & this morning, & could not,—you do not know what pain you give me in speaking so wildly—And if I disobey you my dear friend, in speaking, (I for my part) of your wild speaking, I do it, not to displease you, but to be in my own eyes, & before God, a little more worthy, or less unworthy, of a generosity from which I recoil by instinct & at the first glance, yet conclusively,—& because my silence w^d be the most disloyal of all means of expression, in reference to it. Listen to me then in this. You have said some intemperate things ... fancies,—which you will not say over again, nor unsay, but *forget at once, & for ever, having said at all*,—& which (so) will die out between *you & me alone*, like a misprint between you and the printer. And this you will do *for my sake* who am your friend,—(& you have none truer)—& this I ask, because it is a condition necessary to our future liberty of intercourse. You remember—surely you do—that I am in the most exceptional of positions; & that, just *because of it*, I am able to receive you as I did on Tuesday; and that, for me to listen to 'unconscious exaggerations,' is as unbecoming to the humilities of my position, as unpropitious (which is of more consequence) to the prosperities of yours—Now, if there sh^d be one word of answer attempted to this,— or of reference; *I must not . . I* WILL *not see you again*—& you will justify me later in your heart . . So for my sake you will not say it—I think you will not—& spare me the sadness of having to break through an intercourse just as it is promising pleasure to me,—to me who have so many sadnesses & so few pleasures. You will—! & I need not be uneasy—& I shall owe you that tranquillity, as one gift of many—For, that I have much to receive from you in all the free gifts of thinking, teaching, master-spirits, . . *that*, I know!—it is my own praise that I appreciate you, as none can more. Your influence & help in poetry will be full of good & gladness to me—for with many to love me in this house, there is no one to judge me . . *now*. Your friendship & sympathy will be dear and precious to me all my life, if you indeed leave them with me so long or so little. Your mistakes in me . . which *I* cannot mistake (—& which have humbled me by too much honouring—) I put away gently, & with grateful tears in my eyes,—because *all that hail* will beat down & spoil crowns as well as 'blossoms.'

If I put off next Tuesday to the week after—I mean your visit, . . shall you care much?—For the relations I named to you, are to be in London next week; and I am to see one of my aunts° whom I love, & have not met since my great affliction—& it will all seem to come over again, & I shall be out of spirits & nerves. On Tuesday week you can bring a tomahawk & do the criticism, & I shall try to have my courage ready for it—Oh, you will do me so much good—and Mr Kenyon calls me 'docile' sometimes I assure you; when he wants to flatter me out of being obstinate—and in good earnest, I believe I shall do everything you tell me. The Prometheus is done—but the monodrama is where it was—& the novel, not at all. But I think of some half promises half given, about something I read for 'Saul'—& the Flight of the Duchess—where is she?

You are not displeased with me? *no*—*that* w^d be hail & lightning together—I do not write as I might, of some words of yours—but you know that I am not a stone, even if silent like one. And if in the *un*silence, I have said one word to vex you, pity me for having had to say it—and for the rest, may God bless you far beyond the reach of vexation from my words or my deeds!

Your friend in grateful regard,

E.B.B.

31. R.B. to E.B.B., 24 May 1845

Saturday M^g

Don't you remember I told you, once on a time, that you 'knew nothing of me'? whereat you demurred—but I meant what I said, & knew it was so. To be grand in a simile, for every poor speck of a Vesuvius or a Stromboli in my microcosm there are huge layers of ice and pits of black cold water—and I make the most of my two or three fire-eyes, because I know by experience, alas, how these tend to extinction—and the ice grows & grows—still this last is true part of me, most characteristic part, *best* part perhaps, and I disown nothing—only,—when you talked of '*knowing* me'!—Still, I am utterly unused, of these late years particularly, to dream of communicating anything about *that* to another person (all my writings are purely dramatic as I am always anxious to say) that when I make never so little an attempt, no wonder if I *bungle* notably— 'language,' too, is an organ that never studded this heavy heavy head of mine. Will you not think me very brutal if I tell you I could almost smile at your misapprehension of what I meant to write?—Yet I *will* tell you, because it will undo the bad effect of my thoughtlessness, and at the same time exemplify the point I have all along been honestly earnest to set you right upon..my real inferiority to you; just that and no more. I wrote to you, in an unwise moment, on the spur of being again 'thanked,' and, unwisely writing just as if thinking to myself, said what must have looked absurd enough as seen apart from the horrible counterbalancing never-to-be-written *rest of me*—by the side of which, could it be written & put before you, my note would sink to its proper & relative place, and become a mere 'thank you' for your good opinion— which I assure you is far too generous,—for I really believe you to be my superior in many respects, and feel uncomfortable till *you* see that, too—since I hope for your sympathy & assistance, and frankness is everything in such a case. I do assure you, that had you read my note, *only* having 'known' so much of me as is implied in having inspected, for instance, the contents, merely, of that fatal and often-referred-to 'portfolio' there (Dii meliora piis!),° you would see in it, (the note not the portfolio) the blandest utterance ever mild gentleman gave birth to: but I forgot that one may make too much noise in a silent place by playing the few notes on the 'ear piercing fife' which in Othello's regimental band might have been thumped into decent subordination by his 'spirit stirring drum'°—to say nothing of gong and ophicleide. Will you forgive me, on promise to remember for the future, and be more considerate? Not that you must too much despise me, neither; nor, of all things, apprehend I am attitudinizing à la Byron, and giving you to understand unutterable somethings, longings for Lethe and all that—far from it! I never committed murders, and sleep the soundest of sleeps—but 'the heart is desperately wicked,'° that is true, and tho' I dare not say 'I know' mine, yet I have had signal opportunities, I who began life from the beginning, and can forget nothing (but names, and the date of the battle of Waterloo,) and have known good & wicked men and women, gentle & simple, shaking hands with Edmund Kean and Father Mathew, you and—Ottima!° Then, I had a certain faculty of self-consciousness, years, years ago, at which John Mill wondered,° and which ought to be improved by this time, if constant use helps at all—and, meaning, on the whole, to be a Poet, if not *the* Poet . . for I am vain and ambitious some nights,—I do myself justice, and dare call things by their names to myself, and say boldly, this I love, this I hate, this I would do, this I would not do, under all kinds of circumstances,—and talking (thinking) in this style *to myself,* and beginning, however tremblingly, in spite of conviction, to write in this style *for myself*—on the top of the desk which contains my 'Songs of the Poets—No. 1 M.P.,'° I wrote,—what you now forgive, I know! Because I am, from my heart, sorry that by a foolish fit of inconsideration I should have given pain for a minute to you, towards whom, on every account, I would rather soften and 'sleeken every word as to a bird'° . . (and, not such a bird as my black self that go screeching about the world for 'dead horse'—corvus (picus)—mirandola!)° I, too, who have been at such pains to acquire the reputation I enjoy in the world,—(ask Mr Kenyon,) & who dine, and wine, and dance and enhance the company's pleasure till they make me ill and I keep house, as of late: Mr Kenyon, (for I only quote where you may verify if you please) *he* says my common sense strikes him, and its contrast with my muddy metaphysical poetry! And so it shall strike you—for tho' I am glad that, since you *did* misunderstand me, you said so, and have given me an opportunity of doing by another way what I wished to do in *that,*—yet, if you had *not* alluded to my writing, as I meant you should not, you would have certainly understood *something* of its drift when you found me next Tuesday precisely the same quiet (no, for I feel I speak too loudly, in spite of your kind disclaimer, but—) the same mild man-about-town you were gracious to, the other morning—for, indeed, my own way of worldly life is marked out long ago, as precisely as yours can be, and I am set going with a hand, winker-wise, on each side of my head, and a directing finger before my eyes, to say nothing of an instinctive dread I have that a certain whip-lash is vibrating somewhere in the neighbourhood in playful readiness! So 'I hope here be proofs,' to Dogberry's satisfaction° that, first, I am but a very poor creature compared to you and entitled by my wants to look up to you,—all I meant to say from the first of the first—and that, next, I shall be too much punished if, for this piece of mere inconsideration, you deprive me, more or less, or sooner or later, of the pleasure of seeing you—, a little over boisterous gratitude for which, perhaps, caused all the mischief! The reasons you give for deferring my visits next week are too cogent for me to dispute—that is too true—and, being now & henceforward 'on my good behaviour,' I will at once cheerfully submit to them, if needs must—but should your mere kindness and forethought, as I half suspect, have induced you to take such a step, you will now smile, with me, at this new and very unnecessary addition to the 'fears of me' I had got so triumphantly over in your case! Wise man, was I not, to clench my first favorable impression so adroitly .. like a recent Cambridge worthy, my sister heard of; who, being on his theological (or rather, scripture-historical) examination, was asked by the Tutor, who wished to let him off easily, 'who was the first King of Israel?'—'Saul,' answered the trembling youth. 'Good!' nodded approvingly the Tutor. 'Otherwise called *Paul*,' subjoined the youth in his elation! Now I have begged pardon, and blushingly assured you *that* was only a slip of the tongue, and that I did really *mean* all the while, (Paul or no Paul), the veritable son of Kish,° he that owned the asses, and found listening to the harp the best of all things for an evil spirit! Pray write me a line to say, 'Oh .. if *that's* all!' and remember me for good (which is very compatible with a moment's stupidity) and let me not for one fault, (and that the only one that shall be), lose *any pleasure* .. for your friendship I am sure I have not lost—God bless you, my dear friend! R. Browning

And by the way, will it not be better, as co-operating with you more effectually in your kind promise to forget the 'printer's error' in my blotted proof, to send me back that same 'proof,' if you have not inflicted proper and summary justice on it? When Mephistopheles last came to see us in this world outside here, he counselled sundry of us 'never to write a letter,—and never to burn one'—do you know that? But I never mind what I am told! Seriously, I am ashamed .. I shall next ask a servant for my boots in the 'high fantastical' style of my own 'Luria.'

32. E.B.B. to R.B., 25 May 1845

Sunday

I owe you the most humble of apologies dear Mr Browning, for having spent so much solemnity on so simple a matter, & I hasten to pay it,—confessing at the same time (as why sh^d I not?) that I am quite as much ashamed of myself as I ought to be, which is not a little. You will find it difficult to believe me perhaps when I assure you that I never made such a mistake (I mean of over-seriousness to indefinite compliments), no, never in my life before—indeed my sisters have often jested with me (in matters of which they were cognizant) on my supernatural indifference to the superlative degree in general, as if it meant nothing in grammar. I usually know well that 'boots' may be called for in this world of ours, just as you called for yours,—& that to bring '*Bootes*,'° were the vilest of mal-à-pro-pos-ities. Also, I sh^d have understood 'boots' where you wrote it, in the letter in question; if it had not been for *the relation of two things* in it—& now I perfectly seem to see H O W I mistook that relation; ('*seem to see*,'—because I have not looked into the letter again since your last night's commentary, & will not—) inasmuch as I have observed before in my own mind, that a good deal of what is called obscurity in you, arises from a habit of very subtle association,—so subtle, that you are probably unconscious of it, .. and the effect of which is to throw together on the same level & in the same light, things of likeness & unlikeness—till the reader grows confused as I did, & takes one for another. I may say however, in a poor justice to myself, that I wrote what I wrote so unfortunately, *through reverence for you*, & not at all from vanity on my own account .. although I do feel palpably while I write these words here & now, that I might as well leave them unwritten,—for that no man of the world who ever lived in the world (not even *you*) could be expected to believe them, though said, sung, & sworn.

For the rest, it is scarcely an apposite moment for you to talk, even 'dramatically,' of my 'superiority' to you, .. unless you mean, which perhaps you do mean, my superiority in *simplicity*—&, verily, to some of the 'adorable ingenuousness,' sacred to the shade of

Simpson, I may put in a modest claim, .. '& have my claim allowed.'
'Pray do not mock me'° I quote again from your Shakespeare to you
who are a dramatic poet, .. & I will admit anything that you like,
(being humble just now)—even that I DID NOT KNOW YOU. I was
certainly innocent of the knowledge of the 'ice & cold water' you
introduce me to, and am only just shaking my head, as Flush w^d,
after a first wholesome plunge—Well—if I do not know you, I shall
learn, I suppose, in time. I am ready to try humbly to learn—& I may
perhaps—if you are not done in Sanscrit, which is too hard for
me, ... notwithstanding that I had the pleasure yesterday to hear,
from America, of my profound skill in 'various languages less known
than Hebrew'!—a liberal paraphrase on Mr Horne's large fancies° on
the like subject, & a satisfactory reputation in itself—as long as it is
not necessary to deserve it. So I here enclose to you your letter back
again, as you wisely desire,—although you never c^d doubt, I hope,
for a moment, of its safety with me in the completest of senses: and
then, from the heights of my superior .. stultity, & other qualities of
the like order, .. I venture to advise you .. however (to speak of the
letter critically, & as the dramatic composition it is) it is to be
admitted to be very beautiful, and well worthy of the rest of its kin
in the portfolio, .. 'Lays of the poets,' or otherwise, ... I venture to
advise you to burn it at once. And then, my dear friend, I ask you
(having some claim) to burn at the same time the letter I was
fortunate enough to write to you on Friday, & this present one—
don't send them back to me; I hate to have letters sent back—but
burn them for me & never mind Mephistopheles. After which
friendly turn, you will do me the one last kindness of forgetting all
this exquisite nonsense, & of refraining from mentioning it, by breath
or pen, TO ME OR ANOTHER. Now I trust you so far—: you will put
it with the date of the battle of Waterloo—& I, with every date in
chronology; seeing that I can remember none of them. And we will
shuffle the cards, & take patience, & begin the game again, if you
please—& I shall bear in mind that you are a dramatic poet, which is
not the same thing, by any means, with *us* of the primitive simpli-
cities, who dont tread on cothurns° nor shift the mask in the scene.
And I will reverence you both as 'a poet' & as '*the* poet,'— because it
is no false 'ambition,' but a right you have—& one which those who
live longest, will see justified to the uttermost .. In the meantime I
need not ask Mr Kenyon if you have any sense, because I have no
doubt that you have quite sense enough—& even if I had a doubt, I
shall prefer judging for myself without interposition; which I can do,

you know, as long as you like to come and see me. And you can come this week if you do like it—because our relations dont come till the end of it, it appears—not that I made a pretence 'out of kindness'— pray dont judge me so outrageously—but if you like to come . . not on Tuesday . . but on Wednesday at three oclock, I shall be very glad to see you,—& I, for one, shall have forgotten everything by that time,—being quick at forgetting my own faults usually—If Wednesday does not suit you, I am not sure that I *can* see you this week— but it depends on circumstances. Only don't think yourself *obliged* to come on Wednesday. You know I *began* by entreating you to be open & sincere with me—& no more—I *require* no 'sleekening of every word' or of any word. I love the truth & can bear it—whether in word or deed—& those who have known me longest would tell you so fullest. Well!—May God bless you. We shall know each other some day perhaps—and I am

Always & faithfully your friend,

E. B. B.

33. R.B. to E.B.B., 26 May 1845

Nay—I *must* have last word—as all people in the wrong desire to have—and then, no more of the subject. You said I had given you *great pain*—so long as I stop *that*, think anything of me you choose or can! But *before* your former letter came, I saw the pre-ordained uselessness of mine: speaking is to some *end*, (apart from foolish self-relief,—which, after all, I can do without)—and where there is *no* end—you see! or, to finish characteristically—since the offering to cut off one's right-hand to save anybody a headache, is in vile taste, even for our melodramas, seeing that it was never yet believed in on the stage or off it,—how much worse to really make the ugly chop, and afterwards come sheepishly in, one's arm in a black sling, and find that the delectable gift had changed aching to nausea! There! And now, 'exit, prompt-side, nearest door, Luria'—and enter RB— next Wednesday,—as boldly as he suspects most people do just after they have been soundly frightened!

I shall be most happy to see you on the day and at the hour you mention.

God bless you, my dear friend,

R. B.

42. R.B. to E.B.B., 14 June 1845

[*Saturday*]

June 14, 1845.

When I ask my wise self what I really do remember of the Prize poem,° the answer is—both of Chapman's lines a-top, quite worth any prize for their quoter—then, the good epithet of 'green Europe' contrasting with Africa—then, deep in the piece, a picture of a Vestal in a vault, where I see a dipping & winking lamp plainest, and last of all the ominous 'all was dark' that dismisses you: I read the poem many years ago, and never since—tho' I have an impression that the versification is good, yet from your commentary I see I must have said a good deal more in its praise than that. But have you not discovered by this time that I go on talking with my thoughts away?

I know, I have always been jealous of my own musical faculty (I can write music).—Now that I see the uselessness of such jealousy, and am for loosing & letting it go, it may be cramped possibly. Your music is more various & exquisite than any modern writer's to my ear. One should study the mechanical part of the art, or nearly all that there is to be studied—for the more one sits and thinks over the creative process, the more it confirms itself as 'inspiration,' nothing more nor less. Or, at worst, you write down old inspirations, what you remember of them—but with *that* it begins: 'Reflection' is exactly what it names itself—a *re*-presentation, in scattered rays from every angle of incidence, of what first of all became present in a great light, a whole one. So tell me how these lights are born, if you can! But I can tell anybody how to make melodious verses—let him do it therefore—it should be exacted of all writers.

You do not understand what a new feeling it is for me to have someone who is to like my verses or I shall not ever like them after! So far differently was I circumstanced of old, that I used rather to go about for a subject of offence to people; writing ugly things in order to warn the ungenial & timorous off my grounds at once. I shall never do so again at least! As it is, I will bring all I dare, in as great quantities as I can—if not next time, after then—certainly. I must make an end, print this Autumn my last four 'Bells,' Lyrics, Romances, The Tragedy, & Luria, and then go on with a whole heart to my own Poem—indeed, I have just resolved not to begin any new song, even, till this grand clearance is made—I will get the Tragedy transcribed to bring—

'To bring!' Next Wednesday—if you knew how happy you make me! may I not say *that*, my dear friend, when I feel it from my soul?

I thank God that you are better: do pray make fresh endeavours to profit by this partial respite of the weather! All about you must urge that: but even from my distance some effect might come of such wishes. But you *are* better—look so & speak so! God bless you.

R. B.

You let 'flowers be sent you in a letter,'° every one knows, and this hot day draws out our very first yellow rose—eccola°—

60. *E.B.B. to R.B., 11 July 1845*

You understand that it was not a resolution passed in favour of formality, when I said what I did yesterday about not going out at the time you were coming—surely you do,—whatever you might signify to a different effect,—If it were necessary for me to go out every day, or most days even, it w^d be otherwise—but as it is, I may certainly keep the day you come, free from the fear of carriages, let the sun shine its best or worst,—without doing despite to you or injury to me—and that's all I meant to insist upon indeed & indeed. You see, Jupiter Tonans° was good enough to come to-day on purpose to deliver me—one evil for another!—for I confess with shame & contrition, that I never wait to enquire whether it thunders to the left or the right, to be frightened most ingloriously. Isn't it a disgrace to anyone with a pretension to poetry? Dr Chambers,° a part of whose office it is, Papa says, 'to reconcile foolish women to their follies,' used to take the side of my vanity—& discourse at length on the passive obedience of some nervous systems to electrical influences— but perhaps my faint-heartedness is besides traceable to a half-reasonable terror of a great storm in Herefordshire .. where great storms most do congregate .. (such storms!) round the Malvern hills, those mountains of England. We lived four miles from their roots, thro' all my childhood & early youth, in a Turkish house my father built himself, crowded with minarets & domes, & crowned with metal spires & crescents, to the provocation (as people used to observe) of every lightning of heaven. Once a storm of storms happened, & we all thought the house was struck—& a tree was so really, within two hundred yards of the windows while I looked out—the bark, rent from the top to the bottom .. torn into long ribbons by the dreadful fiery hands, & dashed out into the air, over the heads of other trees, or left twisted in their branches—torn into shreds in a moment, as a flower might be, by a child!—Did you ever see a tree after it has been struck by lightning? The whole trunk of that tree was bare & peeled—& up that new whiteness of it, ran the finger-mark of the lightning in a bright beautiful rose-colour (none of your roses brighter or more beautiful!) the fever-sign of the certain death— Though the branches themselves were for the most part untouched, & spread from the peeled trunk in their full summer foliage,—and birds singing in them three hours afterwards! And, in that same storm, two young women belonging to a festive party were killed on the Malvern hills—each sealed to death in a moment with a sign on the chest which a common seal w^d cover—only the sign on them was not rose-coloured as on our tree .. but black as charred wood. So I get 'possessed' sometimes with the effects of these impressions—& so does one, at least, of my sisters, in a lower degree—and oh!—how amusing & instructive all this is to you! When my father came into the room to-day & found me hiding my eyes from the lightning, he was quite angry & called 'it disgraceful to anybody who had ever learnt the alphabet'—to which I answered humbly that 'I knew it was'—but if I had been impertinent, I MIGHT have added that wisdom does not come by the alphabet but in spite of it? Don't you think so in a measure? non obstantibus Bradbury and Evans?° There's a profane question—& ungrateful too .. after the Duchess —I except the Duchess & her peers—& be sure she will be the world's Duchess & received as one of your most striking poems. Full of various power the poem is .. I cannot say how deeply it has impressed me—but though I want the conclusion, I don't *wish* for it; and in this, am reasonable for once!! You will not write & make yourself ill—will you? or read Sybil at unlawful hours even? Are you better at all?—What a letter! & how very foolishly to-day I am

Yours, E. B. B.

61. *R.B. to E.B.B., 13 July 1845*

Sunday Morning.

Very well—I shall say no more on the subject—tho' it was not any piece of formality on your part that I deprecated; nor even your over-kindness exactly—I rather wanted you to be really, wisely kind, & do me a greater favor than the next great one in degree—but you must understand this much in me—how you can lay me under deepest obligation. I daresay you think you have some—perhaps many,—to whom your well-being is of deeper interest than to me—Well, if that be so, do for their sakes make every effort with the remotest chance of proving serviceable to you,—nor *set yourself against* any little irksomeness these carriage-drives may bring with them just at the beginning; and you may say, if you like, 'how I shall delight those friends, if I can make this newest one grateful'—and, as from the known quantity one reasons out the unknown, this newest friend will be one glow of gratitude, he knows that, if you can warm your finger-tips and so do yourself that much real good, by setting light to a dozen 'Duchesses': why ought I not to say this when it is so true? Besides, people profess as much to their merest friends—for I have been looking thro' a poem-book just now, and was told, under the head of Album-verses alone, that for A. the writer would die, & for B. die too but a crueller death, and for C. too, & D. and so on. I wonder whether they have since wanted to borrow money of him on the strength of his professions. But you must remember we are in July; the 13th it is, and summer will go and cold weather stay ('*come*' forsooth!)—and now is the time of times: still I feared the rain would hinder you on Friday—but the thunder did not frighten me—for you: your father must pardon me for holding most firmly with Dr Chambers— his theory is quite borne out by my own experience, for I have seen a man it were foolish to call a coward, a great fellow too, all but die away in a thunderstrom, though he had quite science enough to explain why there was no immediate danger at all— whereupon his younger brother suggested that he should just go out and treat us to a repetition of Franklin's experiment with the cloud and the kite—a well-timed proposition which sent the Explainer down with a white face into the cellar. What a grand sight your tree was—*is*, for I see it—My father has a print of a tree so struck—torn to ribbons, as you describe—but the rose-mark is striking and new to me: we had a good storm on our last voyage, but I went to bed at the end, as I thought—and only found there had been lightning next day by the bare poles under which we were riding: but the finest mountain fit of the kind I ever saw has an unfortunately ludicrous association. It was at Possagno, among the Euganean-Hills, and I was at a poor house in the town—an old woman was before a little picture of the Virgin, and at every fresh clap she lighted, with the oddest sputtering muttering mouthful of prayer imaginable, an inch of guttery candle, which, the instant the last echo had rolled away, she as constantly blew out again for saving's sake—having, of course, to *light the smoke* of it, about an instant after that: the expenditure in wax at which the elements might be propitiated, you see, was a matter for curious calculation: I suppose I ought to have bought the whole taper for some four or five centesimi (100 of which make 8d. English) and so kept the countryside safe for about a century of bad weather. Leigh Hunt tells you a story he had from Byron, of kindred philosophy in a Jew who was surprised by a thunderstorm while he was dining on bacon—he tried to eat between-whiles, but the flashes were as pertinacious as he, so at last he pushed his plate away, just remarking with a compassionate shrug, 'All this fuss about a piece of pork!' By the way, what a characteristic of an Italian *late* evening is Summer-lightning—it hangs in broad slow sheets, dropping from cloud to cloud, so long in dropping and dying off. The 'bora,'° which you only get at Trieste, brings wonderful lightning—you are in glorious June-weather, fancy, of an evening, under green shock-headed acacias, so thick and green, with the cicalas stunning you above, and all about you men, women, rich & poor, sitting, standing & coming & going—and thro' all the laughter & screaming & singing, the loud clink of the spoons against the glasses, the way of calling for fresh 'sorbetti'°—for all the world is at open-coffee-house at such an hour—when suddenly there is a stop in the sunshine, a blackness drops down, then a great white column of dust drives strait on like a wedge, and you see the acacia heads snap off, now one, then another—and all the people scream 'la bora, la bora!'—and you are caught up in their whirl and landed in some interior, the man with the guitar on one side of you, and the boy with a cageful of little brown owls for sale, on the other—meanwhile, the thunder claps, claps, with such a persistence, and the rain, for a finale, falls in a mass, as if you had knocked out the whole bottom of a huge tank at once—then there is a second stop—out comes the sun—somebody clinks at his glass, all the world bursts out laughing, and prepares to pour out again,—but *you*, the stranger, *do* make the best of your way out, with no preparation at all; whereupon you infallibly put your foot (and half your leg) into a river, really that, of rainwater—that's a *Bora* (and that comment of yours, a justifiable pun!) Such things you get in Italy, but better, better, the best of all things you do not (*I* do not) get those. And I shall see you on Wednesday, please remember, and bring you the rest of the poem—that you should like it, gratifies me more than I will try to say, but then, do not you be tempted by that pleasure of pleasing which I think is your besetting sin—may it not be?—and so cut me off from the other pleasure of being profited: as I told you, I like so much to fancy that you see, and will see, what I do as *I* see it, while it is doing, as nobody else in the world should, certainly,—even if they thought it worth while to want—but when I try and build a great building I shall want you to come with me and judge it and counsel me before the scaffolding is taken down, and while you have to make your way over hods of mortar & heaps of lime, and trembling tubs of size, and those thin broad whitewashing brushes I always had a desire to take up and bespatter with. And now goodbye—I am to see you on Wednesday I trust—and to hear you say you are better, still better, much better? God grant that, and all else good for you, dear friend, and so for R.B. ever yours.

92. *R.B. to E.B.B., 30 Aug. 1845*

Can you understand me *so*, dearest friend, after all? Do you see me,—when I am away, or with you,—'taking offence' at words, 'being vexed' at words, or deeds of yours, even if I could not immediately trace them to their source of entire, pure kindness—, as I have hitherto done in every smallest instance?

I believe in *you* absolutely, utterly—I believe that when you bade me, that time, be silent,—that such was your bidding, and I was silent—dare I say I think you did not know at that time the power I have over myself, that I could sit and speak and listen as I have done since—Let me say now—*this only once*—that I loved you from my soul, and gave you my life, so much of it as you would take,—and all that is *done*, not to be altered now: it was, in the nature of the proceding, wholly independent of any return on your part: I will not think on extremes you might have resorted to; as it is, the assurance of your friendship, the intimacy to which you admit me, now,—make the truest, deepest joy of my life—a joy I can never think fugitive while we are in life, because I KNOW, as to me, I *could* not willingly displease you,—while, as to you, your goodness and understanding will always see to the bottom of involuntary or ignorant faults—always help me to correct them. I have done now: if I thought you were like other women I have known, I should say so much—but—(my first and last word—I *believe* in you!)—what you could and

would give me, of your affection, you would give nobly and simply
and as a giver—you would not need that I tell you—(*tell* you!)—what
would be supreme happiness to me in the event— however distant—

I repeat.. I call on your justice to remember, on your intelligence
to believe... that this is merely a more precise stating the *first* sub-
ject; to put an end to any possible misunderstanding—to prevent
your henceforth believing that because I *do not write*, from thinking
too deeply of you, I am offended, vexed &c &c. I will never recur to
this, nor shall you see the least difference in my manner next
Monday: it is indeed, always before me.. how I know nothing of
you and yours: but I think I ought to have spoken when I did—and
to speak clearly.. or more clearly what I do—as it is my pride and
duty to fall back, now, on the feeling with which I have been in the
meantime—Yours

God bless you—R. B.

Let me write a few words to lead into Monday—and say, you have
probably received my note. I am much better—with a little headache,
which is all, and fast going this morning: of yours you say nothing—I
trust you see your.. dare I say.. your *duty* in the Pisa affair,° as all
else *must* see it—shall I hear on Monday? And my Saul that you are
so lenient to.

Bless you ever—

93. *E.B.B. to R.B., 31 Aug. 1845*

Sunday.

I did not think you were angry—I never said so. But you might
reasonably have been wounded a little, if you had suspected me of
blaming you for any bearing of yours towards myself—& this was the
amount of my fear,.. or rather hope.. since I conjectured most that
you were not well. And after all you did think.. do think.. that in
some way or for some moment I blamed you, disbelieved you,
distrusted you—or why this letter? How have I provoked this letter?
Can I forgive myself for having even seemed to have provoked it?—
& will you believe me that if for the past's sake you sent it, it was
unnecessary, & if for the future's, irrelevant? Which I say from no
want of sensibility to the words of it—your words always make
themselves felt—but in fulness of purpose not to suffer you to hold
to words because they have been said, nor to say them as if to be

holden by them. Why, if a thousand more such words were said by you to me, how could they operate upon the future or present, supposing me to choose to keep the possible modification of your feelings, as a probability, in my sight & yours? Can you help my sitting with the doors all open if I think it right? I do attest to you .. while I trust you, as you must see, in word & act, & while I am confident that no human being ever stood higher or purer in the eyes of another, than you do in mine .. that you would still stand high & remain unalterably my friend, if the probability in question became a fact, as now at this moment. And this I must say, since you have said other things: & this alone, which *I* have said, concerns the future, I remind you earnestly.

My dearest friend—you have followed the most *generous* of impulses in your whole bearing to me—& I have recognized & called by its name, in my heart, each one of them. Yet I cannot help adding that, of us two, yours has not been quite the hardest part, .. I mean, to a generous nature like your own, to which every sort of nobleness comes easily. Mine has been more difficult—& I have sunk under it again & again: & the sinking & the effort to recover the duty of a lost position, may have given me an appearance of vacillation and lightness, unworthy at least of *you*, & perhaps of both of us. Notwithstanding which appearance, it was right & just (only just) of you, to believe in me—in my truth—because I have never failed to you in it, nor been capable of *such* failure:—the thing I have said, I have meant .. always: & in things I have not said, the silence has had a reason somewhere different perhaps from where you looked for it. And this brings me to complaining that you, who profess to believe in me, do yet obviously believe that it was only merely silence, which I required of you on one occasion—& that if I had 'known your power over yourself,' I should not have minded .. no!—In other words you believe of me that I was thinking just of my own—(what shall I call it for a motive base & small enough?) my own scrupulousness .. freedom from embarrassment! of myself in the least of me; in the tying of my shoestrings, say! .. so much & no more!—Now this is so wrong, as to make me impatient sometimes in feeling it to be your impression—I asked for silence—but ALSO & chiefly for the putting away of .. you know very well what I asked for. And this was sincerely done, I attest to you. You wrote once to me° .. oh, long before May & the day we met—that you 'had been so happy, you should be now justified to yourself in taking any step most hazardous to the happiness of your life'—but if you were justified, c^d *I* be therefore justified in abetting such a step,—the step of wasting, in a sense, your best feelings.. of emptying your water gourds into the sand?—What I thought then I think now—just what any third person, knowing you, w^d think, I think & feel. I thought too, at first, that the feeling on your part was a mere generous impulse, likely to expend itself in a week perhaps—It affects me & has affected me, very deeply—more than I dare attempt to say.. that you should persist s o—& if sometimes I have felt, by a sort of instinct, that after all you w^d not go on to persist, & that (being a man, you know) you might mistake, a little, unconsciously, the strength of your own feeling,—you ought not to be surprised; when I felt it was more advantageous & happier for you that it should be so—*In any case*, I shall never regret my own share in the events of this summer, & your friendship will be dear to me to the last. You know I told you so— not long since. And as to what you say otherwise, you are right in thinking that I would not hold by unworthy motives in avoiding to speak what you had any claim to hear. But what could I speak that w^d not be unjust to you? Your life!.. if you gave it to me & I put my whole heart into it; what should I put but anxiety, & more sadness than you were born to? What could I give you, which it would not be ungenerous to give? Therefore we must leave this subject—& I must trust you to leave it without one word more; (too many have been said already—but I could not let your letter pass quite silently.. as if I had nothing to do but to receive all as matter of course *so!*) while you may well trust *me* to remember to my life's end, as the grateful remember,—& to feel, as those do who have felt sorrow, (for where these pits are dug, the water will stand), the full price of your regard. May God bless you my dearest friend—I shall send this letter after I have seen you, & hope you may not have expected to hear sooner.

Ever yours, E. B. B.

102. *R.B. to E.B.B., 13 Sept. 1845*

Saturday M^g

Now, dearest, I will try and write the little I shall be able, in reply to your letter of last week°—and first of all I have to entreat you, now more than ever, to help me and understand from the few words the feelings behind them—(I should *speak* rather more easily, I think— but I dare not run the risk: and I know, after all, you will be just &

kind where you can.) I have read your letter again & again: I will tell you—no, not *you*, but any imaginary other person, who should hear what I am going to avow; I would tell that person most sincerely there is not a particle of fatuity, shall I call it, in that avowal; cannot be, seeing that from the beginning and at this moment I never dreamed of winning your *love*..I can hardly write this word, so incongruous & impossible does it seem; such a change of our places does it imply—nor, next to that, tho' long after, *would* I, if I *could*, supplant one of any of the affections that I know to have taken root in you—*that* great & solemn one, for instance..I feel that if I could get myself *remade*, as if turned to gold, I WOULD not even then desire to become more than the mere setting to *that* diamond you must always wear: the regard and esteem you now give me, in this letter, and which I press to my heart & bow my head upon, is all I can take & all too embarrassing, using *all* my gratitude: and yet, with that contented pride in being infinitely your debtor as it is, bound to you for ever as it is,—when I read your letter with all the determination to be just to us both; I dare not so far withstand the light I am master of, as to refuse seeing that whatever is recorded as an objection to your disposing of that life of mine I would give you—has reference to some supposed good in that life which your accepting it would destroy (—of which fancy I shall speak presently)—I say, wonder as I may at this, I cannot but find it there, surely there: I could no more 'bind *you* by words,' than you have bound me, as you say—but if I misunderstand you, one assurance to that effect will be but too intelligible to me—but, as it *is*, I have difficulty in imagining that while one of so many reasons, which I am not obliged to repeat to myself, but which any one easily conceives; while *any one* of those reasons would impose silence on me *for ever*—(for, as I observed, I love you as you now are, and *would* not remove one affection that is already part of you,)—*would* you, being able to speak *so*, only say *that you* desire not to put 'more sadness than I was born to,' into my life?—that you 'could give me only what it were ungenerous to give'?

Have I your meaning here? In so many words, is it on my account that you bid me 'leave this subject'? I think if it were so, I would for once call my advantages round me. I am not what your generous self-forgetting appreciation would sometimes make me out—but it is not since yesterday, nor ten nor twenty years before, that I began to look into my own life, and study its end, and requirements, what would turn to its good or its loss—and I *know*, if one may know anything, that to make that life yours and increase it by the union with yours,

would render me *supremely happy*, as I said, and say, and feel. My
whole suit to you is, in that sense, *selfish*—not that I am ignorant that
your nature would most surely attain happiness in being conscious
that it made another happier—but *that best, best end of all*, would, like
the rest, come from yourself, be a reflection of your own gift.

Dearest, I will end here—words, persuasion & arguments,—if
they were at my service I would not use them—I believe in you,
altogether have faith in you—in you. I will not think of insulting by
trying to reassure you on one point which certain phrases in your
letter might at first glance seem to imply—you do not understand me
to be living and labouring and writing (and *not* writing) in order to be
successful in the world's sense? I even convinced the people *here*
what was my true 'honorable position in society,' &c. &c. therefore I
shall not have to inform *you* that I desire to be very rich, very great;
but not in reading Law gratis with dear foolish old Basil Montagu, as
he ever & anon bothers me to do;—enough of this nonsense.

'Tell me what I have a claim to hear': I can hear it, and be as
grateful as I was before and am now—your friendship is my pride
and happiness. If you told me your love was already bestowed else-
where, and that it was in my power to serve you *there*, to serve you
there would still be my pride and happiness. I look on and on over
the prospect of my love, it is all *on*wards,—and all possible forms of
unkindness.. I quite laugh to think how they are *behind*.. cannot be
encountered in the route we are traveling!—I submit to you and will
obey you implicitly.. obey what I am able to conceive of your least
desire, much more of your expressed wish—But it was necessary to
make this avowal, among other reasons, for one which the world
would recognize too—My whole scheme of life, (with its wants,
material wants at least, closely cut down,) was long ago calcu-
lated—and it supposed *you*, the finding such an one as you, utterly
impossible—because in calculating one goes upon *chances*, not on
providence—how could I expect you? So for my own future way in
the world I have always refused to care—any one who can live a
couple of years & more on bread and potatoes as I did once on a time,
and who prefers a blouse and a blue shirt (such as I now write in) to
all manner of dress and gentlemanly appointment, and who can, if
necessary, groom a horse not so badly, or at all events would rather
do it all day long than succeed Mr Fitzroy Kelly° in the Solicitor-
Generalship,.. such an one need not very much concern himself
beyond considering the lilies° how they grow: but now I see you
near this life, all changes—and at a word, I will do all that ought to

be done,—that every one used to say could be done, and let 'all my powers find sweet employ' as Dr Watts sings,° in getting whatever is to be got—not very much, surely. I would print these things, get them away, and do this now, and go to you at Pisa with the news—at Pisa where one may live for some £100 a year—while, lo, I seem to remember, I *do* remember, that Charles Kean offered to give me 500 of those pounds for any play that might suit him—to say nothing of Mr Colburn saying confidentially that he wanted more than his dinner 'a novel on the subject of *Napoleon*' !!! So may one make money, if one does not live in a house in a row, and feel impelled to take the Princesses' Theatre for a laudable development and exhibition of one's faculty.

Take the sense of all this, I beseech you, dearest—all you shall say will be best—I am yours—

Yes—Yours ever—God bless you for all you have been, and are, and will certainly be to me, come what He shall please—!

R. B.

103. E.B.B. to R.B., 16 Sept. 1845

I scarcely know how to write what is to be written nor indeed why it is to be written & to what end. I have tried in vain—& you are waiting to hear from me. I am unhappy enough even where I am happy—but ungrateful nowhere—& I thank you from my heart—profoundly from the depths of my heart..which is nearly all I can do.

One letter I began to write & asked in it how it could become me to speak at all if *'from the beginning & at this moment you never dreamed of'*..& there, I stopped & tore the paper,..because I felt that you were too loyal & generous, for me to bear to take a moment's advantage of the same, & bend down the very flowering branch of your generosity (as it might be) to thicken a little the fence of a woman's caution & reserve. You will not say that you have not acted as if you 'dreamed'—& I will answer therefore to the general sense of your letter & former letters, & admit at once that I *did* state to you the difficulties most difficult to myself..though not all..& that if I had been worthier of you I should have been proportionably less in haste to 'bid you leave that subject,' I do not understand how you can seem at the same moment to have faith in my integrity & to have doubt whether all this time I may not have felt a preference for another .. which you are ready 'to serve,' you say. Which is generous in you—but in *me*, where were the integrity? Could you really hold me to be blameless? & do you think that true-hearted women act usually so? Can it be necessary for me to tell you that I could not have acted so, & did not? And shall I shrink from telling you besides .. YOU who have been generous to me & have a right to hear it .. & have spoken to me in the name of an affection & memory most precious & holy to me, in this same letter .. that neither now nor formerly has any man been to my feelings what you are .. & that if I were different in some respects and free in others by the providence of God, I would accept the great trust of your happiness, gladly, proudly, & gratefully; & give away my own life & soul to that end. I *would* do it .. *not, I do* .. observe! it is a truth without a consequence; only meaning that I am not all stone—only proving that I am not likely to consent to help you in wrong against yourself. You see in me what is not:—*that*, I know: & you overlook in me what is unsuitable to you .. *that*, I know, & have sometimes told you. Still, because a strong feeling from some sources is self-vindicating & ennobling to the object of it, I will not say that, if it were proved to me that you felt this for me, I would persist in putting the sense of my own unworthiness between you & me—not being heroic you know, nor pretending to be so. But something worse than even a sense of unworthiness, GOD has put between us! & judge yourself if to beat your thoughts against the immovable marble of it, can be anything but pain & vexation of spirit, waste & wear of spirit to you .. judge!— The present is here to be seen .. speaking for itself! & the best future you can imagine for me, what a precarious thing it must be .. a thing for making burdens out of .. only not for your carrying; as I have vowed to my own soul. As dear Mr Kenyon said to me to-day in his smiling kindness .. 'In ten years you may be strong perhaps'—or 'almost strong'! that being the encouragement of my best friends! What would he say, do you think, if he could know or guess .. ! what *could* he say but that you were .. a poet!—& I .. still worse!—*Never* let him know or guess!—

And so if you are wise & would be happy (and you have excellent practical sense after all & should exercise it) you must leave me— these thoughts of me, I mean .. for if we might not be true friends for ever, I sh^d have less courage to say the other truth. But we may be friends always .. & cannot be so separated, that your happiness, in the knowledge of it, will not increase mine. And if you will be persuaded by me, as you say, you will be persuaded *thus*.. & consent to take a resolution & force your mind at once into another channel. Perhaps I might bring you reasons of the class which you tell me 'would silence you for ever.' I might certainly tell you that my own father, if he knew that you had written to me so, & that I had answered you—*so*, even.. would not forgive me at the end of ten years—& this, from none of the causes mentioned by me here & in no disrespect to your name & your position.. though he does not over-value poetry even in his daughter, & is apt to take the world's measures of the means of life.. but for the singular reason that he never *does* tolerate in his family (sons or daughters) the development of one class of feelings. Such an objection I could not bring to you of my own will—it rang hollow in my ears—perhaps I thought even too little of it:—& I brought to you what I thought much of, & cannot cease to think much of equally. Worldly thoughts, these are not at all, nor have been: there need be no soiling of the heart with any such:—& I will say, in reply to some words of yours, that you cannot despise the gold & gauds of the world more than I do, & should do even if I found a use for them. And if I *wished* to be very poor, in the world's sense of poverty, I *could not*, with three or four hundred a year of which no living will can dispossess me. And is it not the chief good of money, the being free from the need of thinking of it? It seems so to me.

The obstacles then are of another character, & the stronger for being so. Believe that I am grateful to you—*how* grateful, cannot be shown in words nor even in tears.. grateful enough to be truthful in all ways. You know I might have hidden myself from you—but I would not: & by the truth told of myself, you may believe in the earnestness with which I tell the other truths—of you.. & of this subject. The subject will not bear consideration—it breaks in our hands. But that God is stronger than we, cannot be a bitter thought to you but a holy thought.. while He lets me, as much as I can be anyone's, be only yours.

E. B. B.

104. R.B. to E.B.B., 16 Sept. 1845

I do not know whether you imagine the precise effect of your letter on me—very likely you do, and write it just for that—for I conceive *all* from your goodness: but before I tell you what is that effect, let

me say in as few words as possible what shall stop any fear—tho'
only for a moment and on the outset,—that you have been misunder-
stood,—that the goodness *outside*, and round and over all, hides all or
any thing: I understand you to signify to me that you see, at this
present, insurmountable obstacles to that .. can I speak it .. entire
gift, which I shall own, was, while I dared ask it, above my
hopes—and wishes, even, so it seems to me .. and yet could not but
be asked, so plainly was it dictated to me, by something quite out of
those hopes & wishes—Will it help me to say that once in this
Aladdin-cavern I knew I ought to stop for no heaps of jewel-fruit
on the trees from the very beginning, but go on to the lamp, *the*
prize, the last and best of all? Well, I understand you to pronounce
that at present you believe this gift impossible—and I acquiesce
entirely—I submit wholly to you; repose on you in all the faith of
which I am capable: those obstacles are solely for *you* to see and to
declare .. had *I* seen them, be sure I should never have mocked you
or myself by affecting to pass them over .. what *were* obstacles, I
mean: but you *do* see them, I must think,—and perhaps they strike
me the more from my true, honest unfeigned inability to imagine
what they are,—not that I shall endeavour: after what you *also*
apprise me of, I know and am joyfully confident that if ever they
cease to be what you now consider them, you who see now *for me*,
whom I implicitly trust in to see for me; you will *then*, too, see and
remember me, and how I trust, and shall then be still trusting: and
until you see, and so inform me, I shall never utter a word—for that
would involve the vilest of implications. I thank God—I *do* thank
him, that in this whole matter I have been, to the utmost of my
power, not unworthy of his introducing you to me, in this respect
that, being no longer in the first freshness of life, and having for
many years now made up my mind to the impossibility of loving any
woman .. having wondered at this in the beginning, and fought not a
little against it, having acquiesced in it at last, and accounted for it all
to myself, and become, if anything, rather proud of it than sorry .. I
say, when real love, making itself at once recognized as such, *did*
reveal itself to me at last, I *did* open my heart to it with a cry—nor
care for its overturning all my theory—nor mistrust its effect upon a
mind set in ultimate order, so I fancied, for the few years more—nor
apprehend in the least that the new element would harm what was
already organized without its help: nor have I, either, been guilty of
the more pardonable folly, of treating the new feeling after the
pedantic fashions and instances of the world .. I have not spoken

when *it* did not speak, because 'one' might speak, or has spoken, or *should* speak, and 'plead' and all that miserable work which after all, I may well continue proud that I am not called to attempt: *here* for instance *now* . . 'one' should despair; but 'try again' first, and work blindly at removing those obstacles (—if I saw them, I should be silent, and only speak when a month hence, ten years hence, I could bid you look where they *were*)—and 'one' would do all this, not for the *play-acting's* sake, or to 'look the character' . . (*that* would be something quite different from folly . .) but from a not unreasonable anxiety lest by too sudden a silence, too complete an acceptance of your will; the earnestness and endurance and unabatedness . . the *truth*, in fact, of what had already been professed, should get to be questioned—But I believe that you believe me—and now that all is clear between us I will say, what you will hear, without fearing for me or yourself, that I am utterly contented . . ('grateful' I have done with . . it must go—) I accept what you give me, what those words deliver to me, as—not all I asked for . . as I said . . but as more than I ever hoped for,—*all*, in the best sense, that I desire. That phrase in my letter which you objected to, and the other—may stand, too—I never attempted to declare, describe my feeling for you—one word of course stood for it all . . but having to put down some one *point*, so to speak, of it—you could not wonder if I took any extreme one *first* . . never minding all the untold portion that *led* up to it, made it possible and natural—it is true, 'I could not dream of *that*'—that I was eager to get the horrible notion away from never so flitting a visit to you, that you were thus and thus to me *on condition* of my proving just the same to you—just as if we had waited to acknowledge that the moon lighted us till we ascertained within these two or three hundred years that the earth happens to light the moon as well! But I felt that, and so said it:—now you have declared what I should never have presumed to hope—and I repeat to you that I, with all to be thankful for to God, am most of all thankful for this the last of his providences . . which is no doubt, the natural and inevitable feeling, could one always see clearly. Your regard for me is *all* success—let the rest come, or not come. In my heart's thankfulness I would . . I am sure I would promise anything that would gratify you . . but it would *not* do that, to agree, in words, to change my affections, put them elsewhere &c &c. That would be pure foolish talking, and quite foreign to the practical results which you will attain in a better way from a higher motive: I will cheerfully promise you, however, to be 'bound by no words,' blind to no miracle,—in sober earnest, it is not because I renounced once for all oxen and the owning and having to do with them, that I will obstinately turn away from any unicorn when such an apparition blesses me.. but meantime I shall walk at peace on our hills here nor go looking in all corners for the bright curved horn! And as for you.. if I did not dare 'to dream of that'—, now it is mine, my pride & joy prevent in no manner my taking the whole consolation of it at once, *now*—I will be confident that, if I obey you, I shall get no wrong for it—if, endeavouring to spare you fruitless pain, I do not eternally revert to the subject,—do indeed 'quit' it just now, when no good can come of dwelling on it to you; you will never say to yourself—'so I said—' the 'generous impulse' *has* worn itself out.. time is doing his usual work—this was to be expected' &c &c. You will be the first to say to me 'such an obstacle has ceased to exist.. or is now become one palpable to *you*, one *you* may try and overcome'—and I shall be there, and ready—ten years hence as now—if alive.

One final word on the other matters—the 'worldly matters'—I shall own I alluded to them rather ostentatiously, because—because *that would be* the *one* poor sacrifice I could make you—one I would cheerfully make,—but a sacrifice, and the only one; this careless 'sweet habitude of living'—this absolute independence of mine, which, if I had it not, my heart would starve and die for, I feel, and which I have fought so many good battles to preserve—for that has happened, too—this light rational life I lead, and know so well that I lead; this I could give up for nothing less than—what you know—but I *would* give it up, not for you merely, but for those whose disappointment might re-act on you—and I should break no promise to myself—the money getting would not be for the sake of *it*; 'the labour not for that which is nought'—indeed the necessity of doing this, if at all, *now*, was one of the reasons which make me go on to that *last request of all*.. at once; one must not be too old, they say, to begin their ways: but, in spite of all the babble, I feel sure that whenever I make up my mind to that, I can be rich enough and to spare—because along with what you have thought *genius* in me, is certainly talent, what the world recognizes as such; and I have tried it in various ways, just to be sure that I *was* a little magnanimous in never intending to use it: thus, in more than one of the reviews & newspapers that laughed my 'Paracelsus' to scorn ten years ago—in the same column, often, of these reviews, would follow a most laudatory notice of an Elementary French book, on a new plan, which I '*did*' for my old French Master, and he published—'*that* was really an useful work'!—So that when the only obstacle is only that there is so much *per annum* to be producible, you will tell me: after all it would be unfair in me not to confess . . that this was always intended to be *my* own single stipulation—'an objection' which I could see, certainly,— but meant to treat myself to the little luxury of removing.

So, now, dearest—let me once think of that, and of you as my own, my dearest—this once—dearest, I have done with words for the present: I will wait: God bless you and reward you—I kiss your hands *now*. This is my comfort, that if you accept my feeling as all but *un*expressed now,—more and more will become spoken—or understood, that is—we both live on—you will know better *what* it was, how much and manifold, what one little word had to give out.

God bless you—

Your R.B.

On Thursday,—you remember?

This is Tuesday Night—

I called on Saturday at the Office in St Mary Axe—all uncertainty about the vessel's sailing again for Leghorn—'it could not sail before the middle of the month—and only then *if* &c But if I would leave my card &c &c'

106. E.B.B. to R.B., 17 Sept. 1845

Wednesday evening.—

But one word before we leave the subject, and then to leave it finally,—but I cannot let you go on to fancy a mystery anywhere, in obstacles or the rest. You deserve at least a full frankness; & in my letter I meant to be fully frank. I even told you what was an absurdity, so absurd that I should far rather not have told you at all, only that I felt the need of telling you all: and no mystery is involved in that, except as an 'idiosyncrasy' is a mystery. But the 'insurmountable' difficulty is for you & everybody to see,— —& for me to feel, who have been a very byword among the talkers, for a confirmed invalid through months & years, & who, even if I were going to Pisa & had the best prospects possible to me, should yet remain liable to relapses & stand on precarious ground to the end of my life. Now that is no mystery for the trying of 'faith'; but a plain fact, which neither thinking nor speaking can make less a fact. But DON'T let us speak of it.

I must speak, however (before the silence) of what you said and repeat in words for which I gratefully thank you—& which are *not* 'ostentatious' though unnecessary words—for, if I were in a position to accept sacrifices from you, I would not accept *such* a sacrifice .. amounting to a sacrifice of duty & dignity as well as of ease & satisfaction .. to an exchange of higher work for lower work .. & of the special work you are called to, for that which is work for anybody. I am not so ignorant of the right uses & destinies of what you have & are. You will leave the Solicitor generalships to the Fitzroy Kellys, & justify your own nature; & besides, do me the little right, (*over* the *over*-right you are always doing me) of believing that I would not bear or dare to do *you* so much wrong, if I were in the position to do it.

And for all the rest I thank you—believe that I thank you .. & that the feeling is not so weak as the word. That *you* should care at all for *me* has been a matter of unaffected wonder to me from the first hour until now—& I cannot help the pain I feel sometimes, in thinking that it would have been better for you if you never had known me .. May God turn back the evil of me!— Certainly I admit that I cannot expect you .. just at this moment, .. to say more than you say, .. & I shall try to be at ease in the consideration that you are as accessible to the 'unicorn' now as you ever could be at any former period of your life. And here I have done. I had done *living*, I thought, when you came & sought me out! and why? & to what end? *That*, I cannot help thinking now. Perhaps just that I may pray for you—which were a sufficient end. If you come on Saturday I trust you to leave this subject untouched,—as it must be indeed henceforth.

I am yours,

E.B.B.

No word more of Pisa—I shall not go, I think.

109. R.B. to E.B.B., 18 Sept. 1845

Thursday M^g

But you, too, will surely want, if you think me a rational creature, *my* explanation—without which all that I have said and done would be pure madness, I think: it *is* just 'what I see' that I *do* see,—or rather it has proved, since I first visited you, that the reality was infinitely worse than I know it to be .. for at and after the writing of *that first letter*, on my first visit, I believed—thro' some silly or misapprehend[ed] talk, collected at second hand too—that your complaint was of quite another nature—a spinal injury irremediable in the nature of it: had it been *so*—now speak for *me*, for what you hope I am, and say how *that* should affect or neutralize what you *were*, what I wished to associate with myself in you? But *as you now are*—: then if I had married you seven years ago, and this visitation came now first, I should be 'fulfilling a pious duty,' I suppose, in enduring what could not be amended—a pattern to good people in not running away .. for where were *now* the use and the good & the profit and— —

I desire in this life (with very little fluctuation for a man & too weak a one) to live and just write out certain things which are in me, and so save my soul. I would endeavour to do this if I were forced to 'live among lions' as you once said—but I should best do this if I lived quietly with myself and with you. That you cannot dance like Cerito° does not materially disarrange this plan—nor that I might (beside the perpetual incentive and sustainment and consolation) get, over and above the main reward, the incidental, particular and unexpected happiness of being allowed when not working to rather occupy myself with watching you, that with certain other pursuits I might be otherwise addicted to—*this*, also, does not constitute an obstacle, as I see obstacles—

But *you* see them—and I see *you*, and know my first duty and do it resolutely if not cheerfully.

As for referring again, till leave by word or letter—you will see—

And very likely, the tone of this letter even will be misunderstood—because I studiously cut out all vain words, protesting &c:— No—will it?

———————

I said, unadvisedly, that Saturday was taken from me .. but it was dark and I had not looked at the tickets—the hour of the performance is later than I thought: if to-morrow does not suit you, as I infer, let it be Saturday—at 3—and I will leave earlier, a little, and all will be quite right here: one hint will apprise me.

God bless you, dearest friend.

R.B.

114. R.B. to E.B.B., 25 Sept. 1845

You have said to me more than once that you wished I might never know certain feelings *you* had been forced to endure. I suppose all of us have the proper place where a blow should fall to be felt most—and I truly wish *you* may never feel what I have to bear in looking on, quite powerless, and silent, while you are subjected to this treatment, which I refuse to characterize—so blind is it *for* blindness. I think I ought to understand what a father may exact, and a child should comply with—and I respect the most ambiguous of love's caprices if they give never so slight a clue to their all-justifying source: did I, when you signified to me the probable objections.. you remember what.. to myself, my own happiness,—did I once allude to.. much less argue against, or refuse to acknowledge those objections? For I wholly sympathize, however it go against me, with the highest, wariest, pride & love for you, and the proper jealousy and vigilance they entail—but now, and here, the jewel is not being over guarded, but ruined, cast away. And whoever is privileged to interfere should do so in the possessor's own interest—all common sense interferes—all rationality against absolute no-reason at all.. and you ask whether you ought to obey this no-reason?—I will tell you: all passive obedience and implicit submission of will and intellect is by far too easy, if well considered, to be the course prescribed by God to Man in this life of probation—for they *evade* probation altogether, tho' foolish people think otherwise: chop off your legs, you will never go astray,—stifle your reason altogether and you will find it is difficult to reason ill: 'it is hard to make these sacrifices!'—Not so hard as to lose the reward or incur the penalty of an Eternity to come; 'hard to effect them, then, and go through with them'—*not* hard, when the leg is to be *cut off*—that it is rather harder to keep it quiet on a stool, I know very well. The partial indulgence, the proper exercise of one's faculties, there is the difficulty and problem for solution, set by that Providence which might have made the laws of Religion as indubitable as those of vitality, and revealed the articles of belief as certainly as that condition, for instance, by which we breathe so many times in a minute to support life: but there is no reward proposed for the feat of breathing, and a great one for that of believing—consequently there must go a great deal more of voluntary effort to this latter than is implied in the getting absolutely rid of it at once, by adopting the direction of an infallible church, or private judgment of another—for all our life is some form of religion, and all our action some belief, and there is but one law, however modified, for the greater and the less—In your case I do think you are called upon to do your duty to yourself; that is, to God in the end: your own reason should examine the whole matter in dispute by every light which can be put in requisition; and every interest that appears to be affected by your conduct should have its utmost claims considered—your father's in the first place; and that interest, not in the miserable limits of a few days' pique or whim in which it would seem to express itself,—but in its whole extent .. the *hereafter* which all momentary passion prevents him seeing .. indeed, the *present* on either side which everyone else must see—And this examination made, with whatever earnestness you will, I do think and am sure that on its conclusion you should act, in confidence that a duty has been performed .. *difficult*, or how were it a duty? Will it *not* be infinitely harder to act so than to blindly adopt his pleasure, and die under it? Who can *not* do that?

I fling these hasty rough words over the paper, fast as they will fall—knowing to whom I cast them, and that any sense they may contain or point to, will be caught and understood, and presented in a better light: the hard thing .. this is all I want to say .. is to act on one's own best conviction—not to abjure it and accept another will, and say '*there* is my plain duty'—easy it is, whether plain or no!

How 'all changes!' When I first knew you,—you know what followed. I supposed you to labour under an incurable complaint—and, of course, to be completely dependent on your father for its commonest alleviations; the moment after that inconsiderate letter, I reproached myself bitterly with the selfishness apparently involved in any proposition I might then have made—for tho' I have never been at all frightened of the world, nor mistrustful of my power to deal with it, and get my purpose out of if once I thought it worth while, yet I could not but feel the consideration, of WHAT failure would *now* be, paralyse all effort even in fancy: when you told me lately that 'you could never be poor'—all my solicitude was at an end—I had but myself to care about, and I told you, what I believed and believe, that I can at any time amply provide for that, and that I could cheerfully & confidently undertake the removing *that* obstacle. Now again the circumstances shift—and you are in what I should wonder at as the veriest slavery—and I who *could* free you from it, I am here—scarcely daring to write .. tho' I know you must feel for me and forgive what forces itself from me .. what retires so mutely into my heart at your least word..what *shall not* be again written or spoken, if you so will.. that I should be made happy beyond all hope of expression by—Now while I *dream*, let me once dream! I would marry you now and thus—I would come when you let me, and go when you bade me—I would be no more than one of your brothers—'*no more*'—that is, instead of getting to-morrow for Saturday, I should get Saturday as well—two hours for one—when your head ached I should be *here*. I deliberately choose the realization of that dream (—of sitting simply by you for an hour every day) rather than any other, excluding you, I am able to form for this world, or any world I know—And it will continue but a dream. God bless my dearest E.B.B.

R. B.

You understand that I see you to-morrow, Friday, as you propose. I am better—thank you—and will go out to-day.

You know what I am, what I would speak, and all I would do.

115. E.B.B. to R.B., 26 Sept. 1845

Friday evening.

I had your letter late last night, everyone almost, being out of the house by an accident, so that it was left in the letter-box, and if I had wished to answer it before I saw you, it had scarcely been possible.

But it will be the same thing—for you know as well as if you saw my answer, what it must be, what it cannot choose but be, on pain of sinking me so infinitely below not merely your level but my own, that the depth cannot bear a glance down. Yet, though I am not made of such clay as to admit of my taking a base advantage of certain noble extravagances, (& that I am not I thank God for your sake) I will say, I must say, that your words in this letter have done me good & made me happy,.. that I thank & bless you for them,.. & that to receive such a proof of attachment from YOU, not only overpowers every present evil, but seems to me a full and abundant amends for the merely personal sufferings of my whole life. When I had read that letter last night I *did* think so. I looked round & round for the small bitternesses which for several days had been bitter to me—& I could not find one of them. The tear-marks went away in the moisture of new, happy tears. Why, how else could I have felt? how else do you think I could?—How would any woman have felt.. who could feel at all .. hearing such words said (though 'in a dream' indeed) by such a speaker?—

And now listen to me in turn. You have touched me more profoundly than I thought even *you* could have touched me—my heart was full when you came here to-day. Henceforward I am yours for everything but to do you harm—and I am yours too much, in my heart, ever to consent to do you harm in that way— —If I could consent to do it, not only should I be less loyal .. but in one sense, less yours. I say this to you without drawback and reserve, because it is all I am able to say, & perhaps all I *shall* be able to say. However this may be, a promise goes to you in it that none, except God & your will, shall interpose between you & me, .. I mean, that if He should free me within a moderate time from the trailing chain of this weakness, I will then be to you whatever at that hour you shall choose .. whether friend or more than friend .. a friend to the last in any case. So it rests with God & with you—Only in the meanwhile you are most absolutely free .. 'unentangled' (as they call it) by the breadth of a thread—& if I did not know that you considered yourself so, I would not see you any more, let the effort cost me what it might. You may force me to *feel*: .. but you cannot force me to *think* contrary to my first thought .. that it were better for you to forget me at once in one relation. And if better for *you*, can it be bad for *me?*— which flings me down on the stone-pavement of the logicians.

And now if I ask a boon of you,° will you forget afterwards that it ever was asked?—I have hesitated a great deal; but my face is down on the stone-pavement—no I will not ask today—It shall be for another day—& may God bless you on this & on those that come after, my dearest friend.

151. *R.B. to E.B.B., 16 Nov. 1845*

Sunday Morning.

At last your letter comes—and the deep joy—(I know and use to analyse my own feelings, and be sober in giving distinctive names to their varieties; this is *deep* joy,)— the true love with which I take this much of you into my heart, .. *that* proves what it is I wanted so long, and find at last, and am happy for ever. I must have more than 'intimated'—I must have spoken plainly out the truth, if I do myself the barest justice, and told you long ago that the admiration at your works went *away*, quite another way and afar from this hope of you: if I could fancy some method of what I shall say happening without all the obvious stumbling-blocks of falseness, &c. which no foolish fancy dares associate with you .. if you COULD tell me when I next sit by you—'I will undeceive you,—I am not *the* Miss B.—she is upstairs and you shall see her—I only wrote those letters, and am what you see, that is all now left you' (all the misapprehension having arisen from *me*, in some inexplicable way) .. I should .. not begin by *saying* anything, dear, dearest—but *after that*, I should assure you— soon make you believe that I did not much wonder at the event, for I have been all my life asking what connection there is between the satisfaction at the display of power, and the sympathy with—ever-increasing sympathy with—all imaginable weakness?

And since I wrote what is above, I have been reading among other poems that sonnet—'Past and Future'°—which affects me more than any poem I ever read. How can I put your poetry away from you, even in these ineffectual attempts to concentrate myself upon, and better apply myself to what remains?—poor, poor work it is,—for is not that sonnet to be loved as a true utterance of yours? I cannot attempt to put down the thoughts that rise;—may God bless me, as you pray, by letting that beloved hand shake the less .. I will only ask, *the less* .. for being laid on mine thro' this life! And, indeed, you write down, for me to calmly read, that I make you happy! Then it is—as with all power—God thro' the weakest instrumentality .. and I am past expression proud and grateful—My love, I am your R.B.

261. *R.B. to E.B.B., 7 Mar. 1846*

Saturday M^g

You call me 'kind'; and by this time I have no heart to call you such names: I told you, did I not once? that 'Ba' had got to convey infinitely more of you to my sense than 'dearest,' 'sweetest,' all or any epithets that break down with their load of honey like bees—to say you are 'kind,' you that so entirely and unintermittingly bless me,— it will never do now, 'Ba'—(All the same, one way there is to make even 'Ba' dearer,—'*my* Ba,' I say to myself!)

About my *fears*—whether of opening doors or entering people— one thing is observable and prevents the possibility of any misconception—I desire, have been in the habit of desiring, to *increase*

them, far from diminishing—they relate, of course, entirely to *you*—
and only through *you* affect me the least in the world: put your well-
being out of the question, so far as I can understand it to be
involved,—and the pleasure & pride I should immediately choose
would be that the whole world knew our position . . what pleasure,
what pride! But I endeavour to remember on all occasions,—and
perhaps succeed in too few,—that it is very easy for me to go
away and leave you who cannot go. I only allude to this because
some people are 'naturally nervous' and all that—and I am quite of
another kind.

Last evening I went out—having been kept at home in the
afternoon to see somebody . . went walking for hours. I am quite well
to-day and, now your letter comes, my Ba, most happy. And, as
the sun shines, you are perhaps making the perilous descent
now, while I write—oh, to meet you on the stairs! And I shall
really see you on Monday, dearest? So soon, it ought to feel, con-
sidering the dreary weeks that now get to go between our days! For
music, I made myself melancholy just now with some 'Concertos for
the Harpsichord by Mr Handel'—brought home by my father the
day before yesterday;—what were light, modern things once! Now I
read not very long ago a French memoir of 'Claude Le Jeune'° called
in his time the Prince of Musicians,—no, '*Phœnix*'—the unap-
proachable wonder to all time—that is, twenty years after his death
about—and to this pamphlet was prefixed as motto this startling
axiom—'In Music, the Beau Idéal changes every thirty years'—
well,—is not that *true?* The *Idea*, mind, changes,—the general stan-
dard . . so that it is no answer that a single air, such as many one
knows, may strike as freshly as ever—they were *not* according to the
Ideal of their own time,—just now, they drop into the ready ear,—
next hundred years, who will be the Rossini? who is no longer the
Rossini even I remember—his early overtures are as purely Rococo
as Cimarosa's or more—The sounds remain, keep their character
perhaps—the scale's proportioned notes affect the same, that is,—
the major third, or minor seventh—but the arrangement of
these, the sequence—the law—for them,—if it *should* change
every thirty years! To Corelli nothing seemed so conclusive in
Heaven or earth as this

I don't believe there is one of his sonatas wherein that formula does not do duty. In these things of Handel that seems replaced by

—that was the only true consummation! Then,—to go over the hundred years,—came Rossini's unanswerable *coda:*

which serves as base to the infinity of songs, gone, gone— *so* gone by!—From all of which Ba draws *this* 'conclusion' that these may be worse things than Bartoli's Tuscan to cover a page with!—yet, yet the pity of it! Le Jeune, the Phœnix, and Rossini who directed his letters to his mother as 'mother of the famous composer'— and Henry Lawes,° and Dowland's Lute,° ah me!

Well, my conclusion is the best, the everlasting, here and I trust elsewhere—I am your own, my Ba, ever your

R.

269. R.B. to E.B.B., 15 Mar. 1846

Sunday.

How will the love my heart is full of for you, let me be silent? Insufficient speech is better than no speech, in one regard—the speaker had *tried* words, and if they fail, hereafter he needs not reflect that he did not even try—so with me now, that loving you, Ba, with all my heart and soul,—all my senses being lost in one wide wondering gratitude and veneration, I press close to you to say so, in this imperfect way, my dear dearest beloved! Why do you not help me, rather than take my words, my proper word, from me and call them yours, when yours they are not?—You said lately love of you 'made you humble'—just as if to hinder *me* from saying that earnest truth!— entirely true it is, as I feel ever more convincingly. You do not choose to understand it should be so, nor do I much care, for the one thing you must believe, must resolve to believe in its length and breadth, is that I do love you and live only in the love of you—

I will rest on the confidence that you do so believe! You *know* by this that it is no shadowy image of you and *not* you, which having attached myself to in the first instance, I afterward compelled my fancy to see reproduced, so to speak, with tolerable exactness to the original idea, in you, the dearest real *you* I am blessed with—you *know* what the eyes are to me, and the lips and the hair—And I, for my part, know *now*, while fresh from seeing you, certainly *know*, whatever I may have said a short time since, that *you* will go on to the end, that the arm round me will not let me go,—over such a blind abyss—I refuse to think, to fancy, *towards* what it would be to lose you now! So I give my life, my soul into your hand—the giving is a mere form too, it is yours, ever yours from the first—but ever as I see you, sit with you, and come away to think over it all, I find more that seems mine to give,—you give me more life and it goes back to you.

I shall hear from you to-morrow—then, I will go out early and get done with some calls, in the joy and consciousness of what waits me,—and when I return I will write a few words—Are these letters, these merest attempts at getting to talk with you thro' the distance .. yet always with the consolation of feeling that you will know all, interpret all & forgive it and put it right,—can such things be cared for, expected, as you say? Then, Ba, my life *must* be better .. with the closeness to help, and the 'finding out the way' for which love was always noted—If you begin making in fancy a lover to your mind, I am lost at once—but the one quality of *affection* for you, which would sooner or later have to be placed on his list of component graces; *that* I will dare start supply—the entire love you could dream of *is* here—You think you see some of the other adornments, and only too many,—and you will see plainer one day, but with that I do not concern myself—you shall admire the true heroes—but me you shall love for the love's sake. Let me kiss you, you, my dearest, dearest—God bless you ever—

302. E.B.B. to R.B., 7 Apr. 1846

Tuesday.

Dearest, it is not I who am a 'flatterer'—and if I used the word first it is because I had the right of it, I remember, long & long ago. There is the vainest of vanities in discussing the application of such a word .. & so, when you said the other day that you 'never flattered' forsooth ... (oh no!—) I would not contradict you for fear of the endless flattery it would lead to. Only that I do not choose (because such things are allowed to pass) to be called on my side 'a flatterer'— I!—*That* is too much, & too out of place. What do I ever say that is like flattery? I am allowed, it may be hoped, to admire the 'Lurias' & the rest, quite like other people, & even to *say* that I admire them .. may I not lawfully? If *that* is flattery woe to me! I tell you the real truth, as I see the truth, even in respect to *them* .. the Lurias ..

For instance, did I flatter you & say that you were right yesterday? Indeed I thought you as wrong as possible .. wonderfully wrong on such a subject,° for YOU .. who, only a day or two before, seemed so free from conventional fallacies .. so free!—You would abolish the punishment of death too .. & put away wars, I am sure! But honorable men are bound to keep their honours clean at the expense of so much gunpowder & so much risk of life .. *that* must be, ought to be, .. let judicial deaths & military glory be abolished ever so! For my part, I set all Christian principle aside, (although if it were carried out .. & principle is nothing unless carried out .. it would not mean cowardice but magnanimity) but I set it aside & go on the bare social rational ground ... and I do advisedly declare to you that I cannot conceive of any *possible combination of circumstances* which could .. I will *not* say *justify*, but even *excuse*, an honourable man's having recourse to the duellist's pistol, either on his own account or another's. Not only it seems to me horribly wrong .. but absurdly wrong, it seems to me. Also .. as a matter of pure reason .. the Parisian method of taking aim & blowing off a man's head for the sins of his tongue, I do take to have a sort of judicial advantage over the Englishman's six paces .. throwing the dice for his life or another man's, because wounded by that man in his honour. His honour!— Who believes in such an honour .. liable to such amends, & capable of such recovery! YOU cannot, I think—in the secret of your mind, Or if *you can* .. *you*, who are a teacher of the world ... poor world—it is more desperately wrong than I thought.

A man calls you 'a liar' in an assembly of other men. Because he is a calumniator, & on that very account, a worse man than you, . . you ask him to go down with you on the only ground on which you two are equals . . the duelling-ground, . . & with pistols of the same length & friends numerically equal on each side, play at lives with him, both mortal men that you are. If it was proposed to you to play at real dice for the ratification or non-ratification of his calumny, the proposition would be laughed to scorn . . & yet the chance (as chance) seems much the same, . . & the death is an exterior circumstance which cannot be imagined to have much virtue. At best, what do you prove by your duel? . . that your calumniator, though a calumniator, is not a coward in the vulgar sense . . & that yourself, though you may still be a liar ten times over, are not a coward either!—'Here be proofs.'

And as to the custom of duelling preventing insults . . why you *say* that a man of honour should not go out with an unworthy adversary. Now supposing a man to be withheld from insult & calumny, just by the fear of being shot . . who is more unworthy than such a man? Therefore you conclude irrationally, illogically, that the system operates beyond the limit of its operations.—Oh!—I shall write as quarrelsome letters as I choose. You are wrong, I know & feel, when you advocate the pitiful resources of this corrupt social life, . . & if you are wrong, how are we to get right, we all who look to you for teaching. Are *you* afraid too of being taken for a coward? or would you excuse that sort of fear . . that cowardice of cowardice, in other men? For me, I value your honour, just as you do . . more than your life . . of the two things: but the madness of this foolishness is so clear to my eyes, than instead of opening the door for you & keeping your secret, as that miserable woman did last year, for the man shot by her sister's husband, I would just *call in the police*, though you were to throw me out of the window afterwards. So, with that beautiful vision of domestic felicity, (which Mrs Jameson would leap up to see!) I shall end my letter—isn't it a letter worth thanking for?—

Ever dearest, do YOU promise me that you never will be provoked into such an act—never? Mr O'Connell° vowed it to himself, for a dead man . . & you may to me, for a living woman. Promises & vows may be foolish things for the most part . . but they cannot be more foolish than, in this case, the thing vowed against. So promise & vow. And I will 'flatter' you in return in the lawful way . . for you *will* 'make me happy' . . so far! May God bless you, beloved! It is so wet & dreary to-day that I do not go down stairs—I sit instead in the gondola chair .. do you not see? .. & think of you .. do you not feel? I even love you .. if *that* were worth mentioning ..

being your own

Ba

364. R.B. to E.B.B., 19 May 1846

Tuesday.

With this day expires the first year since you have been yourself to me—putting aside the anticipations, and prognostications, and even assurances from all reasons short of absolute sight and hearing,—excluding the five or six months of these, there remains a year of this intimacy: you accuse me of talking extravagantly sometimes. I will be quiet here,—is the tone *too* subdued if I say, such a life—made-up of such years—I would deliberately take rather than any other imaginable one in which fame and worldly prosperity and the love of the whole human race should combine, excluding 'that of yours—to which I hearken'—only wishing the rest were there for a moment that you might see and know that I did turn from them to you. My dearest, inexpressibly dearest. How can I thank you? I feel sure you *need* not have been so kind to me, so perfectly kind and good,—I should have remained your own, gratefully, entirely your own, thro' the bare permission to love you, or even without it,—seeing that I never dreamed of stipulating at the beginning for 'a return,' and 'reward,'—but I also believe, joyfully, that no course but the course you have taken could have raised me above my very self, as I feel on looking back,—I began by loving you in comparison with all the world,—now, I love you, my Ba, in the face of your past self, as I remember it.

.. All words are foolish—but I kiss your feet and offer you my heart and soul, dearest, dearest Ba.

I left you last evening without the usual privilege .. you did not rise, Ba! But,—I don't know why—, I got nervous of a sudden,—it seemed late,—and I remembered the Drawing-room & its occupants.

483. E.B.B. to R.B., 2 Aug. 1846

Sunday morning & evening.

Ever dearest, you were wet surely? The rain came before you reached the front door; & for a moment (before I heard it shut) I hoped you might return. Dearest, how I blame myself for letting you go—for not sending for a cab in despite of you! I was frightened out of all wisdom by the idea of who was downstairs & listening perhaps, & watching—as if the cab would have made you appear more emphatically *you!*—And then you said 'the rain was over'—and I believed you as usual. If this isn't a precedent of the evils of too much belief...!!

Altogether, yesterday may pass among the 'unsatisfactory days,' I think—for if I was not frightened of the storm, (& *indeed* I was not, much!—) of the state of affairs down in the provinces, I was most sorely frightened—uneasy the whole time. I seem to be with you, Robert, at this moment, more than yesterday I was .. though if I look up now, I do not see you sitting there!—but when you sate there yesterday, I was looking at Papa's face as I saw it through the floor, & now I see only yours—

Dearest, he came into the room at about seven, before he went to dinner—I was lying on the sofa & had on a white dressing gown, to get rid of the strings .. so oppressive the air was,—for all the pur-ifications of lightning. He looked a little as if the thunder had passed into him, & said, 'Has this been your costume since the morning, pray?' 'Oh no'—I answered—'only just now, because of the heat.' 'Well,' he resumed, with a still graver aspect .. (so displeased he looked, dearest!) 'it appears, Ba, that *that man* has spent the whole day with you.' To which I replied as quietly as I could, that you had several times meant to go away, but that the rain would not let you,—& there the colloquy ended. Brief enough!—but it took my breath away .. or what was left by the previous fear. And think how it must have been a terrible day, when the lightning of it made the least terror ..

I was right too about the message—He took up the fancy that I might be ill perhaps with fear .. '& only Mr Browning in the room'!!—which was not to be permitted. He was *peremptory* with Arabel, she told me.

Well—we need not talk any more of it—it has made one of us uncomfortable long enough. Shall you dare come on Tuesday after all?—He will be out—If he is not—if my aunt should not be.. if a new obstacle should occur.. why you shall hear on Tuesday. At any rate I shall write, I think. He did not see you go yesterday—he had himself preceded you by an hour.. at five o'clock.. which if it had been known, would have relieved me infinitely. Yet it did not prevent.. you see.. the appalling commentary at seven!—No.

With all the rest I am afraid besides of Mr Chorley & his idea about your 'mysteriousness.' Let Mr Kenyon hold that thread in one hand, & in the other the thread Henrietta gave him so carelessly, why he need not ask you for information—Which reminds me of the case you put to me, Robert—and certainly you could not help a confession, in such possible circumstances. Only, even granting the circumstances, you need not confess more than is wrung from you—need you? *Because Mr Kenyon would undo us—*

Before yesterday's triple storms, I had a presentiment which oppressed me during two days.. a presentiment that it would all end *ill*, through some sudden accident or misery of some kind. What is the use of telling you this?—I do not know. I will tell you besides, that it cannot.. *shall not..* be, by my fault or failing—I may be broken indeed, but never bent.

If things should go smoothly, however, I want to say one word, once for all, in relation to them. Once or twice you have talked as if a change were to take place in your life through marrying—whereas I do beg you to keep in mind that not a pebble in the path changes, nor is pushed aside because of me. If you should make me feel myself in the way, should I like it, do you think? And how could I disturb a single habit or manner of yours.. as an unmarried man.. through being within call—I? The best of me is, that I am really very quiet & not difficult to content—having not been spoilt by an excess of prosperity even in little things. It will be prosperity in the greatest, if you seem to be happy—believe that, & leave all the rest. You will go out just as you do now.. when you choose, & as a matter of course, & without need of a word—you will be precisely as you are now in everything,—lord of the house-door-key, & of your own ways—so that when I shall go to Greece, you shall not feel yourself much better off than before I went—That shall be a reserved vengeance, Robert—

While I write, comes Mr Kenyon,—& through a special interposition of guardian-angels, he has broken his spectacles & carries them in his hand. On which I caught at the opportunity & told him that they were the most unbecoming things in the world, & that fervently

(& sincerely) I hoped never to see them mended. The next word was.. 'Did you see Browning yesterday?' 'Yes.' 'I thought so, I intended to come myself, but I thought it probable that he would be here, and so I stayed away—'

Now—I confess to you that that thought carries me a good way over to your impression—It is at least 'suspicious,' that he who knew you were with me on Saturday & Tuesday should expect to find you again on the next Saturday. Oh—how uncomfortable!—the miracle of the broken spectacles not saving one from the discomfort of the position open to the bare eyes!—

He talked of you a little—asked what you were doing— praised you as usual.. for inexhaustible knowledge & general reasonableness, this time. Did I not think so? Yes—of course I thought so—

Presently he made me look aghast by just this question— 'Is there an attachment between your sister Henrietta & Capt. Cook?'—(put as abruptly as I put it here,) My heart leapt up.. as Wordsworth's to the rainbow in the sky°—but there was a recoil in *my* leap. 'Why, Mr Kenyon!'—I said.. 'what extraordinary questions, opening into unspeakable secrets, you do ask.'

'But I did not know that it was a secret. How was I to know?—I have seen him here very often, & it is a natural enquiry which I might have put to anybody in the house touching a matter open to general observation. I thought the affair might be an arranged one by anybody's consent'—

'But you ought to know,' I answered, 'that such things are never permitted in this house. So much for the consent. As for the matter itself you are right in your supposition—but it is a great secret,—& I entreat you not to put questions about it to anybody in or out of the house'—Something to that effect I believe I said—I was frightened.. frightened.. & not exactly for *Henrietta!* What did he mean?—Had *he* too in his mind...

He touched on Mrs Jameson.. just *touched*.. He had desired my sisters to tell me. He thought I had better write a note to thank her for her kindness. He had told her that if I had any thoughts of Italy they could be accomplished only by a sea-voyage, which was impossible to her—

I briefly expressed a sense of the kindness & said that I meant to write. On which the subject was changed in mutual haste, as seemed to me.

Is not this the book of the chronicles..? And you shall hear again on Tuesday, if the post should be faithful to me that morning.

I might be inclined to put off our Tuesday's meeting, but Mrs
Hedley remains in London for a few days after her daughter's mar-
riage, & 'means to see a great deal' of me—therefore Wednesday,
Thursday, Friday,.. *where* should we look, from Tuesday? but I
must consider & will write. May God bless you! Do say how you
are after that rain. The storm is calm,

& ever & ever I am your own Ba

552. E.B.B. to R.B., 9 Sept. 1846

Wednesday night.

Dearest, you are a prophet, I suppose—there can be no denying it.
This night, an edict has gone out, and George is tomorrow to be on
his way to take a house for a month either at Dover, Reigate,
Tunbridge,.. Papa did 'not mind which,' he said, & 'you may settle
it among you.'—but he 'must have this house empty for a month in
order to its cleaning'—we are to go therefore & not delay.

Now!—what *can* be done? It is possible that the absence may be
longer than for a month, indeed it is probable— for there is much to
do in painting & repairing, here in Wimpole Street, more than a
month's work they say. Decide, after thinking. I am embarrassed to
the utmost degree, as to the best path to take. If we are taken away on
Monday.. what then?—

Of course I decline to give any opinion & express any prefer-
ence,—as to places, I mean. It is not for my sake that we go:—if *I*
had been considered at all, indeed, we should have been taken away
earlier,.. & not certainly now, when the cold season is at hand—And
so much the better it is for me, that I have not, obviously, been
thought of.

Therefore decide!—It seems quite too soon & too sudden for us to
set out on our Italian adventure now—& perhaps even we could not
compass—

Well—but you must think for both of us—It is past twelve & I
have just a moment to seal this & entrust it to Henrietta for the
morning's post.

More than ever beloved, I am
Your own Ba

I will do as you wish—understand.

553. R.B. to E.B.B., 10 Sept. 1846 (1)

Thursday M^g

What do you expect this letter will be about, my own dearest?..
Those which I write on the mornings after our days seem naturally to
answer any strong point brought out in the previous discourse, and
not *then* completely disposed of.. so they generally run in the vile
fashion of a disputations 'last word'; 'one word yet'—do not they?
Ah, but you should remember that never does it feel so intolerable,—
the barest fancy of a possibility of losing you—as when I have just
seen you and heard you and, alas—left you for a time; on these
occasions, it seems so horrible—that if the least recollection of a fear
of yours, or a doubt.. anything which might be nursed, or let grow
quietly into a serious obstacle to what we desire.. if *that* rises up
threateningly,—do you wonder that I begin by attacking *it*? There are
always a hundred deepest reasons for gratitude and love which I could
write about, but which my after life shall prove I never have forgot-
ten.. still, that very after-life depends perhaps on the letter of the
morning reasoning with you, teazing, contradicting.. Dearest Ba, I do
not tell you that I am justified in plaguing you thus, at any time.. only
to get your pardon, if I can, on the grounds—the true grounds...

And this pardon, if you grant it, shall be for the past offences, not
for any fresh one I mean to commit now. I will not add one word to
those spoken yesterday about the extreme perilousness of delay. You
give me yourself. Hitherto, from the very first till this moment, the
giving hand has been advancing steadily—it is not for me to grasp it
lest it stop within an inch or two of my forehead with its crown.

I am going to town this morning, and will leave off now.

What a glorious dream,—thro' nearly two years—without a single
interval of blankness,—much less, bitter waking!

I may say THAT, I suppose, safely thro' whatever befalls!

Also I will ever say, God bless you, my dearest dearest,—my
perfect angel you have been! While I am only your

R.

My mother is deeply gratified at your present.

12 o^{ck}. On returning I find your note—

'I will do as you wish—understand'—then I understand you are in
earnest. If you *do* go on Monday, our marriage will be impossible for
another year—the misery! You see what we have gained by waiting.
We must be *married directly* and go to Italy—I will go for a licence

today and we can be married on Saturday. I will call to-morrow at 3
and arrange everything with you. We can leave from Dover &c *after*
that,—but otherwise, impossible! Inclose the ring, or a substitute—I
have not a minute to spare for the post.

Ever your own
R.

554. *R.B. to E.B.B., 10 Sept. 1846 (2)*

4 p.m. Thursday.

I broke open your sealed letter and added the postscript just now.
The post being thus saved, I can say a few words more leisurely.

I will go to-morrow, I think, and not to-day for the licence—there
are fixed hours I fancy at the office—and I might be too late. I will
also make the arrangement with my friend° for Saturday, if we
should want him,—as we shall, in all probability—it would look
suspiciously to be unaccompanied—We can arrange to-morrow.

Your words, first & last, have been that you 'would not fail me'—
you will not—

And the marriage over, you can take advantage of circumstances
and go early or late in the week, as may be practicable. There will be
facilities in the general packing &c—your own measures may be
taken unobserved—Write short notes to the proper persons,—pro-
mising longer ones, if necessary.

See the *tone* I take, the way I write to *you* .. but it is all thro' you,
in the little brief authority you give me,—and in the perfect belief of
your truth and firmness—Indeed, I do not consider this an extra-
ordinary occasion for proving those qualities—this conduct of your
Father's is quite characteristic...

Otherwise, too, the departure with its bustle is not unfavorable.
If you hesitated, it would be before a little hurried shopping and
letter-writing! I expected it, and therefore spoke as you heard
yesterday. *Now your* part must begin—It may as well begin and end,
both, *now* as at any other time. I will bring you every information
possible to-morrow.

It seems as if I should insult you if I spoke a word to confirm
you,—to beseech you, to relieve you from your promise, if you
claim it.

God bless you, prays your own
R.

555. *E.B.B. to R.B., 10 Sept. 1846*

Thursday.

Dearest, I write one word, & have one will which is yours. At the same time, do not be precipitate—we shall not be taken away on Monday, no, nor for several days afterward. George has simply gone to look for houses—going to Reigate first.

Oh yes—come tomorrow. And then, you shall have the ring.. soon enough, & safer.

Not a word of how you are!—*you* so good as to write me that letter beyond compact, yet not good enough, to say how you are! Dear, dearest.. take care, & keep yourself unhurt & calm. I shall not fail to you—I do not, I will not. I will act by your decision, & I wish you to decide. I was yours long ago, & though you give me back my promise at this eleventh hour,.. you generous, dear unkind!... you know very well that you can do as well without it—So take it again for my sake & not your own—

I cannot write, I am so tired, having been long out—. Will not this dream break on a sudden? Now is the moment for the breaking of it, surely.

But come tomorrow, come. Almost everybody is to be away at Richmond, at a picnic, & we shall be free on all sides.

Ever & ever your Ba

556. *R.B. to E.B.B., 12 Sept. 1846*

1 p.m. Saturday.

You will only expect a few words—what will those be?

When the heart is full it may run over, but the real fulness stays within—

You asked me yesterday 'if I should repent'? Yes—my own Ba,—I could wish all the past were to do over again, that in it I might somewhat more,—never so little more,—conform in the outward homage to the inward feeling: what I have professed.. (for I have performed nothing—) seems to fall short of what my first love required even—and when I think of *this* moment's love.. I could repent, as I say.

Words can never tell you, however,—form them, transform them anyway,—how perfectly dear you are to me—perfectly dear to my heart and soul.

I look back, and in every one point, every word and gesture, every letter, every *silence*—you have been entirely perfect to me—I would not change one word, one look—

My hope and aim are to preserve this love, not to fall from it—for which I trust to God who procured it for me, and doubtlessly can preserve it.

Enough now, my dearest, dearest, own Ba! You have given me the highest, completest proof of love that ever one human being gave another. I am all gratitude—and all pride (under the proper feeling which ascribes pride to the right source—) all pride that my life has been so crowned by you.

God bless you prays your very own
R.

I will write to-morrow of course. Take every care of *my life* which is in that dearest little hand; try and be composed, my beloved.

Remember to thank Wilson° for me.

557. *E.B.B. to R.B.*, *12 Sept. 1846*

Saturday. Sept. 12.
p.m. 4 1/2

Ever dearest, I write a word that you may read it & know how all is safe so far, & that I am not slain downright with the day—oh, SUCH *a day!* I went to Mr Boyd's directly, so as to send Wilson home the faster—and was able to lie quietly on the sofa in his sitting-room down stairs, before he was ready to see me, being happily engaged with a medical councillor. Then I was made to talk & take Cyprus wine,—& my sisters delaying to come, I had some bread & butter for dinner, to keep me from looking too pale in their eyes—At last they came, & with such grave faces! Missing me & Wilson, they had taken fright,—& Arabel had forgotten at first what I told her last night about the fly. I kept saying, 'What nonsense,.. what fancies you do have to be sure,' .. trembling in my heart with every look they cast at me. And so, to complete the bravery, I went on with them in the carriage to Hampstead .. as far as the heath,—& talked & looked— now you shall praise me for courage—or rather you shall love me for the love which was the root of it all. How necessity makes heroes—or heroines at least!—For I did not sleep all last night, & when I first went out with Wilson to get to the flystand in Marylebone Street I staggered so, that we both were afraid for the fear's sake,—but we called at a chemist's for sal volatile° & were thus enabled to go on. I spoke to her last night, and she was very kind, very affectionate, & never shrank for a moment. I told her that always I should be grateful to her.

You—how are you? how is your head, ever dearest?—

It seems all like a dream!—When we drove past that church again, I and my sisters, there was a cloud before my eyes—. Ask your mother to forgive me, Robert. If *I* had not been there, *she* would have been there, perhaps.

And for the rest, if either of us two is to suffer injury and sorrow for what happened there to-day—I pray that it may all fall upon *me!*—Nor should I suffer the most pain *that* way, as I know, & God knows.

Your own
Ba

Was I very uncourteous to your cousin?° So kind, too, it was in him!—Can there be the least danger of the newspapers? Are those books ever examined by penny-a-liners,° do you suppose?—

572. *R.B. to E.B.B., 18 Sept. 1846*

11 1/2 Friday.

My own best Ba—How thankful I am you have seen my blunder°—I took the other company's days for the South Western's—changed. What I shall write now is with the tables before me (of the Railway) and a transcript from *to-day's* advertisement in the Times.

The packet will leave tomorrow evening, from the Royal Pier, S^n, at *nine*. We leave Nine Elms, Vauxhall, at five—to arrive at *Eight*. Doors close *five* minutes before. I will be at Hodgsons° *from* halfpast three to *four* PRECISELY when I should hope you can be ready. I shall go to Vauxhall, apprise them that luggage is coming, (yours) and send *mine* there—so that we both shall be unencumbered & we can take a cab or coach from H's.

Never mind your scanty preparations .. we can get everything at Leghorn,—and the new boats carry parcels to Leghorn on the 15th of every month, remember—so can bring what you may wish to send for.

I enclose a letter to go with yours. The cards as you choose—they are here—we can write about them from Paris or elsewhere. The advertisement, as you advise. All shall be cared for.

God bless and strengthen you, my ever dearest dearest—I will not trust myself to speak of my feelings for you—worship well belongs to such fortitude—One struggle more—if all the kindness on your part brought a strangely insufficient return, is it not possible that this step may produce all you can hope? Write to me one word more—depend on me—I go to town about business.

Your own, own R.

573. E.B.B. to R.B., 18 Sept. 1846

Friday night.

At from half past three to four, then—four will not, I suppose, be too late. I will not write more—*I cannot*—. By tomorrow at this time, I shall have *you* only, to love me—my beloved!—

You *only!*—As if one said *God* only—And we shall have *Him* beside, I pray of Him—

I shall send to your address at New Cross your Hanmer's poems— & the two dear books you gave me,° which I do not like to leave here & am afraid of hurting by taking them with me—Will you ask *our* Sister to put the parcel into a drawer, so as to keep it for us?

Your letters to me I take with me, let the 'ounces' cry out aloud, ever so. I *tried* to leave them, & I could not. That is, they would not be left: it was not my fault—I will not be scolded.

Is this my last letter to you, ever dearest?—Oh—if I loved you less .. a little, little less ..

Why I should tell you that our marriage was invalid, or ought to be—& that you should by no means come for me tomorrow. It is dreadful .. dreadful .. to have to give pain here by a voluntary act— for the first time in my life—

Remind your mother & father of me affectionately & gratefully—& your Sister too! Would she think it too bold of me to say *our* Sister, if she had heard it on the last page?

Do you pray for me tonight, Robert? Pray for me, & love me, that I may have courage, feeling both—

Your own Ba—

The boxes are *safely sent*. Wilson has been perfect to me—And *I* . . calling her 'timid,' & afraid of her timidity!—I begin to think that none are so bold as the timid, when they are fairly roused.

OTHER SELECTED LETTERS

1. R.B. to Euphrasia Haworth, 24 July 1838

Tuesday Evening

Dear Miss Haworth,

Do look at a Fuchsia in full bloom and notice the clear little honeydrop depending from every flower..I have but just found it out, to my no small satisfaction,—a bee's breakfast. I only answer for the *long* blossomed sort, though,—indeed, for this plant in my room. Taste and be Titania,—you can, that is.—All this while, I forget that you will perhaps never guess the good of the discovery: I have, you are to know, such a love for flowers and leaves—some leaves—that I every now and then,—in an impatience at being unable to possess myself of them thoroughly, to see them quite, satiate myself with their scent, bite them to bits..so there will be some sense in that. How I remember the flowers—even grapes—of places I have seen!—some one flower or weed, I should say, that gets some strangehow connected with them. Snowdrops and Tilsit in Prussia go together; Cowslips and Windsor-park, for instance: flowering palm and some place or other in Holland. Now to answer what can be answered in the letter I was happy to receive last week. I am quite well. I did not expect you would write; for none of your written reasons, however. You will see Sordello in a trice, if the fagging-fit holds. I did not write six lines while absent° (except a scene in a play, jotted down as we sailed thro' the Straits of Gibraltar)—but I did hammer out some four, two of which are addressed to you, two to the Queen..the whole to go in Book—perhaps. I called you, 'Eyebright'°—meaning a simple and sad sort of translation of 'Euphrasia' into my own language: folks would know who Euphrasia, or Fanny was,—and *I* should not know Ianthe or Clemanthe. Not that there is anything in them to care for, good or bad. Shall I say 'Eyebright'? I was disappointed in one thing, Canova. What companions should I have? The story of the ship must have reached you 'with a difference' as Ophelia says,—my sister told it to a Mr Dow, who delivered it, I suppose, to Forster, who furnished Macready with it, who made it

over &c &c &c—As short as I can tell, this way it happened: the
Captain woke me one bright Sunday morning to say there was a ship
floating keel uppermost half a mile off; they lowered a boat, made
ropes fast to some floating canvass, and towed her towards our vessel.
Both met half-way, and the little air that had risen an hour or two
before, sank at once. Our men made the wreck fast, and went to
breakfast in high glee at the notion of having 'new trousers out of the
sails,' and quite sure she was a French boat, broken from her moor-
ings at Algiers, close by. Ropes were next hove (hang this sea-talk)
round her stanchions, and after a quarter of an hour's pushing at the
capstan, the vessel righted suddenly, one dead body floating out; five
more were in the forecastle, and had probably been there a month—
under a blazing African sun .. don't imagine the wretched state of
things. They were, these six, the 'watch below'—(I give you the
results of the day's observation)—the rest, some eight or ten, had
been washed overboard at first. One or two were Algerines, the rest
Spaniards. The vessel was a smuggler bound for Gibraltar; there
were two stupidly-disproportionate guns, taking up the whole deck,
which was convex and—nay, look you, these are the gun-rings, and
the black square the place where the bodies lay. Well, the sailors

(All the 'bulwarks,'
or sides at the top, carried
away by the waves)

covered up the hatchway, broke up the aft-deck, hauled up tobacco
and cigars, good lord such heaps of them, and then bale after bale of
prints and chintz, don't you call it, till the Captain was half frigh-
tened—he would get at the ship's papers, he said; so these poor
fellows were pulled up, piecemeal, and pitched into the sea, the very
sailors calling to each other 'to cover the faces': no papers of impor-
tance were found, however, but fifteen swords, powder and ball
enough for a dozen such boats, and bundles of cotton &c that would
have taken a day to get out, but the Captain vowed that after five-
o'clock she should be cut adrift: accordingly she was cast loose, not a
third of her cargo having been touched; and you can hardly conceive
the strange sight when the battered hulk turned round, actually, and
looked at us, and then reeled off, like a mutilated creature from some
scoundrel French surgeon's lecture-table, into the most gorgeous and
lavish sunset in the world: there,—only, thank me for not taking you

at your word and giving you the whole 'story.' 'What I did'? I went to Trieste, then Venice—then thro' Treviso and Bassano to the mountains, delicious Asolo, all my places and castles, you will see. Then to Vicenza, Padua and Venice again. Then to Verona, Trent, Inspruck (the Tyrol) Munich, 'Wurzburg in Franconia'! Frankfort and Mayence,—down the Rhine to Cologne, thence to Aix-la-Chapelle, Liège, and Antwerp—then home.[...]

I shall be vexed if you don't write soon,—a long Elstree-letter:— what are *you* doing—drawing—writing?

Ever yours truly

R Browning.

2. *R.B. to Alfred Domett, 23 Mar. 1840*

My dear Domett,

I was a little way out of Town when your letter arrived— how much it gratified me, blame as well as praise, I cannot tell you, nor need, I hope. The one point that wants correcting is where you surmise that I am 'difficult on system'—*No*, really—the fact is I live by myself, write with no better company, and forget that the 'lovers' you mention are part & parcel of that self, and their choosing to comprehend *my* comprehensions—but an indifferent testimony to their value: whence it happens, that precisely when 'lovers,' one and all, bow themselves out at the book's conclusion... enter (according to an old stage-direction) two fishermen to the one angel, Stokes and Nokes to the Author of 'Venice'° (who *should* have been there, *comme de droit,*° had I known him earlier)—and ask, reasonably enough, why the publication is not confined to the aforesaid brilliant folks, and what do hard boards and soft paper solicit if not *their* intelligence, such as it may be? I wish I had thought of this before— meantime I am busy on some plays (those advertised) that shall be plain enough if my pains are not thrown away—and, in lieu of Sir Philip° & his like, Stokes may assure himself that I see *him*—(first row of the pit, under the second Oboe, hat between legs, play-bill on a spike, and a 'comforter' round his throat 'because of the draught from the stage'—) and unless *he* leaves off sucking his orange at the pathetic morsels of my play—I hold them naught.[...]

3. R.B. to Euphrasia Haworth, May 1840

Thursday Night

My dear Miss Haworth,

Yours received some five minutes since—fancy! But the truth is I am glad to find you have not been indisposed—as I feared. As to *Sordello*—enfoncé!° You say roses and lilies and lilac-bunches and lemon-flowers about it while everybody else pelts cabbage stump after potato-paring—nay, not everybody—for Carlyle .. but I won't tell you what Milnes told me Carlyle told him the other day: (thus I make you believe it was something singular in the way of praise— connu!) All I need remark on in your note is the passage you want cleared up:° 'What are you to be glad of?' Why that as I stopped my task awhile, left off my versewriting one sunny June day with a notion of not taking to it again in a hurry, the sad disheveled form I had just been talking of, that plucked and pointed, wherein I put, comprize, typify and figure to myself Mankind, the whole poor-devildom one sees cuffed and huffed from morn to midnight, that, so typified, she may come at times and keep my pact in mind, prick up my republicanism and remind me of certain engagements I have entered into with myself about that same, renewed me, gave me fresh spirit, made me after finishing Book 3d commence Book 4th; what is involved here? Only one does not like serving oneself as a certain 'Watson'° served Horace in a translation I have: e.g. Book 1. Ode 1. Lines 1 and 2: 'O Mæcenas, descended from Kings (*Tuscan, that is Etrurian*) your Ancestors, (*O you who have proved yourself to be*) both my patron (*since you kindly reconciled me with Augustus*) and a sweet honor to me (*by your Quality and politeness to poor me whose father was nothing but a Freedman*) etc. etc. etc.

You don't know, it seems, that I have announced Three Dramas?— I see—the fly-leaf was left out of your copy. I am in treaty with Macready about one of these°—which I am going to send him, I should say rather—which I think clever and he will think stupid. Don't fear, however, any more unintelligible writing— —

Carlyle is lecturing with éclat—the Macreadys go, and the Bishop of Salisbury, and the three Miss Styles that began German last week. I have still your Tieck, remember.

Ever yours faithfully

R Browning

4. R.B. to Macready, 23 Aug. 1840

Camberwell
Sunday Night

So once again, dear Macready, I have failed to please you! The Druzes *return*, in another sense than I had hoped: for though, to confess a truth, I have worked from the beginning somewhat in the spirit of the cucumber-dresser in the old story (the doctor, you remember, bids such an one 'slice a platefull— salt it, pepper it, add oil, vinegar etc etc and then . . throw all behind the fire')—spite of this, I *did* rather fancy that you would have 'sympathized' with Djabert in the main scenes of my play: and your failing to do so is the more decisive against it, that I really had you *here*, in this little room of mine, while I wrote bravely away—*here* were you, propping the weak, pushing the strong parts (such I thought there might be!)—now majestically motionless, and now 'laying about as busily, as the Amazonian dame Penthesilé'°—and *here*, please the fates, shall you again and again give breath and blood to some thin creation of mine yet unevoked—but *elsewhere*— *enfoncé!* Your other objections I think less material— that the auditory, for instance, know nothing of the Druzes and their doings *until I tell them* (which is the very office I take on myself) that they are men and women oppressed and out-raged in such and such ways and desirous of being rid of their oppressor and outrager: if the auditory thus far instructed (and I considered that point sufficiently made out) call for a previous acquaintance with the Druzes before they will go along with such a desire . . are they not worthy compatriots of the Hyde-park gen-tleman who 'could not think of pulling a man out of the Serpentine to whom he had not been previously introduced'?

I intend to be with you in a day or two under the greenwood at Arden°—but, ask me whence the 'banished Duke' comes, why they banish him and how,—and you confound me . . who yet shall rejoice from my heart when Duke Frederick makes restitution at the end . . so much can 'that one word, banished' (as Juliet says)° effect! Surely such matters are the '*donnés*,' the given quantities, the logical 'be it conceded's, without which there is no working problem of deducing an *ergo*,°—and so it has been from the very dawn and cock-crow-time of the drama (for it is edifying to observe how in some primitive Mystery° (Johan à Tadcastre's or Robert Leicestensis' essay in King John's reign) the courtship of the Sultan of Mesopotamia's daughter by the 'King of Port's' nephew shall have rivetted the attention of all London or St Albans for six hours together.) — And so I could remark on your other 'misgivings'—the sole and simple point, let me say, on which I find you, to my judging, attackable: this note (written 'on a spurt' at midnight and with a sad headache) is from me to you, and for no third overlooker: to the devil all flattery! with the exception of Miss Horton there is not an actor or actress on the stage I can look at without loathing (that's the word) beside yourself: they vulgarize, and bestialize,—no matter, you will not comprehend me: Charles Kean° I never saw (he talks about 'these *hangmen's* hands'—'with a fine burst' (says a paper of yesterday)—and sees 'gouts of *blood*' 'with even a finer'—(I never saw him)—why don't you force the whole herd to run violently down a steep place into the sea? Kean wants to be Macbeth three times a week .. people go to see if he can manage it; *you are* and have been this—how many years?—Macbeth—as everybody knows: why not be something else? Were *I you* (save the mark!)—it should be my first condition with a playwright that his piece should be new, essentially new for better or for worse: if it failed .. who that has seen you perform in some forty or fifty parts I could name, would impute the failure to you who were Iago on Thursday and Virginius° on Saturday? If it did not fail .. were it even some poor *Return of the Druzes*, it would be something yet unseen, in however poor a degree—something, therefore, to go and see. Laugh at all this—I write, indeed, that you may .. for is it not the characteristic of those who withdraw from 'the scene' to 'take on us the mystery of things, as if [we] were God's spies'?—'And we'll wear out, in a walled prison' (my room here) 'sects and packs of great ones that ebb and flow by the moon'!° for tomorrow will I betimes break new ground with So and So—an epic in so many books ... let it but do me half the good 'Sordello' has done—be praised by the units, cursed by the tens, and unmeddled with by the hundreds! God bless you, dear Macready, and send you the man and the Trag[edy] and *how* both of you will be hailed from the back of the boxes, by,

Yours ever

R Browning

5. *R.B. to Alfred Domett, 22 May 1842*

New Cross, Hatcham, Surrey,
May 22. 1842

My dear Domett,

This is the third piece of paper I have taken up to put my first-words to you on—*this* must do, for time is urgent. I cannot well say *nothing* of my constant thoughts about you, most pleasant remembrances of you, earnest desires for you—yet I will stop short with this .. as near 'nothing' as may be. I have a sort of notion you will come back some bright morning a dozen years hence and find me just *gone*—to Heaven, or Timbuctoo, and I give way a little to this fancy while I write, because it lets me *write* freely what, I dare say, I *said* niggardly enough—my real love for you—better love than I had supposed I was fit for: but, you see, when I was not even a boy, I had fancy in plenty and no kind of judgment—so I said, and wrote, and professed away, and was the poorest of creatures: *that*, I think, is out of me, now! but the habit of watching & warding continues and—here is a case where I do myself wrong. However I am so *sure*, now, of my feelings, when I *do* feel—trust to them so much, and am deceived about them so little— (I mean, that I so rarely believe I like where I loathe, and the reverse, as the people round me do)—that I can speak about myself and my sentiments with full confidence. There! And now, let that lie, till we meet again .. God send it!

I shall never read over what I send you,—reflect on it, care about it, or fear that you will *not* burn it when I ask you. So do with me. And tell me all about yourself, straight, without courteously speculating about my being, 'doings & drivings'—(unless there is some special point you want to know)—and by my taking the same course,—(sure you care for all that touches me—) we shall get more done in a letter than when half is wasted. Begin at the beginning—tell me how you are, where you are, what you do and mean to do—and to do in *our* way: for live properly *you cannot* without writing—and to *write* a book now, will take one at least the ten or a dozen years you portion out for your stay abroad. I don't expect to do any real thing till then: the little I, or anybody, can do as it is, comes of them *going to New Zealand*—partial retirement and stopping the ears against the noise outside—but all is next to useless—for there is a creeping magnetic assimilating influence nothing can block out. When I block it out, I shall do something. Don't you feel already older (in the wise sense of the word—) farther off—as one 'having a purchase' against us? What I meant to say was—that only in your present condition of life, so far as I see, is there any chance of your being able to find out .. what is wanted, and how to supply the want when you precisely find it. I have read your poems—you can do anything—and (I do not see why I should not think—) *will* do much. I will, if I live. At present, I don't know if I stand on head or heels— what men require, I don't know—and of what they are in possession, know nearly as little.[...]

6. R.B. *to Alfred Domett, 13 July 1842*

New Cross, Hatcham, Surrey.
July 13. 1842.

My Dear Domett,

[...] I send with this Tennyson's new vol°—&, alas, the old with it .. that is, what he calls old .. you will see, and groan! The alterations are insane. WhatEVER is touched is spoiled. There is some woeful mental infirmity in the man—he was months buried in correcting the press of the last volume and in that time began spoiling the new poems (in proof) as hard as he could: Locksley Hall is shorn of two or three couplets I will copy out from the book of somebody who luckily transcribed from the proof-sheet—meantime *one* line, you will see, I *have* restored—see & wonder! I have been with Moxon this morning, who tells me that he is miserably thin-skinned, sensitive to criticism (foolish criticism)—wishes to see no notices that contain the least possible depreciatory expressions—poor fellow! But how good when good he is—that noble Locksley Hall, for instance—& the St. Simeon Stylites—which I think perfect—Do you (*yes*)—remember our day on the water last year? To think that he had omitted the musical 'Forget-me-not' song, & 'the Hesper-ides'—& the Deserted House—& 'every thing that is *his*'—as distinguished from what is everybodys!—Sir L. Bulwer has published a set of sing-songs°—I read two, or one, in a Review—& thought them abominable. Mr Taylor's affected unreal putting-together, called 'Edwin the Fair,'° is the flattest of fallen—I don't remember anything else since your time.

Dickens° is back, and busy in 'doing' America for his next numbers—sad work—But here is a pleasant circumstance—Sir J. Hanmer°—(you know his pretty poems)—an interesting person—in Parliament this session for the first time, as a Tory (Born so, & bred so—) has, two nights ago, most resolutely recanted on better advisement, & voted against Peel in the matter of the Corn Laws—with a good energetic half dozen words, beside;—so that even political convertites may not be despaired of![...]

7. *R.B. to Arabella and Henrietta Barrett,* *8 Feb. 1847*

Pisa, Feb. 8, '47

I have to thank you, my dearest sisters, for two of the kindest notes in the world. It is an unspeakable delight to me to find that I can sympathize with Ba° in everything, and love most dearly the two whom she loves most dearly. I know, and nobody so well, what you have lost in her—that is, lost for a time—yet your generosity pardons me that loss, while your *woman's* tact and quickness of feeling does justice to the conduct which occasioned it—for both of which, I am, and always shall be most truly and gratefully your debtor. You tell me that the way to pay such debts is to love Ba—but I cannot obey you there—she takes all my love for her own sake—just as you,— whom I was prepared and eager to love for her sake,—you make me love you on your own account. You wish to know how Ba is—from me, as well as from her. I assure you that thro' God's goodness she appears quite well; *weak* certainly, as compared to persons in ordinary health, but with no other ailment perceptible. A few days ago, she seemed to have caught a slight cold—(thro' her kind care of Wilson,° who has been ill, as I am sure Ba will have told you)—but yesterday and to-day the few symptoms of ailing etc. have disappeared. Dr Cook, the physician we called in to Wilson, who had seen Ba just on his arrival, expressed his surprize and delight at the manifold improvement in her appearance—and he observed to Wilson, 'this comes of a visit to Pisa *in time*'—(he is learned in pulmonary disease and has written a book about it)—he has just returned, moreover, from England—'where the cold was intense' he said. Here, also, the cold has been considerable, and we are too indebted to the good already produced by the climate to peril it by going out rashly at this (as we hope) the winter's end: but I t[rus]t and believe that, with the stock of strength *preserved* thro' the winter we shall so profit by the coming fine weather, as to need fear no relapse. Ba sleeps admirably—and is steadily diminishing the doses of morphine, quite as much as is prudent. I daresay she explained to you the cause of the Apothecary's mistake about the prescription, at the beginning—he really believed his morphine to be so superior to what we could get in England that he felt himself bound to diminish the quantity—Ever since, his performances have been unexceptionable—indeed, he is said to be one of the best Chymists in Italy. What, I think, you would be most struck with in Ba, is the strengthened voice—Wilson hears it, she says, thro' her door and ours. I cannot tell you of other qualities that are 'strengthened,' however— no words can convey the native sweetness, unselfishness of that dear nature! Yet I have been used to the kindest of natures, and am by no means likely to err from excess of indulgence to any one.[...]

8. R.B. to Thomas Carlyle, 14 May 1847

Florence, May 14, '47.
My dear Mr Carlyle,—Mr Kenyon writes to me, that, in a letter which ought to have arrived a month ago, he mentioned your kindness in keeping me in mind and wishing to hear news of me! When I read this second letter with my wife yesterday morning, we took it as the best of omens in favour of one of our greatest schemes, which had been discussed by us in its length and breadth only the evening before, and then, not for the first time. We determined that whenever I wrote to you, as I meant to do for the last six or seven months, it would be wiser to leave unsaid, unattempted to be said, my feelings of love and gratitude for the intercourse you permitted since a good many years now—but go on and tell you what an easy thing it would be for you to come to Italy—now, at this time of times, for its own sake and the world's—and let us have the happiness—the entire happiness of remembering that we got ready the Prophet's-Chamber in the wall, with bed and candlestick, according to Scripture precedent. In this country, the wheels of one's life run smoothly—a very simple calculation finds what kind of a carriage, with more or less commodious fitting up, is within your means—and once fairly started in it, you may look out of the windows or ponder the journey's end without further cares about lynch-pins or grease-money (in Germany you must know you are taxed every post for 'Schmiergelt,'° etc.), one man finds you house and furniture for so long—another

contrives you dinner—for so many—you pay what you mean or can, and there is an end of it. Then in this land of solid vast honest houses, built to last—a few rooms cost more than many—or not less—seven or five, nine or seven, it is little matter. You see all I mean, I am sure; and it would not become me to speak more. Only, if ever you are disposed to pass a winter here, we will go to any part you decide for, and be ready for you at any time. I hope it is not wholly for ourselves (for my wife and myself) that I say this—I heard you once allude to Jesuitism—to an intention you had of writing about it: and when I look over the extracts from books on that and similar subjects, as I find them in Newspapers here, I ejaculate (like I don't know what virtuoso, in some great gallery of pretentious painting), '*Raphael, ubi es?*'°—

But in Italy, or in England, I shall ever keep it my first of affectionate prides—something beyond affection and far better than pride—that you have been and are what you are to me—not a 'friend,' neither. I dare believe, on the whole, that there is no better nor sincerer relation than that in which you stand to me. One might fancy I did not profit as I might have done by the facilities you gave me for seeing and communicating with you in England; but I always hoped to be better qualified to profit one day. I don't apologize for writing in this way, and of these things. Here in Italy, it seems useless and foolish to put into a little note any other matter than what comes uppermost (and yet lies undermost).

When I was about to leave England I should have been glad to talk over my intentions with you, respecting my marriage, and all the strange and involved circumstances that led to it. I did not do so, however, not from any fear of your waiving the responsibility of giving counsel, but because, in this affair which so intimately concerned me, I had been forced to ascertain and see a hundred determining points, as nobody else could see them, in the nature of things. And I was nearly as convinced then, as by all that has happened subsequently, that I had the plainest of duties to perform; and there was no use in asking for an opinion which I might know as certainly as I know anything—without giving us both much pain and many words. Through God's providence, all has gone with us better than my best hopes. My wife, in all probability, will become quite well and strong. She only feels weakness, indeed, and may be considered well, except for that. I believe—from the accounts from England, and from the nature of the place in the country to which she was to have been removed a day or two after that on which we determined to leave England—that this winter would have ended the seven years' confinement without my intervention. You will let me say that it could be nobody's true interest that this should be, with an entirely good, unselfish, affectionate creature, in whom during these eight months that I have been by her always, I have never seen an indication of anything but goodness and unselfishness. When I first knew her more than two years ago, we soon found out a common point of sympathy in her love and reverence for you—she told me how you had written to her, given her advice. So that there was one way left for me to love you the more. She is sitting opposite now, and answers (when I ask her, this minute, what I am to say for her), 'But you *know* my feelings'! And I do know them.

Much of what I have written will go to Mrs Carlyle likewise—I never can dissociate you in my thoughts: if we, or *when* we go to England again, I shall try and live near you—as much nearer you as I can. Will you give my truest regards to her? I trust you are both well. You would not suffer by the cold weather I think. It is very hot here just now, but has been cold beyond example.

I see Lely's picture of your Cromwell,° in the Pitti Palace here. I make no doubt you do not want any news now about the reported *cast* of the head; but I will inquire and let you know, on the chance of your wishing it.

Mr Kenyon mentions a note you have given Miss Fuller—and which she will probably bring when she comes here; it is a delight to expect. Let me say, that should you want a *person* to find me, the address is *Via delle Belle Donne*, 4222—but for a *letter* the best direction is to R.B., *Poste Restante, Firenze, Toscana*, simply, as I get such a note duly when I go to the Post Office, and not when it pleases the man to call.—All my space is covered, except to reassure you

I am ever yours,

R. Browning.

9. *Ruskin to R.B., 2 Dec. 1855*

Denmark Hill
2nd December 1855

Dear Mr Browning

I know you have been wondering that I did not write, but I could not till now—and hardly can, now: not because I am busy—nor careless, but because I cannot at all make up my mind about these poems of yours: and so far as my mind *is* made up, I am not sure whether it is in the least right. Of their power there can of course be no question—nor do you need to be told of it; for everyone who *has* power of this kind, knows it—*must* know it. But as to the Presentation of the Power, I am in great doubt. Being hard worked at present, & not being able to give the cream of the day to poetry—when I take up these poems in the evening I find them absolutely and literally a set of the most amazing Conundrums that ever were proposed to me. I try at them, for—say twenty minutes—in which time I make out about twenty lines, always having to miss two, for every one that I make out. I enjoy the twenty, each separately, very much, but the puzzlement about the intermediate ones increases in comfortlessness till I get a headache, & give in.

Now that you may exactly understand the way I feel about them—I will read, with you, one poem—as I read it to myself, with all my comments and questions. I open at Random—Cleon?— no—that's not a fair example being harder than most. The twins?—no—I have made out that—(except the fifth stanza)— so it is not a fair example on the other side being easier than most. Popularity?—yes, that touches the matter in hand.

> Stand still, true poet that you are
> I know you;—let me try and draw you:

(Does this mean: literally—stand still? or where was the poet figuratively going—and why couldn't he be drawn as he went?) Some night you'll fail us? (Why some *night*?—rather than some day?—'Fail us.' Now? Die?) When afar you Rise—(Where?— Now?) remember &c. (very good—I understand). My star, God's glowroom. (Very fine. I understand and like that.) Why 'extend that loving hand.'

(Grammatically, this applies to the Poet. the ellipsis of 'Should He' at first throws one quite out—like a step in a floor which one doesn't expect. Yet locks you safe. How does God's hand lock him; do you mean—keeps him from being seen?—and how does it make him safe. Why is a poet safer or more locked up than anybody else? I go on—in hope. 'His clenched hand— —beauty'—very good—but I don't understand why the hand should have held close so long—which is just the point I wanted to be explained. Why the poet *had to be* locked up.

'My poet holds the future fast.' How? Do you mean he anticipates it in his mind—trusts in it—I *don't* know if you mean that, because I don't know if poets *do* that. If you mean that—I wish you had said so plainly.

That day the earths feastmaster's brow. Who is the earths F.? An Angel?—a Everybody?

The chalice *raising*. This, grammatically, agrees with '*brow*,' and makes me uncomfortable. Others, &c. very pretty I like that. 'Meantime I'll draw you.' Do you mean—his Cork?—we have not had anything about painting for ever so long—very well. *Do* draw him then: I should like to have him drawn very much.

I'll say—'a fisher—&c.'

Now, where *are* you going to—this is, I believe pure malice against *me*, for having said that painters should always grind their own colours.

Who has not heard— —merchant sells. Do you mean—the silk that the merchant sells Raw—or what do you want with the merchant at all.

'And each bystander.' Who are these bystanders—I didn't hear of any before—Are they people who have gone to see the fishing?

'Could criticise, & quote tradition.'

Criticise what? the fishing?—and why should they—what was wrong in it?—Quote tradition. Do you mean about purple? But if they made purple at the time, it wasn't tradition merely—but experience.— You might as well tell me you heard the colourmen in Long-Acre,° quote tradition touching their next cargo of Indigo, or cochineal.

'Depths—sublimed.' I don't know what you mean by 'sublimed.' Made sublime?—if so—it is not English. To sublime means to evaporate dryly, I believe and has participle 'Sublimated.'

'Worth scepter, crown and ball'—Indeed. Was there ever such a fool of a King?—You ought to have put a note saying who.

'Yet there's,' &c. Well. I understand that, & it's very pretty

Enough to furnish Solomon, &c.

I don't think Solomons spouse swore.—at least not about blue-bells. I understand this bit, but fear most people won't. How many have noticed a blue-bells stamen?

'Bee to her groom' I don't understand. I thought there was only one Queenbee and *she* never was out o'nights—nor came home drunk or disorderly. Besides if she does, unless you had told me what o'clock in the morning she comes home at, the simile is of no use to me.

'Mere conchs—.' Well, but what has this to do with the Poet.
Who 'Pounds' *him*?—I don't understand—

World stand aloof—yes—from the purple manufactory, but from
Pounding of Poets?—does it?—and if so—who distils—or fines, &
bottles them.

'Flasked & fine' Now *is* that what you call painting a poet. Under
the whole & sole image of a bottle of Blue, with a bladder over the
cork? The Arabian fisherman with his genie was nothing to this.

Hobbs, Nobbs, &c. paint the future. Why the future. Do you
mean *in* the future.

Blue into their line? I don't understand;—do you mean Quote the
Poet, or write articles upon him—or in his style? And if so—was this
what God kept him *safe* for? to feed Nobbs with Turtle. Is this what
you call Accepting the future ages duty?—I don't understand.

'What porridge'? Porridge is a Scotch dish, I believe; typical of
bad fare. Do you mean that Keats had bad fare? But if he had—how
was he kept safe to the worlds end? I don't understand at all!!!!!!!

Now, that is the way I read, as well as I can, poem after poem,
picking up a little bit here & there & enjoying it, but wholly unable
to put anything together. I can't say I have really made out any one
yet, except the epistle from the Arabian physician, which I like
immensely, and I am only a stanza or so out with one or two
others—in by the fireside for instance I am only *dead* beat by the
41–43, and in fra Lippo—I am only fast at the grated orris root,
which I looked for in the Encyclopaedia and couldn't find; and at the
There's for you—give me six months°—because I don't know *What's*
for you.

Well, how far all this is as it should be, I really know not. There is
a stuff and fancy in your work which assuredly is in no other living
writer's, and how far this purple of it *must* be within this terrible
shell; and only to be fished for among threshing of foam & slippery
rocks, I don't know. There are truths & depths in it, far beyond
anything I have read except Shakespeare—and truly, if you had just
written Hamlet, I believe I should have written to you, precisely
this kind of letter—merely quoting your own Rosencrantz against
you—'I understand you not, my Lord.' I cannot write in
enthusiastic praise, because I look at you every day as a monkey does
at a cocoanut, having great faith in the milk—hearing it rattle
indeed—inside—but quite beside myself for the Fibres. Still less can
I write in blame. When a man has real power, God only knows how he
can bring it out, or ought to bring it out. But, I would pray you, faith,

heartily, to consider with yourself, how far you can amend matters, & make the real virtue of your work acceptable & profitable to more people.

For one thing, I entirely deny & refuse the right of any poet to require me to pronounce words short and long, exactly as he likes—to require me to read a plain & harsh & straightforward piece of prose. 'Till I felt where the foldskirts (fly, redundant) open.'° Then, once more, I prayed; as a dactylic verse, with skirts! for a short syllable Foldskĭrts flў—'as tremendous a long monosyllable as any in the language' and to say, 'Wunce-mur-y'—prayed, instead of 'once more I.'

And in the second place, I entirely deny that a poet of your real dramatic power ought to let *himself* come up, as you constantly do, through all manner of characters, so that every now and then poor Pippa herself shall speak a long piece of Robert Browning.

And in the third place, your Ellipses are quite Unconscionable: before one can get through ten lines, one has to patch you up in twenty places, wrong or right, and if one hasn't much stuff of one's own to spare to patch with! You are worse than the worst Alpine Glacier I ever crossed. Bright, & deep enough truly, but so full of Clefts that half the journey has to be done with ladder & hatchet.

However, I have found some great things in you already, and I think you must be a wonderful mine, when I have real time & strength to set to work properly. That bit about the Bishop & St Praxed, in the older poems, is very glorious. Rossetti showed it me. In fact, I oughtn't to write to you yet, at all, but such is my state of mind at present and it may perhaps be well that you should know it, even though it may soon change to a more acceptant one, because it most certainly represents the feelings of a good many more, besides myself, who ought to admire you & learn from you, but can't because you are so difficult.

Well—there's a specimen for you of my art of saying pleasant things to my friends.

I have no time left, now, for any unpleasant ones—so I must just say goodbye and beg you to accept, with my dear Mʳˢ Browning, the assurance of my exceeding regard & respect.

Ever most faithfully Yours,

J Ruskin

10. *R.B. to Ruskin, 10 Dec. 1855*

PARIS, *Dec.* 10*th,* '55.

My dear Ruskin,—for so you let me begin, with the honest friendliness that befits,—

You never were more in the wrong than when you professed to say 'your unpleasant things' to me. This is pleasant and proper at all points, over-liberal of praise here and there, kindly and sympathetic everywhere, and with enough of yourself in even—what I fancy—the misjudging, to make the whole letter precious indeed. I wanted to thank you thus much at once,—that is, when the letter reached me; but the strife of lodging-hunting was too sore, and only now that I can sit down for a minute without self-reproach do I allow my thoughts to let go south-aspects, warm bedrooms, and the like, and begin as you see. For the deepnesses you think you discern,—may they be more than mere blacknesses! For the hopes you entertain of what may come of subsequent readings,—all success to them! For your bewilderment more especially noted—how shall I help *that?* We don't read poetry the same way, by the same law; it is too clear. I cannot begin writing poetry till my imaginary reader has conceded licences to me which you demur at altogether. I *know* that I don't make out my conception by my language, all poetry being a putting the infinite within the finite. You would have me paint it all plain out, which can't be; but by various artifices I try to make shift with touches and bits of outlines which *succeed* if they bear the conception from me to you. You ought, I think, to keep pace with the thought tripping from ledge to ledge of my 'glaciers,' as you call them; not stand poking your alpenstock into the holes, and demonstrating that no foot could have stood there;—suppose it sprang over there? In *prose* you may criticise so—because that is the absolute representation of portions of truth, what chronicling is to history—but in asking for more *ultimates* you must accept less *mediates,* nor expect that a Druid stone-circle will be traced for you with as few breaks to the eye as the North Crescent and South Crescent that go together so cleverly in many a suburb. Why, you look at my little song as if it were Hobbs' or Nobbs' lease of his house, or testament of his devisings, wherein, I grant you, not a 'then and there,' 'to him and his heirs,' 'to have and to hold,' and so on, would be superfluous; and so you begin:—'Stand still,—why?' For the reason indicated in the verse, to be sure,—*to let me draw him*—and because he is at present going his way, and fancying nobody notices him,—and moreover, 'going on' (as we say) against the injustice of that,—and lastly, inasmuch as one night he'll fail us, as a star is apt to drop out of heaven, in authentic astronomic records, and I want to make the most of my time. So much may be in 'stand still.' And how much more was (for instance) in that 'stay!' of Samuel's (I. xv. 16). So could I twit you through the whole series of your objurgations, but the declaring my own notion of the law on the subject will do. And why,—I prithee, friend and fellow-student,—why, having told the Poet what you read,—may I not turn to the bystanders, and tell them a bit of my mind about their own stupid thanklessness and mistaking? Is the jump too much there? The whole is all but a simultaneous feeling with me.

The other hard measure you deal me I won't bear—about my requiring you to pronounce words short and long, exactly as I like. Nay, but exactly as the language likes, in this case. *Foldskirts* not a trochee? A spondee possible in English? Two of the 'longest monosyllables' continuing to be each of the whole length when in junction? Sentence: let the delinquent be forced to supply the stone-cutter with a thousand companions to 'Affliction sore—long time he bore,' after the fashion of 'He lost his life—by a penknife'—'He turned to clay—last Good Friday,' 'Departed hence—nor owed six-pence,' and so on—so would pronounce a jury accustomed from the nipple to say lord and landlord, bridge and Cambridge, Gog and Magog, man and woman, house and workhouse, coal and charcoal, cloth and broadcloth, skirts and fold-skirts, more and once more,—in short! Once *more* I prayed!—is the confession of a self-searching professor! 'I stand here for law!'

The last charge I cannot answer, for you may be right in preferring it, however unwitting I am of the fact. I *may* put Robert Browning into Pippa and other men and maids. If so, *peccavi:*° but I don't see myself in them, at all events.

Do you think poetry was ever generally understood—or can be? Is the business of it to tell people what they know already, as they know it, and so precisely that they shall be able to cry out—'Here you should supply *this—that*, you evidently pass over, and I'll help you from my own stock'? It is all teaching, on the contrary, and the people hate to be taught. They say otherwise;—make foolish fables about Orpheus° enchanting stocks and stones, poets standing up and being worshipped,—all nonsense and impossible dreaming. A poet's affair is with God,—to whom he is accountable, and of whom is his reward; look elsewhere, and you find misery enough. Do you believe people understand *Hamlet?* The last time I saw it acted, the heartiest applause of the night went to a little by-play of the actor's own— who, to simulate madness in a hurry, plucked forth his handkerchief and flourished it hither and thither: certainly a third of the play, with no end of noble things, had been (as from time immemorial) sup- pressed, with the auditory's amplest acquiescence and benediction. Are these wasted, therefore? No—they act upon a very few, who react upon the rest: as Goldsmith° says, 'some lords, my acquain- tance, that settle the nation, are pleased to be kind.'

Don't let me lose *my* lord by any seeming self-sufficiency or petulance: I look on my own shortcomings too sorrowfully, try to remedy them too earnestly: but I shall never change my point of sight, or feel other than disconcerted and apprehensive when the public, critics and all, begin to understand and approve me. But what right have *you* to disconcert me in the other way? Why won't you ask the next perfumer for a packet of *orris*-root? Don't everybody know 'tis a corruption of *iris*-root—the Florentine lily, the *giaggolo*, of world-wide fame as a good savour? And because 'iris' means so many objects already, and I use the old word, you blame me! But I write in the blind-dark, and bitter cold, and past post-time as I fear. Take my truest thanks, and understand at least this rough writing, and, at all events, the real affection with which I venture to regard you. And 'I' means my wife as well as

Yours ever faithfully,

Robert Browning

11. R.B. to Euphrasia Haworth, 20 July 1861

Florence, July 20. '61.

My dear friend, I well know you feel as you say, for her once and for me now. Isa Blagden,° perfect in all kindness to me, will have told you something perhaps—and one day I shall see you and be able to tell you myself as much as I can. The main comfort is that she suffered very little pain, none beside that ordinarily attending the simple attacks of cold and cough she was subject to, had no presenti- ment of the result whatever, and was consequently spared the misery of knowing she was about to leave us: she was smilingly assuring me she was 'better,' 'quite comfortable—if I would but come to bed—'

to within a few minutes of the last. I think I foreboded evil even at
Rome, certainly from the beginning of the week's illness—but when
I reasoned about it, there was no justifying fear: she said on the last
evening 'It is merely the old attack, nor so severe a one as that of two
years ago—there is no doubt I shall soon recover'—And we talked
over plans for the summer and next year. I sent the servants away
and her maid to bed—so little reason for disquietude did there seem.
Thro' the night she slept heavily, and brokenly—that was the bad
sign. But then she would sit up, take her medicine, say unrepeatable
things to me and sleep again. At four o'clock there were symptoms
that alarmed me,—I called the maid and sent for the Doctor.—She
smiled as I proposed to bathe her feet 'Well, you *are* making an
exaggerated case of it!' Then came what my heart will keep till I see
her and longer—the most perfect expression of her love to me within
my whole knowledge of her—always smilingly, happily, and with a
face like a girl's—and in a few minutes she died in my arms, her head
on my cheek. These incidents so sustain me that I tell them to her
beloved ones as their right: there was no lingering, nor acute pain,
nor consciousness of separation, but God took her to himself as you
would lift a sleeping child from a dark, uneasy bed into your arms
and the light. Thank God. Annunziata thought by her earnest ways
with me, happy and smiling as they were, that she must have been
aware of our parting's approach—but she was quite conscious, had
words at command, and yet did not even speak of Peni who was in
the next room. Her last word was—when I asked 'How do you
feel?'—'*Beautiful.*'

You know I have her dearest interest to attend to *at once*—her
child to care for, educate, establish properly— and my own life to
fulfil as properly,—all, just as she would require were she here. I
shall leave Italy altogether for years—go to London for a few days
talk with Arabel—then go to my father, and begin to try leisurely
what will be the best for Peni—but no more 'housekeeping' for me,
even with my family. I shall grow, still, I hope—but my root is taken,
remains.

I know you always loved her, and me too in my degree. Forgive
my old peevish ways, which came from being too rich,—I shall
trouble nobody with them now—but always be grateful to those who
loved her—and that, I repeat, *you* did.

She was, is, lamented with extraordinary demonstrations if one
consider it: the Italians seem to have understood her by an instinct. I
have received strange kindness from everybody. Pen is very well,

very dear and good, anxious to 'comfort me' as he calls it. He can't know his loss yet. After years, his will be more than mine, he will want what he never had—that is, for the time when he could be helped by her wisdom, and genius and piety: I *have* had everything, and shall not forget.

God bless you, dear friend: I believe I set out in a week: Isa goes with me,—dear, true heart. You, too, would do what you could for us were you here and your assistance needful. A letter from you came a day or two before the end—she made me enquire about the 'Frescobaldi Palace' for you,—Isa wrote to you in consequence. I shall be heard of at 151. Rue de Grenelle, Faubourg St Germ^n.

Faithfully and affectionately yours

Robert Browning.

12. R.B. to Isabella Blagden, 19 Sept. 1862

Ste Marie, près Pornic, Loire Inf:
Sept 19. '62

My Dearest Isa,

Here is your letter, to my great delight, & *there* you are°—to be happy, I hope with all my heart. I could not open your letter for some minutes, took it upstairs & waited awhile before I made up my mind to read it. So all has gone well hitherto journey & difficulties & the getting into a house, all over. You do not tell me *which* Villa yours is—I fail to recognize it by its name but fancy it to be the one where the Kinneys stayed for a time, at the top of the steeper ascent between that to Villa Brichieri & the Columbaja. I have also a confused notion of a new entrance having been made on the side near the Hairdresser's Villa—I forget even his name. Remember to set me right about this. With respect to Florence, I cannot tell how I feel about it, so do I change in my feelings in the course of a quarter of an hour sometimes: particular incidents in the Florence way of life recur as if I could not bear a repetition of them—to find myself walking among the hills, or turnings by the villas, certain doorways, old walls, points of sight, on a solitary bright summer Sunday afternoon—there, I think that would fairly choke me at once: on the other hand, beginning from another point of association, I have such yearnings to be there! Just now, at the approach of Autumn, I feel exactly like a swallow in a cage,—as if I *must* go there, have

no business anywhere else, with the year drawing in.—How thankful
I am that all these foolish fancies never displace for a moment the
solid fact that I can't go but have plain duty to do in London,—
if there could be a doubt about that, I should drift about like a
feather: at times (to give you a notion of what I might do if free
to be foolish) I seem as if I should like, by a fascination, to try the
worst at once,—go straight to the old rooms at Casa Guidi, &
there live & die! But I shake all this off—& say to myself (sometimes
aloud) 'Don't be afraid, my good fellow, you'll die too, all in good
time': so I go on.[...]

13. R.B. to Isabella Blagden, 19 Jan. 1863

[...] Ever since I set foot in England I have been pestered with
applications for leave to write the Life of my wife: I have
refused—& there an end. I have last week received two communica-
tions from friends—enclosing the letters of a certain Geo: Stampe of
Great Grimsby, asking them for details of life and letters, for a
biography he is engaged in—adding that he has 'secured the corre-
spondence with her old friend Hugh Stuart Boyd.'° Think of this
beast working away at this, not deeming my feelings, or those of her
family, worthy of notice—and meaning to print letters written years
& years ago, on the most intimate & personal subjects, to an 'old
friend'—which, at the poor, old blind, forsaken man's death fell into
the hands of a complete stranger, who, at once wanted to print
them—but desisted thro' Ba's earnest expostulation enforced by
my own threat to take law proceedings—as fortunately letters are
copy-right: I find this woman died last year, & her son writes to me
this morning that Stampe got them from him as autographs merely:
he will try & get them back: Stampe, evidently a blackguard, got my
letter, which gave him his deserts, on Saturday—no answer yet; if
none comes, I shall be forced to advertise in the Times, and obtain an
injunction. But what I suffer in feeling the hands of these black-
guards (for I forgot to say, *another* man has been making similar
applications to friends)—what I undergo with their paws in my very
bowels, you can guess & God knows! No friend, of course, would
ever give up the letters: if anybody ever is forced to do that which *she*
would have so utterly writhed under—if it ever *were* necessary, why,
I should be forced to do it, and, with any good to her memory &

fame, my own pain in the attempt would be turned into joy—I should *do* it at whatever cost: but it is not only unnecessary but absurdly useless—&, indeed, it shall not be done if I can stop the scamp's knavery—along with his breath.[...]

14. R.B. to Julia Wedgwood, 27 June 1864

June 27, '64

Dear Friend,

I will call on Thursday at about 4 o'clock. When you most feel the inadequacy of the best we can know on the matter in your mind now, ask yourself fairly how it would be with you if you could suddenly attain to absolute conviction about it, in the sense of your desire—if the whole relations of this world would not be changed to you, and life, as you now find it prescribed, rendered no longer possible: one may assume, then, that for probational or educational purposes to ourselves, more than the yearning we *have*, and the corroborative facts which, by various processes, I think we *may* have, is inexpedient and out of the present harmony: if you object, that one might also reverse the experiment, and see in like manner the whole scheme of our life changed by attaining to the opposite conviction of the nothingness of this hope—I answer that this theory involves, I must think, a crime against humanity, while the other is consistent with wisdom and benevolence—therefore the likelier hypothesis.

Last night I was talking with a friend who read aloud a passage from Dr Newman's° *Apology* in which he says that 'he is as convinced of the existence of God'—an individual, not an external force merely—'as of his own existence:' I believe he deceives himself and that no sane man has ever had, with mathematical exactness, equal conviction on those two points— though the approximation to equality may be in any degree short of that: and looking at the practical effects of belief, I should expect that it would be so: I can see nothing that comes from absolute *contact*, so to speak, between man and God, but everything in all variety from the greater or less distance between the two. When anyone tells me that he *has* such a conviction, I look at a beggar who holds the philosopher's stone according to his profession. Do you see the bearing of all this as I seem to see it? How, remaining beggars—or poor, at least—we may at once look for the love of those to whom we give our mite, though we throw it into the darkness where they only *may* be: fortunately the experiment on our faith is never a very long one.

I am glad that you showed my letter to Mrs Wedgwood. You know well what is the way of the world with any exceptional mode of proceeding: if one wears a white tie instead of a black one, or calls at a house at 10. rather than 5 : p.m.—it has something to say and smile about. It is for you to determine when it is right that I should see you. I thought myself too plainly a sort of tombstone, to be scribbled over when so many blank walls spread on every side: yet a friend of yours and mine did, out of fun, write a silly name on me some months ago, which was read and repeated by various people: to be sure, it came rather of following than departing from the ways of the world, in this instance—seeing that being bidden by our hostess to take a lady down to dinner, I did so—and when the lady told me she would not sit by so and so, I let her sit away from him—whence all this! All I say is, or repeat rather, I shall be happy to have your confidence and your friendship: and when you talk of what may be 'inimical' to it, and of the chances which are natural, I can only remind you that circumstances guard me against many of these—that the veriest weathercock may *rust* and hardly turn again—and that I see a plain line to the end of my life on which I shall walk, unless an accident stop all walking—I shall not diverge, at least. Do not let us talk more about this: but, once for all, and for truth's sake, and because you refer to a doubt again—believe in the complete equality of our relation, and that, from the beginning of my acquaintance with you, I was aware, in proportion to my knowledge of you, that it might greatly interest and advantage me: but of course, it is not, because I may know where pictures are, that I knock at the gallery door daily: now you have thrown it open, let me tell you I like pictures and do not stand before them merely from a wish to wipe the dust from their frames.

And now, this is a letter! and I do not write letters—and I shall not, if you please, write many such, for we can and will talk about everything that interests us: and there is lightness in this, because if you take my arm you must keep my pace, and *hope*: do you know, a phrenologist told me when I was about sixteen that I had absolutely no hope at all in the head of me—and so it really was in those days. But I do think I see light at the far end of the passage. Not that I should like you at all to stand in my place so far on from the entry: you should *live*, step by step, *up* to the proper place where the pinpoint of light is visible: nothing is to be overleaped, the joy no more than the sorrow, and then, your part done, God's may follow, and will, I trust. I am sure you already see much to do, and the comfort of it. Care, too, for your health, in mere fairness to those you love— such sadness grows out of mistake about their interest there! There are people that should know better who hold one's glass heart in their hand, throw it up and catch it again with the pavement underneath. You will not do so: let me find that on Thursday—and know me ever for

Yours affectionately,

R. B.

15. R.B. to Julia Wedgwood, 19–21 Aug. 1864

20th. I went this morning to see the mountain-pass called 'Le pas de Roland'°—the tradition being that he opened a way through a rock that effectually blocks it up, by one kick of his boot, and so let Charlemagne's army pass: it is a striking little bit of scenery, with the clear green river between the mountain-walls, not unlike the Lima at Lucca: but I think I liked best of all a great white-breasted hawk I saw sunning himself on a ledge, with his wings ready. How can you so misconceive of those *above* us, as to fear they may continue to misunderstand? Couched eyes that see none the better for that operation!—Oh, no! Then, it is so easy, wickedly easy, for people indifferent to each other never to quarrel: thence comes it that living in families tends to cretinize one—you find out early all about your fellows, love them always, but have no more curiosity about them, have no hope of improving them in any way, nor indeed desire it— they will *do* as they are: but you yourself will not do as you are, and if you wish another spirit to keep close by you while you go up higher, offences must come, and the wings get in the way of each other: how easily that must be seen by the bird that gets first to the height! Of course I was fortunate through the peculiarity of the relation: in that closeness there could be no misunderstanding: but had there been, I should care nothing about it now.

As for enjoying the sun—all the enviable instants of this life seem when we push out of it into the other, to fall back again fast enough: 'whether in the body or out of the body, I cannot tell': those who *can* tell that they are out of it—do you think they envy you down among the fir-trees? But they may, in a sort, envy you the feeling you will have presently when the dark cloth is suddenly twitched from your face, and fancying yourself lost in the dark, you find yourself at home. 'The whole has no perdition, if some loss.'—This is no chatter nor cant with me, I can tell you, but an instinct which has given worth to many formulas, before I could bear it by itself, truth and force as it is: how these formulas get true and false and then true again when unnecessary! when you can *mean* with Dante 'Thus I believe, thus I affirm, thus I am certain it is, and that from this life I shall pass to another better, there, where that Lady lives, of whom my soul was enamoured.'[...]

16. R.B. to Julia Wedgwood, 2 Sept. 1864

[...] I still see that fault in Enoch Arden:°—if he is to be 'strong and heroic', a fault: nor a natural one, in that way, I think: Could I rule the economy of the piece, it should go thus:—after the return from the peeping in at the window, Enoch should confirm himself in his resolution 'never to let her know', and only admit those other fancies of her learning the truth after his death, and of his children seeing their father once again—as impossible luxuries, to be put down *as* fancies, because destructive, if carried into fact, to what is the only purpose of his life now: and so fancying, and so repressing fancies, he should quietly die in his hole. And then on a mellow autumn evening, the right time for a nutting excursion, should the happy family from the mill sally forth, with a tender reminiscence of old days, toward the well-known brow of the hill, and the hollow where the bushes abound, and there come upon a pauper's funeral, the cart and the four rough planks—and be so set, the party, upon natural speculations. The young man, with the sagacity of his age, should divine that the poor devil could be no other than that odd, disreputable-looking and suspicious character who used to skulk about the ale-house, as if he had reasons enough for avoiding the constable, and—telling on his fingers—wonder whether it could be Giles the Poacher, or Jack the Gypsy that had to do with setting the barn on fire—or peradventure George the Tinker that decamped from his wife and children, leaving them a present to the parish? Thereupon should the Miller, whose thumb is proverbially made of gold—he should 'improve' the occasion, by inculcating on the young ones the evil consequences of self-indulgence—how man is made to conquer his riotous desires, not yield to them 'like this publican', while the Mother, the faithful Annie, though setting a proper example by turning up the white of her eyes, should treat herself to a little retrospective thankfulness—acknowledging that after a little roughness things had come satisfactorily round, and that, worst coming to the worst, dear Enoch's brave death in the storm—was it not better for him, and these beloved ones, than that he should...who can tell?...have lived on, even for such an end as this! And so they should proceed to their nutting, and Enoch, by a series of jolts, to his harbour in the churchyard—and we, to the considerations appropriate to one more view of this world. And now, goodbye till I have taken a stroll—after I have added, though, that the concluding touch in the poem about the fine funeral—which Tennyson gave me to understand was a very pregnant one—strikes me as ambiguous and unlucky—it coincides too exactly with an impudent speech in an old French play, I remember, wherein a gallant thus addresses his mistress, 'And, talking of brute-beasts, how does your husband do? Whenever is he intending to die, that fellow? Let him make haste, and I promise him the finest of funerals!'

By the bye, there is another thing which I want to say, in explanation of something I wrote—about one's family not 'growing', proportionately to one's own growth. I meant *symmetrically*, rather: for they may grow just as you grow, only—here's the fault—you none of you profit by each others' growth, it is not in your direction, but for somebody else to profit by—much as with a cluster of fruits on a common twig: each may bulge out round and red enough in the sun's eye, but the place where all the clustered knobs touch, where each continues to be known to the other, *that* is as hard and green, and insipid as ever, and if peach can only judge of fellow-peach by that place of junction and communion, the result's generally poor enough. Or *is* it generally so? I am inclined to go into extremes, and want, as you say 'we poets do', intensity at price of all other qualities. And now for the woods.

Sept. 3. Yes, the seed of beauty that 'Helen' has scattered all over the world is infinite: I don't know many memorable paintings nor statues of her—but in music, I have been remembering these thirty years and more Glück's overture to 'Helen and Paris',° and wondering whether the rest of the work could keep up to the tone of that—exactly what you remark in Homer—that far-away carelessness of common hopes and fears: I was speaking of it, so, to Hallé° not two months ago, and playing it to him on the table-cloth. In my last good days at Rome, the best in my life, I was meaning to do what I could 'next year', with a subject that struck me—Helen dedicating a goblet, which reproduced the perfection of what Virgil calls 'exsertae mammae',° and was deposited in the temple of Venus—a group of her, bidding farewell to the imperishable beauty, and a young priest receiving the same, and revolving other comparisons: on mentioning this to my friend Rossetti, 'I'll paint it' said he—and there it is, archaically treated indeed. Then, what a strange fancy is that of Euripides° on which he has founded his whole play of *Helena*—'that it was not really Helen, only an apparition of her, that fled to Troy, and caused all the fighting'—the true Helen living sadly and saintly in Egypt, having been stolen by Mercury at the command of Juno and confided to the care of Proteus the King—at whose tomb her husband finds her again, wringing her hands at the world's misconception of her character through the doings of the *eidolon*.° Qy: does this mean, a good poem suffering from the world's misconception of it? There—take your revenge on my *eidolon* for this string of rags and tatters, and be sure that (in Egypt) I am,

ever affectionately yours,
R. B.

17. R.B. to Isabella Blagden, 19 Dec. 1864

19. Warwick Crescent, Upper Westbourne Terr:
Dec 19. '64.

Yes, dearest Isa, it is three Christmasses ago°—*fully* now: I sometimes see a light at the end of this dark tunnel of life, which was one blackness at the beginning. It won't last for ever. In many ways I can see with my human eyes why this has been right & good for me—as I never doubted it was for Her—and if we do but re-join any day,—the break will be better than forgotten, remembered for its uses. The difference between me and the stupid people who have 'communications' is probably nothing more than that I don't confound the results of the natural working of what is in my mind, with vulgar external appearances: poor old Tulk° talked about the teaching he was in the habit of undergoing from his dead wife,— had an idea of her at his ear putting thoughts into his head,—not able to explain it otherwise. By the bye, why did not *he*, in turn, put into his sister's head to remember and make a will,—not leave Cottrell's children without a doit! There was a sale of her effects, & everything of course went to the near relations for whom she did not care a straw,—all for want of a 'nudge' from her brother not to be so careless about those whom she professed to love. She would have told you, dying was the simplest matter in the world, and the last thing she feared at all,—yet,—make her will?—better put that unpleasantness off till tomorrow. Well, for myself, I am certainly not unhappy, any more than I ever was: I am .. if the phrase were to now to be coined first .. '*resigned*'—but I look on everything in this world with altered eyes, and can no more take interest in anything I see there but the proof of certain great principles, strewn in the booths at a fair: I could no more take root in life again, than learn some new dancing step. On the other hand, I feel such comfort and delight in doing the best I can with my own object of life,—poetry,—which, I think, I never *could* have seen the good of before,—that it shows me I have taken the root I *did* take, *well*. I hope to do much more yet: and that the flower of it will be put into Her hand somehow. I really have great opportunities and advantages—on the whole, almost unparalleled ones, I think—no other disturbances & cares than those I am most grateful for being allowed to have.[...]

18. R.B. to Isabella Blagden, 19 Sept. 1867

[...] I am particularly glad you have got the right sense of the Bagni:° those villages,—the hill-roads through the woods,—how I remember them. And the Lima, where I used to bathe, or duck rather. Is old Mrs Stisted still alive and stationed there? It can't well be, yet I have never heard of her death. I think you said the place was little changed. I was there three times. $\alpha\beta\gamma\delta\epsilon\zeta\iota$° There! Those letters indicate seven distinct issues to which I came with Ba, in our profoundly different estimates of thing and person: I go over them one by one, and must deliberately inevitably say, on each of these points I was, am proved to be, right and she wrong. And I am glad I maintained the truth on each of these points, did not say, 'what matter whether they be true or no?—Let us only care to love each other.' If I could ever have such things out of my thoughts, it would not be to-day—the day, twenty years ago, that we left England together. If I ever seem too authoritative or disputative to you, dearest Isa, you must remember this, and that only to those I love very much do I feel at all inclined to lay down what I think to be the law, and speak the truth,—but no good comes of anything else in the long run,—while, as for *seeing* the truth, it seems to me such angelic natures don't—and such devilish ones *do:* it is no sign of the highest nature: on the contrary, I do believe the very highness blinds and the lowness helps to see.[...]

19. Julia Wedgwood to R.B., 15 Nov. 1868

I think both halves of me have read your two volumes,° dear friend, the half that drinks too eagerly to appreciate the flavour, and the half that sips fastidiously and sometimes makes a wry face.

I am not taken in by your efforts to make me think my words of value. 'It is more blessed, etc.'° I detect your application and thank you, but am content with the other end of the divine paradox—the blessing on the poor. Be you content with yours. Still there are some things I want to say, which you will understand and I shall understand, as I say them. Perhaps I am merely indicating my own intellectual limitations; yet if that is all, they are still the limitations, I think, of a fair specimen of the class you address.

You seem to me hardly, if at all, liable in this work to the stock reproach against you; the design is perfectly clear, and there are not many details, if any, that are not equally distinct. You give a stereoscopic view (only it is a case of more than two eyes, so the simile breaks down) and the solidity is quite satisfactory.

Perhaps this very clearness only brings out the grumble which has always mixed itself with my delight in what you utter. Do you remember once saying to me that your Wife was quite wanting in—I am not sure of the exact words, but the sense was, the scientific interest in evil?—I think you said, the physiology of wrong. I feel as if that interest were in you unduly predominant. I well remember your speaking with strong dissent, with which I entirely sympathized, of that kind of moral science which thinks it can fill up the valleys without lowering the hills. I know the depth of the valleys *is* the height of the hills. I know that we can only discern the white against the black. But hatred and scorn of evil, though it be inseparable from the love of good, ought not surely to predominate over it? I know it does with the natural man. One takes the good for granted, one exclaims when it comes to an end, everywhere it is the evil that seems positive. But I look upon the Poet as essentially the *super-natural* man, and I complain of him when he only mirrors our weakness.

Do you remember Bacon's° description of the office of Poetry, in *The Advancement of Learning*?, 'to satisfy the mind' (I forget the exact words) by some shadow of a higher justice than any exhibited in actual life, '*the soul being so much greater than the world*'. This is the element I long for more of in you. You seem to me so to hunger for intensity that you lose the sense of proportion whenever you begin to lay on dark shades. Here, for instance, you have one pure, delicate, soft bit of pearly colouring; but the effect is marred, to my mind, by the black being carried up to its very edge, while its area is needlessly restricted.

The picture of a fribble turned to a man—(the 'swordless sheath filled,'° as you put it elsewhere)—by his first contact with a pure spirit, the quick response to purity that begets trust, and that rarely felt, still more rarely conceived, emotion—the most refined, I think, of this earthly experience—when a woman leans upon a man's dis-interested tenderness and finds a love that ends with itself—all these things, surely, form the core of what you have to say? So much fringe of blackness as brings out this we accept willingly. We need the atmosphere of meanness and cruelty to exhibit fully the luminous soul that centres the picture. But surely, surely we have more of this than that small white figure can bear. One's memory seems filled by the despicable husband, the vulgar parents, the brutal cutthroats, the pathetic child is jostled into a corner. I long for more space for her. In the 3rd and 4th vols I hope we shall have it but still it is not a mere question of the number of printed pages that are occupied with her. There is, what seems to me an absolute superfluity of detail in the hideous portraits, whatever may be bestowed elsewhere. Ther-sites° is brought so fully into the foreground that Achilles can be brought no nearer. It is dangerous to illustrate criticism—very likely any principles of judgment may be wrong, but any illustrations I might bring forward would be still more likely to be so. But, for instance, would not Caponsacchi have touched more lightly on all that was foul while his soul was full of Pompilia? Might not his speech have been free from Swift-like metaphor? An intense pure love does not distance *indignation*—far from it. But that kind of scorn that is mixed with loathing is, I think, wonderfully silenced in its neighbourhood. Would not the narratives of the Crucifixion lose—I do not say grace or beauty but actually *force*, by any elaboration of the character of Judas? I feel it even in that allusion in the *Acts*. The Evangelists were not pleading for their Master before a second Pilate, you may say. Still I think the hypothetical change brings forcibly before one's mind the power of *perfectly* unselfish love (where it is imperfect the effect is sometimes directly opposite) to avert its eye from all evil.

I feel sometimes tempted to be indignant with you for this, because it seems to me you are so bound to give us this which we need. Do you know what an exceptional experience yours has been? I think sometimes the exceptional element in our own fate is hidden from us. I do not, thank God, think it anything exceptional that the power of love should be fully exercised. Except with a poor soon-crushed Pompilia, for whom God keeps the good wine till the last, I believe we are debarred from loving only by our own fault. But love, to most of us, is quite as much the discipline, as the refreshment, of life. We would give our lives for those whose presence is a continual scourge to our taste, or we watch hungrily for the footsteps of those of whose lives we can only think with a blush. Or we deliberately choose companions—perfectly satisfactory to a part of our nature perhaps, but utterly unresponsive to so much, that the joint life seems a starved poor mutilated thing. Does not almost every marriage illustrate some form of this dislocation? But your love had not to split itself up into gratified taste in one direction and exercised severance in another, and intellectual sympathy in a third. One channel held them all.

Did you not thereby contract this debt to us to give some intellectual translation of your experience, and make us feel that love is the principal thing in this world, and the world beyond. Oh, do not leave *scorn* in that prominent rivalry with it! There are more things I should like to say, but I have a notion I have tired out my hearer's patience! I should like to ask why you break down the dramatic framework so often in your characters? That passage about Justinian and the Pandects,° for instance, is yours, and not Franchescini's. But you must have a distinct intention in this, and I can't help always enjoying it, it seems so characteristic of you—though it does seem to me an artistic defect.

I had marked some lines to suggest to you as sounding rugged to my ear, but you must have intended that effect, I think. I can't tell you how wonderfully subtle some touches of Pompilia seem to me. I feel as if they must be a real woman's words. The speech about the *pain of womanliness* is to me a wonderful revelation of apprehension of *our* side of the question, which I can meet with no correlative intuition into yours. I can't imagine what corresponds to it—whether anything corresponds to it. A consciousness of limitation somewhere, I suppose, but I cannot guess where.

Dear old friend, to whom I am no old friend, but glaringly modern, let me have one word in answer to this. If it seems to you hopeless and futile misapprehension, still resolve this diminished seventh which has spread itself all over the instrument, and you can satisfy with three fingers. You know how intensely I listen for all your utterances; if you see nothing else in this letter take it as a clumsy expression of that. I should like to know that life is not all arid to you. But you have your son—and surely much true friendship, even as warm and unchanging as that of

Yours ever affectionately,

Julia Wedgwood.

I have written at night: the daylight hours are spent in the sick room. I mention it as an excuse for diffuseness. One wants time to condense.

20. *R.B. to Julia Wedgwood, 19 Nov. 1868*

I will promise never to spare you of my gratitude if you engage never to doubt whether I think your gifts true gold. It ought to be so, between us. But if you won't *begin* by leaving off, I won't (child-fashion), so I formally tell you I value your criticism, over and above its being an utterance of yours, beyond what words are likely to make you believe. In this case, I think you do correctly indicate a fault of my nature—not perhaps a fault in this particular work, artistically regarded: I believe I do unduly like the study of morbid cases of the soul,—and I will try and get over that taste in future works; because, even if I still think that mine was the proper way to treat this particular subject,—the objection still holds, 'Why prefer this sort of subject?'—as my conscience lets me know I do.

Come next time I will try in other directions. But here,— given the subject, I cannot but still say, given the treatment too: the business has been, as I specify, to explain *fact*—and the fact is what you see and, worse, are to see. The question with me has never been, 'Could not one, by changing the factors, work out the sum to better result?' but declare and prove the actual result, and there an end.

Before I die, I hope to purely invent something,—here my pride was concerned to invent nothing: the minutest circumstance that denotes character is *true*: the black is so much—the white, no more. You are quite justified perhaps in saying 'Let all that black alone'— but, touching it at all, so much of it must be. I have made the most of every whitish tint in the thing's texture: and as, when Northcote asked Reynolds° why he put no red into his flesh, looked awhile earnestly at his own hand and then replied, 'I see no red here'—so I say, 'I see no more white than I give.'

But remember, first that this is God's world, as he made it for reasons of his own, and that to change its conditions is not to account for them—as you will presently find me try to do. I was struck with the enormous wickedness and weakness of the main composition of the piece, and with the incidental evolution of good thereby—good to the priest, to the poor girl, to the old Pope, who judges anon, and, I would fain hope, to who reads and applies my reasoning to his own experience, which is not likely to fail him. The curious depth below depth of depravity here—in this chance lump taken as a sample of the soil—might well have warned another from spreading it out,— but I thought that, since I could do it, and even liked to do it, my affair it was rather than another's.

Just see—you who think I might have lightened the load of bistre—Guido and the four cutthroats did their murder: well? and what more could they do? Why,—(as, depend on it, you are to hear in good or bad time!) Guido's first thought during the flight was, 'Why pay these the money I promised,—which they will never dare claim?' And he would not pay them,—while flying for his life: and they? Behind his back they snatched counsel, each of the other, 'Since he cheats us,—why not kill him and get his money?'—and so all four at once agreed to do: so that, had he not been arrested in his first sleep, Guido would have never awakened at all, since they meant, on their own awakening, to murder him. Again, the Convertites who harboured Pompilia, are you prepared for what they did, immediately after her death, and continued doing when her innocence had been made apparent to the world? They laid claim to all her wealth, declared themselves her heirs to the detriment of her child, 'seeing that all dishonest women consigned to their keeping forfeited to them, in the event of their death while so superintended, whatever property they might have': hence, Pompilia having been nominally given to them as a dishonest woman, they caught at her money with tooth and nail—so that they could only be disengaged by a regular decree of the tribunal that Pompilia, having been altogether innocent, they must let her alone. No, you must fall back on the other charge,—'Why not let all this horror alone?'

The worst is, I can promise you nothing better in what follows: unless the Pope's Judgment (longest book in the poem)° come in as a new light: I did mean it should be so, however. The next book, Pompilia, is all white too: but then come the two buffoon lawyers, and, after the Pope, you have Guido's last display—not pleasant certainly. Also the Augustinian preaches a sermon, and the Priest has a final word to add in his old age. 'I can no more'—as dying operatic heroes sing.

The coarseness—ay, but the man is Italian, noble, and living in 1698, and speaking not to the woman, but against her enemies: all *great* (conventionally great) Italians are coarse—showing their power in obliging you to accept their cynicism. Why is the allusion to Justinian *mine* and not the man's I give it to? The whole of his speech, as I premise, is untrue—cant and cleverness—as you see when the second speech comes: but he was quite able to cant, and also know something of the Pandects, which are the basis of actual Italian law. What are the other escapes from dramatic propriety into my own peculiar self—do tell me that! But I must leave off. So do not you, but continue to help me. I seem not to have begun, even, to say the many things I had in mind to say. Write to me again; your letters will be absolutely alone in the delight they give me.

I leave off to go and dine with Tennyson, who good-naturedly sent this morning to invite me.

Goodbye, dearest friend.

R. B.

You may see I cannot review what I have scribbled. Forgive it all.

21. Julia Wedgwood to R.B., 3 Dec. 1868

Yes, dear Friend, I fear you do not over-estimate the amount of my divergence. I tried to narrow that angle to include the form alone, but as you see it, the form and matter are inseparable, and you doubtless are right. I wish I could apprehend the attraction of this subject to you. I thought I shared your interest in morbid anatomy. I think our issue lies here. You say, 'this is God's world, as he made it for reasons of his own.' I demur. Guido seems to me not at all to belong to the world, as God made it. While yet by a strange paradox *that* world would be exactly the one where Art finds no foothold. It is along the boundary line that its path seems to me to lie—where the waters separate for the two great oceans; on whichever side that watershed is lost sight of, my interest fails. I look to a time when we shall lose sight of the boundary, when this, that we call evil, whether explained or not, shall at all events recede and fade, when we shall partake in God's own calm and need no edge of blackness to tell us what is white. But meantime, in this world any attempt at rendering this seems to me condemned to hopeless futility—so far I go with you. It is the struggle of two elements, the edge of black and white, that seems to me to teach us the meaning of both. Your curious 'depth below depth of depravity' loses sight of this edge. I see no possibility of good in Guido. He seems to me to retain nothing, not only of what God made, but of what—to speak with coarse, super-ficial conciseness—God can use. Here is no energy of hate, a strong instrument for his displeasure—'hateful to God and to his foes'°— one sees no place for such a character on the battlefield.

I think there must be something in the subject to which I am wholly blind, for what I am saying is so obvious; and yet you have chosen it. I shall listen for the old Pope, but except his and Pom-pilia's utterance I fear I shall not find much food in the remaining books. But, oh, be merciful to us in Guido's last display! Shame and pain and humiliation need the irradiation of hope to be endurable as objects of contemplation; you have no right to associate them in our minds with hopeless, sordid wickedness. Having to meet them so often, to travel with them so large a part of the way, we demand of the teacher that he shall help us to endure their terrible neighbour-hood by shewing them as guides towards the light. Do I take too moral a view of the poet's duty? I know you hate this, and I believe I do too. But in this short life, where good fights at such terrible odds with evil—where God hides his face and the Devil shews his—I cannot feel that one of the greatest motive forces we have at our command may rightly act independently of the great battle. We need rest from it—yes, I feel that is the function of Art; it is exactly that the moral sense may go to sleep. But it should awake refreshed.

It was not only in a critical spirit that I complained to myself as I read, for I felt as if I were reading what you had lost in your wife. The sense of good seemed dimmed.

Oh yes, dear Friend, do give us something purely from yourself. Give her a monument more durable than that at Florence—give something that all who read may recognise as the utterance of one who has been taught supremely to believe in goodness by the close neighbourhood of a beautiful soul. I look yet to recognise the sunshine of her presence in the ripe fruit of your mind. I seem to feel in myself the woman's error—the over-tendency to incarnate all things. Ah, well, take it for what it is worth! She must have been your window, even if you could go out and look direct into the face of Heaven. Now that the window is darkened, you will not forget how the room looked. In no sanctuary of Heaven could it be other than keen pain to know that one's gifts were not permanent. What coarse things words are! and perhaps here the meaning is coarse too. Yet I feel as if some rich modulation of harmony or formless melting of colour would best express what I am trying to put into language, and yet perhaps I make a baseless pretence to subtlety in saying so.

I would I knew that I exaggerated the chillness and aridity of your present life. The permanent sense of loss I can[not] quite bear to contemplate. Adieu, dearest friend. How blessed is the etymology of that word! The love deeper than our deepest absorbs all anxiety—for anxiety is born of impotence.

Ever yours,

F. J. W.

22. *R.B. to Julia Wedgwood, 21 Jan. 1869*

I have delayed sending my next volume—you well know why! Still, I do send it at last, though for no bad reason: for, I don't know how, the sending seems a repetition of the old cruel joke of the judge, 'I sentence you', said he to an offender, 'to be whipped from one end of the town to the other!'—'Thank you, you have done your worst!'—'And back again!' added the judge. So, you have thought the worst was over—so, you get this! Accept the willingness on my part to be wrong, if I could but get to think myself, so, which is no fault of yours! 'I like to be' (*so*) 'despised'—quoth Mawworm:° and I take all your blame for better than other folks' praise.

The worst is, I think myself dreadfully in the right, all the while, in everything: apart, of course, from my own incapacities of whatever kind, I think this *is* the world as it is and will be—*here* at least. Shall I dare tell you? I think that in no energetic deed would you attain to a greater general amount of good than you get here,—though the individual qualities (I meant to write, quantities, but my head aches, and the afternoon is dark and confounding), the factors in the sum would be different. Think of your first combination, say, of six people, that do any remarkable thing: there will be nobody to match Guido, whose wickedness does... or rather, by the end, *shall*... rise to the limit conceivable; but is your second, better than Pompilia, your third than Caponsacchi, the others than the Pope, and the two old foolish, rather than wicked-people? I mean, that your good will want as much of the goodness of these, one with another,—as your bad wants of the wickedness of Guido: then, this good (of my lot) comes through—is evolved by—that prodigy of bad: hence its use, hence my poem, hence your blame, hence my kissing the rod, hence this word to beg you to lay it on again and spare not! The buffoon lawyers (not a bit, intellectually and morally, beneath lawyers I have known) serve an artistic purpose and let you breathe a little before the last vial is poured out: Guido 'hope?'—do you bid me turn him into that sort of thing? No, indeed! Come, I won't send more, if you will but lift your finger! There, be you as grateful as a lady who, telling me of her trials last week at a dull dinner-party, where people, whom she had counted on meeting, were absent, added, 'But justice was tempered with mercy, for So-and-so took me downstairs to dinner!'

Well, I like *knowing*, at any price: also, I like the power that comes of it. 'Agnes' ('Where's Agnes?')° chose to call on me the other day— I had not seen her for seven years: my wife would not, or could not, know her, and suffered miserably through her ignorance: in half an hour I gained a victory which, could my wife have hoped, even, to do, would have made her happy indeed—and which she could have gained by no effort that I can imagine: it was as easy to me as 'kiss my hand'—and not altogether unlike it.

By the way, my wife would have subscribed to every one of your bad opinions of the book; she never took the least interest in the story, so much as to wish to inspect the papers. It seems better so to me, but *is* it better? So, the naturalists say that all female beauties are weaknesses and defects except to the male creature, and all real beauty is in *him*, if he could but see! Only, he can't.

Goodbye. You must tell me the amount of stripes due this time, however. Surely, poor Pompilia is prettily done—'a half-penny worth of bread to this intolerable quantity of vitriol!'°

Ever yours,
R.B.

23. *Julia Wedgwood to R.B. 22 Jan. 1869*

No, I don't know why you have delayed sending the 3rd vol., unless to punish me for impertinence! But I have it now. I must write again when I have read it. I have read your letter with many a smile. Is he such a bad Economist as to waste good satire on *me*? No, I answered myself, whatever may be his sins, I cannot think quite so ill of his 'practical reason'. Being emancipated from that coarse theory, which assumes that great souls speak truth, I have a ready alternative. How stupid is our blunder in making the suspicion of fiction an insult! It is the large and generous nature that invents, and who shall say that the fiction may not be a creation? that we may not incarnate a generous hypothesis, so that a Poet becomes an ex post facto Historian? Well, it is a historical fragment in your letter that gave me most lively pleasure. Yet our poor weak nature feeds on fiction too.

All this I write from myself, and yet, I think, a larger half responds, 'I like *knowing* at any price.' It is a heavy price sometimes, leaving us penniless. Yet it is a good bargain. You see I adopt your style and send you the two halves of—the antithesis of Rome. Where is the Tertium Quid to find some grain of truth in each? I hate Tertium Quids! I will have both.

Dear Friend I thank you for some things in your letter from the bottom of my soul. You know what I most care to know about you. It joined on to what else of yours I was reading—the beginning of Pompilia. Yes, it is a lovely Snowdrop growing out of that dunghill, but I can't forgive you for planting it there. No indeed, I vehemently and indignantly deny that half a dozen of any acquaintance beaten up together would yield your quantum of badness—not even if I threw you in as one of them!

But that dainty, lovely, pathetic little picture is an exquisite pleasure to me. It seems like some sudden snatch of melody breaking in on the din of tumult and clamour. How wonderfully you understand the woman's nature! No not *wonderfully*—I retract the senseless adverb—most comprehensibly. You will have another letter, dear friend, to read from

Yours ever,

F.J.W.

24. *Julia Wedgwood to R.B. 30 Jan. 1869*

Pray make haste to send me the old Pope to take the taste of the lawyers out of my mouth!

What a strange mixture it is, that you are so strongly and so incompletely dramatic! You have a photographic impartiality of attention that I cannot understand—you lead us through your picture gallery and your stable yard at exactly the same pace, which impartiality is, I suppose, the test of dramatic, as distinguished from mere lyric, feeling. And yet you never really vary the dialect. I should have thought that very detachment of attention from sympathy would have implied a filtering away of your own thoughts from your own representations, which is the very opposite of what I find with you. Do I make any sort of meaning clear? No doubt the very purpose of poetry is to give an intellectual shape to feelings which are, in ordinary minds, mere diffused colour—yet I chafe against the idea that any blot of mud should afford just as much subject for your pencil as a streak of sunset-remembering in the sky. To bear so much intellectual elaboration feelings ought, it seems to me at least, to be *large*.

It is, I suppose, the consistent dramatic feeling I quarrel with— this readiness to hold a brief for any character or feeling, so it is only individual, to work coldly out any problem, so that it is sufficiently complex without examining the premises. This, I suppose, only shews how narrow and shallow I am. But I am sure the two things together make evil more prominent. I cannot bear to see your thoughts on loan to deck out a sleek pedantic buffoon. When I bring out this edition of your works with which I used to threaten you, I shall only keep enough of Guido and the lawyers to make an ebony frame for that pearly image of Pompilia. Will it not be a terrible punishment for you, if you have to read the work in the other world?

But even with Pompilia I feel here and there what I have said— you seem to me to spoil your pearl in cutting it, once or twice. For instance, look at page 73. Surely the death bed narrative of an illiterate girl should be understandable at once. I may be extra stupid, but I cannot make out the construction of the sentence beginning, 'I did think, do think'°, etc. It seems to me as if it wanted a predicate. It must be some stupidity of mine, but surely the fact that it is possible to puzzle over it in reading it carefully is so far a condemnation of the presentment of the character. It seems to me one of the many instances where your thoughts overflow the dramatic channel. 'Not this man who, from his own soul, re-writes the obliterated charter'...surely that is your idea, not Pompilia's. You said 'It is mine too' when I made the remark about Guido, but I always feel in such passages as if I heard the tune on another instrument. It is your lending so much of *yourself* to your contemptible characters makes me so hate them. I cannot endure to hear your voice in these Advocates' pleadings. Certainly you present us with a wonderful variety of mud; the defence is even more hateful than the attack. The impure medium is wonderfully brought out in the contrast between that sullied image seen through it and the picture in all its native purity. I can not venture to tell you all that Pompilia seems to me. I felt as if it were only half yours, but indeed I do not divide the other influence from your own.

Dear friend, how one says the insignificant, secondary half of one's thoughts! It is as if all utterance were the postscript to some letter that contained all that one really cared to say—the mere refuse after the valuables had been locked up. I doubt if even my postscript is intelligible, or would be to another. I have a wonderful sense that you can drop some grain into these muddy thoughts, that will make them clear—clearer than they are to myself. It seems arrogant after all these years to expect it, but I cannot help expecting it. I rest with a confidence I can hardly justify to myself on your understanding me—on your having always understood me—and that even if you have half-forgotten me, whatever you remember is just. This is a long way from Pompilia, but this blunt pencil of Language always recalls its own imperfections to one's mind when one wants to draw anything subtle, and I went from one imperfection to another.

This is a long letter to give the most impatient man in the world to read, as I believe you are, very nearly. Yet it contains nothing but the mere marginal note of my thought. I must not venture on the text, but I think you know it, you will have understood my delight in renewing my acquaintance with your thoughts. Dear friend, farewell.

Your affectionate,

F.J.W.

25. R.B. to Julia Wedgwood, 1 Feb. 1869

I make haste to say, with unfeigned satisfaction, that you are quite right about the faulty passage at page 73—there is a line dropped out...of my mind, rather than the M.S., a line I will supply° cheerfully, something to the effect that the thought in which P.° will die is—that the proximity to such a man as she describes would be an advantage and nothing to blush about. I have made her go on, you see, on the wings of the thought, till it grew sufficient for itself, demonstrative enough of the fact that she would have begun by enunciating. This being a real blunder, I have the privilege of praising myself under the pretence of making excuse—so, pray you to observe that it has been a particularly weary business to write this whole long work by my dear self—I who used always to be helped by an amanuensis—for, I cannot clearly see what is done, or undone, so long as it is thru' the medium of my own handwriting—about which there is nothing *sacred*—imperative for, or repellent of—change: in print, or alien charactery, I *see* tolerably well: yet I have had to do all this scribbling, and how much more that you will never see! But I 'buckled to', and the thing is done, ill or well: *well*, I think, on the whole.

It is a shame, that when there is anything you contrive to like in it, you cry out, 'It's not yours, you know—only half yours,' and so on: then comes an ugliness, and 'Ah, there you are at home,—there, I see you at work!'—you comment. Unfair,— because, if the good is not mine (as you fancy) in the sense that it is copied from a model,—why may not the uglinesses be copied too, and so not mine neither? I don't admit even your objections to my artistry—the undramatic bits of myself you see peep thro' the disguised people. In that sense, Shakespeare is always undramatic, for he makes his foolish people all clever. I don't think I do more than better their thoughts and instruction, and [improve] up to the general bettering, and intended tone of the whole composition—what one calls, idealization of the characters. What is in the *thought* about the 'charter' impossible to Pompilia, if you accept the general elevation of her character? Besides, it is Italian ignorance, quite compatible with extraordinary insight and power of expression too: I have heard abundant instances of it. For the first instance that occurs,—you would not put into the mouth of an English maid, profoundly ignorant, this phrase, 'She had a certain nobility of mind which, finding in itself nothing of the base and evil, could not credit their existence in others.' Yet that is word for word what Annunziata° said to me of my wife: 'aveva nua certa nobiltà d'animo', etc.

As for the lawyers, why, *Who* is going to find fault with me, in the other world, for writing about what *I*, at least, wish had never been made? But made they are, and just so,—apart, as in the other case, from more shrewdness and learning than they are likely to have,—just so, I have known them: in this present instance, you have the very arguments of the very men: Pompilia's all-but-crime was never conceded—far from it—but was invariably afterward *supposed*, just to show how the clever man could bowl *that* down also, were it set up. Indeed, very reluctantly, I left out one prime passage, 'spared you' indeed, the fine fellows' notion—illustrated wonderfully—of how far appearances may deceive. I hate the lawyers: and confess to tasting something of the satisfaction, as I emphasize their buffoonery, which was visible (they told me at Balliol, the other day) on the sour face of one Dr Jenkins, whilehome Master of the College, when, having to read prayers, he would of a sudden turn and apostrophize the obnoxious Fellows, all out of the discreet words of the Psalmist, 'As for liars, I hate and abhor them!'°—then go on quietly with his crooning.

I will, in a sort, go on with mine, by sending you the Pope in a day or two—ah, and Guido's last dying speech and confession, and so relieve me and you!

Now, in another key, 'Even if you have half-forgotten you, whatever I remember is just'? Are *you* dramatic here, and who is it supposes I half-forget? I think, on the whole, it is probable we shall never meet again, face to face. Depend on it, I keep what I gained, and shall never part with an atom of it. It was foolish of whoever or whatever deprived me of what would have done good to me and harm to nobody: but good remains, as Pompilia says, and I shall use it up to the end of,

Yours,

R. B.

26. *R.B. to Julia Wedgwood, 12 Feb. 1869*

Here is my last trial of your patience, and, as the prayer-book comfortably directs, 'In quires and places where they sing, here followeth the anthem'—*I* help to intone it, I know, profoundly tired as I am of the whole business, but not more dissatisfied with my work, and the immediate effect of it, than one should expect.

I shall begin something else in a different way. Do write to me sometimes. I was startled the other day at a house where I dined for the first time,—the Spottiswoodes',—by hearing that 'the Wedgwoods' were expected afterward: I had to go away elsewhere, and don't know what came true of the promise: I should not like to meet you that way, however.

My son is at Ch. Ch.:° my owl is still on his perch: my book is out: my intention is to hear Joachim° play to-night: my friend is my friend, all the more because of Guido and the Lawyers—'What can I want beside?' as the psalm asks?°

Ever yours,

R. B.

27. *Julia Wedgwood to R.B., 14 Feb. 1869*

I must write to you, my dear Mr Browning, while my delight at the Pope's speech is fresh. Perhaps if I waited to finish Guido it might be too much diluted with remonstrance to do itself justice— and, indeed as it is, the mere subtraction sum performed in concluding the noble utterance and discovering the proportion it bears to the remainder makes me somewhat indignant. But inasmuch as nobody need read Guido's utterance unless he or she please, and no one could have read Innocent's unless you pleased, this is a some exacting and ungracious view of the matter. I feel as if there were more of that which seems to me your special message to us in the Pope's speech than in anything else you have written—it seems to me to leave my mind full of seeds. I say 'It seems' and 'I feel' in this tedious dilution, because after reading it only once I hardly know how far I have taken in *your* thoughts, and how far it is merely my own that are stirred and stimulated. I am sure that it brings us something of that ἔλεγχος σὺ βλεπομενων° that is not less the work of Poetry than the essence of faith. I felt for a while after reading it as if something in me were released and could speak—now when I listen for it the words are all gone, yet I know that sense of everything falling into its place which it gave me and I hardly feel with anything but Beethoven's music—means something large and permanent, which does not wax and wane with this capacity for utterance which it seems to awaken.

There is a sense of the great schism of life being healed in some chords of yours (not by any means in the old strain, ever) that I have never felt equally in any one else. I can feel, as I listen to Innocent,° that this poor little planet is a good inn for our souls to rest in, before they start on the long journey—no, not rest in, that is not the word, but I cannot find another. How truly you say we must speak lies, if we are to use language! If it were merely that one had to use a coarse pencil to delineate those subtle conceptions—but no, words are hopelessly impregnated with false association. But that sense of the wealth and glory of this life, and its insignificance—I can only hurry from one to the other, but you, in some rare flashes, shew me them together. This miserable incompleteness, this straining of the growing plant against the tiny pot, which in prosaic hours seems hopeless misfit and mistake, by *that* light turns into a promise. If we could believe we had an Eternity to work in, as we believe in June thro a snowy day of March! how easy then to bear—not perhaps the sharp ills of life, but all that makes it poor and fretful, all the misconception, thwarted plans, broken work, and that sense of incapacity and poverty within that is harder than all. It would be only then the changed attitude with which one would put away a letter one had tried to read just before sunrise.

I pour out these incoherent ill-expressed feelings, because I feel sure in some way they are the echo to your thoughts, and yet I am aware they take so different a shape that I can fancy you may turn aside almost with irritation. I try to express what your thoughts arouse in *me*. I am sure it is a real effect of your words 'All harmony, all medicine is mine' (I am not quoting Shelley rightly°).—*that*, I feel, just touches the work of poetry. I can believe there is something besides I cannot understand, some more disinterested (so to speak) contemplation of things as they are, in which things foul and hideous have their place—yet this seems to me the ultimate test. I know you feel with me in this, though you admit so much that is apparently inconsistent with it. You do feel that your work is the deliverance of captives, and the opening the eyes of the blind. If those wonderful flashes have ever shewn us a new Heaven and a new Earth, we do not quite go back to the old. Farewell—but I must finish what I have to say by and bye.

Yours ever,

F. J. W.

28. *Julia Wedgwood to R.B., 21 Feb. 1869*

Dear friend,

I feel, after finishing the Poem, as if I could not contemplate it without a sort of a squint. Or rather (for you, of all men, ought to have patience with an elaborate simile) it seems to me that a somewhat slight picture has been put into an elaborately carved frame which represents the same subject under a rather different point of view. I look at the Picture and I see a certain incident; I look at the frame and I see the same incident treated in a more ambitious style and with much greater fullness of detail. The result is that one hesitates which to look at.

For instance, Guido's last speech seems to me the epilogue to a long, dark, complicated elaborate story of intrigue and crime—an intricate web of treachery and cruelty, something of an Iago° history. But Guido's actual part in the drama seems to be one simply of stupid brutality. It is not merely that you enrich him with learning and fancy beyond what he would himself possess—I quite agree with you that tried by that test Shakespear would be undramatic. It is that you give him the kind of mind that fits on to a *different* set of actions. The mere brute, hacking Pompilia to pieces, seems to me to have nothing in common with the keen, subtle, intellectual pagan, sympathising with Virgil, reaching back into a remote past—giving evidence of so subtle and wily an intellect, as well as of such strong powers of hatred, I do not feel this doubleness so much in any other figure, yet I am not sure that there are not two Pompilias though *they* come much nearer together. In short, your subject seems to me too simple for you. This has not struck any one else, so I suppose I am wrong, but still I can't help saying what I think about it.

I do regret that so large a part of your canvas is spent in delineating what is merely hateful. But, of course, my first criticism somewhat cancels the force of the second. In all intellectual wickedness there is something not merely hateful, and so far as you have wandered from your historic theme, your aesthetic variation has gained. Still I *do* want not to have so much ugliness in the picture! Guido says he did not make himself—fit words to be put into the mouth of a liar! You know we make ourselves. I fancy neither you nor I are greatly delighted with this individuality of which so much is owing to the will of each, yet we do not accuse the great artist who sketched a soul we each copy so ill. My longing is to see *his*

work copied—I do not say exclusively; it could hardly be made
evident to us apart from our own scrawls—but at all events that this
be the main thing, that what is presented to us be, on the whole,
God's intention for man, not man's poor blurred distortion of that
ideal. But I believe I am running into repetition of what I have
said before, a course not desirable with the least patient of one's
acquaintance!

Yes, I suppose your first summary of my criticism was true—I
cannot sympathise in your choice of a subject. Surely I must be
wrong here, you cannot have spent all these years on a mistake. I
incline to think my nature is too undramatic, and I want all poetry to
be direct utterance of some congenial feeling—this is narrow. Well,
even this finds something to feed on in the poem in Innocent's
speech and Pompilia's and a little of Caponsacchi's. I think it is very
telling, the way you make the *real* Guido drop all insinuation about
the two. I wish I knew how much historic warrant you have for your
Innocent. I wish I could judge of your translation of Euripides.° I
feel a thirsty yearning towards those few first-hand thinkers of the
world, but I can't get at them.[...]

29. R.B. to Julia Wedgwood, 22 Feb. 1869

You well know I mean nothing by my words about the anthem,
beyond what *you* mean when you hope, 'I did not laugh too dis-
respectfully at your last letter'—why, the very spirit of truth is in
these 'lies', like an odour one has to imprison in an oil, or some such
vehicle: *I* blush (for you) thinking what you please to imply in this
allowance of 'disrespectful laughter', if I be minded to profit thereby:
am I really not to signify never so obliquely that I feel grateful for
your listening so long to what... does not altogether please you? In
another sense, I can believe, for more reasons than one, that you do
and will patiently read what I write: more than that, I know my work
is sincere, and not likely to abound in these days, and is at least worth
examination—even if you did not wish well to my working.

Yes, I got the letter you enquire about, but judged it inexpedient
to clap my hands at the apparition of your praise like a moonrin, till I
was out of the wood—and, behold, I was soon ordained to knock my
head against a tree! How could I expect you to like Guido? See, as
long as you don't like, nay, hate—simply—I sympathise with you:

tell me, 'I hate the deed, and consideration of it'—nay, go on and add, 'I object to anybody else considering such a deed,'—I understand, and, with a limitation, approve. I defend myself when you go beyond and urge, 'And the deed could have no such motives nor circumstances.' You write here—'Guido's part is simply one of stupid brutality'—to which neither does the cultivation, etc. '*fit on*,' nor with the keenness, subtlety, paganism, etc.—nay, even if I understand you, even the treachery, intrigue, and Iago qualities seem inappropriate to the product.

Why, I almost have you at an unfair disadvantage, in the fact that the whole story is *true!* How do *you* account for the 'mere brutal hacking Pompilia to pieces' in a nobleman thirty years long the intimate of Cardinals: is this the case of a drunken operative that kicks his wife to death because she has no money for more gin? But I won't begin and tell my own story over yet another time—I am too glad to get done with it. We differ apparently in our conception of what gross wickedness can be effected by cultivated minds—I believe the gross*est*— all the more, by way of reaction from the enforced habit of self denial which is the condition of men's receiving culture. Guido tried the over-refined way for four years, and in his rage at its unsuccess let the natural man break out.

It seems to me that Napoleon was capable, *mutatis mutandis*, of acting exactly as grossly and abominably as Guido: and that, on the large scale, he *did* act quite as falsely, as selfishly and cruelly. You must consider the matter for yourself: what I could find it in my heart to wonder that you don't see in the work is, that there *is*, or should be, 'an utterance of congenial feeling' all the louder that it is not *direct*—I hoped it would be heard always by the side of, and *above* all, the disgusts and painfulnesses: is there anywhere other than an unintermitted protest (which would be worth nothing were it *loud*) against all the evil and in favour of all the good? Where does my *sympathy* seem diverse from yours so long as we watch the same drama? I quite allow you to refuse to watch. But I don't think that the general interests of the world allow certain other eyes to go and amuse themselves elsewhere. It seems somebody has just written a life of Lucrezia Borgia° on this principle of bidding the eye just see what it likes. He finds this and the other wickedness 'impossible'. *Who* commits the wickednesses that undeniably *are*? Last, I hold you are wrong even in your praise—that is, wrong in thinking that whatever you count white in Pompilia and Innocent could have come out as clearly without the black.

Here shall end my thought and concern about the thing, so far as regards you and your judgment about it. I will try and please you better another time: yes, I have given four full years to this 'mistake,' but what did I do with my fourteen years in Italy? I must go on, busy myself now, and rub my dry stick-like self into a blaze in this cold evening of life. And whatever I write, I will always send you, and you will always like to see it, will always speak your mind about it, and will always be exactly in the relation that you are now to

R. B.

30. *Julia Wedgwood to R.B., 5 Mar. 1869*

Dear friend,

It feels flat and dismal to have no more fuel for my critical fire, and I like to write and tell you so. However, I cannot say that my last stock is quite exhausted yet, but perhaps the smouldering flame finds more to feed on in your MS. than your printed sheets. I am amused to see with what sudden impatience you turn from your production after your long absorption in it. I hardly venture to reply to your last letter (at least, I should not venture unless the alternative of not reading my criticism was open to you)—that I allow you no advantage whatever from the fact of your material being history. 'Tant pis pour les faits!'° if they are not artistic. Fate has no conception of the fitness of things, you must not copy her bungling sketches, full as they are of false perspective and harsh colouring, but give us some relief from her coarse picture gallery by your truer representations.

Yes, truer; in this world I am sure often that what we see with our eyes is false. We have all done things quite out of keeping with our character—at least we seemed to do them, some whiff of strange circumstance coming at the critical moment against the arrow of will; in the world of poetry we must be sheltered from those gusts. However, as I read I mentally analyzed Guido into the historic brute and the fictitious Iago; probably I was wrong. You know how I shall thirst for his successor—or rather, you do not know at all.

I should have felt somewhat mortified to see how little you know, in the allusions which imply that ours has been a mutual relation—only that I think these are lies pure and simple—scentless oil, with no imprisoned odour. You are not really so arrogant, with all your arrogance, as to think that our shares were equal? My dear Friend, do not give me the utterly needless pain of having for a moment to think that you think it. Every act of mine during our short intercourse implied that this *could* not be—that I might merely consider myself. Whether I did wisely or unwisely for myself is not a matter I care to press on you or on any one. I think our common hunger for facts as they are is one thing that has drawn us together; do not let our intercourse be seen by any other light. Indeed, I am not unreasonable. I could bear to have the whole thing fade out of your mind, only not assume such a shape as you suggest (I do not say, design) when you say it was a loss to *you*. You know I turned to you almost as a survivor from some elder race. I stop to smile at my endeavour to turn that pyramid topsy-turvy. To have it copied as an hour-glass, or a figure of 8—! ! !

There there! I know it was all meant in kindness. The last words of your letter saddened me, yet I felt they must be true. The rare glow of your daylight must leave the evening chill, yet for myself I feel such an added preciousness to life with every gained height of thought, I would hope your wide horizon made up to you for almost everything—made up, that is, for all you *can* lose. For is not the best what cannot be lost? It is you who have most given me the sense that the material world is a passing shadow, and that all which binds us each to each is eternal.

I find the British Public° is beginning to like you well, for all minor poets seem to me to taste of you. I don't like you in that form—but I don't know that any one tastes good at secondhand. Adieu.

I am your ever affectionate

F. J. W.

31. *R.B. to Julia Wedgwood, 8 Mar. 1869*

Honestly, I do not understand what you mean, or, at least, *why* you mean what, on the whole, I suppose you may. If I wanted to play at picking out causes of offence, I could charge you with plenty of such, by implication, offence, I mean, in the attributing real falseness to me—the last thing in your thoughts, I well know. There was certainly as great a loss to me as to you—if I treat you as I would be treated, and believe you—in the cessation of our intercourse.° Now, why not? No playing and nonsense—in what respect was I left then with better resources than you? If you even meant such an enormous absurdity as that I saw more company, in one or another way, than you,—first, I doubt the fact—I should not wonder if you had a face to face acquaintance with just as many men and women that count as such, as I had or have: then—resources of the other sort—you do not seriously talk to me in the strain of, 'Ah, my gossip, you are older and more learned (in Guidoism) and a man!'—All I know is, that in some ambiguous way I am motioned to step up on to some pretty sort of pedestal whence I am to observe you somewhere below—which I decline doing.

I lost something peculiar in you, which I shall not see replaced—is that stated soberly enough? I neither can—ever could, nor would, were I able—replace anything I have once had: I think I *have* things thoroughly and effectually and, in a sense, sufficingly; it would be all the worse could I say to myself 'These half-experiences may be expected [to recur] or, if the missing *halves* follow, *that* may do as well, and be novel besides.' But the acquiescence in absolute loss should remove all misconception or scruple as to what proves, when it subsequently presents itself—gain—new and unexpected. You now talk about having 'done' something, 'wisely or unwisely' for yourself: I shall not believe you ever 'did' anything in the matter, but let be, let *do*—wisely, I have no doubt: I think you will not accuse me, after my four years' silence, with saying to the contrary—for I am not given to 'striving and crying.'

Yes, the British Public like, and more than like me, this week, they let their admiration ray out on me, and at sundry congregations of men wherein I have figured these three or four days, I have seen, felt and, thru' white gloves, handled a true affectionateness not un-mingled with awe—which all comes of the Queen's having desired to see me, and three other extraordinary persons, last Thursday: whereupon we took tea together and pretended to converse for an hour and twenty minutes; the other worthies, with the wives of such as were provided, being Carlyle, Grote and Lyell.° This eventful incident in my life—say, the dove descending out of heaven upon my head—seems to have opened peoples' minds at last: and provided the Queen don't send for the Siamese Twins,° the Beautiful Circassian Lady, and Miss Saurin° as her next quartette-party, I am in a way to rise: you see, I am not disposed to contest that some 'resources' *are*!

I think you are in the wrong about the proper treatment of facts—I don't say, as to *my* treatment of them. They want explaining, not altering. As to being 'impatient with what has occupied me for years'—no: it is *done*; I occupy myself elsewhere, or else look else-whither. Goodbye: I wish I could see you again: last Wednesday, I sat at dinner close to an acquaintance of some thirty years—he was very kind, and kept talking so long that I said 'Come, we must go into the drawing- room.' On Saturday he fell, dead. He was wanting me to meet somebody at his house, whom I abstain[ed] from meeting, and he urged that life was too short and uncertain to allow delay in the matter. I was obdurate notwithstanding.

Goodbye, again!

R. B.

32. R.B. to Isabella Blagden, 19 Jan. 1870

[...] I have just been reading Shelley's life, as Rossetti° tells it,—and when I think how utterly different was the fancy I had of him forty years ago from the facts as they front one to-day, I can only avoid despising myself by remembering that I judged in pure ignor-ance and according to the testimony of untruthful friends. Well, I go with you a good way in the feeling about Tennyson's new book:° it is all out of my head already. We look at the object of art in poetry so differently! Here is an Idyll about a knight being untrue to his friend and yielding to the temptation of that friend's mistress after having engaged to assist him in his suit. I should judge the conflict in the knight's soul the proper subject to describe: Tennyson thinks he should describe the castle, and effect of the moon on its towers, and anything *but* the soul. The monotony, however, you must expect—if the new is to be of a piece with the old. Morris° is sweet, pictorial, clever always—but a weariness to me by this time. The lyrics were the 'first sprightly runnings'—this that follows is a laboured brew with the old flavour but not *body*. So with Tennyson—the old 'Galahad' is to me incomparably better than a dozen centuries of the 'Grail,' 'Coming of Arthur,' & so on. I ought to be somewhat surprised to find myself thinking so, since it seems also the opinion of everybody: even the reviews hardly keep on the old chime of laudation.[...]

33. R.B. to Isabella Blagden, 19 Aug. 1871

[...] The strain of London life is too much for me, or rather, *has* been too much, when added to the other strain of cares and fears which, I hope, are over now: I don't know whether I am 'vivacious' as ever, but I am susceptible enough of pain,—perhaps, pain which I make for myself by unnecessary anticipation,—still, pain no less. At this place, I and Pen are alone at a shooting lodge some three rugged miles from the house: he goes away early to sport, and I am blessedly alone till I like to come here—perhaps at 4 or 5 o clock. I have even a piano, books of course—& I find an impulse to write: if I were let alone, I should do far better than I have done. But, NO, dearest Isa,—the simple truth is that *she*° was the poet, and I the clever person by comparison: remember her limited experience of all kinds, and what she made of it—remember, on the other hand, how my uninterrupted health & strength, & practice with the world have helped me. *One* such intimate knowledge as I have had with many a person would have taught her,—had she been inclined to learn: though I doubt if she would have dirtied her hands for any scientific purpose. All is best as it is—for her, & me too: I shall wash my hands clean in a minute, before I see her, as I trust to do.[...]

34. R.B. to Mrs George Henry Lewis, 9 May 1876

Dear Mrs Lewis,

It was some time before I could properly read Mr Fosbroke's poems:° and I confess to having delayed a little the expression of how they strike me. It is hard indeed to have to seem niggardly of praise when one would so gladly give it, to any amount not quite incompatible with telling the truth—as one *sees* the truth, you must remember. For I wish everybody that cares to ask my opinion about poetry to bear in mind that my own claims to be a poet have always been strongly contested, and not altogether by people I despised: so, there is always an appeal from me to a more favourable and presumably competent judge. I cannot expect any great success for the author of these two volumes—that is, success of the kind worth having from the critics worth consulting: there is plenty of the superficial glitter of language, and profusion of figure, to attract another kind of taste: and throughout there is abundant evidence of acquaintance and sympathy with what I should call 'poeticalness';— and these qualities suffice for very many readers—as the extracts from the periodicals, which are appended, prove sufficiently. But somehow it is found that such success neither goes deep, nor strikes root: only creative power does that,—and I cannot, with all the will in the world, see creation here—nor indeed in one out of the dozen volumes of verse which come to me in this way. The misfortune is, that the writers are probably superior in endowment to nine-tenths of their neighbours: they have cultivation, a pictorial and musical faculty, high and fine aims—and yet the wings for actual flight are rudimentary and only distinguish them from the groundlings without availing to make them at their ease in the air. Pray tell this, in your own better—*not* kinder—form to Mr Fosbroke, with sincere thanks for the honour he did me in wishing for the opinion I give with great reluctance: and believe me, Dear Mrs Lewis,—

Yours very sincerely

R Browning

35. R.B. to a Correspondent, 11 May 1876

Dear Friend,

It would ill become me to waste a word on my own feelings except inasmuch as they can be common to us both, in such a situation as you describe yours to be, and which, by sympathy, I can make mine by the anticipation of a few years at most. It is a great thing, the greatest, that a human being should have passed the probation of life, and sum up its experience in a witness to the power and love of God. I dare congratulate you. All the help I can offer, in my poor degree, is the assurance that I see ever *more* reason to hold by the same hope—and that by no means in ignorance of what has been advanced to the contrary; and for your sake I would wish it to be true that I had so much of 'genius' as to permit the testimony of an especially privileged insight to come in aid of the ordinary argument. For I know I, myself, have been aware of the communication of something more subtle than a ratiocinative process, when the convictions of 'genius' have thrilled my soul to its depths, as when Napoleon, shutting up the New Testament, said of Christ: 'Do you know that I am an understander of men? Well, He was no man!' ('Savez-vous que je me connais en hommes? Eh bien, celui-là ne fut pas un homme.') Or as when Charles

Lamb, in a gay fancy with some friends as to how he and they would feel if the greatest of the dead were to appear suddenly in flesh and blood once more, on the final suggestion, 'And if Christ entered this room?' changed his manner at once, and stuttered out, as his manner was when moved, 'You see, if Shakespeare entered, we should all rise; if *He* appeared we must kneel.' Or, not to multiply instances, as when Dante wrote what I will transcribe from my wife's Testament, wherein I recorded it fourteen years ago, 'Thus I believe, thus I affirm, thus I am certain it is, that from this life I shall pass to another better, there, where that lady lives of whom my soul was enamoured.' Dear friend, I may have wearied you in spite of your good will. God bless you, sustain, and receive you! Reciprocate this blessing with

Yours affectionately,

Robert Browning.

36. R.B. to Tennyson, 5 Aug. 1889

My dear Tennyson,

To-morrow is your birthday—indeed a memorable one. Let me say I associate myself with the universal pride of our country in your glory, and in its hope that for many and many a year we may have your very self among us—secure that your poetry will be a wonder and delight to all those appointed to come after. And for my own part, let me further say, I have loved you dearly. May God bless you and yours!

At no moment from first to last of my acquaintance with your works, or friendship with yourself, have I had any other feeling, expressed or kept silent, than this which an opportunity allows me to utter—that I am and ever shall be, my dear Tennyson, admiringly and affectionately yours,

Robert Browning.

NOTES

Notes have been kept to a minimum, but with a writer as allusive and sometimes obscure as Browning this has not proved easy. In general I have limited annotation to matters of allusion, quotation, and (only if unavoidable) explication. Dates of composition and publication are noted, as are comments Browning himself made on his own work. I have not recorded textual variants. All translations are my own, unless otherwise stated. References to Browning's correspondence use the following abbreviations:

Correspondence   P. Kelley and R. Hudson (eds.), *The Browning Correspondence* (Winfield, Kan., 1984–   ).

Dearest Isa   E. C. McAleer (ed.), *Dearest Isa: Robert Browning's Letters to Isabella Blagden* (Austin, Tex., 1951)

DeVane   William C. DeVane, *A Browning Handbook* (2nd edn., New York, 1955).

Hood   T. L. Hood (ed.), *Letters of Robert Browning Collected by Thomas J. Wise* (1933).

Kintner   E. Kintner (ed.), *The Letters of Robert Browning and Elizabeth Barrett Barrett 1845–6* (2 vols. paginated as 1, Cambridge, Mass., 1969).

New Letters   W. C. DeVane and K. Knickerbocker (eds.), *New Letters of Robert Browning* (New Haven, 1950).

RB/JW   Richard Curle (ed.), *Robert Browning and Julia Wedgwood: A Broken Friendship as Revealed in Their Letters* (London, 1937).

Trumpeter   W. S. Peterson (ed.), *Browning's Trumpeter: The Correspondence of Robert Browning and Frederick J. Furnivall 1872–1889* (Washington, 1979)

Pauline

1 Composed between 22 Oct. 1832 (the date given at the end of the poem) and Jan. 1833 (the date at the end of the epigraph). It was published Mar. 1833. Browning saw Edmund Kean act the part of Richard III on 22 Oct. 1832; inspired by the occasion, he conceived a plan to write a series of works in different genres (a poem, a novel, an opera, and so on) and publish each under a different pseudonym. In the event only the first of these projects, the poem, was completed. In a handwritten note, later reproduced in a letter to a friend (*Correspondence*, iii. 265), Browning notes that *Pauline* 'was written in pursuance of a foolish plan which occupied me mightily for a time, and which had for its object the enabling me to assume & realize I know not how many different characters;—meanwhile the world was never to guess that "Brown, Smith, Jones, & Robinson" . . . the respective Authors of this poem, the other

novel, such an opera, such a speech &c &c were no other than one and
the same individual.... Only this crab [apple] remains of the shapely
Tree of Life in this Fools paradise of mine.'

The work was printed privately, using £30 donated by Browning's
aunt; it apparently failed to sell a single copy. Browning sent a copy to
John Stuart Mill, hoping the eminent older man (whom he did not
know personally) would review it, and thereby raise its literary profile.
Mill never wrote his review, but he did return his copy to Browning
heavily annotated. Some of these marginalia, and Browning's own
replies, are reproduced in the notes here; but most devastating for
Browning's sense of himself as a poet was Mill's general observation:
'with considerable poetic powers, this writer seems to me possessed with
a more intense and morbid self-consciousness than I ever knew in any
sane human being...A mind in that state can only be regenerated by
some new passion, and I know not what to wish for him but that he may
meet with a *real* Pauline. Meanwhile he should not attempt to shew how
a person may be *recovered* from this morbid state—for *he* is hardly
convalescent, and "what should we speak of but what we know?"' (For
a full account of Mill's comments, see W. S. Peterson and F. L.
Standley, 'The J. S. Mill Marginalia in Robert Browning's *Pauline*',
Papers of the Bibliographical Society of America, 66 (1972), 135–70.)
Browning was so struck with Mill's criticism, and with the public failure
of the work, that he suppressed it, keeping it out of collected editions of
his work until 1868. One reason for his sensitiveness may be the auto-
biographical provenance of the poem; although Browning always
declared that *Pauline* was 'dramatic' it is nevertheless based closely on
his own youthful experiences, particularly with respect to his crisis of
faith, and the powerful influence of the poetry of Percy Bysshe Shelley
(1792–1822).

1 *Motto*. 'I am no longer what I was | And I know I never shall be again',
   from Clement Marot (1496–1544), *Diverse Epigrams*, 219.

   Epigraph. Browning adapts a passage from the preface of Renaissance
   alchemist Cornelius Agrippa's book *De Occulta Philosophia* ('On Occult
   Philosophy', or 'On Magic', 1531): 'No doubt the title of our book may
   be unusual enough to tempt many to read it, including some with biased
   views, or weakened intellects, or perhaps even hostile intentions, who in
   ignorance, barely even knowing the title, will protest that we are
   teaching the Forbidden, scattering heresies, offending the pious,
   shocking those with enlightened minds:...So conscientious are these
   sorts of people that neither Apollo, nor the Muses, nor an Angel from
   heaven could vindicate me from their execrations: accordingly I counsel
   these people not to read my works, nor try to understand them, nor
   remember them: for they are noxious, poisonous: Acheron's gate is in
   this book, it speaks harshly; let them beware, it will collapse their minds.
   But if you come without prejudice, with the same discretion and pru-
   dence as the honey-gathering bees, then you can read in safety. You will
   receive much learning, and a great deal of enjoyment as well. Still, if you

come across things that don't please you, skip them, don't use them. I AM NOT RECOMMENDING THESE THINGS TO YOU, I AM ONLY TELLING YOU ABOUT THEM. But don't reject the rest for that reason.... So, if I have spoken too freely, please pardon my immaturity, for I wrote this being scarcely even a young man.' After the date, Browning clarifies the last Latin sentence by adding 'V[*ixeram*] A[*nnos*] XX.', which is to say: 'I was 20'.

2 l. 34. *fancy*. The creative imagination (the 'it' of the next line).

4 l. 112. *witch*. Probably without supernatural overtones, meaning only 'a bewitchingly beautiful young woman'.

ll. 112–14. 'A curious idealisation of self-worship, very fine, though' (Mill).

5 l. 142. Mill underlined 'HIS award' and wrote 'what does this mean? His opinion of yourself?'; Browning replied 'The award of fame to Him. The late acknowledgement of Shelley's genius.'

l. 151. *Sun-treader*. Shelley: Browning derives the epithet from Greek (see Aeschylus, *Prometheus Bound*, 791; an appropriate source, in that Shelley completed Aeschylus' drama with his *Prometheus Unbound*). Apollo, god of the Sun, was also god of poetry. There may also be a Greek–English pun on 'Percy Shelley', since the Greek root *persi* means 'destroyer' (i.e. 'treader', in the sense, common in Shelley, of 'trampler' or 'extinguisher'), and *Hele(y)* (without the 's' because Greek has no 'sh' sound) means '*sol*, the sun'.

8 ll. 250–1. *Created by some power... Having no part in God*. The distinction between 'power' and 'God' is from Shelley's writing (for instance, 'Mont Blanc'), where the former quality is the impersonal force of universal Necessity, quite removed from the latter, the personalized, anthropomorphic God of Christianity.

9 l. 313. *These*. The (apparently innate) elements of the narrator's psychological make-up; having detailed their derivation, he now goes on to elaborate 'their course'.

ll. 321–5. *And I myself went... to Tenedos*. The references to Greek myth are not entirely clear, but seem to involve Apollo (the 'god'), Atlas (the 'giant', a rebellious Titan condemned to stand at the western edge of the world supporting the heavens on his shoulders), Orion (the 'old hunter'), and a Greek military leader who took part in the siege of Troy (Tenedos is a small island off the coast from Troy).

10 ll. 334–5. *The naked Swift-footed... Proserpine's hair*. This is uncertain; the messenger of the gods, Hermes, was known as 'swift' (but why 'naked' here?); and it was he who retrieved Proserpine after her abduction by Hades, god of the Underworld.

11 l. 403. *White Way*. The milky way.

l. 404. *man*. Shelley.

12 ll. 433–6. *And I was lonely... key to life.* Browning enrolled in the University of London ('far from woods and fields') in 1828, where his studies may have included Plato. He left the university in 1829 without taking a degree, and this and the subsequent sections of the poem (detailing, as they do, idealism turning into disillusion) may owe something to the experience.

13 l. 479. *Arab birds.* There was a tradition that some types of birds of paradise lacked legs, and lived their entire lives in the air (the tradition derives from bird-catchers' habits of removing the legs from dead birds before exporting them).

14 ll. 497–8. *soul | Yet fluttering.* Another Greek pun: *psuchee* means both 'soul' and 'butterfly'.

l. 505. *erst.* Formerly.

16 ll. 567–71. *that king... coming doom.* In a letter to his friend Thomas Wise (5 Nov. 1886) Browning said of this passage: 'The "King" is Agamemnon, in the Tragedy of that name by Aeschylus, whose treading the purple carpets spread before him by his wife, preparatory to his murder, is a notable passage' (*RB/JW*, 256).

l. 572. *him.* The reference is to Sophocles', *Ajax.* The Greek hero, after the fall of Troy, quarrelled with his colleagues. He went to kill them, but was fooled by the gods into thinking a flock of sheep were his enemies and unwittingly slaughtered the beasts instead.

l. 573. *boy.* Orestes, son of the murdered Agamemnon, who kills his own mother in revenge, and is pursued by Furies as a result (see Aeschylus' *Oresteia*, of which the *Agamemnon* is the first part).

17 l. 624. *harpy.* Rapacious mythological being with woman's face and body and bird's wings and claws; associated with divine retribution.

l. 643. *seraphim.* Heavenly angels. The sense of the whole passage (634–43) is that although in this world reason (which can be abstract) can outstrip love (which must have an earthly object), love unchained from earthly considerations would, and will, far outsoar reason, and rise up to the level of the angels.

18 ll. 648–9. 'Inconsistent with what precedes' (Mill).

l. 656. *Andromeda.* In Greek myth, Andromeda was to be sacrificed to appease a ravenous sea-monster that was threatening Ethopia, but was rescued at the last minute by the hero Perseus. In the passage that follows (656–67), the narrator is describing Caravaggio's painting of Andromeda's rescue, of which Browning possessed an engraving.

ll. 669–75. *I will be gifted... triumph through decay.* In a later handwritten note in the Mill edition Browning identifies this passage as referring to the actor Edmund Kean, whose performance in *Richard III* at Richmond on 22 Oct. 1832 (the date cited at the end of the poem) provided the germ for *Pauline.*

18 ll 678–80. 'Deeply true' (Mill).

19 l. 690. *prejudice.* A pre-formed opinion, without the sense of unwarranted bias.

22 l. 811 *footnote.* 'I'm sorry to say that my poor friend cannot always be perfectly understood in what remains to be read of this curious fragment—indeed, of all people he is the least suited to elucidate what in its very nature can only ever be dream and confusion. Besides which, I am not so sure but that trying to improve the coherence of certain parts of this would only run the risk of damaging the only merit to which so singular a production can lay claim—that of giving a more-or-less precise idea of the sort of work of which this is just a sketch. This unpretentious début, this stirring of passions that rises up and then subsides, these currents of the soul, this sudden return upon oneself, and, more than anything, the quite peculiar nature of my friend's mind, make changes almost impossible. The reasons he gives elsewhere, and some others that are even more compelling, persuade me to look favourably on this writing, which I would otherwise have counselled him to throw into the fire. I don't believe any the less in the great principle of all composition—the principle seen in Shakespeare, Raphael, and Beethoven, that the concentration of ideas owes more to conception than execution. I have every reason to fear that my friend is still a stranger to the former—and I very much doubt whether even with a redoubling of effort he could acquire the latter. The best thing would be to burn this; but what is to be done?

I suppose that in what follows he refers to some examination of the soul (or of his own soul) that he once made, to discover the sequence of those objectives that it would be possible for him to accomplish, each of which, once achieved, would form a sort of plateau from which other goals, other projects, other pleasures would emerge, and these in turn be surmounted. The outcome of this was the idea that forgetfulness and sleep would end everything. This idea, which I do not altogether grasp, is perhaps equally unintelligible to him as to me. PAULINE.'

23 l. 851. *Olivet.* The Mount of Olives, overlooking the garden of Gethsemane, near Jerusalem.

24 l. 860. 'Strange transition' (Mill).

25 ll. 919–21. *one Isle . . . hopes of home. Odyssey* ix relates how Odysseus' crew abandoned their posts and adopted a life of ease amongst the lotus-eaters.

26 l. 951. *The land.* Switzerland

l. 964. *fair pale sister.* The allusion is to Sophocles' *Antigone*, in which Antigone prefers to die rather than allow her brother's body to be dishonoured.

ll. 974–5. Mill underlined 'I shall be | Prepared', and wrote 'he is always talking of being *prepared*—what for?' Browning's reply was: 'why, "that's tellings," as schoolboys say.'

Paracelsus

29 Written late 1834 and early 1835, and published 15 Aug. 1835, the expense of publication being met by Browning's father. By focusing on a historical figure (the alchemist Theophrastus Bombast von Hohenstein, known as Paracelsus, 1493–1541) Browning hoped to distance himself from the charge of 'morbid self-consciousness' he had incurred in *Pauline*. The first edition contained a preface, not reprinted in later editions, in which Browning said that 'instead of having recourse to an external machinery of incidents to create and evolve the crisis I desire to produce, I have ventured to display somewhat minutely the mood itself in its rise and progress, and have suffered the agency by which it is influenced and determined, to be generally discernible in its effects alone, and subordinate throughout, if not altogether excluded: and this for a reason. I have endeavoured to write a poem, not a drama ... a work like mine depends more immediately on the intelligence and sympathy of the reader for its success—indeed were my scenes stars it must be his co-operating fancy which, supplying all chasms, shall connect the scattered lights into one constellation.'

    Paracelsus consists of five acts or parts, of which only the fifth is reproduced here. Part I ('Paracelsus Aspires') is set at Würzburg in 1512, where Aureole Paracelsus is telling his friends, Festus and Michal, of his ambitions; which are, modestly, 'to comprehend the works of God, | And God himself, and all God's intercourse | With the human mind.' The path to this absolute knowledge lies in alchemy, and though his friends warn him of the possible consequences of his hubris, the scene ends with him readying to 'plunge' into his studies. Part II, 'Paracelsus Attains', shifts the scene to the house of a Greek conjurer in Constantinople in 1521. Paracelsus has not uncovered the ultimate secret he was searching for, and he is in gloomy mood ('Time fleets, youth fades, life is an empty dream'). He encounters a young poet, Aprile, and the two exchange perspectives on the world.

> *Paracelus*. I am he that aspired to KNOW: and thou?
> *Aprile*. I would LOVE infinitely, and be loved!

Aprile later dies, telling us that 'God is the perfect poet, | Who in his person acts his own creations.' Although at first contemptuous of Aprile's position, Paracelsus gradually becomes aware of its fundamental truth. By the time of Part III, 'Paracelsus', it is 1526. Paracelsus has returned to Basle to work as Professor at the University. In conversation with his old friend, Festus, he reveals that he detests the students he has to teach, and despite the outward trappings of success feels he has utterly failed. Part IV, 'Paracelsus Aspires' is set in 1528. Paracelsus again aspires, although his aims are now modified by his sense of the necessity of both knowledge and love ('I have tried each way singly: now for both'). Part V sees Paracelsus on his deathbed, summing up the wisdom he has accrued during his lifetime. He is attended by his faithful friend Festus, and sometimes in delirium calls on the (now dead) figure of Aprile, the poet.

31 l. 96. *I am Erasmus*. Festus pretends to be this eminent scholar with hopes of rousing Paracelsus.

32 l. 123. *Jove strikes the Titans down*. Paracelsus (presumably in delirium) conflates two separate myths; that of the rebellion of the Titans against Uranus, and of the rebellion of giants against Uranus' successor as King of the Gods, Zeus (Jove).

l. 126. *plunge*. Phaeton, Apollo's son, took over the business of driving the chariot of the Sun from his father for one day; but he was not up to the task, the chariot ran out of control and would have set fire to the whole earth had not Zeus struck him down with a thunderbolt.

33 l. 148. *empiric*. An untrained doctor or quack (Paracelsus' self-depre-cating assessment of himself).

l. 181. *Galen*. Renowned Greek physician (2nd century AD) and author of medical textbook; in Paracelsus' age Galen's work still commanded a great deal of respect. Browning added a footnote to the text at this point: 'He did in effect affirm that he had disputed with Galen in the vestibule of hell.'

34 l. 187. *Zoroaster*. Persian religious prophet and fire-worshipper, founder of Zoroastrianism.

39 l. 386. *phares*. Lighthouses.

l. 388. *bale*. Burden.

41 ll. 484–5. *canes, . . . fan-trees, tamarisks*. Varieties of tropical vegetations (grass, palm tree, and bush respectively).

43 l. 554. *Azoth*. Paracelsus' sword, in the hilt of which he kept his 'elixir of life' (probably opium); or, according to his enemies, in the hilt of which lived his diabolic familiar.

45 l. 642. *What God is, what we are*. In the first edition, but not sub-sequently, Browning annotated this line with a quotation from Renauldin's biography of Paracelus: 'Paracelse faisait profession du Panthéisme le plus grossier' ('Paracelsus professed the worst sort of Pantheism').

46 l. 666. *psaltress*. Female musician (the psaltery was a medieval stringed instrument).

ll. 672–3. *chrysalids*. Larval insects in their shells.   *dorrs*. Flying beetles.

46-7 ll. 683–719. At the end of his life Browning was to claim that this passage anticipated by twenty years Darwin's *Origin of Species*. Writing to his friend F. J. Furnivall on 11 Oct. 1881 with respect to Darwin, he said: 'all that seems *proved* in Darwin's scheme was a conception familiar to me from the beginning: see in *Paracelsus* the progressive development from senseless matter to organised, until man's appearance (*Part V*)'

(*Trumpeter*, 34). As several critics have pointed out, this is something of a misrepresentation of Darwin.

Pippa Passes

53 Most probably written between summer 1839 and 1840. Published Apr. 1841 as the first in a series of eight pamphlets with the general title *Bells and Pomegranates*. Asked by Elizabeth Barrett to 'tell me what you mean precisely by your "Bells and Pomegranates"', Browning replied: 'The Rabbis make Bells and Pomegranates symbolical of Pleasure and Profit, of the Gay and the Grave, the Poetry and the Prose, Singing and Sermonizing—such a mixture of effects as in the original hour (that is quarter of an hour) of confidence and creation' (letter to E.B.B., 18 Oct. 1845, *Kintner*, 241). The source of the imagery ('the Rabbis') was Exod. 28: 33. The idea behind the undertaking was to produce popular poetry and drama in a cheap format (the pamphlets were paperback and cost sixpence).

Of the origin of *Pippa Passes*, Browning's friend and biographer Mrs Orr (in her *Life and Letters of Robert Browning* (1871), 55) records: 'Mr. Browning was walking alone, in a wood near Dulwich [in London], when the image flashed upon him of someone walking thus alone through life; one apparently too obscure to leave a trace of his or her passage, yet exercising a lasting though unconscious influence at every step of it; and the image shaped itself into the little silk-winder of Asolo, Felippa or Pippa.'

Introduction. The scene is set in the northern Italian town of Asolo, which is located in the region around Trevisio. Browning had visited the town in 1838, and greatly admired its beauty; he was to return frequently, and his last published collection of poetry is called *Asolando*.

55 l. 88. *martagon*. Variety of lily.

l. 89. *St Agnes*. Virgin teenage martyr from the 4th century AD.

l. 90. *Turk bird's poll*. Turkey's head.

56 l. 100. *weevil and chafer*. Types of beetle.

l. 131. *Possagno church*. Designed by Antonio Canvoa (1757–1822). Possagno is near Asolo.

58 l. 181. *Dome*. Cathedral.

59 l. 213. *cicala*. Grasshopper.

Part I. Morning

60 ll. 28 *St Marks*. Cathedral in Venice, about thirty miles distant.

ll. 29–30 *Vicenza . . . Padua*. Italian towns, twenty-five miles south-west and south (respectively) of Asolo.

l. 53. *wittol*. Knowing cuckold.

l. 56. *Black*. Red (from the Italian *vino nero*).

60 l. 58. *Duomo*. Cathedral.

l. 59. *Capuchin*. Friar of the Franciscan order.

61 l. 76. *proof-mark*. A mark on a print or engraving that shows to which print-run it belongs (in general the earlier the print-run, the more valuable the print).

l. 83. *coil*. Fuss.

62 l. 102. *Venus' body*. Italian oath ('corpore di Venere').

64 l. 170. *campanula*. Bellflower

66 l. 235. *double heartsease*. Pansy.

67 l. 294. *Trieste*. Adriatic port not far from Venice.

ll. 299-302. The student's joke depends upon suggesting that the poet ought to have written in a more 'popular' style, and then providing an instance from advertising copy for quack remedies and nostrums.   *Æsculapius*. Greek god of medicine.   *Catalogue of the drugs*. Parody of the Homeric 'catalogue of the ships' near the beginning of the *Iliad*.   *Hebe*. Goddess of youth.   *Phœbus*. The god Apollo.   *Mercury*. Messenger of the gods.   *bolus*. Pill. The word humorously dropped at the end of the speech is 'pox' (to rhyme with 'box').

68 l. 307. *et canibus nostris*. 'And to our dogs' (quoted from Vergil, *Eclogues*, iii. 66-7).

69 l. 358. *fribble*. A trifling person.

l. 362. *Psiche-fanciulla*. Canova's famous statue of Psyche with a butterfly.

l. 365. *Pietà*. Statue of the Virgin Mary holding the crucified body of Christ.

l. 381. *Malamocco*. Island near Venice.

l. 382. *Alciphron*. Greek author from 2nd century AD, renowned as a model of good style. The reference to 'hair like sea moss' comes in his *Letters* 3. 1, and describes a handsome young man.

70 l. 387. *Tydeus*. Greek hero, and one of the seven warriors who attacked the city of Thebes (the 'Seven against Thebes').

l. 390 *Fenice*. The 'Phœnix', a theatre and opera-house in Venice; it had been rebuilt in 1836 and was an important venue for operatic production.

l. 408. *Hannibal Scratchy*. Joke at the expense of Annibale Caracci (1540-1609), Italian painter.

Part II. Noon

72 l. 39. *minion*. Loved one.   *Coluthus*. 'The Rape of Helen', a poem written in the Homeric style by this 6th-century AD Alexandrian poet, remained unknown until it was discovered by Cardinal Bessarion in the 15th century (see l. 40).

72 l. 40. *Bistre*. Dark brown.

ll. 46–7. *He said . . . shaft*. Translation of *Odyssey* xxii. 8. Odysseus has returned home and is about to set about slaughtering the suitors of his wife, beginning with Antinous.

l. 50. *Almaign Kaiser*. German emperor.

l. 54. *Hippolyta*. Queen of the Amazons.

l. 59. *bay-filleted*. Crowned with bay leaves (thought to protect against lightning strikes).

l. 61. *Hipparchus*. Greek tyrant, whose killers hid their daggers in a myrtle tree.

73 l. 92. *Dryad*. Wood-nymph.

77 l. 258. *Kate the Queen*. Caterina Cornaro (*c.*1450–1510) was a Venetian who became Queen of Cyprus; when the Venetians overthrew her reign they compensated by giving her Asolo to rule over.

78 l. 270. *jesses*. Falconer's straps for fastening a hawk's legs.

79 l. 306. *Ancona*. Adriatic town, south of Venice.

l. 328. *Bluphocks*. Browning's note is a quotation from Matt. 5: 45. The name is a joke at the expense of the journal *Edinburgh Review*, whose binding was blue and fox (i.e. reddish-brown), and which was known for its savage reviews of poetry.

l. 329. *Intendant*. Steward of the estate.

80 l. 334. *grig*. Grasshopper.

l. 337. *Koenigsberg*. Capital city of Prussia.

l. 339. *Chaldee*. Aramaic language (the mother-tongue of Jesus). 'Syriac' (in l. 345) is also an Aramaic dialect.

l. 346. *Celarent, Darii, Ferio!* Mnemonic used in the learning of logic. The Latin is meaningless, the point of the words being to encode vowel sounds.

ll. 350–3. *How Moses . . . salaam*. Instead of being something of importance such as Moses bringing a plague of locusts against Pharaoh (Exod. 10: 13–15), or Jonah's fleeing to Tarshish (Jonah 1: 1–3), or Balaam and his ass (Num. 22: 22–34), translating the Chaldean inscription reveals nothing significant.

l. 356. *Beveridge*. 18th-century Calvinist theologian, introduced here for the pun on 'beverage'.

l. 357. *Greek dog-sage*. Cynic philosopher.

l. 358. *Charon's wherry*. Charon's boat, which he used to ferry souls across the Styx (i.e. the Stygian Ferry, l. 362); the fee for this service was one obolus, a small Greek coin.

l. 359. *Hecate*. The goddess of the underworld was sometimes propitiated with offerings of food (such as 'lupine seed').

80 l. 362. *zwanzigers*. Austrian coinage (at the time the Austrians ruled northern Italy, including Asolo).

l. 369. *Metternich*. Conservative and reactionary Austrian statesman (1773–1859).

81 l. 375. *Panurge consults Hertrippa*. He does so about his marriage in Rabelais's *Gargantua and Pantagruel*.   *Believest thou, King Agrippa*. St Paul asks this question (about the prophets) in Acts 26: 27.

l. 395. *Carbonari*. Secret political society.

l. 396. *Spielberg*. Austrian prison.

Part III. Evening.

82 l. 6. *Lucius Junius!* Known as 'Brutus', he drove the kings from Rome in the 6th century BC and founded the Roman Republic.

l. 14. *old Franz*. Austrian Emperor Francis I (he ruled 1804–35).

l. 19. *Pellicos*. Silvio Pellico, Italian writer and revolutionary, who had been in prison 1820–30. He published an account of his incarceration in 1832.

85 ll. 122–3. *Andrea . . . Pier . . . Gualtier*. These fellow conspirators are fictional.

l. 138. *That treaty*. The Treaty of Vienna (1815) which ceded control of northern Italy to the Austrians.

l. 148. *I am the bright and morning-star*. Rev. 22: 16.

l. 149. *to such an one I give the morning-star*. 'And he that overcometh, and keepeth my works unto the end, to him will I give power over the nations . . . And I will give him the morning star' (Rev. 2: 26–8).

86 l. 163. *Titian*. Venetian painter of the 16th century; an altarpiece by him is in the cathedral at Treviso.

87 l. 224. *Python*. Monster slain by Apollo at Delphi.

88 l. 236. *fig-peckers*. Small birds, eaten as a delicacy.

l. 251. *Deuzans and junetings, leather-coats*. All varieties of apple.

89 l. 293. *ortolans*. Another flavoursome species of small bird.

l. 295. *Polenta*. A sort of pudding.

Part IV. Night.

90 l. 4. *Benedicto benedicatur*. A blessing.

l. 7. *Messina*. Sicilian town.

l. 8. *Assumption Day*. Festival in celebration of the Virgin's ascension (15 Aug.).

91 ll. 15–16. *Ascoli, Fermo and Fossombruno*. Italian cities far to the south of Asolo.

91 l. 46. *Correggio.* The Italian painter (*c.*1494–1534) Antonio Allegri; he took the name of his native town, hence Ugo's confusion.

92 l. 65. *podere.* Farm.

l. 91. *soldo.* Small coin.

93 l. 132. *complot.* Conspiracy.

95 l. 191. *Miserere mei, Domine.* 'Lord, have mercy on me'.

Epilogue

l. 2. *dray.* Nest.

l. 5. *hedge-shrew.* Fieldmouse.   *lob-worm.* Lug-worm.

97 l. 70. *Brenta.* River that flows west of Asolo.

l. 88. *mavis.* Song-thrush.   *merle.* Blackbird.   *throstle.* Thrush.

l. 91. *howlet.* Owl.

98 l. 94. *complines.* Evening prayers.

l. 96. *twat.* Browning assumed that the word referred to some part of a nun's attire; Browning was wrong (the word refers to female genitalia).

Dramatic Lyrics

99 This collection was published November 1842 as the third pamphlet in the *Bells and Pomegranates* series.

Cavalier Tunes. Probably written 1836–7, the same period Browning was working on his Civil War play *Strafford.* The three lyrics appeared at the head of *Dramatic Lyrics.*

I. Marching Along

l. 2. *crop-headed.* During the English Civil War (1642–50), anti-royalist 'Roundheads' were distinguished by their short haircuts, pro-royalist 'Cavaliers' by their long hair.

l. 3. *pressing.* Impressing, forcing into military service.

l. 7. *Pym.* Sir John Pym, leading roundhead.   *carles.* Low-born fellows, churls.

l. 10. *pasty.* A sort of meat and vegetable pie.

ll. 13–14. *Hampden...young Harry.* The four men mentioned here were all prominent roundheads.

l. 15. *Rupert.* Prince Rupert of Bavaria, nephew to the king and an important royalist general.

100 *II. Give a Rouse.* The title means 'drink a health to'.

100 l. 16. *Noll*. Oliver Cromwell. His 'damned troopers' were the renowned 'New Model Army.' This lyric relates to a later period in the Civil War than 'Marching Along.'

III. Boot and Saddle

101 l. 10. *Brancepeth*. A castle in north-east England.

l. 11. *fay*. Faith.

My Last Duchess. On first publication in *Dramatic Lyrics* (1842) this poem was paired with *Count Gismond* (see below) under the title *Italy and France: My Last Duchess* was 'Italy', *Gismond* 'France'. The poems were separated in subsequent editions. Scholars have found an original for the narrator in Alfonso II (1533–98), fifth Duke of Ferrara ('Ferrara' is identified as speaker at the head of the poem, a detail Browning first added in 1849). The date of composition is not known exactly, but it may have been early 1842.

l. 3. *Frà Pandolf*. Fictional painter, identified by title ('Fra' means 'brother') as a monk.

102 ll. 45–6. *I gave...stopped together*. Asked to clarify the fate of the Duchess, an elderly Browning 'replied meditatively, "Yes, I meant that commands were that she be put to death." And then, after a pause, he added, with a characteristic dash of expression, and as if the thought had just started up in his mind, "Or he might have had her shut up in a convent"' (H. Corson, *An Introduction to the Study of Robert Browning's Poetry*, 3rd edn. (Boston, 1903), p. viii).

l. 56. *Claus of Innsbruck*. Another fictional artist.

103 *Count Gismond*. Originally entitled 'France' in *Dramatic Lyrics* (1842— see preceding headnote). The date of composition is unknown. 'Aix-en-Provence' is in southern France.

l. 11. *queen*. The narrator, as the most beautiful woman present, has been chosen 'Queen for the day' at the 'Tourney', or tournament.

104 l. 36. *dun*. Dark colouration.

105-6 ll. 86–7. *greaves*. Armoured leggings.   *hauberk*. Armoured plate or chain mail for the torso.   *on the fret*. Fretful, impatient.

107 l. 124. *tercel*. Male hawk.

Incident of the French Camp. Published in *Dramatic Lyrics* (1842) with *Soliloquy of the Spanish Cloister* (see below) as *Camp and Cloister*, this poem entitled 'Camp (French)' and *Soliloquy* 'Cloister (Spanish)'. The poems were separated and given their present titles in subsequent editions. The date of composition is unknown. The French stormed Ratisbon (or Regensburg), a Bavarian town, on 23 Apr. 1809; the incident recorded in the poem is factual.

108 *Soliloquy of the Spanish Cloister*. Published in *Dramatic Lyrics* (1842) as 'Cloister (Spanish), paired with *Incident of the French Camp* (see previous headnote). Date of composition is unknown.

109 l. 10. *Salve tibi!* 'Hail to thee!' (Latin greeting).

l. 14. *oak-galls.* Growths found on diseased oak trees, used in making ink.

l. 16. *Swine's Snout.* Another name for dandelion. The narrator is punningly insulting Brother Lawrence's nose.

l. 22. *chaps.* Jaws or cheeks.

ll. 33–40. *When he finishes ... at one gulp.* The narrator is illustrating (and Browning is satirizing) the religious pedantry of a certain sort of fundamentalist mind: he thinks that crossing his knife and fork in memory of the crucifixion, and drinking his orange juice in three sips in memory of the Trinity (the doctrine of which was heretically denied by the followers of the 4th-century theologian Arius) conclusively demonstrates his piety.

110 l. 49. *Galatians.* There is actually no such text in Galatians, and Browning in later life admitted that this had been an error, saying that he was 'not careful to be correct'. Of course, this fact does nothing to diminish the power and effectiveness of the passage, or the poem as a whole; and the scholars who have expended much ingenuity trying to provide a suitable biblical passage of twenty-nine damnations (or providing the Latin for 'parsley', or 'the Greek name for "Swine's Snout"') are in a sense missing the point—except in so far as their pedantry represents an imaginative entry into the pedantic, indeed obsessive, mind of the narrator.

l. 56. *Manichee.* The Manichaean heresy asserts that Good and Evil, God and Satan, were created together and wield equal power in the universe.

l. 57. *scrofulous.* Corrupt.   *French novel.* Pornographic text.

l. 60. *Belial.* Devil associated with lust.

l. 62. *woeful sixteenth print.* The illustrations of French erotic novels were often very frank. The sixteenth plate in this text is presumably racier than most. It is 'woeful' in the sense that it will result in 'woe' for Lawrence, should he fall under its lustful influence.

l. 70. *Hy, Zy, Hine...* Perhaps the most argued-over, and certainly the most tedious, crux in the whole of Browning. It is not certain what these words represent, but three suggestions carry most weight. (1) They may be supposed to reproduce the sound of the vesper bells to which the narrator alludes in the next line; (2) they may represent a slurred or parodic version of the Latin words of the high Mass; or (3) they may be the beginning of a black-magical invocation of a devil, with which the narrator hopes to form a pact to destroy Lawrence's 'rose-acacia'.

ll. 71–2. *Plena ... Virgo.* The Latin represents a prayer to the Virgin Mary ('full of grace, hail, O Virgin').

111 *In a Gondola.* Composed early 1842; the first seven lines were improvised by Browning at a friend's request sometime before 5 Feb. 1842,

and the remainder of the poem written shortly afterwards. First published in *Dramatic Lyrics* (1842). Browning had visited Venice in 1838.

111 l. 22. *the Three*. Perhaps the woman's husband and two brothers, or her father and two of his sons (see also l. 104 below).

l. 33. *cruce*. Crucible.

112 l. 34. *mage*. Alchemist.

113 l. 72. *sprite*. Spirit.

114 l. 108. *stylet*. Stiletto knife.

l. 111. *saints*. Blesses.

l. 113. *Lido's...graves*. Jews could not be buried in consecrated ground, and were interred in the Lido, a strip of land between Venice and the sea.

115 l. 127. *Giudecca*. A major Venetian canal.

l. 141. *lory*. A kind of parrot.

116 l. 180. *lymph*. Water.

ll. 185–93. Various genuine Renaissance painters are invoked, although the paintings described are probably Browning's invention. *Schidone*: Bartolommeo Schidone (1560–1616), a painter patronized by the Duke of Modena. *Haste-thee-Luke*: Luca Giordano, nicknamed 'Luca-fa-presto' (1632–1705); *Castelfranco*: Giorgiona of Castelfranco (*c*.1475–1510); *Tizian*: Titian (*c*.1485–1576). *Ser*, in l. 191, is an abbreviation of 'Messer' (i.e. 'Sir', or 'Gentleman').

117 ll. 205–6. *Zorzi* and *Zanze* are the names of his and her servants respectively.

l. 222. *Siora*. Signora, 'Madam'.

118 *Artemis Prologizes*. Written Easter 1841, published in *Dramatic Lyrics* (1842). Browning's original plan had been to write a whole tragedy in the Attic style on the story of Hippolytus; but he got no further than this prologue, written in bed during an illness. As he explained to Julia Wedgwood, 'I had another slight touch of something unpleasant in the head...I wrote in bed such a quantity of that *Hippolytus*, of which I wrote down the Prologue, but forgot the rest, though the resuscitation-scene which would have followed, would have improved matters' (*RB/JW*, 102). At the end of Euripides' *Hippolytus* (the plot of which this poem summarizes) Hippolytus dies, preserving to his end his chastity and his powerful animadversion to womankind. Browning's sequel, apart from representing Hippolytus's 'resuscitation', would have detailed his falling in love with a nymph, Arica.

l. 2. *Here*. Greek form of Hera (or Juno), wife of Zeus and queen of the gods.

ll. 4–10. *Though heaven...adore me*. Artemis was goddess of the moon, the underworld ('hell'), and childbirth. She was also a virgin goddess ('the chaste adore me'), who insisted on sexual abstinence from her followers.

118   l. 12. *Athenai.* Athens.

l. 13. *Asclepios.* Aesculapius was a physician of such skill that he could cure even death; he brought Hippolytus back to life, whereupon Zeus decided that he possessed too much power for a mortal and killed him with a thunderbolt.

l. 17. *ounce.* Snow leopard.

l. 22. *Phaidra.* Hippolytus' stepmother, Phaedra, conceived a passion for him; when rebuffed she hanged herself, with a scroll around her neck accusing her stepson of having outraged her.

l. 27. *Amazonian stranger.* Hippolyta, Queen of the Amazons. Her 'race' refers to her son, Hippolytus.

ll. 35–6. *Theseus ... granted three.* Theseus, Hippolytus' father, had been granted three wishes by Poseidon, god of the sea. After Phaedra's suicide, distraught with grief, he used one of these wishes to cause the death of Hippolytus.

119   l. 39. *ai ai.* Greek ('woe! woe!')

l. 42. *Henetian horses.* Horses from Enetia, in Asia Minor, were particularly prized.

l. 75. *cross-way ... honey-cake.* Artemis was worshipped in her underworld aspect as 'Artemis (or Diana) of the Crossways' by having offerings (such as honeycakes) left in crossroads.

120   l. 102. Aesculapius learnt his medical skills from Apollo (the 'radiant' one), Artemis' brother.

ll. 114–15. *rod ... snake.* Then, as today, Aesculapius was represented as holding a 'rod' twined about with snakes.

121   *Johannes Agricola in Meditation.* Written 1835, first published in a magazine (*Monthly Review*) Jan. 1836, when it was paired with *Porphyria's Lover* (see below); reprinted in *Dramatic Lyrics* (1842) as *Madhouse Cells* I (with *Porphyria* as II). Subsequent reprintings gave the text its current title. Agricola (1494–1566) founded the anti-Law or Antinomian sect, who believed (as did the Scottish Calvinists, with whom Browning would have been familiar via his Scottish nonconformist mother) in predestination, that those chosen or elected by God will get to heaven regardless of how badly they act, and that those not chosen are damned no matter what they do. In 1836 Browning appended as epigraph the following passage from Defoe's *Dictionary of all Religions* (1704), although the note does not appear in later editions: 'ANTINOMIANS, so denominated for rejecting the Law as a thing of no use under the Gospel dispensation: they say, that good works do not further, nor evil works hinder salvation; that the child of God cannot sin, that God never chastiseth him, that murder, drunkenness, &c. are sins in the wicked but not in him, that the child of grace being once assured of

salvation, afterwards never doubteth ... that God doth not love any man for his holiness, that sanctification is no evidence of justification, &c. Pontanus, in his Catalogue of Heresies, says John Agricola was the author of this sect, A.D. 1535.'

122 *Porphyria's Lover*. Written 1834 or 1835, and first printed in *Monthly Review* as 'Porphyria', paired with 'Johannes Agricola' (see above). Printed in *Dramatic Lyrics* (1842) after *Johannes Agricola in Meditation* as *Madhouse Cells* II. The stress on madness rather than criminality puts the emphasis on the narrator's state of mind rather than his actions; just as his idealized description of the woman he claims to have just murdered (ll. 44–8, bright blue eyes, blushing cheek) indicates wishful thinking, and gives no sense of how a strangled person would actually appear.

124 *The Pied Piper of Hamelin*. Written 1842 and first published in *Dramatic Lyrics* (1842). The poem was written for, and dedicated to, actor-manager William Macready's young son, Willie, who was suffering with a bad cough.

126 l. 89. *Cham*. The Khan, or Ruler, of Tartary, the land east of the Caspian Sea.

l. 91. *Nizam*. Indian Nabob, or ruler.

127 ll. 123–5. *Julius ... cherished*. The allusion is to a story, well known to schoolboys of the period, that when Julius Caesar's ship was captured at Alexandria he not only escaped and swam ashore, but carried the manuscript of his 'commentary' or history of *The Gallic Wars* with him.

128 l. 133. *train-oil*. Whale-oil

l. 138. *drysaltery*. Shop selling various comestibles.

ll. 139. *nuncheon*. Between-meals snack.

l. 141. *puncheon*. Large flask.

129 l. 177. *Bagdat*. Baghdad.

l. 182. *stiver*. Smallest unit of Dutch currency.

131 ll. 258–60. *heaven's gate ... camel in!* The text is Matt. 19: 24, 'It is easier for a camel to go through a needle's-eye, than for a rich man to enter into the kingdom of God.'

132 l. 296. *trepanned*. Caught in a trap.

Dramatic Romances and Lyrics

133 This Collection appeared 6 Nov. 1845 as the seventh and penultimate *Bells and Pomegranates* pamphlet.

'*How They Brought the Good News from Ghent to Aix*'. Written Aug. 1844 and published as the first poem in *Dramatic Romances and Lyrics* (1845). Browning later claimed that no specific or historical occasion was behind the poem; the 'good news' being delivered is accordingly open to conjecture (presumably it has some military import). Ghent is in the north-west of Belgium, Aix (now Aachen) in modern-day Germany, and all other places named in the poem are Belgian. The route mapped out is not exactly practicable, but the emphasis is more on the immediacy of the ride than any such precise details.

133 l. 10. *pique*. Browning (probably erroneously) meant the term to refer to a pommell or projection on the front of the saddle; 'setting the pique right' means adjusting the saddle correctly.

135 *Pictor Ignotus*. First published in *Dramatic Romances and Lyrics* (1845); the date of composition is unknown. The title is Latin, and means 'Painter Unknown' (a tag often found in Art Museums on unattributed paintings); *ignotus* can also mean 'low-born', and 'overlooked'. Scholars have identified a historical source for the narrator in one Fra Bartolommeo, a painter who gave up art at the prompting of Savanarola and entered a monastery (by the same logic the 'youth' of l. 1 has been identified as Raphael); but such specificity rather undermines the point of the title.

137 l. 67. *travertine*. Limestone.

The Englishman in Italy. Composed in the summer and autumn of 1845 and first published in *Dramatic Romances and Lyrics* (1845) under the title 'England in Italy.' *Piano di Sorrento* is 'The Plain of Sorrento', not far from Naples, a location that Browning had visited in 1844.

l. 1. *Fortù*. The name of the addressee (a diminutive of 'Fortuna').

l. 5. *Scirocco*. The Sirocco, a hot autumnal wind that blows from the South. Browning seems to use the term to refer to a storm.

138 l. 47. *frails*. Baskets woven from rushes.

139 l. 87. *love-apple*. Tomato.

l. 92. *regales*. Choicest morsels of food.

140 l. 122. *medlars*. Types of apple tree.

l. 138. *sorbs*. Service-trees, a sort of pear-tree.

141 l. 157. *fume-weed*. Fumitory, a low-growing weed.

l. 162. *lentisks*. Another name for the mastic tree, an evergreen shrub.

l. 171. *Calvano*. A local mountain (the Vico Alvano).

l. 177. *terrible crystal*. An allusion to Ezek. 1: 22, 'And the likeness of the firmament . . . was as the colour of the terrible crystal.'

142 l. 199. *Galli*. The Galli, or Cockerels, are three rocky islands off the coast from the Piano di Sorrento. The story of the Sirens is found in Homer's *Odyssey* xii. Browning goes on to allude to the tradition that, having failed to lure Odysseus (or Ulysses) to his death, the Sirens hurled themselves into the sea and were metamorphosed into the Galli.

143 l. 250–1. *Feast . . . Virgin*. The Feast of Our Lady of the Rosary was particularly presided over by members of the Dominican order.

143 l. 257. *dizened*. Adorned.

l. 265. *Bellini nor Auber*. Contemporary Italian and French composers, respectively.

l. 269. *Image*. The Image is that of the Virgin Mary.

144 ll. 286–92. *'Such trifles!'... the skies!* The syntax is a little difficult, but the sense is: 'the question as to whether the storm ought to vanish from the skies is akin to the question being debated now in England, whether we should repeal the Corn Laws.' The Corn Laws placed a duty on imported corn as a measure designed to help domestic farmers; but in the face of widespread famine (especially in Ireland) and the unnaturally high price of bread, there was a wide body of opinion (which included Browning) that they ought to be abolished. They were finally repealed in 1846. It is very rare for Browning to allude to contemporary politics in his verse.

The Lost Leader. First published in *Dramatic Romances and Lyrics* (1845); the date of composition is unknown. The 'Lost Leader' is Wordsworth, who had by the 1840s abandoned his youthful radicalism and become a reactionary and establishment figure. The 'handful of silver' refers to Wordsworth's acceptance of a civil list pension in Oct. 1842 (with obvious overtones of Judas's thirty pieces of silver), and the 'riband' alludes to the poet laureateship, which Wordsworth accepted in Apr. 1843. Browning, to his credit, neither abandoned his youthful liberalism nor accepted such establishment tokens. Although his view of Wordsworth mellowed somewhat with age, at the time of writing the poem he was hot against him. Browning wrote to Elizabeth Barrett 22 Aug. 1846, 'I always retained my first feeling for Byron in many respects... while Heaven knows that I could not get up enthusiasm enough to cross the room if at the other end of it all Wordsworth, Coleridge & Southey were condensed into the little China bottle yonder, after the Rosicrucian fashion' (*Kintner*, 986).

145 *The Laboratory*. First published in *Hood's Magazine* (June 1844); reprinted in *Dramatic Romances and Lyrics* (1845). The date of composition is unknown. The subtitle *Ancien Régime* locates the poem in pre-Revolutionary France. The narrator has been identified with the historical poisoner Marie-Madeleine de Brinvilliers (*c*.1630–76).

146 l. 23. *pastile*. Perfumed joss-stick.

l. 29. *minion*. Delicate and weak creature.

147 *The Bishop Orders His Tomb at Saint Praxed's Church*. Written between late 1844, when Browning visited the real Santa Prassede (or St Praxed's) in Rome, and early 1845 when the poem was sent to Hood. First published in *Hood's Magazine* (Mar. 1845) as *The Tomb at St Praxed's*; reprinted in *Dramatic Romances and Lyrics* (1845). The poem was highly regarded in its own day and subsequently as a representation of the Renaissance mind-set; Ruskin's comments (in 1856's *Modern Painters*, IV. xx. 34) are famous: 'I know of no other piece of modern English,

prose or poetry, in which there is so much told, as in these lines, of the Renaissance spirit,—its worldliness, inconsistency, pride, hypocrisy, love of itself, love of art, of luxury, and of good Latin. It is nearly all that I have said of the central Renaissance in thirty pages of the *Stones of Venice*, put into as many lines, Browning's also being the antecedent work.'

147 l. 1. *vanity*...The Bishop is quoting *Eccles.* 1: 2: 'Vanity of vanities, saith the Preacher; vanity of vanities, all is vanity.' 'Vanity' in the biblical context means 'emptiness' or 'futility', although in the poem there is the suggestion of an ironic pun on the more modern sense of the word ('self-love and desire for admiration').

l. 3. *Nephews*. Having taken a vow of celibacy, Catholic churchmen could not openly acknowledge their illegitimate offspring, and often passed them off as 'nephews' or 'nieces' (this is the origin of the word 'nepotism').

148 l. 21. *epistle-side*. That side of the church from which the passage from the New Testament Epistle is read during Mass.

ll. 25–6. *I shall fill...rest*. The Bishop is envisaging a life-sized statue of himself lying on a slab of expensive stone. The 'tabernacle' is a stone canopy over a tomb.

l. 31. *onion-stone*. A cheap marble, so flaky that it was said to peel like onion.

l. 41. *frail*. Basket.

l. 42. *lapis lazuli*. A semi-precious stone of an intense blue colour; a head-sized lump would be extraordinarily expensive. In characteristic fashion the Bishop's greed expresses itself in terms of conventional religious iconography (the beheaded John the Baptist, the Virgin Mary).

149 l. 58. *tripod*. A three-legged stool, from which the priestess of Delphi delivered her oracles.   *thyrsus*. An ornamental spear or rod, associated particularly with Dionysus, god of wine and other licentious things.

l. 60. *glory*. Halo.

l. 66. *travertine*. Limestone.

l. 68. *jasper*. A bright green stone.

l. 77–9. *Tully*. Marcus Tullius Cicero (106–43 BC), whose particular sort of orotund rhetoric was still touted as a model of Latin style in Browning's day.   *Ulpian*. Domitius Ulpianus (170–228), a relatively obscure figure, with accordingly less cachet as a stylist.

l. 89. *mortcloth*. Death-cloth, or pall.

150 l. 95. *Saint Praxed...mount*. The dying Bishop reveals his muddled state of mind, and (perhaps) his ignorance of Church matters, by confusing St Praxed (a female saint) with Christ (who delivered the sermon on the mount).

150 l. 99. *ELUCESCEBAT*. 'He was [a] notable [man]'; the Ciceronian would be *elucebat*.

l. 111. *entablature*. The stone slab on which the Bishop's statue is to lie.

l. 116. *Gritstone*. Sandstone, amongst the cheapest of building materials.

The Boy and the Angel. First published in *Hood's Magazine* (Aug. 1844); reprinted in *Dramatic Romances and Lyrics* (1845). The date of composition is unknown. There has never been a Pope called Theocrite (the name means 'Judged by God'); Browning may have chosen the name because of its idyllic, pastoral associations (from the Greek bucolic poet Theocrites).

153 *Garden Fancies ii (Sibrandus Schafnaburgensis)*. 'Garden Fancies i (The Flower's Name)' and this poem appeared in *Hood's Magazine* (July 1844), and were reprinted in *Dramatic Romances and Lyrics* (1845). The title here is the Latin version of the name of a real-life 17th-century pedant and author of dull books, Sibrandus of Aschaffenburg.

l. 7. *white*. Bright light.   *matin-prime*. Early morning.

l. 10. *arbute and laurustine*. Evergreen shrubs.

l. 19. *pont-levis*. French for drawbridge.

154 l. 32. *Rabelais* (1483–1553), author of the richly (and scatalogically) comic *Gargantua and Pantagruel*, a favourite of Browning's.

ll. 38–9. *de profundis ... Cantate!* The Latin means 'out of the depths, in happy tones, [let us] sing!' A cheerful inversion of the gloomy verse in Ps. 130, *De Profundis clamavi*, 'Out of the depths I have cried unto thee, O Lord.'

155 l. 61. *John Knox*. The Puritanical Scots religious leader (*c*.1510–72) would, of course, have strongly disapproved of the frivolity of a Parisian play or Viennese ballet.

l. 67. *sufficit*. Latin for 'enough'.

156–7 *Meeting at Night and Parting at Morning*. First published in *Dramatic Romances and Lyrics* (1845). These powerfully allusive and ambiguous poems are open to a variety of interpretations. The 'fiery ringlets' of night-time waves in 'Night' may suggest phosphorescence, a phenomenon particularly noticeable in the Mediterranean, which would locate the action there; just as the 'lighted match' (l. 10) locates the time as contemporary. In 'Morning', the 'him' of l. 3 is usually interpreted as referring to the sun of l. 2. (the poem being spoken by the man), although many readers take it as referring to the male partner in the illicit meeting (the poem being spoken by the woman).

Men and Women

157 Published in two volumes 10 Nov. 1855. The title may allude to one of Elizabeth Barrett Browning's *Sonnets from the Portuguese* (1850; sonnet

xxvi contains the lines 'I lived with visions for my company | Instead of men and women'), although the context makes this doubtful, and Browning was in the habit of using the phrase in his correspondence before this date. In a letter to his future wife he contrasted their different poetic techniques as follows: 'You speak out, *you*,—I only make men & women speak—give you truth broken into prismatic hues, and fear the bright white light' (13 Jan. 1845: see below, pp. 594–5). Browning himself thought highly of the volume, but despite some respectful (as well as some dismissive) reviews *Men and Women* was not a great popular success. After a relatively small first print run, no second edition was called for.

157 *Love Among the Ruins.* First published in *Men and Women* (1855). According to a persistent (although possibly apocryphal) story, Browning in late 1851 became disaffected with his laziness in writing poems, and made a New Year's resolution to write a poem a day. The resolution lasted three days; *Love Among the Ruins* being written on 1 Jan. 1852, *Women and Roses* on the 2nd, and *Childe Roland to the Dark Tower Came* on the 3rd. The ruined city described in the poem is probably imaginary, a combination of elements from various antique sites; although since an early draft of the poem was called 'Sicilian Pastoral' (the speaker does seem to be a shepherd, with his reference to 'our sheep', l. 3.), the location may be Syracuse.

158 l. 39. *caper.* Thorny Mediterranean shrub.

l. 41. *houseleek.* Flowering-plant often found in crevices of old walls and roofs.

159 l. 65. *causeys.* Causeways.

Evelyn Hope. First published in *Men and Women* (1855); the date of composition is unknown.

161 *Up at a Villa—Down in the City.* First published in *Men and Women* (1855); the date of composition is unknown. The setting is probably in Tuscany, where the Brownings had rented a villa during 1850.

l. 4. *by Bacchus.* Italian oath ('per Bacco!').

162 l. 28. *pash.* Smash, crash.

163 l. 34. *thrid.* Thread, wind through.

l. 39. *diligence.* Stagecoach.

l. 42. *Pulcinello-trumpet.* Trumpet announcing a puppet show starring the Punch-like character, Pulcinello.

l. 46. *law of the Duke's.* The scene is set in the years of reaction following the failure of revolution in 1848; in 1852, the newly restored Duke of Tuscany Leopold II repealed the constitution and enacted a variety of repressive 'little new laws'.

l. 52. *seven swords.* These represent the seven sorrows of the Virgin Mary.

163 l. 53. Browning wrote to his friend Isa Blagden in 1864 about an article in the *Edinburgh Review*: 'do you see the "Edinburgh" that says all my poetry is summed up in "Bang, whang, whang, goes the Drum?"' (*Dearest Isa*, 196).

164 *By the Fire-Side.* Probably written late 1853, after Browning and his wife visited a ruined chapel amongst the mountains near Bagni di Lucca, an event that is recorded in the poem. Published in *Men and Women* (1855). Whilst not being an autobiographical piece, this poem does contain a higher-than-usual proportion of autobiographical elements; the portrait of 'Leonor' the perfect wife is based on Elizabeth Barrett Browning.

166 l. 43. *Pella.* Piedmontese village on the Lago d'Orta.

l. 58. *boss.* Raised portion at the middle of a circular shield.

l. 64. *freaked.* Streaked, stripy.

167 l. 84. *wattled cote.* Shed made of woven twigs.

l. 92. *pent-house.* A 'penthouse' is a building that leans against or otherwise annexes another building. Here the sense is presumably that the builder has made a cover for the fresco by attaching a structure to the roof-beams.

168 l. 101. *Leonor.* The name of the faithful wife in Beethoven's opera *Fidelio.*

169 l. 132. *Word...new.* Conflating two biblical passages. The 'Word' is God (from John 1: 1, 'In the beginning was the Word'); 'makes all things new' is from Rev. 21: 5, 'And he that sat in the throne said, Behold, I make all things new.'

l. 135. *house not made with hands.* 2 Cor. 5: 1, 'We have a building of God, an house not made with hands, eternal in heaven.'

170 l. 171. *settle.* Bench.

171 l. 185. *chrysolite.* Olive-green precious stone. Associations with fidelity derive, perhaps ironically, from Shakespeare's *Othello* v. ii, 'had she been true, | If heaven would make me such another world | Of one entire and perfect chrysolite, | I'd not have sold her for it.'

174 *Fra Lippo Lippi.* Probably written between winter 1852 and spring 1853; first published in *Men and Women* (1855). For the details of the life of Fra (that is, Brother) Filippo Lippi (*c.*1405–69) Browning studied Vasari's *Lives of the Artists.* Lippi was orphaned at an early age; he was part of a community of Carmelite friars 1421–32; outside the monastery he worked under the patronage of Cosimo de' Medici, and his reputation as a painter spread widely. He was chaplain of the convent of St Margherita until he eloped with one of the nuns (who bore his son Filippino, also to become a painter, in 1457). From 1452–64 Lippi painted his masterpiece, a series of large-scale frescoes in the cathedral at Prato, near Florence; work with which Browning was familiar.

174 l. 3. *Zooks*. 'Gadzooks' (possibly 'God's hooks' or 'God's socks'), a mild oath.

l. 6. *sportive ladies*. Prostitutes.

l. 20. *how you affected such a gullet's-gripe*. 'How you dared grab me by the throat'.

175 l. 41. *take*. Please.

l. 47. *mew*. Cage.

ll. 53–7. *Flower... the thyme*. Lippo provides us with various examples of the short Italian folk-songs known as *stornelli*; the singer is provided with a flower-name (say) and has to improvise a rhyme.

l. 67. *Saint Laurence*. That is, the Church of Saint Laurence.

177 l. 117. *processional and fine*. i.e. dressed handsomely for a procession.

l. 121. *Eight*. Florence had eight magistrates.

l. 130. *antiphonary*. Hymn-book.

l. 145. *black and white*. Black was worn by the Dominican order (the 'Preaching Friars' of l. 140), white by the Carmelites.

l. 148. *cribs*. Pilferings.

l. 150. *safe*. Criminals could claim sanctuary from the civil legal system inside churches.

178 l. 170. *Prior's niece*. We assume the Prior's connection with this young woman is more familiar than familial.

l. 172. *funked*. Died out into smoke.

ll. 175–98. *How?... I ask?* The Prior puts forward a traditional idealist view of painting, the style associated with figures such as Fra Angelico and Giotto di Bondone (ll. 189–90); Lippi represents the new wave of realistic or naturalistic painting that was to supplant it.

179 l. 196. *Herodias*. Actually Herodias's daughter, Salome, whose dance of the seven veils resulted in the decapitation of John the Baptist.

l. 235. *Brother Angelico*. Fra Angelico, or Giovanni da Fiesole (*c*.1400–55) remains one of the most highly regarded of medieval painters.

180 l. 236. *Brother Lorenzo*. Lorenzo Monaco (*c*.1370–*c*.1425) was Fra Angelico's master.

l. 266. *garden*. Eden.

181 l. 276. *Guidi*. Browning erroneously thought that Tomasso Guidi (nicknamed 'Masaccio', or 'clumsy'; 1401–*c*.1428) was Lippi's pupil; in fact he was his master. The error was pointed out to Browning in later life, who refused to accept it: 'I was wide awake when I made Fra Lippo the elder practitioner of Art' (13 Oct. 1866, *Hood*, 104).

l. 307. *cullion's hanging face*. 'The face of that rogue who deserves to be hanged.'

182 l. 327. *phiz.* Face.

l. 328. *Deacon.* St Laurence, the subject of Lippi's painting: Laurence was a martyr, grilled to death on a gridiron. When one side had been cooked he asked his persecutors to turn him over.

l. 334. *pity.* Piety.

l. 347. *cast o' my office.* Example of my work.

l. 351. *orris-root.* The root of the iris was sometimes used to make perfume.

183 l. 358. *Uz.* Job's homeland (see Job 1: 1).

l. 375. *camel-hair.* 'And John [the Baptist] was clothed with camel's hair' (Mark 1: 6).

l. 377. *Iste perfecit opus.* This Latin phrase ('this one made the work') appears on a scroll held by a man in one of Lippi's paintings, although whether the man represented is Lippi himself (as Browning thought) or Lippi's patron (who 'made the work' in another sense) is uncertain.

l. 380. *kirtles.* Skirts.

l. 381. *hot cockles.* Child's game, which involves lying face-down and trying to guess who strikes you from behind. There is a sexual *double entendre* here, as in the previous line.

184 *A Toccata of Galuppi's.* Published in *Men and Women*; the date of composition is unknown. Baldassaro Galuppi (1706–85) was a Venetian composer; a 'toccata' is a rapid keyboard composition characterized by alternating chords and elaborate runs of notes. The speaker is an Englishman like Browning (although l. 9 informs us that he is not Browning), and the poem represents the shifting moods brought about in his mind by listening to the piece of music of the title.

l. 6. *Saint Mark's.* Famous Venetian Cathedral.   *wed the sea with rings.* As a trading city, Venice's wealth depended upon the sea. The city leaders, or Doges, underwent an annual ceremony whereby they 'wed' the sea by throwing expensive rings into the water.

l. 8. *Shylock.* Character from Shakespeare's *Merchant of Venice.*

l. 18. *clavichord.* Ancestor of the modern piano; its strings were hit with metal pins, producing a more staccato sound.

185 ll. 19–21. *lesser thirds.* Two notes, played separately or together as a chord, and separated by three semitones. The song is in a minor key, traditionally a sad or plaintive musical quantity.   *sixths diminished.* Another minor quantity, two notes separated by eight semitones. *suspensions.* A note held over from one chord to another, creating an auditory tension that creates the expectation of resolution. *sevenths.* One tone or one semitone short of an octave; the effect is to create an expectation of harmonic resolution on the full octave. The sense behind all the musical terminology in this stanza is of music in a minor key progressing sadly up the scale, until it hovers on the verge of the

harmonic (and therefore happy) resolution of the theme; this resolution is delayed, creating a sense of suspense, until the beginning of the ninth stanza (l. 25).

186 *An Epistle...of Karshish, the Arab Physician.* Published in *Men and Women* (1855). The figure of Karshish is fictional; his name derives, as the first line suggests, from an Arabic word meaning 'one who gathers'.

187 l. 17. *snakestone.* Charm against snakebites.

l. 28. *Vespasian.* Roman commander who invaded Palestine in AD 66 and became Emperor in AD 70. His son, Titus, also led a military force to Palestine, and destroyed Jerusalem in AD 70.

l. 40. *travel-scrip.* Pouch.

ll. 42–4. *viscid choler.* Sticky fluid.   *tertians.* Fever that recurs every third day.   *Falling sickness.* Epilepsy.

l. 50. *His service payeth me a sublimate.* I have paid for his service (in carrying this message to you) by giving him a drug (a 'sublimate') to cure his 'ailing eye'.

l. 55. *gum-tragacanth.* Salve.

188 l. 57. *porphyry.* The pestle operates in a mortar, or stone bowl, made in this instance out of the hard, marble-like porphyry.

l. 89. *conceit.* Idea, notion. Karshish means that the revived Lazarus was highly suggestible, ready to believe what was told to him.

189 l. 102. *diurnal.* Everyday.

l. 103. *fume.* Hallucination.

l. 106. *tingeth flesh.* The spice saffron does indeed stain skin yellow.

190 l. 161. *pretermission.* Omission.

l. 177. *Greek fire.* Early form of napalm; actually not invented until the 7th century AD.

192 l. 240. *sublimed.* A solid is said to be 'sublimed' if it is turned directly into a gas without passing through a liquid state. Here the idea is that the practitioners, fuelled by ignorance, have gone straight from the disease to a putative cure without passing through the sort of observation and scientific thinking that might actually effect a cure.

l. 247. *leech.* Karshish assumes that Jesus must have been a physician ('leech') to have effected the 'cure' of Lazarus.

193 l. 259. *earthquake.* The earth shook when Jesus died (see Matt. 27: 50–1); Karshish, a little muddled (here as elsewhere) thinks that Jesus was killed by the superstitious and ignorant populace because he was unable to stop the earthquake.

l. 281. *borage.* Medicinal herb.

194 *'Childe Roland to the Dark Tower Came'.* Possibly written in a day on 3 Jan. 1852 (there is evidence both for and against this hypothesis), and

first published in *Men and Women* (1855). Browning claimed the poem came to him in a dream. The subtitle points to one inspiration: Edgar's song in Shakespeare's *King Lear* (III. iv. 182–4), where Edgar (a man feigning madness) sings a mad song in the company of the King (a man really going mad): 'Childe Rowland to the dark tower came, | His word was still, "Fie, foh, and fum, | I smell the blood of a British man."' A 'Childe' is the title given to a trainee Knight.

195 l. 22. *obstreperous*. Loud, vociferous.

ll. 25–30. *As when a sick man...amend*. A grim parallel to Donne's 'A Valediction: forbidding Mourning': 'As virtuous men pass mildly away, | And whisper to their souls to go, | Whilst some of their sad friends do say, | "The breath goes now", and some say, "No,"...'

196 l. 48. *estray*. Stray animal.

ll. 58–9. *cockle...awe*. The weeds ('cockle' and 'spurge') might grow unchecked ('with none to awe them').

l. 64. *It nothing skills*. Nothing is of any use.

l. 66. *Calcine*. Purify or refine by fire (a term from alchemy).

l. 68. *bents*. Coarse grasses.

197 l. 80. *colloped*. A crux. The word may mean 'in folds or ridges'; or, perhaps, 'cut up like meat'. Alternatively, Browning may be thinking of the Greek *kollopos*, meaning 'tightened up' or 'screwed up' (a *kollops* is the peg used to tighten the strings of a lyre or lute).

198 l. 106. *howlet*. Owl.

l. 114. *bespate*. Bespattered.

ll. 130–1. *pad...to a plash*. Trample to a bog.

l. 133. *fell*. Deadly.   *cirque*. Circular space; arena.

l. 135. *mews*. Enclosure (in English towns, people often live in cul-de-sacs or former stable-yards called 'mews').

199 l. 141. *brake*. A toothed-wheel (used for 'breaking' things).

l. 143. *Tophet*. Hell.

l. 149. *rood*. Quarter of an acre.

l. 160. *Apollyon*. A winged devil.

l. 161. *dragon-penned*. Winged like a dragon.

200 l. 179. *nonce*. Moment.

l. 182. *blind as the fool's heart*. 'The fool hath said in his heart, There is no God' (Ps. 14: 1).

l. 192. *heft*. Hilt.

201 l. 203. *slug-horn*. Scholars suggest that Browning was wrong in thinking that 'slughorn' (which they gloss as an archaic version of the word 'slogan', or 'battle-cry') was the sort of horn that could be blown

through; but in fact a 'slug-horn' *is* a sort of horn. If a cow's horn grows stunted or deformed it is called a 'slug' or a 'slug horn' (cf. *OED slug*, sb(2), 5), and the idea of making a trumpet out of a deformed piece of nature has clear resonance for the poem as a whole.

201 *Respectability*. Probably written early 1852 (see l. 22 and note); first published in *Men and Women* (1855). The speaker of the poem is a Parisian man addressing his lover.

l. 15. *Boulevart*. Boulevard. They are walking out of the darkness into a lit section.

202 l. 21. *Institute*. The lovers approach the imposing building of the Institut de France.

l. 22. *Guizot receives Montalembert*. On 5 Feb. 1852, the statesman François Guizot was obliged to deliver a speech at the Institute, welcoming his bitter enemy Charles Montalembert into the Académie Française. Browning was present on this occasion.

l. 23. *lampions*. Lamps (French).

The Statue and the Bust. First published in *Men and Women* (1855); the date of composition is unknown. Browning is here retelling an old Florentine legend.

l. 22. *encolure*. French for 'horses' neck'; here it presumably means 'mane'.

203 ll. 36–9. *a crime...cursed son*. The crime, as the poem suggests, is the 'murder' of Florence's ancient democracy occasioned by the accession to power of the autocratic Medici family, beginning with Cosimo the Elder (1389–1464).

l. 57. *catafalk*. Carriage supporting a coffin during a funeral procession.

204 l. 68. *loop*. Loophole.

l. 72. *ave-bell*. A bell rung for prayers three times a day.

l. 94. *Arno*. The river that runs through Florence.

l. 95. *Petraja*. Located on the outskirts of Florence.

205 l. 100. *leaves*. Comes from.

l. 119. *list*. Choose.

l. 135. *blow*. Bloom.

206 l. 169. *Robbia*. Luca della Robbia (1400–82) was a famous sculptor and maker of terracotta ware.

208 l. 232. *pelf*. Money.

l. 234. *Guelph*. Both a small silver coin, and the name of a powerful Italian family. The sense of the the stanza is: 'Must the game be played with real money? If any token would do, it would be ridiculous to use valuable silver coins.'

209 l. 247. *unlit lamp...ungirt loin*. i.e. the lovers were not prepared, the way Christ abjured his followers to be continually prepared: 'Let your loins be girded about, and your lights burning; and ye yourselves like unto men that wait for the lord, when he will return from the wedding; that when he cometh and knocketh, they may open to him immediately' (Luke 12: 35–6).

l. 249. *we issue join*. We take issue with.

l. 250. *De te, fabula*. The quotation is from Horace's *Satires* (I. i. 69–70): 'Quid ribes? Mutato nomine de te | fabula narratur' ('Why are you laughing? Change the name and it's about you that the tale is told').

How It Strikes a Contemporary. First published in *Men and Women* (1855); the date of composition is unknown. The poem is traditionally seen as a product of the same period of meditation on the nature of poetry that produced *The Essay on Shelley* (1851). Valladolid is a town in north-central Spain; the poet described here is imaginary.

l. 20. *ferrel*. Ferrule (metal tip on the end of a walking-stick to prevent wear).

210 l. 28. *fly-leaf ballads*. Ballads printed on separate sheets.

211 l. 74. *Jewry*. The Jewish quarter or ghetto.

l. 76. *Titians*. Paintings by the Old Master Titian.

l. 90. *Corregidor*. Chief Magistrate.

l. 96. *memorized*. Memorialized.

212 l. 115. *Prado*. Promenade in Madrid.

Bishop Blougram's Apology. First published in *Men and Women* (1855); the date of composition is not known, but it probably stretched over several years between 1850 and 1855. *Apology* in the title means primarily 'justification' or 'formal defence of a position'; and secondarily, and ironically, 'saying sorry for an error'. The worldly-wise Roman Catholic narrator is modelled on (but is not an exact portrait of) two figures. One was John Henry Newman (1801–90), who began life as a vicar in the Church of England, converted to Catholicism, and was made a cardinal in 1879; the other was Bishop, later Cardinal, Wiseman (1802–65), a notable Catholic cleric who had in 1850 been appointed by the Pope to a newly established bishopric of London. The fact that the Pope was able to do this was in itself testament to the fact that the more virulent anti-Catholicism of the previous decades had abated somewhat; but there was still a great deal of suspicion of the Catholic church amongst many English people. The extent to which Browning's poem can be seen as part of this anti-Catholic intellectual climate, and the extent to which it criticizes such bigotry, is open to debate.

l. 3. *Abbey*. Westminster Abbey had been built and consecrated before the Reformation.

212 l. 6. *Pugin*. A. W. N. Pugin (1812–52) was the most famous Victorian architect to espouse the elaborate 'Gothic' style (as embodied, for instance, in the British Houses of Parliament). Pugin was a convert to Roman Catholicism.

l. 12. *You take me*. You understand.

l. 13. *Gigadibs*. The name of the lightweight journalist, the person on the other side of Blougram's heavyweight monologue, may have been suggested to Browning via Victorian horse-drawn carriages. A 'Brougham' is a heavy, closed, four-wheeled carriage; a 'gig' a general term for a light, open-topped two-wheeled one.

213 l. 34. *Corpus Christi Day*. Feast celebrating the Eucharist, held on the Thursday after Trinity Sunday.

l. 41. *their*. i.e. Catholics.

l. 45. *Che che*. Italian idiom; roughly, 'come come!'

214 ll. 52–4. *Goethe*. Johann Wolfgang von Goethe (1749–1832), the great German poet and writer.   *Buonaparte*. The customary spelling for Napoleon Bonaparte's name at this time.   *Count D'Orsay* (1801–52), Victorian dandy, wit, and Bonapartist. In their own way, all three of these people represent individual endeavour.

l. 62. *They can't*. Popes are elected from amongst the cardinals; Bloughram is only a bishop.

214 l. 70. *tire-room*. Dressing room.

215 l. 108. *Balzac's novels*. A complete edition of Balzac's novels in fifty-five volumes began appearing in 1856.

l. 111. *Leipsic*. The German town of Leipzig was famous for its classical publishers.

ll. 113–14. *Parma's pride . . . fleeting glow*. Browning had seen Correggio's painting of St Jerome (known as *Il Giorno*) in the city art gallery at Parma.

l. 125. *overhauls*. Throws overboard.

216 l. 184. *Euripides*. Attic tragedian from the 5th century BC.

217 l. 190. *The grand Perhaps*. 'But, it is said, our religion is gone . . . We quietly believe this Universe to be intrinsically a great unintelligible PERHAPS; . . . All the Truth of this Universe is uncertain' (Carlyle, *Past and Present* (1843), 185). At this point in his book, Carlyle is concerned to discover why it is that 'the Popish Religion . . . flourishes extremely in these years'.

l. 197. *The Way, the Truth, the Life*. Christ calls himself this in John 14: 6.

219 l. 267. *first-cabin*. First-class cabin.

220 l. 315. *Bid . . . they are bread*. In Matt. 4: 3–4 Satan trys to tempt Christ: 'If thou be the Son of God, command that these stones be made bread.'

220 l. 316. *Peter's creed...Hildebrand's*. The difference is that Peter's doctrine asserts the absolute authority of Christ (Acts 2: 36), where Hildebrand (who was Pope Gregory VII, 1073–85) argued that the papacy had political precedence over temporal kings.

221 l. 353. *dock their stump*. Cut short their tail.

l. 377. *winking Virgin*. In his book *Lectures on the Present Position of Catholics in England* (1851) Newman declared his belief in an alleged miracle, that the eyes of a portrait of the Madonna moved.

222 ll. 381–6. *Like Verdi...in his stall*. Rossini (1792–1868) composed over thirty operas, and would therefore be an informed judge of the young Verdi's stumbling beginnings in the genre (probably his *Macbeth*, 1847), whatever the ignorant Florentine audience thought of the piece; also significant is the fact that while Verdi (in 1855) was known only as a composer of secular operas, Rossini had given up writing such works after *William Tell* (1829), and produced instead devotional, religious pieces such as the *Stabat Mater*.

l. 392. *Sixty the minute*. Very rapidly.

l. 397. *demirep*. Immoral woman.

l. 407. *twelve*. A jury.

l. 411. *Schelling*. F. W. J. von Schelling (1775–1854), German philosopher, who suggested it was possible in certain cases to hold two apparently contradictory views at the same time.

223 l. 425. *Peter's chains*. Representing his membership of St Peter's church (i.e. that he is a Catholic).

l. 426. *Noodledom*. Slighting term for the aristocracy; Lord So-and-so has his coat-of-arms embroidered on his coat.

224 l. 466. *The State, that's I*. It was Louis XIV who said 'L'État, c'est moi'; but the sentiment is certainly Napoleonic.

l. 472. *Austrian marriage*. In 1810 Napoleon divorced the Empress Josephine (who had failed to provide him with an heir) and married an Austrian archduchess; 'cant to us the Church' refers to acts such as (Catholic) Napoleon's annexation of the Papal states and emprisonment of the Pope.

l. 475. *Austerlitz*. One of Napoleon's greatest battles.

225 l. 514. *in Stratford town*. Shakespeare retired from play-writing *c*.1610, abandoning the props of the theatre ('the towers and gorgeous palaces', see *The Tempest* IV. i. 152) for a quiet life in Stratford 'dealing in grain and wool' (l. 551).

l. 519. *Pandulph...cardinal*. The line is quoted from *King John* III. i. 138; in the play Cardinal Pandulf excommunicates the wicked King John.

l. 533. *Terni's fall, Naples' bay and Gothard's top*. All examples of beautiful scenery: the waterfall at Terni in central Italy; the bay of Naples; the pass of St Gothard in the Alps.

226 l. 568. *Luther*. Martin Luther (1483–1546) of Germany, pioneering Protestant.

l. 577. *Strauss*. German scholar D. F. Strauss (1808– 74) wrote a life of Christ that challenged the account given in the New Testament (*Das Leben Jesu* was translated into English by George Eliot in 1846, causing something of a stir).

228 l. 626. *What think ye of Christ*. Jesus's question to the Pharisees (Matt. 22: 42).

229 l. 664. *ichors*. (Rhymes with 'liquors'.) Lymph fluid, the bleeding of which was thought at one time to help in the healing of a wound.

l. 669. *box*. Snuffbox.

l. 685. *Ararat*. The mountain on which Noah's Ark came to rest after the flood (Gen. 8: 4).

230 l. 704. *Immaculate Conception*. Pope Pius IX promulgated this doctrine in 1854 (that the Virgin Mary was herself born without original sin, unlike the rest of us; it should not be confused with the Virgin Birth).

l. 715. *King Bomba*. Nickname of the repressive King Ferdinand of Sicily. *lazzaroni*. Beggars.

l. 716. *Antonelli*. One of Pius IX's Cardinals.

l. 728. *Naples' liquefaction*. Newman, in his *Present Condition of Catholics* (see above l. 377 and note), defends the notion that the dried blood of a martyr kept in Naples miraculously liquefies twice a year.

l. 732. *decrassify*. Purify.

231 l. 744. *Fichte's clever cut at God*. German philosopher J. G. Fichte (1762–1814) denied a personal or sentient God, arguing instead 'God' was simply a name for the universal moral order.

232 l. 791. *Scouts*. Dismissively rejects.

234 l. 868. *Pan*. Licentious Greek pastoral God, half man half goat.

l. 877. *Pastor est tui Dominus*. 'The Lord is thy Shepherd' (adapted from Ps. 23: 1).

235 l. 914. *fictile*. Shaped, or moulded.

l. 915. *Anacreon*. Greek lyric poet of the 6th century BC whose poetry celebrates good living.

l. 938. *this war*. The Crimean War started in 1854.

236 l. 942. *drugget*. Cheap cloth, contrasted with the purple silk of the Bishop.

l. 945. *Blackwood's Magazine*. Leading journal and review, founded in 1817.

ll. 946–7. *two points ... Unseized by the Germans*. i.e. you have a critical perspective on Hamlet that even the painstaking German scholars have not chanced upon.

236　l. 951. *Slum and Cellar*. Although now more famous for his novels, Dickens wrote a great deal of shorter journalism that covered this sort of topic, and had titles rather like this.

ll. 972–3. *in partibus . . . nec non*. The Latin means 'In certain regions | Bishop, and also . . .'

237　l. 999. *Oppugn*. Attack.　　　　*fence*. Sword-fighting stroke.

l. 1014. *studied his last chapter of St John*. This last line is open to various interpretations. It may mean 'Gigadibs came to the end of his own study of the Gospels' (with the implication that he had been studying them in depth); or it might mean 'he has studied *the* last chapter of St John' (in which Christ appears for the last time to his disciples, and instructs Peter to 'feed my lambs', a scripture of particular importance for the Catholic church); or perhaps it means that he has been so disgusted with what Blougram has said that he has entirely given over reading the scriptures.

238　*Memorabilia*. Published in *Men and Women* (1855); the date of composition is unknown. The title (which means 'things worth remembering') perhaps alludes to Xenophon's *Memorabilia*, a book containing recollections of another dead master, Socrates. Browning later recalled the incident behind the poem: 'I was one day in the shop of Hodgson, the well-known London bookseller, when a stranger came in, who, in the course of conversation with the bookseller, spoke of something that Shelley had once said to him. Suddenly the stranger paused, and burst into laughter as he observed me staring at him with blanched face; . . . I still vividly remember how strangely the presence of a man who had seen and spoken with Shelley affected me' (*DeVane*, 216–17).

238–9　*Love in a Life* and *Life in a Love* were both first published in *Men and Women* (1855); the date of composition for both is unknown.

240　*Andrea del Sarto*. First published in *Men and Women* (1855), where it was the first poem of the second volume. The date of composition is probably sometime in 1853; the story, possibly apocryphal, is that John Kenyon, the poet's friend, sent a letter from England requesting a copy of a painting by Andrea del Sarto (1486–1531). Unable to obtain this, Browning instead sent this poem. Del Sarto (so called because he was the son of a tailor) was known as 'the Faultless Painter' because of his extremely polished technique. His marriage to the beautiful widow Lucrezia del Fede was not happy, despite his uxoriousness. The poem is set in 1525, whilst Andrea is working on a portrait of Lucrezia that Browning had seen in the Pitti Palace in Florence.

l. 15. *Fiesole*. Village a few miles from Florence.

241　l. 57. *cartoon*. Preparatory sketch.

242　l. 93. *Morello's*. Despite the pronoun in the next line, Morello is not a person but a mountain in the Appenines.

242 l. 105. *Urbinate*. The person from Urbino; which is to say, the great painter Raffaello, or Raphael (1483–1520), who was from that town.

l. 106. *Vasari* (1512–74) author of *Lives of the Artists* (from where Browning derived most of the information for this poem) did indeed know Andrea personally, and may even have been his student.

243 l. 130. *Agnolo*. Michel Agnolo, or Michelangelo (1475–1564), the great Renaissance Master.

l. 146. *fear of . . . Paris lords*. Andrea had worked for a time for the King of France, but had left with some royal money that he never repaid; hence his reluctance to go public in Paris.

244 l. 170. *grange*. Granary.

l. 178. *The Roman*. i.e. Raphael.

245 l. 214. *King Francis*. The French king, from whom Andrea had embezzled money.

l. 220. *Cousin*. Whether Andrea really thinks this waiting person is a cousin or not, we know him to be one of Lucrezia's lovers.

l. 241. *scudi*. Silver coins; thirteen of them represents quite a lot of money.

246 l. 262. *Meted*. Measured.   *reed*. Rod.

In a Year. First published in *Men and Women* (1855); it was probably written (along with a companion poem, 'In Three Days') in July 1852, when Browning and his wife were apart for a little time.

249 *Saul*. The first 96 lines (nine sections) were originally published in *Dramatic Romances and Lyrics* (1845), with the words 'End of Part One' at the end to indicate the fragmentary nature of the work. The completed work appeared in *Men and Women* (1855). The poem expands upon the situation described in the first book of Samuel, where Saul, to quell his evil spirit, summons the shepherd David to play for him: 'And Saul sent to Jesse [David's father] saying, Let David, I pray thee, stand before me; for he hath found favour in my sight. And it came to pass, when the evil spirit from God was upon Saul, that David took an harp, and played with his hand: so Saul was refreshed, and was well, and the evil spirit departed from him' (1 Sam. 16: 22–3).

l. 1. *Abner*. Captain of Saul's army.

l. 9. *Spirit*. The evil spirit sent down by God to trouble Saul.

251 l. 45. *jerboa*. Leaping rodent.

l. 53. *balm-seeds*. Berries from the middle-eastern bush known as 'Balm of Gilead' (although the medicinal attributes associated with 'balm' derive from its resin, not its berries).

l. 58. *arch*. Arrangement of men in battle.

l. 60. *Levites*. Priests.

253 l. 101. *cherubim*. Order of angels; the reference here is to Ezek. 10.

256 l. 179. Ironic contrast to the actual fate of Saul's body. After losing a battle to the Philistines, Saul kills himself; his body is burnt and buried under a tree in Jabesh (1 Sam. 31).

257 l. 203. *Hebron.* City south-west of Jerusalem, built on a mountain of the same name.

l. 204. *Kidron.* In winter, a river east of Jerusalem; in summer a river-bed.

259 l. 244. *dewdrop.* For the dewdrop as an emblem of Divine Grace, see Carlyle, *Sartor Resartus* (1831), II. vi: 'The heart...unvisited by any heavenly dewdrop.'

260 l. 278. *succeed with.* Follow from.

l. 291. *Sabaoth.* Armies; i.e. Saul's might.

262 *'De Gustibus—'.* First published in *Men and Women* (1855); the date of composition is unknown. The title ('About tastes—') is part of a Latin proverb: *De Gustibus non disputandum est* ('There is no arguing about tastes').

l. 9. *Draw yourself...moon.* i.e. step into the shadows, out of the moon-light, so as not to alarm the two lovers.

263 l. 35. *king.* The ill-liked Bourbon King Ferdinand of Sicily ('King Bomba'), who was the subject of more than one assassination attempt.

ll. 40–4. *Queen Mary's saying...'Italy'.* Mary Tudor was Queen of England 1553–8; it was during her reign that Calais, the last English possession in France, was lost to the French. Her dying words were: 'When I am dead and opened, you shall find "Calais" lying in my heart'.

Women and Roses. Possibly written in a single day, 2 Jan. 1852 (see headnote to *Love Among the Ruins*, above); first published in *Men and Women* (1855).

264 l. 15. *unimpeached.* Unprevented.

l. 33. *cincture.* Something that encompasses or encircles.

265 *Holy-Cross Day.* First published in *Men and Women* (1855); the date of composition is unknown. 'Holy Cross Day' is a Catholic feast-day (14 Sept.); the practice of compelling Jews to attend the sermon preached on this day began in 1584, and was not abolished (by Gregory XVI, as Browning's endnote says) until 1846.

l. 1. *bubble and squeak.* Mishmash of fried cooked meat and greens (nowadays potato is used instead of meat).

266 l. 10. *handsel.* Use for the first time.   *the bishop's shaving-shears.* The bishop wants to convert Jews to Christianity; and, for a Jew, shaving would be a sign of such a conversion. The point is that Solomon has converted (or is thinking of doing so) because of the financial advantages it would bring.

l. 20. *acorned hog.* A pig fed on acorns. For Jews, the pig is an unclean animal.

266 l. 23. *chine*. A cut of meat, including the backbone.

l. 29. *quotha?* Did you say?

l. 32. *cog*. Cheat.　　　*Cozen*. Deceive.

l. 38. *Jew ... Turk*. Turks (as simple barbarians) were regarded more favourably by Catholics than Jews (as the 'murderers of Christ').

267 ll. 47–8. *I meddle ... serenades*. The narrator says (perhaps jokingly) that the Bishop has convinced him to give up money-lending; so somebody else will have to finance the Bishop's love-affairs ('serenades').

l. 52. *Corso*. Roman high street. On one occasion Jews were stripped and used instead of horses during the annual race along this thoroughfare.

l. 66. *Ben Ezra's Song of Death*. Abraham ibn Ezra (1092–1167), the famous Spanish Rabbi. Rabbi Ben Ezra did write a 'Song of Death', but the verses printed here are not it.

268 ll. 91–2. *He*. Jesus.　　　*dubious*. His name ('Christ', or Messiah) is 'dubious' because Jews do not regard him as their promised Messiah.

269 *Cleon*. First published in *Men and Women* (1855); the date of composition is unknown. Cleon the Greek poet (the name, ironically, means 'Famous') is fictional; Protus ('First', an appropriate name for an autocrat) likewise. One of the points of the poem is that these two people have been forgotten utterly by history, whilst the obscure Christ has risen to such prominence. The scene is set *c.* AD 50.

l. 1. *the sprinkled isles*. The Sporades, a group of Greek islands off the western coast of Asia Minor (their name means 'scattered' or 'sprinkled').

l. 4. *Tyranny*. Absolute monarchy. In Greek the term *turannos* was reserved for those who had made themselves king by their own efforts (i.e. not hereditary monarchs); the word did not carry the implications of despotism that the English word now has.

270 l. 15. *lyric*. The Greek *lurikos* means simply 'singing to the lyre' (and by extension refers to a lyric poet).

l. 43. *first requirement*. Protus' letter to Cleon contained four enquiries ('requirements') that Cleon, in his reply, answers in turn.

271 l. 47. *epos*. Verse in epic metre (as opposed to lyric metre), although not necessarily of epic length.

l. 51. *phare*. Lighthouse (Greek).

l. 53. *Pœcile*. The Portico in Athens.

l. 60. *moods*. Modes, or musical scales.

l. 83. *rhomb*. Four-sided figure with all the sides, but only the opposite angles, equal.

l. 84. *lozenge*. Diamond-shape.

272 l. 115. *fiction*. In Greek *muthos* means both 'myth, legend' and 'fiction'.

273 l. 132. *drupe*. The word refers to any fruit with a stone; perhaps Browning is referring here to the Greek *druppa*, 'an over-ripe, mouldy olive'.

l. 139. *Homer*. The great epic poet.

l. 140. *Terpander*. Fabled founder of music in Greece from the 7th century BC.

l. 141. *Phidias*. Renowned Athenian sculptor and painter from the 5th century BC, author of the Parthenon. His 'friend' may be Pericles, Athenian statesman; or perhaps another Greek painter.

276 l. 249. *It skills not!* It is of no use.

l. 252. *Naiad*. Water nymph.

ll. 273–7. *The last point . . . painting lives*. Protus' third enquiry concerns immortality, and whether an artist can be said to 'live' through his art.

277 l. 288. *Phœbus*. The sun-god Apollo, eternally young and handsome.

l. 304. *Sappho*. Lesbian poetess, whose lyric poetry was widely admired.

l. 305 *Æschylus*. Great Athenian tragic poet.

278 l. 337. *the rest*. Protus' fourth enquiry concerns St Paul ('Paulus'); Cleon relegates it to a PS.

l. 341. *if Christus be not one with him*. i.e. 'if Christ isn't the same person as Paul'. Cleon is confused because 'Christus' ('Anointed One') is a title rather than a name (like 'Paulus').

Popularity. First published in *Men and Women* (1855); the date of composition is unknown. The unpopular though true poet addressed in the opening line has been variously identified as John Keats, Alfred Domett (one of Browning's friends), and Browning himself; although in all likelihood, no specific poet was intended. Ruskin's letter to Browning (2 Dec. 1855) analyses this poem in great detail (the letter is printed amongst 'Other Selected Letters' below, pp. 686–90).

279 ll. 18–20. *Others give best . . . till now*. A reference to the marriage feast at Cana, near the end of which Jesus turned water into wine: 'And saith unto him, Every man at the beginning doth set forth good wine; and when men have well drunk, then that which is worse: but thou hast kept the good wine until now' (John 2: 10).

l. 24. *Tyre*. Once-great Mediterranean sea-port. 'Tyrian' is used to refer to a purply-blue dye produced in the town from the mollusc known as 'murex', fished off the coast.

l. 29. *Astarte*. Beautiful Semitic goddess.

280 l. 33. *sublimed some pall*. Made some robe look sublime. Purple was a royal colour (hence 'king's ambition') in the next line.

ll. 41–2. *Solomon . . . cedar-house*. See 1 Kgs. 7: 2–3. Solomon built his costly cedar-house for his wife-to-be; its lavish interior decoration was undertaken by Hiram, a man from Tyre, which is why Browning introduces it here.

280 l. 53. *proof.* quality.

281 ll. 61–5. The point of this obliquely phrased final stanza is: Hobbs, Nobbs, Stokes and Nokes, imitative poets who steal the true poet's pioneering techniques, all enjoy great popularity (consuming rich food and drink); but meanwhile what of the man who actually invented the dazzling blue colour (i.e. original poetic genius) by fishing up the murex (the mollusc from which the Tyrian blue dye comes)? Instead of eating turtle and drinking claret, John Keats has to make do with porridge.

Two in the Campagna. Probably written in May 1854 (whilst the Brownings were staying in the Campagna, the plain surrounding Rome) or shortly afterwards; first published in *Men and Women* (1855).

l. 15. *weft.* Web.

283 l. 55. *Fixed by no friendly star.* 'Love is an ever-fixed star | That looks on tempests and is never shaken; | It is the star to every wand'ring bark...' (Shakespeare's Sonnet 116).

A Grammarian's Funeral. First published in *Men and Women* (1855); the date of composition is unknown. The poem is set in 14th-century Italy, at the time when Renaissance scholars were beginning to revive the ancient learning of Greece and Rome. The Grammarian, one such scholar, is dead; and his students sing this song as they carry his corpse to the mountaintop where it is to be buried.

l. 3. *crofts.* Farms.   *thorpes.* Agricultural villages.

l. 12. *Chafes in the censer.* Is heated in the (metaphorical) incense burner.

l. 14. *sepulture.* Burial.

284 l. 22. *warning.* Signal to begin.

l. 34. *Apollo.* God of the sun and poetry; youthfully handsome.

l. 50. *gowned.* Adopted the gown, symbol of scholarship.

285 l. 70. *fabric.* Structure.

l. 86. *Calculus.* Latin for 'stone'; hence gallstones or kidney stones, with a possible pun on 'the stones' (testicles—cf. l. 132).

l. 88. *Tussis.* Cough (Latin).

l. 95. *hydroptic.* Extremely thirsty.

286 l. 129–31. Three Greek particles: *hoti* 'that'; *oun* 'then', 'therefore'; *de* 'to', 'towards'. 'Enclitic' in general means an unaccented particle that affects the accenting of the word to which it is attached; but the enclitic *de*, more specifically, becomes joined to the words it modifies (so 'towards Olympus' is not *de Olumpon*, but *Olumponde*). In other words, the Grammarian has spent his life on relative trivialities of grammar.

286 l. 134. *purlieus.* Haunts.

287 '*Transcendentalism: A Poem in Twelve Books*'. First published in *Men and Women* (1855); the date of composition is unknown. The poem constitutes a piece of advice from an older poet to a younger one, author of the dreary-sounding poem of the title.

l. 6. *prolusion.* Preliminary matter. Perhaps a dig at Wordsworth's recently (and posthumously) published *Prelude* (1850).

l. 22. *Boehme . . . plants.* Jacob Boehme (sometimes spelt Behmen) was a 17th-century German mystic who wrote of his strange communions with plants and flowers.

288 l. 37. *Mage . . . of Halberstadt.* Johannes Teutonicus, 15th-century German magician.

One Word More. Written 22 Sept. 1855, after the manuscript of *Men and Women* had been sent off to the printer; it appeared there at the end of the second volume, looking back on the fifty dramatic monologues of the collection.

289 l. 5. *century of sonnets.* Raphael (1483–1520), although a painter, is said to have written a hundred sonnets to his love, Margherita. Only three of these sonnets survived into Browning's day.

ll. 22–4. *Her, San Sisto names . . . the Louvre.* Lists four Raphael paintings of Madonnas.

l. 26–31. *that volume . . . vanished.* Raphael bequeathed the manuscript edition of his sonnets to his friend and fellow-painter Guido Reni, after whose death the volume was lost.

l. 32. *Dante . . . an angel.* Dante spent his life platonically loving and then mourning the beautiful Beatrice; in the *Vita Nuova* he describes how, on the first anniversary of her death, he began to draw an angel, but was interrupted by 'certain people of importance'.

290 l. 57. *Bice.* Beatrice.

291 l. 74. *He who smites the rock.* Moses.

l. 97. *Sinai-forehead's cloven brilliance.* Moses, uniquely, was allowed to look upon God's glory from a cleft in Mt Sinai; after he had done so his face shone.

l. 98. *rod.* Aaron, in company with Moses, transformed his rod into serpents to convince Pharaoh (Exod. 7).

l. 101–2. *Jethro's daughter . . . bondslave.* Moses married both Jethro's daughter (Zipporah, Exod. 2: 21) and an Ethiopian woman (Num. 12: 1)

293 l. 148. *Fiesole.* Town 3 miles from Florence.

l. 150. *Samminiato.* Church on a hill south-east of Florence.

l. 160. *mythos.* Myth; in this case, the myth is that of the beautiful youth Endymion, with whom Diana, goddess of the moon, fell in love. Keats (see l. 165) wrote a poem on the subject (*Endymion*, 1818).

293 l. 163. *Zoroaster*. Persian religious figure, founder of Zoroastrianism.

l. 164. *Galileo*. Italian scientist (1564–1642) who refined the telescope, and made many observations of the moon.

l. 165. *Homer*. Amongst the Homeric Hymns is one addressed to Artemis, goddess associated with the moon.

Dramatis Personae

295 Published May 1864, the first original work to be published since the death of his wife (Elizabeth Barrett had died 29 June 1861), although there had been a three-volume *Poetical Works* published in 1863. After living in Italy for fifteen years Browning was now settled in London.

Gold Hair: A Story of Pornic. First published in the *Atlantic Monthly* (May 1864), and then in *Dramatis Personae* (1864). It was probably written Aug. 1862. Browning's friend George Eliot was of the opinion that the lady in the poem was drawn with insufficient motivation; Browning took Eliot's copy of *Dramatis Personae* and added three new stanzas to 'Gold Hair' (the present stanzas 21–3). The poem is based on a true story.

l. 2. *Pornic* is a small town in southern Brittany, at the mouth of the river Loire.

l. 7. *seraphic*. Angel-like.

296 l. 38. *degree*. The proper order.

297 ll. 68–9. *dearth | Of frailty*. Lack of things to criticize about her.

298 l. 79. *chased*. Engraved.

l. 82. *gauds*. Toys, trinkets.

l. 84. *pelf*. Money.

ll. 86–7. *O cor...cæca*. The Latin is derived from Lucretius *De Rerum Natura*, 2. 14; it means 'O human heart, blind in its breast...'.

l. 90. *Louis-d'or*. Gold coin.

299 ll. 128–30. *thirty pieces...Potter's Field*. Judas received thirty pieces (of silver though, not gold) for betraying Jesus; after his suicide the priests used the money to buy 'the Potter's Field' to bury strangers in (the phrases in italics are quoted from Matt. 27).

300 l. 131. *Milk that's spilt*. The proverb is: 'There's no use in crying over spilt milk.'

l. 143. *Essays-and-Reviews*. Edited by the Revd H. B. Wilson, *Essays and Reviews* (1860) was a collection of essays on religious subjects by various eminent people. In 1861 a group of bishops, lead by Samuel Wilberforce, denounced the book for its questioning attitude to Christianity; and the synod of the Church of England officially condemned the book in 1864.

300 l. 145. *Colenso*. John William Colenso (1814–83), Bishop of Natal. In 1861 he published a commentary on *St Paul's Epistle to the Romans*, which (amongst other things) attacked the Christian doctrine of everlasting post-mortem punishment.

Abt Vogler. First published in *Dramatis Personae* (1864); the date of composition is unknown. The German composer Georg Joseph Vogler (1749–1814) was called 'Abt' or 'Abbé' because he had taken holy orders. He was famous in his own day for extemporization (he once competed with Beethoven to determine which of them was the better extemporizer). The 'musical instrument of his invention' is the Orchestrion, a sort of portable organ, that he invented in 1789.

l. 1. *structure brave*. Splendid architecture. Vogler is talking about his music.

l. 3. *when Solomon willed*. Solomon was reputed to have a ring upon which was written Yahweh (the 'ineffable Name' of God, l. 7) with which he could command spirits, and using which he single-handedly built a palace at Jerusalem.

301 l. 11. *dispart*. Separate.

l. 16. *nether*. The bottom-most.   *springs*. Place from which everything 'springs' or derives ('the root of things').

l. 17. *minion*. Servant.

l. 19. *rampired*. Fitted with ramparts.

302 l. 34. *Protoplast*. First maker (i.e. God).

303 l. 66. *houses not made with hands*. 'We know...we have a building of God, an house not made with hands, eternal in the heavens' (2 Cor. 5: 1).

304 ll. 91–6. *I feel...this life*. Vogler is describing his extemporizing. In the key of C he moves down in semitones, shifting to a minor key (perhaps A minor), then to C9 (perhaps an octave and one note—a low C and a high D) which is mildly dissonant ('alien ground'), but provides an expectation of harmonic resolution on the C octave, which Vogler finally and satisfyingly provides.

Rabbi Ben Ezra. First published in *Dramatis Personae* (1864); the date of publication is unknown. Browning had on a previous occasion put a poem into the mouth of Ben Ezra (1090–1164), the Spanish poet, scholar and Rabbi (see *Holy Cross Day*), although the placid and optimistic tone of this poem is far removed from the earlier piece.

305 l. 24. *Irks care the...beast*. i.e. 'Are well-fed animals bothered by petty cares?' This line is sometimes cited by scholars as an illustration of the occasionally unharmonious cast of Browning's style.

306 l. 62. *rose-mesh*. The 'mesh' is the net of flesh in which our souls are caught; it is 'rosy' both in colour, and in its pleasures.

307 l. 84. *indue*. Put on.

308 l. 113. *tempt*. Attempt.

l. 124. *Was I, the world arraigned*. 'Was I, arraigned as I was by the world...'. The next line has the same construction.

310 l. 164. *plastic*. Able to be moulded.

311 *A Death in the Desert*. First published in *Dramatis Personae* (1864); the date of composition is unknown. Critics often assert that this poem is a direct reply to certain works of the 'Higher Criticism' that were being published in the early sixties questioning the historical veracity of the Gospels (in particular Renan's *La Vie de Jésus*, 1863, and Strauss's *New Life of Jesus*, 1864); but *A Death in the Desert* addresses the same sorts of questions as Browning explores in earlier works such as *Cleon* or *Karshish*. St John the Evangelist is traditionally said to have died in his nineties at around AD 100; Ebion and Cerinthus aside (l. 329), all the names mentioned in the poem are fictitious.

ll. 1–12. The matter in square brackets explains the provenance and appearance of the parchment; it is a Greek text (as is the New Testament) and it consists of eight pages or paragraphs, each labelled, after the Greek fashion, with letters: running from *epsilon* ('e') down to *mu* ('m'). The narrator tells us, interestingly, that 'm' and 'e' are his own initials, although he dare not actually give us his name.

l. 6. *terebinth*. Turpentine, a good preservative.

l. 23. *decree*. Presumably a Roman decree persecuting Christians.

l. 36. *Bactrian*. The convert is from distant Bactria, a province in central Asia; in other words, he is something of a country bumpkin.

312 l. 39. *Plantain*. A low-growing herb.   *quitch*. Couch-grass, a weed.

l. 50. *nard*. Spikenard, a herb from which perfume can be made.

l. 64. *I am the Resurrection and the Life*. John 11: 25.

313 ll. 82–104. M.E.'s second interpolation attributes to John a very un-Johannine doctrine. In fact, the doctrine of the three (or sometimes two) souls was a persistent heresy that the early Church battled long and hard to stamp out. It is particularly associated with the Gnostic heretic Basilides (fl. 125); St Augustine preached against it in his *De Duabus Animabus* ('Against the Doctrine of the Two Souls').

l. 104. *glossa*. Either 'gloss' (Latin—i.e. an explanatory note'), or else 'word of mouth' (Greek—in the sense of 'I give what I heard by word of mouth from Theotypas').

314 l. 115. *James and Peter*. The two disciples were martyred AD 43 and 67 respectively.

l. 123. *as I have seen*—. John recorded his vision in *The Revelation of St John*, the last book of the Bible. In particular see Rev. 1: 11–17.

315 l. 158. *Antichrist*. 'This is the spirit of antichrist, whereof ye have heard that it should come; and even now already is it in the world' (1 John 4: 3).

315 l. 165. *scorpion...serpent.* Jesus sent out seventy disciples, saying, 'Behold, I give unto you power to tread on serpents and scorpions' (Luke 10: 19).

l. 177. *Where is the promise of His coming?* Quoted from 2 Peter 3: 4.

l. 186. *whole...wickedness.* 'The whole world lieth in wickedness' (1 John 5: 19).

316 l. 227. *optic glass.* Telescope (an anachronism for AD 100).

317 l. 241. *dispart.* Dissipate.   *dispread.* Spread apart.

l. 254. *emprise.* Enterprise (with connotations of chivalric adventure).

318 l. 279. *Prometheus.* Mythical Titan who stole fire from heaven and gave it to mortals (thereby preserving them from extinction) and was afterwards savagely punished by Zeus.

l. 284. *Æschylus.* The great Attic tragedian wrote a trilogy of plays on the Prometheus myth, of which only *Prometheus Bound* survives today. The reference here is to one of the lost plays (*Prometheus the Fire-Kindler*, of which three fragments survive) in which a satyr is so delighted with the new fire that he tries to kiss it, prompting Prometheus' warning: 'Goat, you'll soon enough be mourning your beard if you try that' (Nauck, *Tragicorum Graecorum Fragmenta*, (1856), No. 202).

l. 310. *I forsook and fled.* As did all the disciples (Mark 14: 50).

319 l. 328. *glozing.* Explanation.

l. 329. *Ebion...Cerinthus.* Two 1st-century heretics; they both asserted that Jesus was wholly man and not a god. The historical John entered into a public contest with Cerinthus over this matter.

320 l. 361. *Ephesus.* In south-west Asia Minor (now Turkey).

322 l. 448. *wheelwork.* Clockwork. Another anachronism (see l. 227).

324 l. 530. *heathen bard.* Aeschylus (see ll. 279-86).

325 l. 565. *Atlas.* Titan who carried the world on his shoulders. According to some authorities, on his death he was transformed into a mountain range.

326 l. 623. *God...jet.* The sense is that God alone makes his creations in motion ('at a jet'), unlike the sculptor, who works slowly with static lumps of clay.

l. 625. *pattern on the Mount.* The Ten Commandments, as received by Moses on Mt Sinai.

l. 629. *type.* Prototype.

327 l. 652. *the beasts.* We assume Pamphylax is to be fed to the lions.

328 *Caliban upon Setebos.* First published in *Dramatis Personae* (1864); the date of composition is unknown, but the poem is obviously tied with the intellectual climate of debate that followed the publication of Darwin's

Origin of Species in 1859. The subtitle of the poem makes explicit reference to another work, William Paley's *Natural Theology; or, Evidences of the Existence and Attributes of the Deity, collected from the Appearances of Nature* (1802). In this text Paley argues that the existence of God can be inferred from the world around us (the argument from design), and advances his Watchmaker-God analogy (that if we found a watch upon the ground, its complexity would lead us to infer a watchmaker: the same applies to the complexity of the natural world). This tactic for looking to the outside world and then 'deriving' a God, Browning might suggest, involves looking at things entirely the wrong way round. This is underlined by the epigraph, which is taken from Ps. 50: 21—'But unto the wicked God saith ... thou thoughtest that I was altogether such an one as thyself: but I will reprove thee, and set them in order before thine eyes.' The speaker, Caliban, comes from Shakespeare's *The Tempest*, where he is the bestial, half-human slave of the magician Prospero. The name of his god ('Setebos') also comes from the play.

328–9 ll. 1–23. In the passages in square brackets Caliban is thinking rather than speaking aloud.

328 l. 1. *'Will*. i.e. 'He [Caliban] will'. Caliban talks about himself in the third and first person more or less interchangeably.

l. 5. *eft-things*. Little lizard-like creatures.

l. 7. *pompion*. Pumpkin.

l. 16. *his dam*. Caliban's mother (the witch, Sycorax). That other whom she called God is Setebos.

329 l. 20. *Prosper ... Miranda*. Prospero and his daughter Miranda.

l. 50. *pie*. Magpie.

l. 51. *oakwarts*. Oak-gall; excrescences caused by certain flies on the bark of oak.

330 l. 71. *bladdery*. Bubbling.

l. 79. *hoopoe*. Colourful large-crested bird.

l. 83. *grigs*. Crickets.

332 l. 142. *many-handed*. The cuttle-fish is related to the squid, and has many arms.

l. 148. *hips*. Inedible berries.

l. 156. *oncelot*. Ocelot or jaguar.

l. 157. *ounce*. leopard.

l. 161. *Ariel*. A spirit, Prospero's servant.

l. 177. *orc*. Sea monster.

333 l. 205. *wattles*. Springy twigs.

l. 211. *ball*. Fire-ball (i.e. meteor).

334 l. 229. *urchin*. Hedgehog.

    l. 246. *surprise*. Attack.

    l. 258. *films*. Wings.

335 ll. 287–91. *The wind . . . gibe at Him*. Caliban interprets the storm (with its dusty whirlwind and strikes of lightning) as the wrath of Setebos; Browning may have in mind the appearance of God to the Israelites as 'a pillar of cloud' and 'a pillar of fire' (Exod. 13: 21).

336 *Confessions*. First published in *Dramatis Personae* (1864); the date of composition is uncertain, but must be before 22 Feb. 1860 (when Elizabeth Barrett Browning quotes from the poem in a letter). The 'he' of the first line is a priest come to offer the last rites to a dying man.

337 *Prospice*. First published in *Atlantic Monthly* (June 1864); then, a few days later, in *Dramatis Personae* (1864). The date of composition is unknown, but is presumably soon after Elizabeth Barrett Browning's death in June 1861.

338 *Youth and Art*. First published in *Dramatis Personae* (1864); the date of composition is unknown. The speaker is an opera singer ('Kate Brown'), recalling the passion she once harboured for a sculptor ('Smith') whose studio was opposite her room.

    l. 8. *Gibson*. John Gibson (1790–1866) was a noted sculptor and a personal friend of Browning's.

    l. 12. *Grisi*. Giulia Grisi (1811–69), a famous soprano.

339 l. 18. *Chipped each at a crust*. i.e. polished their abilities.   *Hindoos*. Northern Indians; proverbially hard workers.

    l. 31. *E in alt*. High E.

340 l. 57. *Prince*. Prince Albert, Queen Victoria's husband; he died in 1861.

    l. 58. *bals-paré*. Full-dress balls.

    l. 60. *R.A.* Member of the Royal Academy (the official establishment organization of artists).

341 *A Likeness*. First published in *Dramatis Personae* (1864); the date of composition may have been late 1858 or 1859.

    l. 10. *corns ail*. His corns seem to give him pain (i.e. he is upset by his wife calling his painting a 'daub').

    l. 16. *tandem-lasher*. A sort of horsewhip.

    l. 18. *Tipton Slasher*. A famous boxer of the day (William Perry, from Tipton in Staffordshire), English boxing champion 1850–7.

    l. 19. *cards*. Memorials of accurate shooting (each ace has been shot through the centre).

    l. 22. *Rarey drumming on Cruiser*. J. S. Rarey wrote a book on horsemanship; in it Rarey is pictured astride his favourite horse 'Cruiser'.

    l. 23. *Sayers*. Tom Sayers was English boxing champion 1857–60.

341 l. 27. *remark . . . in it.* i.e. the portrait strongly resembles Jane Lamb.

342 l. 42. *imbroglio.* Confused heap.

l. 54. *Marc Antonios.* Marcantonio Raimondi, a famous 16th-century Italian engraver.

l. 55. *Festina lentè.* 'Make haste slowly' (Italian; i.e. 'stop for a bit').

l. 61. *Volpato.* Giovanni Volpato, an 18th-century Italian engraver.

343 *Apparent Failure.* First published in *Dramatis Personae* (1864); since the events in the first stanza took place in 1856 ('seven years since') the date of composition is 1863. Written to help save the Paris Morgue from demolition, it was successful in so far as the building was not pulled down.

l. 3. *Prince.* Louis Napoleon, only son of Napoleon III. He was baptized in a public ceremony in Paris, June 1856.

l. 6. *Seine.* Parisian river.

ll. 7–8. *Gortschakoff.* Russian foreign minister, who attended the Congress of Paris, Apr. 1856. Cavour, the Italian prime minister, and his opponent Buol, an important Austrian diplomat, were also present.

l. 10. *Doric.* Greek architectural style.

l. 12. *Vaucluse.* Town in south-east France, for a time the home of the famous Italian poet, Petrarch.   *Sorgue.* The river Sorgue rises from a fountain in Vaucluse.

344 l. 39. *Tuileries.* Imperial palace in Paris (a public garden now stands on the site).

l. 43. *leveller.* Political radical (one who advocates the abolition of class).

l. 46. *red.* In stanza V 'red' stands for 'socialist'; here it connotes gambling (the red and black of the roulette wheel), with the implication that one of the suicides killed himself after losing heavily.

345 *Epilogue.* First published in *Dramatis Personae*; the date of composition is unknown, but is likely to be 1863. Critics assume that the unidentified third speaker is Browning himself, who comments upon both the traditionalist High Church ritualism of the first speaker ('David') and the scientific rationalism of the second (spoken under the name of the sceptical French theologian Ernest Renan, whose *Life of Jesus* Browning had read in 1863).

l. 2. *Dedication Day.* The dedication of the temple at Jerusalem (see 1 Kgs. 8 and 2 Chron. 5).

l. 3. *Levites.* The tribe of Levi, who traditionally assisted the Priests at religious ceremonies.

l. 6. *van.* Vanguard (the front).

346 l. 24. *star.* The one present at the birth of Jesus in Bethlehem.

346 l. 26. *Face*. Christ's. The star is 'dwindling' because of Renan's conviction (in his *Life of Jesus*) that there were no supernatural elements attending Christ's life.

l. 29. *gyre*. Spiral.

l. 57. *serene*. The word means 'quiet radiance' (Browning probably found it in Shelley's *Epipsychidion*, 506).

The Ring and the Book

349 Written between 1864 and 1868, Browning's masterwork was published in four monthly parts from Nov. 1868 to Feb. 1870. Its twelve books and 21,116 lines make it a massive work by any standard, although (as Carlyle pointed out) it was 'all spun out of a story but a few lines long' that 'only wanted forgetting'. The first book (reproduced here) explains how Browning came across his source material, 'The Old Yellow Book', in a Florentine flea-market in June 1860. The book in question was a collection of authentic documents (some printed, some handwritten) pertaining to a murder trial that had taken place in Rome in 1698. There was no doubt that the middle-aged nobleman and minor cleric Guido Franceschini had killed his teenage wife Francesca Pompilia; the question was whether this action was (as Guido claimed) justified under the law. Guido insisted that his wife had committed adultery with a young priest, Giuseppe Caponsacchi, in whose company she had run away from his country house. Pompilia (as she lay dying from the stab wounds Guido had inflicted upon her) and Caponsacchi insisted that their relationship had been chaste; the priest had rescued a miserable Pompilia from the violent misuse of her wicked husband. Matters were complicated by the fact that although the impoverished Guidi had married Pompilia with the hopes of a large dowry, it subsequently transpired that Pompilia's parents (Pietro and Violante Comparini) were not only too poor to provide any money (they had themselves thought that Guido was wealthy), but were not even the girl's natural parents. Violante, too old for childbirth, had secretly adopted Pompilia from a local prostitute in order to become eligible for an inheritance that had been left on condition that she produce a child. After Pompilia's flight, Guido and his henchmen had given chase and had caught up with Pompilia and Caponsacchi outside Rome. He took them to law, but was denied satisfaction; and when a heavily pregnant Pompilia was released by the Roman court to the care of her parents, and there gave birth to (Guido was certain) a bastard who would be foistered upon him as an heir, he sought vengeance. With four accomplices he went to the Comparini house, tricked his way into the house by claiming to be bearing a message from Caponsacchi, then stabbed the old couple to death and left his wife with twenty-two stab wounds. Pompilia lingered for four days, giving testimony against her husband before dying. Taken to court, Guido insisted that he had been justified in defending his honour by killing his adulterous wife, and much of the month-long court case

was taken up with the question of Pompilia's guilt or otherwise. On 18 Feb. 1698 Guido was found guilty and sentenced to death; as a minor member of the Church, Guido was able to appeal to the Pope to have his sentenced overturned; but Innocent XII refused to do this, and Guido was beheaded on 22 Feb. (his accomplices were hanged).

Browning's treatment of this source material represents one of the boldest experiments in modern literature. The first and last book of the twelve-book cycle (or 'ring') are told in Browning's own voice, commenting on the provenance and after-story of the trial. The ten books in between each has a different speaker telling the whole story from his or her own perspective. It is not only the repetition inherent in this structure that might have sunk the whole project without trace; each of the monologues is extremely long, even by Browning's own sometimes prolix standards. That the whole works so well is a testament partly to Browning's restless inventiveness and riveting sense of character and local colour (such that the cumulative effect of the whole provides a compelling portrait of human diversity); but also to the overall thematic, imagistic, and structural unity of this massive undertaking, something only relatively recently uncovered by critics.

After the scene-setting first book, the whole is structured in three sets of three monologues. Books II, III, and IV are each spoken by ordinary Roman people, not actually involved in the trial ('Half Rome', 'Other Half-Rome', and 'Tertium Quid', or 'third quantity'). One thinks that Guido should be acquitted, another thinks he should not, and the third assumes that right is probably not wholly on either side. Books V, VI, and VII give us three central protagonists, 'Guido' (a wonderfully grotesque monologue that balances oily obsequiousness to the court with barely suppressed wrath), 'Caponsacchi' and 'Pompilia'. Books VIII and IX are spoken by two clownish lawyers, Dominus Hyacinthus de Archangelis (for Guido) and Juris Doctor Johannes-Baptista Bottinius (for Pompilia), both more concerned with legal pedantries and self-advancement than with the truth. Book X (printed here) concludes the third triad with a more disinterested judge, the Pope himself, who reviews the case and decides that Guido cannot be reprieved. Book XI (also printed here) reintroduces Guido, now awaiting execution in his cell; the mask has slipped, and this monologue is one of the most exhilaratingly savage poems that Browning ever wrote.

349 *Book I. The Ring and the Book*. First published Nov. 1868, in the first of the four monthly instalments of *The Ring and the Book*.

l. 1. *this Ring*. Browning refers to a real gold ring, given to him by his friend Isa Blagden, and engraved with the Italian *Vis Mea* ('my strength'). The firm of Castellani was a famous Roman jewellers; for some of their work they copied antique gold grave-rings from Etruria (in central Italy). Chiusi (l. 6) is one such Etruscan town.

l. 22. *repristination*. Return to an earlier pristine state.

350 l. 36. *ticked*. Pulsed (the 'tick' is the heartbeat).

350 ll. 42–8. *a Square in Florence . . . where they lie.* Florence's Square of San Lorenzo indeed contains all the things Browning mentions here; a statue of 'John of the Black Bands' (a military leader) by Baccio Bandinelli, the Palace of Medici-Riccardi where the influential Riccardi family used to live, and the church of San Lorenzo where they are buried.

l. 50. *knaves.* Servants (archaism).

l. 64. *scagliola.* Stone floor (Italian).

l. 65. *crazie.* Tuscan coin; two of them were worth about one-and-a-half old pence.

l. 68. *Master.* Luigi Ademollo (1764–1849). The prints appear to be of the protagonists of the murder-trial (see ll. 364–7 below).

351 l. 71. *Lionard.* Leonardo (da Vinci).

l. 72. *Joconde.* Now known as the Mona Lisa.

l. 76. *Spicilegium.* Anthology.

l. 77. *Frail one of the Flower.* Dumas's early work, *La Dame aux camélias* (1852).

352 l. 112. *Casa Guidi.* The Brownings lived in this house from 1847 until Elizabeth Barrett Browning's death in 1861.

353 l. 168. *cockatrice.* Mythical beast with the body of a cock and the tail of a serpent; it could kill with a look.

354 l. 192. *tottering ark.* The ark of the covenant (the chest containing the ten commandments) was being shaken by the oxen of Nachon. Uzzah put out his hand to prevent it from tottering over, but touching the ark was such a sacrilegious action that God slew him without further ado (2 Sam. 6: 6–7).

ll. 212–13. *firebrand . . . cornfield.* 'And Samson went and caught three hundred foxes and took firebrands and turned tail to tail and put a firebrand in the midst between two tails. And when he had set the brands on fire, he let them go into the standing corn of the Philistines, and burnt up both the shocks, and also the standing corn' (Judg. 15: 4–5).

354-5 ll. 219–29. This widely ranging list of legal authorities and institutors of various legal codes mostly agree in the severe punishment of adultery.

355 l. 257. *clerkly privilege.* Officials of the church have the right to be tried by an ecclesiastical, rather than a civil, court.

ll. 260–2. The Latin terms are all minor orders in the church: *presbyter*, priest; *primæ tonsuræ*, order of the first tonsure (a 'tonsure' is an ecclesiastical haircut); *subdiaconus*, subdeacon; *sacerdos* also means 'priest'. As scholars have observed, this list is a bit of a jumble.

356 l. 272. *Quality.* The upper classes.

l. 293. *Herodotus.* Greek historian (the 'Father of History') whose history related the defeat of the proud and hubristic Persian empire in its war against Greece.

356 l. 303. *Jansenists, re-nicknamed Molinists*. Cornelius Jansen (1585–1638) and his followers believed that divine Grace flowed directly from God and needed no intermediate priesthood. Miguel de Molinos (1627–96) advanced Quietism, whereby the individual soul should aim for complete passivity, since in this state it would be able to contact God directly. Clearly these two heresies (as the church termed them) have elements in common; Pope Innocent XI, the predecessor to the Pope of the poem, was initially favourable to them both, but later denounced them. The issue was a live one in the 1690s, with Molinism recently declared a heresy; speakers in *The Ring and the Book* generally use 'Molinist' as a term synonymous with 'heretic'.

357 l. 320. *five carlines*. Neopolitan currency, worth about 1*s*. 8*d*. in Browning's day, or roughly 8p today.

l. 341. *chirograph*. Handwriting.

358 ll. 357–8. *Remonstrant . . . all Rome*. i.e. the crowd (according to this writer) expressed its support for Guido, and its disapproval of his punishment.

l. 364. *Ademollo*. See l. 68 and n. above.

359 l. 400. *Gaetano*. Pompilia's child.

l. 408. *proverb*. See the apocryphal 1 Esd. 4: 41, *Magna est veritas, et praevalet* ('Great is truth, and it prevails').

l. 426. *Diario*. Daily paper.

360 l. 427. *French burned them*. The French invaded Rome in 1849.

ll. 439–41. *Manning*. Henry Manning (1808–92) converted from Anglicanism to Catholicism in 1851;   *Newman*. Henry Newman (1801–90) did so in 1845.   *Wiseman*. Nicholas Wiseman (1802–65), the first Catholic Archbishop of London (from 1850).

l. 453. *lingot*. Ingot.

l. 461. *djereed*. Spear (Arabic). An Arab game involves throwing a spear through a series of hoops or rings.

361 l. 476. *Felice-church*. The church of San Felice was famous for its music.

l. 484. *gold snow*. Wealth; see *Iliad* ii. 670.

l. 489. *datura*. A large plant with white flowers.

l. 495. *Arezzo*. The town where Guido lived ('the man's town').

l. 502. *Castelnuovo*. A small town a few miles from Rome. At an inn here Guido and his henchmen caught up with the escaping Pompilia and Caponsacchi and had them arrested.

362 l. 547. *Abate Paul, Canon Girolamo*. These two men were brothers to, and accomplices of, Guido.

363 l. 561. *Prince o' the Power of the Air*. A biblical description of Satan (Eph. 2: 2); here used for Guido.

 l. 566. *Mopping and mowing*. Making faces (see *King Lear* IV. i. 61).

 l. 579. *Saint George*. Patron Saint of England, slayer of a fiery dragon and rescuer of a maiden. Browning altered the actual date of Caponsacchi's rescue of Pompilia from 28–9 Apr. to 23 Apr. because the latter is St George's day.

364 l. 617. *Gabriel . . . Eden-gate*. i.e. when Guido spoke Caponsacchi's name to gain admittance to the house of the Comparini it was akin to the Devil using the name of the archangel Gabriel to gain admittance to Paradise.

365 l. 632. *Tophet*. Hell.

 l. 641. *fell*. Wolf-hide.

 l. 664. *entablature*. Greek architectual order to be found below the roof of a building, but above the columns.

366 l. 678. *favoured*. Ornamented.

 l. 684. *commodity*. Commodiousness (i.e. to make it more portable).

367 ll. 729–30. A lamp was supposed to be lit at all times in the Temple of God (see Exod. 27: 20).

367-8 ll. 737–52. The passage in quotation marks is adapted from Cornelius Agrippa (1486–1535), the Renaissance alchemist and philosopher ('mage'), whose book *De Occulta Philosophia* ('On Occult Philosophy', or 'On Magic') Browning knew and had earlier quoted from as epigraph for *Pauline*. Agrippa was a contempory of Faust, the German alchemist and magician, with whom he was sometimes compared.

368 ll. 753–64. *Was not Elisha . . . eyes opened*. Where Faust only reanimated corpses, giving the appearance of life, the prophet Elisha actually resurrected a dead boy to life (2 Kgs. 4: 29–35).

370-1 ll. 839–74. This passage summarizes the argument of Bk. II of *The Ring and the Book*, 'Half-Rome'.

370 l. 860. *Æacus*. As king of Aegina he demonstrated such probity that after his death he was made one of the three who judged souls in Hades.

371 ll. 875–901. This passage summarizes the argument of Bk. III, 'The Other Half-Rome'.

 ll. 888–890. *Another . . . fountain-sport*. The Piazza Barberini in Rome is centred on a fountain statue of a merman Triton by the celebrated sculptor Bernini.

 l. 894. *caritellas*. Small figures of the Graces.

371-2 ll. 902–34. Summary of Bk. IV, 'Tertium Quid' ('third quantity').

372 l. 927. *girandole*. Branched candlestick.

372-4 ll. 941–1007. Summary of Bk. V, 'Count Guido Franceschini'.

373 l. 971. *his limbs' late taste*... Guido has been tortured by the Court to elicit his testimony.   *the Cord*. The defendant had his wrists tied behind his back, and was then suspended on a rope attached to his arms. He might be suspended for several hours whilst the torturer watched (hence Browning's 'facetious' other title for the procedure 'Vigil-torture'), or else subjected to other procedures (jerking the rope, attaching weights to his feet, and so on).

374-5 ll. 1008–67. Summary of Bk. VI, 'Giuseppe Caponsacchi'.

374 l. 1020. *chrism*. Holy oil.

375 l. 1044. *Tommati, Venturini*. The judges.

375-6 ll. 1068–96. Summary of Bk. VII, 'Pompilia'.

377 ll. 1116–53. Summary of Bk. VIII, 'Dominus Hyacinthus de Archangelis'.

l. 1145. *levigate*. To pulverize prior to analysis.

l. 1147. *inchoates*. develops.

l. 1149. *Ovidian quip*. Ovid's poetry was renowned for its witty vivacity.   *Ciceronian crank*. Cicero's prose was a model of Latin rhetorical elegance. A 'crank' is an elaborate figure of speech.

377-9 ll. 1154–1211. Summary of Bk. IX, 'Juris Doctor Johannes-Baptista Bottinius'.

378 l. 1157. *exordium*. Introduction.   *clap*. Hurry.

l. 1182. *Well done, thou good and faithful*. Matt. 25: 21.

l. 1193. *scrannel*. Screeching, grating.

379 l. 1194. *studio*. Study. Bottinus' practising his speech to the court at home is likened by Browning to a cockerel's tuneless crowing.

l. 1201. *Clavecinist*. Player of the Clavecin, an instrument akin to the harpsichord.

l. 1206. *Corelli*. Arcangelo Corelli (1653–1713), Italian composer, particularly associated with the violin.   *Haendel*. Georg Friedrich Handel (1685–1759), the German composer, is anachronistically invoked here; he was indeed precocious as a composer, but he had no reputation (being aged only 14) in 1698, and he did not come to Rome until 1706.

379-80 ll. 1212–63. Summary of Bk. X, 'The Pope'.

379 l. 1231. *lathen*. Made out of lath (thin strips of wood).

380 l. 1244. *diurnal*. Daily.

380-2 ll. 1264–1321. Summary of Bk. XI, 'Guido'.

380 l. 1265. *Satan's old saw*. 'Skin for skin, yea, all that a man hath will he give for his life' (Job 2: 4).

381 l. 1296. *The enemy.* Satan (see Isa. 59: 19).

l. 1311. *Out of the deeps*...Ps. 130: 1.

382 l. 1320. *Mannaia.* 'Blade' (i.e. the guillotine that will behead Guido).

l. 1332. *sward.* Pasture.

l. 1343. *House of Fame.* Chaucer's poem described how he was brought to the House of Fame in a dream by an eagle.

383 l. 1359. *glass ball with a spark a-top.* The device described here is the 'electric egg': electrical charge is passed across a partial vacuum contained in a glass ball, causing it to fluoresce with a violet colour. A finger pressed to the glass will attract positive ions, causing arcs of light.

l. 1369. *Guy Faux.* Catholic plotter who tried to blow up King James I and Parliament (1605); traditional villain of English folklore, ritually burnt on a bonfire every 5 Nov.

l. 1382. *posy.* Motto.

l. 1383. *O lyric Love.* Epic poems traditionally contain an address to the poet's Muse or Muses; here Browning invokes the spirit of his dead wife, Elizabeth Barrett Browning. There is also a Greek pun involved in this construction; the Greek Muse for lyric poetry was Erato, and *eratos* is Greek for 'lovely' or 'beloved'.

384 *Book X. The Pope.* First published Feb. 1869, in the last of the four instalments of *The Ring and the Book*.

l. 1. *Ahasuerus.* 'On that night could not the king [Ahasuerus] sleep, and he commanded to bring the book of records of the chronicles; and they were read before the king' (Esther 6: 1). 'Shrewd' here means 'cunning' or 'evil-disposed'.

l. 9. *of the making books there is no end.* Eccles. 12: 12.

l. 11. *Peter.* St Peter, founder of the church and first Pope.
Alexander. Alexander VIII was Innocent XII's predecessor.

385 l. 23. *cyst.* Coffin.

385-8 ll. 24–149. The Pope relates one of the most notorious incidents of the early Papacy. Formosus was Pope 891–6; Stephen 896–7; Romanus 897; Theodore 897; John IX 898–900; Sergius III 904–11. The wrangle happened more or less as described here.

386 l. 89. IXΘΥΣ which means Fish. After Christ's promise to the disciples ('I will make you fishers of men', Matt. 4: 19), the Greek word for 'fish' ('ICHTHUS') was taken as an acronym (*Iesus CHristos THeou Uios Soter*, 'Jesus Christ, God's Son, Saviour').

388 l. 150. *which of the judgments was infallible?* Browning alludes to a contemporary debate, especially within the Catholic church, concerning the status of the Pope's pronouncements; since he was God's representative on earth, some theologians argued that he could not be wrong. The doctrine of Papal infallibility was promulgated in 1870.

388 ll. 154–6. *Fear ye not . . . into hell*. Matt. 10: 28.

l. 163. *time wherein to work*. cf. John 9: 4.

l. 169. *assize*. Court.

390 l. 227. *rede*. Interpretation.

391 l. 292. *Swede*. Often identified as the mystic Emanuel Swedenborg (1688–1772), although he was only 10 years old at the time of the monologue. More likely to be a reference to his father Jasper Swedberg (1653–1735), a noted theologian and philosopher of the day, who shared (that is to say, inspired) many of his son's interests.

392 l. 327. *posset*. Hot alcoholic drink.

ll. 329–30. *smoking flax . . . quenches him*. 'The smoking flax shall he [Christ] not quench: he shall bring forth judgment unto truth' (Isa. 42: 3).

393 ll. 375. *He*. Christ. See John 1: 14, 14: 6.

394 l. 382. *Antonio Pignatelli*. Innocent XII's (which is to say, the narrator's) real name; the Pope addresses his earlier self, a self who had travelled widely in the service of the Church.

l. 416. *cirque*. Arena.

395 l. 434–5. *Man . . . please God*. 1 Thess. 4: 1.

l. 448. *portentous*. Sinister.

396 l. 465. *paravent*. Protection against the wind.   *ombrifuge*. Protection against the rain.

l. 470. *sacristan*. Warder of the Church's sacred vessels.

l. 485. *ambiguous fish*. Any fish that lives in the discarded shells of others.

397 l. 509. *soldier-crab*. Hermit crab, which lives in others' shells.

399 l. 578. *gor-crow*. Carrion crow.

l. 588. *curious*. Cunning, unusual.

400 ll. 618–25. *in our Campagna . . . tomb*. The plain around Rome (the Campagna) contains a large number of antique ruins and sites.

l. 640. *Who shall pluck sheep . . . from Thy hand?* John 10: 28.

l. 652. *Aretine*. Pietro Aretino (1492–1555), author of a variety of scatological, obscene, and savage attacks on figures of authority. He also wrote serious works of theology (hence 'incorporate the filth | With cherub faces').

401 l. 689. *preconcerts*. Prepares, makes ready.

l. 695. *the Pieve*. Caponsacchi's church in Arezzo.

402 l. 711. *The lost be saved . . . by fire?* 1 Cor. 3: 15.

l. 712. *Let him, rebuked, go softly . . .* Isa. 38: 15.

403 l. 740. *Murder with jagged knife!* Guido's knife was serrated ('triangular i' the blade . . . with those little hook-teeth on the edge', II. 147–8)

ll. 743–9. Reference to the biblical flood (Gen. 8: 6–11).

ll. 749–51. *'Tis an infant's birth . . . occasion.* The Pope believes that Guido delayed carrying out the murder until Pompilia gave birth because he hoped (via his son) to inherit the estate of Pompilia's parents; had mother and unborn son died together, the estate would have remained with the Comparini.

404 l. 777. *When Saturn ruled.* Mythical golden age, presided over by the father of Zeus, a time of pastoral simplicity. The Pope is being ironic in comparing this idyllic state to the contemporary countryside.

l. 784. *Christ's birthnight-eve.* Guido arrived in Rome on Christmas Eve 1697, but waited until 2 Jan. 1698 to commit the crime.

l. 811. *hebetude.* Dullness, obtuseness.

405 l. 818. *ducat.* Gold coin.

l. 820. *post-house.* Stables. Guido could not escape to Tuscany because he was unable to obtain a pass out of Rome.

l. 832. *Rota.* Criminal court in Florence. This court confirmed a life-sentence upon Pompilia, but the sentence was irrelevant since she was by this time under Roman jurisdiction.

406 l. 893. *Girolamo.* Pompilia claimed that Girolamo made improper advances to her.

407 l. 933. *glebe.* Field.

408 l. 968. *Marzi-Medici.* The governor of Arezzo; despite the similarity of names he was not in fact related to the Medici family (whose head was the Grand Duke of Tuscany), although the Pope seems to think otherwise.

409 l. 983. *Archbishop.* Bishop of Arezzo.

l. 988. *the hireling that did . . . flee.* See John 10: 12– 13.

l. 1007. *Michael . . . armed.* The statue of St Michael on top of the Castel St Angelo, near St Peter's.

411 l. 1080. *Him.* Caponsacchi.

l. 1092. *the other rose, the gold.* The Papacy gave a gift of a golden rose annually to a king or other prominent person who had rendered the Church some notable service. The rose is symbolic of the Virgin Mary.

l. 1098. *leviathan.* Sea-monster of enormous size.

412 l. 1119. *Nard.* Spikenard, an aromatic herb.

413 l. 1141. *pudicity.* Modesty.

l. 1144. *mulct.* Punish (by taxing or fining).

l. 1158. *White-cinct.* Wearing a white belt.

413 l. 1160. *Unchariness of blood*. Willingness to shed blood. The Pope is suggesting that the red colour of a cardinal's uniform signals his readiness to shed blood for his beliefs.

414 l. 1206. *initiatory spasm*. The sense is of a violent rebirth (into a selfless life of service to others).

415 l. 1240. *lynx-gift*. The mythical lynx was renowned for its superb eyesight.

l. 1260. *Perk*. Cheer up!   *pry*. Inquire into.

416 l. 1265. *gyves*. Shackles.

417 l. 1334. *Thy transcendent act*. The incarnation (the birth of Christ).

418 l. 1361. *isoscele deficient in the base*. The Pope imagines an isosceles triangle with two long, equal sides (strength and intelligence) and one shorter ('deficient') side (goodness).

l. 1379. '*I have said ye are Gods*'. Ps. 82: 6.

419 l. 1398. *choppy*. Chapped.   *chymic*. Chemical.

l. 1402. *by God's gloved hand or the bare?* That is to say, via divine myth or unmediated fact.

l. 1411. *probatively*. By trial.

421 l. 1471. *cuticle*. Skin.

ll. 1477–8. *Who was it ... put finger forth?* See above, Bk. I: l. 192 n.

ll. 1483–6. *If foolish virgins ... Bridegroom here*. The foolish virgins omitted to fill their lamps with oil before going to sleep; they were thus unprepared for the arrival of the bridegroom (Matt. 25: 1–13). The bridegroom is interpreted by St Paul as Christ, the Spouse as the Church (Eph. 5: 23–4).

l. 1494. *Monastery called of Convertites*. The convent of Santa Maria della Convertite (set up to help fallen women) was entitled to the estates of immoral women who died intestate. They attempted to obtain Pompilia's estate after her death, but their suit declaring her as adulteress was rejected by the court.

l. 1503. *body*. The convent.

422 l. 1513. *Fisc*. State prosecutor (in this case Bottinus).

l. 1521. *soldiers... . Christ's coat*. Matt. 27: 35.

l. 1524. *woof*. Fabric.   *of price*. Expensive.

423-4 ll. 1584–1608. The Pope refers to a real-life instance of the Church's misplaced zeal in the conflict between the Jesuits in China and the Pope's Vicar Apostolic for the region, Bishop Maigrot. The Jesuits had been in the area for many years, and being 'politic' (l. 1592) endorsed the Chinese word for God. Bishop Maigrot thought it inappropriate. Cardinal Tournon was sent to Peking to sort the matter out.

424 l. 1614. *Rosy Cross*. The Rosicrucians were a quasi-mystical sect, whose 'Great Work' was the alchemic dream of turning base metal into gold.

425 l. 1633. *He*. Christ (Matt. 27: 45).

    l. 1645. *comports*. permits.

    l. 1662. *bard*. Euripides (480–406 BC), the Greek tragedian, who is the supposed speaker of ll. 1664–1784. Browning was particularly fond of Euripides, who was often cited as a 'noble Pagan' by Christian writers because of a passage at the end of his play *Heracles* (also known as *Hercules Furens* or *Mad Heracles*) in which the protagonist denies the various erotic myths associated with the Olympian gods, and insists instead that the true God (singular) was beyond such human desires. (Browning's translation of the passage can be found in *Aristophanes' Apology*, ll. 4976–83).

426 l. 1672. *Machinist*. Engineer (Latin: Machinator). By extension, Zeus (an allusion to the *deus ex machina*, the god lowered by a piece of stage machinery at the end of many Euripidean plays).

    l. 1695. *born to perish*. i.e. because he was born before Christ.

    l. 1701. *When the Third . . . Two*. When Euripides' fame began to rival the older and more traditional Aeschylus and Sophocles.

427 l. 1712. *Felix heard*. Acts 24: 22–7.

    l. 1715. *style*. Punning on 'stylus' (writing implement) and writing style.

428 l. 1756. *tenebrific*. Dark.

    l. 1786. *Paul . . . answered Seneca*. A correspondence (almost certainly forged) between St Paul and the Roman philosopher and dramatist Seneca was discovered in the 4th century. Seneca's Stoic beliefs were regarded favourably by many Christian thinkers.

429 l. 1818. *Druid*. Pagan priest of old Celtic religion.

    l. 1821. *Who is last proves first*. See Matt. 19: 30.

    ll. 1825–7. *gross torch . . . Nero's cross and stake*. The Pope alludes to the persecutions of Nero, which were illuminated by live torches made of Christians.

430 l. 1863. *Molinists*. Heretics (see above, Bk. 1, l. 303).

431 l. 1898. *antimasque*. Burlesque interlude between the acts of a masque. *kibe*. Sore heel.

432 l. 1919. *morrice*. Morris (English folk-dance, involving grown men dressed in white prancing about with bells on their costumes).

    l. 1922. *Augustin*. St Augustine of Hippo (354–430), one of the Church fathers.

    l. 1925. *second in the suite*. Second in line.

    l. 1936. *Loyola*. St Ignatius Loyola (1491–1556), founder of the Jesuit order, and (here) a representative of fanaticism and casuistry.

433 l. 1962–4. *Spare yet . . . bring forth fruit*. See the parable of the fig tree (Luke 8: 8–9).

433 ll. 1980–1. *nemini | Honorem trado*. 'I surrender my honour to nobody' (this was Guido's chief line of defence). This 'right of Him (i.e. Christ, or God)' is so called because of the similarities with a statement of God's (*Gloriam meam alteri non dabo*, 'I will not give up my glory to another' Isa. 42: 8).

434 l. 1998. *Farinacci*. Roman legal expert (1544–1613), whose opinions are often cited by the lawyers in the trial.

435 l. 2037. *coil*. Hubbub.

l. 2042. *tenement*. Building (such as a block of flats).

ll. 2050–1. *Barabbas' self | Was set free*. Offered the choice of whom to release from imminent crucifixion, the Jews chose the thief Barabbas rather than Christ (Matt. 27: 15–26).

l. 2052. *Sabbath close*. Sunday's end. The Sabbath day was supposed to be kept inviolate; here the Pope alludes to the end of his own life.

l. 2055. *silver mallet silent on thy brow*. If a Pope refuses to answer to his name, and does not respond to three taps on his forehead with a silver mallet, he is officially pronounced dead.

l. 2063. *petit-maître*. Foppish, footling.

436 l. 2082. *Priam*. The king of Troy was a very old man when his city was besieged. Virgil has him dressed for battle as the city fell, reproved by his wife Hecuba with the words *non tali | Auxilio* ('such aid is not needed'), *Aeneid* ii. 521–2.

ll. 2094–5. *Quis pro Domino?* Quoted from Exod. 32: 26. Guida had used this scripture to justify his murders (see Bk. V, l. 1542).

l. 2104. *People's Square*. The executions took place in the Piazza del Popolo, 22 Feb. 1698.

437 l. 2123. *sequestered state*. Purgatory.

Book XI. Guido. First published in the final instalment of *The Ring and the Book*, Feb. 1869.

ll. 1–11. Acciaiuoli and Panciatichi are members of the Confraternity of Death, whose duty it is to inform Guido of his sentence. Guido remarks that it was Acciaiuoli's ancestor who founded the Carthusian Monastery Certosa, built outside Florence where the rivers Greve and Ema meet.

l. 14. *Senescal*. Steward of a medieval household.

438 l. 37. *good-hand*. The Italian for 'tip' or 'gratuity' is *buonamano*.

l. 53. *hat and plume*. Symbolic of nobility.

439 l. 76. *coyness*. Disdain.

l. 96. *pricked*. Spurred.   *breathe*. Exercise.

440 l. 105. *pale*. Boundary separating the acceptable from the unacceptable.

l. 114. *springe*. Trap.

440 l. 125. *engine*. Machine—in this case, the guillotine. Guido also describes it as the 'iron tooth' (l. 179).

l. 137. *tacit*. Silent.

l. 141. *shrived*. Administered the last rites.

441 l. 146. *windlestraws*. Dry stalks of grass (i.e. Guido is describing the Cardinal and the Abate).

442 l. 184. *Mannaia*. Guillotine.

l. 186. *Mouth-of-Truth*. A large sculpted head of a Triton, out of whose open mouth water flows, to be found by the Church of Santa Maria in Rome.

l. 206. *Swiss guard*. The Pope's personal bodyguard.

443 l. 243. *elucubrate*. Explain (with the suggestion of pomposity).

l. 261. *cullion*. Fool.

444 l. 270. *Albano*. Franceso Albani (1578–1660), Bolognese painter. 'Florid' applies both to his torrid personal life and his rich painting style.

ll. 292–4. *the silver cord...we're loose*. Guido reappropriates the words of Eccles. 12: 6–7 ('Or ever the silver cord be loosed, or the golden bowl broken...') so that the 'cord' becomes the spinal cord and the 'bowl' the head.

l. 302. *extravasate*. Poured out.

444–5 ll. 302–3. *Roland's sword...Oliver's mace*. Roland and Oliver (here invoked with their favourite weapons) were two great knights from the age of Charlemagne.

445 l. 305. *arachnoid tunic*. Membrane covering the brain.

l. 309. *Fagon*. Famed physician to Louis XIV.

l. 312. *Pistoja*. Italian town of Pistoia, famous for its knives and other cutlery.

l. 324. *Petrus, quo vadis?* 'Peter, where are you going?' Parallels the story told by St Jerome, that Peter left the persecutions of Rome only to bump into Christ, of whom he asked *Domine, quo vadis?* and received the reply: 'I go to be re-crucified.' This was enough to make Peter turn back.

l. 327. *Dorcas*. Raised from the dead by Peter (Acts 9: 36–41).

l. 341. *crib*. Steal.

446 l. 377. *nice*. Picky, particular.   *coy*. Disdainful.

447 l. 400. *crumpled*. Crooked.

448 l. 441. *shag*. Hairy skin (wolf-pelt).

449 l. 491. *looked me low*. Felled me with only a look.

l. 504. *Gorgon shield*. The shield of Athena carried the face of the gorgon upon it, such that anybody looking at it would be turned to stone.

451 l. 546. *try a fall*. Wrestle.

l. 550. *colly my cow!* 'Blimey!' (lit. 'Bash my cow!')

l. 566. *King Cophetua*. Legendary Mesopotamian king who fell in love with (and married) a beggar maid.

l. 583. *Ash*. Ash Wednesday was on 12 February.

452 l. 587. *realize*. Make real (also at l. 595).

l. 623. *Pope's-halberdier*. The Pope's Swiss guard again. A halberdier is a soldier armed with a halberd, which is a sort of combination spear-and-axe.

453 l. 635. *Referendary*. An important Vatican official.

454 l. 680. *tinkle*. The ringing of the bell during Mass to signify that the bread and wine had become the body and blood of Christ.

l. 682. *Trebbian*. An Italian wine.

455 l. 732. *caudatory*. Train-bearer.

l. 733. *caps*. Tips hat deferentially.

456 l. 757. *prodigal son of heavenly sire*. Cf. the parable of the prodigal son (Luke 15: 16–23).

l. 785. *Chap-fallen*. Slack-jawed.

457 l. 798. *compass joy by concert*. Enjoy ourselves together.

459 l. 881. *jaundiced patch*. Jealous fool.

l. 904. *piece*. Painting.

460 l. 913. *horn-blind*. Blind to his wife's infidelity.

l. 914. *lynx*. The lynx is traditionally famed for its superb eyesight.

l. 923. *mote*. Minute, like a mote.

l. 927. *fieldfares*. Thrushes.

l. 928. *bent*. Blade of grass.

462 l. 994. *Esther*. See the story of Esther petitioning the King Ahasuerus on behalf of Jewry, Esther 5: 2 (in the Apocrypha).

l. 1002. *Louis*. Louis XIV was notorious for his philandering.

l. 1022. *wheelwork*. Mechanism.

l. 1023. *proof*. Tempered.

463 l. 1058–9. *endure | The ... hem!* Pompilia initially refused to consummate the marriage.

464 l. 1097. *Provence prodigy*. Spectacular rose, compared with the humble wild rose ('dog-rose') above.

465 ll. 1116–24. *The Etruscan monster...which I slew!* The Chimera ('the Etruscan monster') had a lion's head, a goat's body, and a serpent's tail; it was slain by Bellerophon; an antique bronze statue depicting the scene was discovered at Arezzo in 1554.

465 l. 1138. *wear velvet.* i.e. they are wealthy enough to do so.

l. 1150. *quondam.* Onetime.

l. 1152. *Pantaloon.* A stock clown-figure from Italian comedy.

466 l. 1187. *perdue.* Hidden.

468 l. 1244. *saucy quip.* Presumably that the Cardinal's building is terribly dull: 'lymphatic' (i.e. dull, sluggish) is rhymed with the Cardinal's name in l. 1252.

l. 1272. *transformations of disgust.* Disgusting transformations.

l. 1278. *coil.* Raucous disturbance.

469 l. 1291. *San Lorenzo.* The bodies of Pompilia and her parents were publicly exhibited in this church.

470 l. 1326. *doubles of the hare.* A hare pursued will run zig-zags to try and throw off the predator.

471 l. 1378. *wards.* Inner components of a lock.

472 l. 1408. *Armida.* Female character from the opera *Gerusalemme liberata.*

l. 1415. *zecchines.* Roman coin.

l. 1439. *pleasaunce.* Garden.

473 l. 1460. *gospel-side.* The left side of the altar.

l. 1464. *muzzled ox ... corn.* 'Thou shalt not muzzle the ox when he treadeth out the corn' (Deut. 25: 4).

l. 1474. *high-days.* Holy days; festivals and saint's days.

474 l. 1509. *Anathema!* 'Curse it!'

475 l. 1526. *The letter kills, the spirit keeps alive.* 2 Cor. 3: 6.

476 l. 1601. *tænia.* Tapeworm.

477 l. 1626. *malapert.* Impudent.

478 l. 1645. *hacks and hamstrings.* Disables (literally by cutting the tendons behind the knee).

480 l. 1766. *skull.* The hill on which Christ was crucified was called Golgotha ('Skull').

481 l. 1776. *Jansenius.* Leader of heretical branch of the church.

l. 1803. *Vienna.* Attacked by the Turks in 1683 under the leadership of Mustapha, and successfully defended by Charles, Duke of Lorraine.

482 l. 1834. *gird.* Taunt.

l. 1845. *gaudeamus.* 'Let us rejoice' (Latin).

483 l. 1880. *I go, Sir.* In the parable, the son actually said 'I go, Sir,' 'and went not' (Matt. 21: 30).

l. 1882. *paul.* Italian silver coin worth a shilling in Browning's day (or 5p in modern money).

483 l. 1889. *dollar.* Old European dollar, a silver coin worth about 5*s.* in Browning's day (or 25p today).

484 ll. 1906–15. *ancient Roman-like . . . Etruscan, Aretine.* Guido first invokes the ancient and therefore venerable name of Rome; then substitutes the even older Tuscany, implying that his lineage stretches back even further than Rome. The Etruscans were a pre-Roman civilization who lived in Tuscany; Bk. 8 of Virgil's *Aeneid* describes Aeneas (the founder of what was to become Rome) coming to Italy and being told that the land is inhabited by an ancient people descended directly from 'fauns and nymphs'.

l. 1919. *Jove Ægiochus.* Jupiter of the Dark Aegis (or Shield).

ll. 1927–8. *gules.* Red.   *azure.* Blue.

485-6 ll. 1969–70. *living truth . . . strike Pan dead.* Plutarch's *De Defectu Oraculum* records that at the time of Christ's crucifixion some passengers on a ship heard a voice booming over the water saying 'Great Pan is dead'. Elizabeth Barrett wrote a poem on the subject ('The Dead Pan').

486 l. 1977. *mulct and minish.* Reduce and diminish.

ll. 2000–1. *Those that use the sword | Shall perish by the same.* Matt. 26: 52.

487 l. 2019. *Pontifex.* The Pope.

l. 2028. *Romano vivitur more.* 'We live in the Roman style'. Quoted from Jeremy Taylor's *Doctor Dubitantium* (1660), 1. 1. 5: *Si fueris Romae, Romano vivito more* ('If you are in Rome, live in the Roman style').

l. 2031. *tares.* Weeds (see Matt. 13: 24–30).

ll. 2043–9. *some such fate . . . Let me turn wolf.* Ovid's story tells of feeble Byblis and her passion for her savage brother, Lycaon; Byblis was turned into a fountain (*Byblis in fluvium*), but her brother into a wolf (*sed Lycaon in lupum*: the Latin is quoted from *Metamorphoses* i. 237–9).

488 l. 2051. *Coerced.* Restrained.

489 l. 2093. *who did not make myself.* Guido is quoting Pompilia's words from her speech in Bk. VII.

ll. 2109–10. *daub.* Badly executed painting.   *Rafael.* An old master painting (by Raphael).

l. 2114. *Titian . . . Angelico.* The contrast is between the sensuous and realistic Titian and the idealist, other-worldly Fra Angelico.

l. 2121. *lawn.* Fine cloth.

490 l. 2137. *Paynimrie.* Heathendom ('Paganland').

l. 2142. *furze-sprig.* Shrub twig.   *hauberk-joint.* Joint in a suit of armour.

l. 2151. *demesne.* Archaic spelling of 'domain'.

491 l. 2177. *Olimpias . . . Biancas.* Representative heroines from Italian romance.

491 l. 2178. *Ormuz.* Famous diamond market.

ll. 2191–5. *Sounder than Samson...Delilah dares do!* Delilah discovered that Samson's strength lay in his hair and shaved him, leaving him helpless (Judg. 16: 6–20).

l. 2197. *call-bird.* Decoy.

l. 2204. *Circe.* Enchantress: the daughter of Helios (the Sun), who turned Odysseus' shipmates into pigs (*Odyssey* x).

l. 2206. *honest distaff.* i.e. an honest woman.

l. 2207. *Lucrezia.* Daughter of Pope Alexander VI and sister of Cesare Borgia, with whom she had an incestuous affair; infamous poisoner.

492 l. 2232. *scantling.* A measurement.

492-3 ll. 2253–7. *first the Chamberlain...Seventh on the list.* Guido speculates on who will be made Pope once Innocent is dead (in fact he died within three years); the actual successor was Albano (l. 2332).

493 ll. 2262–3. *fulcrum-stone...move the world.* Archimedes, mathematician from the 3rd century BC, claimed that with a place to stand and a long enough lever he could move the world.

l. 2291. *Saint Peter's bark.* Matt. 14: 24–31.

494 l. 2314. *powers and principalities.* Quoted from Eph. 6: 12, where it refers to the agencies through which evil works in the world.

l. 2326. *Tozzi.* The Pope's physician.

495 l. 2339. *Martinez.* Ambassador to Rome of Leopold, the Holy Roman Emperor.

l. 2355. *halcyon.* Kingfisher.

496 l. 2402. *Athenian who died.* Themistokles, who committed suicide by drinking hot bull's blood (thought to be a posion).

l. 2407. *accursed psalm!* Bk. I (ll. 1311–12) identifies this as Ps. 130, the *De Profundis.*

Fifine at the Fair

498 Composed between Dec. 1871 and May 1862; first published June 1872. This fascinating and complex poem is too long (2,463 lines) to be printed in full here; instead are printed the lyric prologue and epilogue; the remainder of the work is in rhymed alexandrine couplets, and constitutes a dramatic monologue spoken by a modern-day French Don Juan to his wife Elvire, as he attempts to justify his adulterous passion for, and ultimately relations with, a gypsy girl (Fifine) encountered at a fair in Pornic, northern France. Prologue and epilogue are not directly related to the main narrative, but explore the same themes and questions, in particular the binary divisions around which the whole work is organized (body/soul, male/female), and the logic of sexual (and by extension, other) betrayals.

Prologue. Amphibian.

500 l. 53. *Emancipate*. Emancipated.

l. 58. *disport*. Relaxation.

501 l. 73. *she*. Double reference to the butterfly, and the (unidentified) 'certain soul' of l. 33 that it represents. Some critics have taken this to be a reference to the spirit of Elizabeth Barrett Browning.

Aristophanes' Apology

503 Written between Aug. and Nov. 1874 and published Apr. 1875. Another work too lengthy (5,711 lines) to print entire here, it is set in 5th-century BC Greece just after the death of Euripides, and is mostly given over to a debate between a (fictional) champion of the dead tragedian called Balaustion (she had first appeared in *Balaustion's Adventure* of 1871) and the (real-life) Athenian comic poet Aristophanes over the respective merits of Euripides' tragic and Aristophanes' comic art. Balaustion considers Aristophanes' often scatological humour to be smut, and beneath the dignity of an artist; Aristophanes argues that Euripides' plays are too abstract, rather frigid, and also impious in reasoning away the Olympian gods and putting in their place a sort of intellectualized single spirit. Balaustion defends Euripides by reciting the whole of his great drama *Herakles* (Browning's translation of the work is inserted into the text complete); Aristophanes concedes the excellence of the piece, and begins (by way of a reply) to recite a song of his own, 'Thamuris marching'; but he breaks off in laughter before finishing it, and, it now being dawn, he rises to go.

Printed here is 'Thamuris marching' and some of its surrounding matter. Thamuris was a Thracian musician of such skill that he had the audacity to challenge the Muses themselves to a poetic contest. The song has him marching towards this rendezvous; but Thamuris loses the competition, and is blinded and deprived of his gift for song by the immortals.

l. 5183. *psalterion*. Stringed musical instrument, strummed to accompany the performance of lyric poetry in Ancient Greece.

l. 5185. *Sophokles*. Athenian tragedian (495–406 BC), second of the great triad of tragic writers (with Aeschylus and Euripides). Aristophanes cites him as the superior tragedian, and is inspired to sing about Thamuris partly by the fact that Sophocles had written a tragedy called *Thamuris* (this work is now lost).

l. 5189. *Perpend*. Consider.

l. 5194. *Mount Pangaois*. Thracian mountain, famous for its deposits of gold and silver.

l. 5196. *Thessalia*. Thessaly, region in eastern Greece.

503 l. 5200. *Balura*. The river Balyra was so named after Thamuris's contest, because in his blindness and misery he threw his lyre (*Ba*, throw, *lura*, lyre) into it.

504 l. 5220. *Pan*. Pastoral god with human upper half and goat's lower half.

505 l. 5260. *Parnassos*. More conventionally, Parnassus; mountain near Delphi, sacred to the Muses.

l. 5262. *Pieria*. Region on the northern slopes of Mt Olympus; sacred to the Muses.

l. 5276. *Prelude-Battle*. Literal translation of the title of an earlier Aristophanes play, *Proagon*, of which only fragments survived. He says that if Balaustion thought the *Proagon* attacked Euripides ('"best friend"') too much, then he would be fairer in his next play, the 'main fight'. He goes on to describe *Frogs*, one of his most famous plays, in which Euripides descends to the underworld to do contest with Aeschylus for the title of greatest tragedian. Aeschylus wins, in part because his phrases are more weighty (measured literally on a weighing-scale) than Euripides'.

l. 5281. *stray-away*. A straggler. The word is used to describe a sheep that strays away from the herd.

506 l. 5288. *Bacchos*. Bacchus, or Dionysus, was the god of wine and revels; he was also the presiding deity in the Athenian theatre (drama began as religious ritual in a festival devoted to Bacchus). Aristophanes suggests that Euripides' last play, *The Bacchae* ('The Bacchantes') will be sure to win the prize at the next festival (as indeed it did).

l. 5295. *patron-god*. Bacchus (see previous note).

ll. 5298–9. *Athenai breathes … blank*. The poem is set during a period of truce during the long-running Peloponnesian war between the Greek states of Athens and Sparta (and their respective allies). Aristophanes may be thankful for the peace, but it was short lived, and Athens was finally defeated by Sparta the following year (404 BC).

ll. 5301–2. *Arginousai*. Naval battle of 406 BC at which the Athenians had been victorious   *Kallikratidas*. Important Spartan general who died in the battle.

l. 5304. *Dekeleia*. Small town outside Athens which was occupied by a Spartan military garrison 413–404 BC.

l. 5307. *my long labours*. With comedies such as *Peace* and *Lysistrata*, Aristophanes had long been campaigning for an end to the wasteful war.

l. 5310. Theoria (who represents games and festivals) and Opora (who represents plenty and fruitfulness) are characters from Aristophanes' anti-war play *Lysistrata*.

ll. 5313–14. *cates*. Delicacies.   *Collops*. Slices.   *spinks*. Chaffinches.

506   l. 5317. *light Muse*. The Muse of comedy, Thaleia (the name means 'the blooming one').

l. 5318. *Melpomené*. Muse of tragedy (the name means 'the Songstress').

l. 5319. *Amphion*. Legendary poet, who charmed stones with his lyre-playing, and used his talents to build the walls of Thebes.

Pacchiarotto and How He Worked in Distemper, with Other Poems

507   Most of the poems were written in 1876, and the collection was published that year. The title poem is a satirical attack on Browning's critics, in particular Alfred Austin (1835–1913) who had viciously attacked Browning in a review. The collection as a whole contains poems of more personal significance than is usual for Browning.

House. Composed 1 Feb. 1874; first published in *Pacchiarotto* (1876). Critics have suggested that the poem may have been prompted by Browning's disapproval of D. G. Rossetti's 'confessional' and sensual sonnet sequence *The House of Life* (the first part of which appeared in 1870).

l. 3. *pelf*. Wealth.

l. 4. *Unlock my heart with a sonnet-key*. This line is derived from Wordsworth's sonnet, 'Scorn not the sonnet' (1827): 'Scorn not the Sonnet; Critic, you have frowned | Mindless of its just honours;—with this Key | Shakespeare unlocked his heart'. Browning quotes from the poem again at ll. 38–9.

509   *Numpholeptos*. Written Apr. 1876, first published in *Pacchiarotto* (1876). The title is a Greek word, and means 'one possessed by a nymph' (a nymph being a divine spirit associated with nature), 'possessed' in the sense in which we talk of 'possession by devils'. Browning was asked to explain the poem in June 1889, and he replied to his friend F. J. Furnivall (the two italicized terms are in Greek in the original): 'Is not the key to the meaning of the poem in its title—*numpholeeptos* [i.e. nymph-possessed], not *gunaikerastees* [i.e. a woman-lover]? An allegory, that is, of an impossible ideal object of love, accepted conventionally as such by a man who, all the while, cannot quite blind himself to the demonstrable fact that the possessor of knowledge and purity obtained without the natural consequences of obtaining them by achievement—not inheritance—such a being is imaginary, not real, a nymph and no woman: and only such an one would be ignorant of and surprised at the results of a lover's endeavour to emulate the qualities which the beloved is entitled to consider as pre-existent to earthly experience, and independent of its inevitable results. I had no particular woman in mind; certainly never meant to personify wisdom, philosophy, or any other abstraction' (*Trumpeter*, 160). As DeVane laconically comments, 'Browning's explanation is perhaps not so clear as the poem itself' (*DeVane*, 405).

509 l. 20. *Spirit-Seven*. Browning wrote to Furnivall that 'the "seven spirits" are in the Apocalypse, also in Coleridge and Byron: a common image' (*Trumpeter*, 160).

l. 21. *lamp*. Shine like a lamp.

510 l. 60. *Centuply-angled*. Hundred-faceted.

l. 61. *hearted*. At the heart.

l. 73. *blank*. White.

511 l. 84. *bow*. Rainbow.

l. 101. *bickers*. Flickers.

512 l. 121. *smatch*. Trace.

l. 133. *petrific*. With the ability to turn to stone (petrify).

Dramatic Idyls

513 This collection was published Apr. 1879.

Tray. Probably written late 1878; first published in *Dramatic Idyls* (1878). The poem is based on an event actually witnessed by one of Browning's friends in Paris. 'Tray' was the name of one of the dogs Browning's family had owned in his childhood.

l. 2. *Bard the first*. Possibly a dig at William Morris, whose fondness for old-style heroisms and archaic language had been demonstrated by his *Sigurd the Volsung* (1876); possibly the reference is to Swinburne, whose *Poems and Ballads, Second Series* (1878) contain several cod-medieval ballads of this sort.

l. 6. *Bard the second*. More recognizable as the Byron of *Childe Harold's Pilgrimage*, canto III.

Dramatic Idyls, Second Series

515 Published June 1880.

Clive. Written Feb. 1880; first published in *Dramatic Idyls, Second Series* (1880). Robert, Lord Clive (1725–74) engineered in the 1740s and 1750s a series of military victories over the French in India, and then over various Indian armies, the result of which was a British domination of the subcontinent that lasted 200 years. But after his return to England accusations of financial irregularities contributed to his decline; he became an opium addict and committed suicide in 1774.

l. 8. *Plassy*. In North-east India; it was Clive's victory here in 1757 over the forces of Suraj-a-Dowlah that firmly founded the British empire in India.

l. 12. *forthright*. A straight course.   *meander*. A winding course. The narrator is quoting Shakespeare's *Tempest*, III. iii. 3.

515 l. 13. *rood*. A measurement of a few yards.

l. 16. *rummer-glass*. Large drinking glass.

516 l. 27. *smock-frocked*. Wearing farm-labourers clothes.

l. 39. *greenhorn*. Inexperienced person.   *quill-driving clerk*. Clive originally went to India as clerk.

l. 40. *Arcot*. Clive's first military engagement in India, 1750. With just 120 English and 200 native troops he successfully held the city of Arcot against an army of 10,000 during a siege that lasted fifty days.

l. 43. *clouds*. The depression that eventually lead to his suicide.

517 l. 47. *bee's-wing*. Old port.

l. 59. *crashed*. i.e. committed suicide.

l. 69. *Plassy*. When, on his return to England, Clive was given an Irish peerage (the equivalent to a modern life peerage) he chose the name of his greatest victory, and became Lord Plassy.

l. 70. *Pitt*. William Pitt the elder, the prime minister.

517-18 ll. 70–1. The great military leaders mentioned are: Alexander the Great, Macedonian conquerer of Greece, Persia, and India (4th century BC); Julius Caesar, Roman general and emperor (1st century BC); Marlborough, or John Churchill, created Duke of Marlborough after his victory at Blenheim in 1704; Frederick the Fierce (more usually 'the Great'); Prussian military leader and king (1712–84).

518 l. 72. *bore the bell away*. Was the best.

l. 77. *filthy sleep-stuff*. Opium is a powerful narcotic.

l. 91. *factor-days*. Days of being a company clerk.

l. 92. *St David's*. Fort in India.

519 l. 101. *Cock o' the Walk*. Top dog; leading bully.   *scarlet son of Mars*. Mars was god of war; scarlet the colour of the English army uniform.

l. 111. *force*. Cheat at cards (offer the other player free choice of a card when in fact you are tricking him or her into choosing a specific card).

l. 112. *Thyrsis . . . Chloe*. The standard names of lovers in pastoral poetry.

521 l. 147. *flurried*. Flustered.

l. 162. *Rogue's March*. The tune played when a dishonourable soldier is drummed out of the regiment.

523 l. 207. *nick*. Browning's usage is uncertain; perhaps he means 'take, seize' the occasion.

Jocoseria

525 This collection was first published Mar. 1883. Browning took the title from Dutchman Otto Melander's *Jocoseria* (1597), a compendium of

tales and anecdotes, some jokey, some serious. In a letter of 9 Jan. 1883 Browning wrote 'it is a collection of things gravish and gayish—hence the title *Jocoseria*—which is Batavian [i.e. Dutch] Latin, I think' (*Hood*, 213).

525 *'Wanting is—what?'* Probably composed in late 1882 and first published in *Jocoseria* (1883). The cross-shape suggests the pattern poems of George Herbert. The poem was much parodied, for example by Swinburne ('Wanting is—all, | Jargon abundant, | Verbiage redundant, | Splutter and squall'), and by W. R. Hancock ('Browning is—what? | Riddle redundant, | Baldness abundant, | Sense who can spot?').

l. 2. *redundant*. Full, plentiful.

l. 9. *comer*. Christ.

Donald. Written in Aug. 1882; first published in *Jocoseria* (1883). The story originates in an anecdote recorded by Walter Scott in *The Keepsake* of 1832.

l. 5. *bothy*. Highland hut.

l. 10. *trivet*. Device for supporting a kettle over a flame.

l. 12. *Glenlivet*. Scotch whisky.

526 l. 16. *Royal*. King Stag.

l. 42. *Double-First*. At Oxford and Cambridge students are examined in their first and third years; a student who obtains a first on both occasions is said to have a double-first.   *the jigger*. Mild expletive.

527 l. 62. *Mount...Ben*. The latter word is Scots for the former.

l. 76. *burnie*. Small stream.

528 l. 102. *foiling*. Trampling.

l. 103. *callant*. Young lad.

l. 107. *brig*. Bridge.

529 l. 136. *Blondin*. Famous French tightrope-walker (1829–97).

531 l. 206. *clouted*. Patched.

l. 210. *bracket*. Alcoholic drink.

l. 214. *win-penny*. Something that wins a penny.

532 l. 232. *trump*. A person of surpassing excellence.   *Tory*. More usually a term of contempt; if it here implies approbation, this may tell us something of the speaker's political affiliations.

l. 234. *As Homer would say*... See for instance *Odyssey* i. 64: 'escaped through the gate of your teeth'; in this case the periphrasis means 'keeps silent'.

Ixion. First published in *Jocoseria* (1883); the date of composition is unknown. Ixion is a figure from Greek myth, king of Thessaly during his lifetime; he fell in love with Hera (or Here), Zeus' wife and Queen of Heaven, and attempted to seduce her. Zeus foiled his plans by creating a robot Hera out of clouds (on this being Ixion fathered the race known as the Centaurs), and afterwards punished his hubris (arrogance) by having him eternally bound to a flaming wheel in Hades. Browning reimagines him as a sort of Shelleyan Prometheus, unjustly punished by a tyrannical god.

533 l. 28. *Sisuphos*. Sisyphus' punishment was (for ever) to have to roll a large stone to the top of the hill, only to have it roll to the bottom before he reached it.   *Tantalos*. Tantalus was placed in a pool (up to his lower lip) with luscious fruits dangling within reach, only to suffer eternal thirst and hunger (whenever he tried to drink the water would recede, and whenever he reached for the fruit it would sway out of grasp).

l. 33. *throe*. Agonizing pain.

l. 35. *conceited me*. Foolishly thought myself.

534 l. 85. *Olumpos*. Mt Olympus, home of the gods.   *Erebos*. The uppermost region of Hell (Ixion is in effect whirling through the 'sky' of Hell on his fiery wheel).

535 l. 95. *iris*. Rainbow.

l. 112. *Tartaros*. The lowest region of Hell (below Erebos and Hades); the prison of the Titans.

536 *Never the Time and the Place*. First published in *Jocoseria* (1883); the date of composition is unknown. Most critics assume the 'loved one' referred to in this poem is Elizabeth Barrett Browning.

Ferishtah's Fancies

537 Published Nov. 1884. Ferishtah (the name means 'Fairy') is a 'Dervish' or religious teacher, whose twelve 'fancies' or fables inculcate the moral that faith is superior to intellect. Interspersed between the fancies are short lyrics, two of which are printed here; Browning's prologue, which forms an interestingly grotesque and satirical contrast to the generally benign and pious verse of the collection as a whole, is also reproduced.

Prologue. Written Sept. 1883 and first printed in *Ferishtah's Fancies*.

l. 1. *ortolans*. Small birds of the bunting variety; eaten as a delicacy in Italy.

l. 12. *fatling*. Young and luscious animal.

l. 16. *leaf*. Punning on the leaf of a tree and of a book.

l. 31. *peptics*. Digestive organs.

538 l. 38. *Gressoney*. Town in north-west Italy; Browning stayed there in 1883, and (the implication is) consumed ortolans there.

'*So the head aches...*' First published in *Ferishtah's Fancies*; the date of composition is unknown.

538 '*Verse-making was least of my virtues ...*' First published in *Ferishtah's Fancies*; the date of composition is unknown.

Parleyings with Certain People of Importance in Their Day

540 First published Jan. 1887. The journal *The Critic* (2 Jan. 1886) noted that Browning 'dreading his future biographer' had destroyed a large batch of letters, but added on the other hand that Browning was working on an autobiography. When this work appeared it was so unconventional an autobiography that few even recognized it as such. Browning resurrects seven people who may indeed have been important in their day, but who were all of them almost wholly forgotten by the 1880s; he then engages each of them in a conversation (a parleying), and in so doing explores the areas of art and thought that have been most important in his own mental life: philosophy, history, poetry, politics, painting, the classics, and music. Printed here are the prologue to the whole endeavour, and the third parleying with the 18th-century poet Christopher Smart.

Apollo and the Fates: A Prologue. The myth is that of Alcestis; the god Apollo was friendly with the mortal Admetus, and bargained with the Fates (who control human destiny) to allow him to escape death. The Fates agreed, on condition that Admetus found somebody to die in his place. What happened is recorded in Euripides' *Alcestis*, a play Browning had translated entire in *Balaustion's Adventure* (1871); nobody is prepared to die in Admetus' place except his much-loved wife Alcestis. Admetus is mourning her death when the hero Heracles arrives, and it is he who descends into Hades, wrestles with death, and brings back Alcestics alive. The myth had had clear biographical resonance for Browning ever since the death of Elizabeth Barrett Browning. *Apollo and the Fates* is set right at the beginning of the myth, with Apollo wrangling with the Fates for Admetus' life. The epigraph lists the sources upon which Browning has chiefly drawn: the Homeric *Hymn to Hermes*; Aeschylus' *Eumenides*; and Euripides' *Alcestis*.

l. 1. *Parnassus.* Mountain sacred to the Muses and Apollo.

l. 4. *Dire Ones.* The Fates.

l. 6. *Mother.* According to Hesiod (*Theogony*, 217) the Fates were the daughters of Night (Nux).

541 l. 16. *Woe-purfled.* Decorated with unhappiness.   *Weal-prankt.* Embroidered with happiness. Lachesis uses terms from weaving, since she is measuring out the thread of life (the thread comes from Clotho's spindle and is severed by Atropos' shears).

l. 23. *Moirai.* Greek for 'Fates'.

ll. 28–9. *He is slaved for ... a goddess-sent plague.* Apollo was punished by Zeus by being given as a slave to a mortal; the mortal was Admetus, and he treated the god well; hence, Apollo loved him. The 'goddess-sent plague' is a room full of snakes, sent by Artemis after Admetus neglected to sacrifice to her at his bridal-feast.

542 l. 42. *Day's god*. Apollo was god of the sun (as well as of poetry).

l. 58. *forbore*. Was kind to.

543 l. 82. *certes*. Certainly.   *owns*. Concedes.

l. 91. *conceits him*. Imagines himself.

545 l. 127. *Bacchus*. Or Dionysus, god of wine and revels.

547 l. 156. *Semele*. Zeus fathered Bacchus upon the mortal woman Semele.

l. 164. *flambeau*. Lamp.

l. 173. *a cluster*. Of grapes.

548 l. 192. *cummers*. Old women or witches (Scots).

l. 198. *collyrium*. Eye-wash or eye-salve.

549 l. 222. *swound*. Swoon.

l. 229. *bantling*. Bastard.

551 l. 256. *griesly*. Grisly.   *gammers*. Old women.

l. 261. *Pheræ*. Admetus' kingdom. Despite Apollo's optimism here, neither father nor mother were prepared to sacrifice themselves; and when his wife offered herself he accepted (instead of 'spurning the exchange', l. 265).

With Christopher Smart. English poet Christopher Smart (1722–71) lived a fairly mediocre life, and published mediocre poems (see for instance 1752's *Poems on Several Occasions*) until in the mid-1750s he went mad with a sort of religious mania (Samuel Johnson talks of his 'falling upon his knees and saying his prayers in the street, or in any other unusual place'). In 1763 he was confined to a madhouse, where he wrote (with a key upon the wainscot, according to legend) the poems for which he is today remembered. Browning knew and deeply admired his *Song to David* (1763), although works such as *Jubilate Agno* did not come to light until the 20th-century. In this *Parleying* Browning characterizes Smart's madness as a brief interlude, during which he wrote the visionary and inspired *Song to David* and after which he recovered his wits and went back to living his dull life; in fact Smart was mad to the end of his days.

553 l. 40. *Rafael Mother-Maid*. Raphael painted a number of Madonnas; Browning could be referring to any of them here.

554 l. 89. *South*. Italy.   *North*. England.

ll. 90–1. *Rafael touch Leighton, Michelagnolo | Join Watts*. i.e. Combine the best of the old school and the new. Sir Frederick Leighton (1830–96) was, like Raphael, a painter; George Watts (1817–1904) was, like Michelangelo, a painter and sculptor. Both Englishmen were friends of Browning, and both had painted his portrait.

554 l. 93. *supreme.* Used as a noun (i.e. highest point).

l. 94. *Song.* The *Song to David.*

l. 96. *Milton ... Keats.* As with visual artists, so with poets; Milton represents the old style (the 'trumpet-clang'), Keats the new ('flute-breath'), and Smart's poem combines the best of both schools.

555 l. 120. *Hayley.* William Hayley (1745–1820), poet and biographer; here invoked (with 'the rest') as representative of mediocrity.

l. 150. *struck word out.* Produced words (like striking sparks from a flint).

556 l. 153. *swilled.* Washed or rinsed.

l. 159. *him.* By him (the reference is to Adam naming the animals, Gen. 2: 19–20).

l. 180. *bay-tree.* Leaves from the bay were traditionally woven into a crown and awarded to the best poet; hence the tree became associated with poetic endeavour.   *unsightly bough.* The *Song to David*, which was omitted from the 1791 edition of Smart's works.

l. 181. *Horace.* Smart translated the famously urbane and refined Roman poet on two occasions; in prose (1756) and in verse (1767). He represents everything opposite to the frenzied inspiration of the *Song to David.*

l. 183. *sward.* Grass.

557 ll. 198–200. *Wild Virgin's Bower.* Flowering shrub;   *stars.* Flowers;   *faint.* Die off (leaving feathered seeds known as 'old man's beard');   *Purpling ... grey.* The flowers of the Virgin's Bower are purple, the seeds grey. The colours also represent poetry and prose respectively.

l. 210. *text.* As when a preacher recites a biblical text, and then goes on to elaborate a sermon upon it (the 'teaching' of the next line).

558 l. 232. *your function is to rule.* 'Poets are the unacknowledged legislators of the world' (Shelley, *Defence of Poetry*).

l. 235. *Pullulate.* Abound.

l. 255. *Offuscate.* Obfuscate.

Asolando

559 Browning's final collection was published 12 Dec. 1889, the day of the poet's death. He had received advance copies, and was informed late in the day that the volume had been very well received. 'More than satisfied,' he told his son, who brought him the news; 'I am dying. My dear boy. My dear boy.' These were his last words. The title refers to the Italian town of Asolo, which Browning knew well; and also alludes to the cod-Latin *asolare* ('to disport in the open air, amuse oneself at random' as Browning himself defines it; *asolando* would be

the gerund, meaning roughly 'for amusement'). The collection as a whole has the subtitle *Fancies and Facts*, and most of its poems are concerned with exploring this particular dichotomy.

559 *Prologue*. Written Sept. 1889 and first published in *Asolando*.

ll. 1–10. The first two stanzas are supposed spoken by a friend of the poet.

l. 5. *iris-bow*. Rainbow.

ll. 8–9. *uncinct by dower | Of dyes*. Not surrounded by an aura of rich colours.

l. 13. *chrysopras*. Golden-green crystal.

l. 21. *Asolo*. Browning spent quite a lot of 1889 in this picturesque Italian town; it is also the setting for *Pippa Passes* (1841).

ll. 27–8. *Bush | Burning but unconsumed*. God appears to Moses in this guise, Exod. 3.

560 l. 39. *ken*. View, knowledge (Scots).

Bad Dreams. Probably written late 1888, the record (some critics think) of some painful emotional experience of Browning's connected with a wealthy American widow, Mrs Clara Bloomfield-Moore. The obscurity of the pieces is due in large part to their recording dream imagery; and as an exploration of lovers' alienation from one another the work recalls other sequences such as Meredith's *Modern Love* (1862), or Browning's own *James Lee's Wife* (1864).

ll. 1–8. This dream is probably the woman's.

l. 7. *for this*. Because of this.

560-3 ll. 9–93. The man is telling his dream (of a ghastly ball, followed by an encounter with a nameless Something on a throne) to the woman, who replies in ll. 94–108.

561 l. 25. *thwart*. Opposed, contrary.

l. 32. *trulls*. Prostitutes.

562 ll. 53–8. *'Twas a sort of throne...unreconciled*. Recalling the throne of the subterranean spirit Demogorgon in Shelley's *Prometheus Bound* (II. iv. 1–7); 'Panthea: What veiled form sits on the ebon throne?...I see a mighty Darkness | Filling the seat of power'.

l. 62. *Giaours*. Turkish word for the non-Islamic: 'infidels'.

563 ll. 89–90. *Her...she*. The soul is female (Latin *anima*).

l. 103. *ticklish*. Lewd, obscene.   *Anthology*. The Greek Anthology, a collection of short poems and epigrams composed between 700 BC and AD 1000; many of them are sexually explicit.

l. 108. *Hannah More*. A popular writer on moral or religious themes (1745–1833). The point here is that as an answer to the question 'who composed this erotic epigram?', this is about as inappropriate as it is possible to imagine.

563-4 ll. 109–44. The man's dream. The forest recalls Dante's *Divina Commedia*, which begins with the poet's soul wandering through a dark forest.

564 l. 124. *cicatrice*. Scar-like mark.

564-5 ll. 145–89. This is the woman's dream.

564 l. 145. *slab*. Gravestone.

565 l. 159. *halts*. Wavers, stumbles.

l. 168. *Solomon's selected spouse*. The biblical *Song of Solomon* is a man's sensual and sensitive love-poem to his spouse; conventional theology reads it as an allegory of Christ's wedding to the Church.

Inapprehensiveness. Probably written in late 1889, and possibly recording a real incident connected with a visit by Browning's friend Mrs Bronson; first published in *Asolando*. The title is ambiguous; 'inapprehensive' can mean either 'not perceiving', 'not perceiving mentally'; or it can mean 'that does not apprehend danger'.

566 l. 12. *Ruskin*. The great writer and aesthetician (1819–1900) was a personal friend of Browning's. His works often comment on the interrelation of man-made beauty (as in architecture) and God-made beauties (particularly plants and flowers).

l. 16. *distent*. Lit. 'bulging'.

l. 32. *Vernon Lee*. The essayist and critic (1856–1935; her real name was Violet Paget) was just beginning her career in the 1880s. In an essay called 'Ruskinism' (in *Belcaro*, 1883) she takes issue with Ruskin's habit of 'reading' the natural world as if it were a painting.

Development. First published in *Asolando*; this is Browning's last statement on the importance Greek literature and myth always had for him.

l. 3. *siege of Troy*. Homer's *Iliad*.

567 ll. 6–7. *Priam*. Aged king of Troy.   *Helen*. The most beautiful woman in the world, Helen ran away from her ageing husband Menelaus with the handsome Trojan youth Paris. The Greeks put together an armed force to retrieve her, and the siege of Troy began.

l. 11. *Atreidai*. Menelaus (Helen's husband) and Agamemnon (military leader of the Greek's expedition) were the sons of Atreus.

l. 13. *Achilles*. The greatest warrior of them all, Achilles got into a huff when a beautiful slave woman Briseis was taken from him; but when his best friend Patroclus (wearing his armour) was killed, he ended his sulk and went into battle, killing the Trojan Hector.

l. 30. *Pope*. The translation of Homer by Alexander Pope (which appeared in 1715–20) is still very highly regarded.

568 l. 43. *Buttmann*. Author of a standard schoolboy Greek Grammar.

568 l. 46. *Heine.* More usually Heyne, editor of the *Iliad* (1802).

l. 57. *Scio.* Chios, a Greek island with a good claim to being Homer's birthplace.

l. 58. *Hymns.* The *Homeric Hymns* are today not thought to be by Homer.

l. 59. *Battle of the Frogs and Mice.* The *Batrachomyomachia*, a burlesque epic, probably not by Homer.

l. 60. *Margites.* Homer's great lost comic epic, named after its prot-agonist (whose name means 'Greedy-gluttonous').

l. 64. *Wolf.* Friedrich August Wolf (1759–1824), the great German philologist, whose *Prolegomena in Homerum* (1795) advanced the (now generally accepted) theory that the Homeric poems were not written by a single man, but were the culmination of a lengthy oral tradition.

569 l. 81. *Ulysses.* Latin name for Odysseus, hero of the *Odyssey*.
Hector and his Spouse. Trojan military leader and his wife, Andromache.

l. 82. *Achilles and his Friend.* The friend was Patroclus.

l. 84. *Browning says.* In effect, Browning spends the whole of *Asolando* saying just this; that 'fancies' are preferable to 'facts'.

l. 88. *nonage.* Youth.

ll. 100–1. *Peleus' son.* Achilles.   *loathe . . . a lie as Hell's Gate.* Quoted from *Iliad* ix. 312.

l. 109. *Ethics.* Aristotle's *Nichomachean Ethics*, a dry treatise on morals.

l. 113. *Stagirite.* Aristotle was born at Stagira.

570 *Epilogue.* First published in *Asolando*; the date of composition is unknown. 'One evening, just before his death-illness, the poet was reading this [the third stanza of this 'Epilogue'] from a proof to his daughter-in-law and sister. He said: "It almost sounds like bragging to say this, and as if I ought to cancel it; but it's the simple truth; and as it's true, it shall stand' (from *Pall Mall Gazette*, 1 Feb. 1890).

l. 6. *yet so mistaken*; yet you (the person addressed in l. 2) are mistaken in pitying me.

Uncollected Poems

571 *Helen's Tower.* Printed privately in a pamphlet along with a poem by Tennyson of the same title; the occasion was the building of a tower by the Marquis of Dufferin at Clandeboye in Ireland to honour his mother, Helen, Lady Dufferin and Countess of Gifford. Browning then pub-lished the sonnet in the *Pall Mall Gazette*, 28 Dec. 1883, but he did not reprint it during his life.

Epigraph. From *Iliad* iii. 145; it means 'Helen on the tower'.

l. 2. *Scaean gate.* Gate of Troy, from which Helen watched Trojan warriors going out to do battle with the Greeks (*Iliad* iii. 145).

571 ll. 13–14. *God's self…stars together sang*. God says to Job 'Where wast thou when I laid the foundations of the earth?…When the morning stars sang together, and all the sons of God shouted for joy?' (Job 38: 4–7).

'*Oh Love, Love*'. Written Dec. 1878, as a translation of the opening of the first chorus from Euripides' *Hippolytus* (525–44), at the request of Professor J. P. Mahaffy. Published in Mahaffy's *Euripides* (1879), but not reprinted during Browning's lifetime.

ll. 8–9. *Aphrodité*. Greek goddess of love and sex.   *Love*. Eros (the Greek *eros* means physical love) was the son of Aphrodite and Zeus.

572 l. 10. *Alpheian river*. In the Peloponnesus.

l. 11. *Pythian shrines of Phoebus*. Apollo (Phoebus) was worshipped as the Pythian at Delphi, where oracles were given out in the name of the god.

l. 12. *Hellas*. Greece.

Why I Am a Liberal. Published in Andrew Reid's collection of statements of political affiliation, *Why I Am a Liberal, Being Definitions by the Best Minds of the Liberal Party* (1885); not reprinted during Browning's lifetime.

To Edward FitzGerald. Written on 8 July 1889; published in the *Athenaeum* 13 July 1889, and not reprinted in Browning's life. Browning was sitting in a friend's garden flipping through the recently published *Letters and Literary Remains of Edward Fitgerald* (ed. W. Aldis Wright, 1889), when he chanced upon (vol. i, pp. 280–2) the following: 'Mrs Browning's Death is rather a relief to me, I must say: no more Aurora Leighs, thank God! A woman of real Genius, I know: but what is the upshot of it all? She and her Sex had better mind the Kitchen and their Children; and perhaps the Poor: except in such things as little Novels, they only devote themselves to what Men do much better, leaving that which Men do worse or not at all.'

573 l. 7. *were yourself alive*. Fitzgerald had died in 1883.

Prose

574 *Introductory Essay [Essay on Shelley]*. Edward Moxon, the publisher of Browning's *Bells and Pomegranates* series, purchased a series of letters by Shelley at auction in May 1851. He intended to publish these letters as a pendant to his earlier collection of Shelley's prose (*Essays, Letters from Abroad, Translations and Fragments*, ed. Mary Shelley, 1840), and approached Browning to write an introduction to the volume. Browning wrote the essay in Paris during Dec. 1851, and Moxon's volume, *Letters of Percy Bysshe Shelley, with an Introductory Essay by Robert Browning* emerged in 1852. It swiftly transpired, however, that the letters were mostly forgeries, the work of George Gordon Byron, who styled himself 'Major' and claimed to be the illegitimate son

of Lord Byron the poet (in all likelihood he was no such thing). Moxon swiftly withdrew the volume, and only a few copies survive. Browning's essay was reprinted in 1881 as a separate volume by the Browning Society (the basis of the text printed here) and by the Shelley Society in 1888, but was otherwise not republished during Browning's life. Both the importance of Shelley to Browning's own poetic development, and the comparative rarity of any piece of critical prose by the poet, lend the 'Introductory Essay' a particular importance.

574 l. 31. ποιητης. The Greek (*poieetees*) means 'one who makes, a maker' and by extension 'a poet'; strictly speaking, it should have an acute accent on the second eta.

578 l. 166. *Homerides*. 'Homeridai' was the collective name for those poets from Ancient Chios who claimed to be the descendants of Homer.

580 l. 250. *The 'Remains'*. That is, the poetical remains; in this case the poems produced by Shelley from 1812 until his death by drowning in 1822, 'a period of ten years' which includes all his acknowledged masterpieces.

581 l. 308. *'E pur si muove'*. 'And yet it does move'; reputedly said by Galileo (1564–1642) just after the Inquisition has persuaded him to renounce as heretical his idea that the earth moved around the Sun, and not (as the Church insisted) vice versa.

ll. 318–19. *certain charges against his private character and life*. Browning's eventual disillusionment with Shelley hinged on his learning about Shelley's abandonment of his first wife Harriet (who subsequently committed suicide) and his running away with the underage Mary Wollstonecraft without her parents' permission. It is not certain how many of these circumstances were known to Browning at the time of writing the 'Introductory Essay'. The issue of Shelley's atheism may also be alluded to here.

584-5 ll. 435–43. Quoted from Shelley's *Julian and Maddalo*, ll. 409–17.

586 l. 498. *leaving the dead to bury their dead*. Christ's instruction to his disciples (Luke 9: 60).

586-7 ll. 509–15 and ll. 519–22. Quoted from Shelley's *The Boat on the Serchio*, ll. 7–17 (omitting four lines) and ll. 30–3.

587 l. 523. *David*. Reputed author of the biblical psalms.

l. 534. *Junius*. Pseudonym of influential 18th-century writer and political commentator, who remains unidentified. Byron's opinion, in his *Vision of Judgment* (1822), was 'that what Junius we are wont to call | Was *really, truly*, nobody at all' (ll. 639–40).

l. 534. *Rowley*. The (fictitious) medieval monk under whose name Chatterton (1752–70) tried to pass off his forged manuscripts.

l. 537 n. *Andrea Verocchio*. Or Verrocchio; Italian sculptor (1435–88); his sarcophagus for Piero and Giovanni de' Medici in the Old Sacristry

of San Lorenzo in Venice was his own work and not an antique frag-
ment, whatever Shelley may have thought.   *fancifully character-
ising*. In *Julian and Maddalo*, ll. 98–140. The landscape as described by
Shelley (for instance, the 'windowless, deformed and dreary pile', l. 101)
does not precisely resemble the reality, as Browning notes.

587 ll. 540–1. *Guido*. Guido Reni, Italian painter (1575–1642).   *Carlo
Dolce*. Carlo Dolci, a little regarded Italian painter (1616–86). Shelley
did indeed prefer these artists to the more famous Michelangelo.

l. 541. *Divine Being*. Browning alludes to Luke 12: 10.

588 l. 554. *Julian and Maddalo*. Written in 1818, a more mature production
than *Zastrozzi* (1810), Shelley's youthful Gothic romance.

l. 566. *his own note to 'Hellas'*. The quoted words are not in any note to
Hellas, nor any of Shelley's other published notes or prefaces. Browning
may be thinking of a passage from Mary Shelley's preface to her edition
of Shelley's *Poetical Works* (1847): 'His imagination has been termed too
brilliant, his thoughts too subtle. He loved to idealize reality... few of
us understand or sympathise with the love of abstract beauty, and
adoration of abstract good, the *to agathon kai to kalon* of the Socratic
philosophers, with our sympathies with our kind. In this, Shelley
resembled Plato; both taking more delight in the abstract and the ideal
than in the special and tangible.' The Greek quoted here means 'the
Good and the Beautiful'.

ll. 578–84. Browning quotes the whole of *Fragment: Igniculus Desiderii*
(1817), ll. 1–7.

589 l. 603. *lapidary*. Expert in precious gems.

l. 606. *Koh-i-noor*. The famous diamond.

ll. 615–16. Quoted from *Epipsychidion*, ll. 128–9.

Selected Letters

591 The letters are arranged in two sections; first, letters chosen from the
courtship correspondence between Browning and Elizabeth Barrett
1845–6; secondly, various letters from Browning to other correspond-
ents, ranging over the length of his life. Annotations are identified by
the date of the letter and the addressee.

Courtship Correspondence

John Kenyon (1784–1856), the son of a wealthy West Indian plantation
owner, was friendly with both Elizabeth Barrett and Robert Browning,
and it was through him that Browning first contacted and then (on 20
May 1845) met his future wife. Elizabeth Barrett was 38, and more-or-
less invalided, spending most of her time in her bedroom in her father's
Wimpole Street house. Mr Barrett's extreme overprotectiveness meant
that he would not permit his daughter, or any of his children, to marry;

and when Robert and Elizabeth finally eloped together in Sept. 1846 he refused to have anything more to do with her.

From May 1845 until Sept. 1846 Browning and Elizabeth Barrett exchanged letters, mostly every day and sometimes several in a single day; Browning also visited regularly. The courtship correspondence is of very great interest as the profile of a developing love-affair, but in addition to its emotional validity it contains the two poets' thoughts on poetry, often couched in terms of specific criticisms of their poems.

Forty-five letters are here reproduced from a correspondence of 573, mostly single letters of interest but with one or two runs of several letters (for instance, the first ten letters exchanged by the two poets) to give some sense of the continuity of the sequence as a whole. Each letter is identified by a number that corresponds with the numeration in the standard edition, Kintner (ed.), *The Letters of Robert Browning and Elizabeth Barrett Barrett 1845–46*, 2 vols. (Cambridge, Mass.: Harvard University Press, 1969).

591 1. R.B. to E.B.B., 10 Jan. 1845.

your poems. Elizabeth Barrett's two-volume *Poems* (1844).

592 2. E.B.B. to R.B., 11 Jan. 1845.

so excellent a thing in women. 'Her voice was ever soft, | Gentle and low, an excellent thing in woman' (*King Lear*, v. iii. 274–5).

593 3. R.B. to E.B.B., 13 Jan. 1845.

594 *'Alla cara...O tu'* 'To the dear memory—of—Torquato Tasso— Doctor Bernardini—has offered—the following poem—*O thou*'

Mr Fellows. The archaeologist Charles Fellows had recently discovered the Xanthian marbles in Lycia (they are now in the British Museum).

595 4. E.B.B. to R.B., 15 Jan. 1845.

headlong. 'testa' (head) and 'lunga' (long) do not together constitute a proper phrase in Italian.

596 *Mr Horne.* Richard Hengist Horne (1802–84) was a poet and writer, and friend of Elizabeth Barrett.

εἴδωλον. The Greek means 'a shape, image, spectre'.

597 5. R.B. to E.B.B., 27 Jan. 1845.

'Bells'. That is, *Bells and Pomegranates* VII ('Dramatic Romances and Lyrics').

598 *Bertha...the Page.* All poems by E.B.B. ('Bertha in the Lane', 'A Drama of Exile', 'Rhyme of the Duchess May', 'The Romaunt of the Page').

BRADBURY AND EVANS. The printers used by Browning's publisher, Moxon, who would require a legible manuscript to work from.

599 6. E.B.B. to R.B., 3 Feb. 1845

his romances. Horne's *New Spirit of the Age* (1844), in which E.B.B. is characterized as 'in constant correspondence with many of the most eminent persons of the time'.

grand scene in Pippa Passes. Part I, ll. 1–282 (the Ottima–Sebald scene).

κ.τ.λ. Greek for 'etc.'

600 *Atalanta-ball.* The beautiful but rather savage Atalanta challenged suitors to a race, promising to marry any winner and kill any losers. Hippomenes won the race by throwing three golden balls in her path, which she stopped to pick up.

601 *nobler sons than he.* The mother of Brasilides, the 5th-century BC Spartan general, said so on his death.

602 μηδέπω 'εν προοιμίοις. Quoted from Aeschylus, *Prometheus Bound*, 741: 'not yet reached the prologue'. Prometheus recites a long list of sufferings to Io, but concludes with this phrase, whereupon Io bursts into tears.

rash and sudden. Romeo and Juliet, II. ii. 117–18.

7. R.B. to E.B.B., 11 Feb. 1845

603 *going to press.* Carlyle's *Oliver Cromwell's Letters and Speeches* was published Nov. 1845.

masoretic. The original Hebrew text of the Bible consisted only of consonants. The Masoretes were 6th–10th-century AD scholars who added vowel points to this text, sometimes materially affecting the interpretation of passages.

tant de façons. 'The many formalities'.

Alfred over the sea. Alfred Domett had emigrated to New Zealand in 1842.

604 *Rialto where verse-merchants most do congregate.* See *Merchant of Venice* I. iii. 50.

decamp to the crows. 'Sod off' (an Aristophanic phrase).

605 *Cornelius Agrippa.* The 15th-century alchemist, whose *De Occulta Philosophia* ('On Magic') provided Browning with an epigraph to *Pauline* (1833) and a passage in the first book of *The Ring and the Book* (1868).

go softly all their days. Isa. 38: 15

does as they bid him. See also Browning's letter to Alfred Domett, 13 July 1842, printed below.

break off in the middle. Butler, *Hudibras*, 'argument' to Canto 1.

606 8. E.B.B. to R.B., 17 Feb. 1845

606 *Mr Landor.* Walter Savage Landor (1775–1864), poet and writer, was acquainted with both Browning and Elizabeth Barrett.

607 *gr-r-r-you swine.* Last words of Browning's 'Soliloquy of the Spanish Cloister' (1842).

608 *my soul among lions.* Ps. 57: 4.

Professor Wilson. John Wilson, who wrote (under the pseudonym of 'Christopher North') swingeing attacks on Tennyson's early poetry, amongst other things.

Discourse on Poetry. Sidney's *Defence of Poetry*, which in fact does not mention Shakespeare because it was written (in 1579–80) before his career had begun.

609 *calculating machine.* Babbage's proposed machine was the forerunner of modern computers.

science creuse. 'Hollow science'.

confiteor tibi. 'I confess to you'.

610 *geese are in the Capitol.* The Ancient Romans kept certain sacred geese in the Capitol; on one occasion their hissing alerted the Romans to an invading force.

9. R.B. to E.B.B., 26 Feb. 1845.

611 *an amber-drop enwraps a bee.* Donne's 'To the Countess of Bedford', l. 25.

Lycophron. 4th-century BC Greek poet and tragedian.

612 *Charlie is my darling.* Song of the Jacobites, who opposed the reigning royal family and its Protestant succession on the grounds that the Catholic Charles Stewart ('Bonny Prince Charlie' or 'the young Cavalier') was the rightful king, as indeed he was. In the 18th century two rebellions were mounted on behalf of the Jacobite cause.

Polidoro's perfect Andromeda. Browning had an engraving of Poliodoro de Caravaggio's painting (of Perseus rescuing Andromeda) in his study.

John Mill. See the headnote to Browning's *Pauline* (1833), above.

613 *I throw… mildly sweet.* Quoted from a fragment preserved in Henry Kirk White's posthumous *Remains* (1808). Kirk White wrote his poetry on the back of his mathematical papers.

10. E.B.B. to R.B., 27 Feb. 1845.

turtle. Turtle-dove (see Song of Solomon 2: 12)

614 *thymele.* Altar to Dionysus, centrally placed in Ancient Greek theatre.

directing it by your will. E.B.B. translates from *Prometheus Bound*, 286.

judge what I say. 1 Cor. 10: 15.

Thou canst not say I did it. Macbeth III. iv. 50.

615 *novel-poem.* Looking forward to *Aurora Leigh* (1856).

616 16. R.B. to E.B.B., 15 Apr. 1845.

Cellarius. A sort of waltz.

617 *fuori di me.* 'Outside of myself'.

Syrenusa. 'Siren Isles', three small islands off the coast of Italy known as the Galli (see 'The Englishman in Italy', ll. 199–228 and notes, above).

17. E.B.B. to R.B., 17 Apr. 1845.

618 *Lamia.* Serpent woman (the 'viperine she-fiend' of letter 16).

619 18. R.B. to E.B.B., 30 Apr. 1845.

story of D'Israeli's. Benjamin Disraeli's first novel, *Vivian Grey* (1827–8); Browning goes on to refer to an episode from Bk. 5, ch. 15.

620 *Alfieri.* Vittorio Alfieri (1749–1803), Italian poet; he wrote nineteen tragedies, including *Saul* (1782).

19. E.B.B. to R.B., 1 May 1845.

621 *Flush.* Elizabeth Barrett's lap-dog.

622 20. R.B. to E.B.B., 3 May 1845.

sound speech not to be reproved. Tit. 2: 8.

Phoibos Apollon. More conventionally, Phoebus Apollo. In the first book of the *Iliad* Apollo sends arrows of plague-death amongst the mules and dogs, and then the men.

ὤμοι. (Greek) 'alas!'.

623 *subaudire.* (Latin) Supply a missing word.

Odorosi fioretti . . . gigli. 'Sweet-smelling flowers, roses of red, lilies of the whitest'.

When one should . . . atmosphere. Shelley, *Marenghi*, ll. 7305.

Monte Calvano. Mountain near Sorrento.

'Niursi—sorbi!' 'Yessir—apples!'

Piedigrotta fête. The festival of the Madonna of Piedigrotta, celebrated 8 Sept. *Volanti* are silver-gilt coaches, driven by the aristocracy to the festival in honour of the Virgin.

624 *Hood in his emergency.* Thomas Hood, editor of *Hood's Magazine* was ill (in fact he died the day this letter was written).

625 30. E.B.B. to R.B., 23 May 1845. Browning's sixteenth letter (subsequently destroyed) seems to have proposed marriage. This is E.B.B.'s reply.

626 *one of my aunts.* Jane Hedley, E.B.B.'s maternal aunt.

627 31. R.B. to E.B.B., 24 May 1845.

Dii meliora piis. 'May the gods grant better things to the upright' (Virgil, *Georgics*, iii. 513).

628 *spirit stirring drum. Othello* III. iii. 353.

the heart is desperately wicked. Jer. 17: 9.

Edmund Kean. The great actor had died in 1833. *Father Matthew*, Irish Franciscan temperance preacher; he had visited London and preached in 1843, where Browning had heard him. *Ottima.* Murderous and adulterous character from *Pippa Passes*.

John Mill wondered. Another reference to Mill's annotations of *Pauline* (see headnote to that poem, above).

Songs of the Poets—No. 1. M.P. It is not clear to which poem Browning refers here; perhaps 'Songs of the Poets, No 1. M.P.' refers generally to Browning's output. 'M.P.' may stand for 'Mad Poet' (a review of *Pauline* had referred to Browning as 'the mad poet of the batch'), or perhaps *me poeta* (see *Kintner*, 77).

sleeken every word as to a bird. Elizabeth Barrett, 'A Portrait', ll. 53–4.

corvus (picus). A bird of the crow family. *mirandola.* A pun on the Italian philosopher Pico della Mirandola (1463–94), whose name is also Italian for 'looking at her'.

629 *Dogberry's satisfaction.* It was actually Pompey (in *Measure for Measure* II. i. 136) who said 'I hope here be truths', not Dogberry from *Much Ado About Nothing*.

son of Kish. See 1 Sam. 9 and 16.

630 32. E.B.B. to R.B., 25 May 1845.

Bootes. The constellation, also known as 'the Waggoner'.

631 *Pray do not mock me. King Lear*, IV. vii. 59.

Mr Horne's large fancies. In his *New Spirit of the Age* (on E.B.B.'s polymathy).

cothurns. Buskins, the boots symbolic of tragedy.

633 42. R.B. to E.B.B., 14 June 1845.

the Prize poem. Tennyson's 'Timbuctoo' won the Chancellor's Medal at Cambridge in 1829; it contains all the elements quoted here by Browning, as well as an epigraph attributed to Chapman.

634 *flowers be sent you in a letter.* E.B.B. wrote a poem called 'A Flower in a Letter'.

eccola. 'Behold!'

60. E.B.B. to R.B., 11 July 1845.

Jupiter Tonans. The thunder.

Dr Chambers. Physician to Queen Victoria and one of the most famous doctors of the day.

635 *non obstantibus Bradbury and Evans.* Bradbury and Evans notwithstanding.

61. R.B. to E.B.B., 13 July 1845.

637 *bora*. Cold north wind.

sorbetti. Iced drinks.

638 92. R.B. to E.B.B., 30 Aug. 1845.

639 *the Pisa affair*. A reference to E.B.B.'s proposed visit to Pisa, for which she was trying to gain the approval of her father.

93. E.B.B. to R.B., 31 Aug. 1845.

640 *You wrote once to me*. R.B. to E.B.B., 1 Mar. 1845, not reproduced here.

641 102. R.B. to E.B.B., 13 Sept. 1845.

letter of last week. E.B.B. to R.B., 31 Aug. 1845 (No. 93, printed above).

643 *Mr Fitzroy Kelly*. Recently appointed Solicitor-General.

considering the lilies. Matt. 6: 28.

644 *Dr Watts*. Isaac Watts (1674–1748), hymn-writer. R.B. quotes from his version of the 92nd Psalm.

651 109. R.B. to E.B.B., 18 Sept. 1845.

652 *Cerito*. Fanny Cerrito, noted ballerina of the period.

655 115. E.B.B. to R.B., 26 Sept. 1845.

656 *a boon*. E.B.B. is asking for the return of a love-letter R.B. had sent her after their first meeting, and which she had sent back to him as inappropriate (see above, letter 30). The letter was eventually returned and destroyed.

151. R.B. to E.B.B., 16 Nov. 1845.

657 *Past and Future*. E.B.B.'s 1844 sonnet suggests that its author is resigned to the idea that life is over for her.

261. R.B. to E.B.B., 7 Mar. 1846.

658 *Claude Le Jeune*. 16th-century French musician.

659 *Henry Lawes* (1596–1662), the musician, highly praised by Milton (who wrote a sonnet about him); he composed music for the verses of almost all the major poets of his day.

Dowland. John Dowland (1563–1626), world-famous composer for the lute.

661 302. E.B.B. to R.B., 7 Apr. 1846.

such a subject. E.B.B. and R.B. had been discussing, and disagreeing on, the subject of duelling.

662 *Mr O'Connell*. Daniel O'Connell (1775–1847), the Irish political leader, once killed a man in a duel in 1815 and vowed thereafter never to do so again.

664 483. E.B.B. to R.B., 2 Aug. 1846.

666 *in the sky*. See Wordsworth's 1807 lyric 'My heart leaps up'.

667 552. E.B.B. to R.B., 9 Sept. 1846. R.B. and E.B.B. are now planning their marriage (which took place on 12 Sept. 1846) and elopement to Italy. Events are complicated by Mr Barrett's plans to move his family to the seaside for a month's holiday.

669 554. R.B. to E.B.B., 10 Sept. 1846 (2).

my friend. Captain James Pritchard. In the event he could not attend, and his place was taken by another of Browning's friends, James Silverthorne.

670 556. R.B. to E.B.B., 12 Sept. 1846. E.B.B. and R.B. are now married (secretly), although E.B.B. is still staying at Wimpole Street.

671 *Wilson*. E.B.B.'s maid, who witnessed her marriage.

557. E.B.B. to R.B., 12 Sept. 1846.

672 *sal volatile*. Smelling salts.

your cousin. James Silverthorne, Browning's witness.

penny-a-liners. Newspaper hacks, who were thought to routinely examine church registers for gossip-column material.

572. R.B. to E.B.B., 18 Sept. 1846.

my blunder. Browning had given the wrong time to catch the train (on 19 Sept.) that would take E.B.B. and R.B. to the ferry.

Hodgsons. A bookshop.

673 573. E.B.B. to R.B., 18 Sept. 1846.

Hanmer's poems... books you gave me. Sir John Hanmer (1809–81), politician and poet. The 'two dear books' are probably, rather unromantically, *Scholia in Aeschyli tragoedias* (1820) and a facsimile of the 1603 *Hamlet*.

Other Selected Letters

For ease of annotation, these letters are also given a number, although in this case the numeration only refers to the present edition. Provenance for each letter is given in terms of printed source rather than manuscript: a full list of the sources here referred to only by short title can be found at the head of the notes.

675 1. R.B. to Euphrasia Haworth, 24 July 1838. *Hood*. Euphrasia Fanny Haworth (1801–86), minor poet and close friend of Browning.

absent. Browning had travelled by boat to Italy earlier that year.

I called you, 'Eyebright'. In *Sordello*, iii. 967 ('My English Eyebright'). The name 'Euphrasia' derives from the Greek *euphraino*, 'to cheer or gladden, to gladden the eye'.

677 2. R.B. to Alfred Domett, 23 Mar. 1840. *Correspondence*. Alfred Domett (1811–87) was a minor poet and a close friend of Browning's. He

emigrated to New Zealand in 1842, where he eventually became Prime Minister.

677 *Stokes and Nokes to the Author of 'Venice'.* Domett himself was the author of *Venice* (1839); Stokes and Nokes are fictitious persons, presumably standing for critics.

comme de droit. 'By right'.

Sir Philip. Sir Philip Sidney (1554–86), author of *Apologie for Poetry* (1595).

678 3. R.B. to Euphrasia Haworth, May 1840. *New Letters.*

enfoncé! An emphatic word of dismissal.

the passage you want cleared up. Sordello iii. 967 f.

Watson. David Watson, author of *Odes, Epodes and Carmen Seculare of Horace, translated into English prose* (1741).

one of these. Browning's play *The Return of the Druses*, which (as he anticipates here) Macready did not like (see the next letter).

679 4. R.B. to Macready, 23 Aug. 1840. *New Letters.* William Charles Macready (1793–1873), actor and theatrical impresario, who staged (and acted in) Browning's *Stafford* (1837), which was written for him.

Penthesilé. Queen of the Amazons. Browning may be alluding to Spenser's *Faerie Queene*, v. vii. 31: 'Full fiercely layde the Amazon about, | And dealt her blows unmercifully sore.'

at Arden. The wood in Shakespeare's *As You Like It.* Browning is referring to Macready's home, Elm Cottage, at Elstree; he continues the allusion to Shakespeare's play in the following lines.

as Juliet says. Romeo and Juliet, III. ii. 113–14.

ergo. Therefore.

some primitive Mystery. The authors and titles of plays Browning goes on to cite are his own invention.

680 *Charles Kean.* This actor (1811–68) was Macready's most hated rival.

Virginius. Noble Roman protagonist of James Sheridan Knowles's *Virginius* (first produced 1820).

take on us ... by the moon! King Lear, v. iii. 16–19.

681 5. R.B. to Alfred Domett, 22 May 1842. *Correspondence.* Domett had emigrated for New Zealand in Apr. 1842.

682 6. R.B. to Alfred Domett, 13 July 1842. *Correspondence.*

Tennyson's new vol. Tennyson's *Poems* (1842) was of two volumes, the first containing revised versions of earlier works and the second new work.

a set of sing-songs. Bulwer's *Eva: The Ill-omened Marriage, and Other Tales and Poems* (1842).

682 *'Edwin the Fair'*. Henry Taylor, *Edwin the Fair: An Historical Drama* (1842).

Dickens. Charles Dickens's experiences during his American tour shaped his portrait of that country in his travel book *American Notes for General Circulation* (1842) and, more savagely, in *Martin Chuzzlewit* (1843–4).

J. Hanmer. See note to 573 (E.B.B. to R.B., 18 Sept. 1846) above.

683 7. R.B. to Arabella and Henrietta Barrett, 8 Feb. 1847. *New Letters*. Elizabeth Barrett's sisters, Arabella being seven years her junior and Henrietta three years.

Ba. Elizabeth Barrett's nickname.

Wilson. Elizabeth's maid.

684 8. R.B. to Thomas Carlyle, 14 May 1847. *Hood*. Carlyle (1795–1881) was one of the most eminent of Victorian men of letters.

Schmiergelt. The road toll.

685 *Raphael, ubi es?* 'Raphael, where are you?' (i.e. this is all rubbish—where is the great master?).

686 *your Cromwell*. Carlyle had published his two-volume *Oliver Cromwell's Letters and Speeches* in 1845.

9. Ruskin to R.B., 2 Dec. 1855. David DeLaura (ed.), 'Ruskin and the Brownings: Twenty-five Unpublished Letters', *Bulletin of John Rylands Library*, 54 (1972), 324–7. John Ruskin (1819–1900), the famous critic and art historian, was an acquaintance of both the Brownings. R.B. sent him a copy of *Men and Women* (1855), and he replied with a series of questions concerning passages he could not understand, relating in particular to the poem 'Popularity' (printed above), which Ruskin quotes and analyses line by line. Browning's reply is printed below.

688 *Long-Acre*. Street in London, near Covent Garden, famous for its artists, artisans, and artists'-supplies.

689 *orris root . . . six months*. See 'Fra Lippo Lippi', ll. 351 and 345.

690 *Till I felt . . . open*. 'Saul', l. 20.

691 10. R.B. to Ruskin, 10 Dec. 1855; from Collingwood, *Life and Work of John Ruskin* (1900).

692 *peccavi*. 'I have sinned'.

Orpheus. The mythical poet, whose singing was so wonderful it charmed rocks and trees.

693 *Goldsmith*. Oliver Goldsmith (1730–74), poet and playwright.

11. R.B. to Euphrasia Haworth, 20 July 1861. *Hood*. Browning is writing immediately after the death of Elizabeth Barrett.

Isa Blagden. See next letter and note.

695   12. R.B. to Isabella Blagden, 19 Sept. 1862. *Dearest Isa*. The Brownings
met the energetic Isa (pronounced 'eesa') Blagden in Florence in the
1840s. After E.B.B.'s death, she and Browning exchanged monthly
letters, mostly filled with gossip and chit-chat.

there you are. Blagden had just moved from London back to Florence.

696   13. R.B. to Isabella Blagden, 19 Jan. 1869. *Dearest Isa*.

Hugh Stuart Boyd. A youthful E.B.B. had corresponded with the much
older Boyd (1781–1848) in the 1820s, and after his blindness in 1828
had become his reader. There may have been the possibility of romance
between the two of them, but it never came to anything.

697   14. R.B. to Julia Wedgwood, 27 June 1864. *RB/JW*. Browning began
his friendship with confirmed spinster Julia Wedgwood in spring 1864,
and the two corresponded energetically. Critics have assumed that
Wedgwood reminded Browning of his dead wife. Wedgwood broke the
relationship off in March 1869, for reasons that remain obscure.

Dr Newman. John Henry Newman (1801–90). His autobiography *Apo-
logia pro vita sua* (1864) detailed his religious life, and in particular his
conversion to Catholicism.

699   15. R.B. to Julia Wedgwood, 19–21 Aug. 1864. *RB/JW*.

pas de Roland. At Bayonne in the French Pyrenees. Roland was the
semi-legendary warrior of the Holy Roman Emperor Charlemagne.

700   16. R.B. to Julia Wedgwood, 2 Sept. 1864. *RB/JW*.

Enoch Arden. Tennyson's poem came out in 1864. Enoch returns after
shipwreck to find his wife happily remarried; rather than disturb the
domestic bliss he lies down and dies. The last lines of the poem are: 'So
passed the strong heroic soul away, | And when they buried him the
little port | Had seldom seen a costlier funeral.'

701   *Gluck's . . . 'Helen and Paris'*. The composer C. W. Gluck (1714–87) first
produced his *Paride ed Elena* in Vienna, 1770.

Hallé. Sir Charles Hallé (1819–95), pianist and conductor.

702   *exsertae mammae*. 'Thrusting breasts' (from Virgil, *Aeneid* i. 492).

strange fancy is that of Euripides. Browning refers to this myth in *Fifine
at the Fair*, ll. 306–20.

eidolon. Image.

17. R.B. to Isabella Blagden, 19 Dec. 1864. *Dearest Isa*.

three Christmasses ago. Since E.B.B.'s death.

Tulk. An old friend from the Brownings' days in Florence.

703   18. R.B. to Isabella Blagden, 19 Sept. 1867. *Dearest Isa*.

the Bagni. Isa was at the Bagni ('Baths') of Lucca.

$\alpha\beta\gamma\delta\epsilon\zeta\iota$ The first seven letters of the Greek alphabet. It is difficult to
identify precisely which seven issues Browning has in mind here, but

the list probably includes spiritualism, Napoleon III, and the best method of raising Pen.

704   19. Julia Wedgwood to R.B., 15 Nov. 1868. *RB/JW*. Browning sent Julia Wedgwood copies of the four volumes of *The Ring and the Book* as they were published (Nov. 1868–Feb. 1869). In this and the following twelve letters she offers her opinions on Browning's masterwork, and he replies.

two volumes. Containing the first six books of *The Ring and the Book* (up until Bk. VI, 'Giuseppe Caponsacchi').

It is more blessed, etc. i.e. 'to give than to receive'.

705   *Bacon.* Francis Bacon (1561–1626). His philosophical treatise, *The Advancement of Learning*, was published in 1605.

swordless sheath filled. Quoted from Browning's 'The Statue and the Bust', l. 15. Julia Wedgwood is referring to Browning's portrait of Caponsacchi.

Thersites. The base-born butt of Homer's *Iliad*, contrasted with Achilles, the most perfect warrior (i.e. from one extreme to the other).

706   *That passage...Pandects.* See Bk. V, 'Count Guido Franceschini', ll. 1781 f.

707   20. R.B. to Julia Wedgwood, 19 Nov. 1868. *RB/JW*.

708   *Northcote asked Reynolds.* James Northcote (1746–1831) and Joshua Reynolds (1723–92), two eminent painters.

709   *(longest book in the poem).* Actually, the longest book is not Bk. X, 'The Pope', but Bk. XI, 'Guido'.

21. Julia Wedgwood to R.B., 3 Dec. 1868. *RB/JW*.

710   *hateful to God and to his foes.* Quoting Dante ('A Dio spiacente ed a' nemici sui').

711   22. R.B. to Julia Wedgwood, 21 Jan. 1869. *RB/JW*.

Mawworm. Hypocritical character from Bickerstaff's comedy *The Hypo-crite* (1768).

712   *('Where's Agnes?')* The title of one of Elizabeth Barrett's poems.

a half-penny worth...vitriol! Adapts Prince Hal's comments on Falstaff's tavern bill (which includes two gallons of 'sack', or burnt sherry, but only an obol's worth of bread): 'O monstrous! but one halfpenny-worth of bread to this intolerable deal of sack!' (*1 Henry IV*, II. iv. 519–21).

713   23. Julia Wedgwood to R.B., 22 Jan. 1869. *RB/JW*.

714   24. Julia Wedgwood to R.B., 30 Jan. 1869. *RB/JW*.

I did think, do think. Bk. VII, 'Pompilia', ll. 1494 f. 'Not this man... obliterated charter' (below) is also quoted from this section of *The Ring and the Book*.

716 25. R.B. to Julia Wedgwood, 1 Feb. 1869. *RB/JW*.

I will supply. Browning altered Bk. V, ll. 1494–5 for the second edition (1872).

P. Pompilia.

717 *Annunziata*. The Italian maid who was with the Brownings when Elizabeth died.

words of the Psalmist . . . abhor them! Ps. 119: 163, 'I hate and abhor lying: but thy law do I love'.

26. R.B. to Julia Wedgwood, 12 Feb. 1869. *RB/JW*.

718 *Ch. Ch*. Christ Church, Oxford.

Joachim. Joseph Joachim (1831–1907), the famous violinist.

the psalm asks. Perhaps Ps. 23: 1, 'The Lord is my shepherd, I shall not want.'

27. Julia Wedgwood to R.B., 14 Feb. 1869. *RB/JW*.

ἔλεγχος σὺ βλεπομενων. 'That by which invisible things are proved'; this is the definition of Faith in Heb. 11: 1 ('the evidence of things not seen' in the Authorized Version).

719 *Innocent*. That is, the Pope of Bk. X (Innocent XII).

(I am not quoting Shelley rightly). Indeed. Shelley wrote: 'All prophecy, all medicine are mine' ('Hymn of Apollo', l. 34).

720 28. Julia Wedgwood to R.B., 21 Feb. 1869. *RB/JW*.

Iago. The brutal villain from Shakespeare's *Othello*.

721 *translation of Euripides*. The Pope imagines Euripides addressing the modern world, Bk. X, ll. 1669–1789.

29. R.B. to Julia Wedgwood, 22 Feb. 1869. *RB/JW*.

722 *Lucrezia Borgia*. W. Gilbert, *Lucrezia Borgia* (1869); a review of this book appeared in the *Spectator* immediately after a review of *The Ring and the Book*.

723 30. Julia Wedgwood to R.B., 5 Mar. 1869. *RB/JW*.

Tant pis pour les faits! So much for the facts!

724 *British Public*. Alluding to Bk. I, 'The Ring and the Book', l. 1379, where Browning addresses the 'British Public, ye who like me not'.

31. R.B. to Julia Wedgwood, 8 Mar. 1869. *RB/JW*.

cessation of our intercourse. Browning and Wedgwood did not communicate from March 1865 to late 1868, for reasons which are not clear.

725 *Carlyle, Grote and Lyell*. Thomas Carlyle (1795–1881), George Grote (1794–1871), author of an influential *History of Greece*, and Sir Charles Lyell (1797–1875), geologist.

Siamese Twins. Chang and Eng, the original Siamese Twins, were joined at the waist, and exhibited themselves for a living until their death in 1874.

725 *Miss Saurin.* Woman at the centre of a cause célèbre in 1869, when she brought charges (for malicious conspiracy and libel) against the Mother Superior of a convent.

726 32. R.B. to Isabella Blagden, 19 Jan. 1870. *Dearest Isa.*

Rossetti. William Michael Rossetti, whose 1870 edition of Shelley's poetry included a memoir of the poet.

Tennyson's new book. The Holy Grail and Other Poems (1869).

Morris. William Morris published his connected cycle of epics, *The Earthly Paradise*, 1868–70.

727 33. R.B. to Isabella Blagden, 19 Aug. 1871. *Dearest Isa.*

she. E.B.B.

34. R.B. to Mrs George Henry Lewis, 9 May 1876. *New Letters.* Elizabeth Lewis was the German wife of a prominent London lawyer, and society hostess.

Mr Fosbroke's poems. John Baldwin Fosbroke, friend of Mrs Lewis and minor poet, author of the narrative poem *Rheingold* (1872), and *Erlinthule, King of Ithol, and Lyrics of Greenwood Tree* (1873). The poetry is awful.

728 35. R.B. to a Correspondent, 11 May 1876. *Hood.* An (unidentified) lady had written to Browning, believing she was dying, to thank him for the solace she had derived from his poetry, particularly 'Rabbi Ben Ezra'.

729 36. R.B. to Tennyson, 5 Aug. 1889. *Hood.*

FURTHER READING

Modern Collected Editions

Richard Altick (ed.), *The Ring and the Book* (Harmondsworth: Penguin 1981).

Ian Jack *et al.* (eds.), *The Poetical Works of Robert Browning* (Oxford: Oxford University Press 1984–). Five volumes have so far appeared.

Roma King *et al.* (eds.), *The Complete Poems of Robert Browning* (Athens: Ohio University Press 1969–). Nine volumes have so far appeared.

John Pettigrew and Thomas Collins (eds.), *Robert Browning: The Poems* (2 vols., Harmondsworth: Penguin 1981).

John Woolford and Daniel Karlin (eds.), *The Poems of Browning* (Harlow: Longman 1991–). Two volumes have so far appeared.

Letters

Browning's letters are at the moment dispersed between a large number of separate volumes and collections. The complete *Browning Correspondence* is currently being edited (by Kelley and Hudson, see below), but it will be a number of years before this is completed (in forty volumes).

Thomas Collins (ed.), *The Brownings to the Tennysons* (Waco, Tex.: Wedgstone Press, 1971).

Richard Curle (ed.), *Robert Browning and Julia Wedgwood: A Broken Friendship as Revealed in Their Letters* (London: John Murray and Jonathan Cape, 1937).

Clyde DeVane and Kenneth Knickerbocker (eds.), *New Letters of Robert Browning* (New Haven: Yale University Press, 1950).

Thurman Hood, *Letters of Robert Browning* (New Haven: Yale University Press, 1933).

Philip Kelley and Ronald Hudson (eds.), *The Brownings' Correspondence* (Winfield, Kan.: Wedgstone Press, 1984–). Eleven volumes have so far appeared.

F. G. Kenyon (ed.), *The Letters of Elizabeth Barrett Browning* (2 vols., London: Smith and Elder, 1898).

Elvan Kintner (ed.), *The Letters of Robert Browning and Elizabeth Barrett Barrett, 1845–46* (2 vols. paginated as one, Cambridge, Mass.: Harvard University Press, 1969).

Edward McAleer (ed.), *Dearest Isa: Robert Browning's Letters to Isa Blagden* (Austin: University of Texas Press, 1951).

——(ed.), *Learned Lady: Letters from Robert Browning to Mrs Thomas Fitzgerald 1876–1889* (Cambridge, Mass.: Harvard University Press, 1966).

Michael Meredith (ed.), *More Than Friends: The Letters of Robert Browning to Katharine de Kay Bronson* (Waco, Tex.: Wedgstone Press, 1985).

William Peterson (ed.), *Browning's Trumpeter: The Correspondence of Robert Browning and Frederick J. Furnivall, 1872–1889* (Washington, DC: Decatur, 1979).

Criticism, Biography, Scholarship

Isobel Armstrong, *Victorian Poetry: Poetry, Poetics and Politics* (London: Macmillan, 1993).

Joseph Bristow, *Robert Browning* (New York: Harvester, 1991).

David J. DeLaura, 'The Context of Browning's Painter Poems: Aesthetics, Polemics, Historics', *PMLA* 95 (1980), 367–88.

W. C. DeVane, *A Browning Handbook* (2nd edn., New York: Appleton-Century-Crofts, 1955).

Philip Drew, *The Poetry of Browning: A Critical Introduction* (London: Methuen, 1970).

William Irving and Park Honan, *The Book, the Ring and the Poet: A Biography of Robert Browning* (London: Bodley Head, 1974).

Daniel Karlin, *Browning's Hatreds* (Oxford: Oxford University Press, 1993).

Philip Kelley and Betty Coley, *The Browning Collections: A Reconstruction with Other Memorabilia* (Waco, Tex.: Armstrong Browning Library, Wedgstone Press, 1984).

Roma A. King, *The Bow and the Lyre: The Art of Robert Browning* (Ann Arbor: University of Michigan Press, 1957).

—— *The Focusing Artifice: The Poetry of Robert Browning* (Athens: Ohio University Press, 1968).

Robert Langbaum, *The Poetry of Experience: The Dramatic Monologue in Modern Literary Tradition* (New York: Random House, 1957; 2nd edn. 1963).

Loy D. Martin, *Browning's Dramatic Monologues and the Post-Romantic Subject* (Baltimore: Johns Hopkins University Press, 1985).

J. Maynard, *Browning's Youth* (Cambridge, Mass.: Harvard University Press, 1977).

J. Hillis Miller, *The Disappearance of God: Five Nineteenth-Century Writers* (Cambridge, Mass.: Harvard University Press, 1963).

William O. Raymond, *The Infinite Moment and Other Essays in Robert Browning* (Toronto: University of Toronto Press, 1950; 2nd edn., 1965).

Clyde de L. Ryals, *Browning's Later Poetry, 1871–1889* (Ithaca, NY: Cornell University Press, 1975).

—— *The Life of Browning: A Critical Biography* (Oxford: Blackwell, 1993).

E. A. W. St George, *Browning and Conversation* (London: Macmillan, 1993).

W. David Shaw, *The Dialectical Temper: The Rhetorical Art of Robert Browning* (Ithaca, NY: Cornell University Press, 1968).

—— 'Browning's Murder Mystery: *The Ring and the Book* and Modern Theory', *Victorian Poetry*, 27 (1989), 79–98.

E. Warwick Slinn, *Browning and the Fictions of Identity* (Totowa, NJ: Barnes and Noble, 1982).

—— *The Discourse of Self in Victorian Poetry* (London: Macmillan, 1991).

Mary Rose Sullivan, *Browning's Voices in The Ring and the Book: A Study of Method and Meaning* (Toronto: University of Toronto Press, 1969).

Herbert F. Tucker, *Browning's Beginnings: The Art of Disclosure* (Minneapolis: University of Minnesota Press, 1980).

William Whitla, *The Central Truth: The Incarnation in Robert Browning's Poetry* (Toronto: University of Toronto Press, 1963).

John Woolford, *Browning the Revisionary* (London: Macmillan, 1988).

INDEX OF TITLES

INDEX OF FIRST LINES